Eddie Collins

Eddie Collins

A Baseball Biography

RICK HUHN

McFarland & Company, Inc., Publishers
Jefferson, North Carolina, and London

LIBRARY OF CONGRESS CATALOGUING-IN-PUBLICATION DATA

Huhn, Rick, 1944–
Eddie Collins : a baseball biography / Rick Huhn.
p.   cm.
Includes bibliographical references and index.

ISBN-13: 978-0-7864-3287-5
softcover : 50# alkaline paper ∞

1. Collins, Eddie, 1887–1951.   2. Baseball — United
States — Biography.   I. Title.
GV865.C65H84   2008   796.357092 — dc22 [B]   2007046245

British Library cataloguing data are available

On the cover: Dick Perez, *2B Sentinel*, oil on canvas,
www.dickperez.com (courtesy of the Philadelphia Phillies)

Manufactured in the United States of America

McFarland & Company, Inc., Publishers
Box 611, Jefferson, North Carolina 28640
www.mcfarlandpub.com

To my parents Lester and Myrtle

Acknowledgments

How does a publisher decide where to place the acknowledgments page? Should it be at the beginning or end of the work? In the former case the author acknowledges that he started out with a blank page and could not have accomplished that which follows but for the considerable help he received from those he is about to thank. In the latter case he looks over that which he has written, is thankful for all the help he received in producing it, and wishes to gratefully acknowledge those who provided that help. I've decided it does not matter. Given all the help and inspiration I received from those who answered my call in connection with this book, placement is not an issue. I could neither have started nor finished it without their help.

I had so much assistance from so many people in researching, writing and editing this book that I must keep each thank you brief. That in no way lessens my gratitude. If I do fail to thank you, please understand that I will be reminded someday and I will be eternally embarrassed.

First, let me say that in researching and writing this book I relied in the main on factual and statistical information from Baseball-Reference.com, Retrosheet.com and *Total Baseball* (8th edition). I commend the editors and the contributors to these sources for providing such a thorough body of work. A special thanks to Sean Foreman of baseball-reference.com for permitting me to use his website's compilation of Collins' career statistics in an appendix. I also thank the Office of the Commissioner of Major League Baseball and particularly Charlyne A. Sanders for permission to reproduce portions of the American League Black Sox Scandal papers. A huge thank you must be directed to Steve Gietschier for opening the archives of the *Sporting News* to me and allowing me to comb through the publication's vast clippings and photo files. And my continuing thanks go to the Society for American Baseball Research (SABR), an organization which opens the door to baseball researchers, writers and enthusiasts of varying interests and provides them with a treasure trove of resources, enabling them to delve into the lives of baseball players like Eddie Collins and his contemporaries. Eileen Canepari of SABR deserves special thanks for unerringly fulfilling my many research library requests.

My description of the early portion of Collins' life and baseball career was aided and enriched in large part by Diane Keonig (genealogist), Joseph Poillucci, Jay Reynolds, Jim O'Malley, John Flanagan, Jennifer Doyle, the North East Historical Society (Millerton, N. Y.), the Dutchess County (N. Y.) Historical Society, Sara Mascia and other volunteers at the Tarrytown (N. Y.) Historical Society, Bill Cribbs (Irving School), Jocelyn K. Wilk and staff of the University Archives and Columbia Library (Columbia University), the staff of the Butler Library (Columbia University), Colleen Pelletier and the staff of the Plattsburgh (N. Y.) Public Library, Alex Beswick-Couturier of the Rutland (Vt.) Free Library, and the staff of the Hartford (Conn.) Public Library. A special thanks to my longtime friend Sharon Kettyle and her son, Jack Barnhardt, for suggesting I contact Khalil Blake, who helped me complete my search through the Columbia University student newspapers published during Collins' stay at Columbia.

My research into the baseball career of my subject was given a terrific boost by Gabriel Schecter, Claudette Burke, Freddy Berowski, Anne McFarland, Tom Schieber, and others on the staff of the National Baseball Hall of Fame Library. I believe the story of Collins' lengthy baseball career is enriched by the photographs of Collins and others which were provided with the assistance of Bill Burdick and later Pat Kelly of the library. In addition, I owe a large measure of gratitude to baseball researcher Russ Wolinsky of the Hall. At several stages during my early efforts he provided valuable information concerning Collins. Toward the end he reviewed the manuscript and pointed out factual errors on a number of issues. This type of help is invaluable in any attempt to render a true account of an individual's life.

Coverage of the Philadelphia portion of the Collins' life was aided by members of the Philadelphia Athletics Historical Society, in particular David Jordan and Ernie Montella. Early on Bill Kashatus and later others like Bill Burgess, Tom Swift, Peter Morris, Ray Robinson, Lee Lowenfish, Pete Cava, Tom Barthel, and Dr. Charles Alexander offered invaluable help. A special thanks to Norman Macht for providing a large number of newspaper articles written by Collins, and to Connie Mack's daughter, Ruth, for taking the time to speak with me about Collins. There was an enormous amount of newspaper microfilm to comb through from Eddie's two stops in Philadelphia. I could not have come close to reviewing it without some local help from Michael Quate. Mike spent numerous hours working on my behalf, and his father, Allen, pitched in as well. The staffs of the Urban Archives and the Samuel Paley Library at Temple University were quite helpful in any number of ways, as were the staffs of the Cleveland Public and the Columbus and Worthington (Ohio) Public libraries. And an emphatic thanks to the staff of my local Westerville (Ohio) Public Library for their help with inter-library loans. Cheryl Fulton and Evan Struble saw me heading to the circulation desk on numerous occasions and never visibly winced.

Collins in Chicago represented a separate challenge. I could not have covered that segment of Collins' biography in as much detail without help from knowledgeable people like Gene Carney, who set aside time to review my treatment of the Black Sox Scandal and add his valuable insight. In addition, Susan Dellinger, Dan Levitt, Richard Lindberg, Mark Rucker, and Bernard Weisberger each added something important to the mix. The Chicago Historical Society provided valuable information and ProQuest Historical Newspapers — available at the time through SABR — permitted broad access to the *Chicago Tribune* and other newspapers of great value.

When I reached the last two decades of Collins' life, I directed my attention to his family and to his days in Boston. The most difficult family member to trace was his older son Paul, a member of the Episcopal clergy. I received more information than expected by contacting Carl Knirk, an old and dear friend who works for an Episcopal diocese. He contacted church archivist Diane Wells and the information was in hand in days. Those who helped on the "Boston period" include Bill Nowlin, as well as Boston Public Library staffers Mary Beth Dunhouse and Aaron Schmidt. SABR member Dick Bresciani and Debbie Matson bent over backwards in providing me photographs, as well as information which enabled me to contact former Red Sox players who were in the organization at the same time as Collins. Thanks, as well, to those players for their time in permitting me to interview them.

Any writer knows that when the first draft is done the job is still a long way from completion. Writing a baseball biography filled with statistics and anecdotes and events from well over one-half century ago can be angst-ridden unless you have expert editing assistance along the way. In this case I received terrific support from baseball historian Steve Steinberg. In addition to supplying a number of articles that gave unique perspectives of Collins from other parts of the country, he gave the manuscript a detailed once-over and then offered his insight on a number of issues. This help coupled with the aforementioned efforts of Russ Wolinsky and thorough edits from two friends, local Columbus author Lee Caryer and longtime English teacher Linda Eddy of Marietta, Ohio, I felt ready to turn the work over to the publisher. I cannot thank these four enough for providing their expertise.

For this writer no acknowledgment would be complete without recognizing the essential part his family played in completing the work. My principal colleague was my daughter, Kimberly Huhn Bumgarner, who totally rearranged her schedule to allow time to work for her father. I was afforded an opportunity to spend quality time with her and to marvel at her editing and computer skills. Our partnership enriched my writing experience and increased my love and admiration for her. Thanks to her husband Rob for readily allowing her to team up with me. And finally I thank my wife, Marcia, who inspires all I do and who once again provided her total support and guidance from beginning to end.

Table of Contents

Acknowledgments   vii

Introduction   1

Prologue   5

1	Family Ties	9
2	Columbia's Finest	15
3	Summer Job	27
4	Meeting Mr. Mack	37
5	A Baseball Education	42
6	Yannigan No More	52
7	Signature Season	65
8	$100,000 Infield	77
9	Keystone King	92
10	Switching Sides	112
11	War Clubs	131
12	Sour Series	149
13	Clean Sox	166
14	Trials and Tribulations	184
15	Trade Talk	196
16	Leader at Last	215
17	Hot Seat	229
18	A's Redux	243
19	On the Line	255
20	Junior Executive	270

21   Building Blocks   283

22   Missed Opportunities   294

23   Parting Shots   308

Appendix One: Transcript of Eddie Collins' Statement
   to Leslie N. O'Connor, Chicago, February 19, 1921   319

Appendix Two: Eddie Collins' Career Statistics
   (as Player and Manager)   325

Chapter Notes   333

Bibliography   347

Index   355

Introduction

The seeds for this book were planted in the early 1950s on the living room floor of my family's home in the small town of Marion, Ohio. I was about nine at the time and baseball was my game. Like most young boys of that era I enjoyed playing baseball outdoors, finding a sandlot game wherever and whenever I could, and just hitting the ball around or playing catch when I could not. And like so many of my friends, I was also interested in the major leagues. My passion, however, was such that I wanted to do more than just watch or play baseball, so I took my game inside. I became a big league manager — the board game variety.

Although I would graduate to more sophisticated board games like APBA or Strat-O-Matic, at this point in time I played the Cadaco All-Star Baseball Game. It depended on slotted player cards that fit conveniently over a metal spinner. These player cards were divided into numbered sections, the numbers corresponding to the different results an at-bat might bring. Then I carefully picked my lineup. As each player came to the "plate," I would spin and he would bat. If the spinner magically stopped on the section at the top marked number "1," my batter had smashed a home run. The size of each section corresponded roughly to how a player hit in real life. Thus, Babe Ruth's home run section was larger than anyone else's. There were sections for each of the various base hits, as well as for sacrifices, ground outs, and fly balls. Space appropriate to each player was even provided for stolen bases. The game board was a diamond; the base runners, tiddlywinks. It was simple, but fun.

The opposing teams in this league were but two: an all-star roster made up of current players and a team consisting of all-time greats. Since I was an only child, I managed both squads. By now it should be no surprise that the regular second baseman on my old-timers' team was none other than Eddie Collins.

It is fair to ask "Why Collins?" when cards for second base legends such as Napoleon Lajoie and Frankie Frisch were also included. The answer is simple: I could easily pronounce Collins' name. The last names of the others presented a problem. In my league, I was more than just an owner and a manager. To ensure the integrity of the game, and much to my parents' chagrin, I also announced each contest out loud in the homespun fashion of Jimmy Dudley, then radio announcer for my favorites, the Cleveland Indians. I whiled away most rainy-day afternoons, and many sunny ones too, sitting Indian-style on the thick carpet, an imaginary microphone inches from my face.

So at nine I was already an Eddie Collins fan, but only to a point — the very narrow point of a metal spinner. Almost every kid knew the legendary feats of earlier stars such as the Babe, Lou Gehrig, and Ty Cobb, but my knowledge of Eddie Collins was limited to a name and some numbers on a little white card. It would remain so for many years. During those years I knew that Collins was a member of baseball's Hall of Fame. I could add that the home run section on his card was narrow; all other hitting and base running categories were quite wide. That was about it. I do not recall ever seeing a picture of Collins. In my mind, however, based only on his card, I saw a rather dashing razor-sharp young man built for speed and grace. Then one day while I searched through photographs for a biography on Hall of Famer George Sisler, another of my board game regulars with an easily pronounceable last name, I found a picture of the two contemporaries shaking hands. I was shocked. Collins was not at all as I had pictured him. Next to the handsome, graceful presence of "Gorgeous George" stood a rather short, floppy-eared man with a sad, angular face, dressed in a baseball uniform at least two sizes too large. This star of stars looked anything but a big-time star. Yet because of my earlier familiarity with his name and my renewed interest in baseball history, I made a note to check back on Collins.

It was about a year later before I found some time to do a little digging into the person behind the Eddie Collins card. By then my work on Sisler was completed and on its way to a publisher. Since I was interested in writing about another important player or baseball personality, it was important that the individual's life or career be such that it deserved full biographical treatment. As with Sisler, I also did not want to write a biography if others had already tilled the field. I determined to date that no one had written about Collins.

Next I did some initial reading about my potential subject. I quickly found that during a record-setting 25-year baseball playing career from 1906 to 1930, Collins batted .333 and became a member of the exclusive 3,000 hit club—rarified air, indeed. I then went to the latest *Baseball Abstract* written by Bill James to find out where in his revered ranking system Collins fell. James, a creditable baseball historian, combines his unique mathematical formulas with a keen analysis of what wins baseball games. He then uses his findings to compare different players from different eras and establishes a ranking by position. Whether one always agrees with him or not, Bill James has a way of cutting reputations down in size. Recalling that the section at the top of my old Collins' card indicated he seldom hit home runs, I thought perhaps Eddie would be low on the list after all these years. I did expect him to be included, since his card showed a knack for frequently getting on base in all manner of ways— statistics the James-system favors. Even then I was surprised when I located the *Abstract*'s list of second basemen and found Eddie Collins ranked second all-time, trailing only former Cincinnati Reds slugger Joe Morgan. That ranking in itself satisfied my criteria that Collins deserved full biographical treatment. However, since numbers alone do not good stories make, I investigated further.

After concluding my research, I realized that Eddie Collins was not only one of baseball's most consistently good batters, but also perhaps its best bunter and hit-and-run man, as well as one of its craftiest base runners and finest defensive second basemen. In addition, during his career he was repeatedly referred to as the game's smartest player, both on and off the field. I wondered why. He was certainly one of the game's highest-paid performers, a source of much irritation throughout the years to lesser-paid players such as Chicago White Sox teammates Chick Gandil and Eddie Cicotte. I discovered that writing about Collins permitted me to learn about his playing days at Columbia University, where he starred as team captain in baseball as well as the starting quarterback in football. Then there was his professional career, first with the Athletics, then the White Sox, and finally the Athletics again— teams which for many of the Collins years dominated the baseball landscape, giving rise to his frequent World Series heroics and reputation as one of baseball's best "money" players. Weaving in and out would be Collins' storied bosses, Connie Mack and Charles Comiskey, as well as teammates with names like Frank "Home Run" Baker, "Stuffy" McInnis, "Chief" Bender, "Shoeless Joe" Jackson, Ty Cobb, Tris Speaker and Mickey Cochrane. There would be an opportunity to take another look at the fabled Zimmerman boner in the 1917 World Series and the "Black Sox" scandal—this time from the perspective of one who did not conspire to defraud Chicago owner Charles Comiskey, but who played with this disparate bunch who many believed might be baseball's greatest team. Finally there was an opportunity to view and analyze Collins' post-playing career days as a general manager, vice president, and part owner of multi-millionaire Tom Yawkey's Boston Red Sox. Here Collins scouted and signed Hall of Famers Ted Williams and Bobby Doerr, but stood by as the Red Sox turned away Jackie Robinson. The Red Sox became the last organization to sign an African American baseball player when they might have been the first.

When I finished my course on Eddie Collins, I was convinced he was a lot more than a set of numbers on a slotted card. He was a fierce competitor whose "game" belied his appearance and gave credence to his oft-repeated title as the "King" of baseball second basemen. I wanted to learn more and then write his biography. My decision, at least to me, should not have come as a surprise. I guess when I think back on it, this book was in the "cards" all along. It just took me a while to realize it.

Prologue

A careful check through major league baseball's record books will find nary a mention of Eddie Sullivan. Yet a young man known by that name to his Philadelphia Athletics teammates played for the team on September 17, 1906, and for several games thereafter, giving a fair account of himself. That he appeared on the field of play at all was no mean accomplishment considering that less than a week earlier young Sullivan was ready to throw in the towel.

Sullivan, all 5 feet, 9 inches of him, had joined the Athletics while they were finishing a homestand against their American League rivals, the Boston Red Sox. A strong summer of semiprofessional baseball in New England convinced Athletics manager Connie Mack that Sullivan and teammate Dave Shean deserved a major league look. These two were part of a youth movement initiated by Mack when his defending league champions appeared to be out of the running for a second straight pennant.

Upon reporting to Philadelphia, the 19-year-old Sullivan was told to join his new teammates in morning workouts but not to appear for the afternoon games. That first morning workout afforded the youngster an experience he would never forget.

"I put on a uniform that did not fit me too well," he said years later. "Gosh, I weighed about only 140 pounds. I was self-conscious among all those big fellows — men like Waddell, whom I had read so much about. Waddell had been warming up on the sidelines."[1]

"Waddell" was none other than George Edward "Rube" Waddell. "The Rube," as he was generally known, was once described by noted baseball historian Lee Allen as one who sported "an unruly shock of blonde hair, a flat nose, and a dimpled chin, and threw the ball so hard with his left arm that the leather of the catchers glove would scream."[2] In Allen's opinion Waddell was "[t]he most improbable person ever associated with big league baseball...." In 1903 he began the "year sleeping in a firehouse at Camden, New Jersey, and ended it tending bar in a saloon in Wheeling, West Virginia. In between those events he won twenty-two [*sic*] games for the Philadelphia Athletics, played left end for the Business Men's Rugby Football Club of Grand Rapids, Michigan, toured the nation in a melodrama called *The Stain of Guilt*, courted, married and became separated from May Wynne Skinner of Lynn, Massachusetts, saved a woman from drowning, accidentally shot a friend through the hand, and was bitten by a lion."[3]

In the vernacular of the game, Waddell had great "stuff." Enough that in a 13-year career, he won 193 games, lost 143 and carried a 2.16 earned run average (ERA). When Rube spotted the wide-eyed kid with the billowy uniform step onto the field, the veteran's eyes lit up, and he broke into a Cheshire–cat grin. He was, he realized, about to feast on the rawest of rookies. Immediately, he yelled for Sullivan to grab a bat so he could throw him a few.

"I thought that was great — I was about to bat against the great Rube. But I didn't know what Waddell was up to. With more fear than confidence, I took my stance at the plate. He threw me three curves that looked as if they had dropped off a table. I missed all three. I thought I'd never make good if they had that kind of pitchers in this league and I started to walk away. Rube must have noticed how downcast I was, for, he walked out of the box, patted me on the back and said, 'Don't mind, kid. I do that to all of 'em.'"[4]

Still, Sullivan remained so dejected that he considered heading home. Over the next day or two, however, talks with Connie Mack and veteran first baseman Harry Davis convinced him to stick around for a few more morning workouts. In those workouts Mack must have seen something he liked. When the team completed its series with the Red Sox on September 15, the tall, slender manager asked his new find to accompany the team by train as it headed to Chicago for a series with the White Sox. Sullivan, if not fully recovered from his experience with the Rube, agreed after first checking with his parents.

The White Sox were in the midst of a miracle season. Burdened by weak hitting, the team somehow had a slim first-place lead of one and one-half games over the New York Highlanders, a lead they would not relinquish as they became better known as "the Hitless Wonders."

The first game with the Chicagoans was set for September 17. In those days the White Sox played their home games at old South Side Park, located at Thirty-Ninth Street and Wentworth Avenue. With the White Sox battling for a pennant and the Athletics in third place not all that far behind, "Sully," as his teammates were now calling him, did not expect to play. He was in fact relaxing in the dugout before the game when Mack turned to him and told him he was starting the game at shortstop. The words "electrified" him. His "legs quivered" as he prepared to take part in his first major league contest. And before he even had time to take a deep breath, he was thrown into the fray.[5]

On the mound for the White Sox to face Sullivan in his debut was Ed Walsh. A master of the spitball and, like the Rube, a future Hall-of-Fame hurler, Walsh was the holder of a lifetime ERA of 1.93 and only two years from a 40-win season. At 6 feet 1 inch and 193 pounds, "Big Ed," as he was known, was an imposing figure. He loomed especially large for a pint-sized freshman in a uniform a couple of sizes too big for him. No one could blame Sullivan if he backed down a bit. However, Sully did not back down, not one bit. When the dust cleared from an 11-inning dual between Walsh and Waddell, the rookie could hold his head high. In five appearances at the plate, batting sixth in the lineup, he had singled and sacrificed. At shortstop he was flawless, including two putouts and four assists.[6]

The next day the *Philadelphia Inquirer* carried a report on the game, finding little to fault Mack's youngsters for in a 5–4 loss. "If one of the youngsters whom Manager Mack, with his eye looking toward the future is now trying out, had committed either actual errors of commission or errors of omission which led to the triumph of the White Sox, some consolation might have been obtained from that fact. But the youngsters never figured in the game except in a meritorious way."

Regarding Sullivan in particular, why his performance "may be only a flash in the pan, but he was called upon to do a little bit of everything that may be expected of a shortstop and he was there every time. He ran up on them and he backed for them. His catch of Hahn's short fly to left was a regular Monte Cross [the A's regular shortstop] catch."[7]

The next day Sullivan again found himself in the starting lineup. Once again his team lost, this time 7–0, in the face of four-hit pitching by the Sox's Frank Owen, a 22-game winner. But again Sullivan held his own, slapping a line drive single to center in the fifth inning and fielding without a hitch. The rookie did provide a bit of comic relief on an otherwise bleak day when he assumed the center fielder made a shoestring catch of his line drive in the fifth and headed toward the dugout. He was saved further embarrassment when "a whole flock of Athletics ran out from the bench and pulled him back onto first base."[8]

In the third and final game of the White Sox series, Eddie Sullivan finally tasted victory for the first time as a major leaguer, but in order to do so his teammates had to overcome his own shoddy fielding. In the first inning he fumbled a ground ball that eventually resulted in a score. In the ninth a second costly error led to two more Chicago runs. Still, it was not enough and the Athletics bested the Sox and pitcher Nick Altrock, 4–3. Altrock, in the midst of one of his finest seasons in the big leagues, would earn more notoriety in the ensuing years for his entertaining clown act from the coaching box. On this day, however, Sully added a single and a sacrifice to what now was a modest three-game hitting streak.

Their work in Chicago complete, the Athletics headed for St. Louis where they were joined by Simon Nicholls, a 24-year-old shortstop brought to the club from the Southern League. Manager Connie Mack, perhaps sobered by Sullivan's bobbles in Chicago, started Nicholls against the Browns. Eddie watched from the bench as the locals blasted the A's, winning three of four.

Actually, Sullivan did not see action again until the team arrived in Cleveland for a three-game series with the Naps. In that series Sully made an unsuccessful pinch-hit appearance in game one and in game three reached base on a pinch-hit grounder that the shortstop bobbled. A walk, passed ball, and single later, Sullivan scored his first major league run. The score came at the expense of Nap pitcher Addie Joss, a brilliant but tragic figure in the sport who would later die from tubercular meningitis at the unseemly age of 31. Sullivan's run was not enough as the A's fell to the Naps, 5–3.

Eddie next found the field on September 28, in his team's second contest in Detroit, when he played third base and batted third in a 7–4 A's victory. This time around Eddie fielded his position but was the only starter who did not hit safely. He did, however, aid his team's course in the third inning when his sacrifice kept a rally alive. Later he reached base on a fielder's choice and scored a run. This game in Detroit would serve as the last time the name Eddie Sullivan ever appeared in a major league box score. For when the A's left Detroit and arrived in New York for a season-ending four-game series with the Highlanders, young Eddie Sullivan was not with the team. Although the Mack youth brigade continued its march to the 1906 finish line, Sullivan was no longer in formation.

All told in 1906 Eddie Sullivan played in six games, appearing at the plate 15 times with three hits for a .200 batting average. All three hits were singles and did not produce a run batted in (RBI). He scored two runs.[9] Two of the pitchers he faced, Walsh and Joss, were eventually enshrined in baseball's Hall of Fame. He committed two errors in one of the games, but otherwise fielded admirably. Although not a spectacular debut, it was in no way an embarrassing one. If his manager, the peerless Connie Mack, found fault with the rookie's performance, he never voiced it. Indeed, it seemed at 19 years of age the youngster's entire athletic career lay before him.

Why then did Eddie Sullivan never appear in another major league game? In fact, the boy did play again. And not just one season, either. When he retired after 25 seasons, no twentieth century major leaguer had ever played longer. Yet Sullivan's name does not appear in the eighth edition of *Total Baseball* or in other books documenting in detail the statistical records of the game. How could such an oversight occur? The answer is most certainly there, but for that you need to read the rest of the story.

CHAPTER 1

Family Ties

"My folks say that I was born with a baseball bat in my mouth instead of a silver spoon."
— Eddie Collins[1]

The Hudson Valley village of Millerton, New York, between 900 and 1,000 inhabitants strong, is 98 miles and more than one far cry from New York City. For those city dwellers seeking a weekend retreat and who do make the two-hour drive north or the equivalent train ride on the Metro-North Harlem Line from Grand Central Station, the lodging of choice is the Simmons Way Village Inn. The highly regarded "bed and breakfast" is stately and serene; enough so, that it once graced the cover of an issue of *The New Yorker* magazine featuring country inns of the Northeast. The inn itself was originally built around 1854 by E.W. Simmons, and thus its name.

In the mid–1800s and beyond, E.W. Simmons was a prominent figure in Millerton in both height, at 6 foot 3 inches, and in community affairs. He was originally an educator who conducted an academy which served as the first business establishment in the village. In 1876 the business failed. Simmons, by then over 50 years old, was admitted to the local bar. He then proceeded, in no particular order, to practice law for the next thirty years, play a mean game of backgammon, and frequent the local saloon. In addition, he buried one wife and married another.[2]

The second marriage of lawyer Simmons was to Sarah (Meade) Trowbridge. Sarah was a widow with a daughter named Mary, also often called "Matie." The Trowbridges were a prominent family in North East, the larger town immediately adjacent to Millerton, who could trace their ancestry to England in 1135. The first American settler in the family, Thomas Trowbridge, came to Dorchester, Massachusetts, in 1636. Mary's grandfather Alexander was a prosperous farmer, a captain in the militia, and co-owner of the Millerton Hotel. His first wife bore him seven children. Their son Perry married Sarah Meade. Their daughter Mary was born in 1855. When Perry died, his widow became the second Mrs. E.W. Simmons.[3]

On June 21, 1880, the newspapers in nearby Amenia, New York, reported the marriage of Matie M. Trowbridge to John R. Collins, the assistant general freight agent of the Harlem Railroad, a division of the powerful New York Central Railroad. The wedding was held in Millerton. The ceremony had been performed the previous Wednesday by a minister.[4]

Almost eight years later, Mary Trowbridge Collins found herself at the Simmons house, home of her mother Sarah and her step-father E.W. She was in the late stages of a pregnancy. Whether Mary came to the house merely to visit her family or with the specific intent to seek their assistance and shelter in giving birth is unknown. What is known is that on May 2, 1887, while at her parents' home, she gave birth to a son, Edward Trowbridge Collins.

It is often written that Edward Trowbridge Collins was an only child. Indeed, he was the only child of Mary and John Collins. There was, however, the matter of young Mr. Collins' half-sister, Grace. An explanation for that rests with his father John.

John Rossman Collins was born in New York City on August 12, 1839, the son of John I. Collins and Catherine Rossman. As a boy he sold newspapers, much the same as Al Smith, the former governor of New York and unsuccessful presidential candidate in 1928 who grew up in the same area of the city. While still a youth, John joined the Volunteer Fire Department, becoming a part of the rivalry that existed between the fire companies of Lower Manhattan. The goal was to be the first company to get water on the fire. These were the days before steam, when the water was pumped by hand.

Later, John R. Collins hired in with the Harlem Division of the New York Central Railroad, at the time a one-track operation without stations. Residents with homes adjacent to the tracks were paid by the railroad to serve the purposes of a station.[5] In time, Collins was elevated to the position of assistant freight agent. In the hierarchy of railroads, the position was one of substance and esteem, offering a good wage. John lived and worked in the city where he met, and on June 5, 1866, married Annie M. Holden of Boston. On March 7, 1867, the couple gave birth to Grace Rossman Collins. For at least ten years, the small family remained in New York City, but then tragedy struck. In 1876 Annie Collins passed away, leaving a 37-year-old husband and a nine-year-old daughter. In 1880 John remarried Mary and lived in the Millerton area. It appears that after her mother's death, Grace lived part-time with John's parents in Nyack, New York.[6] It is less certain whether or how much Grace resided with her father and his new wife for the seven or so years between the date of their marriage and the birth of their son Edward. However, it seems likely she lived with them for a time, since in 1890, when she was 23, Grace Collins married Philo Reed Cline of Millerton and remained in the village the rest of her life.[7]

By 1890 Grace's half-brother, no longer Edward, but forevermore Eddie, was a robust three-year-old and a precocious toddler at that. Already he was showing a flair for sports, particularly the one with the small round horsehide ball. In fact, according to Eddie, "I can't remember the day that I didn't have a bat, glove and ball."[8]

According to his mother Mary, "When Eddie was very small, not more than five or six years old, we used to go in summertime to the shore of Lake Ontario. The fishermen there used to watch him play ball and were quite struck with the strength and agility he showed for one so young. 'Where is that ballplayer,' they would say; 'bring him out and let's see how far he can throw that ball. He's a natural player; he'll be in the big leagues some day.'"[9]

Eddie's recollection of his early interest in baseball, as well as his mother's remarks on the subject, contradict a number of writers who state that early on Collins showed little interest in baseball. For example, Hugh Fullerton, the noted baseball writer writing for the magazine *Liberty* as if from an interview with Collins, told readers that Collins "played little baseball as a youngster preferring foot racing and football" until he began school.[10]

If Eddie was developing a budding interest in baseball, it was not all that unusual, especially for a youngster growing up in baseball crazy Dutchess County, which included Millerton and its environs. In the late 1800s the county produced a Hall-of-Fame ballplayer in "Big Dan" Brouthers of Wappinger Falls, one of the game's earliest sluggers. The county even housed a professional team in Poughkeepsie, which played in the Hudson River League as early as 1886. The team and the league were short-lived, but in 1894 a team from that city joined the New York State League. By that time, however, the Collins family had relocated.[11]

In the early 1890s John Collins was elevated to the position of freight agent of both the Harlem and the Hudson River Divisions of the New York Central Railroad. As such, he maintained an office in the Grand Central Terminal in New York City. Although his work required him to be in the city on a daily basis, it also required that he live in the Hudson River Division. His initial choice for relocation was White Plains in New York's Westchester County, but when he found it outside the required boundary, he chose nearby Tarrytown, then a community with a larger population than White Plains. The location, approximately 25 miles from New York City, offered a daily train commute of an hour or less.

Located on the east bank of the Hudson River at its widest point, some three miles from shore to shore, Tarrytown was Mohegan Indian country until Henry Hudson, an Englishman, arrived in 1609. Sailing on commission by the Dutch West India Company to find the long sought Northwest Passage to the Pacific, Hudson was temporarily fooled when he saw the wide expanse of the river at Tarrytown. Thinking this portion of the river, later named the Tappan Zee (Dutch for "sea"), would open into another ocean, he pushed on, exploring the river all the way to Albany before realizing, much to his disappointment, it was merely a river.

The Dutch, however, saw a lot to like in what they referred to as New Netherland. Before long Peter Minuit was appointed the director-general of the company, a position he held when he purchased Manhattan Island for a handful of trinkets and beads. Soon it became apparent that in order to cement the Dutch influence and keep out the English who were settling New England and Virginia, there was a need for settlement in the Hudson Valley. As an incentive to prospective settlers, large deposits of land along the river were granted to company members who brought settlers with them. These members were known as "patroons." The patroon system smacked of medieval feudalism, but at least initially the system helped to populate the area. Of course, with the settlers came the associated problems with the neighboring Indian tribes. By 1645, however, a treaty was in place and peace ensued. In turn that same year the first white homestead appeared in what became known as Tarrytown.[12]

The first great land owner in the area was Frederick Phillipse. In addition to his land, Frederick accumulated wealth from shipping and trading. In time he became the richest man in New York.[13] By 1800 the Tarrytown area claimed approximately 3,000 residents. These numbers increased as wealthy families, businessmen and financiers from New York City moved their families to the area. In the process they "built palatial mansions, rode in ornate, horse-drawn carriages and maintained magnificent ocean-going steam yachts."[14]

The most famous resident of Tarrytown was the author Washington Irving. In his *Legend of Sleepy Hollow*, named for the town which sits to the immediate north of Tarrytown, Irving adds to the controversy surrounding the derivation of the name Tarrytown by writing that the local housewives of the area had a part in it because their husbands had a tendency to "tarry" at the local village tavern on market days. This is disputed by at least one historian, who claims there was a local family of that name. A third, perhaps more reasonable version, is that the Dutch word for wheat is "terwe." Wheat being an important crop in the area, it was not long before this commercially viable location along the Hudson became the mispronounced offspring of Terre (wheat) Town.[15] Whatever the derivation of its name, in 1892 a residence on Wildey Street in the village of Tarrytown, New York, became the permanent home of John Collins and his family.[16]

For a young man of five, this larger town, situated as it was on a slope that rises in height to give a panoramic view of the widest expanse of the Hudson, must have seemed wondrous. In the winter deep snows engulfed the town, affording opportunity for snow forts and snowball fights. Then too there were the sleigh rides and, in this last era before the automobile, the carriage rides. In an area sprinkled with the rich and powerful, many of the carriages could only be described as ornate.

For Eddie Collins, Tarrytown was where he "played baseball with the kids in the neighborhood every possible chance."[17] It was also where he received an excellent education. Unlike most of his friends, he was enrolled in a local private college preparatory school, the Irving Institute.

The institute, later known as the Irving School, was the oldest private school in Westchester County, established in 1837 by William P. Lyon and his brother Charles. Washington Irving was a patron and the head of the school's board of examiners. Other well-known Americans, such as Daniel Webster, then Secretary of State William Cullen Bryant and Dr. William A. Duer, the president of Columbia University, served on the school's board of directors. As the years passed, the school developed a reputation as an English classical boarding school, and the sons of the wealthy from all over the nation arrived in Tarrytown by stagecoach and steamboat to attend the school.[18]

In 1891, four years prior to Eddie's arrival at the school, the Reverend John Myers Furman became owner and headmaster. He would serve the school until his death in 1933. Under his guiding hand, student enrollment increased. By 1927 the student body numbered 125. In general, the student's ages varied from 12 to 20 and most made the school their home. Since Eddie was a local boy and his parents, while certainly of some means, were not in the class of wealth of the majority of students enrolled, it is likely that for at least part if not all of the eight years he was schooled at Irving, he lived at home.

John and Mary Collins made whatever sacrifices necessary to afford their only son the opportunity for an education at the Irving School. The "object of the School" was stated thusly: "to develop strong, manly characters combined with general culture, and to provide through instruction in the studies leading to entrance at college; it has sent the representatives yearly to the leading universities and scientific schools."[19]

During the years Eddie attended the Irving Institute, it was located on Pocantico Street. Classes at the school were designed to be small enough to serve individual needs, yet large enough to encourage an *esprit de corps*. The school was Christian, but non-sectarian. The students attended either the Episcopal or the Reformed Church.[20] The course of study emphasized the classical and the scientific as a preparation for college.

Although the students at the institute carried a heavy workload, both time and facilities were provided for sports. There was a gymnasium and a ball field. And, despite its small student body, the institute fielded interscholastic teams, including a baseball team. Unfortunately, little is known of Collins' activities and accomplishments at the Irving Institute. What little baseball news graced the local newspapers concentrated on the public schools, particularly the Washington Irving High School in Tarrytown. As F.C. Lane, writer and eventual editor of *Baseball Magazine*, so eloquently put it, "Echoes of this period of his [Collins] life are few and meager."[21]

Although it is generally accepted that Collins was a shortstop in high school, a brief article which appeared locally in May 1903, his senior year, stated the following: "The Irving Institute baseball team suffered defeat at the hands of the Yonkers High School team on Saturday by a score of 11–10. It was a 10 inning game. Collins and McCormick were the battery for Irving."[22]

The notion of Eddie Collins, the pitcher, is not that far-fetched. In an interview with a reporter for the *New York Evening Telegram* in July 1918, Eddie confirms that, indeed, in those early days he was at times a pitcher. In one summer sandlot game, he even made some spare change for his troubles.

> It was less than a dollar, I believe. I don't recall the name of the opposing nine in that first game for which I received money for playing. It was one of the local "kid" aggregations and the battle was nip and tuck until the end. I was hit pretty hard on the mound, but finally my mates got the range of the opposing pitcher and we forged into the lead and held it until the end.

The foe got something like a dozen hits off me and bunched a lot of them in the third inning. I recall vaguely how I felt when we were so far behind, and it would not have taken much coaxing to have me abandon baseball forever. But luck changed in the after innings and we crept up until we finally went into the lead....

The Tarrytown Terrors was one of the kid teams with which I played in those days and one year — I do not recall the exact date — we made a run of twelve victories and considered ourselves quite unbeatable. I played every position of the nine during that run of victories.[23]

On one occasion some years later in an article in which noted sportswriter Hugh Fullerton discussed Collins' fiery temperament and competitive spirit, marveling at how he kept it under control, he revealed that there was one time the younger version of the baseball player lost it entirely — while pitching.

He was then pitcher for Irving School — pitcher, first batter, captain, and everything else. They were playing a Tarrytown team and winning until late in the game, when the Tarrytown boys discovered that the third baseman of the school team was about as good a fielder as a Stoughton bottle. They started hitting, bunting, and pushing the ball toward that poor third baseman and every ball went through him.

Collins, pitching harder and harder, was getting mad, and when the sixth bounder went through the third baseman Eddie threw a stone at the unfortunate player, chasing him out of the grounds. He probably has felt that way many times since, but either controlled his temper or failed to find a stone.[24]

In addition to baseball, Collins played football for the Irving Institute. During the fall of 1902, he was the school's right half back during a successful season.[25] His accomplishments at the school were such that sometime not long after his graduation, a medal was named in his honor, awarded annually to an Irving student who exhibited all-around proficiency in the classroom and on the playing fields; a prize that years later inspired another young baseballer at Irving who would play a big part in the Eddie Collins saga.

The 1903 prep baseball season was the last for Collins at the Irving Institute. Although little is known of his time at the school, there is no doubt the education he received there, both inside and outside the classroom, played an important part in the development of Eddie Collins, the man. At the school the youth studied alongside, played with, and befriended the future captains of industry and government of the land. In so doing it is likely he breathed in a good deal of aristocratic air, a substance which gave him a quiet confidence, even a trace of aloofness, which would not go unnoticed as he moved along life's path. Through similar processes he developed the characteristics of a leader. He began to nourish an interest in the management side of corporate life, one who manages as opposed to one who is managed. In short, during his time at the institute, he became "an Irving man."

As Eddie experienced significant change during his eight years of preparatory education, his parents John and Mary Collins experienced significant change as well. They were religious people, attending the First Baptist Church in Tarrytown for many years. During this time the family moved from their original Wildey Street residence to 90 North Broadway, the main business street in Tarrytown.[26] In addition, in 1900 John retired from the New York Central Railroad after more than thirty years. Over those years he built a solid reputation, even befriending Cornelius Vanderbilt, the railroad tycoon, and Chauncey Depew, a United States senator and chairman of the board of the New York Central. But the time had come to move on, for an opportunity beckoned to pursue a job closer to home. John became the registrar of the Tarrytown Board of Water Commissioners, a job he held until his death. One of his duties was to issue the bills for water service to the utilities customers. As such he became a well-known figure in town and a member of many local organizations, including the Masons and the Lyceum. An outgoing man with a muscular physique and an erect bearing, Eddie Collins' father "ate everything and smoked cigars all his life."[27]

In the spring of 1903, John and Mary looked on with justifiable pride as their son Eddie received his high school diploma from Irving. It was now time to put those many years of college preparation to work. In a matter of weeks, Eddie Collins would become a fixture in the classroom and on the playing fields of another institution, matriculating to one of the nation's largest and most prestigious schools, Columbia University.

CHAPTER 2

Columbia's Finest

"Joe McGinnity pitched for the Giants; I got a base hit off him. That hit meant more to me then than any hit I have ever made since.... It fired me with the ambition to play big league ball.

— Eddie Collins[1]

In miles traveled, Eddie Collins did not go far to obtain his college education, but the twenty-five or so miles from Tarrytown to the campus of Columbia University felt as if they were several continents removed. In 1900 Tarrytown was a mere village, while New York City was a metropolis in a constant state of population explosion. In contrast to the almost pastoral setting of Collins' small hometown on the Hudson, the streets of the city that would become his new home for most of the next four years were lined with tall buildings, large factories, museums, fine restaurants, and theatres, and offered residence to a vast mixture of humanity of every race, religion, and ethnic origin.

In 1903 Columbia, the biggest school in the nation's largest city, was second nationally only to Harvard in size and widely considered among the country's finest centers for higher learning. Founded in 1754 as King's College, it owed its existence to charter by the King of England. Shortly after the American Revolution, the college received its present name. After several moves the main campus relocated in 1897 to the area of the city known as Morningside Heights at 116th Street and Broadway. This was its location in the fall of 1903 when Collins arrived on campus hoping to make his mark academically and athletically. It did not take him long to establish the latter. By mid–October Eddie was listed among a group of 11 men reporting to Coach Richards for freshmen football practice. A schedule of five games was on the season's bill of fare.

Despite his decidedly small stature — he was at least an inch shorter than his stated 5 foot 9 inches and he weighed less than 140 pounds — Collins' interest in football was intense. He played the sport in high school and he intended to play it in college, as well. He truly loved the sport. In fact, "[at] that time I liked football better than I liked baseball...."[2]

On October 21 Collins, a halfback in high school, saw his college action at quarterback for the frosh, and also handled kickoffs in a scoreless tie with DeLaSalle. His first score came when he kicked a point-after-touchdown in a close win over Horace Mann. While several of the games were with local teams, both high school and prep, the big game for the Columbia freshmen was the November 3 clash with major-college rival Penn. Although Eddie was listed as slightly injured prior to the game, he shared quarterback duties in a 5–5 tie.

The final game of the season for the Blue and White undoubtedly carried special meaning for Eddie. Not only was he now the captain of his team, the first of many such captaincies for the athlete, but his team's opponent was none other than his alma mater, the Irving

School. If the Columbia quarterback felt nostalgia as he lined up against some of his former schoolmates and teammates, it did not show in the score, a 24–0 Columbia victory. In the game Collins kicked four extra points for his new charges. The victory ended the season for the freshmen at 2-1-2. The 1903 Columbia varsity was 9–1, including seven shutouts.

Now that football season was over, Collins could turn his full attention to his school work. Although Columbia provided studies in degree tracks for science, mechanical engineering and several other majors, Eddie was listed as a student in the "college," indicating a general course of study. If he entered college with an intended course of study, he kept it to himself, although from time to time he indicated the possibility of a law career, a career track favored by his parents. It seems from comments made during his stay at Columbia that Collins was a serious student; nonetheless, his campus activities were not limited to the classroom and the playing field. He soon joined his school's Alpha Alpha Chapter of Beta Theta Pi fraternity.

Studies and fraternity life kept Collins busy until the spring of 1904 when he made his first imprint on a college baseball diamond. It was February 4 and the Columbia coach, Howard J. Earle, a former player-manager for a minor league professional team in the New York State League, was receiving candidates for both the varsity and the freshmen baseball squads. Collins reported with the freshmen to a tryout that was held in the gym due to inclement weather. The first game with Pratt Institute was more than seven weeks away. During that time Eddie must have done a great deal to catch his coach's eye as he earned a starting slot on the varsity squad. He did it the hard way. During a practice game between the

freshmen and the varsity, he banged out three hits against the school's top hurler and covered enough ground in the field to convince his coach he was ready. It was a move the men of Morningside Heights would not regret.

On March 30 Collins, no longer a pitcher, was the left-handed hitting and right-handed throwing starting shortstop on the Columbia varsity as it defeated Pratt, 14–4. Brown-haired, blue-eyed Eddie, not yet 17 and still wet behind his very large ears, did not hit safely, but reached base enough to score two runs and do "particularly good work at short-stop, accepting three almost impossible chances without an error."[3]

Despite his solid play, Collins did not appear in the next game, a lopsided win over New York University. Against Trinity he appeared briefly, as a late-game replacement at second base. Before that game the young infielder received some pointers from Billy Lauder. In 1902 and 1903, Lauder was a third baseman for the New York Giants of the National League. In the spring of 1904, he was sharing his expertise with the Columbia nine.

South Field was the home field for Columbia in 1904. On April 13 Columbia took both its gear and its home field advantage to the Polo Grounds, the home of the Giants, where they faced off against

Collins as a senior at Columbia University, New York City. He graduated in 1907 (University Archives and Columbiana Library, Columbia University).

a strong Yale squad. This was the fourth version of the famous ball yard. The configuration was such that the occupants of carriages could watch the game from their coach. It is not certain anyone in a carriage watched this particular game, but if they did, they saw that Collins was back in the lineup batting second and once again playing second base. The Eli pitcher, Mackey, however, was a good one, and neither Eddie nor his teammates could generate a run, falling 1–0. Eddie was not one of the Columbia players with a hit and, in fact, was removed in the bottom of the ninth for a pinch-hitter.

The next day is one for the Eddie Collins' scrapbook, if he kept one. Eddie and his mates took on the major leagues' New York Giants. This time the turf, as well as the game, belonged to the professionals. When all was said and done it was no contest. The Giants prevailed, 9–1. Still this was not a giveaway. The Giants played some of their regulars and this 1904 team was one of the organization's best. At season's end they would possess 106 wins and a National League flag. There was no World Series that season or they might well have added that trophy to their honors. But Eddie Collins for one was not stared down. Playing second base again and hitting sixth, he stowed away a lifelong memory.

The boys from Columbia were spared one hurdle that sunny afternoon; they did not have to face the great hurler Christy Mathewson. Their challenge, however, was almost as daunting. They faced another star pitcher, Joe McGinnity, in the midst of a 35–8 season in which his earned run average was 1.61. Since it was an exhibition game, McGinnity gave way to Hooks Wiltse, himself a 13–3 thrower in 1904. And as was the case in exhibition games in those days, the Giants' regulars for the most part were on the field the entire game to stare down the collegians.

Collins recalled that their big league opponents fielded "many Giants in ability as well as in stature...." In addition to Mathewson and McGinnity, the roster included recognizable names like Bresnahan, Dahlen, McGann and Taylor. The collegians could only touch the Giants' pitching for a pair of hits, but Eddie garnered one of them and left the playing field feeling "quite a hero."[4]

Front and center for Collins' performance was the great Giants manager John McGraw. Although McGraw was an astute judge of talent, Eddie apparently did not impress him with the hit. Perhaps it was the freshman's two errors.

The remainder of Columbia's 1904 baseball season was not quite as exciting from a big-league aspect, yet overall it was quite satisfactory for the team and for its freshman infielder. The final season record was 11–3. Season-ending wins over Syracuse and Penn were highlights. As the season progressed, Collins settled in at shortstop and often found himself hitting in the lead-off slot. He also found his batting eye. In a 6–1 win over Rutgers, he had two hits, including a lead-off home run. Against Syracuse he had three hits and scored two runs.

A victory over Manhattan was deceiving. In the last half of the ninth with two out, a runner on third and Manhattan ahead 4–3, it appeared the Columbia batter watched a called third strike to end the game. The umpire seemed to signal as such, then reversed and said it was ball three. While the Manhattan team and many of its rooters stormed the field to argue with the umpire, the Columbia runner scored from third to tie the game. Manhattan protested and left the field, forfeiting the game to the Blue and White by a score of 9–0.

All in all for Eddie Collins, 1904 served as a great launching pad for his college baseball career. In summarizing the 1904 season, *The Columbian*, the school yearbook, commended freshman E.T. Collins for "doing particularly good work."[5]

Having established himself as a football player by both captaining and quarterbacking the 1903 freshmen squad at Columbia, Eddie Collins had a bright future in football as well as baseball, as the varsity prepared for its 1904 gridiron schedule. However, when the list of candidates for football was issued, Collins' name was not among them. Nor did he join the team at a later date. Whether this inactivity was due to health, grades, parental restriction, or some other less obvious reason, remains a mystery. It does not appear that Collins' physical condition played a role since on November 3, 1904, he participated in the freshman and sophomore track meet and tied for first in the 100-yard dash in a time of 11.2 seconds.[6]

If Collins' football career was finished, or just on hold, the exact opposite was true of baseball. On February 15, 1905, when Columbia met for its first spring workout, Eddie was present, ready to renew his claim as the team's shortstop and lead-off batter. When the candidates reported, there was one big change from the previous year. The Columbia varsity was now coached by Billy Lauder, the former big leaguer who began assisting the team in 1904.

Eddie Collins could have drawn much worse for a coach than William Lauder. Born in Norwalk, Connecticut, or thereabouts, in February 1874, Billy was college educated, graduating from Brown. After a stint in the old Connecticut League, he joined the Philadelphia Phillies of the National League in 1898, becoming one of the first college boys to play major league baseball. He played third base for the Phillies in 1898 and again in 1899, when he appeared in 151 games, drove in 90 runs and batted .268. In 1901 he jumped to the fledgling American League and its Philadelphia Athletics franchise, where he appeared in only two games. He then returned to the National League and spent 1902 and 1903 with the New York Giants as their third baseman. In 1903, his last year in organized baseball, he appeared in 108 games, drove in 53 runs, stole 19 bases and batted .281. Why he left the game at the highly serviceable age of 29 is open to conjecture, but in 1904 the steady, slick-fielding Art Devlin took over at third base for the injured Roger Bresnahan and held that position for the Giants until 1911.

As the coach at Columbia, Lauder had much to offer a young infielder such as Collins. The new coach had knowledge of the professional game in all its aspects, as an infielder, a base runner and a batter. A mastery of each of these fundamentals of the game was particularly important in this, the era of the "dead ball." In its heyday, dead ball baseball emphasized strategy over power. A player made his mark in the sport by knowing how to steal a

Collins starred at the plate and in the infield for Columbia University from 1904 to 1906. He was elected team captain for 1907. However, prior to that season he was declared ineligible by the university for playing semipro baseball during the summer of 1906 (University Archives and Columbiana Library, Columbia University).

base, execute a hit-and-run play, and lay down a sacrifice bunt. These plays permitted a base runner to advance an extra base or two, thus scoring a run that carried added value in a day of low scoring against powerful pitching. Billy Lauder understood the intricacies of this game, as well as what it took for a collegian to enter and survive the rough and tumble professional game of the early 1900s. Before he was through, Lauder's ability to bring the game of baseball to young men found him also head coach at his alma mater, Brown, as well as Williams and Yale. He was not Eddie Collins' first baseball coach and he would not be his last, but in later years Eddie would name Billy Lauder as one of the three most influential men in his initial development as a baseball player.[7]

It is not so surprising that Lauder would choose Columbia for his first post-baseball employment. Although the term "Ivy League" would not be coined until the early 1930s, baseball had long been played at the schools that eventually made up the league. In addition to Columbia, this included Harvard, Princeton, Yale, Cornell, Dartmouth, Brown, Penn, and, until 1945, army. Furthermore, the level of play at these schools was so strong that practice games, like the one between the Giants and Columbia in 1904, were frequent. As a result, over the years a number of ball players from these schools found themselves in the major leagues in short order. One such player from Columbia was future Hall of Fame member John Montgomery Ward, who played his professional ball for New York's National League teams in the late 1800s and later used his Columbia law degree for the betterment of the individual player versus management.

It is uncertain whether or not Billy Lauder thought he had any Hall of Fame prospects on his 1905 edition of the Columbia baseball team. He did have a good number of candidates for the squad, 30 for the varsity and 15 freshmen, enough in fact to form two teams and let them square off against each other for playing time. He also instituted a training table for 15 of his players, including Collins. The players met daily in the Commons for lunch, as much to discuss baseball as to manage their diet. Previously, the training table at Columbia was limited to the football team.

The first game of the season, on April 1, saw a lopsided 25–0 win over Polytechnic Institute. Lead-off hitter Collins hit safely twice and scored five of those runs. He scored three more in a 14–5 win over Xavier in the next outing, getting three hits. On April 11 the Blue and White were scheduled to play the New York Highlanders of the still-maturing American League. The game was postponed due to rain. The game against a tough opponent, a team now better known as the Yankees, might have helped Lauder's team prepare for its first real regular-season test against a powerful Yale team. That game was played in New Haven on April 15 and at least 100 students accompanied the Columbians to cheer them to victory; however, the extra support was not enough. Collins led off the game by striking out, setting the tenor in a 2–1 loss. Eddie did collect one of two Columbia hits. Attendance for the game was an impressive 3,000. Following the game, the *New York Times* advised readers that "Collins, the popular short stop of last year's team, is about the only man who is sure of a permanent position...."[8]

Collins continued to impress as his team reeled off consecutive wins over New York University, West Point, Penn and Syracuse, the last three on the road. In each of these games, the young Columbia shortstop played errorless ball. Batting out of the third slot against NYU, Eddie tripled.

Columbia's modest four-game streak came to an end on May 7 at Ithaca, New York, when the men from Morningside Heights were shut down by Cornell, 5–0. One of the four Columbia hits was another Collins triple. On May 9 Coach Lauder took his charges for a workout at American League Park, home of the Highlanders. The practice proved worthwhile as his squad ran off consecutive wins against Wesleyan, Crescent A.C. and Penn, the latter a

The 1905 Columbia University varsity baseball team. Collins is seated on the ground to the right. The other players are not identified (University Archives and Columbiana Library, Columbia University).

10–0 success at American League Park. The same venue saw the Columbians face off in a rematch with Cornell. Despite the repeat opportunity, however, Columbia lost again, this time 3–2. Collins had a hit but also committed one of his few errors of the season.

The Blue and White returned to its winning ways with victories over Montclair and Fordham. In the latter game, a 5–4 victory over the cross-town rivals, Eddie hit a home run in the first inning.

The remainder of the 1905 season was played out on the road during a trip through New England. On the whole, despite stops at several picturesque campuses, the venture was a disaster, resulting in two wins and five losses. The victories were at Amherst and Andover, while the losses included a double-bill bashing at Dartmouth and single disappointments at Vermont and Harvard. The final contest was an embarrassing 9–0 loss at Brown. That defeat left the Columbia team at 13–8 as the season came to a close.

If the 1905 college baseball season was not all Billy Lauder wanted for his team, it was an important year in the development of Eddie Collins. By season's end, he was established as a star of the team. Although actual statistics are not available, it is said he batted .400 for the year.[9] Furthermore, his performance caught the eye of more than just his coach. The Columbia team trainer in 1905 was Mique (Mike) Martin, a Latin American who doubled as a trainer for the Highlanders during that time. Later, for many years, he was the trainer for the Washington Senators. Although Clark Griffith would eventually become a fixture in Washington, in 1905 the future Hall-of-Famer was the manager of the New York Highlanders and Martin's boss. Years later Martin told this story:

"Why, I am the trainer at Columbia in 1905, and we have a little second baseman who is muy fast, muy hitter. Bueno! I am close to Señor Griffith, which is then the manager of the New York Yankees. I recommend this little second basemen, which his name is Eddie Collins. Si, the same Collins.

"Mr. Griffith says: 'this college boy, he varee [*sic*] much too small for the American League.' This pains me varee much...."[10]

Señor Martin was not the only one recommending Collins to the Highlanders. Tom McAvoy, once a police commissioner of New York City and a contractor involved in building the first Highlanders' ballpark in Manhattan, heard about Collins and went to the Columbia campus to watch him play. Once a great Giant fan, McAvoy was now a staunch Highlander supporter. Liking what he saw of Eddie, McAvoy too approached Griffith.

The glowing recommendations of both Martin and McAvoy brought Collins a brief morning workout. Perhaps it was just his size as Martin claims, or maybe there was something else about the young man that failed to impress Griffith, but after a short time the former pitching star waved the erstwhile candidate off the field.[11] Would it have made a difference if the exhibition game between Columbia and the Highlanders had taken place as scheduled on April 11? No one will ever know for sure.

What the fans of Columbia athletics did know was that Eddie Collins was a fixture on their baseball team. Football seemed a thing of the past for their baseball star as the varsity gridiron squad met in late September 1905 to practice in preparation for what many were calling the toughest football schedule in school history. When the coaching staff greeted approximately 39 candidates for the varsity, Collins was once again not among them. The four quarterbacks who would perform for head coach William R. Morley included a lad named William J. Donovan, who won the starting slot.

The season began for Columbia with shutout wins over Union College and Seton Hall. In a follow-up story to the Seton Hall tussle, the *New York Times* reported a disturbing number of injuries sustained by players during the game, pointing to a disparity in size between the much lighter Seton Hall players and the heavier Columbians as the culprit. There were reports in 1904 of an increase nationally in football injuries. The alarming trend was now spreading into the 1905 season. Many in the nation were concerned about the so-called brutality of football. There were reports of at least 18 deaths at all levels of the sport in 1905, as many as three in the college game. That concern reached all the way to the White House. President Theodore Roosevelt, a Harvard graduate, invited the presidents and athletic representatives of football's "Big Three," Harvard, Yale and Princeton, to a meeting at the White House in October 1905, where he urged serious consideration of reforms at the next annual meeting of the Football Association. The president's call, though meritorious, was met with much skepticism by the college administrators. Charles W. Eliot, Harvard's president, felt it would be particularly difficult to bring about the reform "through the very men who have long known about the existing evils and have been largely responsible for their continuance."[12]

The power structure at Columbia, at least the academic base, shared these concerns, as well as a concern that the sport of football was a distraction from what many still considered the main reason for attending college: an education. Therefore, on October 11, three members of the 1905 Columbia varsity were dropped from the team, including the team captain, who was also dismissed from school. There were rumors that another eight players were on the verge of ineligibility. The *New York Times* called the school's action a "wholesale slaughter of Columbia's football hopes...."[13]

It is mere conjecture, but it is reasonable to assume that the academic upheaval in the Columbia program, plus the continuing loss of manpower due to injury, led to the appearance of Eddie Collins at the varsity football practice on October 16. The school newspaper announced that the former quarterback of the freshman team "was out for practice and showed up well in running the scrub [sic]."[14] At the time Columbia's record stood at 3-0-1 by virtue of a scoreless tie with Wesleyan and an 11–5 win over Williams.

Collins' first opportunity for varsity play was a scheduled clash with Amherst on October 21. A big crowd was present on a fall Saturday made for football. Although William Donovan started for the Blue and White and played most of the game, Coach Morley must have seen something in Collins that caught his fancy. Even though Eddie had practiced less than a week, Morley inserted him into the lineup at quarterback in the second half with Columbia down 10–7. Collins quickly asserted himself, moving the chains for a first down on a quarterback keeper. When the drive stalled, he punted out of bounds on Amherst's 25-yard line. Then, with less than a minute to play, Amherst fumbled on the 28-yard line and Columbia recovered. There was just enough time for a field goal. The Columbia kicker sent it through the uprights for a tie as time ran out, and the students mobbed the field.

Now the schedule toughened. As Collins recalled it, "We had a hard schedule that year and we met unusually strong opposition. That was the season that both Yale and Penn had championship teams. Both if I remember were unscored on through the season."[15]

First up, however, was another tough nut in Princeton. Before that game could be played, controversy struck Columbia yet again when the *New York Times* reported that Coach Morley was under investigation by the Columbia school authorities for an incident that occurred during the Wesleyan game. Morley was a consensus All-American quarterback and team captain at Columbia during his college days. While standing on the sidelines coaching during the Wesleyan game, Morley thought he saw a Wesleyan player jump upon one of his Columbia players after that player was already down. In an effort to defend his player, Morley ran onto the field and jumped into the fray, arms swinging. Later, the beleaguered coach claimed he was only trying to separate players from the two teams. Whether or not he struck the Wesleyan player as alleged was never fully determined, but the incident was widely reported and condemned.[16] Although the investigation did not result in discipline for the coach, it was additional fodder for those in the Columbia administration who felt football's glass was overflowing and creating an unsightly mess for their beloved university.

Still, by the following Saturday, the only thing that mattered was the big contest with Princeton. William Donovan started as the Columbia signal caller, but he was again replaced by Collins in the second half, this time due to a knee injury. As was often the case in those days, since the forward pass was not yet legal, quarterbacks ran and kicked. Eddie did both, but unlike Amherst the result was not so good. The final score saw Columbia on the losing end, 12–0.

On the Monday following the Princeton game, the majority of varsity players were given the day off. Collins, on the other hand, now due for more playing time because of Donovan's injury, was asked to report for duty. At the session he was given instruction in punting and drop kicks. He showed accuracy with regularity at 35 yards. On November 1 the lineup for the upcoming game against powerful Yale indicated the Columbia quarterback as Eddie Collins. A simple line in the November 4 school newspaper mentioned the switch at quarterback was one of several contemplated lineup changes. No reason for the change was furnished, but there is indication that Donovan still suffered from a wrenched knee.

When Yale and Columbia met in New York on Saturday, November 4 before a crowd estimated at 10,000–15,000, it became quickly apparent Coach Morley did not bestow favor upon his new quarterback. The game was no contest. Columbia's offensive attack consisted mainly of punts to the opponent after a series of unsuccessful drives. Collins added to his squad's distress when he fumbled a punt. He did return two others for 12 and 30 yards, respectively, but that was about it for the first-time starter. When the final whistle blew with Columbia on the short end of a 58–0 score, Coach Morley must have issued a sigh of relief. When the statistics were totaled, Columbia's rushing attack showed six yards for the afternoon, none in the second half. As to Eddie Collins, however, the *New York Times* was kind, telling readers, "there were one or two little shafts of light which lighted this dark picture. One of them was the thirty-yard quarterback run of the auburn-haired Collins, after the Yalens had failed to bring him down when he had caught a punt."[17]

The *New York Times* had spotted something. It was the same thing Coach Billy Lauder recognized, and more recently Coach Morley. As a vastly undersized football player even for the era, Collins exhibited an air of self–confidence and pluckiness that would continue to serve him throughout life. It became his trademark, and it began as much as any day on that fall afternoon in 1905. An unidentified witness to the game saw Collins run that "30 yards against Yale through men who loomed about him like sequoias," never signaling for a fair catch, though it was the wise thing to do, but instead keeping his balance by churning his quick feet and when finally brought down, arising quickly from the mass of humanity ready for the next play.[18]

Collins' quick ascension on the football field, however, was not the only thing creating some extracurricular excitement in the fall of 1905. The hometown Giants of baseball's National League, those same Giants Collins and Columbia faced only one year before, were embroiled in a World Series battle with the neighboring Philadelphia Athletics under the direction of Connie Mack. Even though it required missing a class and a football practice, Eddie decided to attend Game Two at the Polo Grounds on October 10. Although he had played baseball for years by now, this was the first professional game he ever attended. A Giants fan, he was bitterly disappointed as he watched a Chippewa Indian named Chief Bender completely throttle the Giants with a four-hit, 3–0 shutout. Eddie, who sat in the bleachers, like most young athletes must have imagined himself on that field, yet as he said later, "little did I dream that I would one day be an actor in a drama of like character...."[19]

Back on the football field, two games remained on Columbia's schedule. Next up was Cornell, after a week off. During that time Collins further solidified his hold on the quarterback position. Donovan, still undoubtedly hampered by his injury, was now clearly the backup. If this discouraged the college senior, it did not show up in the long run. In fact, down the road much would be heard from William J. Donovan. Nicknamed "Wild Bill" by his Columbia teammates, the moniker stuck throughout the years as Donovan went on to earn a Columbia law degree and become a World War I Medal of Honor winner. Later, as a member of a prestigious Wall Street law firm and an intimate of a fellow Columbia Law graduate named Franklin Delano Roosevelt, "Wild Bill" served during World War II as head of the Office of Strategic Services, better known as the OSS. As such, he was essentially in charge of the United States' intelligence community during the war. Since the OSS was the predecessor of the Central Intelligence Agency, "Wild Bill" Donovan is commonly considered its father. There is no question "Wild Bill" Donovan put together a brilliant resume. But in 1905, as the Columbia football team prepared to regroup and meet Cornell, Donovan sat while Eddie Collins played.

In order to meet Cornell, the Columbia team and about 100 students traveled to their opponent's home field in Ithaca, New York. Collins' leadership, kicking and running were the basis of an important victory. "[W]e were repaid in some measure for these setbacks (Yale and Princeton) by a hard-fought victory over Cornell by the score of 12–6. This was the best game that I [Collins] ever played."[20]

One game remained on the schedule: powerful Penn. The only mar on Penn's season to date was a tie with Lafayette. Practices were particularly intense. The game stirred interest in the Columbia student body as well. The last practice, a session at American League Park, the site of the next day's contest, drew more than a thousand student supporters, who practiced the songs and cheers to be used during the event.

On Saturday, November 25, this same student contingent arrived at the stadium via special subways. Their enthusiasm was dampened only by the game itself. During the week between the Cornell game and this one, much of the luster faded from Collins' game, most notably his kicking. As a result, Columbia frequently ceded field position to the Quakers. Even a fake punt resulted in only a few yards. He fared only somewhat better on his punt returns. The overall result was a devastating 23–0 loss, leaving Columbia's record for 1905 at 4-3-2. Still, prospects were good for 1906, with most of the team, including their newfound

quarterback, returning. In Collins' opinion, "[p]rospects at Columbia looked good...." Football, not baseball, was Collins' real game. "The most pleasant memories I have of college sports are of that year of varsity football."[21]

Thus, it must have come as a severe blow to Collins when, a mere three days after the loss to Penn, Columbia president Nicholas Murray Butler announced that the school was abolishing football. The decision by one of the nation's largest and most important universities shook the sports world and reverberated from coast to coast. The determination was based on not only the many injuries suffered by the 1905 Columbia squad — only three regulars, including Collins, escaped some type of reported injury — it took into account the sport's negative impact on academics. And, quite frankly, the latter issue had been irritating the school's academicians for some time.

Columbia's problems with football began as early as 1899, involving payment for services of players and an accompanying coverup. In 1902 a squabble broke out between a football committee and a faculty committee over disqualification of a star player. And then in 1905 there was, of course, the charge against Coach Morley for allegedly striking an opposing player in the Wesleyan game. Even if Coach Morley's actions were well intentioned, they were unacceptable to school administrators and represented another large nail in the program's coffin.[22]

Football was Collins' first love. Pictured here in his Columbia football gear, he showed real promise in 1905 as a varsity quarterback. However, at the close of the season his football career ended as the sport was banned by the university (University Archives and Columbiana Library, Columbia University).

Columbia, however, was not the only school taking a hard look at football in 1905 as a continuing intercollegiate entity. Teddy Roosevelt's concerns have been discussed. Even President Butler initially tried to reform the sport with a gentle push from within by contacting Harvard president Eliot and urging him to work with Walter Camp's Rules Committee, the existing authority for the sport, to institute significant change. But Eliot was firm in his refusal to join in any effort to reform the sport through that committee.

Now that Columbia's bold stand was front-page news, other schools quickly joined the fray. New York University called a meeting for December 8, 1905, at a New York City hotel to discuss whether the game of football as presently constituted should be abolished. Columbia attended the meeting along with 12 others and attempted to convince those others to vote in the affirmative. Union, NYU, Stevens and Rochester agreed; the remaining universities did not. More importantly, Harvard, Yale and Princeton, those major powers, did not even attend the meeting. Instead, Harvard took a leadership position in traveling a different path. A separate committee was formed that eventually negotiated with the Camp Committee. The result was a set of rules and reforms which satisfied Harvard and left only one major football school out in the cold: Columbia.

As one would expect, the decision to abandon any sport, particularly such a popular sport as intercollegiate football, did not sit well with the Columbia student body. The staff of the student newspaper reacted immediately. On November 29 the editorial staff of the *Columbia Spectator* agreed that "sweeping changes" to the sport were needed to reduce the risk of serious injury. In the newspaper's opinion, the university was well within its rights to recommend such changes, "but to absolutely abolish the game is not necessary and is uncalled for." The newspaper called for a mass meeting of students in order to issue a formal protest.[23]

President Butler, by letter dated December 1 to the alumni and students of the university, responded by saying those in charge of formulating the rules of football permitted it to become a profession rather than a sport. "It demands prolonged training, complete absorption of time and thought and is inconsistent — in practice at least — with the devotion to work which is the first duty of the college or university student." Furthermore, "the experience of years has shown that the rules [Camp] committee do not desire to reform it."[24]

The Columbia student body remained unconvinced. A mass meeting of students was set for December 5; Coach Morley and team members were asked to appear. Over 800 students filled Earl Hall on campus for a meeting which aroused great passion and resulted in a resolution asking the administration to reconsider its action. In what now appears to be an obvious effort to avoid serious unrest, the school agreed to consider the petition carefully. As mentioned, however, on December 8 representatives of Columbia attended the NYU Conference in New York City and asserted their conviction to abolish the sport on their campus. Just in case that vote did not send a clear enough message, another was sent in a letter to the editor of the *Columbia Spectator* from the Student Board of Representatives. The lengthy letter, printed in the December 18 edition of the student paper, refused to consider a request by the students to buy more time until a final decision was made. Thus, when the University Council met on December 19 to discuss and vote on the students' petition for reconsideration, the die was already cast. The students' frustration was further fueled when the administration delayed announcing its final ruling until most of the students were off-campus for the Christmas holiday. The decision was formally announced on December 21, 1905, with the University Council adopting the previous recommendations of the various controlling powers within the school and abolishing the sport. In a few short weeks, the school rode full circle from an attempt by its president to enlist the support of Harvard in reforming football from within, to a decision abolishing it in the face of serious efforts, albeit delayed, by Harvard and the vast majority of other schools to initiate radical reform. Football did not reappear on the Columbia agenda as an intercollegiate sport until 1915.

The loss of football, a game he dearly loved, came as a serious blow to 18-year-old Eddie Collins. After totally scrubbing the sport in 1904, he had returned to the game and had become a major player at quarterback. Prospects for his final year were promising. Now his football career was ended just as abruptly as a career-ending injury.

In sum, Eddie's varsity college career totaled fewer than four games. Interestingly, over the years the written accounts of Collins' limited gridiron exploits were repeated and grew more effusive each time, until those achievements fell just short of All-American status. Given his final year of eligibility, perhaps that might have happened. That it did not, in the long run, did little to lessen his stature. In the future Collins would be forced to confine his athletic endeavors to the baseball diamond. It was not as much fun for him as football, but it would just have to do.

CHAPTER 3

Summer Job

> "I thought the affair was a joke, and believed the scout in question was someone who was trying to kid me; but at any rate I did no business with him."
>
> — Eddie Collins[1]

If the hierarchy at Columbia was seriously concerned about the intrusion of sports into academics, and they were, they did not need to concern themselves with Eddie Collins. Eddie was a serious student who was thinking about a career in law. The short baseball tryout and quick dismissal by the Highlanders did little to foster a belief that a career in baseball was the answer.

Eddie studied hard, but he liked to have some fun, too. The story is told that one snowy winter day Collins, now an upperclassman, spotted a lowly freshman student walking across the Columbia campus wearing a brown derby. Apparently the custom of the day was for freshmen to wear caps at all times. In the opinion of Collins and his friends, a black derby might pass the test, but this fellow's brown derby clearly did not. Seeing the poor fellow and his hat from a distance some 75 yards away, Eddie packed a snowball and flung it with unerring accuracy, cleanly striking the derby off the stunned wearer's head. According to the storyteller, Collins was no bully. It was not his style. He was, however, "the only man who could throw that far."[2] This was an interesting comment since in future years, Collins was often criticized for having an average arm.

In the spring of 1906, Coach Billy Lauder was back, and so was his prized junior shortstop Edward T. Collins. The weather in March did not cooperate with Lauder's baseball program, so practices were held indoors, resulting in a lot of cage work and little else. The season opened with a bang on April 5 with an easy win over the Pratt Institute at Columbia's South Field. Four days later Collins enjoyed a big day at the plate with a pair of doubles against an improving NYU team. Columbia won easily, 14–5.

Over Easter vacation the Columbia baseball players made a "southern" trip which took them to the Baltimore-Washington area. The trip included a stop at Annapolis for a 7–5 win over navy. Eddie had another big day, stealing six bases. One of his opponents, Robert A. Theobald, the captain of the Middies and later a Rear Admiral during World War II, recalled years later that Collins was perfect at bat, going 6-for-6.[3]

The southern excursion continued with a win over Johns Hopkins. In that one Collins continued his rampage on the bases with two more thefts. Columbia's record now stood at 4–0, but any visions of grandeur were dampened when the team traveled across Baltimore to meet that city's entry in the professional Eastern League and received a 20–0 lesson. Eddie stole another base in the exhibition game and two more in a trip-ending 5–3 win over George Washington. All told Eddie stole 11 bases on the trip.

Now the intercollegiate competition stiffened. First up was Rutgers at South Field. Once again Collins was a terror with a pair of hits and two stolen bases in a 6–4 victory. Wins over West Point and Penn followed. Eddie was on fire, his batting average to date residing at .594. The next highest Columbia regular was at .333. Then came Yale, a definite thorn in Columbia's side. The game was scheduled for April 28 at American League Park. A notice in the student newspaper proclaimed that it was each student's "duty" to attend the big game because, since "the abolition of football by the faculty, baseball has become the leading major at Columbia and should be supported in the same way football was supported."[4]

For six innings the Blue and White fought gamely and the score was tied at five. Then in the seventh the Columbia hurler lost his control. Seven runs later, Columbia sustained its first loss of the season. Collins for once did little to help his team's cause. In six at-bats he walked once, sacrificed successfully and scored a run, but committed an error.

Its initial loss sent Columbia into a tailspin. They lost 13 of their next 15 games, winning only one and tying the other. The season tally, including the exhibition with Baltimore, was a deflating 9-15-1. Throughout the losing streak, however, Collins held his own or better, continually getting on base or moving a runner along. By season's end his batting average for a second season hovered around .400. At the end of the season he was honored by his teammates with his selection as captain for the forthcoming 1907 campaign.

By now it was apparent to Columbia coach Billy Lauder that his star pupil, Collins, possessed big league potential. The kid could hit, run and throw with the best of them. Moreover, he seemed to understand the strategy of the game, excelling at laying down a bunt to move the runner, as well as taking an extra base. Best of all, he had something one could not really coach: great speed. All that he needed to play at the professional level was some extra seasoning. In order to help Eddie obtain that seasoning, Lauder turned to Billy Lush, coach of the Yale team that forced his Blue and White into such a sharp nose dive.

Like Coach Lauder, Billy Lush entered the college coaching circle at the end of a professional baseball career. By 1906 he was 32 years old. The native of Bridgeport, Connecticut, played all or part of seven seasons of major league ball, five in the National League with Washington and then Boston and a year each at Detroit and Cleveland of the American League in 1903 and 1904, respectively. He also had extensive minor league experience. Oddly enough, his most productive major league season was his last when he racked up a career high in hits and runs batted in. Always a light hitter, but useful as a speedy base runner who could field most every position, Lush was a good man to counsel an emerging talent like Collins. The two were alike in a number of ways. Both were small in physical stature; Lush was 5 feet 7 inches and 160 pounds. Both were Irish-American. And both had an early interest in law, Lush taking courses at Yale Law School. Before his college coaching career was completed, Lush was a baseball coach at Yale, Columbia, Fordham, the U.S. Naval Academy and St. John's College. He also coached basketball at Yale, the Naval Academy, NYU and St. John's College.

In 1906 Billy Lush took the bit from his friend Billy Lauder, making a proposition to Eddie Collins. He asked him to play summer ball for him on a semiprofessional team at Plattsburg, New York. The proposition was intriguing to young Eddie, but it carried a degree of risk. Most colleges frowned on their athletes receiving money for summer play. Some, however, looked the other way. It was doubtful that Columbia, given its track record on football, would be one of the lenient ones. Still Eddie accepted Lush's proposal. The reason was simple. He started playing for pay in 1906 because he needed expense money for his last collegiate year.[5]

With his decision to play for money made, Collins prepared to head to Plattsburg. On the way he took a detour. He stopped in Red Hook, New York, home of another semiprofessional club. One of his teammates there was Heinie Zimmerman. Collins would run into or, perhaps more precisely, away from Zimmerman many years later.[6] Another teammate on that Red Hook team, one who became a lasting friend, was Jack Coffey, who later became athletic director at Fordham. Eddie's stay in Red Hook, a small Dutchess County farming community a couple of hours north of New York City and even less distance from his birthplace in Millerton, was a short one. For his troubles he was paid $5 per game, his first real pay for play. By late June he was on his way to Plattsburg.

The arrival of the college hot shot from Columbia in this New York town situated on the west banks of sparkling Lake Champlain, just north of the Adirondack Mountains, was eagerly anticipated. Billy Lush signed a number of college players that summer for play in the Northern League in which Plattsburg belonged. The league itself was not affiliated with Organized Baseball. It was thus often termed an "outlaw" league. Still, there were no Jesse James sightings, and games proceeded in a civilized manner. Other league members were Mont-Barre, representing the cities of Montpelier and Barre, Vermont; Rutland, Vermont; Burlington, Vermont; and Ottawa, Canada. The majority of Rutland players were Holy Cross baseballers, while Eddie recognized several Penn players when he faced off with Burlington. Ottawa's lineup included collegians from Georgetown and Illinois, as well as players with previous professional and semiprofessional experience. In addition to Collins, Lush's team included players from Yale, Cornell, Brown and Dartmouth. But even among all these players, Collins was considered an important catch. Shortly after his arrival the *Plattsburg Daily Press* advised readers that "Collins at short is one of the best ever seen in this city, and will certainly become popular with the fans."[7] This time around Eddie received a bit more pay; he was set to earn $40 per week.

Despite the excitement over the prospects for a summer of highly competitive baseball in Plattsburg, there were storm clouds on the horizon. The team was organized and owned by a group of enterprising citizens known as the Base Ball Association. Funds to maintain and operate the franchise were dependent in the main on the sale of raffle tickets for an automobile. In order to raise enough money to support a full summer of semiprofessional baseball in the city, the sale of 1,500 raffle tickets was required. While the tickets were selling, there was no certainty that the goal could be reached. There was, fortunately, funding to begin the season. The first game was played on June 23, minus Collins and the rest of his squad. The team members either had not yet arrived or were not ready to play. Plattsburg's 6–0 loss was no surprise since the team was comprised entirely of members of the Plattsburg High School team.

On June 25, fully stocked with signed talent, the locals fared no better, succumbing to Burlington by a 5–1 count. The loss merely served to turn on the faucet for a string of similar defeats. Collins recalls he "played about fifteen games, as near as I can remember, and lost thirteen of these."[8] A review of local newspapers of the time supports Collins' memory. Although Eddie smacked the ball all over the diamond and held his own at shortstop, his new team "wasn't good, and that's being charitable."[9]

One team whose performance against Plattsburg was particularly galling was Rutland. On June 28 the Vermonters shut out the New Yorkers, 11–0. On the mound for Rutland was Fordham product Dick Rudolph, a right-handed spitballer who spun a three-hitter. One of the three hits was a triple by Collins. On another day the two would face off in another forum. In later years, Rudolph plied his trade in the National League for the Giants and later the Boston Braves, where he remained until 1927. His record included 122 regular-season wins, plus two in the World Series coupled with a 0.50 ERA. His appearance on the mound in the

Northern League in 1906 evidences the high caliber of play and goes a long way in explaining why the draw of the league was more than just the money. In addition to honing one's game against keen competition, there was always the chance of discovery. There were even reports that summer that Jimmy Collins, the great third baseman and then manager of the Boston Americans (Red Sox), was scouting the league.[10]

Some, but certainly not all, of Plattsburg's problems could be attributed to the late arrival that summer of Billy Lush. The manager did not arrive in town until July 1. When his team faced off against Rutland and Rudolph again on July 5, Lush and Collins formed the keystone combination and the team won, 6–5. Eddie garnered two of his side's seven hits in aiding the cause. A loss to Montpelier the next day dampened the enthusiasm and left the team with a 2–6 record. The main fault, according to local scribes, was weak pitching. Despite the losses, the local press was impressed with Collins' efforts. In a loss to Ottawa, the *Daily Press* lauded the steady play of Lush at second base, but told readers "it was for Collins to electrify the crowd in the fifth with a three bagger ... beyond the right field fence...."[11]

The losses, nevertheless, continued to mount in what for Collins and his teammates was becoming a discouraging experience. Some of the frustrations surfaced on the field. In an 11–4 loss to visiting Burlington on July 14, a game marred when a Burlington player hurled a baseball into a group of young boys cheering against him on the sideline, Eddie failed to hit and committed two errors. Two days later, his personal results were better, but not his team's, when Plattsburg fell again. The team's 2–13 record placed it dead last, six games behind fourth-place Mont-Barre and eight behind league-leader Burlington.

On July 18 a meeting was held in Burlington that should have cheered the heart of any man like Collins, who was trying to eke out a college payment plan with a summer of Northern League baseball. At the meeting league representatives voted to abolish the limit on the salaries of its players. There was, on the other hand, a serious cautionary note: Plattsburg's representative voted "no" on the proposal. A second cautionary note: Billy Lush was no longer the manager.

The managerial change did nothing to slow Plattsburg's fall. Collins hit well on July 20 in a 5–1 loss to Ottawa, but two days later he was the shortstop for Rutland. The reason: "Plattsburg has quit the Northern League for good. Manager Harry Gibbs had lots of confidence but no financial backing...."[12]

The loss of Plattsburg was not fatal. The Northern League continued to operate as a four-team league. Eddie Collins continued to play as well. The move to Rutland, a small town in central Vermont near the New York border, was not a major deal for a summer vagabond and, unlike Plattsburg, Eddie's new team had a winning record. His immediate insertion into the Rutland starting lineup was eased by the transfer of Dave Shean, a slick fielder and swift base runner, to second base. Collins and Shean quickly became friends, initiating a long and warm association.

Proceedings at Rutland, however, did not get off to a smooth start. In his first game, a 5–1 loss to Burlington, Collins committed a pair of errors and went hitless. He was only a bit better in a win over Ottawa, committing another error, but providing a hit.

Unlike Plattsburg, the Rutland team was run by a board of directors elected by shareholders. A few days after Eddie's arrival, reports surfaced that the team's manager, P.F. McMann, was on the local griddle. The board of directors thought their manager "too extravagant in signing so many men...." There was thought of releasing the popular manager, a move the local newspaper and the team opposed. According to the paper, by bringing in new men, McMann was "giving what the fans have been calling for — a strengthening."[13] There was talk the team was prepared to refuse to practice or play for a different manager.

There was little doubt as to the focal point of the dispute between the board and manager. On July 25 the *Rutland Daily Herald* reported that Eddie Collins "turned down an offer of $275 a month made by Ottawa to come to Rutland. He was out of a job after Plattsburg disbanded less than three minutes. [Montpelier-Barre] wanted him also...."[14]

As the summer stretched into late July, Collins became more comfortable with his team and they with him. On July 25 he helped defeat league leader Burlington with a pair of hits, a steal and flawless fielding. Dave Shean was getting his share of hits and stolen bases, too. Still it appeared that Rutland was in for a roller coaster ride. On July 27 a note appeared in the *Rutland Daily Herald* that Billy Lush, Eddie's manager in Plattsburg, was now playing third base for Rockville, Connecticut. On August 2 the paper reported attendance for a home game with Montpelier-Barre was 534, a season low. The team's record stood at 12–11.

Even though many of the players in the Northern League were college players, they were paid for their trouble. In the eyes of the Rutland fans, they were professionals. As such they could quickly go from the town heroes to the town bums. One Rutland fan wrote to the local newspaper, "What do you think of three professional baseball players that will walk up to the slab, and let a poor 'comrade' die on third? Why, you could go out to the hay-field and get three men that would do that well."[15]

Although it is uncertain whether or not Collins was the target of the acid letter writer, he was the target of one local paid scribe after an August 6 loss to Ottawa. Even though he punched out a double and single, his fielding at shortstop, which continued to be much worse in Rutland than in Plattsburg or even back at Columbia, was a sticking point. According to the report, "the players couldn't stop a ground ball with a steam shovel nor hit a balloon with a snow shovel. Collins and Bagley made the infield slow, the former with a couple of errors...." And later it was suggested "[s]omebody connected with the team ought to purchase a 'hook.'"[16]

Perhaps this type of talk fired up Collins. In a 13–2 win over Montpelier-Barre on August 13, Eddie had a pair of hits and scored four runs. He and double-play partner Shean turned in a perfect day in the field. Rutland's pitcher that day was Stan Yerkes, who had pitched in 1901–1903 with St. Louis of the National League. The win, nevertheless, did little to quiet fan discontent. After all, the team's record at 14–17 remained dismal. Attendance, still quite poor, was blamed on poor team play. On the same day as the win over Montpelier-Barre, the team's stockholders met at the local Bardwell House to decide whether the team should continue. It was decided to continue the season, albeit with "changes to the team."[17] Those "changes" were not delineated.

The next game for Rutland was August 15. This time Dick Rudolph was on Eddie's side and Rutland prevailed over Ottawa, 7–3. According to reports, "Collins covered more ground than any shortstop ever seen since the Northern League was born." More importantly, at least for the two involved, Eddie Collins and Dave Shean were under the watchful eye of the "big fellows."[18]

The "big fellows" in this case were the Philadelphia Athletics of Connie Mack and the American League. Mack recalls, "I sent one of my extra players, who was a good 'mixer' and made friends easily, to get acquainted with the collegian. He got on good terms with him, but could not do business with the player."[19]

The loquacious gent referred to by Connie Mack was Jimmy Byrnes, a 26-year-old catcher who played all ten of his big league games for the A's in 1906. He was but 5 feet 9 inches, 150 pounds himself and not put off by Collins' size. Byrnes was not shy, and it did not take Collins long to discover his interest. Eddie was non–plussed.

"The league was in a bad way late that summer. The boys were having a lot of fun, kidding and joking. One day a fellow showed up and watched me play. Paddy Duff, who was a great kidder, and Billy Lush told me he was Byrnes, a catcher, who was scouting for major league talent. They told me he had come to watch me. I suspected a joke and dodged.

"When Byrnes wanted to talk to me about playing professional ball I thought the fellows had framed me and it took him two days to persuade me he was on the level. I had no idea I was good enough to be a big league player, having looked up to them so long as a kid I thought they could do anything. I wouldn't listen to Byrnes...."[20]

While it is clear Byrnes was favorably impressed by what he saw of Collins in summer 1906, just who tipped Connie Mack off about Collins in the first place is somewhat unclear. As a former major leaguer, Billy Lush had some credibility as an evaluator of talent. He also knew Mack was one of the few managers then interested in college players. Perhaps, he thought, there might be a few bucks in it for him. According to at least one report, he sent Mack a letter and Byrnes' trip to the North Country followed shortly.[21]

Connie Mack and one of his players remember it quite differently. The player was Andy Coakley, a major league pitcher for most of 1902 through 1911 in a career that included work for the Reds, Cubs, Yankees and A's. In 1905, Andy won 18 of his career 58 wins, losing 9–0 to Christy Mathewson in the Giants-A's World Series of that year. The graduate of Holy Cross later became a baseball coach at Columbia and tutored Lou Gehrig. Coakley remained at Columbia for over 35 years. In 1906, however, he was with the A's. In a strange set of circumstances, his path crossed that of another Columbia Lion, Eddie Collins.

"I actually found Eddie while I was on my honeymoon. I was married in 1906, and Mack gave me a week off, and we went to Vermont. I hired a buggy with the missus one day, and we rode to Montpelier. A ball game was going on, and, of course, I had to have a look. I was impressed with a little infielder, who was as fast as lightning. It was Collins. When I went back to the Athletics I told Mack about this boy."[22]

At any rate at this point, it made no difference who sent Jimmy Byrnes; Collins was not interested. There were 22 games remaining on Rutland's schedule and Eddie planned to remain the team's shortstop.

Perhaps spurred on by the A's interest, Collins began swinging a hot bat. At the same time his team perked up. By August 18 Rutland's record stood at 17–17, including a close win over Burlington. Baseball in Rutland was suddenly becoming fun. Then in almost a repeat performance of Plattsburg's swan song, Rutland's season abruptly ended as well. This time, at least on the surface, the reason seemed different. It was said the players themselves caused cessation of play by disbanding. The underlying reason, however, was in reality the same. The players were concerned they would not receive pay for their play. Hearing rumors that the team was running short of funds, team members refused an upcoming road trip to Burlington unless they received a written guarantee of their salary in full or the cash equivalent. Instead of complying, the stockholders of the team voted to fine the players for insubordination and disband the team.

A second meeting was held in short order. At that meeting a committee of three players from the team, including Collins, presented their side of the argument. It was their position that while the team members felt their actions were justified at the time, their stand was probably hasty. Despite this verbal peace offering, the stockholders refused to back down. Thus Collins and his teammates were finished at Rutland, with loss of pay to boot.[23] Collins related the experience tongue-in-cheek.

Finally, as things were looking blue and there was considerable back pay coming to me, I interviewed the manager one Saturday night and asked for my money. He informed me that while I had some technical claim for the cash, the attempt to extract blood from a turnip had in all ages proved a failure, and that for all practical purposes the Rutland Club was in the turnip class. He claimed, however, that all our troubles would vanish on Labor Day. The admiring throng that would surely crowd the grounds on that date would enable the club to meet its bills and we would not be losers. Some of us debated this question but found it too uncertain. For aught we could foresee, it might rain on Labor Day and the treasury be as empty as ever. It seemed advisable, all things considered, to pocket our loss, since we could not pocket the money, and seek fresh pastures and better filled grandstands elsewhere. The club owed me, as I remember, somewhere in the neighborhood of $77, which I was obliged to donate to the score of sad experience.[24]

Still the Rutland experience was by no means a total failure. During his time at Rutland, Collins batted .302 in 18 games played. Although his 13 errors at shortstop did not add to his luster, his spirited play had attracted interest from some important people.

Because it was not yet Labor Day, there were more baseball fields to plow in summer 1906, especially for players of the caliber of an Eddie Collins. A call from Billy Lush sent Eddie, plus teammates Dave Shean and a Rutland first baseman/pitcher named "Snakes" Wiltse, the older brother of New York Giants ace pitcher "Hooks" Wiltse, packing off to Rockville, Connecticut. Collins was once again under Lush's umbrella.

Look on a map today and one will be hard pressed to find Rockville, Connecticut. It is now part of the city of Vernon. Unlike Plattsburg and Rutland, whose teams played in a league, Rockville was an independent in the semipro ranks, totally separate from the well-respected Connecticut State League.

It probably did not take much coaxing by Lush to get the Rockville team management to spring for Collins and his friends. Baseball in Connecticut in the early 1900s was a sizzling commodity and Rockville was a major player. Local businessmen would invest significant dollars to bring the best talent to their town. In Rockville's case the incentive was an opportunity to play against and top their chief rival, Manchester, a nearby city that also fielded an independent team.

What Michigan is to Ohio State and Texas is to Oklahoma, Manchester was to Rockville. In the early 1900s the series was dominated by Manchester — a situation Rockville's investors were hell-bent to remedy. As such, Collins felt the heat as soon as he arrived in town.

"There was a strong rivalry between this town [Rockville] and the neighboring city of Manchester. Upon this rivalry hinged the profits, in fact the very existence of the baseball team."[25]

In fact, when Collins and his teammates arrived in Rockville in the third week of August, the baseball scene was already literally "soaked" in controversy. Earlier that month Rockville accused Manchester of soaking a ball for one of its pitchers, making it heavier and thus more difficult to hit. When Manchester came to play Rockville in late August, the locals demanded that Manchester's board members leave their customary perches on the team bench and relocate to the grandstand. Insulted, the Manchester board returned the complementary season tickets previously offered by Rockville. Tempers flared on both sides.

The rivalry between Manchester and Rockville was not limited to the players, owners and fans of the two cities. Even the local newspapers took up their respective team's cause. Local reports emanated from Manchester that Rockville was stacking the deck by using 28 players during the season, while Manchester was able to win five of the eight contests (there was one tie) with only 15 on its roster.[26]

Into this melee rode Sir Edward T. Collins. After arriving in Rockville and unpacking his bags, he did not take long to make his presence known. On August 25 he punched out three hits as Rockville's bolstered lineup, which now also included outfielder Doc Carney of Holy Cross, topped Manchester, 8–2. The season series now stood at five games to three, Manchester. In a game against Massachusetts foe Fitchburg, also a Rockville win, Eddie impressed local fans with a sensational catch. Another game with Fitchburg followed closely, but Collins was absent for the win, due to tonsillitis.

In view of the spark Collins, most prominent of the new players, was bringing to Rockville, his illness caused concern about the upcoming three-game Labor Day series with Manchester. If Rockville wanted to overtake Manchester, a series sweep would be required. Concerns about Collins' availability were quickly allayed as he appeared and played well in yet a third straight Rockville win over a reeling Fitchburg.

Now the stage was set for the Labor Day series. One game was scheduled for Saturday in Manchester, with a Monday morning game in Rockville and a second game after that in the afternoon in Manchester. Even under normal circumstances the late-season series would peak fan interest and intensify the inter–city rivalry. This time, in view of the soaked ball controversy and the allegations of player stacking, the piano wire was stretched that much tighter. Manchester's response to these issues was the addition of several new players of their own, including a "league battery" for the first game of the series.[27]

Match-ups between Rockville and Manchester rarely concluded without at least one flare–up. Saturday's game had yet to start before the water boiled over. A stunned Manchester crowd of 3,000 looked on as "Rockville drew the color line, and refused to play because Manchester had secured Pitcher William Holland of the Brooklyn Royal Giants, colored, to occupy the box. Manager Lush of Rockville withdrew his team from the field."[28]

The Manchester team and its management were furious. Quickly, they surveyed their options. They could stand on moral ground, claim a forfeit and refund the admission fee, or they could continue the game with another pitcher. The lure of a big gate was too much. They substituted a white pitcher and lost, 11–3.

On Labor Day Monday, September 3, the controversy continued. The morning game was played as scheduled in Rockville, with Manchester bringing in a pitcher from the New London team of the Connecticut State League to enhance its chances. It was to no avail. Rockville won again, 3–0. Collins was at his best, going 4-for-4.

The real trouble started in the afternoon tilt set for Manchester, the scene of Saturday's tiff. Given Rockville's victories in the first two games of the holiday series, the teams now stood at 5–5. The game would provide a season winner. Another crowd of 3,000 was present. At the end of five innings with Rockville up 3–2, Manchester's manager inserted the black pitcher Holland. As he did on Saturday, Billy Lush took his team, including Collins, off the field. This time neither team would budge. Manchester was awarded a forfeit. Its fans rushed onto the field and hoisted Holland on their shoulders.

Following the game as could be expected, accusations flew back and forth between the two cities. Rockville accused Manchester of inserting the black hurler because they knew it would end the game, sparing yet a third straight defeat and loss of the season series. The argument totally ignored the painful fact that 41 years after the end of the American Civil War, a team in a Northern state refused to take the field on the basis of an individual's race.

Who was to blame for the incident? An argument can be made it was Billy Lush, who came to Rockville from Plattsburg mid–season with his infusion of new talent. He was the one significant factor in the new make-up of the Rockville team. Lush's position is particularly vexing, however, when one takes a close look at his actions upon his arrival in Rockville. On August 22, just two days after Collins and the other Northern Leaguers arrived in town, Lush trotted his team, including the newcomers, onto the field for a game with a team described as the "New York Colored 'Champs.'"[29] The game was won by the all-black team, 4–2. The winning pitcher was William Holland, who twirled a three-hitter. This is the very same

Holland whose color stopped a holiday ball game just over a week later. The team was none other than Holland's Brooklyn Royal Giants.

Thus, Lush's decision to halt play when Manchester brought Holland on to pitch seemed particularly inconsistent. The Rockville manager's actions in that regard were, of course, quickly brought to light. Pitcher Holland was quoted on that subject a day after the first occurrence.

"I cannot see why they [Rockville] should object to playing with me in the game as they have played nine of us in Rockville and I have pitched against them."[30]

In removing his team from the field on this first of two occasions, Billy Lush apparently acted on his own. At least that is how one member of Rockville's board of directors viewed it. Immediately after Saturday's game the director told a reporter, "If at tonight's meeting of the director's the only reason for leaving the field is said to be the objection to Pitcher Holland I will move that we disband our team at once as I consider it a mean act and one the directors of the Rockville Baseball Association should feel ashamed of."[31]

But manager Lush had a voice, too. He claimed his position was not at all inconsistent. He did not object to playing exhibition games with blacks; after all, big-league teams did it all the time and so did he. But playing in a game with a single colored player was just not done, particularly in the "league."[32]

Lush's position was indefensible, but unfortunately factually correct. And, despite the statements of the lone Rockville board member after Saturday's game, not only did Lush receive the unanimous approval of the Rockville board of directors for his actions over the Labor Day weekend, but also that of the association members. Instead of covering themselves in shame, it seems that Lush and his team were now town heroes. A crowd of 500–1,000 supporters greeted them upon their return from Manchester on September 3, and they were feted at a banquet a few days later.[33]

What the Manchester–Rockville affair came down to was not right or wrong or even adherence to the misguided policies of the "league." It was later revealed that Lush had played in games with a single black player.[34] It came down to playing the race card for money and inter–city glory. In Saturday's game Manchester inserted William Holland knowing there was little to lose. If Lush permitted Holland to pitch, Manchester's fortunes would have been bolstered by a top-flight pitcher who only days before practically shut Rockville down. If on the other hand, as expected, Lush protested on the basis of race, Manchester could take the high moral ground and still play the game. After all, they would never give up a heavy day's receipts. When the game was played out without Holland, just as Manchester feared, the rejuvenated Rockville team was a winner. Still Manchester accomplished something; they had forced Billy Lush's hand. They now knew exactly where he stood. He would not allow Holland to play.

On Monday morning Manchester lost again. The season series was on the line in that day's afternoon game. Another sizable crowd was in place in Manchester to see the outcome. The game was started. After five innings with Rockville ahead, Manchester made its move by inserting Holland. It took Dr. F.J. Bailey of Hartford, a disinterested spectator that day, to lay it all out.

"The fact was Rockville positively refused long before the game to play if Holland were to pitch. Manchester knew this, but put him in the fifth inning. Why didn't they [Manchester] let him start the game? Simply because they wanted the big gate receipts. 'Fans' pay to see baseball not to see half a game and a squabble of managers."[35]

As a result of the weekend, both sides claimed victory — Rockville because it led 3–2 at the end of five, Manchester due to forfeit. In terms of what the affair said for the state of human dignity, neither side could claim victory. For his part, in discussing his summer in

New England to various scribes over a number of years, Eddie Collins never uttered one word of this bleak incident.

Instead, Rockville moved ahead and Collins with it. There were, of course, no more contests with Manchester. There were games with Bridgeport and Holyoke of the Connecticut State League, a loss and a win respectively, and a final game against Thomaston. In that one, an 18–2 rout, Collins contributed a pair of doubles to the victory total.

And in the background of a waning summer, there was Connie Mack, who appeared in Springfield in late August to see a Connecticut State League game between league leaders Springfield and Norwich. According to the *Hartford Daily Times,* the A's manager was "on the lookout for 1907 material...."[36] The next day a follow-up note mentioned that Mack watched the game but was unimpressed with the talent on display.[37] Perhaps that is why before Collins left Rockville, Jimmy Byrnes made a second stab at him. This time Eddie was much more firm.

"I told him that I had another year in college, and, furthermore, had no intention of following baseball as a profession. With that the scout left and I dismissed the matter from my thoughts."[38]

It could not be any clearer. Faced with a fork in the road, college to the right and professional baseball to the left, Collins decided to go right, a direction taking him back to Morningside Heights to captain Columbia for his senior year. But when he arrived in New York, he did not turn hard right. Instead, he took a round-house left and headed downtown. It was a directional shift that drastically changed his life.

CHAPTER 4

Meeting Mr. Mack

"He was not the star of the Columbia University [baseball] team. He was the Columbia University team."

— *New York Evening Journal*[1]

Connie Mack liked college baseball players on his team and he liked what he heard about Eddie Collins. He once said, "These boys, who knew their Greek and Latin and their algebra and geometry and trigonometry, put intelligence and scholarship into the game."[2] Collins fit that bill, and the A's leader wanted him. Mack either wired Collins directly or spoke by telephone long distance with Billy Lush, asking for Eddie to meet him in New York, where Mack's A's were finishing a series with the Highlanders. The date was September 9, 1906.

"The season [in Rockville] closed after Labor Day, as I remember it, on a Friday. I believe we played some sort of a barnstorming exhibition game on the Saturday immediately after and on the Sunday which followed I journeyed to New York in the company of Billy Lush, and met Connie Mack at the old Fifth Avenue Hotel. Up to that time I had no definite idea of becoming a professional baseball player. I had not supposed I was good enough.... I was like most undergraduates at college, merely living from day to day, with no settled prospects, waiting for something to turn up which should indicate the subsequent turn of events."[3]

This was Eddie's first encounter with the man everyone called Connie Mack, but who was born in East Brookfield, Massachusetts, as Cornelius Alexander McGillicuddy. By the time he met with Collins, Mack was 43 years old, a wizened veteran of the baseball wars as player, manager and franchise owner. One of his many nicknames, the "Tall Tactician," says as much about his size and bearing—a paper-thin 150 pounds on a 6-foot 1-inch frame—as his unmatched skills as baseball's Merlin the Wizard.

It is sometimes hard to imagine that the stately Mack, as refined in dress and manner as any international diplomat, once crouched behind the plate as a catcher in the rough-and-tumble baseball world of the late 1800s, but that is exactly what he did for 11 major league seasons, beginning in 1886.

One of seven children of Irish immigrants, Mack played town ball early on; he then graduated to the Connecticut State League, the same league he mined for talent in late summer 1906. In 1886 he was sold by Hartford, an Eastern League team, to Washington of the National League, where he became popular with the fans, even though he was never much of a hitter.

In addition to Washington, where he spent the majority of three and one-half seasons, his playing days included stops in Buffalo for one season in the aborted Player's League and six in Pittsburgh. During this time Mack played a number of positions, but primarily he was a catcher. It was while crouching behind the batter, peering out on the wide expanse of the ball field that a man "fragile" in build and perhaps ill-suited for the position "became celebrated for his defensive skill, his knowledge of the game, and his alert and winning disposition."[4] In addition, underneath Mack's refined manner there burned a fire, the desire to win that is found in all great competitors. He was, as one writer put it, "a cute operator as a catcher."[5] He bent the rules almost to the breaking point, talking incessantly to distract the batter, becoming skilled at making a slapping sound when a batter missed a pitch in hopes the umpire would signal a foul tip caught for an out, and even tipping the hitter's bat to throw off his swing.

Toward the end of the 1894 season after over three seasons in Pittsburgh as a player, Mack was appointed the team's player-manager. For the next two seasons, he sharpened his managerial skills for a team that won more than it lost but did not finish anywhere close to the top. At the end of the 1896 season, Connie was told his contract would not be renewed. He played but sparingly his last years in Pittsburgh; thus, his career as a player was essentially coming to an end as well.

One man read the reports of Connie Mack's demise with interest. His name was Ban Johnson, a former columnist for a Cincinnati newspaper. In the fall of 1893, Johnson and his good friend Charles A. Comiskey, a well-known player and then Cincinnati's National League manager, formed the Western League in an effort to challenge the 12-team National League's monopoly as "the" major league. The move proved successful, and in 1896, Johnson was in the market for a manager for his Milwaukee club. He offered the job and the potential for partial team ownership to Mack, who readily accepted. In short order Mack was in charge of all facets of the Milwaukee franchise.

In 1899 when the National League reduced to eight teams, Johnson made his move. In October he renamed his league the American League. Although for a short time it remained a minor league, by 1901 Johnson had shed any remaining pretense that he sought less than equal footing with the National League. One of his first moves was expansion into the East, the very territory covered by the Nationals.

One of the cities in which Ban Johnson determined to place a team for his revamped league was Philadelphia. On January 28, 1901, the final touches were implemented to give the American League its face for the future. Teams were set in place in eight cities, including Baltimore, Boston, Chicago, Cleveland, Detroit, Milwaukee, Washington and Philadelphia.

The man Ban Johnson chose to manage the new club in Philadelphia was Connie Mack. The choice made sense. Through his association with Pittsburgh, Mack was a known quantity in Pennsylvania. In addition, the Tall Tactician enjoyed some success during his time in Milwaukee, never finishing below fourth and improving steadily along the way.

In its original form, the new Philadelphia Americans were funded by Charles Somers, a wealthy Cleveland businessman who backed several of the American League franchises. In order to entice Mack to leave Milwaukee for Philadelphia, Johnson offered Connie one-quarter interest in the franchise for between $5,000 and $10,000. Somers put up the rest, but soon Mack was able to interest others in the venture. A primary contributor was Benjamin F. Shibe. Almost 70 at the time, Shibe was a partner in A.J. Reach and Co., a large sporting goods concern. His partner, Al Reach, was then part owner of the main competition in town, the Philadelphia Phillies of the National League. Mack not only offered Shibe a one-half interest in the new club, he also further whetted the man's appetite by indicating the Reach baseball would then become the official ball of the new league. Eventually Shibe accepted. The other one-quarter interest in the team was purchased by a pair of sportswriters, Samuel "Butch" Jones of the Associated Press and Frank Hough of the *Philadelphia Inquirer*. The pair had worked with Mack to locate a spot for a new ballpark. On February 19, 1901, Ben Shibe was elected president of the Athletics, the same name as that of the city's first outstanding ball club in 1860, as well as that of its representative in the first professional league in 1871.[6]

Early on, the club picked up a second appellation when John McGraw claimed they would be "the white elephants of the league."[7] Mack liked the nickname "White Elephants" and his club proudly adopted it. He and his crew then set about the task of proving McGraw wrong, finishing first in both 1902 and 1905 and second in 1903, the same year the American League and the National League reached an agreement officially placing the two leagues under one mantle and on equal footing. They also finished fourth in 1901 and fifth 1904.

Thus, when Connie Mack greeted Eddie Collins in early September 1906, his White Elephants were a highly respected club and its Tall Tactician a familiar figure, on his way to becoming a national icon. But if Collins was in awe of the man with the chiseled face and deep-blue eyes, he did not show it. From the start he was charmed by this older, wiser man, yet he negotiated at arms length, a heady businessman already.

"From the very first I was favorably impressed. He seemed to have a fatherly air about him, he was so affable without being artificial, and he seemed to convey that he was very much interested in me. He asked me questions about my college and what I planned to do after my graduation, which was the next year. When I told him that my future course was undecided, he then wanted to know if I would sign to play with him next year, but insisted that I graduate first and not join his club until June."[8]

At first Collins did not bite. "I was extremely anxious not to bind myself to a contract that should inconvenience me in any other plans I might have. It was flattering to be approached by the manager of a major league club, but I knew something of the way in which recruits, though signed by the majors, are often farmed out or transferred to small clubs in the minors, and I was anxious not to be farmed out in this way.

"So Connie listened, readily enough, to the proposition I made him and drew up an agreement which specified that during the following year I should not be traded or sold to any other club without my consent."[9]

Thus, in 1907 Eddie Collins would get his opportunity to play big league ball. For the time being, he would return home to visit his parents and await the start of school. But, according to Eddie, Mack had a different idea.

"His [Mack's] next words were: 'What are you going to do between now and the time your college opens in the fall?' When I told him I had nothing in view, he suggested that I take a trip West with the Athletics, and said he could arrange it so I could play under an assumed name and no one would know my identity."[10]

All that was left for Collins was to travel home to Tarrytown and break the big news to his folks. "I succeeded in getting the consent of my indignant mother and, much more easily, that of my father, and then went over to Philadelphia to report to Mr. Mack."[11]

Mack's recall is different. In a syndicated autobiographical series in 1930, he states it was Collins' idea to play in 1906 and that he was not aware of Eddie's desire in that regard until the youth showed up at Columbia Park.[12] At any rate Collins arrived in Philadelphia a few days later, around September 13, as the A's were preparing for a home series with Boston's Red Sox. By now Milwaukee and Baltimore of the original eight American League teams were gone, replaced by the St. Louis Browns and the New York Highlanders, respectively.

Since the Athletics' inception in April 1901, the franchise played its baseball in Columbia Park. Located at 29th and Columbia near many of the city's breweries, the capacity of the park on Collins' arrival was 13,600.[13] When he reported to Mack's office located under the stands, he was in for a surprise. The A's manager was talking with a man, later identified as Tim Murnane, a baseball writer for the *Boston Globe*. Upon noticing Collins, Mack quickly broke off his conversation and turned toward Eddie.

"'Hello, Sullivan. Glad to see you,' he [Mack] shouted meanwhile pushing me through the door and into the corridor. He closed the door behind him, drew a deep breath, then explained.

"'The reason I did that was because I was afraid Murnane would recognize you. He must have seen you play against Harvard at some time.'"[14]

Tim Murnane was no ordinary reporter. For some eight seasons, primarily from 1872 to 1878, he played baseball. His stints in the major leagues included time with the original Athletics of the National Association of Professional Baseball Leagues and Boston's first National League entry. Some students of the game credit him for the derivation of the term "bunting." He managed and scouted as well and was literally a fount of baseball knowledge. Given his continuing interest in the game, the former collegian from Holy Cross might well have seen Eddie Collins doing his bit as a college player against one of the New England collegiate nines.

Therefore, Eddie Collins was now a Philadelphia Athletic by the name of Sullivan. Mr. Mack, as everyone called him, had lived up to his part of the bargain; he had protected Eddie's collegiate eligibility. Now it was up to Eddie to do his part and show his new employer he could perform on the field. After the scary start with the flaky Rube Waddell, Sully did perform reasonably well, as did his summer friend Dave Shean. Still, when the road trip was over and the A's

In late 1906 Collins first played for the Philadelphia A's under the name Eddie Sullivan. He remained with the club through the 1914 season. Here Eddie appears in uniform during those early days (George Grantham Bain Collection, Library of Congress, Prints & Photographs Division, LC-DIG-ggbain-14025).

returned to face the Highlanders on October 2, Shean continued to play out the season while Eddie returned to Columbia. To his "surprise, when the trip was over Connie gave me a check for a full month's pay, and at the rate of salary that my 1907 contract called for."[15] His 1907 contract called for payment at $400 per month.[16] For a young college guy, it was a grand sum.

When Collins returned to Columbia in the fall of 1906 to begin his last year of school, prepared to serve his captaincy for the Blue and White, he was a professional baseball player in every sense of the word. Still all seemed normal as he progressed toward graduation. He remained a Beta and served as a member of the school's athletic council. In late March 1907 he reported to South Field to begin preparations for his senior season. As so often the case, muddy conditions delayed a scheduled contest with City College of New York, but when the game was played and won by Columbia on March 26, Eddie Collins was not in the lineup. That same day the University Committee on Athletics announced Collins was ineligible to further represent Columbia athletics. He had violated the "summer baseball" rule. The report in the school newspaper indicated Collins planned to fight the decision. The paper reported that according to Collins, under the rules of the Amateur Athletic Union, he was still eligible to play collegiate baseball.[17] It was a weak argument, however, and not even technically correct as the A.A.U. had already revoked his registration card.[18]

A number of chroniclers of this portion of the Collins' saga assign Eddie's disqualification to his play for pay with the Athletics. This is not the case, although different versions of the story by Collins himself have added to the confusion. The *New York Times* got it right about the reason for the ruling. Calling the senior captain "the best ball player Columbia ever had," the paper stated the decision was based on his play in Plattsburg and Rockville, where the teams "played for a gate and were considered professional...." The article went on to say that in "vigorously" protesting the committee's ruling, "Collins denies that he received a cent of money, and [claims] that he even paid his own expenses."[19]

Collins' version of his response to the charges differs from the version in the *Times*. He claims he immediately confessed when called before the university's athletic committee and questioned about Plattsburg. He was not asked and did not mention his association with the Athletics. The committee was "gracious," but permanently barred him from further baseball play for the school. Instead they appointed him to coach; a paid position which served to cover his expenses. Thus he remained in school and coached at Columbia throughout the spring of 1907, but as commencement neared Eddie skipped the ceremony, reporting instead to the A's at the end of May.[20]

It might seem odd that Columbia, a school which only a little over a year before had taken a definitive and almost singular stand against the professional aspects of intercollegiate athletics, on one hand declared Collins ineligible to play ball due to taking money and on the other hand immediately found a job for him coaching its eligible amateur athletes. But Columbia's decision is not nearly so surprising when taken in the context of the times, an era when many colleges permitted athletes who played in the same summer leagues Eddie played in to maintain their college eligibility. Would Columbia have felt the same had they known of Eddie's performance for the Athletics of Philadelphia? The answer is anyone's guess. At any rate, when the Columbia class of 1907 graduated on June 12, Eddie Collins was not there to receive his diploma. He was already off to Philadelphia. Had he stayed around to check the "senior class statistics," the results of balloting by his classmates, he would have discovered he was voted the "best athlete" in the class and, among categories which included "laziest," "noisiest," and "most conceited," he had been voted the "grouchiest" member of the senior class.[21]

But whatever terms his classmates used to describe him, Eddie Collins, no longer a Sullivan, was officially a big league ball player in name, as well as form.

CHAPTER 5

A Baseball Education

"[T]he following year I had a hard time convincing Socks Seybold and Murphy that it [Sullivan] wasn't my right name."

— Eddie Collins[1]

Under the direction of Connie Mack, the Philadelphia Athletics were a lot like a volatile common stock. The club's performance could be charted. The team was either on a long upswing or a long downswing in value depending upon when you happened to look. These increases and decreases were logged in terms of years rather than days or months. Like a patient investor, a fan of the A's who held his interest in the team through the bad times usually found good times ahead. In June of 1907 the A's were in a bit of a trough, having followed their American League triumph of 1905 with a disappointing fourth-place finish in 1906. During that season the team was in first place until mid–August before slumping. By the time Collins joined up, the squad stood third on their way down. Still the team's losses were, in effect, Eddie's gain. Otherwise, it is doubtful Mack's lineup would have carried an Eddie Sullivan.

In 1906 there was a noticeable drop in the pitching excellence enjoyed during the 1905 championship season. Rube Waddell's 27 wins shrunk to 15, Eddie Plank's from 24 to 19 and, in a disastrous decline, Andy Coakley's from 18 to 7. Only 15-game winner Albert "Chief" Bender, the Chippewa who owned the only A's win in the 1905 World Series, and Jack Coombs, another Mack collegian from Colby College, improved their records on the 1906 pitching staff. Thus, based on such a shaky foundation, there was no telling what 1907 held in store for the Mackmen, as they were often called.

The regular lineup for the 1907 A's was merely serviceable, led by first baseman Harry Davis, a perennial league leader in home runs and runs batted in, and outfielder Socks Seybold, a .316 batter in 1906. The infield was anchored by Danny Murphy. At age 30 Murphy was solidly entrenched at second base, although his three errors in Game Three of the 1905 World Series contributed to his team's defeat. In 1906 he hit .301 with 60 RBIs, the highlight a two-out triple to end a then record-setting 24-inning contest with the Red Sox.

On the left side of the infield, third base and shortstop respectively, were weak hitters John Knight and Monte Cross. In 1906 Knight shared his position with Rube Oldring, who now manned one outfield post, along with Seybold and Topsy Hartsel. Although Knight was only 21, his anemic .194 average in 1906 offered little encouragement. Cross was at the other end of his career. Over 15 years, which included four seasons across town with the Phillies, Cross made his reputation with his glove. In 1906 an injury to Cross opened the door for Collins' late summer tryout. It was here at shortstop that Mack hoped to place Collins upon his arrival in 1907.

One player who was not on the 1907 Athletics was Eddie's friend Dave Shean. He would, however, resurface in 1908 in Philadelphia, but with the Phillies on the way to a nine-season major league career. Good friends for life, Shean and Collins never played on the same team again.

Connie Mack's first opportunity to try Collins out came on June 4 at Columbia Park. Mack started the youngster at shortstop in place of Cross, whose back was injured during a recent series in Washington. Danny Murphy was also injured, replaced at second base by Simon Nicholls, a young speedster. At the time the A's stood 20–19 on the season in fifth place. Although the usually reliable Eddie Plank started for the A's, he was not effective and the team fell to the defending world champs, 10–6. Neither Collins nor Nicholls was of much help. Each went 0-for-3 with an error, but according to the *Philadelphia Inquirer*, "[t]hese new men were no more responsible for the loss of the game than some of the older bunch...."[2]

Mack needed Nicholls and Collins again for the next tangle with the White Sox on June 6. This time Rube Waddell shut down the Sox and their hurler Ed Walsh. Both Nicholls and Collins fared better this time around with two hits and one hit, respectively. But once again Collins was shaky in the field, committing his second error.

The next day, in an effort to bolster his team's hitting and add experience to the lineup, Mack traded the youngster John Knight to the Boston Red Sox for Jimmy Collins. The future member of the Hall of Fame, no relation to Eddie, was on the far downside of a career which also saw him managing the Red Sox until August 1906. For Eddie Collins, the acquisition meant added confusion, as he was sometimes mistaken as the veteran's brother and even at times for the star infielder himself. As for the A's Jimmy added a bat and at 37 a wise hand to a team with youth waiting in the wings.

The experiment of Eddie Collins as the A's regular shortstop in 1907 was brief. Once Monte Cross returned, he shared the position with Simon Nicholls, who gave a good account of himself at the plate, hitting .302.

Although Collins had failed to take advantage of the opportunity at shortstop in 1907, there might be a logical explanation. When the season started, he was still in college and, therefore, unable to take part in the A's annual spring training. In addition, unlike the previous summer when he joined the team after a full calendar of baseball, in the spring of 1907 Collins sat and watched his college teammates struggle through another disappointing season. Thus, in addition to his general lack of big league experience, Eddie was rusty when he arrived in Philadelphia and was inserted into the lineup almost immediately.

Now, due to his lackluster performance, Collins would mostly sit and watch as his teammates began a slow upward climb into the pennant race. On July 1 he was a late-inning replacement at shortstop in a loss to Boston. Cy Young, the winningest pitcher in baseball history, was on the mound, but Eddie did not get to the plate. He did bat three times without success in the second game of a double-bill with the Highlanders before a large American League Park crowd. In that one, a 7–3 loss, he played errorless ball.

There followed a number of pinch-hit appearances by Collins over the course of the next several weeks, mostly unsuccessful. Then in early August, Mack made a move which was quite surprising, given the circumstances surrounding the signing of Collins. When Eddie signed with the Mackmen, the agreement required the A's to keep him for the full season. Yet in August Mack was approached by a friend, Walter Burnham, the manager of the Newark Bears, a minor league franchise. The Bears were approaching a crucial series with one of their chief rivals, Jersey City, minus an important player. Could Mack help Burnham out by lending him one of his players for the series? Mack looked at his bench and there sat Collins, accumulating little but serious splinters. But Mack was a man of his word. What would he do?

"Mack approached me on the subject and made the suggestion that I go to Newark. He said: 'You can leave Saturday and meet us in the West,' and he gave me my ticket.

"So I went to Newark and played four days. It so happened that I had remarkable good fortune at the bat those four days. If I remember, I made something like twelve or fourteen hits during the four games and received a good deal of favorable comment from the local sporting sheets.

"On one occasion, in particular, I had an odd experience. As I remember, I made four hits and as many errors during that game. Nearly all my errors contributed to a score by the opposition, while on the contrary nearly all my hits were equally valuable to our club. The game seesawed back and forth, an error of mine now turning the tide in favor of the opposition when one of my hits would turn it back again. Eventually we won, but it was a strange game. Fortunately, the memory of my hits drowned out the memory of my just as numerous errors.

"When Saturday came I was naturally anxious to get the train for the West to meet the Athletics. The manager had tried to induce me to stay over Sunday, as he thought on the strength of the week's showing and the press agenting I had received I would be something of a drawing card. But I had told him I should have to leave. In the dressing room, as I had no regular locker, I had given my watch, money and railroad ticket to the manager to keep for me, and after the game when I inquired for him I was much surprised to find that he had gone to Providence. I was immediately impressed with the notion that a plot had been worked against me and that he had taken my possessions temporarily so as to make my presence with the club on the profitable Sunday a certainty. This view which, by the way, was doubtless a wholly erroneous one, so incensed me that I vowed I would not play for Newark under any circumstances.

"The son of the manager then approached me and offered me fifty dollars if I would stay over Sunday and play for the team, but I refused, at the same time calling down various misfortunes on his father for making off with the personal belongs I had entrusted in his care.

"He heard me through and then said, 'You needn't worry about that. He has left for Providence, alright, but before he went away he gave your things to me to return to you and as you won't play here to-morrow you may have them now.'

"That was the close of an odd episode and the only time I ever played with a regular minor league team."[3]

Eddie's recall of the events in Newark, if not his hitting numbers, was good. The records show seven hits in 16 at-bats in the four games played, all but one lost to Jersey City.[4] His poor play at shortstop was accurate as well. At Newark at the time was Paul Krichell, who one day became the New York Yankee super scout. A terrific judge of talent, Krichell took a look at Newark's borrowed infielder and ventured that Collins was a "[t]errible looking player, at least as shortstop."[5]

By the time Collins returned to the A's on August 11, the team was in second place. Under these circumstances there was little chance for him in Mack's current scheme, so he once again sat and watched. Then Mack recalled Collins' earlier successes versus Eddie Walsh. On August 20 Collins was inserted as a pinch-hitter in the ninth but was not charged with a time at bat in a 4–1 loss to Walsh and his White Sox. Collins next appeared as an unsuccessful pinch-hitter in the second game of a double-header split with the St. Louis Browns on August 24, a 6–4 loss. The A's, however, were now in first place and in a dog fight with both Chicago and the Detroit Tigers. The A's good fortune continued until September 24, when they lost to Walsh and Chicago again, 8–3. Waddell was the loser for the A's. Collins appeared as a pinch-hitter in the ninth but could not help the cause. That loss dropped the A's to second.

Nothing much was heard from Collins again until a late September series with the Detroit Tigers. By then the teams were practically in a dead heat for first place in the league race. The first game of a scheduled three-game series went to the Tigers, 5–4. The next day rain forced a doubleheader. It would be the last time the two teams would meet for the season. The crucial twin bill, of course, drew major fan interest. Columbia Park at that time was a typical ballpark with wooden grandstands extending down both the first and third base lines. These grandstands were covered, while open grandstands or bleachers continued down each foul line. In left field was another stand of bleachers. There was a dressing room for the A's in a small clubhouse underneath the stands. The visitors dressed at their hotel, taking trolleys or horse-drawn carriages to the park. The players sat on wooden benches on each side of the playing field since there were no dugouts. Adding to the close-knit atmosphere was the aroma of hops from the nearby breweries. Connie Mack obviously liked his workplace; he lived right across the street. Many of his players lived in the area as well.[6]

On September 30 the ballpark, which normally held a little over 13,000 spectators, burst at the seams with an estimated 24,000 crazed fans, at least 7,000 more than attended the first game. According to the *Inquirer*, "if the big enclosure could only have been stretched like India rubber there's no question that 50,000 persons would have gladly passed through the turnstiles."[7]

Through the years there were probably many more than 50,000 fans who claimed they were there to watch one of the classic games in Columbia Park history. What was supposed to be the first game of two started out in fine fashion for the A's. They jumped on Tigers pitcher "Wild Bill" Donovan — no relation to Collins' quarterback competition at Columbia — for a 7–1 lead. Unfortunately for the Mackmen, baseball is a nine-inning game. The Tigers had not forgotten that fact and inning by inning cut into the A's lead. In the ninth a young outfielder by the name of Ty Cobb hit a Rube Waddell serving over the right field wall to tie the game. In those days a home run was an infrequent sight; many of those recorded round-trippers were of the inside-the-park variety, but not this one. In only his second full season and a mere 20 years old, Cobb was already showing a flair for the dramatic.

When the A's were unable to score in their half of the ninth, the game spun into extra innings. Then in the bottom of the fourteenth, it appeared that the A's were back in business when their first basemen, Harry Davis, the first man up, stroked a pitch from a tiring Donovan into the crowd standing behind the rope in left-center field. Under normal circumstances Davis' effort represented a ground-rule double, but when Detroit center fielder Sam Crawford claimed interference by a policeman, umpire Silk O'Loughlin bought it. When he did, the A's Monte Cross, who was not even playing that day, and Tiger first sacker Claude Rossman began fighting. Allegedly, Rossman's anger was fueled by Cobb's remark that Cross had called Rossman a "Jew bastard."[8]

The two combatants were soon joined by their teammates, and after a great deal of pushing and shoving, order was restored. Rossman was evicted from the game. Much more significantly and, it would seem unjustly, Davis was called out. When the next batter, Danny Murphy, hit a single which would have scored Davis or placed two on base with nobody out, the frustration was amplified. The A's failed to score and the game continued.

By the bottom of the seventeenth inning, the game was approaching four hours in length and the remaining daylight in short supply. Due up was A's center fielder Rube Oldring, who batted from the right side. Since "Wild Bill" Donovan threw from the right, Mack looked down his bench for a left-handed hitter. One who fit that description was Eddie Collins. Eddie had yet to hit safely as a pinch-hitter in 1907. Thus, when Mack told him to pick up a bat, it was either an act of supreme confidence in the ability of his young charge or an act of

Collins of the A's looks skyward as he takes a hefty swing at a pitch (George Grantham Bain Collection, Library of Congress, Prints & Photographs Division, LC-DIG-ggbain-17858).

desperation. At any rate, Eddie came through, stroking a single. When he died on the base paths, the game was called. Detroit left town in first place, a lead which in the end won them a league pennant.

After the game the normally placid Mack blistered the umpires. "If ever there was such a thing as crooked baseball, today's game would stand as a good example."[9] For Mack the game served as a resounding defeat, a lost opportunity for a team he thought was on the upswing. For Collins, however, despite the loss in a game which stood as one of his all-time favorites, there was gain. In the most important game of the season, he had been called upon in a pressure-packed situation to perform on a large stage and he had delivered. That hit did wonders for his confidence, as well as for Mack's ultimate confidence in him.

Now Eddie Collins was on his way as a big-league ballplayer. He next appeared on October 4 in game number one of a critical double header with the Washington Nationals. On the mound for Washington was the "Big Train," Walter Johnson, at the time like Collins a 19-year-old right-handed newcomer struggling to get his fifth win of a career total 417. Near the end of his career, Collins would marvel at the pitching speed and motion of the man he now faced for the first time.

"You just swung, that was all. Either you did or you didn't, and more often you didn't.

"Walter's style of pitching is the poetry of motion. His effortless windup, the sway of the body, that beautiful side-arm delivery, all make a picture to be remembered."[10]

Collins got his first look at that tall powerhouse as a pinch-hitter in the eighth inning with his team down 1–0. Of course, Johnson was not the pitcher he eventually developed into, nor was Collins the hitter. On this particular occasion the hitter won out, as Eddie laced a triple. He was later thrown out at the plate on a ground ball by left fielder Topsy Hartsel. However, later in the same inning, the A's tied the score, sending the game to extra innings where they lost in the tenth. The loss put the team in serious trouble. A win in the second game was of little comfort. The A's went into the last day of the season needing to win both games of their second double-bill in a row with Washington and for St. Louis to win all three of their weekend games from league leader Detroit.

The scenario would only play out if the A's held up their end of the bargain, which they did winning both games, 4–2 and 4–0. Collins played shortstop in both contests, getting two hits in each. His wild throw in game one led to a Washington run. But the Tigers did not do their part. They beat St. Louis, 10–2, in the first game of their series to clinch the pennant. In the end the Athletics finished the 1907 season a mere one and one-half games behind the Tigers. They could argue with the umpires about that tie on September 30; however, they would need to confront higher authority to complain that the game was never played out.

In the early 1900s the teams did not always play their full schedule due to rainouts or in this case a tie. The season was not extended to make sure each team played an equal number of games. In 1907, for example, the Tigers played 153 games (three ties) in ending the season 92–58, while the A's played only 150 (five ties). Their final total was 88–57. As a result, they were seriously hindered in their championship quest when the last three-game series of the season with the Tigers was reduced to one game (and a tie). That series with the Tigers was scheduled in Philadelphia for Friday, Saturday and Monday. No ball was played in Philadelphia on Sundays by virtue of a Blue Law enacted by the Pennsylvania State Legislature in the late 1700s to prevent sporting and its questionable moral attachments from occurring on the Lord's Day.

The state of Pennsylvania and its largest city, Philadelphia, certainly did not stand alone in barring Sunday baseball. However, as early as 1902, the cities of Chicago, St. Louis and Cincinnati permitted their baseball franchises to play games on the day. The A's, of course, took part when their games were scheduled on a Sunday in those cities. Philadelphia did not and would not budge on this issue for a long time. The first lawful Sunday baseball game in Philadelphia was not played until April 8, 1934, and involved the Phillies. By then Sunday baseball was already a staple in all the other major league cities. Thus, in 1907 when Saturday's game with Detroit was rained out, the second and third games of the series were forced onto Monday. When the first game ended in a tie due to darkness, the A's were deprived of two opportunities to tame the Tigers. A win in each and the A's would have been champions of the American League.

Still, the future looked bright for Mack and his Philadelphia Athletics. Despite the ban on Sunday games, attendance reached a record 625,581. The future appeared bright for Eddie Collins as well. For the season he appeared in 14 games, batting 23 times. His eight hits left him with a batting average of .348, which if nothing else proved he took advantage of his limited opportunities. His fielding left more to be desired. In six games at shortstop, he committed four errors. The fact that two of his starts came on the last day of the season showed he was in Mack's plans. Collins had even learned a lot when he was sitting and merely watching play unfold.

"I was in for a wonderful course of training on the bench. Day after day he [Mack] had me sit beside him."[11] Collins was still in school, only not Columbia. The class was baseball, and Mack had a Ph.D.

In 1908 that training process would continue, starting with the benefit of a full diet of spring training. If all worked out by mid–April, there would be a Collins at short, as well as at third. There was only one problem with this forecast: Eddie Collins never made it to spring training. He contracted pneumonia and required bed rest for eight weeks. As a result, he was unavailable to the team until after the start of the regular season.[12]

Although his exact arrival on the scene is uncertain, Collins' first official appearance for the A's in 1908 occurred when he received a walk as a pinch-hitter on April 28. The home loss to Washington left his team in fourth place, one and one-half games out of first.

The team Collins met in Philadelphia in April differed from the 1907 squad in one significant regard. Rube Waddell now pitched in St. Louis for the Browns. Despite a highly successful 1907 campaign in which he won 19, lost 13 and struck out 232 batters, Waddell's eccentricities finally got to Mack and he was forced to focus on the player's status with the team when several A's threatened not to report to spring training if he was still on the squad.[13]

Although Eddie was not one of the A's involved in scuttling Waddell, his take on the man was summed up years later when he called George Edward Waddell "the oddest character I ever met...."[14]

Waddell was replaced by another Rube, this one much more placid but also much less talented. Joining Eddie Plank, Jimmy Dygert, Chief Bender and Jack Coombs in the regular rotation was Canadian-born Rube Vickers, a 2–2 pitcher in 10 games in 1907.

Collins' return to the A's in 1908 brought with it a couple of questions. Did he have a future with the club and, if so, at what position? The questions arose shortly after his return when Mack was interrogated about reports he sought Jack Barry, a college phenom from Holy Cross who just happened to play shortstop. Although Simon Nicholls was holding down that position for the time being, Mack acknowledged that he along with several other managers tried to sign Barry, but the youth was adamant about returning to college for his final year. Mack claimed his efforts stopped there as, "I am very well satisfied with my utility infielder, Eddie Collins. He has not been very well this spring, but he showed me enough last fall to warrant the prediction that he is a great player."[15]

The response was clear enough; Collins was Mack's shortstop designee. It was therefore surprising that one day after Mack's remarks about Collins and Barry appeared in print, Eddie found himself in unfamiliar territory as the A's right fielder against the Browns on May 16. As the A's bested the Westerners, Eddie played errorless ball while aiding the cause with a double and a game-winning single that broke a scoreless tie in the tenth.

Simon Nicholls remained at shortstop and, based on his performance in the first game against the Browns, Collins was again the A's right fielder in a 12–10 A's win. Eddie shone at the plate for a second time in a row with three hits. He did commit an error in right field, but this didn't keep him out of the lineup for a third game against the Browns in a 5–2 loss. He responded with a hit and successfully fielded the position.

Although Collins did nothing seriously wrong during his brief time in the outfield, neither did he cover himself in glory. Soon he was back in the role of pinch-hitter. Then in late May, regular second baseman Danny Murphy became ill. On May 28, Mack inserted Collins into the lineup as his second baseman versus Detroit. It was Eddie's first major league start at that position. The game was not a good one for the A's; they lost, 10–2, but according to the local paper, "Collins covered second, and he covered it in splendid style," even if hitless at the plate and exhibiting a bit of "over-ambition."[16]

Since Murphy was still unable to play, Collins again was at second for both ends of a twin-bill split with the Highlanders on May 29. In the first contest, a 6–5 loss, he went 2-for-5, but he did commit an error. His triple, however, did not go unnoticed by the Tall Tactician.

One game remained on Collins' tour at second base. He was present and accounted for with two hits and another errorless game as the A's bested the Nationals on June 1. Murphy was back for the next game, but Eddie's bat kept him in the lineup, now in center field, for three games. Again he was errorless, but good fielding involves more than merely avoiding errors. Range, arm strength, foot speed and instinct play an important part as well.

Connie Mack's inability to find a place for Collins in 1908 did not go unnoticed. Jimmy Isaminger, the well-known Philadelphia sports writer, recalled a scene in Mack's office involving a veteran reporter.

"He [Collins] can't field anywhere," he told Connie after Eddie had been tried in several positions in one week.
"We'll see about that. Just give him a chance," Connie replied.
"That runt can't hit, either."
Mack's eyes blazed with anger at that remark. He departed from his usual soft spoken voice to roar out: "There's where you are wrong. If Collins can't hit why then I don't know anything about baseball and I'm going to quit and become a five cent insurance agent."

Isaminger finished his story by telling readers, "So far as known, no householder was ever called to the door and asked by a long, lean, wistful looking man to take out a $200 life insurance policy."[17]

Given Mack's thinking, therefore, it was clear that Collins would continue to play even if his middle initial might be "u" for utility rather than "t" for Trowbridge. The next time Collins found the field other than as a pinch-hitter was June 11 when he played shortstop in a 7–0 loss to the White Sox and again the next day in another loss. He was in center field on June 14 versus Detroit. By now the flagging A's were in fifth place, dangerously close to sixth. It appeared that if there was a season for Mack to experiment, this was it. And that was exactly what Connie Mack did over the next several games with Eddie Collins. He was in center field for a game or two, in left for a game or two, and then on June 21 he went back to shortstop. This time, however, the move carried more significance. In a switch akin to a three-player trade, regular second baseman Danny Murphy was placed in right field, shortstop Simon Nicholls moved into Murphy's place at second base, and Collins was inserted at short. And there he would stay, or so it seemed.

At 31, Daniel Francis Murphy was still a serviceable ballplayer, one who by 1908 was in his seventh season with the A's, all at second base. He was a steady if not spectacular infielder, and a better hitter. Murphy was a fan favorite and a noted stealer of opponent's signs. In June of 1908, Mack decided Danny Murphy was well suited for his outfield, thus the switch to right field. It was now up to Collins to prove the Tall Tactician right.

All told, between June 23 and the second game of a doubleheader with Chicago on July 15, Collins played shortstop for 18 games. What happened was not all that pretty. As Eddie undoubtedly cringed and A's fans frowned, local headlines reported, "A Miscue by Eddie Collins,"[18] "Wild Heave by Eddie Collins Lets in Two Runs in the Eighth,"[19] and "[A's] Lose Opener in Double-Header by Poor Fielding by Eddie Collins and Nichols [sic]."[20] This last one, reporting on the first game played with Chicago in Philadelphia on July 15, did the trick. Mack had seen enough. The A's still lingered in fifth, seven games behind league leader Detroit, when Mack made his move. He switched Collins, who despite his poor fielding still carried a strong bat, to second base. But instead of switching Nicholls back to short, he inserted his latest college recruit, Jack Barry, at the position. This was the same fellow the reporter questioned Mack about earlier in the year, the hot prospect that Mack felt sure was eventually heading elsewhere, the same prospect Mack had long coveted and now possessed. Eddie Collins' run at shortstop was over. Not used to failure, Collins' lack of success mystified him.

"Mack began by playing me at shortstop. He kept me there for only a few days. I then realized that there must be something the matter with me as a shortstop. What it was, I did not know; even to-day [1914] I do not know."[21]

The Tall Tactician explained his reasoning, telling his biographer, Fred Lieb, he was "never quite satisfied with his [Collins] shortstop play, so I tried him at third base, and in a few games in right field ... I soon had to get him out of there, a couple of fly balls almost hit him on the head.

"So I got another idea. I thought, why not put my second baseman, Danny Murphy, in right field, and see what Eddie could do at second base? Though Danny had been my second baseman since my first pennant winner in 1902, he never was a really great second baseman. He didn't pivot too well on double plays, but Murphy always was a sweet hitter."[22]

Collins agreed with Mack's assessment of his situation in 1908. He had played several positions and excelled at none. That is, until he was placed at second. "There I found my haven."[23]

In retrospect Connie Mack probably decided Eddie Collins was his second baseman before all that outfield discomfort, back when Murphy was first injured in late July and Collins held up well at the position over the course of a four-game stretch. But Mack was a deft handler of men. He knew that switching Danny Murphy to right for a bumbling, unproven Collins would anger Murphy's many fans and place added pressure on the kid to perform well in the field. Instead, he turned the valve and slowly released some steam by first inserting Nicholls there. By that time Mack considered Nicholls, who was struggling at the plate, as a player with a limited future with his club. On the other hand, Mack liked Collins' bat as well as his foot speed. He "showed me he was a real ball player."[24]

After 1908 Nicholls played only 21 more games for the A's and 24 total in the major leagues. Although Nicholls' major league playing career was undoubtedly affected by his untimely death from typhoid fever and peritonitis in March 1911, the choice of Collins over Nicholls did nothing to harm Mack's reputation as a superb judge of talent and molder of men who played the game at a very high level. Eddie Collins did not just like his new position; he loved it. More importantly, he thrived there not only offensively, where Mack expected it, but defensively as well.

"I would rather play second base than any other position. It is curious, but when I'm in the infield, right on the edge of the grass, down on the first line of defense, I am able to hit better than if I played the outfield.... In the infield it seems that one is keyed up to a higher pitch of tension than is possible standing way out in the outfield...."[25]

Of course, the transition from gopher boy to second sacker supreme did not occur overnight. Nor did it happen without the assistance of others. Like his boss, Collins recognized he was replacing a fan favorite. Initially the A's faithful were unhappy, but Murphy took his position change in stride. He found Collins a grateful student.

"I took to the position naturally and really found myself there, but Murphy played a great part in helping to mold me into ... a good second baseman."[26]

Collins was unlike some baseball players who come by their talents naturally. Other than his speed and his quickness, he worked hard to develop his other skills, including hitting, as well as fielding.

Andy Coakley, who saw Collins early on but was gone from the A's by 1908, recalls that before he left the team, he worked with Collins to improve his ability to bunt. "I used to buggy whip and switch him across the shins when he didn't stand in perfect balance while drilling on bunts. He was a perfectionist. He wanted every move correct."[27]

Now Collins had Murphy helping him in much the same way as Coakley and it began to pay off. Even though Eddie missed a number of games at the end of the season, more than likely due to an injury, his final tallies showed appearances in 102 games. In 330 at-bats he hit safely 90 times for a .273 average, compared to the A's team average of .223 and the league average of .239. In addition, he drove home 40 teammates and even hit his first major league home run.

As for Connie Mack, he saw his team end the season in sixth place, its worst American League finish to date. That placed the A's 22 games off the pace set by the Tigers, who were defeated in the World Series by the Chicago Cubs. Nonetheless, Mack believed his mid-season moves would eventually bear fruit. And, at the same time he was constructing a team on the field, Connie was involved in another construction project. This one involved concrete and steel. For when second basemen Eddie Collins lifted a fly ball to Boston center fielder Tris Speaker to end a 5–0 loss to the Boston Red Sox on October 3, it was the last out of the last game ever played by the Philadelphia Athletics in Columbia Park. A new baseball park would greet Mack and his Mackmen when they in turn greeted the 1909 season.

CHAPTER 6

Yannigan No More

"There are two remarkable things about Collins — his fiery temper and fighting spirit — and his control of both."

— Hugh Fullerton[1]

When Eddie Collins arrived in New Orleans on March 10, 1909, for his first spring training, he joined a team that was still in transition. During the off-season Connie Mack acquired catcher Ira Thomas from the American League champion Detroit Tigers. He joined catcher Doc Powers, who appeared in 62 games for the A's in 1908 but sported little punch. In his 10 big league seasons, Powers' career average was .216 with four home runs and 199 runs batted in. In addition, he was 38 years old. Thomas was 29 and in 1908 batted .307, albeit in only 101 at-bats. At an imposing 6 foot 2 inches and 200 pounds, Thomas soon became someone Mack depended on, although he was never a workhorse and never batted .300 again.

Toward the end of the 1908 season, Mack experimented with any number of players besides Collins, whose own job was anything but secure. One such prospect was John Franklin Baker, a 22-year-old third baseman from Maryland whom Mack brought in from Reading, Pennsylvania, of the Tri-State League. Connie liked what he saw during the Marylander's nine-game stay and planned to give him a longer look while the team trained in Louisiana.

Already figuring prominently in the mix was Jack Barry, the college flash. Despite hitting a meager .222 in 1908, he had shown enough promise during his 40-game stint to earn a much longer look. Although he played more games at second base than at shortstop during his initial season, Barry was now penciled in at short in Mack's master plan.

The one fixture in the A's infield was native Philadelphian Harry Davis, the team captain who was beginning his ninth season as an original Athletic. Mack thought so much of Davis as a thinker and strategist — he was another master at stealing signs — that he permitted Davis to manage the club in Mack's absence. Davis was more than just an "old head" to a kid like Collins. Much the same as Andy Coakley and Danny Murphy, Davis played a significant part in Collins' development. And like Coakley, Davis quickly realized Eddie was in pursuit of perfection.

"He [Collins] was a great fellow for asking questions. He was a pest in that respect — asking you point-blank on the field — instead of waiting till after the game."[2]

But even though an infield was taking shape with Davis at first, Collins at second, Baker at third and Barry at short, Mack was not finished. On January 8, 1909, an article on the sports page of the *Philadelphia Inquirer* reported the A's had been awarded John McInnis by the National Commission, baseball's ruling body. McInnis, then 18 and claimed as the property of the minor league Haverhill club, was now the property of the A's, his position yet to be determined.

On March 11 when the regulars lined up for a morning workout, Collins must have wondered whether Connie Mack was having second thoughts. Although the youngsters Barry and Baker manned shortstop and third base respectively, Danny Murphy stood on second. The outfield consisted of Topsy Hartsel, Rube Oldring and a newcomer, Heinie Heitmuller, a 25-year-old right-handed hitter from California.

The *Inquirer* took notice, telling its readers that "Collins was looking in better health than last year, so that it is certain to be a problem where to place him. If he hits as well as in 1908, it seems likely that he is due for a place."[3]

It was clear to most that the 1909 spring training season would be a pivotal one in determining the long-term stock market report on the A's of Connie Mack. According to A's part-owner Frank Hough, writing a column for the *Inquirer* as the "Old Sport," the Tall Tactician faced "an embarrassment of riches in the way of infielders," with at least three candidates at each position. As to Collins, "His ability to reach first may more than offset any slight defect in his fielding, and justify his selection as guardian of second base."[4]

On March 17 Mack set up an intra-squad match that only he could pull together on that early date. He fielded a team of collegians against a team of non-collegians. The non-collegians were victorious in a hotly-contested rivalry, 5–2. Collins led the college boys with three

If Collins had a weakness in the field it was the strength of his throwing arm. He often joked about it. However, he made up for any inadequacies by his ability to quickly position himself in front of ground balls and make accurate throws (National Baseball Hall of Fame Library, Cooperstown, New York).

hits, including a triple and a double. He also fielded second in fine fashion. His play in that game bought him a shot with the big fellows on March 21, when the A's met the locals from New Orleans. It was the final game at their spring base, and the A's won, 6–3. Eddie was the hitting star for the big league club. He banged out three singles and a triple, scoring twice. The triple, with the bases loaded, was the game's major blow. Nonetheless, he remained a member of Mack's "Yannigans"—in baseball's sometimes strange lexicon, a spring training second stringer. When it came to Collins as a member of his regular infield, unlike Barry and Baker, Mack remained unconvinced.

When the A's prepared to break camp and play their way north, Mack unveiled a plan. He divided the roster into two separate squads, the regulars and the Yannigans. The logical step was for Mack to accompany the regulars and assign someone else for the second team, but Mack had other ideas. He assigned John Shibe, the son of majority owner Ben, to manage the regulars. His eyes and ears on the field would be team captain Harry Davis. As the regulars advanced north, so would Mack, only the manager would be guiding a crew that included Collins, John McInnis, who was filling various infield slots, pitcher Harry Krause, a promising left-hander of 21, and a pair of young outfielders named Amos Strunk and Joe Jackson.

At age 19 Jackson made his first appearance with the Athletics toward the end of 1908. That start, which actually encompassed five games beginning on August 25, was interrupted by a trip home due to homesickness. It was a rocky beginning, to say the least, for the obviously talented hitter and fielder from Greenville, South Carolina. Unlike most rookies, Jackson arrived with a reputation as a legendary hitter. The advance publicity angered many of the A's veterans, who gave him a hard time. The fact Jackson was illiterate only served to stir the pot more. According to one of Jackson's many biographers, Donald Gropman, those A's who were bitter toward Jackson "made him the butt of all their yokel tricks. One night in the hotel dining room they tricked him into drinking the water in the finger bowl and then laughed him out of the room."[5]

Whether it was hazing of this type or merely frustration over his play— he hit only .130—the teenager returned home once again. He did not return in 1908. Nevertheless, Mack knew what a talent he had in Joe Jackson, and with help from those close to the youngster, he was able to convince him to return in 1909. When nothing changed, Jackson left the team once more. At least in the spring while the Mackmen played in the South, he was giving major league baseball another try. Now like the rest of Mack's Yannigans, Joe Jackson was heading north, his final destination Philadelphia.

Eddie Collins spoke often about Connie Mack's decision to divide his squad in 1909 and its effect on the development of the team. As it turned out, there was more to Mack's plan than just coaching a bunch of young prospects from the bench during the games. According to Collins, "We were clay in the hands of a baseball wizard."

Each day the youngsters gathered around their wise teacher, listening as he gently analyzed their mistakes, taking care to ensure their enthusiasm was genuine. During each session additional intricacies of the game of baseball were revealed, understood, and filed away.[6]

The daily meetings became a club ritual and continued into 1909 and every season thereafter. Before long many other teams copied the idea. Collins described the A's routine:

"Every morning at 10, we gather in the club house; if the team is on the road, we meet in Connie's room in the hotel. We are never in session less than ten minutes or rarely more than half an hour. But in that time the game to be played that afternoon is sometimes won. Every point of the defensive and offensive strength of the opposing team is discussed. Mack will mention the pitcher that our opponents will probably use, and instantly a scheme of attack is devised. This attack varies as we meet different pitchers. Always in those morning meetings, Mack goes over the entire situation, plans the battle."[7]

The trip north could not have gone better for Collins. After a win in Montgomery, Alabama, and one in Birmingham, in which Eddie, now the captain of the Yannigans, led the team's offense with a triple and two singles, the team headed to Nashville. There the winning streak continued, as did the heat in Collins' bat. In Louisville Mack was confronted by angry team management, upset at his nerve in parading a group of wide-eyed rookies through town instead of bringing his regulars. Nonetheless, the Yannigans won easily, 15–2. A day later they won again, 6–4, much to Mack's delight and local management's dismay. Collins stroked five hits in those two contests and scored four runs.

In early April while the regulars prepared to play the annual "city championship" with the cross-town Phillies, the Yannigans stopped in Indianapolis, where their winning streak was halted at seven. A loss at Columbus followed. When the Yannigans reached Reading, just outside of Philadelphia, one of the members made a U-turn and headed south. Joe Jackson had acquitted himself well during the spring. He fit into Mack's plans for his outfield. Yet after the game in Reading, the team, including Jackson, stood on the station platform awaiting a train to Philadelphia to prepare for the start of the regular season only a few days away. As he stood there, Jackson spotted some empty milk cans. One of the cans was painted red. The color indicated the can was to be returned to a plant located in the South. Jackson told Mack he wished he would tie him to that can and send him to the South as well. Mack took him at his word, sending Jackson to Savannah in the South Atlantic League.[8] According to Eddie, "Joe brightened immediately...."[9]

Unlike Joe Jackson, the remaining Yannigans boarded that train in Reading eager to join their mates and begin a brand new season. However, in April 1909, there was much more awaiting them at home than just an opening day match with the Boston Red Sox, and the city of Philadelphia was pulsating in anticipation.

By 1909 Philadelphia was a city of about 1,500,000 inhabitants. Even the casual observer knows that the "City of Brotherly Love" was settled by William Penn on Quaker principles of tolerance and harmonious living. Less are aware that the city was configured in grids and without fortification. Although Penn's vision called for a community of farmers, the introduction of a port soon transformed the city into a trading hub second only to New York City. The willingness of the Quakers to encompass those with different beliefs and of different races resulted in the rise of substantial pockets of Italians, Irish, Eastern Europeans and Asians. A significant migration of blacks began after the Civil War. These diverse groups were drawn to the factories that formed and increased in size as the country entered the Industrial Revolution. At the same time, a rising merchant class eschewed a simple Quaker existence, preferring more public entertainment in the form of restaurants, theater, dancing, and similar cultural pursuits. Two forms of entertainment the working and merchant classes shared in common were the city's pubs and its baseball.

By 1908 the success of American League baseball in Philadelphia necessitated a search for a new home for Benjamin Shibe, Connie Mack and their Athletics. Although Columbia Park was a mere eight years old, its wooden stands and small capacity were inadequate to house an increasingly popular team in an increasingly populated city. Overflow crowds were not uncommon at Columbia Park. A shining example was the mashed throng of 28,000 that jammed the park to see the return of Rube Waddell and his newly adopted St. Louis Browns in May 1908. Since the lease on Columbia Park was coming to a close, it was high time to move. It was up to the majority shareholder, Ben Shibe and his family, to take the first step.

That step was taken in 1908 when A's ownership formed a separate corporation that eventually became the owner of a new ballpark. After a series of negotiating sessions with the city, the new company began purchasing land at 21st and Lehigh, an area which at that time was some distance from the center of town. The location, in an area with many vacant lots and even some woods, raised eyebrows. To make matters worse, right across the street was the Philadelphia Hospital for Contagious Diseases. This was where those unlucky souls who contracted smallpox were treated. Although plans were already in place to close the facility, it still caused passersby to cringe.

The owners of the Athletics, however, were visionaries. They realized that by planning a ballpark at 21st and Lehigh they were taking a risk, but the location was near trolley lines and took less than 15 minutes to reach from city hall.

The standout feature in the design of the new park was the choice of the materials used to build it. This was to be the first full steel and concrete baseball stadium erected for a major league club. Ground breaking occurred on April 13, 1908. It took two months to grade the land, with sod for the playing field being imported from Columbia Park after the 1908 season.

It took less than a year to complete construction of what was to be named Shibe Park. A feature was its domed tower at the main entrance on the corner of 21st and Lehigh. The facade was French Renaissance and the tower housed a pavilion. The park seated 23,000, but there was room for an additional 10,000 who could stand on banked terraces behind outfield ropes. The double-decker grandstand introduced for the first time folding chairs for 10,000 fans between the first and third base lines. Bench seats provided the remaining 13,000 with their view from uncovered concrete bleachers that ran to the left and right field corners. The aisles were wide enough that an additional 7,000 could squeeze in, making the theoretical capacity of the facility 40,000.

A clubhouse for the Mackmen was constructed under the grandstand on the third base side and provided thirty lockers, three showers and a small trainer's room. A tunnel ran from the clubhouse area, which consisted of four rooms, to the dugout. The visitor's clubhouse was a bit smaller and located on the first base side.

The dimensions of Shibe Park included a 12-foot-high wall which enclosed the outfield. The distance from home to center was 515 feet, from home down the left field line 378, and from home down the right field line only 340 due to the 20th Street boundary.

Additionally, there was a spacious press box and offices inside the park for the team's executives and staff. There were drinking fountains throughout the stadium and attendants in both the men's and women's restrooms. There was a garage for 200 cars and parking spaces set aside for more, in recognition of a growing trend. And finally there were stores and restaurants along the Lehigh Avenue and 21st Street sides of the first floor of the park. In short, Shibe Park was state of the art and then some.[10] In the words of author Bruce Kuklick, there was in the new ballpark "an abiding element; it was 'a lasting monument,' built to endure with a grandiose beauty that should express continuing prosperity and assured advance."[11]

Now in the second week of April, Connie Mack and his Yannigans were back in town, as were the A's regulars. All that remained was for the park to open on April 12. The fans, of course, were in frenzy — and not just the upper classes. According to William Weart of the *Philadelphia Evening Telegram*, the new stadium was "built for the masses as well as the classes...."[12]

The players were ecstatic about opening in a brand new ball park, too. In that regard Mack had a few surprises up his sleeve. Collins recalls that based on the 1908 results, "the Philadelphia fans were not optimistic about a successful season for the Mackmen. So Connie filled up the newspapers with tales of what a wonderful collection of youngsters he had. On one or two occasions before the opening of the season, he hinted at changes. He suggested that when the Athletics took the field for the first official game of the American League campaign, that there would be many new faces in the line-up. Yet, in the exhibition games, he kept in all the old regulars. In this way he created a keen feeling of anticipation on the part of the Philadelphia fans. Every fan was wondering which of the old Athletics would lose their jobs; what youngsters would win them."[13]

Collins vividly recalls the opening game and the new park, firm in his conviction that "Connie had gone about the fashioning of a team to fill it as methodically as the architects had gone about their job."[14]

In truth Connie's hand was somewhat forced for the opener since Baker, a youngster Mack intended to start at third, was injured. It is reasonable to assume that Jack Barry was also injured or he too would have started. He had played well in the spring, was tabbed to work his way north with the regulars as a shortstop, and once in the lineup remained the shortstop for 124 games. The lineup and batting order (with age in parentheses) that Mack did use for the opener was Hartsel (35) in left, Nicholls (26) at third, Collins (21) at second, Murphy (32) in right, Davis (35) at first, Strunk (20) in center, McInnis (18) at short, Powers (38) catching, and Eddie Plank (33) on the mound.

At game time Mack's mix of young and old were greeted by 35,000 boisterous fans who jammed the crevices and thousands of others who climbed upon surrounding housetops on 20th Street to secure their view. By then the multitude, many arriving to form lines as early as seven that morning, had already stood to sing "America," watch and listen to various officials of the government and the sport before seeing bands and players march to center field where Ben Shibe and Ban Johnson raised both the American flag and an Athletics pennant. They all then sang "The Star Spangled Banner." There followed a ceremonial ball toss by Philadelphia Mayor John Reyburn and umpire Tim Hurst's cry, "Play ball." The christening of Shibe Park was underway.

After all the pomp and circumstance, the actual game might have been a letdown. Perhaps it would have, if the hometowners had succumbed, but they did not, besting a Boston team that featured Tris Speaker in center, 8–1. Collins upheld his end with a pair of singles, scoring a run. He was also gunned down at the plate, trying to score on one of Danny Murphy's four hits.

Pitching was expected to be a strength for the A's in 1909 and lefty Eddie Plank provided confirmation by scattering six hits. Another of Mack's "college boys," he graduated from Gettysburg College and did not join the Athletics until 1901, when he was already 25. In 1909, this initial win — one of 326 in a hallmark career — was just the first of 19 against 10 defeats.

Collins always loved to discuss Eddie Plank, describing him as "a man of fine character and intelligence" who, unlike Rube Waddell, "was not as famous for his eccentricities as his pitching skill." According to Eddie, "On the slab he [Plank] was nervous, irritable, superstitious, off the field restless and capricious."

Plank's routine included a variety of "poses, gyrations and other motions.... The umpires fussed, the players raved, but Eddie ignored them all. He pitched as he pleased — and won."[15]

For Eddie Plank there would be many more games and many more wins. For battery mate Doc Powers, his appearance on opening day 1909 was tragically his last. Powers, known as a defensive stalwart, was like Plank an original member of the A's and quite popular with the fans and players. Doc performed well in the game on April 12, scoring a run. However, after the game in the clubhouse, he suffered acute indigestion and was rushed to the hospital. Despite three surgeries, he developed peritonitis and died two weeks later on April 26, 1909. According to speculation at the time, the veteran catcher consumed a cheese sandwich right before the game. Perhaps the food failed to properly digest due to his extended crouching behind the plate during the game.[16] In an ironic twist, "Doc" was not just a nickname; Powers was a practicing physician. His death shocked his team and its fans, but no one more than Connie Mack, who became tearful on learning of the loss and later called Powers one of his greatest catchers.

It was fortunate for the A's that when it came to the position of catcher, their cupboard was not bare. Mack had recently obtained the competent Ira Thomas from Detroit. In addition, as the season wore on, Jack Lapp, a 24-year-old left-handed hitter with a decent batting eye, and Paddy Livingston, 29 and better behind than at the plate, shared time with Thomas.

The Athletics, with Thomas now behind the plate and Collins solidly entrenched at second, were nevertheless floundering at 5–8 by early May. A four-game losing streak following Powers' death was costly. However, on May 6 the Mackmen defeated Washington, 2–1, behind a fine performance from Chief Bender. The win ignited the fortunes of a team given little chance by prognosticators to contend for the pennant. They won nine of the next ten, including a 10–2 pasting of league leader Detroit on May 19. During the streak Collins carried his weight, hitting close to .290. His triple in the twelfth inning in a May 17 game with the White Sox drove in Frank Baker with the winning run. By that time Jack Barry was the shortstop, and Mack's infield was set. Moreover, Eddie was making a name for himself stealing bases. His emergence in that regard reflected one of the ways Connie Mack was such an effective manager.

"One day when I had not been with the club long, he [Mack] said to me: 'Eddie, did you ever notice how Cobb slides? Pretty nice, isn't it?'

"That was all. I didn't need a bludgeon to be told my sliding was wrong. So I went out and practiced it quietly, and presently the nod and smile that he gave me were so genuine that it paid for all the bruises, and bumps sustained by flinging oneself into a dirt pit."[17]

The added dimension of Collins, the base stealer, greatly increased his value. In 1909 his 67 steals were second only to Cobb's 76 on the American League leader board. The pair continued to battle each other for theft laurels throughout their careers.

In addition, Collins' play was showing marked improvement in another facet; he was becoming an excellent second basemen. The *Inquirer* recorded one stellar play while reporting the A's 8–4 victory in Detroit on May 21.

"Collins' play on [Wild Bill] Donovan in the fourth was about the greatest ever made on the sacrifice. He ran to cover the sack for [Harry] Davis. Davis slipped and the ball got past him. Collins threw himself at the ball, nailed it and tagged Donovan on the leg just in front of the bag."[18]

Although Collins was often accused by Mack and others of possessing a weak throwing arm and almost as often described as fielding like an old woman, no one after 1908 accused him of being anything but a superb second sacker.

According to the esteemed sports writer Bob Broeg, "Afield, he could relax until he seemed to droop. At times he even seemed to loaf when a ball was hit to him. But though never as graceful as, say, Lajoie or Charley Gehringer, two other outstanding second basemen, he always seemed to be in front of the ball. For one thing, he played hitters both wisely and well with his massive hands."[19]

Bolstered by the strong arm of Eddie Plank and three hits each from Collins and Jack Barry, by now a fixture at short, the A's beat the Tigers, 7–1. With their three wins in the four-game series, the A's were now running neck and neck with Detroit. And for one brief moment, Mack's mix of whiskered veterans and whiskerless youngsters rested in first place in the American League. The Mackmen of 1909 were now in a race for the flag and there they would stay.

A good deal of the credit for the Athletics' success in 1909 must go to their excellent starting pitchers. Plank and Chief Bender, in the midst of fashioning an 18–8 campaign with a 1.66 ERA, were the anchors. They were joined by right-hander Cy Morgan, over from the Red Sox and a nice complement to the Chief; Harry Krause, surprising everyone on his way to a sparkling 18–8, 1.39 season; and Jimmy Dygert, no slouch himself in stacking up a 9–5, 2.42 mark. Simply put, on any given day the A's opponents faced "shut-down" pitching.

Already enthralled by their new ball park, Philadelphians began flocking to this sparkling palace in increasing numbers, eager to see a contender. The crowds, congregating as they were in an area of the city unaccustomed to such attention, brought accompanying problems. On May 29 as the team prepared for a twin-bill killing of Boston, the city experienced what was probably its first gridlock. Traffic on Lehigh Avenue approaching the park came to a standstill. For several hours prior to the start of the action, no cars moved in either direction. Nevertheless, 14,269 of the faithful made their way into the ball yard in time to see Collins go 4-for-4 and steal two bases, one a double steal executed with Danny Murphy.

The traffic problems, nevertheless, were hampering attendance. The congestion on May 31, before Boston rebounded with two wins of its own, was described thusly:

"All roads led to Shibe Park yesterday, alright, but the going, the hoofing, the pedestrianizing, as it were, was mighty tough on Shank's mare. Anything and everything that was on wheels, from the great big truck down to the humble little furniture car, was pressed into service by energetic hustlers in quest of the nimble dime and quarter, but the great majority of those who witnessed the games were compelled to utilize the locomotion with which they were originally endowed. And they seemed to enjoy it, for a better natured bunch of enthusiasts could hardly be imagined — that is going in to the park. In the morning the attendance was 8,760 and in the afternoon it footed up 17,792 — a total for the day of 26,552. What the attendance would have been under normal transportation facilities can only be conjectured, but it is not extravagant to say that it would have been in the neighborhood of 50,000."[20]

Through June and July the A's stayed in the hunt, either in second or in third. They were as far out as seven games in late June, but an eight-game winning streak brought them to within one-half game of the lead on July 9. By then they were sporting a respectable record of 44–26. During this span Collins continued to make himself an indispensable part of the A's machinery. His hitting out of the number three spot in the lineup was particularly timely in several instances and flat out spectacular in others. On June 11 the A's won an extra-inning home tilt with the Browns, 2–1, when Eddie went 4-for-5, including a triple. His single in the eighth brought pinch runner Rube Oldring in with the tying run and his infield single in the eleventh eventually brought Eddie across the plate with the winning tally. He had a 4-for-4 day, again including a triple, on June 28 in a 2–1 loss to the Highlanders. Through the first 62 games, Collins set the batting pace in the American League at .367. He was no longer Connie Mack's secret.

On July 3 a large contingent of Eddie Collins' Columbia "fan club" attended a doubleheader in New York. The A's won both games and Collins did not disappoint his friends. He was 5-for-9 on the day with a triple and a double. In addition, he scored a run in each game.

According to the Old Sport, Collins' real strength was that "he does not bat in streaks, nor is he confined to any particular style of batting or handicapped by a change from a right-hander to a left-hander. He can line them out or dump them down, just as the emergency demands, and appears to hit left-handers, with just as much freedom as he does right-handers.... Then with all his physical excellence he has got a head and no end of nerve, forming a combination that is almost ideal."[21]

Of course, there were those in the league not as taken with Collins' newfound status.

On July 13 the *Inquirer's* sports editor wrote that "Collins has incurred the dislike of many old-timers. So long as he was playing at the speed which he showed last season, but which suggested the tremendous gait that he has developed this, he was let alone, but since he has gained the batting premiership, passing such great sluggers as [Napoleon] Lajoie, Cobb and [Sam] Crawford, he has aroused the jealousy of many of the ancients, who see in the rapid rise of youngsters like Collins their own decline. On more than one occasion runners have gone into second in a way not justified by the exigencies of the occasion, but up to date none of the thugs has succeeded in getting him." In passing, the writer noted that Baker was another of the "youngsters whom the opposition are after."[22]

In short order, the aforementioned assessment would prove amazingly prescient, but perhaps there was more for the opposition to dislike about Collins than merely the fact he was becoming an outstanding hitter. Eddie had earned the nickname "Cocky" as he performed on the field of play, but that is also how he was known by his teammates. Most attributed the choice of nickname merely to Collins' air of self-assuredness rather than to an offensive attitude or bearing. Still, the degree of confidence and the outward manner by which it was exhibited in one so young certainly affected those around him, especially those who now opposed him and more and more frequently experienced defeat at the hands of his rising A's.

One did not have to look far to find examples of Collins' competitive and, at times, combative spirit. On base at the end of a double-header loss to the Browns on July 17, the A's newest base-running threat stole second, stole third, and then attempted to steal home, where he "was declared out by Umpire Perrine, but not until he had made a vigorous protest."[23]

On July 30 Collins and his infield mates pulled off a triple play against the Cleveland Naps in a 7–1 win. At the plate with runners on first and third and no outs, the Naps' first sacker, George Stovall, hit the ball toward Eddie, who "wriggled his body like a professional contortionist" and caught the ball, surprising both base runners. A throw to Frank Baker at third caught one; his subsequent throw to Davis at first completed the feat.[24] The win was their seventh in a row.

Then a few days later on August 3, Collins was involved in another altercation. This time he picked on the wrong umpire. A decade prior to the advent of the American League, Timothy Carroll Hurst, a short, stocky fellow with a quick wit and colorful disposition, made his debut as an umpire in the National League. Stories about Tim Hurst's days in that league abound. Although one must question many of these tales, it does appear that Hurst was dismissed from his service with that league when an irate fan tossed a beer stein at him and he tossed it back into the stands, injuring an innocent bystander. Despite this and any number of other incidents which gave pause regarding Hurst's ability to stay out of trouble, he had a reputation for fairness. He often was called upon to referee prizefights. Thus, when American League President Ban Johnson encountered a need for new umpires for his league, he hired Hurst, who continually stirred up fans, players, owners, and Johnson himself.[25] But Hurst survived and was umpiring a doubleheader at Shibe Park on August 3 between the White Sox and the A's. The A's won both ends of the afternoon's card, including the second game, 10–4, but there are two totally different versions of an altercation that occurred between Collins and Hurst in game two.

According to a muddled description of play in the bottom of the eighth in the August 4 edition of the *Inquirer*, Collins was called out at second by Hurst, "took exception, and must have said something offensive to Hurst for the latter spat in his face." This, of course, ignited the crowd of over 16,000, who continued to hoot and howl at Hurst throughout the game-ending top of the ninth. After the game "a crowd of excited fans got after him [Hurst]. He walked over to the tunnel and pushed and jostled, but before any of the more excited spectators had a chance to do him harm, he was surrounded by the Athletic players and a number of officers and rushed to cover."[26]

A second version, totally at odds with the first, was told to baseball writer Fred Lieb, who related it in an article about Hurst, which appeared in a 1961 issue of *The Sporting News*, the national baseball weekly.

> Tim got into his big scrape with Collins largely because of his penchant for calling out runners at first base before the ball reached the first basemen's mitt.
>
> We'll let Joe Ohl, road-secretary of the Athletics in their early championship years, take it from here:
>
> "Knowing of the way Hurst called out runners long before they reached base, Cocky Collins and our veteran first basemen, Harry Davis, decided to have a little fun at Tim's expense," said Joe.
>
> "It was our first year at Shibe Park, now known as Connie Mack Stadium, and if memory serves me correctly, we were playing Washington. The Athletics were well ahead, and a slow-footed Senator batter hit an easy grounder to Collins. As soon as Cocky let go what seemed to be a throw, Hurst called the runner out.
>
> "Collins never let go of the ball, and Davis completed the act by pretending to catch the phantom throw. When the Washington coach yelled at Hurst, 'Davis hasn't got the ball,' and Collins sheepishly showed he still held the ball, Tim realized he had been taken for a ride.
>
> "The madder he got the more the Athletics, and even the Washington players, laughed. The fans also were in convulsions in the stands. From the start, Hurst's indignation was directed almost entirely at Collins. He called Eddie everything he had in his dictionary, and then grew so angry that when Collins approached him he spat at our crack second basemen."[27]

Under both versions and even under a third version, which had Collins approaching Hurst and stepping on his foot with his spiked shoes, the result was the same. Ban Johnson fired Hurst and he was finished as an umpire. But even here there is some confusion. Although witnesses were in almost total agreement that Hurst did spit on Collins, neither Collins nor Mack ever preferred charges. According to an editorial in *The Sporting News,* Hurst was officially discharged for failing to file a timely report of the incident, a habitual problem.[28] In his biography on Ban Johnson, author Eugene Murdock writes that when Hurst's report finally arrived, it contained no defense of the spitting. Later when Johnson questioned Hurst about it, he merely replied, "I didn't like college boys."[29]

Of course, it takes two to tango, but Collins escaped the incident with all but his reputation as a "cocky" customer unscathed. When the Hurst incident occurred, the A's were in the midst of an upswing that, following three straight home wins in early August over Detroit, saw them tied with the Tigers on August 10. In game two of that series, an incident occurred involving Collins and Tiger catcher Oscar Stanage, which turned up the heat just enough to make what happened in subsequent Tigers-Athletics clashes that year more understandable. In the bottom of the first inning, Collins stood on third when Harry Davis hit a dribbler toward that base. Eddie took off for home, but as he reached Stanage, who moved almost 20 feet up the line to stand guard, the Tiger catcher caught the A's speedster with an elbow, knocking him down and out. When Eddie recovered, play was continued with the umpire calling him safe and the A's prevailing, 5–3. Fortunately, Collins was not seriously hurt and, in fact, drove in three runs and scored two in the clash, but the Philadelphia faithful gave Stanage an earful until he was removed from the game in the fifth with a hand injury. By his actions, however, the Tiger catcher delivered his message. The defending champs were in no mood to roll over for the upstart A's. And this was only a beginning.

Despite the warning the A's remained in first, or tied for first, with the Tigers over the next several weeks. As tight as the race for the flag, so was the race for the league batting title.

This one involved the A's and the Tigers as well. Although his average was off from earlier in the season, Collins still led the league at a robust .347. Gaining was the two-time defending American League batting champ, Ty Cobb, now clearly the game's top hitter. In addition to raising his average to .339 after a slow start, the Georgia native, every bit a Tiger on the base paths as well as at the plate, led the league in thefts with 52.

The contenders next met in Detroit on August 24 with the A's riding a five-game win streak. In those games Collins' glove was almost as hot as his bat. Just prior to the Detroit series in a win over Cleveland on August 21, he leaped high for a streak off the bat of outfielder Bris Lord, knocked the ball down with his gloved hand and caught it with the other before it touched the ground, turning a somersault in the process.

On August 24 when the A's entered Bennett Park, home of the Tigers, one game ahead of the Detroiters, the home team was on a five-game win streak of their own. Harry Krause and the Tigers' Ed Summers were the hurlers. It took less than one inning to bathe the game in controversy. In the bottom of the first, Cobb walked, then stole second. Krause then proceeded to walk center fielder Sam Crawford, but as ball four headed for the plate, Cobb sprinted for third, drawing a throw from A's catcher Paddy Livingston. As Cobb approached third with a hook-slide left, A's third sacker Frank Baker reached across the bag to tag him with his bare hand, meeting Cobb's spikes, which opened a small cut. Cobb was an easy out. However, the A's stormed the umpires claiming Cobb's action was a deliberate spiking for which he should be ejected. At the time only a pair of umpires worked each game. The two umpires in charge on this particular day ignored the protest. Baker was bandaged and stayed in the game, little worse for wear.

Later in the game Cobb doubled. This time he again hit the dirt, his slide upsetting Collins at second, as once again the A's fumed. They were even more upset at the score, as Detroit won, 7–6. There followed two more losses to the Tigers, the latter a 6–0 pasting at the hands of George Mullin, number 22 for the Tigers' pitching star. These losses knocked the A's off their tenuous perch and they left Michigan two behind the new leaders. The matter might have rested there, one the A's and their fans wanted only to forget; however, the furor was only beginning. Ty Cobb's actions had stirred the bees under Connie Mack's normally placid bonnet. He was beside himself with rage, telling reporters Cobb was a troublemaker whose "tactics ought to be looked into by the American League." Mack pledged to bring the matter of Cobb's actions in the first game to the attention of league officials.

"Other players have rights as well as Cobb. He should not be permitted to vent his spite upon them. I know that Cobb has threatened to get Baker, Barry and Collins. He did spike Baker and knock Collins heels over head yesterday trying to do the same to him. He may be a great player, but he is a pinhead in this respect. Organized baseball ought not to permit such a malefactor to disgrace it. You can take this straight. I am going to take steps to stop it."[30]

This statement, coming as it did from someone as respected and laid back as Mack, stung Ty Cobb. The charges stemming from this incident, especially given that Baker and Collins were seen as young, rising stars with clean records, probably did as much as anything to foster the notion, eventually held by many, that Cobb was a dirty player. Years later Cobb talked about the incident, denying he was out to get anyone. "Of the scurvier stories marketed and remarketed about me, the one that hurts as much as any, concerns Frank Baker."[31]

The day after hearing about Mack's charges, Cobb was more vociferous, calling the position of the A's manager "most ungentlemanly" and stating he "never spiked a man deliberately." He then went further, charging Eddie Collins with knocking out Tiger Oscar Stanage in an earlier game and stating Collins "goes into the bases the same way that I do and he has hurt as many men as I have." According to Cobb, "that is baseball and if we get hurt we take our medicine and don't go around crying over it."[32]

True to his word, Connie Mack did approach the league's president, Ban Johnson, to lodge his complaint. After issuing an initial warning, Johnson backed off in deference to the umpires and then viewed a photo that showed Baker off the base, reaching across for the tag and decided that was enough evidence to totally clear the Tiger star.[33]

The incident with Cobb was like a magnet with its polar opposites, drawing any number of opinions for and against. Unlike many baseball writers across the country, Collins, who considered Cobb the most "dynamic" player ever, did not blame his rival for Baker's injury, saying years later that Cobb never "went out of his way to spike opposing players." To the contrary, Collins felt Cobb, who always played all-out, was such a skilled slider he was able to slide away from the tag "rather than adopt football tactics."[34]

If the Tigers were upset about the charges against their teammate, it seemed to inspire them rather than dampen their spirit. By the time they next hit the road, their most recent homestand showed 15 wins with but two defeats. When they arrived in Philadelphia on September 16 to begin a four-game set, they brought a four-game lead, leaving the A's in desperate need of a sweep.

By now Philadelphia was a city of Cobb-haters; their antipathy fueled even further by an incident some two weeks prior when their nemesis brawled with a black elevator operator in Cleveland. The incident was widely reported and Cobb faced arrest for drawing a knife during the fight and slashing out at the operator. When Cobb finally arrived in the City of Brotherly Love, he was the recipient of at least a dozen threatening notes and letters. As the big series approached, the sportswriters of Philadelphia stoked the fire; in particular Horace Fogel of the *Evening Bulletin* and Frank Hough, the *Inquirer's* "Old Sport," who accused Detroit manager Hugh Jennings of introducing the "homicidal instinct" to Cobb's base-running style.[35] Indeed, at this point it was difficult to tell just who was the most worked up about Ty Cobb—the players, the fans, or the press.

Certainly Connie Mack was aware of the importance of beating the Tigers. "I never wanted to sweep a series so badly in my life."[36] He almost got his wish.

On September 16 playing in front of almost 25,000 fans and an extra large contingent of 180 policemen, a number of them surrounding the Tigers bench, the A's and ace moundsman Eddie Plank drew first blood, 2–1. An understandably jumpy Ty Cobb came up dry in four tries at the plate, delighting the multitude when he struck out with the bases full of Tigers in the fourth inning. Collins supplied a double to the A's cause and scored a run but was injured when his ankle was hit by the Tigers' fine shortstop, Donie Bush, as Bush slid hard into second. After the game Eddie's ankle swelled.

During the season Collins boarded at the home of Harry Davis and his family. Mack accompanied the A's trainer to the Davis home after the game. They worked on the ankle during the night, enabling Collins to play the next day, albeit not at his normal pace.[37] He was 0-for-2 in that second game of the series, a devastating 5–3 defeat. Over 27,000 witnessed the contest and even Cobb received applause several times, including when he stole third and Baker shook his hand to signify a truce, when he dove into the crowd behind the roped-off area in right field to one-hand a Davis fly ball in the fourth, and finally the next inning when he handed five dollars to the fan whose hat he had stepped on the previous inning when he went beyond the ropes. The A's rooters were now of the opinion Ty Cobb was not such a bad sort after all.

The final two games of this crucial series went to the Mackmen. In game three, a 2–0 victory when Chief Bender fashioned a three-hitter, Collins was back in form at the plate.

"Wild Bill" Donovan, the Tigers' moundsman, was almost as effective as the Chief, giving up four hits. Collins had three of them, including a double and run scored. Cobb was relatively quiet with only a single. The crowd of over 35,000 was believed the largest to date in baseball history. Many others, in what was becoming a local custom, watched from the rooftops of the adjacent row houses.

After a Sunday break to observe Pennsylvania law, the series resumed on Monday. Once again Plank answered the bell, winning 4–3. By now the *Inquirer* noted Collins, who doubled and scored a run in four trips, was a clear fan favorite, as were the Mack's "schoolboys," as the opposition called Collins, Baker, Barry, and left fielder Heinie Heitmuller. Of course, Cobb could not leave town without depositing at least one more imprint. In the fourth he spiked Jack Barry in a play at second, breaking skin. Barry was forced out of the game, requiring stitches. The injury was so serious that Barry did not play again in 1909. The incident might have proved incendiary, but Barry, who knew what might otherwise happen, gestured to the fans that his contact with Cobb was purely accidental. Cobb, who added another hit, managed to leave town in one piece, satisfied that his Tigers still held a two-game lead.

The A's went 8–6 in their remaining games and never closed the gap. In the estimation of Connie Mack, a 2–1 loss to the seventh-place Browns the day following the Tigers' departure from Philadelphia sealed his team's doom. In that one, Collins' failure to lay down a bunt with the bases full in the eighth was the golden opportunity squandered. Even the Tigers' split with Washington the same day inserted salt in the wound. Mack lamented that his A's "had planned, schemed, worked, and sweated to cut two games off Detroit's lead, and little [Bill] Bailey put us two and a half games back again. We never could make it up, and that was the margin by which we lost the 1909 pennant."[38]

Still, the A's second-place finish, with a sparkling record of 95–58, spoke volumes for the future. The fact that by season's end five regulars were under 30 years of age only added to a prognosis of good health. The attendance figure of 674,915, which stood with Boston as the American League's best, was testament to the vision of Benjamin Shibe, Mack and the remaining owners in creatively planning and financing their new ball park, one which could accommodate over 120,000 fans in that one pivotal four-game series with the Tigers.

For Eddie Collins, 1909 was a season of solidification and amplification. Entering spring training, he was fighting for an infield position. He closed the year a bona fide star, finishing second in the American League in hits (198), bases on balls (62), stolen bases (67), batting average (.347), and on-base percentage (OBP) (.416). He was third in runs scored (104), total bases (257) and slugging percentage (.450). The fact that Cobb led him in most categories and would in most cases throughout their careers was merely further proof of the distance traveled, for it was no great shame to finish second only to the game's greatest star. Edward Trowbridge Collins had arrived. Yet for him and for the White Elephants, the best was yet to come.

CHAPTER 7

Signature Season

"'That man [Collins] is the best ball player I ever saw,' Evers told me after the fifth game. 'He has no faults of any kind. Mechanically he is as near perfect as any player could be, whether at bat, or the bases, or in covering second base, and he has the best kind of a thinking head to top it all.'"

— Johnny Evers to Hugh Fullerton[1]

Given their accomplishments in 1909 and the exhausting campaign just completed, one would think in the fall of 1909 that it was time for Connie Mack and his Mackmen to rest. Such was not the case. In mid–September it was announced the team planned a western swing through the United States, eventually hooking up on the West Coast with a team of all-stars.

Mack was not finished molding his team. In spite of their high standard of play, at least in Mack's mind, there were still many skills to master and combinations to try out. For a lot of the young men, the extra money was a boon as well. It was reported that those who made this trip and played in the games, about a dozen players in all, would earn nearly as much money as the losers of the World Series would earn from their four-game share.[2] If true, the runner-up A's made as much as their bitter rivals, the Tigers, who lost the World Series to the Pittsburgh Pirates in seven games.

The A's 1909 barnstorming tour was the first for Collins. Although it was not his last, he did not avail himself the opportunity to barnstorm nearly as much as did many other premiere players of his day. The term "barnstorming" relates to the practice of playing exhibition games in various locales, usually in a city or town that did not have its own ball club or was the home to a minor league club. The term was borrowed from the fields of entertainment and politics, where one would perform or appear wherever one could, even if it meant a barn.[3]

Prior to heading west, the A's played a number of games in the East, including in Hartford, Connecticut, and Perkasie, Pennsylvania. On October 8, the same day as Game One of the World Series, Eddie and his mates faced off in front of 3,000 fans in Trenton, New Jersey, against the Philadelphia Giants, a black team. Collins had a hit and scored a run in a 5–2 Athletics' triumph. In 1909 the Giants were champions of their Eastern League. Their star pitcher in 1904 was the great Rube Foster. Foster was no longer with the team, but the Giants were still a powerhouse. The first baseman the day they met the A's in Trenton was Emmett Bowman, a sometimes pitcher, full-time jack-of-all-trades who was an early star in the Negro leagues. The shortstop was John Henry "Pop" Lloyd, the Hall-of-Famer who was discovered by Foster and played for several of his teams. In right field was Spottswood Poles, called by some the black Ty Cobb and an eventual decorated World War I hero. Catcher Bruce Petway, who possessed a strong arm, was one of the first to throw accurately to second base from the squat position, and once nabbed Ty Cobb all three times he attempted to steal in a game.

Several other area games ensued over the next week as the team tread water awaiting the close of the World Series. In Reading local favorite Frank Baker pitched the last inning, much to the delight of his adoring fans. The A's pre-tour record was 13–0. Collins played in all of the games until the last game in Shamokin, Pennsylvania, on October 17. He missed that one to return to New York, where he picked up his mother, who would make the trip to California with her son and his team. According to Mary Collins, "I was not anxious to have him [Eddie] become a ball player. I had hoped he might choose some other profession. But all that is passed now a good while ago. We watch him play whenever we get the opportunity and we have been glad to see him succeed as he has done. We are good fans now, his father and I."[4]

Thus Eddie and his mother were among those who boarded the train at 8:45 A.M. at Philadelphia's Broad Street Station, heading for the West Coast with a stop or two along the way. One of those stops was in Chicago, where on October 19 Chief Bender twirled a two-hit shutout and Collins out-hit the National League Cubs by one, including a three-base hit, in a 2–0 victory. By October 24 the A's barnstormers were all the way to Spokane, Washington, where they defeated a national all-star team that included the New York Giants' Fred Snodgrass and Larry Doyle. Additional games were played in Washington and in California, the tour extending into the first week of November. A highlight for the fans of Seattle was the appearance of Walter Johnson, a westerner himself, on the mound for the all-stars on October 27. Undaunted, the A's won, 5–3.

During the extensive trip the Athletics more than held their own. Mack could not have planned it better. In his mind his "boys" were ready for a fast launch in 1910. "I had a feeling what our club could do," he remarked. "From the time we reported at Virginia Hot Springs for training [in 1910], I felt we were pennant-winning material."[5]

Before the A's could truly talk pennant, however, there was still much work to do — road work, that is. During the ten-day stay at Hot Springs, the team's conditioning program called for a good deal of hiking. In addition, there were the hot baths, a gentle way to soothe tired muscles. The plan called for the regulars to train here first, before joining Mack and the younger group in Atlanta. The team's hotel in Hot Springs was ideal for their purposes, surrounded by mountains with roads extending outward. The first real opportunity to hit those roads was March 1; Danny Murphy and Topsy Hartsel took advantage. Collins, who was no longer a Yannigan, joined Harry Davis, Jack Coombs, Eddie Plank and Chief Bender in an afternoon round of golf on the hotel's famous links. Sometime earlier, President William Howard Taft had toured the same course in record-setting fashion.

The next day, however, the whole team hit the roads and the 1910 training season began in earnest. About ten days later, as scheduled, the camp moved to Atlanta. The Mackmen, who lined up as the regulars for the first exhibition game in that city on March 14, were essentially the same who finished 1909 in such fine fashion. Collins batted third, this time behind Rube Oldring and once again ahead of Frank Baker. The A's fared well against the competition, mostly the minor-league variety. One important aspect of the spring was the continued development of youngsters John McInnis, still carried as a utility infielder, and outfielder Amos Strunk. Another was the significant development of the middle infield combo of Barry and Collins. During an exhibition game in Atlanta on March 19, the *Inquirer* noted that "both men played with greater confidence than on any previous day."[6]

The secret, according to Collins, was hard work. And as for Barry and Collins, all that hard work really began to pay off in the spring of 1910. Although throughout the years some observers of Jack Barry questioned his ability as a shortstop, Collins was definitely not one of them.

"Jack Barry could go farther to his right for a ball and be in better position for a throw as he fielded it, than any shortstop I have ever seen."

Collins felt the key to infield compatibility was the ability of each member of the infield to completely understand the other. In this regard he and Barry reached the point that "(a)bout the only signals we employed was a closed hand for Jack to cover second on an attempted steal and the open palm for me."[7]

Although in 1910 the Barry-Collins combo was still very much a work in progress, in time it would come to the point where the pair performed in symmetry comparable to circus performers on the high wire. Collins cited an illustration stemming from a game with the Red Sox.

Batting with a man on third and the infield playing him straight away, Harry Hooper smashed a grounder to the first base side of second. Collins thought it was a certain base hit, but stretched just far enough to knock it down. Knowing he could not make the throw, he slapped the ball toward second. This is exactly what Barry had anticipated. He grabbed it and threw to first, nabbing a bewildered and frustrated Hooper.[8]

Spring training was, of course, more than just work. There was time for a few more rounds of golf. From the frequency he hit the course, Eddie was apparently developing a fondness for the game, although he was not on the level of Jack Coombs, considered one of the best at chasing the little white ball.

While the A's worked hard, at least most of the time, the Tigers, in particular, their manager Hughie Jennings, chaffed at the absence of Ty Cobb. The star, who made it a habit of skipping a good deal of the spring festivities, was still not on board by late March.

As Cobb continued to cut his own path, the A's topped Atlanta in a tight contest and headed north. The first stop on their northbound train ride was Greenville, South Carolina. It would have been a fitting homecoming for the local hero, Joe Jackson, but for one slight glitch; Joe was no longer with the club. In 1909 he was brought back to Philadelphia near the end of the year, appearing in only five games. By late March 1910 he was gone. The *Inquirer* claimed the problem was conditioning.[9] There were others who said he was still unhappy with the A's. Whatever the reason, by the time the team stepped off its train in Greenville, "Shoeless Joe" was on loan to New Orleans of the Southern League.

Despite their disappointment in missing Joe Jackson, the baseball fans of Greenville were enamored of another Mackman: Eddie Collins. If further evidence was needed to justify the assertion that Eddie was now a legitimate star, his reception in Greenville provided it. According to the *Inquirer*, "A record crowd of natives were on hand and heartily received the men [A's]. All were anxious to get a peep at Eddie Collins, but he was too wise and incidentally too modest and he jumped into a hack and made a hasty trip to the hotel."[10] Instead, Eddie made his case the next day with a pair of hits and a run as his team spanked the locals, 6–1. The next day he hit an inside-the-park home run in another A's victory.

On April 1 the Mackmen arrived in Philadelphia for what proved to be Collins' first inner-city series with the Phillies. Such affairs were common pre-season and post-season events in many two-team cities during baseball's early days. In addition to stirring fan interest, the games provided additional revenue for the clubs and players. The Phillies of 1909 and 1910 were a middle-of-the-pack bunch who hovered around the .500 mark. They were led by outfielder Sherry Magee, who hit a National-League-leading .331 in 1910. Therefore, many of the A's fans, confident that this was their year, must have shuddered when the six games were evenly divided.

Then on opening day in Washington, the team took another blow; this one counted. After watching President Taft become the first U.S. president to throw out a ball to inaugurate a baseball season, the White Elephants effectively continued to watch as Walter Johnson spun a one-hit shutout in a 3–0 loss. The final score could have been considerably more lopsided but for several stellar plays at second by Collins. The next day the A's found their bats and won their first game, behind Chief Bender. Mack's ace would be 23–5 for the season with a sparkling 1.58 ERA.

Collins and Bender were always close. When it came to American League hurlers, Eddie placed the Chief in his top five because "he made pitching a fine art." According to Collins, both Smoky Joe Wood and Walter Johnson were faster, the A's own Jack Coombs and "Death Valley" Jim Scott of the White Sox threw better curves, and the Naps' Addie Joss and White Sox hurler Doc White possessed better "slow balls." However, in Collins' estimation, he "never saw anyone who could toss all styles with the skill that 'Chief' exhibited."

Collins was also impressed with Bender's knowledge of each batter, his control and, perhaps most of all, his courage. The Chief thrived on matching up with baseball's best teams. Connie Mack obviously shared Eddie's opinion of the hurler. If Mack needed one pitcher for one key game, his choice was easy. He would not hesitate to go with Chief Bender.[11]

Thus, it was fitting that in a season of many important wins, the Chief won the first. However, despite their promise, the 1910 A's were only 5–4 on the season following a loss to the Highlanders on April 28. Collins played well during the stretch, including a three-hit effort in an eleven-inning win over Boston on April 23 in which he scored the winning run and another effort two days later when he hit his fifth major-league home run over the left field seats in Boston. The win on April 30 in New York brought the team home with four wins in their last five outings, just a game out of first. A good homestand might well solidify their position. Thus, a win in the home opener against the Red Sox was key. Chances for that seemed slim entering the home ninth inning as the A's trailed the Beantowners, 6–2. First baseman Harry Davis started the inning off right with a single that got things moving, and in rapid style the A's closed the gap to 6–5 with two men still on base. Nonetheless, there were two outs when Eddie Collins finally reached the plate to face Smoky Joe Wood, the magnificent Boston righty who was in relief of starter Eddie Cicotte. Wood, who pitched with an over-arm motion that put such a strain on his shoulder that it caused Walter Johnson, his main rival for pitching supremacy, to cringe, was described by *Baseball Magazine* in 1912 as "faultlessly clever, brilliantly fast, a marvel of pitching grace."[12]

It was, therefore, no surprise that when the first two offerings from Wood were called strikes that "the crowd started to make for the gates, having given up hope." But the spunky Collins had not. He took a "wasted" pitch from Wood; then on the next offering, he "seamed the sphere in the middle of his bat with a resounding clash." The ball slid between second and first into right field, and the base runners, Amos Strunk from third and Rube Oldring from second, scampered home. Oldring just beat a good throw with the game winner. Those loyalists remaining rushed the field and tried to lift Collins to their shoulders, but in typical fashion he "ducked the issue and sought safety in his dressing room." According to the *Inquirer*, "it was the greatest rally the Athletics ever made at Shibe Park."[13]

Of course, at that point in team history, the A's stay at Shibe was only one season and a few games long, but it was a great comeback, nonetheless. It served as the second and perhaps most important victory of a 13-game win streak and one of 15 out of 16 wins (with one tie) that propelled the A's into a solid position as front-runner, turning the still-powerful Tigers into the pursuer rather than the pursued. Except for a few days in second place in the first half of June, the Mackmen led the pack the rest of the way.

Because of clutch performances like the one against Smoky Joe and the Red Sox, Collins was in increasing demand for interviews. Despite his shyness and reluctance to appear in the spotlight, he consented to a request for an interview with Fred Lieb, a reporter gaining a reputation for himself by writing biographies of top-ranking ball players for *Baseball Magazine*. Interviews, today all too common, were much rarer in those days. Little did Collins know that he was "the first top name in baseball that I [Lieb] interviewed face-to-face." Lieb met with Eddie a few blocks from Shibe where he still boarded with Harry Davis and his wife. After talking to Lieb about his days at Columbia on both the football and baseball fields, Eddie told his interviewer he felt the A's could win the pennant in 1910. Then the subject turned to the unlikely topic of razors.

> The manufacturer of a new safety razor then on the market had sent Collins one of the new razors, and he was delighted with it. He became the interviewer. I told him I still used a straight razor, one my father had given me when I was old enough to shave. Eddie said, "Take it from me; get rid of it and buy one of the new safety razors. You'll never regret it. You never have to be afraid you'll cut yourself; it really makes shaving fun." I took Collins' advice and never regretted it.
>
> As we left together for the ball park, Mrs. Davis called after us, "you fellows win today. Hit a home run, Eddie." Collins seemed a bit annoyed at the order and grumbled to me, "She should know by this time that I don't hit home runs." He hit only three in 1910.[14]

Collins was right about the home runs. Actually, his home run total for 1910 was about average. He never hit more than six in a season, but in 1910 not many others were hitting home runs with greater frequency, and Eddie was anything but a wilting flower with a bat in his hands. He often finished the season in the league's upper echelon in doubles and triples.

A major reason for the success of Collins as a hitter was revealed in his statement to Mrs. Harry Davis, recorded that long ago day by Fred Lieb. Early on, Eddie realized that his size and weight, seldom more than 160 pounds during his prime, did not offer the luxury of an effective big swing. In response he choked-up on his bat, learned to lay down a deadly drag bunt, and concentrated on spraying the ball to all fields.

Over the years many observers described Collins as a "fidgety" batter. But that was just the part that was visible to the eye. It was the part of the batting process that took place under the hat that set Collins apart from most others. Late in his career, when he talked about the makeup of the great hitter, he might have been discussing himself when he attributed 50 percent of a batter's success to confidence, 40 percent to ability and 10 percent to luck.

"It is not 'how' but 'where' the hits go that counts. If a fellow up at the plate 'feels' that 'they can't get me out'—'feels' it, I say, not simply says it, that is true confidence and he makes a lot of hits — when they are worth while."[15]

When Collins described the art of hitting, he left out one less familiar facet: superstition. Many ball players are quite superstitious when it comes to hitting; Collins was no exception. Yet his routine was one of the strangest. Eddie did not smoke or chew tobacco, but he did chew gum. When he came to the plate, he took the gum from his mouth, sticking it onto the bottom of his cap. If he were two strikes down, he reached for the gum, popped it back in his mouth and chewed vigorously as he fidgeted and fumed, awaiting the next pitch.

According to Eddie, his "pet hobby" began quite by accident. Always a gum chewer, he found himself one day without a stick. When he asked around, he found no one else had a stick for him to borrow, either. Upset, he vowed never to find himself in that position again. He sent someone, presumably a bat boy, to locate a new stick of gum. In the meantime he removed the piece he was currently chewing and stuck it on the bottom of his cap, just in case he needed it later.

"Shortly thereafter, not that time at bat but in a few days, I was batting against some tough pitcher and after missing two swings I thought of my gum and took it off the cap and started chewing. I made a hit, and that was that. I don't know what effect the gum has; of course, none, except in my mind, but I feel better if after missing two strikes I have it where it belongs."[16]

Fred Lieb's biographical treatment of his interview with Collins came out in June, 1910. In addition to a thorough discussion of Eddie's background and history to date, it showed a more personal side of the budding star. In particular it noted, perhaps the first time in print, that Collins was an intelligent person both on and off the field, already writing his own newspaper articles about his team, including a series of 1910 spring training articles for the *Philadelphia Evening Bulletin*. Collins did enjoy writing and more was to come. In addition, Lieb talked about his subject's industriousness, including work as a salesman for a sporting goods company and as a fledgling civil engineer.[17]

There was probably some truth to Lieb's assertion that Collins sold sporting goods. Many ball players of that era took off-season jobs and selling sports equipment does not seem out of line. Lieb's assertion that Eddie not only planned to one day work as a civil engineer, but also in fact already performed as one, seems much more unlikely. Although Collins often spoke of his early interest in a law career, this seems the only mention of an engineering career that would have required extensive additional training beyond Eddie's general education. Mr. Lieb was accurate, however, in reporting that "Lucky Eddie" Collins was now a permanent resident of Philadelphia and that "a young lady dwelling in one of the suburbs was quite a frequent visitor at Shibe Park last season [1909]."[18] In fact, Eddie's newest and biggest fan was 21-year-old Mabel Harriet Doane, and the feeling was mutual.

But in 1910, personal matters aside, there was still a lot of baseball to be played. On May 19 the A's 13-game skein ended. The fact that the team that ended it was the Tigers, in the first meeting between the front runners, caused the tongues of baseball's board of "experts" to wag. In their opinion, the Mackmen were still just a group of upstarts. One writer who agreed with the majority was the esteemed Hugh Fullerton. He felt that other than Collins, Rube Oldring and strong pitching, the A's were a group of "mediocre" players.[19] But the Tigers' victory did not mean the end of the line for the White Elephants. They won the next two games by the scores of 5–2 and 7–4, as their march to the pennant continued. Collins, who heard boos for his sloppy fielding in the opening 14–2 roasting, was cheered lavishly when he "pulled the gang out of their seats with a hair-raising one-hook stab of [Sam] Crawford's smash...."[20]

In the early part of 1910, Collins' batting was down a bit as his average settled into the upper .260s, but he continued a base-stealing trend that started the previous season. His 14 stolen bases in 24 games trailed Ty Cobb by a single digit. As the season progressed, Eddie's batting average began to improve, though it never reached 1909's heights. On the other hand, his impressive base-stealing pace not only continued, but it stepped up a notch. In that regard, Connie Mack certainly liked what he saw and talked about it some years later.

"Eddie surely ran for me that season.... We still were playing for that one run, and if Collins got on and stole second or third, we had good men in Baker, Davis, and Murphy to drive him home. It was the kind of game I liked best, when the home-run era came in I adjusted myself to that kind of an attack, but I derived much more personal pleasure out of directing a base-running offense, as when Collins was stealing all those bases."[21]

For a time New York joined the A's as a pretender to Detroit's throne. However, a lengthy series with the Highlanders during mid–June and early July in which the A's won nine of twelve took care of that nuisance. During the games Eddie played well enough to earn yet another nickname — "The Tarrytown Terror."[22]

One of the real surprises in 1910 was the emergence of Jack Coombs, the 27-year-old right-hander, as a dominant pitching force. Entering the year, winning 35–35 in his four seasons with the A's, the Colby College graduate with the devastating drop ball dramatically improved to 31–9. His marvelous 1.30 ERA was second only to Ed Walsh of the White Sox. The win total would represent almost 20 percent of his career total 158 victories. His 13 shutouts established the existing American League record. Like many of the Mackmen, Colby Jack, also dubbed "Kennebunkport Jawn" by the local press, would manage in his post-playing career in both the major leagues [Phillies] and in college [Duke] before his death in 1957.

In July the Tigers were a wounded animal, and Hugh Jennings and Ty Cobb brought a steaming pot to an overflowing boil by charging that the A's were quitters, intimating that the race for the pennant was far from over. The city of Philadelphia, or rather its press, reacted as expected. In his column in the July 29 *Inquirer*, the Old Sport reminded the Tigers to look to themselves on the subject of quitting. Referring to a recent series in which the A's swept their accusers in four and Collins' triple in the ninth tied the score, leading to a 9–8 win, the columnist penned his retort, asking readers, "Was there ever a more abject case of quitting than the Detroiters showed here in the last series, when they dropped four games to the Athletics? Certainly no one in Philadelphia ever saw a player curl up so quickly and completely as did Cobb when he deliberately quit on Collins' long drive, enabling Eddie to get all the way in and tie the score. About the size of it is when the Detroiters are winning Cobb is the best winner in either league, but when he is 'collared,' as the horsemen say, he chucks it like the veriest dunghill. And he has shown it on more than one occasion in this city."[23]

Lost in all this rhetoric was what at the time seemed like an extremely minor deal. On July 30 Connie Mack dealt Joe Jackson to his old friend, Charley Somers, the owner of the Cleveland Naps. The deal, which had Cleveland sending outfielder Bris Lord to Philadelphia, involved a number of maneuvers to get Jackson around existing trade restrictions. In retrospect, the transaction was one of the steals of the century. The Mackmen were the victims. At the time, however, the trade made sense. The regular A's left fielder was an aging Topsy Hartsel, 10 years Lord's senior. His average was a meager .221. Meanwhile, Jackson was hitting the tar out of Southern League pitching, but was an unhappy camper every time he came near the Athletics.

"I knew exactly what I was doing when I let Jackson go to Cleveland. Lord, of course, helped me at the time. I said our players didn't like Jackson, but that isn't why I traded him. I also knew Joe had great possibilities as a hitter. At the time, things were going none too well for Charley Somers in Cleveland, and I was anxious to do him a good turn in appreciation for the way he had helped us out in Philadelphia in the early days of the league. So I let him have Jackson."[24]

In Bris Lord, a 26-year-old who played for the A's from 1905 through 1907, the A's were getting a known quantity. Nicknamed the "Human Eyeball" because of his keen vision, Lord gave Mack another right-handed batter and an outfielder with a good arm. Immediately, he was inserted in center field, Oldring moving to left, and proved Mack's faith in him was well placed. When he arrived from Cleveland, Lord carried a .219 average, but in 70 games with the A's, he added spark to the lineup, batting .280.

In early August the A's went on an eight-game winning spree. Mixed in, however, was a tie. In that one, on August 4 in Chicago, the highlight was the performance of Jack Coombs. The A's workhorse—he led all American League pitchers with 45 appearances—pitched 16 innings of three-hit ball, striking out 18. Ed Walsh was almost as good for the White Sox, limiting the A's to six hits and also flinging a shutout, as the game ended in a scoreless tie. Collins joined his mates in frustration, hitless in seven trips to the plate. He had better luck a few days later in a pair of wins against the Browns with seven hits in 10 at-bats. He had seven more in a pair of games in Cleveland in mid–August. By August 20 his average was up to .330.

The winning streak in August, coupled with a number of other victories, gave the Mack-men a stranglehold on first. A win over Chicago on August 20 brought their record to 76–34. They led runner-up Boston at that point by 14 games in the loss column, New York and fading Detroit by 15. With this type of lead, it did not take local scribes long to start glancing across the aisle at the National League to begin to compare the A's chances with that league's powerful Chicago Cubs.

The Athletics put their final stamp on the 1910 season during a series in Detroit, beginning September 15, winning three of four. This gave them the season series with the Tigers, still their toughest opponent, 13–9. Collins put his own stamp on the Detroiters in the third game in Cobb-like fashion when he singled, stole second, went to third when the catcher's throw sailed wide, and scored when the relay there was no better. The play was so close at the plate that the umpire called Eddie out and then reversed his call when he found Tiger catcher Oscar Stanage dropped the ball. Collins celebrated the play two innings later with a rare home run.

On September 21 in Cleveland, the White Elephants won the American League pennant without scoring a run or winning the game. At the end of 11 scoreless innings of three-hit baseball twirled by Jack Coombs, the A's found that despite a tie, their only remaining contender, the New York Highlanders, were eliminated from contention by suffering a third straight defeat in Chicago. For Eddie Collins and many of his teammates, it was their first championship of any kind. For Connie Mack and the A's, it was another opportunity for glory.

Although the Athletics could now begin to look forward to the World Series with a clear conscience, there were a few matters worth attending to before the end of the regular season. On September 30 they took one step when the team set a new American League record of 99 wins as Jack Coombs won his 30th victory in defeating the Red Sox, 4–1. Collins added a triple to the festivities. The short-lived old record of 98 was set by Detroit in 1909. The A's ended at 102–48. The next closest competitors were the New York Highlanders with 88 wins, 14½ games behind. Detroit fell to third, trailing the "quitters" by a full 18 notches.

Now it was on to the World Series, or was it? The American League season concluded on October 9. Their older brethren, the Nationals, had agreed to extend their league's season to mid–October at the urging of Cubs owner Charley Murphy. Mack was upset, the fans were upset and the press was upset, but it did no good. The reasons for the change were never clear, although the idea, perhaps, initially stemmed from Squire Ebbets of the Dodgers, who felt Columbus Day could provide the league's franchises with as big a gate as July 4, if only the schedule were extended to include it.[25]

Whatever the reason the A's faced a gap of several days before the start of championship play and Mack needed to fill it. First, however, on October 5 he collected a thirty-horse power Bergdoll touring car, a gift from his players. Collins watched from the stands as his team lost to the Highlanders, taking a rare game off to rest in preparation for the days ahead.

As he sat with the "bugs," as baseball fans were often called in those days, Collins reflected on another highly successful season. Although his average was down 23 points from 1909, at .324 he still stood fourth in the league. Furthermore, there were improvements in two other areas of significance. His RBI total increased from 56 the previous season to 81 in 1910, good for third in the league, and his stolen bases total of 81 led both leagues.

The effects of Collins' stellar base-running exploits on his team's equally stellar performance did not go unnoticed by one experienced observer. Hugh Fullerton was of the opinion that the "test of the ball player is his ability to run bases. In that part of the game, more than any other, the player has the opportunity to prove his mental caliber, and the smartest and brainiest ball players always have been the best runners. For running the bases requires quickness of thought, of eye, of decision and judgment, more than of foot. Brains plus speed are needed."[26]

Fullerton thought Eddie Collins had the appropriate mix of brains and speed. Given his view that Collins' 1910 A's were overall a mediocre bunch, he put his theories about base stealing and about Collins' ability in that regard to a test.

> I investigated to discover how they [the A's] had won so easily. The secret was revealed in the base running of Collins, who by his stealing alone won at least seventeen games that otherwise the Athletics would have lost. I discovered this fact by securing a file of the most reliable Philadelphia paper for the entire season. That paper, in its daily accounts, gave Collins individually credit with winning forty-one games. In twenty-seven of the accounts of games it was specifically stated that Collins won them by his daring base running. Of these twenty-seven games I have thrown out ten — not because the accounts of the game proved Collins did not win it but because they did not clearly explain how he won it. In the remaining seventeen cases it was explained how his base running turned the tide and won for the Athletics.[27]

Given Fullerton's assessment of Collins' contributions to a pennant winner, one would think the A's star a strong, if not the strongest, candidate for league most valuable player laurels. But such was not the case in 1910. In those days there was no most valuable player award in the sense there is today. Instead, the Chalmers Automobile Company awarded one of their prized iron horses to the player in each league with the highest batting percentage. In the waning days of 1910, the battle for the prize in the American League was waged between Ty Cobb and Cleveland's star Napoleon Lajoie. As with most things involving Cobb, there was significant controversy. The Tigers' slugger, thinking his lead was safe, sat out his team's last game. Lajoie, easily the more popular figure among the players as well as the fans, played both ends of a twin bill in St. Louis. The Browns, deciding to give Lajoie some help, stationed their third basemen so deep that the Cleveland star bunted safely several times and ended the day with eight hits, appearing to win both the batting title and the car. When official league figures were released indicating Cobb was the actual winner by an ever-so-slight margin — a figure proved incorrect years later — the auto manufacturer in a public relations coup awarded both men vehicles. Though they each had a car, perhaps the real league MVP had something much more coveted: a date with the Chicago Cubs.

The same could not be said for Eddie's outfield teammate Rube Oldring, who had enjoyed a fine regular season, batting .308, second only to Eddie, and tying for the team lead in home runs with four. He broke his leg in August, replaced for the remainder of the year by the youthful Amos Strunk.

The Cubs were without one of their best as well. In early October Johnny Evers, the middleman of the legendary Tinkers to Evers to Chance infield combo, and Collins' counterpart at second base, broke his fibula, knocking him out for the duration. His place was taken by Eddie's old friend from his semipro days at Red Hook, Heinie Zimmerman, who provided a better bat but less fielding and leadership than Evers.

Even without Evers, the Cubs were a powerful lot with first baseman-manager Frank Chance, shortstop Joe Tinker, Frank "Wildfire" Schulte and a veteran backstop in Johnny Kling. On the mound they were even better, led by future Hall-of-Famer Mordecai "Three-Finger" Brown, Orvil Overall, Ed Reulbach and a rookie sensation by the name of Leonard "King" Cole. Many of these players were veterans of the Cubs' 1907 and 1908 World Series championship teams. If the A's were proud of their 102 wins, the Cubs were just as proud of their 104. Clearly, they were the favorites over the upstart Mackmen.

While the A's awaited what many thought was an obvious fate, they made good use of their time. They kept their engines softly purring by engaging in a series of contests with a team made up of the American League's finest. The all-stars included Ty Cobb and several Washington Nationals, namely Walter Johnson, base-stealing great Clyde "Deerfoot" Milan, catcher Gabby Street, fire-brand infielder Kid Elberfield, and baseball's reigning clown prince Herman "Germany" Schaefer. Boston's smooth-gliding Tris Speaker manned center field.

Cobb was not present for the first exhibition, a three-hit win for Walter Johnson, due to automobile problems totally unconnected with the Chalmers controversy. His place in right field was taken by the weak-hitting Schaefer, who mollified the right field bugs, upset by Cobb's absence, with a running comedy routine.

The A's did not fare well in the series with the all-stars, losing four. To make matters worse in game four, Collins wrenched his knee while making the turn at first following a single and was unable to finish the game. He recovered quickly, however, remaining firmly in Connie Mack's first-game plans.

By the time Game One of the World Series, scheduled for October 17 in Shibe Park, arrived, the city of Philadelphia was almost chaotic. Some of the furor was stirred up by the proximity of the game itself, some over a decision by local authorities who ordered residents living adjacent to Shibe Park who possessed convenient rooftop perches not to use them to view the games. The invitations were extended anyway and many looked on from the top of buildings as Chief Bender and the Cubs' 12-game winner, Orvil Overall, locked horns. Overall's record of 12–6 was a bit deceiving in that he was a three-time World Series winner for the Cubs, once over the Tigers in 1907 and twice in 1908. In 1910 he was battling a sore arm and, despite a most respectable ERA of 2.68 for the season, it showed. The A's reached him for two runs in the second, another in the third. He was replaced by Harry McIntire in the fourth, as the A's won, 4–1. The Cubs did not touch the Chief for a run until the ninth inning, garnering only three hits. Collins singled in two official at-bats and scored a run when his distracting antics at first following a walk brought a wild pick-off throw that sent him to third. Frank Baker's double, his second of the game, brought Eddie home with the last run. Over 26,000 fans in the stadium, as well as a roof-top crowd nearby, and thousands of others who stood in front of the offices of the *Inquirer* watching play develop on a giant scoreboard, were sent away happy.

The next day the Mackmen took their second step toward a world title, besting the Cubs and their mound ace, Three Finger Brown, 9–3. They won despite a sub-par performance by Jack Coombs, who walked nine batters and escaped disaster by frequently getting the key out with Cub runners dotting the bases. He stranded 14 Cubs along the way.

The A's attack in Game Two was led by Eddie Collins as he "stepped into the limelight ... and gave a wonderful exhibition of gilt-edge baseball.... He was a whirlwind on the runways, stealing second twice ... while he wrapped out two doubles and a single in four trips to the plate.... He covered ground around second in a speedy, unerring way that made even the Chicago rooters join in the acclaim that greeted his wonderful performance."[28]

One of Collins' hits that day drove in two runs to put the A's on top. One defensive play in particular caught Hugh Fullerton's eye. At least when he described it in 1911, he felt Collins' effort was "[t]he greatest play I believe ever made on a ball field ... and broke the Cubs entire system of play." According to Fullerton, going into the series, Cubs manager Frank Chance felt he could run on the A's catchers. In Game One it did not work. The next day Chance switched to a hit-and-run attack. The first Cub up was left fielder Jimmy Sheckard, who worked Coombs for a walk. Next up was right fielder Frank Schulte. The A's expected Sheckard to steal, and twice Coombs pitched out. Each time Collins edged toward second to accept a throw. He did so a third time, but suddenly the Cubs pulled a hit-and-run, and Sheckard sent a sharp grounder between A's first baseman Harry Davis and Collins. Davis, a slow man in Fullerton's view, gave up on the ball. Sensing this, Sheckard prepared to round second and head for third.

But unlike Davis, Collins did not give up on the ball. Instead, Fullerton watched as just when it appeared the ball was through the gap, Eddie "stuck down his hands, and the speeding ball struck in his glove and remained there. Up to that point the play might have been made by anyone, with speed enough and luck enough. The great part of the play was that which followed. Almost any other player would have been satisfied to toss the ball to first base and retire Schulte, but Collins was the exception. Pivoting like a ballet dancer as the ball struck his hands, he threw with perfect accuracy and terrific force to Barry on second base, forcing Sheckard by a step," the relay almost doubling Schulte. The play stopped Chicago's rally. They did score a run in the inning, but in Fullerton's estimation, they would have scored several more, driven Coombs from the box and evened the series. Now just the opposite had occurred, and "the Cubs seemed at sea during all the remainder of the Series, their confidence shaken and the Athletics revived."[29]

Adrian "Cap" Anson, the long-time Cubs first baseman and eventual member of the Hall of Fame, took in the Series. After Game Two he observed, "The principal feature of the game was the excellent all-round play of the Athletics' star second basemen, who in my opinion has no superior as an all-round ball player. I can candidly express the opinion that he can be compared with the old-timers, Bid McPhee, of the old Cincinnatis; Fred Pfeffer, of the Anson Colts, and Fred Dunlap," and "will stand comparison with ... Johnny Evers, or the Clevelander's Larry Lajoie, and as an all-round valuable man to a team I do not even think Cobb is superior."[30]

Clearly, no game did more to both establish and solidify Eddie Collins as a baseball star than Game Two of the 1910 World Series. After the game he even found time to write about it for a local newspaper.

A pair of victories carefully tucked away in their back pockets, the Mackmen now turned to Chicago as the venue for Game Three. After a day of travel, Mack, perhaps in search for the real Jack Coombs, trotted his iron man to the mound once again. The Cubs turned to Ed Reulbach, a 6 foot 1 inch, 190-pound right-hander with a swift delivery. The Chicago twirler, who like Collins groomed for the majors by playing in the Northern League, was no stranger to World Series competition. In 1906 he pitched a one-hitter in the World Series, the first time that feat was performed. From 1906 to 1908, he led the National League in winning percentage, but in 1910 he was 12–8 and his normally miniscule ERA rose to 3.12.

The Cubs were undoubtedly hoping for rain, which would have permitted them to start the more reliable Three Finger Brown again. The best they got was an early morning rain and a mist that persisted throughout much of the game. A chilly northwest wind added to the gloomy proceedings, which became even gloomier for Chicago fans when the Mackmen jumped on their favorites for a 12–5 win. The A's opened quickly, knocked Reulbach out after two innings, and buoyed by a five-run third, led 8–3 at that point. The big blast was a three-run disputed home run by Danny Murphy. Umpire Tommy Connolly rubbed salt in Chicago's wounds when he ejected Frank Chance for overstating his argument that Murphy's blast, which hit a distant fence after clearing the overflow crowd in right field, was merely a double. The ejection was the first ever in a World Series game. Coombs collected the win and Collins went 1-for-5, singling and scoring a run.

The Mackmen, needing only one more game to claim the title, were now poised on October 21, waiting to move in for the kill. However, it did not happen. The continuing rain forced a postponement. The next day the Cubs, behind rookie righty King Cole, eked out a 4–3 win that took 10 innings. Cole was not all that sharp — he allowed 10 hits — but he was sharp enough. The A's behind the Chief actually entered the bottom of the ninth inning leading 3–2, but the Cubs tied it on a Schulte double and Chance's clutch triple, then won it in the tenth on catcher Jimmy Archer's double and Sheckard's timely single. Collins again went 1-for-5, scoring another run. Their backs to the wall, the Cubs were forced to use Three Finger Brown in the last two frames.

If the A's were frustrated by falling three short outs from the first four-game sweep in World Series history, it did not show. They simply set down their bats, removed their gloves and waited another day.

So far only two pitchers — Bender and Coombs — had performed for the Mackmen. Since Connie Mack had three games remaining and needed but one win, would he choose to rest his staff by sending 18-game winner Cy Morgan or 16-game winner Eddie Plank to the hill? He did not. When Game Five began October 23 in Chicago, Jack Coombs touched the rubber for a third time. This time the man they called Colby Jack was sharper. He gave up nine hits, but only two runs as the A's won the game and the World Series, 7–2, and four games to one. On the mound for the Cubs was a tired Three Finger Brown. The usually reliable Brown, who gained his nickname the hard way when his right hand was caught in a farm implement, resulting in loss of most of his forefinger, a mangled middle finger and a crooked little finger, was at age 33 still a most effective pitcher. His best pitch, probably aided by his deformity, was an overhand or "hook" curve, which broke sharply down and outward. This plus a fastball and an assortment of other deliveries brought him 25 victories — almost one-fourth of the Cubs' wins in 1910. His 1.86 ERA was second in the National League. For his career the man teammates preferred to call "Miner," because he once worked in one, was 239–130 with a 2.06 ERA. But he was also human. In a desperate move to save the series, Frank Chance had used Brown the day before in relief of King Cole. He had helped win that game, but now he proceeded to lose this one by giving up five runs in the eighth to seal the Cubs' fate.

In the clincher, Eddie Collins had another big day. He went 3-for-5, including two doubles, two steals and two RBIs. For the series he batted .429 (9-for-21), stole four bases, scored five times, batted in three teammates, and played errorless ball. He was at the very least a cornerstone of the A's upset of the previously invincible Cubs. In dispatching the favorites, the A's used but two pitchers in the entire series, while their hitters set a World Series' record by averaging seven runs per game.

The next day the Athletics and their Tall Tactician arrived by rail at the Broad Street station in Philadelphia where they were greeted by a huge throng. A banquet followed at the Bellevue Stratford Hotel, attended by men and women in formal evening attire. Of course, not everyone could attend and thousands amassed outside the hotel as the celebration continued inside. Naturally, Connie Mack spoke and heaped praise on his team collectively and individually, especially Captain Harry Davis. Jack Barry, Frank Baker and Collins sat side-by-side, taking it all in. Cap Anson spoke, as did Tim Murnane. If the Boston scribe had not known who Eddie Sullivan was a mere four seasons ago, he indeed knew now.

When the furor, if not the vivid memories, settled down, each member of the team found an additional $2,062.74 in his pocket. That represented the winner's full share for the 1910 World Series, the year in which the Athletics won their first world championship and Eddie Collins proved he was truly a money player.

CHAPTER 8

$100,000 Infield

"But this is Eddie Collins' stock in trade. 'Doing the unexpected,' is the secret of his success."

— Fred Lieb[1]

On November 3, 1910, less than two weeks after his team's World Series triumph, Edward Trowbridge Collins exchanged marriage vows with Mabel Harriet Doane of Clifton Heights, Pennsylvania. Writer Fred Lieb had been correct several months earlier when he told readers that Eddie had a girlfriend and a serious one at that.

Like many things in Collins' life since his formal introduction to Connie Mack in 1906, his marriage to Mabel Doane was in no small part due to the match-making attributes of the Tall Tactician. There are several versions describing how the couple met, Mack figuring in them all. Connie and the bride's father, C.P. Doane, a prominent businessman, were childhood friends reunited when Mack came to Philadelphia, where Doane ran the Kents Woolen Mill in Clifton Heights. As Collins' stardom ascended, Doane became a fan of the A's second sacker and sometime in 1908 or 1909 asked Mack for an introduction. The two became friends. Later, Collins visited the Doane's residence and became acquainted and then attracted to his only daughter, Mabel, a pretty brunette in her early twenties who was already an accomplished musician.

Another version, perhaps a bit more romantic, has Doane and his daughter visiting Mack's home near Columbia Park in 1908. Collins, who boarded nearby with Harry Davis and his family, saw Mabel there and asked her out.

In either event a match was made and the couple became engaged. On November 3 their family and friends gathered at the Doane's home to watch Eddie's friend, the Reverend George H. Ferris of the First Baptist Church in Philadelphia, perform the ceremony. Mabel's father gave her away. Arthur Lee, Jr., a friend of Eddie's from Columbia, was the best man. Albert [sic] Cline, his step-sister's husband, served as an usher.

A number of the world champion Athletics attended the wedding. Unfortunately, the chemist who mixed the formula was absent. The Tall Tactician had recently taken a wife of his own. He and Katherine Hallahan, his second wife, were honeymooning when Collins was wed.[2]

There is little doubt Mabel Doane came from a family of means, but by the time of his marriage, Collins was a man of some means himself. Based on his strong play in 1909, he signed a new contract in January 1910, raising his salary from $2,400 to $4,000, a princely sum for the day, particularly when combined with his World Series bonus. Another increase in February 1911 raised his pay to $6,000, well above the salary of most of his contemporaries, both in and out of baseball.[3]

Collins' increasing status on the national baseball scene afforded additional advantages. By 1910 baseball players were finding a number of ways to use their increasing popularity. In September 1905 the "Flying Dutchman," Honus Wagner, star shortstop for the Pittsburgh Pirates of the National League, signed a contract with what later became the Hillerich & Bradsby Co., out of Louisville, Kentucky, giving that company the right to use his signature endorsement on one of their popular baseball bats. Ty Cobb gave his permission in 1908. On April 16, 1910, Collins gave his permission as well.[4] Given Collins' starring role in the most recent World Series, his bat was certain to be a hit — no pun intended.

When it came to bats, Collins had his preferences. According to Henry Morrow, the players' contact with the Louisville Slugger folks, Eddie was "another who was fussy about his bats. He wanted every one made from the wood of the 'heart' of the tree — the center cut. This always made his bats red on one side and white on the other."[5]

Supplied with a slew of bats made to his personal order — he used this type throughout his career — Collins left for spring training in 1911 on March 1. Accompanying Eddie was his bride, Mabel, about to experience her first spring training. As before, the veterans reported to Hot Springs, Virginia. Mack and the younger players reported to Savannah.

Three weeks prior to his spring trek, Collins, along with Harry Davis and Sherry Magee of the Phillies, was a guest of honor at the Hotel Walton in Philadelphia for a dinner banquet hosted by that city's sportswriters. Eddie spoke briefly to some 400 in attendance.

Once again hiking and golf were activities on the Hot Springs agenda. One afternoon Danny Murphy led a group on a hike over the mountains. Only catcher Jack Lapp and Collins were able to finish, returning to tell whoever was listening, "Never again."[6] True to his word, Eddie turned back at the halfway mark the next day when the group tried a seven-mile journey to Flag Rock, the highest peak in the area.

The stay at Hot Springs, with the golf and the hiking and holiday atmosphere, was all part of Connie Mack's spring training philosophy. The Tall Tactician avoided the tendency of some managers to bring their teams to peak efficiency in the spring, fearing a team so trained would wear thin by mid-season. Therefore, once the regulars made camp with the youngsters, they followed a rather laid-back physical routine with the emphasis on "shaping up the batting eye and getting the whips in shape and letting the physical condition of the men take care of itself."[7]

Collins put it this way. "Down south, Mack shows attention to young pitchers but not the slightest to his veterans. Indeed he generally lets the veterans take care of themselves."[8]

The team that Mack fielded for 1911 was essentially the same one that propelled the franchise to the top in 1910. This included team mascot Louis VanZelst, a tiny hunchback who was adopted by the A's fans as well as the team. He came to the A's in 1910 — some say he was discovered by Collins — and since the team just happened to win it all that year, he was given a great deal of credit for the accomplishment. After all, didn't the players rub his back for good luck?[9]

Collins took no credit for the acquisition, saying that the little fellow the players called "'Little Van' ... just drifted into the park one morning and saying never a word to anybody minded our bats."[10]

Perhaps it was Mack's spring training philosophy, or maybe it was the foul spring weather that played havoc with the exhibition schedule, but the world champs did not start well in 1911. In fact, it was their sixteenth game before they even reached the .500 mark.

Given the A's 3–2 dispatch of a good Phillies team in a five-game city series, one would have expected more at the start. At least 20,000 A's rooters thought so when they attended the home opener, only to see a fine performance by Chief Bender squandered when the A's

American Leaguers who formed an all-star roster to play the Cleveland Naps on July 24, 1911, in Cleveland. The game was played for the benefit of the family of Addie Joss, the Naps' pitcher who died mid-career from tubercular meningitis. Those pictured are (back row, left to right) Bobby Wallace (Browns), Frank Baker (A's), Joe Wood (Red Sox), Walter Johnson (Nationals), Hal Chase (Highlanders), Clyde Milan (Nationals), Russ Ford (Highlanders), Collins; (front row) Germany Schaefer (Nationals), Tris Speaker (Red Sox), Sam Crawford (Tigers), Jimmy McAleer (Nationals' manager), Ty Cobb (Tigers, in Cleveland uniform), Gabby Street (Nationals), and Paddy Livingston (A's) (National Baseball Hall of Fame Library, Cooperstown, New York).

fell to the Highlanders and Jim Vaughn, 2–1. Collins was up to his old tricks, at least in that one, electrifying the crowd in the first inning by beating out an infield hit, stealing second and then third when the throw to nail him was bobbled.

In the spring the Mackmen were stunned by the death of former teammate Simon Nicholls. By that time a minor leaguer, Nicholls was a victim of typhoid fever at 29. Now, only a few weeks later and mired in their early-season slump, the A's were saddened by another most untimely death. On April 14 Addie Joss, the 31-year-old pitching star of the Cleveland Naps, succumbed to tubercular meningitis. Collins considered the right-hander "very puzzling" and one of the best he faced. The mystery of Joss, at least to Collins, was how he was able to throw his change of pace with the exact same motion he used for his fastball, making it "the best slow ball that ever floated under my bat."[11]

The loss of the popular Joss set all of baseball back on its heels, but as does life, the season continued. Individually, the early-season A's had their days. Collins was no exception with three hits and three RBIs in an April 18 loss to Boston, and another three-hit effort in a win over the same club several days later on April 24. On April 25 the Mackmen and the city of Philadelphia celebrated as Governor John Tener, later the National League president, raised the American League banner over Shibe Park. Then the A's continued the celebration by topping Washington, 11–2.

In 1910 the A's were able to string together several long winning streaks, thereby thrusting themselves to the top. Early on in 1911, those prolonged win streaks were not part of their scheme. However, in late May the White Elephants won seven in a row and, after a loss, another seven straight. Then following another single loss, they ran off six more victories. By June 16, this 20 out of 22 stretch took them to second, only two games behind first-place Detroit. This was no mean feat considering the Tigers started the season in similar fashion, also winning 20 of their first 22.

There were a couple of reasons for the Athletics' recovery. One was the continued hot bat and base-running exploits of Eddie Collins. On May 14 American League figures showed him batting .431, ahead of Ty Cobb (.390) in that department. In steals Collins was just ahead of Cobb as well. Ahead of both gentlemen was a lesser-known quantity, the Athletics' John McInnis, the second reason for his team's ascent. McInnis, who was finding the field more and more, this time subbing at short for an injured Jack Barry, was batting an astronomical .455.

In mid–May Collins missed three games with an injury but was back in time for his team's first series with Detroit, a four-game face-off which the rivals divided. Collins' four hits in the second loss went for naught, but the A's victories in the last two games of the series ignited them to the first of their many streaks and eventually led to their lengthy hot streak. Though the A's looked to be back in the thick of things, their prospects suffered a major setback in mid–July when they lost four in a row in Detroit, falling more than five games behind the vengeful Tigers.

During mid-season, subtle changes were once again afoot in Mackland. For over two seasons now, the infield of Baker, Barry, Collins and Davis provided a solid basis for a championship mix. Barry and Collins were trumpeted to be without peers. Frank Baker, at 25 the A's cleanup hitter, was better known for his bat than his glove. The A's third sacker appeared clumsy at times, an unfair assessment in Collins' opinion.

"Frank Baker ... was probably the most misjudged man in baseball. He was often called a poor fielder and it was said he was kept on the team only because of his hitting. Baker was a very capable fielder and was able to stop many balls that other third basemen would pass up. He had a wonderful arm and was able to rifle a ball across the infield at such a clip that base runners many times were fooled."[12]

The fourth member of the inner core, Harry Davis, however, was now 37 and showing wear and tear. Always a strong hitter whose long suit was power, Davis was hitting the ball less frequently and with less sting. From 1904 to 1907, he led the league in home runs. He had a career high of 12 in 1906. Thereafter, his production fell each year until he hit but one in 1910 in 492 at-bats. In 1910 he batted .248, well below his career .277. By June 1911, the previous year's figure seemed lofty.

On June 7 the A's were at Shibe tangling with the Tigers. Davis was at his usual spot, a healthy Jack Barry back at short. Mack was for some reason not on the bench that day and Davis was the acting manager. In the eighth with Detroit in front 3–1 and two out, Collins was on second. Davis was due up. Instead, Davis inserted John McInnis, the utility infielder with a hot bat, to hit for him. McInnis promptly sliced a single to left, Collins scored, and the A's rallied in the ninth to win, 4–3. McInnis, previously used only at short, third and once in the outfield, finished in foreign territory at first base.

Whether the move was the "little bit of impromptu strategy" as the *Inquirer* termed it, or part of a master plan hatched by an intriguingly absent Tall Tactician, only the actors can tell.[13] Nevertheless, on June 12, the A's and their fans celebrated Harry Davis Day (an earlier one in late May was canceled due to inclement weather), and in the game that followed, McInnis was once again a replacement for Davis at first. The next day McInnis started at first against those same Browns and was thereafter the newest member of what was soon to become better known as "the $100,000 Infield."

Mack's choice of 20-year-old John Phalen McInnis, better known as "Stuffy" because as a youthful player in hometown Boston, those who marveled at his play often shouted, "That's the stuff, kid," caused many to scratch their head. Although there was no doubt the youth had talent with the bat, at 5 foot 9 and one-half inches he was considered by most as too short to play the initial sack. That spot was usually reserved for taller players, who were able to provide a longer reach and stretch for the throw-over. Yet Mack and McInnis proved the "experts" wrong. Collins agreed.

"He [McInnis] was the best target in the league to throw at. He stretched further, leaped higher, covered a lot of ground and never lost the direction of the bag when he had to get a bad throw."[14]

Now McInnis was a regular as the A's tried to recover from their bitter defeats in Detroit.

"The $100,000 Infield" helped the A's to American League pennants in 1910, 1911, 1913 and 1914. They are shown here with outfielder Danny Murphy, who played second base before Collins took over. Pictured (left to right) are Stuffy McInnis (1B), Murphy, Frank "Home Run" Baker (3B), Jack Barry (SS), and Collins (George Grantham Bain Collection, Library of Congress, Prints & Photographs Division, LC-DIG-ggbain-15514).

Part of the reason for the Tigers' resurgence was the dazzling performance of Ty Cobb, on his way to a career-defining season that would see him bat .420 on a then-record 248 hits, while driving in 127 runners and reasserting himself as a stolen base king with 83. But despite Cobb's heroics, the A's lineup, finally solidified, began playing a steady brand of winning baseball, keeping pace with the Tigers and biding their time.

In maintaining that pace, the A's were forced to overcome one significant blow. In the second inning of a July 1 contest in Washington, Collins and right fielder Danny Murphy both closed in on a shallow fly ball. Eddie called for the catch and was in an exposed position while making the grab when Murphy collided with him head on. The force of the collision dislocated Eddie's left elbow. There was concern of ligament damage. Both men left the game. Estimates that Collins was out for a month were incorrect, yet he did not return until July 17. In the interim he missed 15 games, his place taken for the majority of those contests by Claud Derrick, a 25-year-old right-handed batter. The team went 8–7 during that time.

The time away from the game, however, did serve one purpose: it allowed Collins to truly savor a personal moment. On July 3 Mabel and Eddie welcomed their first child, Paul Doane Collins.

On July 17, when Collins returned, he did so with some authority, garnering three hits and proving there was little dust on his glove in an 8–6 win over the Browns in St. Louis. Interestingly, on that date Philadelphia had a team in first place, but it was the long-starved Phillies, not the A's, who enjoyed the distinction.

On July 24 Collins joined a veritable host of future baseball Hall of Famers and other well-known players in Cleveland to play a benefit game to raise money for the widow and children of the late Addie Joss. There are some who call this gathering baseball's first true all-star game. That is arguable. What is not is the magnitude of American League talent on the field at Cleveland's League Park. In addition to Collins, the all-star contingent alone included Ty Cobb, Tris Speaker, Clyde Milan, Frank Baker, Sam Crawford, the Highlanders' slick-fielding first baseman Hal Chase, St. Louis Browns shortstop Bobby Wallace, Washington catcher Gabby Street, the A's and Cleveland native Paddy Livingston, Smoky Joe Wood, Walter Johnson and Highlanders pitcher Russ Ford. The Naps countered with no less than Nap Lajoie, no longer managing, Joe Jackson, who was now a star and Cobb's rival for top batting honors, and the aging Cy Young, at 44 no longer a pitching menace, but still very much a presence.

The game, like most all-star match-ups, was anti-climactic. Played before over 15,000, the all-stars won, 5–3. Collins hit safely twice, one a triple, and scored a run. Of much more importance, he and his fellow ball players raised over $12,000 for Addie's family.

The A's closed the gap a bit in a five-game series with Detroit that began on July 28, winning the first three and losing a pair at the end. The first game of the series, part one of a double bill, was a classic viewed by what many called the largest crowd to date in Shibe Park history. In the eleventh inning Bender and Ed "Kickapoo Chief" Summers of Detroit were hooked in a scoreless duel. Summers was still fashioning a two-hitter when he walked his fellow moundsman to lead off the inning. By virtue of a sacrifice, Bender stood on second with two out and Collins swinging the lumber. Like most of his brethren, Eddie was hitless in four attempts, but not for lack of trying. In the sixth Ty Cobb stabbed a Collins' liner, robbing his rival of certain extra bases. This time Eddie made certain the Georgia Peach was not involved. He laced a Summers' offering to right for a double, driving in the Chief with the game winner, and the fans celebrated. Collins did too, with four hits the next day in an 11–3 A's victory. The Mackmen were clearly holding their own, but if they expected a repeat trip to the series, they still needed some help. They received an unexpected boost from the Tigers themselves. It seemed that after the series at Shibe, Hugh Jennings' charges lost some steam, much of the hissing sound caused by the New York Highlanders, who defeated the Tigers with frequency. In the meantime the A's habit of winning three in a row here and four there began to pay dividends. On August 4, only days after the disappointing ending to the Detroit series, a double victory at Shibe boosted the team into first, a perch they protected like the robin and its tiny egg for the remainder of the season.

By late August Connie Mack was feeling confident. A six-game lead over the Tigers in the loss column helped steel his confidence as he told reporters in Cleveland, "We are going to win the American League pennant again and we are going to win the world series, too."[15] Strong words from the normally reserved leader of the Mackmen, but the real clincher was on the field when the A's ran off 10 straight in September to secure the pennant.

The A's of 1911 were a scrappy bunch, none scrappier than Collins. In a loss to Detroit on August 29, a ground ball bounced up and hit the second sacker on the nose, knocking him out of the game. There was significant bruising, but according to the treating physician, no break. After missing an exhibition game the next day in Worcester, Eddie was back in the lineup, "presentable" according to Mack, his large floppy ears still his one standout feature.[16]

The sore nose did little to hold Collins back. On September 5 he gave a major assist to his team's 10–4 victory over Washington with three hits, a walk, a stolen base and four runs scored. On September 22 at Shibe in a 2–1 extra-inning win over the Browns, the A's won their eighth straight in their 10-game (with one tie) streak and Collins again proved his value to his team. In the field he went high to snare a line drive and he turned a rally-ending double play in the eleventh. In the fourth inning he stroked the first pitch to him to center for a single, immediately burgled second, took third on a wild pitch, and scored on a force out, exhibiting Dead Ball Era baseball in all its grandeur.

The A's dotted the "i," so to speak, on the 1911 regular season when their late-season win streaks placed them in a position to clinch the American League pennant by beating the Tigers. This they did on September 26 when the Shibe faithful watched their warriors win convincingly, 11–5, for their 96th victory on the season. Collins tripled and knocked in a run to aid Jack Coombs, who was in the midst of a 28–12 season. The final total was 101 wins versus 50 losses, the victory total only one fewer than the record the A's set in 1910.

Although not considered a signature season in Collins' career, as injuries limited his play to only 132 games, 1911 actually was impressive in several ways. For one thing his batting average, .365, was the highest of his career, though well below his early .400-plus pace and only fourth-best in an offensive season dominated by Cobb and Jackson. His 73 RBIs were third-best on his team. His on-base percentage (OBP), which included 62 walks, trailed only Jackson and Cobb. In addition, he continued to field with the best. His overall value was recognized when he finished third to pitcher Ed Walsh and run-away winner Ty Cobb in the Chalmers voting conducted by one writer from each league city.

At this point all eyes turned to the National League to determine the A's opponent. They did not have long to wait. On October 4 the New York Giants shut out the Brooklyn Dodgers, 2–0, to clinch a piece of cloth of their own. The Cubs, still reeling from the 1910 post-season, finished in second. In their stead the A's would be batting against the likes of Christy Mathewson and Rube Marquard, as well as hitting to Fred Merkle, Larry Doyle and Fred Snodgrass. Mack would be facing off against his old rival, John McGraw. Mack was delighted at the prospect. The Tall Tactician and his A's had taken a beating from the Giants in 1905 and the bitter taste remained. But this was 1911 and Mack saw an opportunity for a payback. In his mind Mathewson, despite his continuing brilliance (26–13, 1.99), was the key.

"Matty still is a great pitcher," Mack told Harry Davis. "But he's six years older than he was in 1905, and I'm sure he's not as fast. And I think we have better hitters than we had in that earlier series."[17]

Despite their excitement and anticipation, the A's again faced a layoff, due to the staggered schedule. For Collins it was a shame since he ended the regular season with a hot bat, including an inside-the-park homer against Washington on October 4 and a double and pair of triples, one with the bases jammed, versus the Highlanders on October 6.

Not one to tinker with success, Connie Mack once again set up a series with a group of all-stars, including the ever-present Cobb, the "Prince of First Base" Hal Chase and others. The all-stars smashed the cover off the ball in a couple of the games, but the A's won a pair themselves and Collins' bat stayed hot with four hits in one game and three in another. In his mind the tune-ups were important.

"These games did a world of good to our club [the A's], as we had gone stale after we had clinched the pennant in the middle of September, and the beatings the 'All-Stars' administered to us acted as a fine tonic, and really put us on our feet again and into our true stride, so we entered the fray perfectly fit to meet the Giants."[18]

Well, almost perfectly fit. Although he played a few experimental innings against the all-stars, Stuffy McInnis could not shake off the effects of a right arm and wrist injury sustained over three weeks prior when struck by a George Mullin delivery. Harry Davis, retirement gifts on the shelf, was back at first.

A crowd of almost 40,000 jammed the Polo Grounds on October 14 for Game One. On the mound for the Giants was their "Big Six," the same Mattie who stilled the A's bats in 1905. The A's countered with Bender, their own cinch pick, painting the game with the same mound face-off fans saw in the 1905 finale. To complete the image, McGraw, playing psychological chess, bedecked his team in the same black and white uniforms with white belts they wore when they vanquished the A's six years prior.

For a while it was 1905 all over again as the dust settled on a 2–1 Giants win. Bender pitched quite well, showing more than enough stuff to win. He struck out 11 and gave up only five hits. Some say it was his best World Series effort. The A's were able to knick Mathewson for six hits. The winning run came home in the seventh when Josh Devore, the Giants left fielder and lead-off man, singled to drive in Chief Meyers. As for Eddie Collins, the hero of 1910, he figured as the goat in Game One as he bobbled an easy two-out roller by Giant third sacker Buck Herzog, allowing the runner on second, Fred Snodgrass, to round third to score. Eddie's throw appeared to arrive in time to nail the Giants' center fielder, but catcher Ira Thomas failed to block the plate, Snodgrass sliding around him to tie the score. Collins was 0-for-3 at the plate, further confirming that this was a different season and a new World Series.

The scene for Game Two shifted to Shibe Park. After a one-day delay due to rain, the Series resumed on October 16. When it was over, the A's fans cheered a new hero. If 1910 was the coming out party for Eddie Collins, 1911 was the same for John Franklin Baker. Although it did not all happen at once, for during the season Frank socked 11 homers to lead the league, his 1911 World Series performance was dramatic, to say the least. In the sixth inning of Game Two, with the Giants' 26-game winner Rube Marquard pitching and two out, Collins came to bat. The *Inquirer* of October 17 described play as follows:

It was Eddie's third time at the plate. On his first visit he had singled and on the second attempt he raised a fly to Devore. But his third effort was more successful. He drove the ball along the left field foul line and landed safely on second base. Then came the mighty Baker to the plate. Indian Chief Meyers and pitcher Marquard held a conference. To the crowd it looked as though it had been decided to present Baker with a pass to first base. But something in the arrangements slipped a cog. Instead of pitching out Mr. Marquard proceeded to serve his enemy with a swift curve ball, and as one of these came cutting across the plate Baker swung at it, and the crack of the bat as it connected with the sphere must be still ringing in the ears of the entire team. Murray, the auburn-haired right fielder, ran bravely to the fence as soon as the ball began its flight through space, but suddenly came to a dead stop when he realized that it was beyond his reach. Every one of the Giants turned to look where the ball was going, and Marquard, crestfallen and gloomy, bowed his head after a glance had shown him that the ball had gone over the fence. So terrific was the drive that the force of the ball almost carried with it one of the boys who sat on the fence.

For several minutes the crowd howled with glee, and when the noise died out it became apparent at once to all the spectators that this home-run drive had taken all the spirit out of the Giants, and thereafter they were helpless before the superb pitching of Plank.[19]

In that same *Inquirer* appeared a column written by Christy Mathewson, syndicated for publication for newspapers throughout the country. By 1911 baseball, previously quite popular, was gaining even more momentum. Certain players and managers gained name recognition beyond the big league cities where they regularly performed. Fans everywhere, not just in New York or Philadelphia, craved words of wisdom from those select few. Mathewson was one such "name" player. He and other stars such as Ty Cobb, Tris Speaker, and Collins suddenly appeared as "reporters" on the World Series. Did they write these articles, or were they "ghosted" by the regular press or others? The debate has raged for years and neither answer may be totally incorrect.

Now here, following Game Two, was a column allegedly from Matty describing and critiquing the play of his team and his teammates contemporaneous with series play. In the article Mathewson claimed that following his double, Collins stood close to his bag at second so he could steal the signal from Giants catcher Chief Meyers to pitcher Marquard. Meyers saw what was happening and approached the mound. This, according to Mathewson, is what Meyers told Marquard and what transpired:

"Pitch him two curve balls no matter what I sign for."
A big leaguer knows only two kinds of balls, a curve and a fast one, the latter ball coming up to the plate with all the speed the pitcher possesses. Myers [*sic*] crouched down and gave the sign for a fast one for the benefit of Collins and "Rube" broke a curve off the edge of the plate which the umpire called a ball. Myers then signaled for another fast one to throw Collins off, and Marquard broke a curve over the plate for a strike.
But those two had exhausted the Indian's reserve supply, and he had to go back to straight signs, hoping to have thrown Collins off by this time with his "phoney" signals. But Collins and Baker were too clever. Marquard thought that he could sneak a fast one over the plate after pitching the two curves, but Baker was up there all set and waiting for it. Collins had evidently tipped him right, and it was clever work on the part of both of them. Baker hit the ball over the right field fence, and that cost us the game.[20]

Tris Speaker, or at least whoever wrote for him in his own syndicated column that year, agreed.[21] Matty and Speaker were most likely partially correct in their assessment of the situation. Collins, who never accepted tip-offs on pitches himself, is generally conceded to be one of the greatest sign stealers of all time. On the other hand, in his discussions of baseball strategy, he often said he looked for the pitcher, not the catcher, to tip the pitch.

Mathewson's article did not stop there, however. In a rather startling statement, especially for the times, Matty revealed that in Game One he realized it was best to deliver slow curves to Frank Baker, not fastballs. He claimed he warned Marquard before Game Two, but the advice went unheeded. Although he was otherwise most complimentary toward his pitching mate, Marquard did not take kindly to the remarks and said so publicly. The series may have been tied, but trouble brewed in Giants territory.

For Game Three the show returned to the Polo Grounds, where on October 17 newspaper columnist Christy Mathewson took the mound to test his recently stated theories on pitching to Frank Baker. The A's choice was Jack Coombs. The iron man needed an iron arm for what turned out to be an 11-inning duel. For eight and one-third innings, Mathewson and the Giants held sway, 1–0. Then Matty tried out his theory on Baker and paid for it dearly when Frank cleared the fence with his second home run of the series. For the Mackmen it meant a tie game and a new life. For Mr. Baker it meant that a man who never hit more than 12 home runs in a season and 96 for a career forevermore carried the nickname "Home Run."

Coombs blanked the A's in the ninth. The game remained locked until the top of the eleventh, when with one down, Collins got his second single of the day, then reached third when Herzog threw wild trying to nail Baker on a close play at first. Baker took second. Eddie then scored when shortstop Art Fletcher bobbled Murphy's grounder. Davis followed with a single to score Baker, boosting the A's lead to 3–1. An unearned run in the ninth, due to Eddie's second muff of the day and third of the series, did not prevent a 3–2 A's victory.

Collins recalled what happened after the game as the New York fans reacted to the loss. In those days ballparks with clubhouses, or even lockers and showers, for visiting teams were rare. In New York City the A's stayed at the Hotel Alamac and their rooms served that purpose. Normally the players took buses to and from the stadium, but this was the World Series, so they hired taxis. The ride to the park was smooth, but the trek back to the hotel after the game became rocky after their win.

"The cabs were tomato-smeared by the time we arrived back at the Alamac."

The team learned its lesson and retained policemen for the ensuing trips to the ball yard during the series. They rode in the front of the cab. This put a stop to the vegetable assault, but not the invectives. Still, "words are easier to take than over-ripe vegetables, so none of us [the A's] suffered by the actions of the New York fans."[22]

The match now seesawed back to Philadelphia. In his *To Everything a Season*, author Bruce Kuklick describes what happened next.

"With the A's up by one in the series, it rained for five days. In his tower office Connie Mack looked out at the grey surroundings every morning and hoped for the weather to break. In the Shibe Park lunchroom a vendor's nightmare occurred. Employees removed the sandwich meat from between the two pieces of bread and put it on ice. They gave the bread to orphanages. After two days, they discarded the meat itself, and the franchise worried about its profits. On the sixth day the rain stopped, but grounds keepers spent the day drying out the water logged field with cans of burning gasoline."[23]

In addition to the rain and the players' stampede to the press to report and critique one another, there was one other matter unrelated to the games themselves. The Giants were upset when attendance figures were announced. Believing the newly constructed stands in New York held 50,000 fans, a number of the Giants' players were upset when a crowd of 38,281 was announced for Game One. Feeling the owners were understating the figures to reduce the players' share of the proceeds, Chief Meyers and others took their case to the National Commission. Mack and the A's stayed out of it.

If that wasn't enough, a Cobb-like feud erupted between the teams in the third game when Fred Snodgrass spiked Frank Baker in the thigh as he slid into the A's third basemen spikes held high. Given Baker's heroics, the A's and their fans saw red. "It was a willful offense," said Collins.[24] But the rain dampened all and when the series finally resumed on October 24, everyone looked forward to just playing ball. Once again Mathewson and Bender faced off. Matty had told reporters in his latest column that now that the A's had used up their power, the key was keeping their speed off the bases. "Take Barry and Collins out of that team and they would look like a pretty bad lot of base runners, wouldn't they?"[25]

This time the A's did get the base runners, clipping Big Six for 10 hits, his relief Wiltse for one, and beating the Giants' ace, 4–2. Matty was kind to the victors, telling readers it was "a case of too much Baker and Collins." More particularly it was "the hitting of Baker [2-for-3 with two doubles, one run scored, one RBI] and Collins [2-for-3, one score] combined with Collins' defensive play that cost us the game." Mathewson described Collins' theft of a sure-fire Larry Doyle hit in the eighth as a rally killer, as Eddie turned it into a double play. "Collins was on the ball so fast that many of the spectators thought it was a hit-and-run play and he was going in to cover the base."

Finally, Matty thought Collins "ought to have at least been credited with an assist" when the A's infield pulled some trickery with one out in the top of the sixth. It occurred when Baker trapped a foul ball hit by Red Murray, the right fielder. The play occurred just outside the line and Doyle, who was on first at the time, headed toward second thinking it was fair and safe. Barry took it all in at short and bluffed as if it were a grounder. At second Collins shouted "throw the ball here," causing Doyle to bear down on second even harder.[26] When Baker tossed to first for the double play, Doyle looked the fool and the fans let him know they agreed.

In Game Five played on October 25 at the Polo Grounds, a New York crowd saw its share of heroics and controversy, as well. Trailing three to one in the game count and 3–1 in the score with two down in the ninth, the Giants fought back gamely to tie, before winning it in the bottom of the tenth on a wild play at the plate.

The pitchers, for what could well have been the final game, were Marquard and Coombs. The big blow, a three-run homer by Rube Oldring in the third, knocked Marquard from the game. McGraw's choice for a reliever, Leon Ames, paid off, however, as the righty with the great curveball shut down the Mackmen for the next four innings, keeping his team within striking distance. Jack Coombs, sailing along as he did in Game Three, suddenly caught his spikes and pulled ligaments in his groin. He gamely trudged on, but was not nearly as effective. It didn't help that Collins, 0-for-3 in the contest, bobbled a ball in the seventh that helped the Giants score a run, making it 3–1.

In the ninth the Giants finally got to a pained Colby Jack. In retrospect, Mack waited too long to make a pitching change. The inning ended with the score tied. In the bottom of the tenth, Mack had Plank on the mound and two out. Larry Doyle stood on third when Fred Merkle lifted a fly into right. Murphy caught it along the foul line and Doyle flew toward the plate, sliding and beating the throw. A's catcher Jack Lapp picked up the ball, left the field, and the crowd went wild, their Giants the victors, 4–3.

After the game Bill Klem, a National League umpire who worked more World Series contests than anyone else and is enshrined at Cooperstown, said that Doyle missed the plate. If Lapp had only tagged Doyle, he would have called him out and the inning was over. Later both Mack and Harry Davis claimed they saw Doyle fail to touch the rubber but remained silent because it might have precipitated a riot if they appealed the call at that point.[27] McGraw, too, saw the miss and admitted such to Klem.[28] It seemed just about everyone but poor Jack Lapp recognized the situation. Now he and his mates still needed to win one more game.

That win came the very next day in Philadelphia as the A's won the entire package in convincing fashion before a delighted crowd, 13–2. Collins, who went 0-for-4 but scored a run when he reached base safely on Merkle's hurried throw as a result of a deft bunt, was the only everyday player to fail to hit. Bender, returning a game earlier than many expected, pitched four-hit ball and overcame five A's errors to gain the win. John McGraw, who brought back Leon Ames to start, despite his four innings in Game Five, left his normal coaching perch on the sidelines before the game was finished to avoid the catcalls from exuberant A's fans, as their team scored seven runs in the seventh inning.

For the series Eddie Collins went 6-for-21 for a .286 average, well below his 1910 results. In addition, despite a number of spectacular fielding plays, he committed several costly errors. Nonetheless, he was now recognized as a team leader on a club that was a repeat champion.

Even Collins, however, recognized that the heroes of the 1911 World Series were Frank "Home Run" Baker and Chief Bender. Writing under his byline, Eddie told readers, "For iron nerve, craftiness, control and general all-around ability I don't think he [Bender] has an equal in the game today." As for Baker he termed the third baseman's home run in Game Three "the turning point" of the series. Christy Mathewson was a "great pitcher" and along with Bender, "Two of the craftiest, hardest and capable slab artists that the game has ever produced." Finally as to this year's series, by comparison "last year's World Series was like a picnic," in that this year it was "close, hard-fought and nerve-wracking throughout."[29]

Did Collins write these words, or did someone write them for him? Only Collins and, if there was one, his "ghost" knows for sure. It does seem certain that Collins, a college-educated man who did not hide his pride in that achievement, wrote many of the articles attributed to him during his career and, perhaps, he wrote them all. In addition to articles under his singular byline, there are any number of articles in which Collins is listed as a co-author and others where he told his story to someone else clearly identified as the author.

At least one noted writer thought Collins authored his own material. In an article in *The Sporting News* in 1949 on "ghostwriting" in baseball, H.G. Salsinger of the *Detroit News* wrote that "[a]s far as we can remember, the only player who ever wrote the stories published under his name was Eddie Collins, when he was with the Philadelphia Athletics at the peek of his playing career. Collins, a very literate man, wrote his daily contributions in longhand and insisted upon them being published just as they were written."[30]

Issues surrounding writing by baseball players, in general, and Eddie Collins, in particular, swirled for years, but for now Eddie and his team were the talk of the baseball world. Entering the 1912 season, instead of cast with doubt as was the case in 1910 and 1911, the Mackmen were the overwhelming favorites, and with good reason. Except for Danny Murphy (33) and Eddie Plank (36), their primary players were in their twenties. Harry Davis, the valued veteran, was now in Cleveland, where he was still playing a bit and managing. The new captain of the A's was Danny Murphy.

The infield of Baker, Barry, Collins and McInnis was now commonly referred to as "the $100,000 Infield." It is hard to believe in a day when the minimum salary for a single player is three times that amount, but the monetary value attributed to the group signified they were priceless. In the spring of 1912 at their new training site in San Antonio, the quartet honed its skills. Collins liked to talk about the group.

"Those were the golden days, those years with 'Stuffy,' 'Jack,' and 'Bake.'"

Even practice was fun for this motley crew. McInnis kept things lively, challenging his infield mates to make errant throws so he could stretch for them or dig them out of the dirt. There were plenty of laughs, but in the end it was the group's willingness to work that made the difference.

"We were out early and late. It was practice all the time, but we were regular prima donnas in regard to the way the workouts were conducted."

They were almost dictatorial in directing those who hit infield practice for them. Pitcher Jack Coombs was their favorite and, thus, anyone else was in for a very critical review.

"Harry Davis ... tried it once but only once." On that occasion Davis, who had a knack for hitting the ball so as to get a bad hop, caused Collins and crew to bark loudly as his habit altered their workout plans. Davis, a funny guy, yelled back, "Once a .300 hitter, always a .300 hitter."

Collins remembered, "He won that argument but he never batted for us again."[31]

In 1912 the work ethic of "the $100,000 Infield" paid off. Before long there were some calling the group the best of all time, and there is no doubt, even today, they are among the best. By 1930, estimates were made that the $100,000 value had increased to a million; by 1950, two million. Today that amount would be in multiples. This is particularly amazing when one realizes that this "priceless" infield cost Connie Mack practically nothing. He picked off Collins and Barry from college, Baker and McInnis from the minors, all at a bargain.

Mack's low-cost, high-caliber infield was at the top of its game in 1912 in the field and at the plate. McInnis hit a solid .327, driving in 101 runs. Baker batted .347, drove in a league-leading 130 runs and lived up to his nickname, stroking 10 home runs to tie Tris Speaker for the league lead. Jack Barry, never the hitter by comparison, hit a respectable .261 and drove in 55 runs. Collins led or tied for the team lead in numerous categories: batting (.348), on-base percentage (.450), games played (153), runs scored (137), walks (101) and stolen bases (63), among others.

Given these numbers and strong pitching performances by Jack Coombs (21–10, 3.29) and Eddie Plank (26–6, 2.22) and a credible effort by the Chief (13–8, 2.74), one would envision a fine season and repeat pennant-winning performance by the A's. Connie Mack thought so. He felt the 1912 Mackmen formed "his greatest team." The "club had speed, hitting power, pitching skill, and more brains than one ordinarily finds on three clubs ... ."[32]

But the season plays out on the field, not on paper. A glimpse at what was to come was gleaned, perhaps, by the results of the six-game City Series, a four games to two rebuff by a mediocre Phillies team. The only real highlight for the A's was engineered by Collins and his mates when they pulled off a rare triple steal in game one of that series.

The Mackmen started fast in 1912, winning their home opener over Washington, 4–2, before 18,000 fans, and then won two more. By June 1, however, the record stood at 17–17. Although at the time the players did not realize it, or perhaps more accurately would not admit it, they were trailing a Boston Red Sox team that they could not catch. Mack summed up 1912 best to biographer Fred Lieb.

"There was talk of our having a monopoly on the pennant, like the later-day talk about the Yankees. The whole attitude of the league was that we would win again in a walk. That became so contagious that our players caught it. They became puffed up and believed themselves unbeatable. If ever a club suffered from overconfidence, it was my 1912 team."[33]

Collins, who thought that in 1912 the team was as good as in 1911, agreed with Mack that overconfidence played its part. "There's no explaining our collapse — if it could be called that — of 1912. Perhaps deflation is a better word. Perhaps we had grown a bit too cocky. Perhaps we had taken our success too much for granted. Maybe we were beginning to believe those many nice press notices."[34]

If one were given to excuses, the A's had theirs. For example, there was Jack Coombs and his bad back, as well as Ira Thomas and his illness, which limited him to 48 games. There was also Danny Murphy's injured shoulder, which limited him to 36 games; some early season arm problems for Collins, rumored to be rheumatic in origin; and minor injuries to others, like McInnis and Baker. But these health issues alone did not account for the A's decline. Mack's assessment and Collins' as well were much closer to the mark.

Still, the season was not without its moments. One occurred on May 18 when Collins and his teammates faced off against a makeshift lineup of "Tigers" playing in place of the regulars, who were on strike protesting the suspension of Ty Cobb for a fracas that occurred in New York a few days earlier. The precipitating factor was a boisterous fan who finally went too far when he used a racial slur, sending Cobb into the Hilltop Park grandstand, where he beat up the man. It did not help Cobb's case that when the event took place, Ban Johnson was in attendance, nor that the rowdy fan was missing one hand and several fingers on his other. Nonetheless, when Cobb was indefinitely suspended, his fellow players played one game against the A's without him, then sat out the next game in what amounted to the first player strike. The lineup the A's faced instead included semipros and collegians from the Philadelphia area as well as 42-year-old Tiger coach Joe Sugden at first and fellow coach Jim "Deacon" McGuire, 48, behind the plate. On the mound was a seminary student from St. Joseph's College.

The game, understandably, was a farce; the A's eked out a 24–2 win. Collins piled up five hits in six appearances at the plate and stole five bases. It was nothing for the A's nor baseball to brag about. By the fourth inning many of the 15,000 in attendance were scattering to the exits. Mercifully, the next day's contest was canceled and then, after Cobb urged his teammates to return with a fine and accepted a 10-day suspension and his own fine, the strike was over.

On May 27 Collins had a standout day against a legitimate lineup when he singled twice, doubled twice, walked, stole two bases (including home) and scored three times in a 12–6 A's win over the Red Sox.

Collins never admired the Red Sox more than in 1912. The Bostonians, including their famous "Golden Outfield" of Duffy Lewis, Tris Speaker and Harry Hooper, "played consistent ball all season. I guess they deserved to win."[35]

In a double-header with the Tigers in Philadelphia on July 19, Collins hit safely three times in each game and stole home. Nevertheless, his efforts were overshadowed by the ever-present Cobb, who hit safely seven times on the day and stirred up his usual serving of controversy when the A's accused him of violating the rules by stepping out of the batter's box to meet the ball. The umpire ignored the protest.

During his career Collins seldom failed to finish a game he started, but on August 17 in Philadelphia against the White Sox, his temper topped his common sense. Umpire Jack Sheridan tossed him in the fourth for protesting a close call at second. Eddie felt the tag was in time and argued too long and too much. He was having a good day at the plate to boot. When the A's lost a close contest, 5–4, the *Inquirer*'s Old Sport, despite agreeing that Collins' beef was righteous, took him to task:

"The self-immolation of Collins was unnecessary.... There is such a thing as a player being too mealy mouthed, but then there is the other extreme; he may become too pronounced in his kicks, and do his team more harm than good by kicking himself out of the game.... He [Collins] is needed in every minute of play between now and the time when the final disposition of the flag is assured."[36]

It was one of the few times the Philadelphia press found public fault with Collins. But there was more than just Collins' temper to worry about. The A's, accustomed to winning the close ones, were now on the other end of that spectrum, and three straight losses to the Red Sox at the end of August had them reeling, 13 and one-half games out of first and in third place behind Washington, as well.

To their credit the Mackmen continued to play hard, Collins in particular. Playing against Ty Cobb seemed to bring out the best in Eddie. On September 11 in Detroit with Cobb drawing fire again for stepping up and out of the box, this time for a called out, Collins stole six bases on a 3-for-5 day at the plate. The six steals, which included another theft of home, set a new modern (post–1900) record. It was a wild day. Umpire Tommy Connolly was struck by a bottle thrown by an irate fan and, of course, Cobb and his teammates did not take kindly to Cobb's disqualification on a technicality he had impugned with regularity in earlier contests.

Eleven days later Collins proved his road show on the bases in Detroit was no fluke. In the first game of a double-bill with St. Louis, he stole another six bases as follows: a steal of second in the first inning, another in the fifth and seventh, followed in that same inning by a double steal of third with McInnis, then a steal of second and of third in the eighth. He was 5-for-7 at the plate in the two games.

The six stolen bases are still a major league record and stood almost eighty years until tied by Otis Nixon of the Atlanta Braves in Montreal on June 16, 1991. It remains the American League record for single-game steals. When told he had tied Eddie Collins' record, Nixon said, "I don't even know who that guy is."[37]

In 1912 opponents definitely knew who Collins was, but by the time of his base-stealing heroics, it was too late. Boston was a winner with an American League-record 105 victories. A highlight was the remarkable pitching performance of Smoky Joe Wood, who went 35–4. The A's finished in third at a respectable 90–62, one behind Washington. The A's might have finished in second, but in typical fashion Mack tried out a number of youngsters at the end, including 20-year-old outfielder Eddie Murphy and a trio of young pitchers with names that would become familiar: Joe Bush, Herb Pennock and Stan Coveleski. The Red Sox followed up their regular season success by besting the Giants in the World Series.

Individually, another fine year at the plate for Collins earned him sixth place in the voting for the Chalmers Award, won by Tris Speaker. Collins 137 runs scored led the American League.

The year, however, was not over. Since both the A's and the Phillies sat idle, their owners decided a post-season City Series was in order. The A's and Collins played well, taking five of six. A few weeks later on October 28, Eddie and Mabel were off on an adventure of a different type as members of a party of 20 A's players and their wives who joined John Shibe on a trip to Cuba to play 12 games against that island's best. Since the A's were still the biggest draw in baseball by virtue of their back-to-back titles, the people of Cuba eagerly looked forward to the visit. On their way to Key West to catch their ship, the Mackmen played four games in the South, including a November 1 date in Miami.

The games in Cuba were played in November with the A's taking matters seriously, winning 10 of 12, including eight straight. The losses were attributed to the departure of Jack Barry during the tour and, perhaps, to Eddie Plank's ineffectiveness due to a bout of the "grip." At the end of November, a weary bunch of Mackmen returned stateside, less than three months away from a new season and a fresh start.

CHAPTER 9

Keystone King

"He [Collins] is the greatest man in a pinch that I ever saw."
— John McGraw[1]

Connie Mack did not join his team for its fall excursion to Cuba because he was welcoming a new addition to the Mack tribe at home. Both before and after the trip, however, the Tall Tactician left his imprint in preparation for a more productive 1913 season. Collins recalled the scene in the clubhouse after the last regular season game when Mack told the club he felt they " 'were the best team of the lot.'

"Those words haunted us all that winter and when the next spring came along we were a sober, serious and determined squad, bound closely by an avowal to win back the laurels we had forfeited through careless and sometimes sloppy play of the year before."[2]

Mack was at it again as soon as his team returned from Havana, bringing each of the players back to Philadelphia for a talk. His instructions: keep in shape during the winter layoff with light work, physically prepared to engage in full scale spring drills in San Antonio in early February. If conditioning had been a problem in 1912, Mack meant to rectify it in 1913.

Over the winter there was at least one other change, this one involving the structure of team ownership. Based on his success there was interest in bringing the Tall Tactician to other franchises. The New York Highlanders approached him. In order to secure Mack's continuing presence, majority A's owner Benjamin Shibe began a series of complicated maneuvers, including the sale of Shibe Park to the company that owned the Athletics and a loan to Mack, which enabled Connie to purchase the one-quarter interest of Messrs. Hough (the Old Sport) and Jones and become a 50-percent co-owner with Shibe. That piece of business completed to Mack's satisfaction, he and Shibe could turn their attention to bringing the world title back to Shibe Park.

Another piece of that puzzle remained firmly in place. On February 21, 1913, Eddie Collins renewed his contract with the A's at $6,000, remaining one of baseball's better paid performers.[3]

Arriving at camp in shape was never a problem for Collins, for he believed in keeping in shape over the winter. Upon arrival in Texas in late February, he was ready to go. The team he greeted was essentially the same, with only minor repairs. Over the winter outfielder Bris Lord, a .238 hitter in 1912, was sold to the Boston Braves of the National League. His place in the pasture was taken by Eddie Murphy, a solid-hitting youngster known to his teammates as "Honest Eddie." In 33 games toward the end of 1912, he impressed Mack with his bat and his speed. During this particular spring Mack also found a new catcher in Wally Schang. Up from Buffalo, the switch-hitting youngster at age 23 offered promise of a better bat than either Ira Thomas or Jack Lapp.

The spring sessions progressed smoothly on the field, with at least one significant bump off of it. On March 13 as the players rested in their bunks on a train taking them from Austin, Texas, to Waco for their next encounter, their Pullman car broke loose. When the engineer realized what happened, he slowed down and the uncoupled Pullman collided with the coupled car in front of it, ramming a number of the players' heads against the walls next to their bunks. Fortunately, no one was seriously injured and the A's, barely fazed, defeated Waco, 9–2. More rail problems ensued in late March on the team's trip north when a flood hit Louisville, shutting down all rail traffic and stranding the Mackmen for several days. The players killed time in their hotel, playing cards and relaxing one last time before taking on the Phillies in a renewal of their cross-town rivalry.

In that series the A's served notice by their spirited play against the Phils that they were prepared for a faster start in 1913. They won five games and lost none, one ending in an 18-inning 2–2 tie. In a surprising move, Danny Murphy, who was running the club in Mack's absence, allowed the A's pitcher, Carroll "Boardwalk" Brown, a promising 26-year-old righty, to pitch all 18 innings. Brown later attributed this overuse to arm troubles which cut short his promising career.

The season opener was in Boston on April 10 with over 22,000 fans on hand to greet the world champions. The A's wasted no time reminding them that this was a totally new season. In the first inning Collins, batting in his usual number three position, behind new lead-off man Eddie Murphy and Rube Oldring, singled the pair home against starter Joe

Collins' first stay in Philadelphia as a member of the Athletics ran from late 1906 through the 1914 season. Here he and several A's teammates await their turn for a few batting practice swings. They are (left to right) Jimmy Walsh, Jack Lapp, Wally Schang, unknown player, Collins, Rube Oldring, Frank Baker, and Danny Murphy. Those identified were all members of the A's 1913 World Championship club (Philadelphia A's Historical Society).

Wood. On the day Eddie was 5-for-5 and also scored a run as the A's won, 10–9. Of concern was the poor pitching performance of Jack Coombs, as well as that of Chief Bender in relief. It was left to the old-timer Eddie Plank to save the game. It would be a trend for Mack this season, using his veterans in relief as he began starting several of his younger moundsmen, including Boardwalk Brown (17–11, 2.94), Joe Bush (15–6, 3.82), Herb Pennock (2–1, 5.13) and another new find, Bob Shawkey (6–5, 2.34).

Concern over the condition of Colby Jack Coombs grew when Mack started him again two days later in part two of the Boston series. He was wild and was removed in the first inning. Again Plank saved the day, the A's winning, 5–4. Collins' single in the first was his sixth consecutive hit to start the new season.

The A's continued their jump start when they defeated the Browns on May 8 for their sixth straight. They now stood 15–3. The news about pitching stalwart Jack Coombs was not nearly so good; the diagnosis: typhoid, a highly contagious and in those days at times fatal bacterial infection passed by man through unsanitary conditions in food and water. Colby Jack was finished for the year, if not for his career. It was a severe blow to a team with an aging staff.

Like his team, Collins was off to a particularly good start in all facets of his game: hitting, stealing bases, and scoring runs in bunches. In a 4–0 win over the Highlanders on April 25 in Philadelphia, the *Inquirer* reported that Eddie "appropriated the afternoon for a regular personally conducted swat fest all his own, busting the ball on the beezer for three doubles and a single out of his four trips to the plate and adding a pair of stolen bases to his string for good measure."[4]

A day later yet another double and a triple raised Collins' average to .515. By now, based on the sustained excellence of his hitting and fielding, Collins was drawing comparisons with Napoleon Lajoie and Johnny Evers as the best second basemen then playing ball, if not the best ever. Perhaps the first outwardly visible sign for Collins was in 1912 when Eddie appeared in his own advertisement. Under the caption "Brainy Collins," the advertiser asked readers to "Read what one of the sensations of 2nd base in the whole history of baseball says about Coca-Cola."[5]

Then there were comments like that of Oscar Vitt, the Tiger infielder who ventured a comparison of Collins with his own teammate, Ty Cobb. In a column in a San Francisco newspaper, which he may or may not have written himself, Vitt called Collins "the most valuable ball player in the world," saying while "Cobb is a remarkable ball player ... I do not think he is as valuable to a club as Collins." Conceding that Cobb is the much more colorful player and "therefore, more popular with the fans, Cobb is essentially an individual player.

"Cobb will try to steal a base no matter whether his club is five runs behind. This Collins will not do. It is not the kind of ball playing that will win games. Cobb catches the eye quicker than Collins, but I think the latter gets better results for his club."[6]

Flattering comments such as this would have merely brought an embarrassed shrug and brush off from Collins. In his mind there was no comparison; Cobb was the best of all-time and Eddie maintained that opinion throughout his life. A comparison of second basemen was another topic entirely. An interesting take on that subject came from F.C. Lane of *Baseball Magazine*. Writing in December 1912 in an article entitled, "The Greatest of All Second Basemen," an 11-page treatment of the subject, Lane whittled his choices to three — Lajoie, Evers and Collins — and tried to even out their differences in age.

By way of background, by 1913 Napoleon Lajoie was a 38-year-old veteran of both the National and the American leagues. The right-handed hitter and thrower at 6 foot 1 inch and 195 pounds was a man of exceedingly good looks, composure and grace. One of the all-time greatest pull hitters, his late-season chase with Cobb for the Chalmers Award remained an epic tale. In 1901, the first season for the American League, he hit a record .426. Until the emergence of Collins, he had no American League peer at second base.

On the other hand, Lajoie's National League counterpart Johnny Evers, like Lajoie a future member of the Hall of Fame, was slight of build at 5 foot 9 inches and 125 pounds. By 1913 he was 31 years old, still playing with his only benefactor, the Chicago Cubs. Evers made up for his lack of size with a volatile temper. Never a hitter of Lajoie's caliber, Evers was nonetheless at his best in the big games, carrying a lifetime .316 average in the World Series. His highly successful approach to grounders — he sidled toward them — earned him the nickname "the Crab." In 1912 he enjoyed his top season at the plate, hitting .341 and compiling an on-base-percentage of .431, which was second in his league.

In comparing his second-base subjects, F.C. Lane first set out the criteria. "A second baseman, is a fielder first and a batter second," whose "duty ... is to stop all drives which fall anywhere within his territory and get his man." While "finish and ease in fielding at least count for something," the more important aspect is "ground covering ability." In that regard, Lane pointed out that great fielders normally have lower fielding averages, because they "cover so much ground that they accept chances which do not logically belong to them."

Other features Lane deemed important for great second basemen include the "ability to field almost equally well on both sides of his position," as well as "cover the bag," and his ability in "tagging the runner who is trying to steal the bag."

When it comes to hitting, timeliness and the ability to get on base with a walk were high on Lane's list. And, perhaps, most important is "that quality of mind which gives certain players the reputation of being brainy in distinction from others who are merely good mechanical workers."

After polling a number of veteran players who named Lajoie, Evers and Collins most frequently and in various order as the best, Lane proceeded to make his comparisons. Between Lajoie and Collins, he found the latter:

> has not the superlative merits which characterize Lajoie's flawless work at second base, but he is a much faster man and covers doubtless considerably more ground. And if he can not pick up a grounder with one hand or pull a high drive out of the air with the inimitable ease of the Cleveland star, he can at least do it in some fashion; and is not that the main thing to be considered? In other words, is it of such great importance how a man stops a ball and gets it to first base so long as he does stop it and get it there in time to cut off a runner? Spectacular, true; but the work of the greatest of second basemen is built upon more substantial things.
>
> Collins is nervous, excitable and lacks the finish of Lajoie, but he knocks down far more than his just share of hard hit balls and fields them rapidly if not so brilliantly as his great rival. He plays the game with a dash and an energy which Lajoie has never shown. He is, in short, a live wire.... He [Lajoie] outhits Collins and is unquestionably the better batter of the two, but Collins' speed more than makes up for the difference. Collins is a wonderful base stealer and that is important; Lajoie is not. Lajoie has no superiors, probably no equals in the art of putting the ball on the base runner at second; but Collins, in the judgment of two people out of three accomplishes more real work in the course of a season, does more real benefit to his team than Lajoie.

On the other hand at least in 1912, where Lane recalled Collins was a bit below par and Evers at his best, Johnny Evers was Lane's choice as the best.

"The two [Evers and Collins] compare very favorably at almost every point, but the difference where it is perceptible at all favors the National League player. Take Collins out of the Athletics' line up and the club is still remarkably strong. Take Evers out of the Cub line up and the injury is all but irreparable."[7]

And what did Johnny Evers think about all of this comparison business? When it came to Lajoie versus Collins, to Evers, never one to mince words, the choice was clear. In the same article he was quoted as saying, "A man can not be a great second baseman who is afraid to dirty his pants." In his opinion Lajoie fielded a ball standing, or he did not field it at all. "Collins runs full speed to one side, then falls flat on his face and manages to reach the ball by stretching full length after it...."[8]

Of course, in 1913 Collins was a mere 26, thereby making any comparisons with older players somewhat skewed. But one who saw them both and gave his honest appraisal was the great Cy Young. In the end he was unable to choose.

> I was at the end of my career when Collins was at his best, while I was at my peak against Lajoie. I had an opportunity to see both of them. And you know — I just can't compare 'em. They are like two saddles we had down on the farm, the western saddle and the English saddle. They were both great, but for different kinds of ridin.'
>
> Lajoie was one of the most rugged hitters I ever faced. He'd take your leg off with a line drive, turn the third baseman around like a swinging door and powder the hand of the left fielder. Collins, on the other hand, was what you'd call a "cutie," punching hits here and there when you weren't looking.
>
> They were the same on the field; Lajoie was smooth, Collins jackrabbity. But they both got over the fence, if you know what I mean. They both got there. Lajoie, however, had one thing in his favor. He was the Babe Ruth of our day.[9]

All comparisons aside, Collins' early-season heroics in 1913 sparked his A's to an early league lead, where they remained. Although the A's took most of the mystery out of the league race, there were still enough hi-jinks to keep everyone happy. One wild scene took place in St. Louis on May 9 when the umpires, Charles Ferguson and Silk O'Loughlin, showed enough indecision to cause both teams to howl and scratch their heads. In a close play at first base, Ferguson called Rube Oldring out, then reversed his decision, calling him safe. O'Loughlin, the plate umpire, overruled Ferguson and once again Oldring was out. Collins, standing at the plate awaiting his turn at bat, went wild, throwing his cap into the air and his bat after it. Ira Thomas rolled his catcher's mask to the mound. All this hubbub caused O'Loughlin to think. He turned around and called Oldring safe. Now it was the Browns who were howling. After another 10 minutes, order was restored and Eddie hit a weak roller back to the pitcher, who threw him out to quietly retire the side and restore order. The A's lost, 7–3.

By virtue of their league lead, their winning ways since 1909, and their bevy of stars, the A's were easily the top draw in the circuit. In Cleveland, for example, a May 18 date with the A's brought a record crowd of 23,617 to the park. Bender, now relieving more games than he started, pitched the last seven innings for a 4–2 A's victory.

As Collins' stature as a player grew, so did his air of confidence. More and more frequently he lived up to his nickname "Cocky." He would not hesitate to scold a teammate for less than stellar play. A case in point was Byron Houck, who in 1913 came to the aid of a struggling A's staff with a 14–6 record (4.14 ERA) in 41 appearances. On June 12 in the late innings in Philadelphia, Houck fielded a grounder but failed to toss it to Collins covering first, "for which oversight he was soundly berated by the aforesaid Mr. Collins."[10] The misplay eventually led to the tying run and the A's came up short in the end, 5–2.

In Collins' mind his occasional "instructional" tirades did nothing to hurt team unity. Recalling the "good old days" in Philly with the Mackmen, Eddie said, "There was friendship off the field as well as on. We were more than a team: we were a club."[11]

If his second baseman's directional interactions with fellow teammates bothered Connie Mack, he never mentioned it, instead often praising Collins as his manager on the field. Eddie's confidence in himself and his teammates, particularly his fellow infielders, allowed him and Jack Barry to devise a method for blocking the double steal, an important and frequently executed offensive tool in the days of the dead ball. Collins readily admitted the maneuver was developed to cover for his weak throwing arm.

"It required extraordinary effort for me to get the ball to the plate, in time to head off a fast man, when I took the throw at second, so I proposed to Barry that with runners on first and third, I should cut in behind the pitcher when the man on first started for second. If the runner on third remained there I would open up my hands and Jack could catch the ball and get the runner going into second."[12]

The maneuver worked well, but not always. One of the shakier moments occurred in the early going for the pair. The A's were hosting Detroit when Barry paid too much attention to the runner and not enough to the ball, which bounced up and smacked him in the gut.

"After that experience Jack said he would remember to keep his eye on the ball and let me watch the man at third. He did, and we pulled the play successfully several times before we left home."[13]

While this was going on, the Tall Tactician was doing some maneuvering of his own. As the season wore on, Jimmy Walsh, a 27-year-old left-handed batter, was playing a lot in the outfield with the youngster Eddie Murphy. Since neither player was all that experienced, Mack, scorecard in hand, waved the cardboard to signal the positioning he wanted, thus utilizing his superior knowledge of the strengths and weaknesses of each opposing batsman. The strategy worked and the image of the erect, dapper man in the dugout in a business suit, cupping his scoreboard while directing his troops, is a lasting image of one of baseball's legendary field generals.

By mid–July the A's led second-place Cleveland by 11 games in the loss column and third-place Washington by 17; even opposing managers were conceding the pennant. According to Frank Chance, the former "Peerless Leader" of the Cubs who was now managing the Highlanders, "There's only one real club in big league baseball today and that is the Athletics."[14]

It was in 1913 that Collins began to establish his image as an iron man. In August the *Inquirer* noted that "gritty Eddie Collins is sticking in the conflict with a boil on his leg that would have many a guy pulling faces at himself in the privacy of his own bedroom."[15] Teammate Rube Oldring had already noticed Collins' willingness to play through pain. In 1911 Eddie sprained his ankle while sliding home for an inside-the-park home run against Boston and Smoky Joe Wood. According to Oldring:

> We helped him [Collins] hobble to the Athletic bench. We cut off his shoe and noticed the ankle was black and badly swollen.
> Although Connie Mack wanted several of us to carry Collins to the club house, Eddie dissented. He looked at the ankle, cussed a couple of times and then told us to "strap that damn thing up." We did, and Collins put on a bigger shoe and went out to finish the game. He accepted every chance that came his way during the next four innings without an error. We won that game, 1–0.[16]

It was good that Collins was playing an iron man role. Several of his teammates, including Stuffy McInnis and Boardwalk Brown, were out with injuries as the team approached the end of the season. Harry Davis, back after one unsuccessful season managing Cleveland, filled in for Stuffy at first. However, McInnis was back on September 22 as the A's clinched their third pennant in four years with a pair of shutout wins over the Tigers at Shibe. In the first game "Bullet Joe" Bush lived up to his nickname, giving those doubting the ability of the A's pitching staff to weather a World Series storm something to think about.

The A's finished their season at 96–57, six and one-half games in front of second-place

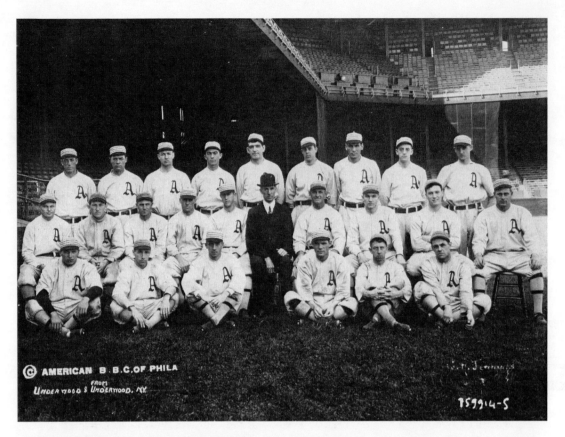

The 1913 World Champion Philadelphia A's. They are: (Back row, left to right) Eddie Plank, Harry Davis, Byron Houck, Ira Thomas, Boardwalk Brown, Chief Bender, Weldon Wycoff, and Herb Pennock; (center row) Amos Strunk, Jack Lapp, Tom Daley, Wally Schang, Joe Bush, Connie Mack, Danny Murphy, Bob Shawkey, Billy Orr, and Rube Oldring; (bottom row) Jimmy Walsh, Doc Lavan, Jack Barry, Eddie Murphy, Collins, and Stuffy McInnis (Photo Collection, Cleveland Public Library).

Washington, who received an enormous boost from Walter Johnson. "The Big Train" had one of the great years any pitcher ever had by winning 36, losing 7 and posting an ERA of 1.14.

During the 1913 season Collins batted .345, hit three home runs, drove in 73 teammates, and led the league in runs scored for the second straight season with 125. In stolen bases his 55 ranked third behind Washington's Clyde Milan and Danny Moeller, as well as Cobb, who had 51. His on-base percentage was .441, which stood third in the league. He finished third in the Chalmers balloting to Walter Johnson and former teammate Joe Jackson, who enjoyed a .373 season at the plate.

Clinching the pennant early allowed Mack to give his players, including Collins, a few games off to rest up for yet another confrontation with the New York Giants. It is doubtful, however, that Eddie could totally relax. Several days before the teams were set to open in New York, he fell into the middle of a controversy involving players planning to write articles about the World Series under their bylines. Collins had already dabbled in such matters in previous years. In 1913 he planned to expand his efforts, contracting with the Wheeler Syndicate for daily reports on the Fall Classic. Then the National Commission, unhappy with a practice which in many cases was a certain sham and perhaps under pressure from the legitimate press, issued a ban on all such articles. The National Commission went further than that, however, issuing an edict to the effect that if any of the Giants or A's players continued the practice, they would cancel the World Series. This, of course, affected Collins. It also affected a number of others, including Giants manager John J. McGraw and players Christy Mathewson, Rube Marquard, Larry Doyle and Chief Meyers. In addition to Collins, teammate Frank Baker was identified as a potential violator. Non-participants who planned to report on the series included Ty Cobb and his manager, Hughie Jennings, and Rabbit Maranville of the National League's Boston Braves.

Some, including Collins and McGraw, were under contract at the time the ban was announced. McGraw greeted the news with his usual bombacity, saying he would fulfill his contract. While never denying that someone else wrote his columns, he stated "nothing goes out over my name which does not contain my own views."[17]

While the controversy continued to brew, McGraw and the players received support from David Fultz, a former A's player who was now president of the fledgling Baseball Player's Fraternity, one of the earliest attempts to form a players' union. His group, always searching for ways to gain a foothold with the players, was available if needed.

For his part Connie Mack promised to abide by the National Commission's decision. If Baker and Collins did not cease and desist, they would not appear in the series. Fortunately, he did not have to make that move. When the edict was first issued, Ban Johnson, American League president, was on vacation in Michigan. Upon his return he termed the commission's position regarding cancellation of the series merely a suggestion, telling reporters, "The purpose of the commission is not to prevent players earning extra money in any legitimate way, but to stop the faking which is bound to do baseball a serious injury unless it is curbed."[18]

Johnson, who specifically referred to Collins and Baker, offered an alternative. If a player wanted to write, he must go to the headquarters of the National Commission after a game and dictate his story to a stenographer. It is uncertain if anyone took Johnson up on his offer. What is known is that the 1913 World Series moved forward and Collins and most of the others wrote about it in detail. After the series the National Commission asked to see the contracts of each player-writer. If the contracts were signed before the commission issued its position, then no further action by way of fine would be taken. Until that review was completed, neither the Giants nor the A's would receive their share of the World Series proceeds. No fines were reported.[19]

According to Collins, his manager did not take the National Commission's threats seriously. Mack did approach Eddie and explain the commission's compromised position and Ban Johnson's proposal.

"I told Mack that I would willingly comply with that part of the arrangement, as I always wrote whatever appeared over my signature and that as far as the rest I was under contract to a certain paper and did not wish to break my contract since the agreement was entered into in good faith, prior to any opposition from outside sources."[20]

All this fuss began in New York on October 7. Since managers Mack and McGraw each had one series victory versus the other, 1913 served as the rubber match. Although Mathewson was now 33, the Giants entered the series with a bolstered pitching staff, featuring a pair of right-handers, 24-year-old Jeff Tesreau (22–13, 2.17) and 29-year-old Al Demaree (13–4, 2.21). The team won its third straight National League pennant by 12 and one-half games over the Phillies.

After the dust settled on a first-game duel between Rube Marquard and the Chief, the A's owned a 6–4 win. Bender was not sharp, allowing 11 hits, but the A's found Marquard and Crandall for 11 more-timely hits of their own. Taking up where he left off in 1911, "Home

Run" Baker hit another this day and, as before, Collins was on board. Eddie joined Baker as the A's hitting star with three hits, including a triple and a stolen base. He scored three runs.

The show moved back to Shibe Park for Game Two on October 8. For this one Mack and McGraw trotted out their wisened veterans Plank and Mathewson. The pair, despite their advancing age, did not disappoint. Through nine innings neither team scored. In the bottom of the ninth, Mack may have overplayed his hand, permitting Plank to bat for himself with Barry on third, one out, and fine hitters like Murphy, Schang and Walsh available on the bench. Plank hit a grounder, Barry was trapped and then retired at third, and the rally fizzled. In the tenth the Giants reached a tiring Plank for three runs and a 3–0 victory. Collins was 1-for-4 against the Big Six, but he struck out twice — an unusual occurrence — and committed an error.

After the game in his daily syndicated column, Collins gave Mathewson his due. "He [Mathewson] is one ball player who must command the respect of the most partisan of Athletics' fans." At the same time Collins felt frustration for his old friend, Eddie Plank. "If a pitcher ever deserved a win, it was the old master Plank." Before he closed, Collins issued a bold prediction. Based on his 1911 experience with Mathewson, "the more we hit against him and the oftener he goes against us, the less effective he is."[21]

Back in New York on October 9 for the third game, the big mystery was who the Tall Tactician would send to the mound to face McGraw's choice, Jeff Tesreau. The veterans Bender and Plank were not well rested. Perhaps it was time to choose one of the youngsters and gently shove him onto the big stage. Mack's choice for that honor was "Bullet Joe" Bush, a hurler who earned his nickname because of the speed of his fastball, not his proficiency with firearms.

Bolstered by the A's early hitting heroics — they scored five times in the first two innings — Bush came through. Although only 20, Bush pitched a five-hitter, winning 8–2. Collins was the A's hitting star. His play hatched a story for Hugh Fullerton, who began his tale by calling Eddie "one of the greatest hitters, from a scientific standpoint, who ever stepped to a plate."

According to Fullerton, during the World Series he met umpire Bill Rigler, who stopped him to ask a question.

"Say, is this fellow Collins a kidder?"

"Anything but that," I replied.

"He pulled a funny one on me today," said Rigler. "He came up after the Athletics had the game won by a big score and said 'Mr. Umpire, I wish you'd watch this one closely; I'm trying to hit a homerun into that right field stand.' I told him to do the batting and I'd do the watching, and he said, 'this fellow is pitching me slow balls inside the plate. I can't hit one of them into the stand except right on the foul line.' I told him I'd be careful. He hit the first ball pitched into the stand, foul by a foot or two; the next one hit the foul line just in front of first and went foul, and the third one was a home run — fair by inches."[22]

Although the story reads better if Collins had hit a homer, it was actually a triple, driving in a run. It was one of three hits on a day when the little second sacker drove in three and scored twice. After the contest, McGraw still "dictating" or "reviewing" or whatever it was he did before his articles appeared in print, called Collins "the heart and brain of the Philadelphia team" and "the greatest man in a pinch I ever saw."

The scratchy field general some called "Muggsy," others the "Little Napoleon," often was charged with negligence in failing to land Collins for his own while Eddie was attending Columbia just a few miles away from the Polo Grounds. In this same piece McGraw told readers he "always thought perhaps he [Collins] would come to the Giants after he finally finished college. Many times since I have felt as if a great ball player was slipped out from under my nose."[23]

The fact is that, despite rumors that McGraw saw Collins play a lot while he was in college, the only time McGraw ever saw Collins play during that period was the day the Columbians played exhibition ball with the Giants. Collins never worked out for McGraw as he did for the Highlanders' Griffith. "There has been for years an impression that John McGraw scouted me while I was playing for Columbia and passed me up. That isn't so."[24]

According to Collins, Mack's decision to pitch Bush was anything but last minute. It was no "hunch." The team had recognized during an exhibition game in 1912 that the kid was special when he struck out a veteran of the Columbus, Ohio, team several times on three futile swings. Mack quickly learned about Bush's self-confident temperament and played to it by telling him days ahead of time that he would start in the World Series.

Collins recalled that, "[O]n the day of his World Series game, Bush had an air as though he were going to face some easy minor league club in an exhibition match."[25] When Game Three was over and Bush had polished off the Giants, that was just about the size of it.

Mack drew from a more familiar well in Game Four, sending Chief Bender to the mound. McGraw, anticipating a lengthy series, went with Al Demaree. Immediately prior to the start of the game, Mack fooled everyone by sending Bob Shawkey and Boardwalk Brown onto the field to warm up. Bender did not appear until moments before the start. Once again he was not sharp, but this time pitched well enough to win, 6–5. Collins was not a factor in this one, with Jack Barry, Rube Oldring and Wally Schang carrying the big lumber. The A's carried a six-run lead into the seventh and then held their breath as the Giants put on a furious rally.

Collins wrote that the Chief "grew a little careless, so he admitted to me after the game." But Eddie assured his readers that Matty, pitching with less rest than his age now required — "he is no 'spring chicken' " — would not be able to stop the A's from closing out the series.[26]

Collins' assessment of Mathewson was on the mark. The A's did have better luck against Matty the second time around. Still, the Big Six was a tough nut to crack, allowing but three runs and six hits. It was enough, however. That was because Eddie Plank pitched a brilliant two-hitter, losing a shutout only because he collided with Baker on a simple infield popup, extending an inning in which he gave up one of his two hits, allowing a run. Plank's performance earned him a ride on the shoulders of his teammates as the Mackmen celebrated yet another world championship with a 3–1 win.

In nailing their final victory in the series, the Mackmen aided Plank's cause with some fine hitting. Baker, who loved to play the Giants, had two hits, raising his series average to .450. Collins went one-for-three, sacrificed, and helped turn a pair of nifty double plays. For the series he batted .421.

Once again the city of Philadelphia prepared to celebrate a grand victory. This time, however, the excitement was quickly tempered by news of the death of Harry Davis, Jr., the first baseman's son. The young man was a familiar site around the ballpark and the news saddened the Mackmen. At the boy's funeral, the $100,000 infield acted as pallbearers.

After the National Commission resolved its concerns about those players who wrote about and played in the series, the players on the participating teams received their individual shares. Each of the Mackmen received $3,243.94, a significant sum. The Giants each received $2,162.92.

Eddie's post-season plans in 1913 included a hunting trip with teammate Bob Shawkey, former teammate Ben Egan, and Jack Dunn, the manager of Baltimore's minor league franchise. The group planned to hunt near Shawkey's home in Forest County, Pennsylvania, and the adjacent Allegheny National Forest. Eddie, who had developed a real passion for the sport, now made these excursions a regular part of his off-season program. In addition, it was reported that the A's star, now living with his family in the Philadelphia suburb of Lansdowne, planned to "settle down for the winter thumping the typewriter with hands and brains for a newspaper syndicate."[27] The fruit of that labor was a bi-weekly column on baseball strategy, carried by a local newspaper. It seemed Collins' run-in with baseball's authorities over his writing habits had made little impression.

In late November Collins' name appeared in the press in an entirely different context. A small article in the *New York Times* and other newspapers across the country on November 26 revealed that the A's star had turned down a reported offer for $15,000 a year over three years made by the fledgling Federal League. The money would be guaranteed by placing the total sum in a bank to earn interest, thus giving it an actual value of $50,000. In rejecting the offer, Eddie praised Connie Mack and declared he would not consider any proposition which involved abandoning his A's.[28]

Collins' suitor, arriving on the scene only months before, was the new game in town. The American League considered the Federal League and its organizers "outlaws," ignoring the fact that not so long before the A.L. also was considered an outlaw league. At any rate as originally organized, the Federal League did not appear a serious threat. Clubs were established in Chicago, St. Louis, Cleveland, Pittsburgh, Indianapolis and Cincinnati, and did little to bother the existing player contracts of those in Organized Baseball. However, by November the composition and influence of the league was changing. Of most importance was the ascendancy of wealthy Chicago businessman James A. Gilmore to the league presidency. His entry gave the league instant credibility. Soon other men of substantial wealth, such as Charles Weeghman, who owned a chain of Chicago eateries, and oilman Harry Sinclair, were on board. In addition, the league expanded from six to eight ball clubs, adding Buffalo, Brooklyn and Baltimore, while deleting Cleveland. There were now five Federal League clubs competing in National League cities and three in American League territory. Although by November there was still little evidence the "outlaws" were signing major league players to their teams' contracts, reports of such a large offer to a player of Collins' stature certainly raised eyebrows, even though he quickly rejected it. The fact it coincided with the appointment of a new man to lead the league offered a broad hint of things to come.

As 1913 came to an end, the A's were in Collins' words "just one big happy family."[29] However, families live in dwellings, and in 1914, the A's dwelling was beginning to show cracks in the edifice.

For Collins the cracks in the stucco began early. Following his graduation from Columbia in 1907, Eddie maintained a close affinity with the school and it with him. Often when the A's played in New York, excursions were organized for Columbia students to attend and cheer their famous alum. In 1912 interclass baseball teams at his school competed for "Eddie Collins medals." In early 1914 there was some question whether Billy Lauder would return to coach the Blue and White. Collins promised to assist the collegians by donating a couple weeks of his time to coach them, prior to heading south for spring training. When Connie Mack heard about it, he issued an emphatic "no." Collins was needed in camp; there would be no coaching his alma mater that spring. Columbia was not without help, however. Billy Lush and Andy Coakley, old Collins' mentors and friends, came to the university's rescue.

The team that arrived in Jacksonville in early March was essentially the same group that brought a title back to Philadelphia in 1913. By now Wally Schang and Jack Lapp were handling the bulk of the catching duties, but Ira Thomas was still very much a presence. Jack Coombs was still out, but Bob Shawkey and Joe Bush were ready to take on more of the responsibilities. Those two, along with right-hander Weldon Wycoff, at 22 in his second season with the club, Herb Pennock, and newcomer Rube Bressler, at 19 a left-handed pitcher and later a lifetime .301 hitter as a position player, offered more depth to the staff than available in previous seasons. Boardwalk Brown was a mid-season casualty of the arm problems he developed the previous spring.

Herb Pennock was the most interesting of the lot. The son of a family of some means from nearby Kennett Square, the future pitching star showed promise but would earn most of his kudos in Boston and later New York. While he was with the Mackmen, however, he and Collins became fast friends. In time, Collins would consider Pennock his closest friend.

Shortly before the team headed south, there was one personnel change of some significance. Danny Murphy, his role diminishing by the year due to age and knee problems, was sold to Baltimore of the International League. Although Mack guaranteed that his former captain would receive his normal salary despite the change, Murphy was unhappy and soon landed with the new Brooklyn club of the Federal League. The move upset Mack and, given Murphy's popularity and influence with the Mackmen, may have placed a "chicken in the hen house" when it came to the new league's influence on the remaining A's stars.

Now Mack needed to name a new field captain. Collins seemed the logical choice. Instead, Mack selected Ira Thomas, who was by now a close confidant. The *Inquirer* reacted to the move.

"Thomas selection as captain was a decided surprise to those who had picked out a new leader for the Mackmen. Many thought Eddie Collins would get the job, but Mack evidently figured that Thomas, being a shrewd cool judge of the game and a veteran of many years standing, besides being a diplomat, would fit in better than the fiery Collins as the field leader."[30]

Perhaps the newspaper was correct, but it is just as possible to venture that the Tall Tactician felt the interest exhibited by the Federal League in his star second baseman was not as one-sided as it appeared on the surface. In view of the increasing reports of player defections, the idea was not so far-fetched.

If Collins was upset by Mack's choice of a field leader, he did not voice it publicly. Instead, he played hard and hit well in Jacksonville until felled by a severe cold.

One gets the idea that a month or so in a warm climate each year was a bowl of cherries for the veteran players assured of a spot on the squad, but that was not always the case. For example, as the team played their way north in late March, they reached Charleston, South Carolina, by train in early morning. Several players spent the day sightseeing while several others posed for a "moving picture drama" at the local ball park. The squad dressed for the game at their hotel and then arrived early at the park to workout and play. Following a 5–0 win, they rushed to the hotel, washed up and ate a hurried dinner at 6:30 P.M. They were then driven in buses to the station to catch a 7:20 P.M. train for a game the next day in Wilmington, North Carolina, versus Baltimore's International League club.

The game in Wilmington on March 25 was of note as the A's faced a schoolboy lefty by the name of Babe Ruth. The A's reached him for 13 hits, including a Collins single, but Ruth limited the big league champs when it counted, winning, 6–2. The A's took a second peek at Ruth in Baltimore three days later. This time they scored early and knocked him from the box. Collins' double in the first drove in a pair.

On April 1 the entire baseball world, particularly the Mackmen, were saddened by the death of Rube Waddell, who succumbed to tuberculosis at age 37. Mack was quite shaken by the untimely loss of his former star hurler, commenting that Rube "was more sinned against than a sinner."[31]

While the A's were taking care of the Phillies in the City Series by a 4–3 game count, all of Organized Baseball was keeping an eye on legal proceedings in Grand Rapids, Michigan, where the Federal League sought an injunction to keep Phillies catcher William Killifer from returning to that team after he had signed a contract to play for Chicago's Federal League entry. On April 10 the court denied the injunction but declared Organized Baseball's treasured "reserve clause," which bound a player to his team for the next season, invalid. The judge scolded both the new league and Killifer, but it was clear as the case went on appeal that the tug-of-war for top talent was just beginning.

The regular season opener for the A's was in New York on April 14. Unlike the previous year, the Mackmen were left in the starting blocks. The 8–2 loss was followed by several more. No one was hitting. By the time the team returned to Shibe Park for the home opener on April 23, the record stood at 2–3, not including a pair of ties with the Red Sox.

A stiff cold wind blew inside Shibe for the home opener. A crowd of 10,000 braved the weather, hoping to give the locals a lift. It was to no avail. The Highlanders prevailed, 5–3.

By 1914 Collins was becoming more involved in product endorsements. In April he added an A.J. Reach and Company fielder's glove to the list, which already included endorsements for baseball bats and Coca-Cola. When he wasn't hitting, as was the case in early 1914, the trusty glove was Eddie's steadying influence. The box scores were replete with descriptions of a great stab here, a great throw there, and the increasingly smooth artistry of the $100,000 infield.

In May the A's began playing like the Mackmen of old, giving chase to a Tiger team that grabbed the early lead. There was even talk of a return by Jack Coombs, although it proved premature. By mid–May the hits began to fall more regularly for Collins, and his average, which had hovered uncharacteristically around the .250 mark, now edged toward .300.

On May 16 Collins impressed the Chicago White Sox and their owner Charles Comiskey with a perfect day at the plate and a signature day in the infield as the A's clipped the Sox, 4–3. On the day Eddie was 3-for-3, including a triple, on which he scored when the throw to third went astray, and a walk. In the field he nailed a runner at the plate with a perfect throw. He also knocked down a line shot from his second base counterpart, Lena Blackburne, and then with his back to the plate, wheeled and fired to first to catch the Chicagoan.

During the team's early season struggles, a stated goal was to reach first place by June 1. As May turned to June, the improved play of the A's earned dividends. On May 29 a double-header sweep of the Highlanders at the Polo Grounds pushed the Philadelphians into first, reaching their goal a couple of days early. Except for a brief slip or two, the A's remained the frontrunners for the remainder of the season.

In late May the Federal League announced that a number of major league players stood ready to jump to the new league. Several of the teams, including a St. Louis entry owned by ice-machine magnate Phil Ball, were starving for star players to draw fans to their struggling franchises. There was a strong movement to sign these upper echelon performers to future contracts. It was then no surprise that on June 18, a small article appeared in the *Inquirer*, dateline Chicago, reporting that sources in that city with the Feds were neither confirming nor denying that Collins, Baker and McInnis of the A's were negotiating with the league. Mack, when asked, made light of the matter. "Oh the Feds. Are they still playing? You see, we don't hear much of them."[32]

Collins, who remained silent at the time concerning the allegations, opened up about it in early 1915 to F.C. Lane of *Baseball Magazine*.

"Last summer Mr. [Robert B.] Ward, president of the Brooklyn club had a conversation with me in which he mentioned certain high figures, though nothing definite was decided upon. His talk, I believe, was in the nature of a feeling-out process, as he told me it would be necessary to lay the matter before the executive department of the Federal League.

"Later, in Chicago, president Gilmore asked me to see him for a conference and set a date when I was to meet him. He was called away, however, and unable to keep the appointment.

"That is all the dealings I have had with the Federal League, with the exception of a meeting with president Gilmore, in which he said that had he not been called away to Indianapolis and had met me as he intended to do, he would have made me such an offer as would have induced me to materially alter my plans. However, I can say nothing as to that, as the meeting never occurred, and the offer in concrete form was never made."[33]

President Gilmore of the Feds essentially agreed with Collins' version, saying he sent Hal Chase, a high profile Federal League recruit, to explain that he had been called away and expressed considerable regret he was unable to meet with Eddie since it opened the door for Connie Mack to stick a finger in the dike.[34] And act quickly Mack certainly did.

"We tore up some contracts in mid-season, wrote new ones, entered into three-year agreements with Eddie Collins, Frank Baker, and other key players."[35]

Collins confirmed the timing but not the length of the contract. "It was shortly after this [the aborted meeting with Gilmore] that Connie Mack approached me with the proposition that I sign a five years' contract with the reserve clause stricken out and certain other modifications, which would make it strictly binding. I do not know whether or not he was hastened in this resolve by rumors that the Federal League were endeavoring to get me. In fact, I know nothing of the circumstances which induced him to make such a contract at that time. In any case, he did so and as the terms were agreeable I signed the contract without question."[36]

It seems Collins was correct. The deal he inked with Mack was for five years, 1914 through 1918 and, though not publicly stated at the time, it was for $11,500 per year. The new figure was a huge boost for Collins. He had already received a significant increase, from $6,000 to $8,333.33, when he signed a new three-year deal less than five months earlier on February 17. This new figure lifted him into the upper tier of player salaries. In addition, it contained a clause, believed rare if not unique for the time, that Collins "shall not be transferred to any other club without his consent."[37] And he owed it all to the market created by the Federal League.

The entire scenario begs the question: Would Eddie Collins have jumped to the Federal League? In short, it is highly doubtful. In the first instance, Collins loved the American League so much it is unlikely he would have ever considered a jump to even the National League. Second, he loved Mack as a father and his teammates as brothers. As such he would have found it exceedingly difficult to exhibit disloyalty and voluntarily abandon them for money alone. Nonetheless, he was a shrewd businessman. While still a college student he showed Mack he could drive a hard bargain. The Federal League in its pursuit of him presented an opportunity, through increased bargaining power, to increase his earnings and he took it. If, however, there was ever any doubt what Collins would have done with a Federal League offer, he cleared it up years later.

"I never contemplated for a moment signing with a Federal League club. The fact that I was loyal to the American League in thought and action need not be stressed, for I had an iron-clad contract. If the terms did not suit it was my fault, but the fact is they did."[38]

Now that he and others were securely tied to the A's it was time to get back to matters of bats, balls and gloves. In July the A's actually solidified their vice grip on first place with a 12-game win streak, perhaps fueled by the raising of their championship flag in a ceremony at Shibe on July 15. Even a threatened players' strike did little to slow down the A's momentum. As the wins piled up, so did Collins' statistics. By July 12 he was batting .320 and moving up the chart. By August 9 he was at .350. Efforts like the one on June 29 helped his cause. In a twin-bill split with Washington, he counted a home run, single, two walks, two runs scored and a stolen base in one game, and a pair of hits, a walk, an RBI and a stolen base in the other. By July 28, when the 12-game run came to an end with a loss to Detroit by a 4–3 score, the A's lead over the Red Sox, now in second place, was eight full games in the loss column.

The defeat in Detroit, however, did little to alter the A's pace. They won 12 of their next 14 and, when they looked again, stood 68–34 on the season, with the Red Sox 11 behind. They were clearly on their way to their fourth pennant in five years. All was well. Or was it? After a brilliant August (23–5), the A's experienced a mediocre September and October (17–15). As a result they finished the season only eight and one-half games ahead of the Red Sox. Even more disturbing, they lost the season series to the Red Sox, 12–9, including nine in a row at one point.

According to Collins, "late in the season, we all fell into a slump. It hit everybody. We couldn't bat, field, run nor pitch. And the odd part of it was that we couldn't revive ourselves in the face of what we knew was to be stiff opposition."[39]

Mack was concerned as well. In Cleveland on September 22, he dropped the slumping Frank Baker from his cleanup spot to sixth in the order, inserting Amos Strunk behind Collins. Strunk responded with three hits; Baker, with only one. The A's got the message, at least that day, winning, 14–3.

In Collins' opinion, one source of his team's hitting woes, including his own, was the increasing use of trick pitches, particularly the "emery" ball. This pitch by definition describes a baseball which is roughed up with an emery board, cloth, or similar rough-edged material so as to scuff it up, making it move or curve more erratically. The inventor of the pitch is often said to be Russell Ford, an effective pitcher with the New York Highlanders from 1909–1913. While with the Highlanders, Ford taught his pet pitch to others, including Ray Keating. As his team struggled against the effects of a roughened ball in an 8–8 tie versus Boston on September 11, Collins decided he had seen enough.

"In 1914 we were playing the last game of a series in Boston and we were fighting all through the game over the condition of the ball. Tommy Connolly and Bill Dinneen were umpiring and we ruffled Tom's sense of dignity with impunity. We went from Boston to New York and who should appear to umpire but Connolly and Dinneen."

On the mound for the Highlanders was Ford's student, Ray Keating. The A's first two batters each struck out on three pitches. As Collins strode to the plate, the previous batter, Rube Oldring, suggested he check the ball. Eddie stepped to the plate and asked umpire Connolly to take a look. He would not do it, whereupon Eddie refused to hit until the ball was examined. At that point Connolly ordered Keating to pitch and three pitches later Eddie was called out on strikes.

"'Will you look at the ball now?' I [Collins] demanded, as the teams were changing sides."

Connolly did just that and after he was finished he asked to see Keating's glove. Inside it he found a tiny strip of emery paper. It covered a hole cut in the palm of the mitt.

"Connolly rolled the ball to Dinneen and kept the emery paper. He sent both emery paper and ball to league headquarters and I understand they were used as exhibits in the conference which eventually led to the ban on all sorts of adventitious aids to pitching."[40]

On September 27 the A's clinched the pennant on a 6–0, four-hit shutout of St. Louis by Chief Bender, one of his 17 wins versus three losses in another terrific season on the hill. The next day Collins and Frank Baker did not play, heading east. They missed the first regular season performance of Jack Coombs, who was hit hard in a 7–1 loss to the Brownies.

Although the papers indicated Collins was headed home for a rest, that was not the case. Instead, Mack sent him and perhaps Baker as well to look over the A's surprise World Series opponents, the upstart Boston Braves. Supposedly, Mack also asked Chief Bender to scout the Braves, but the Chief did not follow through.

The Braves were picked by no one to win the 1914 National League race. Until July 18 they lived up to their subterranean billing by languishing in the league cellar, more than 11 games behind the Giants. Their 35–43 record was deceiving, however. They were winners of nine of their last 12 games by that time and, although no one then knew it, on their way to the top. After July 4 the Braves were 68–19 and quite the stunner. The Tall Tactician needed a scouting report on the Braves because so little was known about them.

What Collins saw was a famous second sacker, Johnny Evers, late of the Cubs; a slap-happy shortstop named Walter Maranville, who lived up to his nickname "Rabbit" with quickness and great leaping ability; a tall young catcher named Hank Gowdy, in his first full season in the majors; and a pair of right-handers who were enjoying outstanding years in the persons of Bill James (26–7, 1.90) and Dick Rudolph (26–10, 2.35). Their only .300 hitter among the regulars was outfielder Joe Connolly at .306. The group was managed by George Stallings, a gentleman off the field, but a foul-mouthed scratcher on it. It is said Stallings liked nothing less than a base on balls.

Collins was impressed with the Braves, but few agreed with him. Most saw a quick end to the conflagration and they were right; only, it was not at all as predicted.

Game One of the 1914 World Series took place in Philadelphia at Shibe Park before just over 20,000 fans, all certain that over the last several weeks their team was just treading water while awaiting the arrival of their next National League victim. It took less than six innings to dispel that belief as a stunned crowd watched the Chief, their series stalwart, walk from the mound, his head bowed, and his team down, 5–1. It was the first time Bender had ever been knocked out of a World Series contest. In this one he was bested by Dick Rudolph, who pitched a five-hitter in defeating the Mackmen, 7–1. Collins went hitless in three at-bats while Hank Gowdy, the Braves' catcher, had three hits. According to Eddie, "Rudolph had us guessing. He had us biting at bad balls and letting strikes go across the plate unmolested."[41]

The A's and their fans were naturally disappointed but certainly not discouraged. It was only one game, but the Braves were proving to be a scrappier bunch than anticipated. In particular, their manager was kicking up a fuss, directing his barbs at none other than the kindly Connie Mack. The uproar was caused by Mack's refusal to allow the Braves to work out in Shibe Park on the two afternoons prior to the start of the series. Mack offered his opponents the mornings for this purpose since the A's played their last regular season game on one of the afternoons in question and because he wanted to use the park on the only other remaining afternoon for his own team. Stallings was furious. He wanted his men to use the field in the afternoon to allow them to get used to the light and the shadows they would face during actual game conditions. When Mack refused to budge, Stallings publicly called his managing colleague a cheapskate and said when he arrived in town, he planned to punch him in the nose. The fight never took place, but the Braves verbally abused the Mackmen throughout the series.[42]

Ban Johnson took in the games in his official capacity as American League president and saw firsthand the treatment the Braves hurled at the A's.

"During the first game the Boston players became very abusive. Mack's men were not used to that in the American League and it disconcerted many of them, I think. Eddie Collins was the only member of the Mack team, as I recall, who had the courage to fight back. The Boston behavior was reported to the National Commission and I immediately called the attention of the umpires to the condition."[43]

This then was the atmosphere as the A's and Braves faced off in Game Two. Instead of switching cities after each game, this season the first two games were played at Shibe. On the mound for the A's was the old but reliable Eddie Plank. His opponent was the much younger Bill James. When the game was over, Collins could only shake his head in amazement.

"The second game Plank was great, as he usually is, but at that I do not think we would have defeated James. He was too good. To me he seemed by all odds the best pitcher of the series. We were able to do nothing with his delivery and while Plank lost by an odd succes-

Collins receives a new Chalmers automobile at Shibe Park in Philadelphia during pre-game festivities for the 1914 World Series. A car was awarded annually at the time to the ballplayer selected as the most valuable player in each league. Collins was the American League winner, while Johnny Evers of the Boston Braves was selected in the National League (Transcendental Graphics).

sion of breaks, I believe he was inevitably headed for defeat, solely through the strength and invincibility of his rival."[44]

The only run in the game came in the top of the ninth when Boston's Les Mann, batting with two outs, dropped a short fly to right, just beyond the fingertips of a sprinting Collins, scoring a runner from third. The final score was 1–0, James fashioning a two-hitter. Collins had one of the hits, a single; Wally Schang doubled for the other. Through the two games in their home park, the Mackmen were almost totally shut down, with only seven hits and one run.

The scene now shifted for Game Three to Fenway Park, which the Braves were using since their own ball park was on its last legs and considered too small for World Series action. By now the A's knew firsthand that the Braves could do more than just bench jockey. They promised their full support for Mack's mound choice, Joe Bush. The A's didn't exactly live up to that promise in what turned out to be a crushing 12-inning 5–4 defeat, but they did perform much better than in the previous two games with eight hits. They even staked Bullet Joe to a two-run lead in the top of the tenth, but the youngster could not make it stand before Boston's Royal Rooters Fan Club and 35,000 other raucous Bostonians.

The Braves started Lefty Tyler, but when the chips were down in the eleventh and twelfth innings, Bill James was back on the mound. The hitting of Hank Gowdy was again a difference maker. He had two doubles and a tenth-inning home run. Collins, who singled, walked and stole a base, but was not a real factor, still felt "with all fairness, we ought to have won."[45]

By now it seemed inevitable the A's would lose the series. Their one hope was a well-rested Chief Bender. After all, the Chief had won 15 straight at one point during the regular season. Certainly he would not lose to the upstart Braves again, and he didn't. In fact, he never touched the field. Mack decided instead to go with Bob Shawkey. Since Shawkey had started eight more games during the season than Bender, the decision to start him instead of the Chief could not be deemed a shocker. But in view of Bender's history of clutch performances, one wonders if Mack was listening to the rumors floating around about Federal League defections and, therefore, already committed to a totally different course for his ball club when he threw Shawkey into the fire instead of turning to the Chief?

Actually, the A's 23-year-old 15-game winner did not pitch a bad ball game. Instead, when he retired after five innings pitched due to a hand problem, his team was still in it, trailing only 3–1, the final score. Herb Pennock finished up and between them the Braves had only six hits. The A's had seven, including a Collins single in four trips.

The loss meant the A's now wore the ignominious crown of being the first team in World Series history to lose four straight since, in 1907, Detroit's four losses included one tie. To make matters worse, the shortened series meant less money for the A's and Braves franchises since the players' shares were subtracted from proceeds of the first four games, but not the rest.

Collins, by now a seasoned businessman as well as a player, recognized the manner of his team's defeat carried beyond the ball field and up the stairs to the executive offices.

"By the time the fourth game arrived we had caught the habit and were defeated, as a matter of course. I was sorry to lose four straight, not only because such an overwhelming defeat had never before been recorded against a club in a world series, but also because the owners lost heavily by the shortened series. It was a grand demonstration of the inherent honesty of baseball, but an unfortunate ending to a season that had not been financially profitable."[46]

The series was a personal low for Collins on the field. He hit .214, a career World Series low, with three singles in 14 at-bats, no runs scored, and only one RBI. This following a season in which he batted .344 (2nd in A.L.), boasted a sterling on-base percentage of .452 (2nd) and OPS (the combination of OBP and slugging percentage) of .904 (2nd), and was first in runs scored with 122. He was also second in stolen bases with 58.

Baseball writers and historians often mention that Collins was "frequently a bridesmaid never a bride" when it came to his league's batting title. Interestingly, in 1914, Collins once again finished second to Cobb in the race for that title. Cobb was injured on at least two occasions during the season. He earned his title with 345 appearances at the plate in 98 games. In 1914, this qualified him for the title. Under current minimum at-bat requirements, however, the Georgia Peach would not have qualified for the batting title, making Collins the 1914 league leader.

Unlike some seasons, Collins' work in 1914 did not go unrecognized. His grand regular season, coupled with the A's pennant victory, earned him an automobile as he was voted the winner of the league's Chalmers prize, almost doubling the votes for second-place finisher Sam Crawford. The National League recipient was also a second baseman as well as a World Series opponent: Johnny Evers. These were the last Chalmers Awards. It was 1922 before the American League recognized a most valuable player again.

Over the years, particularly in view of subsequent events in World Series play, there are those who feel the Athletics took a dive in losing the 1914 Series to the Braves. This is only natural given the A's overwhelming odds. Some bettors had it 8–5. As a result, many people who bet — and more and more people were betting on baseball every year — lost heavily, while a select few won big. There is, nonetheless, no hard evidence the A's conspired to throw this series. There is only mere supposition, such as that interposed by author William Kashatus in his biography of Chief Bender. Kashatus, who agrees documentary evidence is lacking, alleges Bender took a dive in Game One.[47] In support of his theory, he cites a post-series Collins quote that Bender "lost interest."[48] There is, however, a great deal of difference between losing interest, or perhaps one's focus, and taking a dive for money or otherwise. Instead of shunning Bender, as one might expect if Collins thought he was on the take, Eddie continued to consider the Chief his friend. He even hired him as his assistant years later. In addition, during the 1913 World Series, Bender had also performed with less than his usual flair, yet no one yelled fraud then. A much more reasonable explanation is that in 1914 Bender once again simply had a bad game.

On the other hand, in contrast to the red-hot Braves, there is ample evidence the A's were a struggling team both on and off the field during the latter portion of the 1914 campaign. They were quite average by season's end. One off-the-field controversy involved Collins and once again, at least on the surface, it involved his penchant for putting pen to paper. In late November or early in December, Ira Thomas, while he was out on the West Coast on a barnstorming tour managing at the behest of Mack, gave an interview to the *Los Angeles Examiner*. In the article which followed, Thomas was quoted as criticizing Collins:

[He] has tipped many things that he should have kept quiet about in the articles he has written. He did not give away our signs or tell much about the inside workings of our club, but he did something that was just as bad. For years our players have been grabbing the signs of other clubs, the peculiarities of the different players and their weaknesses. Very little of this was gathered by Collins, but naturally, with the rest of the players, everything was told him. He used this information in the articles, telling of how we knew what was coming from a certain pitcher because he always did a peculiar wind-up when he was going to throw a curve ball. Naturally, the players heard about this and started to remedy their defects. Certain signs that had been used a long time by other clubs were changed. With the information we had at our disposal we would have been able to win pennants for the next six years. But this was all changed. The other clubs are watching us keenly and we no longer have the big edge over the visiting teams."[49]

While there is reason to believe Thomas was not the only A's player who felt Collins should keep his thoughts on baseball strategy to himself, the timing of the comments is intriguing. Eddie had been writing articles about the A's and their strategies for years. Although some baseball commentators claim Thomas was referring to articles written for *American Magazine* in 1914 for the reported sum of $2,000, there were in fact but two, and neither gave away anything of substance. A more revealing article, one which discussed details about how the A's studied the pitcher and not the catcher for tip-offs, was written by Collins for *Pearson's Magazine* in June 1910. It was entitled "Outguessing The Pitcher."[50]

After Thomas' allegations came to light, Christy Mathewson came to Collins' defense. He found the idea that anything Eddie revealed had affected the A's chances for winning "ridiculous" since the "secrets" were generally known to all.[51] Others like catcher Gabby Street, who played with Collins in the Addie Joss game, felt just the opposite. "It was not until Eddie Collins wrote a series of magazine articles that we learned where the A's got their dope and then we smartened up."[52]

It seems that despite Street's comments, there exists a more logical explanation for the timing of those sharp remarks by Ira Thomas, as well as his targeting of Collins. There is reason to believe that some of the Mackmen were not pleased with the Tall Tactician's selection of Thomas as captain. After the 1914 season, an unnamed Athletics player told a *New York Times* reporter that the team was never the same after Ira's ascendancy as "he was not a regular player, and the other fellows always liked to see one of the regulars in the Captain's position." The player also felt Thomas, who apparently had Mack's ear, forced former captain Danny Murphy off the team. This was an exceedingly unpopular move, especially when Thomas succeeded him as captain and began to "call down many players who knew more baseball than Ira Thomas will ever know."[53]

Perhaps Collins was one of those players Thomas had "called down." An article by editor William G. Weart of the *Philadelphia Telegraph* referred to a report that said, "One of the [A's] stars is reported to have gone through the entire season without speaking to Ira except when absolutely compelled to do so during a game."[54]

There is nothing to indicate whether the player referred to in Weart's piece was Collins. There is, however, the additional information in that piece that Thomas had further alienated himself from team members by refusing to support the fledgling Player's Fraternity. Just maybe Thomas was using the allegations against Collins to deflect attention away from himself. Whatever the reason, it seems from the timing of the remarks, that is, after the season when it was much too late to make a real difference, the statements were merely the public airing of an internal feud and sour grapes at that.

Nonetheless, couple this internal flailing with the amazing fact that despite their poor play at season's end, many on the A's roster, particularly Bender, considered the Braves an inferior opponent, and one has the formula for a major upset. Collins heard the rumors of discontent with the A's performance and firmly cast them aside, specifically addressing the rumors of a fix some 13 years later in 1927.

"In 1914 ... on account of the Braves' quick victory many wild tales went the rounds, none of which were true. The truth is that we were lucky to win the American League pennant and if the season had been two or three weeks longer, probably we would have lost."[55]

Thus, for Collins, by any measure, 1914 was a mixed bag. Nevertheless, at 27 he was in his prime and considered by many the best at his craft. There would be many more years in an A's uniform. After all, despite this minor setback, the Athletics were still baseball's best team. There was no reason to believe the Mackmen were not here to stay, or was there?

CHAPTER 10

Switching Sides

Magnates don't care for the mon'....
They're in the game for the fun —
That is why Collins was sold."

— Ring Lardner[1]

Sometimes even a blue chip stock loses some of its attractiveness, giving truth to the old adage, "Beauty is in the eye of the beholder." While most pundits felt the collapse of the Athletics in the 1914 World Series was merely a temporary glitch, that segment of society that really mattered — the A's fans — had lost interest in the club some time ago. To the fans by 1914, the Athletics, good, bad, or indifferent, were yesterday's news.

Attendance figures for the A's bore this out. In 1910 as the A's battled for their first title under Mack's "kiddie" program, the team led the league in attendance with 588,905 fans. In 1911 they repeated as league attendance kings and champions with 605,749. In 1912, despite returning a team everyone expected to excel, they fell to third in attendance at 517,653. In 1913 there was a brief revival when the team drew 571,896 fans, second in the league draw, as they climbed back to the top of the league standings. Then in 1914 with essentially the same squad, they proved "familiarity breeds contempt," by drawing only 346,641, fifth out of the league's eight teams.

The Old Sport read the signs in October, telling the *Inquirer's* readers, "the fans had for so long been accustomed to see the Athletics win that some of the spice of victory was taken out of the game which was reflected in the gate receipts of the season."[2]

The Tall Tactician read the signs as well, and upon reflection believed a team that contended, one where each contest was in doubt, formed a more anticipatory and enthusiastic audience than one that won most of the time and constantly garnered championships.

"When your club is fighting to the top the fans come out to the park...; but pennant winners get to be an old story."[3]

Never was this truer than in 1914. Here Mack had built a true baseball dynasty, only to see a significant loss in revenue from ticket sales in the midst of seeming prosperity. To compound the problem the war between the so-called "major leagues" and the Federal League meant increased player salary demands. Already Mack had experienced the downside when he found it necessary mid-season to significantly increase Collins' salary and renegotiate contracts of others like Frank Baker. Then to make matters even worse, the team's destruction in the World Series significantly reduced the A's expected revenue. Unlike teams with independently wealthy owners, Mack was not an otherwise rich man. He owned half of the A's and it was his lifeblood. According to author Bruce Kuklick, Mack's "thrift was explainable. He did not have other income to offset baseball losses."[4]

Given all these problems, no one should have been surprised at what came next, yet most were, particularly the players involved. The first real inkling that wholesale changes were on the immediate horizon occurred in early November when Mack asked waivers on Chief Bender, still only 30, Colby Jack Coombs, then but 31, and 39-year-old Eddie Plank. While the moves raised eyebrows, the fact Coombs was still in limbo following his health problem and Bender and Plank were seriously dickering with the Feds made the moves understandable and did not necessarily portend more. This was borne out when in early December Bender signed with Baltimore of the Federal League and Plank eventually with the St. Louis Terriers of that league. Coombs ended up with Brooklyn of the National League.

Even rumors that surfaced in mid–November alleging that either Collins or Ira Thomas was headed to New York to manage the Highlanders were met with a shrug. Perhaps Thomas was involved, but it was much harder to believe the talks included Collins.

The shocker occurred on December 8 when Connie Mack announced the sale of Eddie Collins to the Chicago White Sox for $50,000, the largest such transaction to date. A deal of such magnitude was not consummated overnight, nor are details of the whys and wherefores totally consistent. The sale, however, when viewed with the backdrop of the Federal League wars, offers insight into the unique position of power brandished by Ban Johnson, his then-strong friendship with his hunting buddy Charles Comiskey, the president and owner of the White Sox, and the bargaining chips held by a sharp-dealing star like Collins.

Collins first heard about the deal from his wife, Mabel, who told reporters about hearing the phone ring at their Lansdowne home and giving the caller a hard time.

"'Hello,' said the voice. 'This is Mr. Johnson, president of the American League. I want to talk to Mr. Collins.'

"Eddie was out at the time. 'Quit your kidding,' promptly replied Mrs. Collins, sweetly enough. 'You're one of those practical jokers who is always calling up. If Edward finds out who you are he will put a stop to it.'

"Bang! went the receiver.

"In a few minutes the telephone rang again.

"'I want to speak to Mr. Collins,' said the voice.

"'Who is this?' asked Mrs. C. 'I suppose that it is President Wilson this time.'

"'It is Mr. Comiskey, president of the Chicago club,' replied the speaker.

"'Did your friend, Mr. Johnson, who called a few minutes ago, lose his voice?' asked Mrs. Collins. 'Stop your joking.'

"Bang! went the receiver again.

"'I've a good mind to cut that telephone off altogether if they don't quit that,' said Mrs. Collins.

"Again it rang.

"'Well?' she said. 'Who are you this time?'

"'It is Connie Mack,' replied the speaker. 'Is Eddie home?'

"Mrs. Collins recognized the voice of the Philadelphia manager.

"'Did Mr. Johnson and Mr. Comiskey really telephone?' she asked, surprised.

"'Yes,' answered Mack.

"'Eddie is at a friend's house, but I'll get him right away.'"[5]

It was an amusing story about a serious call. It is apparent the Collins deal was on Connie Mack's mind for some time, even before the rumors surfaced of talks with the New Yorkers. Perhaps it began as early as when he first heard Eddie was tinkering with the Feds, or maybe when he signed the star to a big-money contract; certainly from the end of the World Series when Mack's financial woes worsened. At any rate, the seed was firmly planted by Mack in a discussion with Ban Johnson. The league president claimed he took over from there.

"I engineered the deal for the White Sox.

"Comiskey's club had finished in seventh place and Mack said he wanted to sell Collins. At first I was very much interested in having him go to New York. I wanted a strong team there. Ruppert and Huston had become interested in the Yankees and I went to them and told them it was possible to get Collins.

"But they were new to baseball and the idea of paying $50,000 for a ball player stunned them and they did not jump at the proposition. But Mack wanted to sell Collins and, as the White Sox had made a bad showing I went to Comiskey and told him it was possible to get Collins, and we went to Philadelphia and saw Mack and Collins.

"Eddie told us that he would prefer to play in Philadelphia, that he did not want to play in the West. I told him I would personally give him $5,000 if he would consider the proposition to go to Chicago and he said he would think it over.

"At the next meeting at New York, at the Belmont Hotel, he said he would go to Chicago if his terms were met. Comiskey did not see him at the meeting at all. I did all the talking to Collins. On the way to the meeting Collins met John Lannin of Boston and Lannin wanted him for the Boston club; but I told Lannin that he already had a good club in Boston and that Collins was scheduled to go to the White Sox.

"Collins wanted $15,000 a year for five years and a check for $10,000 for signing. That was satisfactory and Comiskey agreed.

"But Collins said: 'Of course that $5,000 you promised me goes too, Mr. Johnson.' I replied that I thought, in view of the fact that he was to get $10,000 from Comiskey for signing, that he would forget the $5,000 I had offered him; but he insisted on getting that also and I signed my personal check for $5,000. He was a great ball player and always gave his best."[6]

The individual most shocked by the transaction was, of course, Eddie Collins. His career at its peak, the self-assured young man had developed a real love affair with the city of Philadelphia, the Athletics and the Tall Tactician. He had heard the trade rumors but totally disregarded them.

"Had an earthquake shaken Philadelphia I could not have been more surprised than I was when I realized that I was no longer a member of the little band with whom I had spent eight exceedingly happy years. My home was in Philadelphia. I had been first introduced to Mrs. Collins by Mr. Mack, who was a lifelong friend of her father, and I had, somehow, always supposed I was forever going to remain 'at home.'"[7]

Moreover, if Collins were to leave Philadelphia, Chicago was not his first choice. He told Johnson he preferred New York. "He informed me, however, that the affairs of that club [the Highlanders] were in a very unsettled state, as indeed they were at that time. He said that the club could not pay anywhere near the salary Mr. Comiskey was prepared to offer...."[8]

There are credible baseball historians who doubt Ban Johnson ever approached prospective Highlanders owners Colonel Jacob Ruppert and Tillinghast Huston with a proposition to buy Collins for their new franchise. They believe the pair was financially able and willing to spend money to improve their team, and it seems totally out of character for these gentlemen to turn away from an opportunity to purchase one of baseball's best at the outset of their venture.[9]

Nonetheless, regardless of the sequence of events leading up to the transaction, the result was the same: Eddie Collins was on the move. At the time of his sale, Collins had a comfort level, the likes of a horsehide-covered cocoon, suddenly ripped asunder. That he kept his cool, acted with reason and bargained from a position of strength in an era when many of his fellow ball players were still treated as mere pawns and responded accordingly, says something about his strong will, as well as his business acumen. Eddie discussed his thought processes with writer Jim Nasium of the *Philadelphia Inquirer* on the same day his sale was announced.

The first news that any deal was under consideration was conveyed to me Sunday morning, in a telephone message from the Bellevue-Stratford, in Philadelphia, when Ban Johnson called me up at my home with instructions that he and Mr. Comiskey desired my presence at a conference. I went to the hotel and held a meeting with Comiskey and Johnson, at which I was asked by Mr. Comiskey if I wanted to go to Chicago. I told him no, as my property and friends and my wife's friends and all of our affiliations were and had always been in the East.... Then Mr. Johnson told me to consider it until Tuesday morning. At which time I was to meet he and Mr. Comiskey in New York and give them my final decision. I then talked it over with Mr. Mack and Connie told me to consider the matter carefully and come to New York and whatever I did in the matter, if I decided not to accept, he would fulfill his contract with me...., that Mr. Mack had no desire to severe our connections except for financial reasons.

So I met Mr. Johnson and Mr. Comiskey at the Hotel Belmont this morning.... The terms they offered me were so flattering that I could not refuse.... I am pleased to say that I am getting more money than I ever thought I would be able to earn in my life.[10]

The Tall Tactician, particularly in his public pronouncements, was not all that clear as to his reasons for selling Collins. A few months after the deal, he denied the issue was financial and blamed the Federal League for forcing his hand with Collins and the others in what, before it was through, amounted to an almost total purge of his championship club, leaving the A's the worst team in the American League, if not all of baseball.[11] Sounding much the same as he did when he claimed he sold Joe Jackson to Cleveland to repay a debt to Charlie Somers, Mack told his biographer Fred Lieb, "I sold Eddie to Chicago to save him for the American League."[12] And as stated previously, there was reason for the league and its owners to be concerned, for on December 4, 1914, the best pitcher in baseball, Walter Johnson, had signed a three-year contract with the Chicago Whales. Two weeks later, however, he was back with the Nationals.

Mack vehemently and consistently denied he sold Collins to Chicago because of the rumored animosity with Ira Thomas over the newspaper articles.

"I [Mack] would like to say that the reported trouble between Ira Thomas and Collins had nothing to do with the sale, that being too picayune a thing to pay any attention to."[13] Nor did he sell his players because of rumors of gambling influence, which according to Mack "had nothing to do with it."[14]

In Collins' opinion, bottom line, he was peddled to Chicago because of the A's financial troubles, first, and the Federal League threat, second. "Besides being a great baseball general Mr. Mack is a businessman. Compared with most of his associate club owners he was not wealthy at that time and the offer he received from Mr. Comiskey was too tempting and meant too much in various ways to be turned down. Had the series with the Braves lasted six games, I have always believed, however, that he would have refused the Chicago offer."[15]

It seems hard to argue with Collins' reasoning. Mack blamed the Federal League, but that league's aggressive tactics intruded on his control of player salaries. Any way you cut it, the sale of the A's Chalmers Award winner at the height of his career came down to the almighty dollar. By receiving $50,000 from Comiskey, Mack both eased his financial pressure and eliminated a source of discord on his club. Comiskey received a star player to stave off inroads by the Feds into his fan base in the Windy City. Ban Johnson made an adjustment in player personnel that balanced team strength in his league much as a general balances troop strength during war. In retrospect, when the established leagues and the Federal League finally made peace, it could easily be said Eddie Collins was a casualty of their war, as well as a richer person for it.

Of course, there is always room for a slightly different slant. According to one columnist, who wrote for the *New York Evening Journal* and called himself "Right Cross," it was

Collins' nature that led to his sale. Shortly after the deal the Tall Tactician filled his gaping hole at second base by obtaining the still popular, but no longer nearly as effective Napoleon Lajoie from Cleveland. According to the *Journal's* columnist, Mack's situation in Philadelphia was clearly monetary. After pointing out that Lajoie at this stage was not as "valuable" as Collins, the writer asserted Mack "finally came to the conclusion that a wonderful baseball team was not a guarantee of gate receipts.... Connie is not in baseball to promote art but to promote his bank account." Mack needed to look no farther than Detroit for an answer to his dilemma. The Tigers, despite having no real chance at the pennant, were a better draw than the A's. Why? "[T]he Tigers had Cobb and Crawford, and the Athletics did not. They had Collins, who is fully as useful a man as Cobb, but the crowd will not come out to see him ... Collins is a businessman and Cobb is character..... The Dear Old Public does not, as a rule, go dotty over Lajoie, but he is better stuff for a popular idol than Collins," who "plays baseball — and nothing more."[16]

It was one man's view, probably shared by others, but it was not the popular cry in Chicago. The city was ecstatic over its new star, as local newspapers blared out the front page news "Eddie Collins a Sox" and, in a scoop quickly denied by Comiskey, that the new acquisition "May Manage Team."[17]

The reaction to the deal in the *Tribune*, the *Daily News*, the *American* and the other Chicago newspapers was uniform: it was a steal. But despite the giddiness of the entire city over the purchase of a star of Collins' brilliance, the most popular man in town was Charles Comiskey. Of course, the man his friends called "Commy" and many others called the "Old Roman," due to his physical makeup and personal traits, was highly popular in Chicago long before he decided to plunk down serious change for Eddie Collins. Born in Chicago in 1859, Comiskey was in his mid-fifties when he bought Collins and was already one of the major forces in the game. Before he became an owner, Commy was a manager and before that a player. He began playing professionally, as a pitcher, then switched to first base, where some say he put his stamp on the way the game is now played by becoming the first to play off the base to increase his fielding range. Whether the change in positioning was actually the result of an 1883 rule change eliminating the one-bounce out on balls hit into foul territory, and whether Comiskey perfected the strategy all on his own or as others say Cap Anson did so, Comiskey was soon a player-manager for the St. Louis Browns. Under his tutelage the Browns won four straight American Association titles from 1885–88. Eventually he became player-manager of the Cincinnati Reds, where he remained until 1894. While in Cincinnati he became friends with a local sportswriter, Ban Johnson.

When Johnson organized the Western League, Commy gathered all his resources and became owner of the Sioux City franchise, which he eventually brought home to Chicago's South Side. His club, renamed the White Stockings in 1899, became a gem of the new American League when the circuit was formed in 1900. When Collins took his first taste of professional ball, he faced off against one of Commy's greatest teams, the 1906 Chicago White Sox, better known as the "Hitless Wonders." But the fortunes of baseball success are fleeting. Commy's organization found little to brag about following its 1906 triumph. By the end of 1914 the Sox owner was hungry for another World Series winner. In Eddie Collins he felt he had fashioned a start toward that goal. Although it was the most money ever paid for a baseball player, Commy had no problem justifying the then-extravagant expenditure.

"It's this way. I have been paying out sums like $18,000, $15,000 and $12,000 every year for players who are nothing more than a gamble. As a matter of fact, none of the players I have paid fancy sums for ever made good. Only my bargains like [Ed] Walsh, [Reb] Russell, [Buck] Weaver and one or two others ever came through.

"So I reasoned that instead of paying $18,000 for a bush leaguer, whose ability to make good nobody could foretell, it would be better business to pay three or four times that sum and get a star whose skill was uncommon and well-known."[18]

And why Collins, when there is Cobb, Speaker and many others? "I [Comiskey] secured him for the White Sox fans simply because I considered him a premiere, all-round player in batting, base running and fielding.

"Still another advantage in Collins is his quick-thinking brain, a most essential talent in the ball club contending for a pennant."[19]

The Collins' transaction was not just a topic of conversation in Chicago and Philadelphia. All of baseball was abuzz. Almost the entire March 1915 issue of *Baseball Magazine* was devoted to Collins and the effect his sale might have on the forthcoming season. Some of the talk concerned the financial enormity of the deal. In one article William Phelon, the longtime baseball reporter and magazine writer, wrote that given Collins' many talents, "he'll pull back that $50,000 through Comiskey's gates in half a dozen Sundays."[20]

In a second article Phelon took a much closer and lengthier look at Collins the man and Collins the player.

[Collins] is a self-made man, gaining education, fame and riches without influence and with only his own intrinsic ability to advance him.... He is of Irish blood, therefore a big card with the old-timers who still maintain that all good things in muscular endeavor must be of Celtic race. He can actually write, and write well, ... and thus endears himself to the world of scribes as a player-writer who is not a rank fake and palpable fraud....

If there is any criticism to be made of Collins, it is strangely that he is too uniform, too evenly balanced — therefore he does not afford as much good copy, as many "human interest stories" as most of the famous players....

Wherefore, 1915 will be, to Collins, just like any other season: only one more year of unequaled achievements by the man who was the best ball player, and the worst publicity agent, of them all!

On the other hand, whereas Collins the man was "just like an everyday ordinary person," Collins the player, especially as an infielder, had a style "all his own." As a second basemen, "Collins is not an Apollo of grace as he fields the ball, but nobody could ever say that he was awkward, clumsy, or fell over his own feet.... He can't make one-hand grabs like [Johnny] Evers; he can't do a lot of things other stars have done — but his own individual ideas are the real thing at all stages!"

As Phelon tells readers, Evers, who considered Collins the "greatest," once told him, "darned if I can explain, why he is, but he IS, just the same."[21]

One who had a possible explanation for Evers' difficulty in explaining Collins' ability was Jack Kofoed, like Phelon a frequent contributor to magazines and one who worked in Philadelphia while Collins played there. Kofoed, who in comparing Collins to Cobb opined that "a great infielder is of more value than an outfielder who is equally famous," felt he had his finger on the secret to Collins' success.

He is not a big man. There is nothing in the wiry length of him to suggest abnormal quickness of brain and muscle; less in the leisurely slouch he affects. His tanned face is lean, and there are tiny wrinkles spraying out from the corners of his hawk's eyes. It is something aside from his physical qualities, however, that makes you realize that he is no 'average' man; that he would be a leader in whatever vocation he might turn his versatile powers. I think, myself, that illimitable self-confidence has placed Edward Trowbridge Collins on the highest seat in baseball's realm. He has no brooding fear of failure; only a belief that brooks no opposition.[22]

All opinions and praise aside, all that was left was for Collins to change his frame of reference from Philadelphia to Chicago. He would keep his home for the present in Lansdowne but ply his trade in the Midwest. He did have one concern: the wind. He was aware that the White Sox were reputedly a weak-hitting franchise. Given his positive outlook, he refused to buy into it.

"In my own experience I have always found that that prevailing winds at Chicago seemed to favor the pitcher and seemed always to be blowing against the batter.... Whether or not the new environment will interfere with my own batting eye I can not say, but I do not see why it should.... I see no reason why a batting record should suffer in a White Sox uniform."[23]

The "new" environment Collins referred to was Comiskey Park, home of the White Sox since 1910. When Eddie played his first game against the Sox in 1906, the team was housed at South Side Park, an older edifice which seated only 15,000. Given the success of Shibe Park and its concrete-and-steel construction, Commy decided to build one of his own. Although his architect recommended a "classic" design similar to Shibe that eliminated the use of view-obstructive posts, Commy, who certainly was economical if not down-right cheap in many aspects of the business, chose the less expensive design that included the posts. The park was built in a working-class neighborhood in South Side Chicago at West 35th Street and South Shields Avenue. When the park opened on July 1, 1910, it seated 32,000 fans. It consisted of a covered two-decker grandstand which continued down each baseline for 30 feet and two detached single-deck covered stands which continued down each foul line. Beyond the outfield were uncovered bleachers which held 7,000 of the park's seats. When the park opened, these seats went for 25 cents each, an attractive price in the neighborhoods of the South Side.

The original dimensions of the park were 363 feet from home plate down each foul line and 420 feet to center. The distance to center gave outfielders plenty of room to run down long fly balls. The fence in right and left stood 10-feet high and was 11-feet in center.[24]

Besides the stadium's massive size, a distinguishing facet of the design was the letter "C" pressed into the brick on the stadium exterior. According to White Sox historian Richard Lindberg, "It was the only unique characteristic distinguishing the baseball plant from any number of factories and warehouses in the surrounding Bridgeport neighborhood."[25]

Collins now had a new ball club and a new ball park. What he did not have was a manager. Following a long and arduous 1914 season that saw the ChiSox finish with a record of 70–84, Commy intended to unload his current field general, James "Nixey" Callahan. Nixey, a former player-manager, was at the end of a downhill slide which saw his team finish in fourth in 1912, fifth in 1913 and tied for sixth in 1914. It was not surprising then that speculation included Collins among the team's management prospects. But Commy was apparently not interested in going that route and neither was Collins, telling a friend in a letter, "I don't want to have any such job as long as I am good enough to be in the batting order regularly. I believe that one end or the other is bound to suffer as a result."[26]

When Commy did name his choice, it was a real surprise to just about everyone. In fact, Collins, who was on a hunting trip on December 17 when club secretary Harry Grabiner made the announcement, had never heard of him. Again, it was Mabel Collins who broke the news when Eddie arrived home.

"'Well, Edward, I see you have a new boss.'

"'Who is it, 'Kid' Gleason?' inquired Edward.

"'No,' answered his wife, 'a man named Rowland.'

"'You must be wrong,' replied 'Eddie.' 'I never heard of any such man in baseball.'"[27]

The man Collins had never heard of was Clarence Rowland, and he did have some baseball experience — of the minor league variety. As a player he was a reserve catcher, then later a manager in the Three-Eye League. In 1914 his Peoria team won that league's pennant. Commy was attracted by his new manager's ability to pick out young talent. In 1909 he had tipped the White Sox's owner to Larry Doyle, but Commy ignored the advice and missed out on the eventual Giants star.[28]

Rowland came to the White Sox with a couple of strikes against him in addition to his lack of big league experience. He was young — at 35, not that much older than several of his players — and to sophisticated big city folks, he was merely an Iowa "busher." Then there was his nickname, earned in his semipro days when he wore his father's blue knickers. It was hard for people to take someone called "Pants" all that seriously. But level-headed players such as Collins would take a wait-and-see attitude. Early in the spring of 1915, he told friends that "Rowland has the goods. He knows baseball and he knows players and he knows human nature."[29]

In many ways when a baseball player is sold or traded, he arrives at his new destination carrying a clean slate. The same was true of Collins, with one exception. The local press was aware of the rumors of dissension among the Mackmen as a result of Collins' way with words. They suspected it had something to do with his availability. Thus in an editorial column on December 12, the *Chicago Tribune* asked, "[W]ill Collins continue his newspaper writing?" Naturally the paper shared its view, telling readers the writing caused dissension in Philadelphia and it would do the same in Chicago.

"'The *Tribune*' believes the White Sox need ball players…. 'The *Tribune*' does not believe the White Sox need authors….

"There is also an ethical side to this writing. A player can not write all he knows and be fair to his teammates. He can not conceal what he knows and be fair to his readers. Collins is too big a man to have to make such a choice."[30]

Just in case Collins was not aware that there was pressure on him to perform in Chicago, the *Tribune* made sure. On December 20 a cartoon appeared surrounding a likeness of Eddie under a headline declaring he was the "Highest Priced Player in Baseball World." Just below it a subheading stated the former A's star, "Must Increase Attendance at White Sox Park 1,000 Per Game to Repay Salary and Purchase Money."[31]

One person who would not be around to see whether or not Collins could increase attendance was William Gleason. The popular and knowledgeable White Sox coach and assistant manager under James Callahan was given his unconditional release on December 29. Brought to the White Sox at the request of Callahan, the man they called "Kid" was deemed expendable with Rowland now at the helm.

Now it was 1915 and before the ink was dry on the *Tribune's* editorial asking Collins to refrain from putting so much in writing, he was back in the news again, this time for something he put into a personal letter to his new teammate, pitcher Eddie Cicotte. According to *The Sporting News*, Cicotte shared the contents of a letter he received from Collins in which he told Cicotte he was happy to be out of Philadelphia. Coming in the face of any number of statements Collins made extolling the virtues of his time in the City of Brotherly Love, the release of the contents of the letter proved quite embarrassing at the very least.[32]

Less embarrassing was a letter Collins wrote his new manager, Pants Rowland.

"I had a fine letter from Eddie Collins and he declared he would do everything in his power to make the White Sox a success."[33]

Eddie was in the news one more time in early 1915 when rumors flew in New York following Walter Johnson's return to Washington and the American League. The stories suggested with the reason for Collins' purchase by Commy now moot and his presence no longer needed in Chicago, Collins was on his way to New York to play for a Highlanders' team now more popularly known as the Yankees. Comiskey quickly shot that idea down, saying his new star was purchased to win a pennant.

"I can't believe that the new owners of the Yankees expect me to give Eddie Collins to them. If they have any such thoughts in mind they will be disappointed. Eddie Collins will be with the White Sox."[34]

Collins' first spring training with the White Sox took place in Paso Robles, California, in 1915. On the way out the White Sox were scheduled for an appearance at the Panama-Pacific International Exposition in San Francisco on February 20. Their special train, which included Mabel Collins, left Chicago's LaSalle Street station on the evening of February 16. Eddie and Mabel had arrived in Chicago a few days earlier so he could be fitted with his new White Sox uniform. Now 28, Collins was a veteran and one of the older Sox regulars. A rookie on trial from Milwaukee of the American Association was 23-year-old Oscar "Happy" Felsch. Collins, Felsch, and several others were part of a White Sox rebuilding program which began shortly after Comiskey's return from the world tour his team and John McGraw's Giants took at the end of the 1913 season. The trip covered over 38,000 miles and included visits to several continents. It reinvigorated Commy. By the spring of 1915, his efforts were starting to take shape and, hopefully, return dividends.

Despite their losing record in 1914 and the loss of first baseman Hal Chase to the Federal League, the White Sox were not without talent. Their catcher was another Milwaukee find, Raymond William Schalk. Purchased in 1912 at age 19, Schalk, who was considered small for a catcher, was already a proven backstop with a great arm and a rapidly expanding knowledge of the game. In 1914 he appeared in 136 games, hit .270 with an OBP of .347, and so impressed the scribes that he finished sixth in voting for the Chalmers Award won by Collins.

A catcher with a good head and bat was an important start. But Comiskey had more in place by 1914 than just Ray Schalk. At shortstop that year was 24-year-old George "Buck" Weaver. A White Sox regular since 1912 and current team captain, Weaver was sturdy with a bat, but at the same time perhaps out of position at shortstop. Still, positioned alongside a first-class second baseman such as Collins, the middle infield would be adequately manned.

In the outfield John "Shano" Collins, a 29-year-old veteran from Massachusetts, was a fine complementary player, with his defensive skills a strength. If necessary he could also play first base. Once Hal Chase left for the Federal League, first base was primarily manned in 1914 by Jack Fournier, the top returning batsmen. Unfortunately, fielding was a challenge the career .313 hitter could never overcome.

By the end of 1914, the White Sox were no longer dependent on over-worked Ed Walsh. Between 1906 and 1912 the 11-year veteran had won 168 of the 357 games in which he pitched. His arm was now essentially dead. Even without him, however, the White Sox possessed a solid pitching staff, including right-handers Joe Benz, Jim "Death Valley" Scott, Collins' pen-pal Eddie Cicotte, and lefty Reb Russell. Cicotte, picked up on waivers from the Red Sox, was the elder statesman at age 30 and threw another of the trick pitches, the "shine" ball. Added to this group was a young spitball pitcher named Urban "Red" Faber. Commy found him in Des Moines, Iowa, of the Western League. He was in the early portion of a long and illustrious career.

The cupboard therefore was not bare on the team Collins met and trained with in spring 1915. There was more than just a new group of players to adjust to for Eddie that first year. Unlike Connie Mack, Eddie's new boss, Comiskey, trained his teams hard in preparation for each upcoming season. There was extensive road work and little time for golf and relaxation, as the team conducted two-hour workouts in the morning and afternoon. Still the formula seemed to agree with Collins, especially since Rowland quickly took him into his confidence, and his new shortstop, Buck Weaver, and others seemed to readily accept him.[35] In order to make room at second for Collins, weak-hitting Lena Blackburne (.222 in 1914) was moved to third base. Early in the training period manager Rowland installed Collins in his familiar third slot in the batting order. Eddie responded by hitting at a good clip, including several four-hit efforts. By the time the team arrived in St. Louis for the season opener against the Browns on April 14, "Pants" declared them fit and equipped to vastly improve on their sixth-place 1914 finish.

It took 13 innings in the opener, but the White Sox prevailed, 7–6. In the contest Collins pulled off several sparkling plays. In addition, as Commy and Ban Johnson sat together in a field box, they watched Eddie step in front of Buck Weaver in the bottom of the eleventh to keep the angry shortstop from ejection as he balled his fists and threatened mayhem over a close call at second.

Early in the season as the White Sox struggled on the road, an article by Harvey T. Woodruff appeared in the *Tribune* and shed light on Collins' financial dealings with Connie Mack in 1914 and later with Comiskey. Entitled "Eddie Collins of Sox Worth More than His Weight in Gold," Woodruff declared that Collins' last contract with the A's waived the "ten-day clause," a standard paragraph in baseball contracts of the day which permitted a team to dismiss a "reserved" player on 10 days notice. It also called for him to earn $11,500 per year. In exchange for Eddie's agreement to eschew his desire to remain in the East and to play for the Sox, his annual figure was increased by Comiskey to $15,000 per year, plus the $15,000 signing bonus. Since the price paid for Collins was $50,000, the total cost to Comiskey to complete the deal was $140,000. Based upon Collins' current playing weight of 160 pounds, Woodruff figured Eddie cost Commy $875 per pound. The current cost of gold was $248.04. Therefore, Woodruff concluded, "Collins cost more than three and one-half times his weight in gold." In the writer's opinion, if Collins can help Commy win a pennant, "it is a cheap investment."[36]

At least 22,000 fans were convinced Commy had invested wisely as they saw a vintage Collins performance on the base paths in their team's home opener at Comiskey Park on April 22 against the Browns. In that one the Sox scored five in the ninth to rally for a 5–4 win. Three singles, two triples and a pair of passed balls in that ninth nailed the victory, none more important than a two-strike grounder to deep short which Eddie legged out for a hit. A passed ball and he was on second. A ground out later he stood on third, but now two were out. Then Shano Collins lined a triple and Eddie crossed home with the tying run. Another passed ball and the "other" Collins scored the game-winner, the first of seven in a row. A new, improved White Sox team was on the prowl. By May 22 the team was in first place, a position they held by virtue of two nine-game winning streaks. However, when they met the Boston Red Sox in a five-game series at Comiskey Park beginning on July 17, they lost four of those games and their lead.

As the Sox were winning, Collins' new teammates were able to get a close look at his growing list of superstitions. They covered the gamut — before, during and after the game. Collins dressed in ritualistic fashion. He removed his street hat and immediately replaced it with his baseball cap. Forget to do it and a hitless afternoon was certain to ensue. He still chewed gum and stuck it to the bottom of his cap, but he also always picked up the baseball bat at the end of the row which was in front of the bench. His bat always had to be on the end and no one else's could touch it. In addition, no two bats should ever cross. If they did, the opponent would get a hit. When an out was recorded, by custom, the infielders would throw it "around the horn." When they did, Collins insisted he get the ball last to toss it back to the pitcher. Failure to do so would result in runs. Finally, if he failed to hit three times in a row, Eddie made sure he touched a bench player before his fourth at-bat. It worked, did it not? He got a triple one day right after doing so.

After the game there occurred perhaps the strangest routine of all. As he changed back to street clothes, Collins always put on his shirt collar, tie, hat and coat before he put on his trousers. Failure to follow through meant a loss the next day.[37] In the end, as long as it worked, it all made sense and, apparently, it worked for Eddie more often than not. Of course, like any superstition, that was not always the case. Take May 11 in Chicago when he fanned with the bases loaded in a 2–0 loss to the Nationals, a team regularly called the Senators.

One of the more amazing aspects of the White Sox's early-season pennant push was the respect garnered for the team's new skipper, Pants Rowland. Observers were surprised at how a veteran like Collins quickly fell into line with Pants as his leader. It appeared the new manager was proceeding in a thoughtful manner. Though no one would have questioned the move, it was probably wise that Rowland did not appoint a team captain. The logical choice would have been Collins, and Comiskey even indicated as much soon after Eddie's acquisition. But the choice of Eddie or anyone else at that point might have indicated weakness and a willingness to abdicate power on the part of the new Sox manager. In addition, the non-decision avoided potential conflict between Collins and Weaver. In fact, the two continued to get along and even played some golf together. Still, the *Tribune* saw Collins in a leadership role, pointing out that he "acts if occasion demands."[38]

On June 17 Collins returned to Philadelphia for his first visit in an opposing uniform. A mid-week crowd of 5,000, large for the struggling A's, greeted its former hero. Many of those in attendance stood in the stands next to the field prior to the game in order to shake hands with him. If he was at all nostalgic, Collins did not show it once the game started, as he singled his first time up. As Death Valley Scott shut out Mack's boys, Eddie added two doubles and a walk to his total on the day. On June 19 a formal celebration was held as 8,000, the biggest crowd to date for the season, showed up for "Eddie Collins Day." Again the White Sox won the game, 8–2, but Collins was not quite as menacing at the plate. He did walk twice, stole a base and scored, but was 0-for-3 in his other plate appearances.

In late June Collins nursed a leg injury but managed to keep playing. On June 28 he got his first look at the Browns' new pitching star, George Sisler, like Collins a former collegiate star. The White Sox won, 4–2.

By mid–July, even though their team was playing well, Commy and Pants realized the team's youth would eventually catch up with it. A five-game losing streak which began on July 2 in Detroit drove the point home. Therefore, they began a search for help. On July 7 they picked up 23-year-old outfielder Nemo Leibold. A steady fielder, he batted from the left; over the next several years, he was handy as a platoon hitter who batted in the lead-off position against right-handed pitchers. An important aspect of Leibold's game was his ability to coax walks.

Just over a week later on July 15, the White Sox pursued another left-handed batter, Eddie Murphy, from the A's. Still only 23, Murphy played in 137 games in 1913 and 148 games in 1914 and hit well. He was expendable, of course, because Connie Mack was still cleaning house.

The ChiSox brass was not done. However, before they could do more, tragedy struck their city. On Friday, July 23, the White Sox were in town celebrating their third straight win over the Yankees, as they put any remaining visions of the disappointing series with the Red Sox out of their minds. Early the next morning some 2,572 passengers — employees of Western Electric, their families and friends — boarded the excursion steamer *Eastland*, docked between LaSalle and Clark Streets along the Chicago River. The group was headed to Michigan City, Indiana, for the annual company picnic. Moments later at 7:28 A.M., while still at the mooring, the ship slowly tipped over and 844 passengers perished. The city, state and nation were stunned.

The city of Chicago had seen other major disasters since Father Marquette, the French-born missionary, and Louis Jolliet, the Canadian explorer, first eyed its eventual site in 1673. During the War of 1812, Fort Dearborn, erected at the mouth of the Chicago River, was destroyed and many of its occupants killed by attacking Indians. Despite this terrible loss, the fort was rebuilt. In 1833 a town was incorporated at the location, taking the name "Chicago," an Indian name some believe denoted strength or greatness. By 1837 the town, once 350, growing ever more populated, was incorporated as a city of over 4,000 inhabitants. In October 1871 a fire of unknown origin began in a cow barn and spread to the city's business district. By the time the flames subsided, 300 citizens were dead and 90,000 homeless. Once again the city and its people proved their vibrancy and Chicago was literally rebuilt. By 1900 the Bureau of the Census counted 1,698,575 Chicagoans, more than one-third born abroad.

In 1903 Chicago experienced yet another disaster when the Iroquois Theater, filled to capacity, caught fire. Some 600 people, many children, died. Now just over a decade later, what quickly became known as the Eastland Disaster was the worst loss of life the city had ever known. The event's cause was epitomized by the line, "Somebody made a big mistake."[39]

Chicago was a city in mourning. In deference to the families of the deceased, Charles Comiskey canceled a doubleheader with the New York Highlanders. Over the next week or so, the White Sox played listless baseball. Perhaps it was a reaction to their city's loss, perhaps not, but they lost seven of their next nine games, including six in a row. They were now in third place, three and one-half behind league-leading Boston.

It was obvious Commy's troops needed more reinforcements. In June they tried to pry shortstop Ray Chapman from Cleveland. They failed but did get Leibold. In July the White Sox missed out on Jack Barry when the Fourth of July holiday delayed the mail carrying Mack's announcement that Collins' old keystone-combination buddy was on the market. In the interim the Red Sox gobbled him up.

The setbacks only seemed to whet Commy's appetite. On August 21 the White Sox acquired "Shoeless" Joe Jackson from the Cleveland Indians for cash and three lesser talents named Braggo Roth (outfielder), Larry Chappell (outfielder) and Ed Klepfer (pitcher). Bidding for the hitting star among American League rivals was reportedly fierce, with Boston, New York and Washington in the hunt. The White Sox won out because Commy sent Harry Grabiner to Cleveland with instructions to raise the ante until all the others backed off. The *Tribune* reported the cash outlay for the deal as $15,000, but subsequent descriptions of the transaction set the figure at $31,500. Although the players dealt to Cleveland were not big names, Braggo Roth, then 22, went on to lead the American League in home runs that same season with seven. At the time of the transaction, regular White Sox first baseman Jack Fournier was out of the lineup due to a fractured arm and Jackson was capable of playing first base. Nonetheless, it was decided John Collins would remain at that position.

Why was Jackson on the market? He seemed to love playing baseball in Cleveland and had blossomed into a major hitting star while there. The answer was simple. He was available for the same reason Collins had become available: money. Indians owner Charles Somers was in a serious cash crunch; his team was drawing poorly. In 1914 attendance was in the 185,000 range. In 1915 the popular Lajoie was now residing in Philadelphia and the team's attendance, as well as their record, continued to flag. Then, of course, there was the ever-present Federal League. Shoeless Joe was an obvious target for them, as well. On August 16 in order to ward off the Feds and in a move similar to Mack's with Collins, Baker and the others, Somers inked Jackson to a three-year contract for 1917, 1918 and 1919 at a reported $6,000. Then he dealt him away.[40]

Now it seemed the White Sox were fortified for the stretch run. Unfortunately, it did not work out that way. The addition of Jackson did little to stem the team's late-season decline. Their record stood at 67–44 on the date of the trade. Sporting a new lineup with Jackson batting cleanup, their record for the remainder of the year was 26–17. It was nothing to be ashamed of, but not enough to catch the pennant-winning Red Sox. The team actually lost ground in the pennant race. The fact Jackson's production fell after the trade did not help. He was hitting .327 at the time of trade, .272 thereafter. By season's end the White Sox trailed the pennant winners by nine and one-half games, Detroit by seven.

The White Sox of 1915, however, were a vastly improved product over the 1914 brand. Their final count of 93–61 was a 23-game improvement, due largely to increased run production. In 1914 the club was dead last with 487 runs. In 1915 they scored 717 and jumped to second. Given a continued good showing from a fine pitching staff, the future for the White Sox was definitely brightening. If rebuilding a baseball team is a bit like tilling a new plant bed, Charles Comiskey was proving to be quite a gardener.

One plant that was already producing flowers stemmed from Commy's investment in Eddie Collins. In 1915 the new Sox second baseman batted .332 to finish second in the league, though a far cry from Cobb's .369. His OBP of .460 was also second, as was his runs scored total of 118. His 119 bases on balls stood first and his 46 base thefts were third. His 77 RBIs were seventh. He led his team in most hitting categories. Last, but certainly not least, his fielding continued to win kudos throughout the league.

In Chicago at the end of each season, it was customary to schedule a City Series for early October with the Cubs. One would think the players would find such an event, coming as it did at the end of a grueling pennant chase, a drudgery just as easily avoided. This would be especially true for one like Collins who had already played in a number of World Series. On the contrary, Collins, a regular participant in the annual Phillies-A's clashes, found the Chicago City Series a good experience.

"One is wonderfully lucky to have a chance to play in even one world series [sic] ... as I have. Then the city series, here in Chicago, are almost like those for the championship. Fans are enthusiastic and keyed up. It's fine to play in such games and fortunately, when so stimulated, I always play better."[41]

In 1910 Collins feasted on the Cubs in the World Series, and he did so again in 1915 as his White Sox took the series from the northsiders, four games to one. In game one alone he singled twice, doubled, tripled, drove in three runs and stole two bases to spark a 9–5 win. The games drew fans, over 75,000 in all. They also attracted controversy. The players shared the proceeds in only the first four games. The White Sox's winning share was $420 per player; the Cubs', $300. Both figures were well below previous years. The players were upset, particularly with Comiskey, who forced the teams to play two of the games in the bitter cold before smaller crowds, saving a Sunday game and its big crowd to fill the coffers of the ball clubs alone. An unnamed Cub player who felt he knew who to blame did not hold back his disgust in a comment to the *Tribune*.

"They always told me Comiskey was a friend of the ball player. I understand he was responsible for our playing on two cold days. Consequently he gets the big money from the Sunday crowd and the ball player gets his little mite which came in on the cold days."[42]

Commy did not respond to the charge, but interestingly one of the *Tribune* writers recalled the owner "expressed great disappointment after employing a lot of high salaried players only to have them beaten out of the pennant."[43]

When it came to his club's home attendance, Commy had reason to complain. In 1914 with a sixth-place team, his White Sox finished second in league attendance, drawing just over 469,000. In 1915 despite a vastly improved ball club which fashioned a third-place finish, the team remained second in league attendance, improving to 539,461. For Commy, faced with a much higher payroll, it meant he was not yet reaping the benefit of his expenditure. For Collins, the 70,000 fan jump in 79 home contests meant he was not drawing at the rate at least one local sports writer believed he needed to draw in order to prove his worth.

In fairness to all concerned, baseball in Chicago in 1915 was a three-team affair. The Federal League's Chicago Whales finished first in their league, drawing fans from a weak Cubs franchise, as well as from the more popular White Sox. Led by player-manager Joe Tinker, formerly with the Cubs, the Whales edged the St. Louis Terriers by .001. On December 22 that threat to Commy's bottom line, as well as to the rest of major league baseball, was eliminated. The magnates, the owners of the American and National league franchises, reached an agreement with the Federal League by which that league ceased to do business. In exchange for the agreement, the Federal League received a sum of money, about $600,000, to be distributed to its eight owners, many of whom were in serious need of much more. Also, a lawsuit pending before a Federal judge, Kenesaw Mountain Landis of Chicago, charging anti-trust violations, was dropped, although Baltimore later initiated a separate litigation. The initial suit filed by the Federal League was in limbo anyway as Landis, a baseball fan, was slowly starving the litigation by delaying his decision. In addition, two of the Fed team owners were permitted to purchase major league clubs. Phillip DeCatesby Ball bought the St. Louis Browns of the American League while Charles Weeghman purchased the Chicago Cubs of the National League. Weeghman Park, now known as Wrigley Field, became the home of the Cubs. Finally, the wayward players who jumped to the new league were permitted to return to Organized Baseball.

During the baseball season Collins rented an apartment in Chicago. After the season he returned to Philadelphia and Lansdowne where he, Mabel and their son Paul maintained their home. On the way he stopped to watch Philadelphia in the World Series. But it was not the A's he watched that year. It was the Phillies. The A's, without the core of their world championship team, were now the American League's cellar dweller, sporting a miserable 43–109 record. Only 146,223 fans paid their respects, putting a dent in the Tall Tactician's theory that struggling teams draw more fans than successful ones.

In both 1915 and 1916, the former Mackmen were still favorite topics of conversation. One of those former A's, Frank "Home Run" Baker, was now a member of the New York Yankees. He had sat out the 1915 season in a contract dispute with Connie Mack, who then sold Baker to the Yankees. During the 1916 season he saw a precipitous drop in his batting average, if not his overall production. Yankee manager Bill Donovan attributed Baker's struggles to a sudden eagerness to swing at pitches, even bad pitches, early in the count. Others, including Hughie Jennings of the Tigers and Fielder Jones of the Browns, thought the problem stemmed from the absence of Eddie Collins, in the past batting just ahead of Baker in the lineup. In their opinion, Collins was on base so much when Baker reached the plate that it constantly put opposing pitchers "in the hole."[44]

In February 1916 just before the White Sox headed for their new spring training playground in Mineral Wells, Texas, Collins spoke to a church group in Palmyra, New Jersey. Collins, who was known to swear with the best of them when provoked on a ball field, did not drink or smoke. In a day when the forces of the Anti-Saloon League were gathering across the nation, he gave the audience of over 500 a bit of his philosophy of life.

"Baseball business and the world itself will be better off when John Barleycorn is dumped overboard. Temperate living is necessary for success in any field of action.... Cut out the booze, don't be intemperate in eating, and you've won half the battle."[45]

Speaking of baseball business, Collins was experiencing a little of the executive side of the game himself by that time. In March it was announced that Collins and Jack Dunn, the long-time Baltimore baseball official who introduced Babe Ruth to the professional game, had filed incorporation papers at Annapolis, Maryland, for the formation of a company to own the Baltimore Orioles. Dunn and Collins, who were frequent hunting buddies, and others such as Fritz Maisel of the Yankees, were now shareholders in the minor league club. Eddie, still in his twenties, was now a baseball magnate.

Given Commy's reported disappointment with his team's results in 1915, there was speculation during the off-season that Pants Rowland might be gone. Commy put that speculation to rest in December. On March 12 Rowland and his squad, including late arrivals Eddie Collins and Eddie Murphy, stepped on a train southwest bound.

One of the first orders of business for Rowland in 1916 was finding a third baseman. In 1915 Lena Blackburne played the bulk of the games at that spot and provided a weak bat, hitting only .216. By early April, Zeb Terry, a 25-year-old right-handed batter who could field well enough to cover shortstop, provided a solution. Buck Weaver was moved to third and Terry inserted at short, where he quickly formed a smooth combination with Collins.

At first base the club continued to wince at the fielding exploits of Jack Fournier, but his team-high five home runs and his .322 average kept him in the lineup. Jack Ness, who batted from the right side and had a 49-game hitting streak in 1915 at Oakland of the Pacific Coast League, was added to provide an extra bat and, hopefully, a steadier glove.

Eddie Collins hit well that spring with several four-hit outings. Apparently, he did not miss the company of his wife who, along with most of the spouses, stayed home per the desires of none other than Charles Comiskey. No written order was issued and, according to sports scribe I.E. Sanborn of the *Tribune*, none was needed. Commy sought to limit the distractions and potential for discord which might accompany the presence of the so-called "better half." The players knew their owner's stance and most wisely chose not to disregard it.[46]

One of the things that Collins liked about Pants Rowland was his thinking-man's approach to the game. In 1916 the manager decided to play to his team's strength, a stronger fielding aggregate, and to re-sod the infield at Comiskey Park to make it faster. His group could

Collins, a left-handed batter, takes a swing and watches the flight of the ball during a batting practice while with the Chicago White Sox. He is wearing a home uniform. The styling indicates the photograph was taken during either the 1915 or 1916 season (National Baseball Hall of Fame Library, Cooperstown, New York).

still get in front of the hot bangers while his hitters could get some shots past opposing infields less equipped to handle the heat.

On April 12 Rowland prepared to test his theories in the home season opener versus the Tigers. A crowd of 31,000, the largest ever for a ChiSox opener, stormed Comiskey Park, eager to watch what promised to be a strong team. The Tigers did not cooperate. Sox starter Reb Russell only lasted into the second inning and his team fell, 4–0. Collins' bat, so hot all spring, was ice cold. He went 0-for-4.

Hours after the disappointing loss, Pants Rowland received an important endorsement. Speaking at a banquet, his boss announced Pants would be his manager "as long as I am owner and president of the club."[47] The fact that the statement was made by Commy during a speech to the Woodland Bards gave it even more weight.

The Boston Red Sox had their fan club, the Royal Rooters. In 1916 the White Sox had the Woodland Bards. The core of the group consisted of a number of Commy's hunting pals. Commy loved to hunt and fish and was seldom happier than doing so with a group of friends. Frequent expeditions into northern Wisconsin for this purpose led in 1907 to construction of a hunting lodge on property Commy owned near Mercer, Wisconsin. The compound became known as Camp Jerome. In 1910 Joseph C. Farrell, a Chicago songwriter, press agent and friend of the Sox owner, organized those who went to the camp into a group. There were initiations for new members, and Farrell encouraged the membership to write verse. When they did they became known as the "Woodland Bards" in keeping with the spirit of the most famous bard, William Shakespeare. The original membership was less than 40, but over the years it increased to 250. Soon there was a club room in Comiskey Park. "[A]s time passed, membership in the Woodland Bards was regarded as a symbol of attainment in the Chicago sporting world."[48]

In the early going in 1916, the White Sox saw one administrative change that affected their on-field work. On April 19 Eddie Collins was appointed the White Sox's team captain. Only one season before, Rowland had determined no captain was needed. Now with a youthful shortstop and a position change at third, as well as the expected fielding lapses at first, Commy and Pants felt a steadying influence in the field might help. They would get no argument from Eddie. After watching while Danny Murphy and then Ira Thomas were nominated by the A's instead of him, the appointment was an honor and a welcome show of confidence. How it was, and in the future would be, received by his teammates was yet to be determined.

Clearly in the short term the addition of a captain did little to ignite the team's initial thrust. By June 22 Commy was probably hoping the Woodland Bards were too drunk to recall his ringing endorsement of his "busher" manager. The team sat mired in fifth place, about to fall to sixth after a double loss to the lowly Browns. Their record of 26–28 mirrored their listless play. One of the problems was the hitting of the new team captain. Although his position was as safe as any, there were rumors in mid–May of shakeups in other portions of the lineup, including first base, where Fournier's miserable fielding was raising even more eyebrows. The *Tribune*, however, was particularly critical of Collins. "Incredible as it seems, Collins is swinging at bad balls persistently." In a game in New York he fanned three times in succession. According to the paper, on the fourth at-bat, "It looked almost as if he was desperate to the point of recklessness."[49]

During his career, slumps were essentially foreign to Collins, but like any player he did incur them from time to time. When he did, his philosophy was simple.

"I have no set rule for climbing out of a slump except to 'bear down hard.' I always give myself a careful self analysis. I try to put my finger on the hidden cause of my slump. And when I have located that cause I exert myself to get out of the slump."[50] There was always a saving grace. "Slumps, the worst of them, pass in time."[51]

Just a few days later, as the Sox endured several days of rain in Boston, the squad was fired up by reports in the local Boston newspapers claiming dissension on the team, particularly between Collins and Rowland. The articles intimated that the team had already closed shop for the season. When Collins refused to allow a cartoonist to make a drawing by hiding behind a newspaper when the artist approached, that unflattering image became the cartoon, adding to the embarrassment and further fueling the anger.

In short order, one change was made. Outfielder John Shano Collins switched places with Fournier at first base, keeping the latter's bat in the lineup but muting the clinking sound of his steel glove. Four days later Pants changed direction and placed Jack Ness at first, shifting Shano back to the pastures. Fournier became odd man out. Although Rowland blamed the weak start on overconfidence, he continued trying to find the right combination by shifting gears and players. On May 24 he benched Shano Collins in favor of Eddie Murphy. The *Tribune* wondered if the benching of Eddie Collins and Ray Schalk was to follow.

During the slump one issue remained clear. The White Sox of 1916 wanted Pants Rowland to remain their manager. On May 26 a day after a game with the Washington Senators ended in a tie, the team asked Rowland to give them some time alone while it gathered for a team meeting. No one knows exactly what occurred. The team did not immediately end its struggles, but less than a month later they began to play much better. Any idea there was quit in this team's vocabulary was quickly dismissed.

Collins finally broke out of his season-long slump on June 16 as part of a 7–4 Sox win over the Red Sox. On the day, Eddie was 3-for-5 including a walk, a bunt single, a double, a triple, two runs scored and two RBIs. He continued his hot hitting as the White Sox won seven in a row from June 27 through July 3 and raised their record to 36–29.

One of Collins' closest friends and allies on the White Sox was Ray Schalk. In mid–July the team was in Philadelphia for a series, and Eddie and Mabel entertained Schalk and Pants Rowland at the Collins' home in Lansdowne.

The pennant race in 1916 was hotly contested. By July 25 the recharged White Sox showed a 49–40 record but still rested in fourth behind New York, Boston and Cleveland, in that order. Still they were only two and one-half games out, and on August 4, as a result of a nine-game winning streak, they jumped to first. Unfortunately, they could not hold the lead. For the month of August, their overall record was 14–15. As a result, they hovered between second and fourth.

In mid–August, despite his public comments endorsing Rowland, Commy quietly rehired Kid Gleason as a coach. The "Kid," by now not so coltish at age 50, had enjoyed a long playing career, mostly in the National League, which saw him not only pitch, but play second base among other positions. In the 1890s he was one of the game's best. A leader on the field, he served as captain of the Giants and the Tigers, as well as the Phillies. His nickname was earned as much for his boyish enthusiasm as for his diminutive size. This was his second time around with the White Sox, and upon his return the *Tribune* found his best attribute his "fighting spirit which possesses him from the start to the finish of a ball game."[52]

Perhaps Commy felt his club needed some of Gleason's fighting spirit as they approached crunch time. In 1916, unlike 1915, the team played much better down the stretch. A seven-game winning streak in early September kept them in the thick of the battle. Their fans in ever-growing numbers came on board. On September 17 a record crowd of 40,000 turned out at Comiskey Park on a Sunday to watch Red Faber, in the midst of a fine season that saw him win 17 against nine losses and post a 2.02 ERA, go up against Babe Ruth. This was the same youngster whom Collins saw a couple years earlier when Ruth was pitching for Baltimore. The older version was on his way to a 23-win season and league leading 1.75 ERA. His Red Sox were in a familiar position: first place. The ChiSox were looking for a second consecutive win over the league leaders, having won the previous day behind their own young pitching star, Lefty Williams. A win would boost Commy's guys into first. However, it was not to be, as Ruth gave up two runs early, including a Collins' score after a single, but then shut out the White Sox on two hits the rest of the way for a 6–2 victory.

The rubber game of the three-game series was on September 18. Again the White Sox went with Williams, one of the most pleasant surprises of the 1916 season. Purchased from Salt Lake City of the Pacific Coast League after a stellar season, he started 26 games for his new club in 1916. The 23-year-old left-hander would finish the year at 13–7 with a 2.89 ERA. One of his losses unfortunately was on the 18th to the Red Sox by a 4–3 count. Despite a fine effort by the rookie, especially since he was pitching on one day's rest, the Bostonians left town in first.

The mid–September series with the Red Sox was the last crack the White Sox had at their rivals. They really never overcame it. They played credible baseball to the end, but not enough to win. A 2–0 loss to the Cleveland Indians in the first game of a doubleheader on the last day of the season eliminated the White Sox from the race. They finished at 89–65, winning four fewer than in 1915, but only two games behind a Red Sox team that won its second consecutive World Series, defeating the Brooklyn Robins in five games.

The City Series in 1916 was really no match. Playing against a Cubs team which won only 67 games and finished 26 and one-half games behind the Robins, the White Sox took four straight. An interesting sidelight about the fourth game, played on a Saturday, was the betting. Over the years there was an increased interest in betting in baseball. Gamblers were an increasing presence at the ball park. Betting pools or syndicates were increasingly popular among the general population. It was telling that in the midst of a World Series where betting interest was at its annual peak, there were still large stakes placed on a city series between an also-ran and a second-place finisher. In its coverage of the fourth game, the *Tribune* noted that by sweeping the series, the White Sox "scored one for the honesty of baseball." Why? Because gamblers were betting that club owners would make sure that the series extended to a fifth game to ensure a Sunday contest and a big gate.[53]

Despite another reasonably successful season, as the schedule played out, rumors continued to circulate that Pants Rowland's job was in jeopardy. The Chicago press it seems had yet to embrace the White Sox leader. One rumor, quickly put to rest, even had John McGraw heading west to take the helm. It might have helped dampen the speculation if the club's owner had commented clearly about the situation. Comiskey's silence fueled the speculation that Collins or Schalk might be in line, but nothing came of it.

Collins was not interested in his team's managerial position at that point. He was too busy trying to figure out why his hitting was below par, at least for him, during the past season. On the year Eddie led his team in only two categories, games played (155), in which he was tied with Joe Jackson, and on-base percentage (.405). Most of the other categories were headed by Shoeless Joe, who fashioned a fine campaign, including a .341 batting average. Still, Collins' .308 figure was sixth in the league and his 86 walks third. His OBP was third. In reality it was a season which would disappoint only an elite star.

When he looked back on 1916, the highlight for Collins took place off the field. On November 23 Eddie and Mabel welcomed their second child, Edward Trowbridge Collins, Jr.

Just as there was reason for joy in the Collins family, as the Christmas season approached there was reason for joy for certain members of the White Sox family as well. On December

During the off-season Eddie Collins enjoyed spending time with his family. Here he is shown in late 1921 outside his Lansdowne, Pennsylvania, home with his sons Paul (standing), age 10, and Eddie, Jr., age five (Harry Ransom Humanities Research Center, University of Texas at Austin).

19 Commy announced Pants Rowland would return. A number of the Sox players were ecstatic, including Collins, Jackson and Buck Weaver, all of whom wrote to Commy to express their pleasure at his decision to retain their manager. Nothing was said about the return of Gleason or about Collins' position as captain, but the owner took a back-handed slap at Eddie's performance in that department.

"I [Comiskey] might have gone out on first base myself last year and maybe we would have won the pennant. Anyway, I know of one or two instances when I would have been under some fly balls, whether the captain forgot to holler who was to take the ball or not."[54]

Was someone complaining and blaming Collins for the team's failure to win it all? It is hard to tell, for the comments were made while Commy was in a jovial mood. He had just received a gift of a golf bag and clubs from Ban Johnson as the pair and their wives prepared to vacation in Excelsior Springs, Missouri.

Still, Commy had brought Collins and Jackson to Chicago, not to come close, but to win a pennant for his organization and for the city. Their price was high, and Commy was not a frivolous sort. Even though attendance continued to climb (679,923 — 1st in the A.L.), his club must win it all in 1917 or heads would roll. Under that sort of pressure cooker, one way or the other 1917 would be a season worth remembering.

CHAPTER 11

War Clubs

"While we played and frolicked, our fellow-men on the other side of the Earth suffered and died. While we tossed baseballs, they tossed hand-grenades; while our 'attack' consisted of a rally in the ninth, with bats and balls as the ammunition, our fellow-men in Europe rallied to save their homes and their families from ruthless aggressors, with death and devastation the price for failure."

— Eddie Collins[1]

If there is truth in the old adage that baseball championships are forged in the off-season, the 1917 Chicago White Sox are a fine example. Heading into the season Comiskey had a winner, but not a champion. Some tinkering was still needed. He solved his first base puzzle on February 25, just a short time before the team headed south for training camp, by purchasing Arnold "Chick" Gandil, who had played for the team in 1910. The White Sox eyed Gandil in 1915 when he was with the Senators, but in 1916 the Indians purchased him for $7,500. In 1917 the Indians placed him back on the market and the White Sox paid $3,500 to obtain his services. The fact a fine fielder and handy batsman with a lifetime .277 average was so available at age 29 should give one pause. Perhaps Commy blinked a couple of times, but the Sox were in need of a contributor at first, and Gandil fit the bill. It was left for Pants Rowland to deal with Gandil's shady side — he was friends with gamblers — and the rough edges honed while a boxer in his early years.

At shortstop the Zeb Terry "experiment" was a failure. One might consider looking beyond his anemic hitting (.190, 17 RBIs), but not his disappointing fielding (27 errors, .935 fielding average). Another solution was needed. The White Sox thought perhaps they found it when they purchased Charles "Swede" Risberg, a 22-year-old infielder from Vernon, California, of the Pacific Coast League. In fact, other than a strong arm, at the time of his purchase Risberg seemed to offer little more than Terry. Moreover, like Gandil, he was a fellow with a gritty demeanor. For now at least, he permitted the White Sox the luxury of keeping Buck Weaver at third.

One additional piece to the puzzle had been added on the pitching side in 1916. During that season as in the rebuilding years preceding it, the one constant for the ball team on Chicago's South Side was its pitching. In 1916 the hurlers led by Red Faber, Eddie Cicotte, Lefty Williams, Reb Russell and Joe Benz led the American League in ERA at 2.36. The staff grew stronger with the addition of left-handed reliever Dave Danforth. Called "Dauntless Dave" for continuing to pitch despite arm troubles, Danforth was later the subject of controversy and was even suspended for a time for throwing "doctored" baseballs. But in 1917, a time when relief pitching was still a step-child, Danforth came to the rescue often enough (over 40 relief appearances) and with such success (9 saves) that he made a real difference.

His team's roster in place, Commy announced that this would be an intensified spring.

In order to be better conditioned for their campaign, the White Sox planned to arrive in Mineral Wells one week earlier than normal.

There was to be another difference in spring 1917. For three years a war had raged in Europe. More and more it appeared it was a conflict that would eventually engulf the United States. In recognition and preparation, plans were in place for baseball players to conduct regular military drills. There was talk a drill sergeant would be assigned to run the White Sox through their paces in spring training and throughout the regular season.

When the team finally reported, one face was missing. The great Ed Walsh, in Collins' opinion the best of all the spitballers, was no longer with the club. During his 13 seasons with the White Sox, his record was 195–125, his ERA less than 1.82. In 1917 he played a limited role for the Boston Braves as he completed his career.

The team held its first workout on March 6. Collins, who was still the team's captain, had every reason to miss that first practice — his trunk did not arrive with the others — but when the men hit the field, there he was in a variety of clothes borrowed from various teammates.

On March 10 the White Sox's organization followed through with their plans to provide the team with a military presence. A White Sox, BNG Company (Baseball National Guard) was formed, led by Sergeant Walter Smally, a member of the country's armed forces. He in turn nominated White Sox team members Pants Rowland, James Scott, Ray Schalk, Reb Russell and Eddie Collins as corporals to lead their mates in various drills. In view of the rampant rumors concerning a draft which would include conscription of ball players and a shortened season, the drills were a minor inconvenience at worst and probably a welcome exercise. In this way the players felt they were doing their part, at least in some small way.

In between the military drills the Sox prepared for a pennant run. In order to bring along several youngsters, Commy scheduled to play only minor league clubs during spring training. It made for a scary situation early on as a wild pitcher, perhaps nervous in the face of major leaguers, hit Collins twice, once on the foot and then in the head. Eddie left the game but was not seriously injured.

On April 6 the U.S. declared war on Germany. The Americans were in to stay in what now was a world war. Wartime disposition of professional ball players was no longer hypothetical. An article in the *Tribune* in early April indicated that a number of Sox regulars would be draft-eligible under current plans, including Faber, Williams and their rising outfield star, Happy Felsch.[2] Collins was not mentioned.

The 1917 season opened in St. Louis on April 11 and the Sox were ready. They won behind a good performance by Jim Scott, 7–2. Collins was 1-for-3 and walked. New first baseman Gandil went 3-for-4, including a double. After a loss, Eddie Cicotte took the mound and pitched a no-hitter, winning 11–0. Collins went 2-for-3 and scored three times.

Cicotte's mastery of the Browns did not surprise Collins. His "best assets were his control and cleverness. Always a spitball pitcher, he nevertheless was constantly experimenting. Dave Danforth, who originated the so-called 'shine ball,' gave him his best lead. Cicotte, watching him, worked at it until he had it all but perfect. Thereafter he was almost unbeatable."[3]

Collins' description of Cicotte's invincibility, at least in 1917, was not far from wrong. Rubbing the ball on his uniform to achieve a smoothness or "shine," Cicotte increased the effectiveness of his curve, with a concomitant increase in his results. By season's end the pitcher's record was 28–12, his league-best ERA a pleasing 1.53.

The home opener on April 19 saw the Browns involved again. Over 27,000 fans braved a rainy day and watched the Sox take one on the chin, 6–2. The highlight was the pre-game military exercise performed by a much-improved group of White Sox marchers. Major General Barry of the army and Ban Johnson watched from the stands as the team, dressed in full army uniform and each member carrying a Springfield rifle, marched to the sounds of a band whose beat was drowned out by the throaty roar of the surprised crowd. After Major General Barry inspected his "troops," they changed clothes and played some ball.

Collins felt that the drills were a benefit to his team. Writing in the *Tribune*, he acknowledged that his group marched like "rookies" at the start, but improved more rapidly because of the "discipline of the ball field." The "coordination so necessary for successful team work was undoubtedly a great aid." Instead of a detriment to preparation for their season, "we were more fit for ball playing after a week of drill than we would have been without it."[4]

Perhaps the drills did help. There is no denying the White Sox enjoyed some early-season success in 1917. By the end of April their record stood at 10–6. Collins' early pace was not quite as fast, hitting only .233.

In early May it seemed the entire White Sox club caught Collins' hitting illness. On May 5 the Sox found out what it was like to be on the negative side of a no-hitter when Ernie Koob, a former collegiate pitching star, repaid the favor of Eddie Cicotte's gem with one of his own. The Browns won, 1–0, when Swede Risberg, learning on the job, dropped a pop fly that led to the game's lone tally off a George Sisler single. Losing pitcher Cicotte only allowed five hits.

The next day the White Sox were no-hit and lost again, 3–0, this time by former Federal Leaguer Bob Groom. The fact that this was the second game of a twin bill and they garnered nine hits in the opener did little to alleviate the embarrassment since they lost that one as well, 8–4. The White Sox did not panic, however. Pants Rowland kept his lineup intact, despite the unnerving fact his team now stood 11–10 and the expected front-runner, Boston, was on top.

Rowland's calm approach to his team's brief slump worked. On May 12 his boys defeated the Yankees, 2–1, and proceeded to win eight straight during a home stand that included two out of three wins from the Red Sox. The latter victories were fueled by the team's negative reaction to false reports that Commy was about to replace Pants with former Red Sox manager Bill Carrigan.

Overall, the team compiled a 17–7 record in May. Although Collins was still not hitting at his usual clip, he made up for it by working pitchers for even more walks than usual. In addition, he provided stellar glove work in stabilizing the Sox's infield. And in the May 19 win over the Red Sox, a team now managed by his friend, Jack Barry, Collins' bat finally heated up as he went 3-for-5, including a triple, two runs scored and an RBI.

A 2–1 loss to the Red Sox on May 20 behind submariner Carl Mays ended the eight-game streak. Perhaps a bean ball delivered by Mays that struck Happy Felsch kept the White Sox from digging in at the plate.

In June the White Sox went on an extended road trip. They were playing well, despite the loss of pitchers Faber and Scott to injury. When they arrived in Boston for an important four-game set with the Red Sox beginning June 15, their record stood at 33–17 and they were in first place by a game and one-half. The initial game went to the Chicago bunch, 8–0, behind a Lefty Williams shutout. A Joe Jackson triple in the fourth which followed Collins' single was all the left-hander needed to complete his task. Nothing in that game, however, prepared Organized Baseball for what happened the next day.

On June 16 Eddie Cicotte and Babe Ruth faced off in what promised to be a tense, hard-fought game. By way of background, in late May the defending world champion Red Sox were in the midst of a ten-game (with one tie) win streak, looking every bit an odds-on favorite to repeat as champs. Then while playing at home where they entered every game a favorite, they lost nine of 13. The defeats cost the Boston gambling establishment, and a large and active contingent it was, a lot of money. As a result, they were in a nasty mood. With the White Sox ahead 2–0 and a light mist turning to rain, the gamblers saw an opportunity to cut yet another loss. Because of the rain, a portion of the crowd moved into the covered pavilion area where the gamblers regularly sat; then they stormed the field hoping to delay the game until it could be called due to the increasing effects of the rain. Instead, the umpire called a time out. In the ensuing melee, which resulted when several of the White Sox's players fought off the rioting ticket-holders, Buck Weaver was hit by a bottle. Because of a lack of police presence in the park, the fracas lasted longer than need be, but eventually the game continued and the White Sox won, 7–2. Warrants were issued for the arrest of Weaver and White Sox utility infielder Fred McMullin for allegedly assaulting fans. Nothing came of the charge, but a civil suit was filed by allegedly aggrieved fans.

The cause of the riot, not the riot itself, served as a warning sign to at least one observer, sportswriter James Crusinberry of the *Tribune*. The next day he wrote that unhappy gamblers incited the crowd to riot and "unless the American League or both major leagues take some decisive action to stamp out gambling in the ball parks in Boston, there are likely to be repetitions." He then asked why "the betting ring is allowed in Boston and not tolerated in other cities."[5]

Ban Johnson answered back by admitting that a problem existed, at least in Boston, and while "friendly wagers, with often a dinner or a cigar as the stake, do no harm," baseball will go after "the men who try to make a business of establishing themselves at the daily games and taking bets from all comers."[6]

Just how hard would Johnson and baseball's owners go after the gambling establishment? And, if they did, was it already too late to overcome the deeply embedded stranglehold the wagering community had over the game? These are questions that only time would answer. For now, as authors Warren N. Wilbert and William C. Hageman related in their study *The 1917 White Sox*, "the warning bells were ringing loud and clear."[7] As such, there could be little excuse on the part of ownership or players for what happened later.

Following the raucous events on June 16, the Red Sox fought back, winning a twin bill two days later. It might have signaled the demise of a lesser club, but this White Sox team was for real. One of the reasons was solid infield play; the insertion of Risberg at shortstop was finally paying dividends. Despite making a lot of errors, he possessed an uncanny ability to range far and wide for ground balls. Weaver was a tower of strength at third and Collins gave him his just due.

"'Buck' Weaver liked to play ball better than anyone I have ever seen. It has always been said that Jimmy Collins was the greatest artist at third of all time. I don't dispute it, but I'd rather have had 'Buck' on my team. He played great ball at short, but was a trifle erratic there and preferred third.

"He was a wonder on hard-hit balls and bunts. Those hit with moderate speed gave him what little trouble he experienced. Though he was great as a fielder he was still better as a batter and base runner. He batted equally well right or left-handed."[8]

Fortified by a properly positioned Weaver, the Chicago Americans remained in first place until a pair of losses to the Tigers on July 5 and 6 knocked them into second. During June Collins' bat remained relatively cool. At the midpoint in the season, he was hitting just .260. Weaver led the club at .281. Still, Collins was able to come through with timely hits. On June 20 he was responsible for all three runs in a 3–2 win over the Indians as he tripled to drive in two and scored one himself. On June 29 he supported a strong Red Faber performance with a pair of hits, including a triple in another close win over the Tribe, 3–1.

In 1917 Red Faber won a number of important games and exhibited the form which eventually landed him a spot in the Baseball Hall of Fame. Collins considered Faber the real successor to Ed Walsh. While he praised Faber's control of the spitter, as well as his array of pitches, and felt Faber did not always receive the proper recognition, he most admired his "unbounded courage and incorruptible integrity."[9]

On July 8 the White Sox regained the league lead with an 8–4 win over another weak Athletics team. For the next month or so, the White Sox played well enough to hold the lead, although the Red Sox remained close at hand and occasionally jumped into first. The front runners met thirteen times and the White Sox won seven. One game ended in a tie after 15 innings.

The Chicagoans finally obtained some breathing room on July 23 when they defeated the Red Sox at Comiskey, 5–3. The win gave the White Sox a four and one-half game cushion. The hitting star was not Collins — he went 1-for-4 — but Hap Felsch. By now Felsch was an important cog in the White Sox machinery both at the plate and in the field. When it came to Felsch's ability to play the game, Collins spared few words.

"'Happy' Felsch was the greatest right-hand hitter I have seen since Lajoie. I think as a fielder he ranked next to Speaker, which is the best compliment I can think of.... For throwing, ranging over a vast territory, coming in and fielding ground balls, Felsch never had an equal except 'Spoke.'"[10]

The performance of the White Sox during the 1917 season is remarkable for more than just the team's overall result. In assessing the season it is important to keep in mind the schedule was played against the backdrop of a worldwide conflagration; one in which many of these still young and fit athletes were expected eventually to participate.

On July 21 in the midst of one of the crucial series with the Red Sox, Buck Weaver learned he drew a low number in the draft lottery, meaning he might be one of the first married men called to serve. Up until that time married players such as Schalk, Collins, Gandil and Weaver had less to worry about. Unlike Weaver, Collins had a high draft number and was, therefore, well down the list for any type of call-up. The number of married players meant the White Sox would remain essentially intact for the remainder of the season. While Weaver and others awaited their fate, Jim Scott did not. He enlisted and awaited assignment.

Despite the tense situation, the season brought its usual share of amusing incidents. In one of the July wins over the Red Sox, Buck Weaver fouled off 17 balls before he finally flied out. Play was stopped for a time because the umpires ran out of balls. Weaver sat down on the ground and Collins, the on-deck hitter, returned to the bench. There was a real concern the game might be called for darkness before Weaver completed his lengthy at-bat.

If the Red Sox, a team powered by the hitting of outfielders Harry Hooper and Duffy Lewis and the pitching of Babe Ruth, Dutch Leonard and Carl Mays, hoped to catch the White Sox, the guys wearing the pale hose put the idea to rest with an impressive spurt in late August and early September. Beginning August 23 and ending September 14, they won 18 of 19 to salt away a pennant. The game that may have given them the confidence for such a run occurred three weeks earlier on August 1. It was a 4–0 shutout over those Red Sox fashioned by Reb Russell. The victory stopped a four-game losing streak and, coupled with a 7–1 gem over Boston the next day by Red Faber, sent Comiskey's boys on their way. Collins made himself useful in each game with a hit and a run.

There were a few reversals before the team went on its victory surge. On August 10 against the Senators, Buck Weaver slapped a hard tag on Washington catcher Eddie Ainsmith and broke the index finger on his glove hand. The injury knocked the valuable third sacker from the lineup until September 24. His place was taken by Fred McMullin.

Then on August 17 the White Sox lost to the A's in a 12-inning, 9–7 defeat. The frustrating loss temporarily cost the White Sox the lead. More significant, it was the last appearance for Jim Scott, as a few days later he became the first major league player called to active duty. Already in service was Hank Gowdy, who had enlisted.

These setbacks did little to alter the White Sox's course. By the time Scott left for boot camp the win streak was in full swing, having started in rather remarkable fashion on August 23, a day when the team marched in full military dress as part of its effort to win Ban Johnson's $500 prize for the best marching baseball squad in the league. The White Sox may not have won the final prize in that competition, but a bigger prize awaited.

Between August 23 and September 14, the only defeat suffered by the White Sox was a 6–3 loss to the Browns at Comiskey on September 1. At the end of the day, the White Sox led the Red Sox by three and one-half games, although both teams were even at 47 in the ever-important loss column. Next on the schedule came the Tigers for back to back doubleheaders on September 2 and 3. The Tigers were fighting the Indians for third-place money.

The four-game set with the Tigers, seemingly only one in a number of important series during the season, goes down as one of the most analyzed and discussed four-game regular season series in the annals of baseball. In the 1920s there were allegations the series was fixed. In 1917 it saw the White Sox, in the midst of a terrific hot streak, beat the Tigers four straight over a Labor Day weekend. The first game was won by the White Sox, 7–2, on September 2. The second game that day went 10 innings, the White Sox a 6–5 winner. The next day the White Sox ruled again, 7–5 and 14–8.

In this particular series the scores, actually fairly close, did not tell the whole story. In the series the White Sox, a team which at times ran poorly during the season, stole 20 bases, seven in one game. They also were walked 22 times, and the Tigers fielded miserably, committing 10 errors. Yet coming as it did, in the midst of a pennant race, the games were reported and nothing more.[11] The critical analysis was for later — much later.

The White Sox had the Tigers' number in 1917, winning 16 of the 22 times they met. On the other hand, the Tigers fared the best of any American League team against the Boston Red Sox. Their 12–9 record over the defending champs was one better than Chicago's 12–10. This too would become a matter for discussion and controversy at a later time.

After the White Sox tamed the Tigers, their lead was six and one-half games. In short order the organization was accepting applications for World Series tickets. They would have little problem selling the ducats. For quite some time the crowds at Comiskey, often supplemented by men in khaki uniforms, were large and vocal. The White Sox were, for the time being, the only show in town.

Now talk turned to just when the Pale Hose might clinch the pennant. Even before that happened, talk reached Pants Rowland that the team was planning a banquet to celebrate. Pants feared overconfidence. Writer James Crusinberry reported that the manager was upset about the banquet until he heard Collins and Eddie Murphy talking about all the alcohol they planned to consume at the event. Realizing the two were teetotalers, he and the others on the team knew it was all a big joke. According to Crusinberry, "All who knew these two athletes [Collins and Murphy] expect to see them going arm and arm that night [after the team clinches] across to the drugstore to celebrate with an ice cream soda."[12]

Most observers were more confident about the team's pennant chances than its manager. Rowland and Collins were offered an opportunity to write about the forthcoming World Series for a New York syndicate. They even told Pants someone would write his material for him, but he politely declined. Collins, who would write his own copy anyway, did not divulge his plans.

The White Sox put Pants at ease on September 21 with a 10-inning win over the Red Sox in Boston. It was the start of a three-game series with the Beantowners. The White Sox lost the next two, but it did not matter. They were the new flag holders. At the conclusion of the game, Rowland announced that with only eight games remaining, he would rest several of his regulars, including Collins. But Eddie remained in the lineup, perhaps because he was in the midst of a long streak of consecutive games played.

When the season ended on October 1 with a 4–2 loss to the Yankees and the White Sox a full nine games in front of the Red Sox, Collins could look back on a regular season that saw him struggle, but as was so often the case, still play his best ball at crunch time. His .289 batting average was well below his career figure, but the fact it was at or near his season-high offered proof of his strong play during the White Sox's hot streak. Overall, he had over forty multi–hit games and bunted, stole bases and walked with his usual skill and timeliness. His OBP of .389 was sixth best in the league. His 91 runs fourth. His 89 walks and 53 stolen bases were second. Only two American Leaguers reached base more times than Collins. All this on what some called an "off year."

As the season played out, plans were announced by the Woodland Bards for a banquet, this time for real, to honor the team. Arguments were made for a gala event for over 1,400 persons at the Edgewater Beach Hotel. The price for fans to see their heroes was $10 a head, a hefty price at the time. On the ballfield arrangements were made for a pair of post–season exhibition games with the Indians to keep the American League champions sharp.

Collins did not play in that first exhibition against the Indians. He, as well as Eddie Cicotte and coach Kid Gleason, the guy many observers credited with the White Sox's success, were in New York scouting their team's World Series opponents, an old Collins' favorite, the New York Giants.

Although they were still managed by John McGraw, this was a decidedly different Giants team than Collins faced in 1913. Gone were Matty and Marquard, replaced by another Rube, this one named Benton (15–9, 2.72), and by Ferdie Schupp (21–7, 1.95), Pol Perritt (17–7, 1.88) and Slim Sallee (18–7, 2.17). Jeff Tesreau was still around, but not quite as effective at 13–8, 3.09. The hitting attack was led by an outfield consisting of George Burns, Dave Robertson and the Ty Cobb of the Federal League, Benny Kauff. Then there was Collins' counterpart at second base, Buck Herzog, who was coming off an injury which hampered his season. And finally, at third base was an old friend from Eddie's semipro days in Red Neck, New York, the irrepressible Heinie Zimmerman, who had played the bulk of his career for the Chicago Cubs, leading the National League in hitting and home runs in 1912 at .372 and 14, respectively. The Giants, winners of 98 games in 1917, were nothing to be trifled with, but then neither were the White Sox. Most thought the series a toss-up, although some felt the Giants' experience as a World Series entrant gave them the edge.

The lineup Rowland penciled in for Game One, an October 6 affair in Chicago, contained one change. In Weaver's absence Fred McMullin played a solid third base and fielded well. Upon Buck's return McMullin remained at third, Weaver moved back to short, and Risberg was benched.

Based upon his fabulous regular season (28–12, 1.53), the White Sox's choice of Eddie Cicotte for the opening game starter was easy. The Giants countered with lefty Slim Sallee. Both pitchers flashed strong performances, each team being held to seven hits. The difference was that Cicotte's game effort was backed by a Happy Felsch solo home run in the bottom of the fourth and a sensational play in the outfield by Joe Jackson, robbing Giants first baseman Walter Holke of a probable triple. As a result, the Chicagoans won, 2–1, sending over 32,000 home happy. Collins was happy with the victory, if not his hitless performance.

The 1917 Chicago White Sox were winners of the American League and the World Series. They are: (back row, left to right) Eddie Collins, Buck Weaver, Eddie Murphy, Chick Gandil, Joe Benz, Ted Jourdan, Swede Risberg, and Red Faber; (middle row) Fred McMullin, Mellie Wolfgang, Joe Jenkins, Manager Pants Rowland, Eddie Cicotte, Byrd Lynn, Reb Rusell, and Happy Felsch; (front row) Ziggy Hasbrook, Lefty Williams, John "Shano" Collins, Nemo Leibold, and Joe Jackson (National Baseball Hall of Fame Library, Cooperstown, New York).

Game Two took place the next day, also at Comiskey. Once again the Sox were the winners, this time 7–2. Red Faber was the pitching star, shutting down the Giants' attack after the second inning. Ferdie Schupp, another lefty, started but was ineffective and departed in the second inning. Joe Jackson was one hitting hero, driving in a pair in a five-run fourth inning. Collins' single in that inning, one of two on the day, drove in a run, and he swiped a pair of bases before the books were closed. Another 32,000 smiled and basked in the sun on this beautiful fall day.

The series switched to New York for Game Three and with it the White Sox's fortunes. After another day's delay due to rain, the contests resumed on October 10 with a rested Cicotte facing Rube Benton. Once again Chicago's shine-ball ace was terrific, yielding but two runs. But New York was better, limiting the Sox to five hits and no runs. For the second game in a row, Collins was 2-for-4. Game Four is best described as the "Benny Kauff Show." The Giants' outfielder, an early day Joe "Willie" Namath in the manner in which he flashed his broad smile and flashy clothes on the Great White Way, seared his brand into World Series lore by hitting a pair of home runs to lead the Giants to a 5–0 victory and knot the series at 2–2. Red Faber, like Cicotte not so fortunate on his second go-round with the Giants, took the loss. Ferdie Schupp, to the contrary much more effective than in his first outing, gained the win. His shutout raised the White Sox's string of scoreless innings to 22. Collins was 1-for-3 and stole a base.

Comiskey Park was the site for the pivotal Game Five, played before 27,000 White Sox faithful on October 13. What they saw in the first two innings was not to their liking as the Giants knocked surprise starter Reb Russell from the box, taking a 2–0 lead while their starter, Sallee, extended the White Sox's string of futility to 24 innings. Now Cicotte was on the mound, followed by Lefty Williams, and they did little better. In the middle of the seventh, the Sox trailed, 5–2, having ended their scoreless streak with a tally in the third and another in the sixth. Then the White Sox rallied. Singles by Jackson and Felsch and a Chick Gandil double scored two. Later in the same inning, Gandil scored on a delayed double steal when Herzog botched the throw to second. The game was tied. The Sox broke it open with three in the bottom of the eighth and won it, 8–5. The White Sox now were but one away from a world championship. When it was over, Collins, who had three hits and a walk in five trips and scored a pair, stated, "I have been in many a world series game, but never in one like this one today."[13] Years later he would say, "To my mind, this was the deciding game."[14]

Perhaps Collins had never been in a World Series game like Game Five in 1917. However, when the White Sox arrived back in New York City for Game Six, he was about to play in one that his fans and baseball historians, for that matter, would remember a lot longer. For this one Pants went back to Red Faber, Cicotte having toiled for six innings in the previous contest. McGraw chose Rube Benton as his starter. The teams were scoreless through three. As was true throughout this series, the fourth frame was an impact inning. Since a play that developed in that fourth inning was Collins' most famous, it bears analysis from his vantage point.

At the time Collins was resting on third base. He reached there by virtue of a two-base throwing error by third baseman Heinie Zimmerman, followed by right fielder Dave Robertson's misplay of a Joe Jackson fly ball. Jackson now stood at first. When the next hitter, Happy Felsch, hit back to Benton on the mound, Eddie edged off third toward home, hoping just to draw a throw and avoid a double play. It worked. Benton tossed the ball to Giants catcher Bill Rariden, and the fun began.

As Rariden held the ball, Collins sashayed back and forth along the base path between third and home. Rariden was standing outside the base path by the time he tossed the ball to Zimmerman. When Eddie turned he alertly saw home plate was uncovered and tore for the plate. Zim took the only course now open to him. He gave good chase, but was unable to catch the speedy Collins.

"In a World's Series game when you see a base uncovered you run for it. You don't waste time. Believe me I [Collins] didn't waste any time on that play. If the clear path to the plate struck me as amazing, I didn't let it cause me any worry or stop to ponder on the miracle. Zimmerman wasn't even close as I crossed the plate.

"At least two, possibly three other men could have covered the plate on that play. It just happened they didn't. Why they didn't I'll never know. As I look back on that play I'm sorry to see Heinie made the goat — for he was the least to blame."[15]

Now the Sox led 1–0, with Jackson on third and Felsch on second. That meant later, when Chick Gandil singled to center, the score climbed to 3–0. The Giants, who scored two in the fifth, were never able to overcome the lead. The White Sox, behind another strong performance from Faber — he won three games in all — were world champions. The feat was accomplished with Faber and Cicotte pitching all but two innings in the six games played.

It was the fourth World Series championship for Collins in seven seasons, the first for many of his White Sox teammates. Once again Eddie lived up to his reputation as a money player, hitting .409, scoring four times and stealing three.

And, of course, there was that "Zim" play. The next day the play was the talk of the town and the country. Ignoring the fact Zimmerman's biggest mistake was his wild throw which put Collins on second in the first place, as well as paying scant attention to the other active culprits in the misguided scenario such as Rariden and first baseman Walt Holke, the sports scribes had a field day. They ignored Collins' attempts to excuse the actions of a friend. Instead, as the dust settled around that third base bag, they hopped aboard the best line of all, spun off the typewriter of the ever-creative Ring Lardner, who had Zimmerman barking out, "Who the hell was I going to throw the ball to, Klem [the home plate umpire]?"[16]

The headline over Hugh Fullerton's article in the *Atlanta Constitution* summed it up for the scribes. It read: "Heinie Zimmerman's Bone One of History's Classics."[17] Fullerton, who felt the better team won the game and the series, had earlier noted the intensity of the combatants, predicting the clubs were on the edge of a free-for-all several times during the games, based upon the bench-jockeying and rough play. In one instance, he recalled Collins and the Giants' Art Fletcher jaw to jaw until the umpires pulled them apart.[18] Perhaps then no one should have been surprised at John McGraw's reaction to Pants Rowland's attempt to console him after the last game. When he was approached he told Pants, "Get away from me, you god — damned busher."[19]

It might surprise some that in Eddie Collins' opinion, the 1917 White Sox were "the greatest team ever assembled."[20] This is a rather remarkable statement when one recalls that Collins participated in a number of other World Series and had the opportunity to later play against some of the great Yankee powerhouses. He voiced this opinion almost 25 years later, and it was his final say on the matter.

At least in 1917 in the Deadball Era, it was hard to argue the point. There was the White Sox's record that year, 100–54, for one. Then there was the fantastic pitching, including Faber and Cicotte in their prime, accompanied by Reb Russell and the skyrocketing Lefty Williams, plus Dave Danforth to mop up if needed. As to the regulars, there was that infield, now solidified, which boasted Weaver, Gandil, Risberg and Collins himself. And in the outfield, besides Happy Felsch, a .308 hitter with good power and wonderful fielding acumen, there was the great Joe Jackson, at 27 in the prime of an already illustrious career. Behind the plate was Ray Schalk.

Collins never could say enough about Schalk. The catcher was admittedly small in stature, but it was a deficiency "he more than made up for in guts, gumption and grit." Eddie saluted the way Schalk blocked the plate and his ability to shoot the ball like a bullet to any base to cut down a potential theft. But perhaps most of all he marveled at his friend's durability.[21]

Schalk and the rest of the world champs arrived in Chicago by train on the afternoon of October 17, the welcome mat out. Brass bands and a number of speakers joined hundreds of fans at the station to greet the conquerors. Commy had arrived the day before to the cheers of the Woodland Bards. He sang the praises of Rowland, Collins and the others. All in all, the Sox seemed just one happy family — a troupe whose members were about to take home a World Series share of $3,669 a piece.

The Sox, however, almost didn't get a portion of their money. One day after the series the two participants lined up at Camp Mills on Long Island for an exhibition game for the soldiers. A highlight of the game, won by the White Sox, 6–3, was a recreation of the "Zim boner" with Fred McMullin and Germany Schaefer, baseball's playing-comedian, acting as the participants. The game was part of a planned barnstorming trip between the two teams, but the National Commission felt such a trip took away from the glamour and importance of the World Series and withheld $1,000 to ensure no further games would be played. The White Sox got their share on time only because Charles Comiskey put up the amount involved in order to guarantee compliance.

Comiskey was a paradox of sorts. While to the outside world he seemed an exceedingly generous man, some of his players saw him in a different light. They saw attendance at Comiskey Park soar to over 680,000, once again the league's best following. They knew what that meant on the deposit side of their owner's bank account. They saw his generous side and how much he gave to charity. For example, in 1917 10 percent of his gross receipts, an amount in excess of $17,000, was sent to the Chicago Chapter of the Red Cross for European war relief.[22] Yet at the same time, many team members felt they were given short shrift when it came to contract time and were underpaid. In addition, they could grouse at their owner and complain among themselves when it came to reimbursement for their expenses, including the fact their boss would not foot the bill to launder their uniforms. In fact, many of the players on the White Sox decided, perhaps to save money or maybe out of defiance, to forgo the washing process. Eventually their white socks became black from the dirt on the playing fields. Some observers jokingly began calling the team the "Black Sox," the name of a Chicago National League entry in the 1800s, as well as a term that would one day assume a new and quite different meaning for the city's American League franchise.

In truth, many baseball historians now believe that in the late teens the individual salaries paid the White Sox were reasonably commensurate with those paid other ball players of that era. Also, Commy's policy regarding expenses, including laundry, was really no different than that of other ball clubs. What Commy did face, perhaps forcing him to take a closer look at his bottom line, was one of the higher payrolls in baseball due to the higher number of quality ball players he had accumulated to build a championship team. And one of these ball players was making a lot more money than any other player on the team.

In 1915 when Eddie Collins was sold to the White Sox, he took a hard line and wisely negotiated a lucrative long-term contract for himself. His salary of $15,000 per year became public knowledge. Everyone knew what Collins was making. Only players like Ty Cobb of the Tigers and Tris Speaker, formerly of the Red Sox and now the Indians, were making more. There was certainly wage disparity on their teams as well, but the makeup of the White Sox made for differences in their acceptance and the response to the circumstance.

The difference in salaries on the White Sox, when coupled with the team's success, bred serious discontent. In the days following the peace agreement with the Feds, baseball salaries were shrinking, not rising, as owners no longer were required to look across the street to see what the competition was paying. Collins' salary, however, was locked in until 1920. On some clubs the players would look at the value Collins added to their team and adapt to it. They would bide their time, play hard and hope their performance would enable them to increase their salary base in the future. A number of the players on the White Sox did just that, but a number of others did not. Players like Chick Gandil were not the type, when aroused by envy, to back down. Gandil is described by the authors of *The 1917 White Sox* as one who "didn't smile much, was quick to draw a line in the dirt over what he perceived to be assaults on his manhood, and was in the forefront of every battle *mano a mano,* in which the Sox were involved."[23]

Chick Gandil did not like Eddie Collins. It is said his problems with the man pre–dated their days on the White Sox, stemming from a fielding play in 1912 when Gandil was with Washington and Collins with the A's. Gandil went into second base and Eddie's tag broke his nose.[24] It was probably one of those times Gandil drew a line in the dirt, but it is possible the pair would have eventually clashed anyway once they were thrown together on the same team. The educated and by now quite wealthy and refined Collins was the polar opposite of the rough and tumble Gandil. Eddie would fight given significant cause; Gandil would fight just to fight. Collins, as team captain and by nature a leader, had a good number of supporters, but Gandil had his as well, which included the young, impressionable, but also rough-cut, Swede Risberg. Then there was Buck Weaver, in great need of money and unhappy over his lot, who had declared bankruptcy just a few months earlier. And there was Joe Jackson, an uneducated man, who respected Collins but felt ostracized by him and others like him while in Philadelphia. He was friends with Lefty Williams, another who felt underpaid, along with Eddie Cicotte and Hap Felsch.

The word "cliques" might be an oversimplification, but loose-knit lines were forming behind Collins and Gandil, and Gandil's group was unhappy even in the face of triumph in October 1917. Commy's determination to hold the wage line in 1918, as he feared the effects of war on baseball in general and his team in particular, only made matters worse. In his study of the White Sox teams of that era, baseball scholar Robert Cottrell discusses the end of 1917, Commy's broken promises and White Sox salaries for 1918.

"In the midst of the 1917 season, Comiskey promised a team bonus if the White Sox won the pennant. The actual payoff was a case of poor-quality champagne, which enraged his entire squad. Even following the World Series triumph, Comiskey proved no more generous. Weaver, for example, was forced to accept the same $6,000 salary he had first secured three years earlier, when he was a far less skilled batter and fielder. The great Joe Jackson received the same pay [$6,000], Schalk a mere $1,000 more and Cicotte $1,000 less. Felsch was paid but $3,750, first baseman Chick Gandil got only $4,000, and Williams signed a contract for the 1918 season that set his salary at $3,000. Meanwhile, Eddie Collins, whom Weaver despised for refusing to sharpen his spikes during the World Series like the other White Sox, was paid $15,000 a year."[25]

Weaver's reaction to Collins, much like Gandil's, seems out of proportion to Collins' alleged conduct. It seems more appropriate to posture that Gandil, Weaver and the others were really condemning Eddie for achieving what they all sought — top dollar for their performance on the ball field. The fact that Collins achieved that goal, their goal, and they to date had not, made him a "company" man in their eyes, Commy's "man," so to speak. The fact he was college-educated and by nature somewhat reserved and aloof only added to that image, further separating him from that faction of his team. In reality, Collins was not Commy's "boy." The two respected each other at least in their early relationship but were never close.

Collins was no fool. He felt the rising animosity on the White Sox squad. Perhaps that was one of the factors, patriotism the more obvious, which led him to write league president Ban Johnson in mid–December 1917 telling the executive he was thinking of entering the service.

Despite his correspondence with Ban Johnson, when it came time for spring training in 1918, Collins was still a civilian. Instead of basic training during the off-season, he spent time hunting with Jack Dunn, touring in his automobile and playing some golf. In February he attended the baseball winter meetings in New York City and ran into Pants Rowland, who told reporters, Eddie "looked fine. [He] had been skating and shoveling snow all winter and is eager for the start."[26]

No trades involving the White Sox were made at the winter meetings. No one wanted to help the prohibitive favorites capture a second straight pennant and world title. The main concerns for White Sox management entering the new season were, first, whether or not there would even be a season in view of the war, and second, which players would be available for the season. At present Collins was on the roster. Since he had yet to enlist, he was placed in Class 4 as a married man, his presence in uniform required only if the service ran out of eligible single men.

The team left for Texas in mid–March but missed its first day of training when the tender of the locomotive pulling their train jumped the track east of Weatherford, Texas. Fortunately, the railroad cars themselves did not derail and the only result was a three-hour delay in the team's arrival time.

In spite of the dissatisfaction of several Sox players with their new contracts, the only early spring holdout was pitcher Reb Russell. Early on, the team received another jolt when a vehicle carrying Schalk, Cicotte, Jackson and Gandil was in a collision. The group was returning from a golf outing. Cicotte's neck was wrenched and Gandil complained of back problems. When Commy heard about the affair, he was so upset he banned golf and motoring for the duration of the camp.

Collins was late in arriving that spring, staying in Philadelphia to help Ray Thomas coach the University of Pennsylvania team. By March 30 he was with the Chicago team in Houston, banging out three hits in an easy White Sox win. It was, nevertheless, a short training stint for the Sox's second baseman, for on April 11, after the team played a game in Wichita, Kansas, he fainted while being examined by a doctor for a severe cold. The diagnosis: tonsillitis, aggravated by the damp, cold sleeping conditions in the Pullman cars the team slept in along the tracks as they played their way north. Commy assigned Eddie Cicotte to accompany Collins ahead to Kansas City to rest and await the team.

If the train wreck, the auto accident and Collins' tonsils were not enough, the White Sox sustained the temporary loss of Buck Weaver due to the death of his father and Kid Gleason due to a squabble with Comiskey. Yet by April 16 all, except for Gleason, were ready and in place for another run at a flag.

Collins announced to Pants Rowland that he was fit as a fiddle for the home opener, but in the early going his abbreviated spring affected his play. In the opener his wild throw in the fifth led to two St. Louis runs and a Sox defeat, 6–1. On April 18 Lefty Williams threw a four-hit shutout to get the Pale Hose into the victory column.

Williams was now a mainstay of the White Sox staff. Collins considered him a "truly great pitcher.... His control was unusually good. He had a real fast ball, a fine curve, was smart and didn't know what it was to be afraid.... For cold, sublime nerve he never had a superior."[27]

The White Sox's split left them at .500 after two outings. Two months later few thought they would still be playing at such a pace, but that is exactly where matters stood. The team was troubled, tied for fourth, six out of first and saddled with a record of 27–27. In a season of few highlights, there was at least one for Collins. On April 26 the Sox faced off against the Browns in St. Louis with Collins in the lineup for his 473rd consecutive game.[28] The streak started on October 5, 1914. At one time it was the longest by a second baseman. However, it did not last long. On May 2, against Detroit, Eddie was not in the starting lineup due to a knee injury he sustained in a spiking incident in a game with the Indians, but he batted for Red Faber in the fourth inning and singled. It was his 478th straight game. When he did not play against the Tigers the next day, the streak ended. In his absence Swede Risberg played second and continued to do so for the next nine games until Collins returned on May 13. In the interim Eddie was permitted to travel home to Philadelphia where he could meet the team when they traveled east.

The 1918 season was, of course, an extremely difficult one, played as it was in the face of the uncertainties of war. Unlike 1917, when the vagaries of war really had little effect on baseball, in 1918 there were real concerns that the season would be canceled, followed by concerns the season could not be completed, all intermingled with the ever-changing status of individual players as interpreted by the U.S. government. In sum, as the season progressed there were no assurances about anything when it came to the business of baseball. During this season, marching in military formation, bat or sometimes rifle on shoulder was not going to be enough. Nor was Ban Johnson's offer to enlist.

One of the first players to feel the heat from the spotlight the government was beginning to put on baseball was Joe Jackson. Like Collins, the White Sox's right fielder was a married man and therefore in Class 4. In early 1918 the government sought additional manpower. On May 1 Jackson's local draft board in Greenville, South Carolina, changed his status to Class 1, making him eligible for the draft. On May 3 the *Tribune* speculated that Jackson would finish the season since his selection number was far down the list. Nonetheless, a few days later on May 11, Jackson took his military physical while the team was in Philadelphia. He passed the physical and learned he would be drafted in a matter of weeks, perhaps by the end of the month. Thus on May 13, only 17 games into his season, Jackson advised the White Sox he was leaving to take a job at Harlan and Hollingsworth Ship Building Company in Wilmington, Delaware. The company was involved in the defense industry and, not coincidentally, fielded a baseball team. In fact, a number of industries in that area fielded teams and were stocking them by actively recruiting from the major and minor leagues. The fact they were to be paid for the privilege of continuing to play baseball did not detract from the players' incentive to jump their professional teams. Jackson was just one such recruit, although perhaps the first and definitely the most high profile of the lot.

Just a few days later Jackson's move proved prophetic. On May 18 U.S. Secretary of War Newton D. Baker issued a "work or fight" order. In conjunction with the order was a ruling that baseball was a form of entertainment and, therefore, a "non–essential" occupation. As a result all ball players aged 21 to 31 were required to register for the draft or secure employment in a shipyard or defense plant by July 18. The order was later modified to permit the two leagues to play into early September, but for Joe Jackson the damage was done, even though the government's ruling legally stayed his draft status. Ban Johnson, Charles Comiskey and many newspapers in and outside Chicago leveled their verbal artillery, calling the players, who switched to industry, draft dodgers and the like.

Johnson held little back, declaring that players who took such jobs to evade military service should be "yanked into the Army by the coat collar. The American League ... does not approve of players trying to evade military service."[29]

Commy, obviously distressed at the prospect of losing many of his prize players, took the opportunity to wax patriotic when Lefty Williams and backup catcher Byrd Lynn left the team on June 11 to work and play ball at Jackson's shipyard.

"I don't consider them fit to play on my ball club. I would gladly lose my whole team if the players wished to do their duty to their country, ... but I hate to see any ball players, particularly my own, go to ship yards to escape military service.

"There can be no other reason for their act, as they can not honestly earn as much building ships as they can playing ball."[30]

While all this was going on, the White Sox suffered additional reversals. Collins continued to play injured, forced to do so because on May 15 Buck Weaver tore cartilage in his right foot. Then on June 4 pitching ace Red Faber announced plans to enlist in the navy. He would be around for a while, but his departure coupled with the loss of Lefty Williams spelled doom. To be sure other teams were losing players as well, but no team, even one with exceptional talent like the White Sox, could withstand such a series of blows. And the Sox did not. They fought gamely — their record at the July 4 mid–way point was 34–35 — but by the end of July they stood seven games under .500 at 43–50. Even when their pitching was good, the timely hitting, so important to their success the previous season, was just not there.

A hallmark of the White Sox's success for some time had been their pitching. In 1918 the staff was in shambles. Eddie Cicotte went from 28–12 to 12–19, his ERA over a run per game higher. Faber and Williams appeared in only 11 and 15 games, respectively. Dave Danforth went from 11–6, allowing 2.65 runs per game, to 6–15 and 3.43. To pick up the slack, management brought in 19-year-old right-hander Frank Shellenback. He threw the spitter and went 9–12 in 28 games. They also brought in the veteran John Picus Quinn, another righty. At 34 Quinn was toiling away with the Vernon club in the Pacific Coast League, having last seen major league service in 1913. In the interim he played two seasons for Baltimore of the Federal League. The White Sox were able to purchase him because the Pacific Coast League, like most minor leagues, disbanded in mid–season due to the war. Before making the purchase, Commy checked with the National Commission and learned he could deal directly with the player. When Quinn pitched well — he went 5–1 with a 2.29 ERA — the White Sox decided they wished to keep him. However, although the National Commission had decided that for 1918 minor leaguers were free agents, they also decided the players would return to the rosters and ownership of their former minor league clubs once that league's operation resumed. Since the players were still owned by that club, it had the right to sell him. Unbeknownst to Commy, the New York Yankees had purchased Quinn from the Vernon club for the 1919 season. Commy protested and the case went before the National Commission, which consisted of the National League president, the supposedly neutral member Garry Herrmann (team president of the Reds) and American League president Ban Johnson. On April 26 the Commission ruled against the White Sox, awarding Quinn to the Yankees for 1919. They were apologetic, conceding the advice they gave Commy was misleading and inadvertently kept him from dealing directly with the Vernon club to purchase the pitcher.

Commy was furious. Even though he knew the Commission was a three-man operation, he blamed Ban Johnson for the ruling. The two men had a long history, at times stormy. In the beginning their friendship gave birth to the American League. Later there were disputes over supposed slights and gags that went too far when the men were together on their hunting trips. From time to time there were also disputes over the handling of issues related to baseball, including personnel. According to Johnson's biographer Eugene Murdock:

> Ban and Commy were both proud, strong-willed men. They fought hard for what they believed was right, and when things went badly for them, they did not accept defeat gracefully. As long as their interests did not conflict, there was little danger of a serious dispute. However, because of their respective positions, friction was bound to arise. Ban as league president had to govern in the interest of all eight clubs. Comiskey as president of one of those eight clubs had to guard his team's interests. If Chicago became involved in a dispute with another club, Johnson had to resolve the matter as fairly as he could, and he sometimes ruled against the White Sox. It was not the petty hunting gags that drove these men apart. It was the critical clashes over baseball policy — occasionally fanned out of proportion by the press — that were responsible for the deep-rooted and most unfortunate hatred.[31]

However, for almost ten years, from 1908 to 1918, the relationship between the pair was peaceful, if at times shaky. The men and their wives traveled together and as was seen during the holiday season in 1916, even exchanged gifts. Now in 1918 the feud resurfaced; it never ended. As Murdock described the Quinn debacle and its aftermath, he reasoned that "like so many other incidents in the Ban-Commy relationship, the final break resulted from an unintentional oversight and misunderstanding."[32] It did not help that Quinn pitched until he was 49 and enjoyed a number of productive seasons before he finally rested his arm.

While the Quinn dispute raged, the White Sox defections continued. On July 1 Happy Felsch left the team to take a $125-a-week job with the Milwaukee Gas Company and play

White Sox owner Charles Comiskey (left) and American League president Ban Johnson during a more amicable time (National Baseball Hall of Fame Library, Cooperstown, New York).

baseball on Sundays. There was no certainty the job carried an exemption from active service. It was later said Felsch left the team over an argument with Collins. As it stood, Hap played in only 53 games for the season.

Throughout 1918 Collins struggled at the plate. His .276 batting average was second only to his .273 in 1908 as a career low. Still, Collins, who played in only 97 games during the season, proved his value by getting on base. His on-base percentage of .407 was third in the league, bolstered by 73 bases on balls, which stood fourth. His stolen base production was down, though, as he finished with 22, tenth in the league.

Of course, given the war and the team's performance, there was a precipitous decline in attendance. Only 195,081 passed through the turnstiles at Comiskey in 1918, just three American League teams faring worse. The news media shared the fans' frustration. After one game in July, James Crusinberry, taking a leaf from Secretary Baker's book, wrote in the *Tribune*, "The kind of baseball played by the Sox at times today is neither essential or productive."[33] A few days later Crusinberry's description of a single game at Comiskey Park really summed up the state of the wartime game not only in Chicago, but throughout the country.

"It was about as quiet a victory as ever was won on the South Side grounds. Not many more than 2,000 persons were present and they seemed afraid to cheer, for they didn't know just how Secretary of War Baker would take such actions. Under such a strain baseball has lost its chief merit, for it can't even furnish mental relaxation and recreation to the tired citizens."[34]

It was this same Secretary Baker, however, whose staff had met with the leaders of baseball and extended the work or fight order, but only until September 1. Organized Baseball could have plodded along after that date with undrafted players, but they chose to cut mounting losses at the gate and end the season early. Ban Johnson was ready to shut everything on August 20 and start the World Series at that point. However, since there was a 10-day grace period, the owners, led by a defiant Charles Comiskey, overruled Johnson and voted to play until September 2 and then hold the World Series. Nonetheless, that prospect only put off the inevitable and Collins, for one, finally decided to seriously explore his options. Perhaps his eventual decision was influenced by an announcement from Washington on July 31 that those working in the shipyards who were designated Class 1 must prove they were indispensable to continue their deferment. Although not specifying ball-playing ship workers, the order was certainly aimed in their direction.

At any rate on August 13, it was announced that Eddie Collins' last game was to be the August 15 clash with the Red Sox at Fenway. By then the military was no longer accepting enlistments, but when Collins was in Philadelphia several weeks earlier, he made his plans. He sat down with his wife and talked things over. A decision was made. Eddie Collins would become a Marine.

"If I thought I had troubles as a rookie in baseball, I hadn't lived until I discovered the troubles a rookie Marine has."[35]

As a Marine, one of the highest paid players in baseball was now about to make a little over $30 per month. In addition, Collins, who unlike Jackson still enjoyed an exemption with his local draft board as a married man and was unlikely to be drafted, turned down a job with the YMCA, as well as the opportunity to play shipyard ball for more money. As such, unlike Jackson and many others who were vilified for their actions, Collins was accorded a hero's send-off. Instead of derogatory remarks from team management and the league office, Eddie received the Old Roman's congratulations and best wishes. Instead of negative national press, in its August 22 issue *The Sporting News* published a photograph and short story about Collins under the heading, "One Who Wants to Fight."[36]

In his last game of 1918 on August 15, Collins played well, helping his team to a 6–2 win over a Red Sox team which later replaced the Pale Hose as world champions with a six-game conquest over the Chicago Cubs. On that date the White Sox's record was 53–55 and they rested in fifth place. Following Collins' exit, there were only sixteen remaining games on the White Sox's schedule. Playing the majority of them with Johnny Mostil at second base, the White Sox won four and lost twelve to finish the season in sixth place at 57–67.

Collins sadly summed up the season and its lost promise. "[T]he stress of war had laid a heavy hand on each member of that club — and we never showed to our best advantage."[37] Now that he had fielded all the plaudits, it was time to deal with the real life aspects of military life.

> I was a buck private when I entered.... I suffered every drudge any enlisted Marine suffered, but I learned from that bunch the meaning of spirit and determination....
> Mostly it was drill and exercise and guard duty on the wind-swept piers of the Philadelphia Navy Yard in the dead cold of winter. Or it was drill and target practice on a snow-swept field with a snarling sergeant standing behind you.
> But it was an experience of which I am proud. Outside of my accomplishments on the baseball field and my membership in the corridors of baseball's great and warm halls, I am next most proud of my one-time membership in the greatest of all military units — the United States Marines.[38]

Unlike the major leaguers who matriculated to the shipyards, Collins did not plan to play baseball for the Marines. Yet he was not without a big reputation as a ball player, and the Marines were as competitive, or even more competitive, than most.

One day, shortly after I became just another number among the horde of military men Uncle Sam was assembling in the first World War, I was summoned to the Office of the Commanding General of our unit, General Radford.

I wondered what was up as I proceeded toward the headquarters.

As I entered his office and saluted, General Radford appraised me with eyes that looked suspiciously like those of a mackerel. He glowered and held himself stiff and erect.

"I'm told you were a ball player as a civilian," he said. "I have an assignment for you. Go to Villanova and report to Lieutenant Hill. The Marines are playing a baseball game and I want you to play there. We want to win. And," he added somewhat ominously as I shuffled nervously on the floor before the desk, "I HOPE [*sic*] you give a good account of yourself."

I reported to Lieutenant Hill and was inserted into the lineup. The General's "hopes" were realized. I had a good day—though, I dare say I don't believe I could have had anything but a good day, with his words imprinted on my mind.

I played two or three other games for Lieutenant Hill's team, and we won them all as I recall. I got quite a kick out of that "baseball detail"—unfortunately those "details" didn't come often enough.[39]

Although Collins chose military service over work in an essential, war-related industry, he was also one of the lucky ones. He remained stateside, and on November 11 he celebrated with the rest of the nation when an armistice was signed and peace restored.

For a time baseball remained on the back burner of the national conscience. Soon, however, there began the questions about the place of the sport in a post–war America. More specifically, when it came to the White Sox there was the question of their manager and the shipyard players. Would Rowland, a manager with a constant question mark hanging over his head even while his team was winning a championship, be able to maintain his position after a year of dashed hope? And would Commy, that most vociferous critic of the players who chose to work and play ball rather than be drafted, take those same players back on his team? More particularly, what about the playing status of Eddie Collins? Would he be discharged in time to report for spring training, or even be able to play at all in 1919?

The answer to this latter question was still uncertain in early December. Collins told reporters he had no idea how long his services would be required and doubted his availability for the start of the season. As to the shipyarders, after an aborted attempt to ban them by Tigers owner Phil Navin, it was left to each owner to determine his players' fate. Commy was taking it under advisement. At least there would be baseball in 1919, even as the season was reduced to 140 games as the magnates took baby steps in response to the disastrous attendance levels in 1918.

Questions notwithstanding, as 1918 came "peacefully" to an end, the future still held great promise for the country, its national pastime and for the Chicago White Sox. In every good way possible, 1919 promised to be a season to remember.

CHAPTER 12

Sour Series

"I was to be a witness to the greatest tragedy in baseball's history — and I didn't know it at the time."

— Eddie Collins[1]

The drama of 1919 actually began on the last day of 1918 when Charles Comiskey made a surprise announcement. Pants Rowland was out; William "Kid" Gleason was his new manager. The announcement of the change, made on December 31, was even more surprising since it was generally believed that following their falling out the previous season — perhaps money-related — Commy and Gleason were not speaking. The White Sox's owner had reportedly done something similar when he hired Fielder Jones more than a decade earlier. The Fielder decision worked out well and Comiskey felt this one would as well.

Commy did not specify his reasons for dismissing Rowland, who was still only one year away from having secured his boss a championship, but it is likely he saw the cliques forming on the squad and felt Pants was not in control. Although Rowland was constantly under intense scrutiny and criticism from the Chicago press and White Sox fans, he now received quite a bit of sympathy from both sectors. After all, the war, which saw his team ripped apart, was not his fault. For one of the few times, Commy felt the sting of criticism, even though Rowland's four-year tenure was almost as long as that of Fielder Jones, who managed for Charles Comiskey from 1904–1908 and also won a world title.

Although Collins enjoyed playing for Rowland, who now purchased an interest in Milwaukee's American Association club, and constantly sang Rowland's praises during the manager's time at the helm, he was effusive in his praise of his new field general.

"Kid Gleason, manager of the White Sox! That's the best New Year's present I could think of. Mark it down that in view of the fact that Gleason has been made chief skipper of the Sox, I would not change places with any one on any club in the American League. By this I mean to say that the White Sox look to me the one best bet for 1919."[2]

Those words were spoken days after Gleason's appointment. Years later Collins would express his admiration for Kid Gleason, the manager and the person. By Eddie's measure Gleason was an "old school" guy "whose character glistened and gleamed despite the rough edges...." He would do anything for his players. They recognized this and loved him for it. Collins felt not only admiration, but love for the old bird. "He was one of the best and truest friends I ever had."[3]

The feeling between Gleason and Collins was mutual. Shortly before he was named manager, the Kid talked about the star infielder to American League umpire and frequent sports page contributor Billy Evans. Calling Eddie "an ideal man for a captain," he added that "Collins is the greatest player I have ever seen in my long career, and I have seen a lot of them. Never saw him do a dumb thing in his life, and incidentally he is forever keeping some of his

149

Over the course of his career the colorful William "Kid" Gleason (right) both coached and managed Collins (left) while he was with Chicago White Sox. Later the pair, who became great friends,
coached together under Connie Mack in Philadelphia (George Grantham Bain Collection, Library
of Congress, Prints & Publications Division, LC-DIG-ggbain-30961).

teammates from making a slip. With Collins to direct the play on the field, with that gang making base hits and runs, I think I could sit on the bench and handle the club from there without much trouble. There is a ball club [the White Sox] worth managing."[4]

Now Commy had given Kid Gleason that very opportunity. There was only one problem: Eddie Collins was still a Marine. That problem, however, was resolved on February 6 in Philadelphia when Collins was granted an honorable discharge. The private with the floppy ears completed his service with the Quartermaster's Department, having served his entire time in Philadelphia just a few miles from his home and family. Although his active service was completed, Eddie served in the Marine Corps Reserve for a full four years until his discharge on August 19, 1922.[5]

When he returned to civilian life, Collins was entering the fifth and last year of his original contract with the White Sox. He made immediate plans to leave with the team when they left for their camp at Mineral Wells, Texas, on March 21. The fate of some of his teammates was less certain. The contracts of White Sox players like Joe Jackson were terminated by Comiskey when they went to the shipyards. Given the owner's comments about Jackson and others like Lefty Williams and Byrd Lynn, would Commy take them back? And then there were the fans. What reception would they accord the players who chose the route to the docks and similar occupations?

As to Commy's position, there was little doubt. He thirsted for another championship, as well as the increased attendance such success drew to his stadium. In addition, when Kid Gleason accepted the Chicago job, it was with the new manager's understanding the core of the team would return. Therefore, given the right price, the disaffected could return. In February Joe Jackson was back on the club, his $6,000-per-year contract the same as before. Holding the line on salaries, giving an inch only when forced to do so, Commy took back the rest one by one.

The fans and the local press were the tougher sell. Some would resist cheering for someone who in their opinion shirked his duty. Others would realize that in the end all Jackson and the others did was work in a war-related industry, nothing more or less than the secretary of war had ordered.

Players such as Risberg, Gandil and Weaver initially attempted a spring holdout. They quickly folded their cards and reported for duty, no doubt unhappy but with few viable options. As the spring wore on, only Fred McMullin was a serious absentee and eventually he rejoined the team as well.

While there were few changes in the team that reported to Mineral Wells in March, there was one significant addition to the pitching staff. A left-handed rookie, Richard "Dickie" Kerr, joined the squad from the American Association. Standing only 5 feet 7 inches and weighing 155 pounds, the 25-year-old hurler from St. Louis was a reliable starting pitcher for Gleason by season's end, even though little had been expected.

Although Collins showed some rust in the early going, by the end of the first week of April, he was reaching mid-season form. The infield was rounding into shape as well, turning a triple play against Houston's minor league team. In that one Collins hit safely three times and scored three runs.

On the surface it appeared all was well with the Pale Hose as they prepared for 1919. In reality nothing had changed. If anything, the situation was worse than before; the animosities of 1917 and 1918, apparently smoldering as war ravaged Europe and beyond, flamed anew.

> Never in all history has a team been racked with the troubles of that [1919 White Sox] club. Discord was the keynote of the day — every day. There were cliques and personal jealousies. I [Collins] guess there were even hatreds....

Little did I think that such an eventful year faced me when I entrained from Philadelphia for the training camp of the White Sox late in February of 1919, fresh out of the Marine Corp[s].

From the very moment I arrived at camp I could discern that something was amiss. We may have had our troubles in other years, but in 1919 we were a club that pulled apart, rather than together. There were frequent arguments and open hostility.[6]

Collins' major nemesis continued to be Chick Gandil, but the problems went beyond just Eddie and Chick.

"Gandil and I didn't speak to each other for two years while playing side by side. Some of the pitchers didn't like Schalk. Many a time bad throws or wrong throws were written into the records because the thrower didn't care for the guy he was throwing to and wouldn't give him a chance to make the catch."[7]

Given Collins' intimate knowledge of his team's internal strife, one would think Collins would readily disagree with those who included the White Sox, along with the Red Sox, Indians and rising New York Yankees as pennant contenders. Not so.

"[T]he White Sox of '19 had the greatest possibilities of any baseball combination ever assembled."[8]

"Whoever it was who said harmony and unity are essential to the success of a championship team wasn't acquainted with ... the 1919 White Sox....

"In spite of all this [discord], we started off the season on a winning note and, except for

The 1919 Chicago White Sox infield is known for two things — they played quite well together and they did not get along on or off the field. Left to right: Buck Weaver (3b), Swede Risberg (ss), Eddie Collins (2b), and Chick Gandil (1b) (*The Sporting News*—Zuma Press).

a brief period in mid-season, led most of the way. We may not have been each others' 'dearest friends,' but once we took the field we suddenly jelled into a formidable unit."[9]

Collins' brief capsule of the season was essentially accurate, but before the season even started the ChiSox gave evidence of what was to come when they stopped in Cincinnati for a pair of final "warm ups" with a Reds team which showed intriguing promise. In the first game young Dickie Kerr held the Reds for 10 innings as his mates carved a 3–1 victory. In the second contest Lefty Williams and Eddie Cicotte combined to again thwart the Reds, 5–3. Anyone watching the contests gave the edge to the White Sox, but the games were hard fought, the scores close. Clearly, the Reds were a team to watch.

In the season opener played in Sportsman's Park in St. Louis, the White Sox served notice, defeating an improving Browns team, 13–4. Collins let everyone know he was back with a three-run home run in the fourth inning. The team's record was already 6–1 when it returned to the Windy City for its home opener on May 2. A crowd of 12,000 watched prior to the game as Eddie Collins and a squad of Marines marched around the field, then proudly presented a new flag for the park and ran it up the pole. That was the highlight as the team came a cropper, 11–4.

Such lowlights were few in 1919 for the White Sox. They started in first and remained there until mid-June. On May 30 doubleheader wins over their chief competitor, the Cleveland Indians, boosted their record to 23–7. One of the highlights was the return to form of Red Faber, another ex-serviceman. On May 7 he was on the mound as the Sox tamed the Tigers, 9–3.

When the White Sox weren't fighting with each other, they were in physical combat with their opponents. In one early June contest, a 5–3 loss to the Tribe, Gandil tangled with the Indians' Tris Speaker. During the fight both men were badly bruised, suffered spike injuries, and Gandil's shirt was ripped to shreds. The bleacher crowd, excited to fever pitch, began throwing bottles onto the field until Gleason and a cadre of policemen restored order. The fracas, which resulted in a five-day suspension for Gandil, seemed to sidetrack the Sox. They lost five of their next six. By June 12 they were in second for the first time all season. The lone win during that string was a 5–1 victory over the Yankees at the Polo Grounds. In attendance that day was a squad of Marines and a Marine band, sent to the park to honor Collins. Not wishing to disappoint, Eddie delivered a bases loaded inside-the-park homer in the top of the eighth to bust the game open.

The next day Collins, still in an expansive mood given his clutch blow the previous day, stopped by the team hotel to see if anyone needed a ride to the ball park. He was driving the Twin Six his wife brought over from Philadelphia. Finding most of the players already departed, he gave a ride to part-time catcher Joe Jenkins and several of the writers who were still hanging around the lobby. It was for naught; the game was called for rain, but the scribes enjoyed their ride enough to write about it.

Collins did some more motoring a few days later while the team was in Boston for a series. This time he and fellow teammates Nemo Leibold, Buck Weaver and Joe Jenkins drove to Brae Burn to watch a golf tournament. It seems perhaps at least Weaver and Collins, whose wife on occasion was photographed sitting together with Mabel Collins at the ball park, were on speaking terms, if no more.

A great deal of the blame for the woes of the White Sox on their road trip in June, which dropped them from the top of the league, was attributable to a dose of quiet bats. At one point, 11 games into the excursion, Happy Felsch was batting just .138. Collins was not much better. He was able to provide only eight hits to the cause in thirty at-bats. Jackson and Weaver were only slightly more productive. A lineup change resulted. Collins moved up to the number two slot in the order and Weaver dropped to third.

When the White Sox hit Shibe Park in mid–June, Collins, who always stayed at his residence when he was in town, was able to get some home cooking. It did little to help his average, but the team fed off the weak A's fare and won three in a row. The wins put them on top of the standings once again.

In Washington the team received a lift from veteran Grover Lowdermilk, a right-hander obtained from the Browns in mid–May in order to bolster the starting rotation. An effective curveball brought victory for Lowdermilk and the Sox over the Senators on June 19.

Much was written about the 1919 baseball season. The regular season, however, was really not all that remarkable. The White Sox bounced back and forth between first and second, occasionally falling to third, as they progressed through June. Then in early July, while at home, a block of 10 wins out of 11 contests vaulted the team into first. Although the Indians stayed quite close and the Yankees and Tigers contended, the Pale Hose remained in first the rest of the season. Collins' slump in June was not indicative of his overall performance in 1919. Frequently, he combined his fine hitting with a dash of daring on the base paths. He led the league in steals for the second time in his career, accumulating 33. An example of Collins on the run occurred at Comiskey on July 14 in a 9–3 win over the Red Sox. In that one Eddie hit a three-run home run. Like many of his four-baggers, this one was a classic inside-the-park gem. In the fourth inning two runs were in and two Sox on base when Collins came to the plate. He picked on a Sam Jones' pitch, sending it to the wall in right center. When he reached third, it appeared he would stop since the second baseman already had the ball, ready to fire it to the plate if needed. But Collins kept going and the pitcher, who never thought the White Sox second baseman would be so daring, reached up and cut off the throw to the plate. It would be one of four round-trippers for Eddie during the season.

Of course, Collins was not doing it alone. Joe Jackson was in the midst of a banner season in which he hit seven home runs, drove in 96 runners and hit .351. As a team the White Sox's batting average of .287 led the league. On the mound, Cicotte (29–7, 1.82) and Lefty Williams [23–11, 2.64] were highly effective workhorses, pitching in 40 and 41 games, respectively. Only Red Faber, plagued by injuries and later a bout with the flu, was a notch or two down from his normal high level at 11–9 and 3.83 in 25 games.

One man who was enjoying the performance of the White Sox was owner Charles Comiskey. And it was easy to see why. As the team continued its winning ways, the fans flocked back to his park. On July 20 the largest crowd to date, 30,000, watched Cicotte throttle the Yankees, 2–1. When Joe Jackson ended the suspense with a dramatic game-ending home run, the crowd cheered and cheered. All was forgiven. Shoeless Joe was once again their hero and baseball their pastime. The White Sox would draw over 625,000 fans in 1919, second best in the league. Commy and the rest of his fellow magnates could rest easy; baseball was back in business.

In late July the business side of the game reared its ugly head in another player transaction that further fractured the relationship between Commy and Ban Johnson, as well as Johnson's standing with several of the other owners. The game which precipitated the battle — though hardly the underlying cause of the matter — occurred in Chicago on July 13 when Carl Mays, the sometimes brilliant and often controversial Boston Red Sox hurler with a nasty temper, left the game and his team in the second inning, down 4–0. Over time any number of reasons have been asserted for Mays' actions, including poor support by his teammates, frustration at being hit in the back of the head when his catcher attempted a throw down to second, and that catch-all phrase: "personal problems."

Since Mays was a fine pitcher when in the proper mood, a number of teams including the White Sox expressed interest in acquiring him from Harry Frazee's Red Sox. Since Mays walked away from the team, Ban Johnson felt discipline was in order. As such he let it be known he would not approve any deal for Mays. However, two weeks later, in Mays' continued absence, Frazee traded him to the Yankees.

Ban Johnson immediately suspended Mays indefinitely. Colonel Jake Ruppert, along with Tillinghast Huston, owners of the Yankees, protested, arguing that the discipline at this point penalized their team. They also accused Johnson of a conflict of interest since he was a shareholder in the Cleveland Indians, a loser in the bidding for Mays. The accusation was ironic in view of Johnson's admitted meddling when Connie Mack placed Collins on the market and the Red Sox, Yankees and Comiskey expressed interest. In friendlier days Commy got a boost from Ban on that one. Here the Yankees' owners, certainly encouraged by Commy's support, sought and obtained a temporary injunction restraining Johnson and the American League from interfering with Mays' services for New York.

Now the plot thickened. Having secured legal backing, the Yankees scheduled a meeting of owners and invited Johnson — a clear reversal of the American League "way" during the Johnson era. Interestingly, only Boston's Frazee and Johnson's enemy, Comiskey, attended. The sides in the American League were now aligned for future discussions about league affairs, including any reorganization of the National Commission.

The next move involved the league's board of directors, a five-man group which included the three maverick owners. They voted to reinstate Mays in good standing. The matter dragged on for some time in and outside the courthouse. Eventually the temporary injunction became permanent and Mays remained a Yankee. In the end Ban Johnson's presidency and the continued viability of the National Commission were struck crippling blows. Commy was the early victor, but Ban Johnson was not dead yet.

In the midst of all this backyard brawling, the pennant races moved into the stretch. As the Sox advanced toward the pennant, one group they could count on for unwavering support was the Marine Corps. A scheduled clash with the Yankees on August 23 was declared Marine Day by Commy. Captain L.W. Putnam endorsed the event on behalf of the Marine Corps.

"Eddie Collins was a Marine and the Marines as a corps are White Sox rooters."[10]

Before they played in front of the Marines, the Sox met the Red Sox in Chicago on August 16. They watched as Babe Ruth, now playing regularly in the outfield on his way to a record-setting season with 29 home runs, blasted a tape-measure drive that stood the entire White Sox team in its tracks as the white pellet sailed over the fence.

The Marines came ashore on August 23, 2,000 strong, and watched as their adopted team blasted the Yankees, 10–2. Prior to the game a group of Marine "scouts" stormed the dugout and "captured" Eddie. They then hoisted him on their shoulders and carried him to their welcoming brethren in the grandstand, handshakes all around. In the ensuing contest their hero singled, walked and scored a run. The victory was number nine in a 10-game win streak that all but sewed up the pennant.

Less than a week later Commy was arguing against a proposal to lengthen the World Series to nine games. Club owners, particularly those in the National League, favored the addition of two games. They had misjudged fan support and reduced the 1919 season to 140 games. An extra two games might help recoup some of their lost revenue. Commy opposed the idea, seeing no reason to change a system which worked just fine in the past. He denied a lengthened series further exposed an already thin pitching staff which would enter the series without Red Faber, battling injuries and experiencing weakness from his bout with the flu.

Meanwhile, in early September with pennant prospects bright, Gleason and a number of his players traveled to Chicago's north side to take in a Cubs' game. They were not there to cheer on the locals. They were far more interested in the Cubs' opponent, the Cincinnati Reds, surprise leaders of the National League.

In August, in an attempt to bolster their pitching staff, the White Sox purchased an experienced right-hander from the Red Sox in the person of 32-year-old Bill James, a member of the Tigers in 1917. On September 9 the spitballer proved his worth by shutting out the Senators and Walter Johnson, 2–0. A few days later on September 12, another newcomer, this time 26-year-old Roy Wilkinson, shut out the Athletics, 7–0. The additional pitching helped but could not totally hide the fact the Pale Hose were only 13–10 in September and ended the season losing six of seven, including four straight.

These last games were deemed academic when the Sox bested the Browns in Chicago on September 24, 6–5. The victory clinched the second pennant in three years for the White Sox. Collins was not around to celebrate on the field at the end of the game, however, having been ejected for arguing when he was called out on a close play at the plate.

Still the four straight losses, especially the last three at home to Detroit, later raised eyebrows. Although each game was close, 10–7, 7–5 and 10–9, respectively, Collins later admitted that despite the fact Detroit was still battling for third-place money, "there was what might be termed a considerable lack of interest in the games on the part of the White Sox."[11]

At season's end, despite limping to the finish line, the 1919 White Sox's record stood at 88–52. Cleveland finished three and one-half games behind. Despite Detroit's three wins at Comiskey, the Tigers finished a half-game behind the third-place Yankees.

On an individual basis in 1919, Collins, much like his team, was back on track. He hit .319 and finished seventh in the league in OBP at .400. He was sixth in runs scored with 87. His 80 RBIs were ninth. The league-leading 33 stolen bases represented one more than his current age. In late September he celebrated 13 years in the major leagues.

On a team which led the league in hitting at .287, including Jackson's .351, the lowest average in the lineup was Risberg's .256. Their starting pitching, though lacking in depth, was still spectacular. Since Faber had not started since mid–September, in the World Series Gleason planned to call upon Dickie Kerr, whose 13–7 record and 2.88 ERA gave the White Sox manager at least some comfort.

As it turned out, the visit by the White Sox to the Cubs' ball park several weeks prior turned out to be fortuitous, for their World Series opponents were, indeed, the Cincinnati Reds. Winners of 96 games versus 44 defeats, the team some considered upstarts finished a full nine games in front of the Giants. Fielding a lesser-known group of players than the White Sox, the Reds' manager was Pat Moran, a former Phillies' leader and briefly a Giants' pitching coach who was in his first season as the Cincinnati skipper. Their star player was Edd Roush, who played briefly for the White Sox in 1913. In 1919 Roush, still a youthful 26, enjoyed a fine, although not his finest, season. His league-leading batting average was .321 and his 71 RBIs ranked second in the National League. He was also a superb center fielder.

Another fine hitter for the Reds was their third baseman, Heinie Groh. A lifetime .292 hitter, Groh was an excellent batsman who could lay down a bunt and was frequently among the league leaders in walks.

While the Reds' position players were solid, pitching depth was the team's hidden strength. The Reds could go five or six deep and lose very little sleep in that department. In order of most games started, there were Hod Eller (19–9, 2.39), Lefty Dutch Ruether (19–6, 1.82), Jimmy Ring (10–9, 2.26), left-hander Slim Sallee (21–7, 2.06), and Ray Fisher (14–5, 2.17). In addition, Dolph Luque (10–3, 2.63) appeared in 30 games and started nine.

On paper the Reds looked mighty good, but their record and pitching depth were dismissed by many experts and, in the early going, by a number of bettors as the October classic approached. After all, the American League, which was striving for its fifth consecutive World Series championship, was considered the stronger league. And, to boot, the 1919 White Sox, their 1918 season quickly dismissed as a casualty of the war, were considered one of the greatest teams, if not the greatest, of all time.

In umpire Billy Evans' opinion, the series could be tied to the performance of "the greatest money ball player in the world.

"If the Cincinnati Reds are able to stop Eddie Collins in the big show, then the National leaguers need not worry about the outcome of the baseball classic."[12]

What did Evans, who was assigned to umpire the series, think? After issuing a disclaimer that given his position he would not pick a winner, he stated he "leans strongly" toward Chicago with a healthy Red Faber. On the other hand, he compared the confidence of the Reds to that of their league's last winner, the 1914 Boston Braves. "[N]o National League club that has met the American league entry in the big series in the last ten years entered the classic with a better chance to win than the Reds. On paper the Reds do not shine, but on the field they perform most brilliantly, and it is on the field that ball games are won."[13]

The field in this case, at least for Game One, was Redland Field, which stood at the corner of Western Avenue and Findlay Street in Cincinnati. Over Commy's objections, the series was scheduled for nine games, with the first team to five wins taking home the prize. The first game was set for October 1. On the mound for the Sox was Eddie Cicotte. Moran decided to open with Dutch Ruether in order to use his left-handed deliveries to still the bats of left-handed hitters Eddie Collins and Joe Jackson. Before his stellar season in 1919, Ruether had won only three games in the majors.

As the game neared, the betting odds, in a series which promised to spawn heavier betting than any before it, began switching from the White Sox to the Reds. A published reason was a rumor that Cicotte was nursing a sore arm. The exact condition of that arm remains uncertain. It is clear, however, that the 1919 World Series was not Mr. Cicotte's shining moment.

The first inning of Game One is one of the most analyzed innings in baseball history.* It started calmly enough. Right fielder John "Shano" Collins lined a single to center to lead off the game but was out at second when Eddie's attempt at a sacrifice was unsuccessful. Eddie now stood at first. When Buck Weaver stepped to the plate, Collins, sensing an early opportunity to test the arm of Cincinnati catcher Ivy Wingo, claimed he flashed Weaver the hit-and-run sign. Weaver either missed the sign or chose to ignore it, and Eddie, running with the pitch, was an easy out. Weaver then flied to Roush in center to end the inning.

In the dugout, Collins is said to have asked Weaver, "Were you asleep?" Weaver, who was by now clearly no friend of Collins, replied, "Quit trying to alibi and play ball."[14] The confrontation gave lie to a sub-heading in the October 2, 1919, edition of *The Sporting News* advising readers, "It's a Happy Bunch [of players] in Chicago on Eve of World Series."[15]

In the bottom of the first, Cicotte took the mound. The Reds' second sacker, Morrie Rath, stepped in. Cicotte's first pitch was on the money for strike one. Then, in perhaps the most analyzed pitch of this or any series, the left-hander reared back and flung a ball which struck Rath in the back, up between his shoulder blades. Many believe the errant pitch was a signal to bettors of things to come. Rath eventually scored the first run.

The White Sox tied the game in the top of the second. Their demise, however, in the

---

*Note—The discussions in this book of the 1919 World Series and its aftermath will focus on the play of Eddie Collins, as well as his actions and reactions to the subsequent controversy surrounding the series. There are entire books and hundreds of articles discussing the events which came to be commonly known as the Black Sox scandal. A fair sampling of these treatments is listed in the bibliography at the end of this book.

form of a five-run Reds' uprising, came in inning number four. The big blow was a two-out, two-run triple by pitcher Dutch Ruether. One run was already in and two more followed. The outcome might have been seriously altered when earlier in the inning with no one out and Pat Duncan, the left fielder, on with a single, shortstop Larry Kopf hit the ball right back to Cicotte. There were reports, though highly varied, that the Sox pitcher hesitated before throwing to Risberg to force Duncan at second. When Risberg reportedly stumbled over second while attempting to double Kopf at first, the chance for a double play fell through.

Ruether was not only the hitting star of Game One with two triples, a single and a walk, but he fashioned a six-hitter to boot. The Reds won easily, 9–1. Collins, batting in his now customary second slot in the lineup, was 1-for-4 in the game, while hitting star Jackson was 0-for-4.

For this World Series Collins was back on the sports beat, writing a daily column which appeared in the *Chicago Daily News*. He was joined in this endeavor by Ray Schalk, who wrote a separate column appearing in that paper. Prior to Game One, Collins had expressed certainty that his team was eager to play and ready to win it all. In his mind Gleason was the catalyst. "[Y]ou would rather take a good beating any day than not win for him."[16]

Not much changed in Collins' tune after the opening loss. Certainly on that day the Reds were the better team, but a clobbering is often easier to take than a close game and still counts as only a single loss. Eddie told readers he spoke to Cicotte in the clubhouse after the game and "he had no excuses to offer."[17]

The "man on the street," particularly the betting man, was not quite as upbeat about Collins' team. The odds, already leaning toward the Reds, swung even more in that direction. In addition, rumors were swirling that the outcome of this series was in the hands of big-time gamblers and the White Sox were in the midst of throwing this one to the Reds.

"Naturally we of the club heard these reports. But we shrugged them off as preposterous. 'Just a lot of idol gossip,' I felt, and so told inquirers."[18]

Over time it would be revealed that this was only the tip of the iceberg. There would be tales of shouting matches between Ray Schalk and his pitchers, as well as Gleason and the players, both individually and as a team in at least one team meeting. There would be various versions of tip-offs to Charles Comiskey and to Ban Johnson and machinations against each other as their hatred expanded into an all-out power struggle — one where the need for one to squash the other trumped the need to act for the good of the game. But years later Collins claimed that going into the series, even though he had not fraternized with Gandil, Risberg, Cicotte and the rest, he admired their ability and never dreamed they would betray their teammates by conspiring to throw a game, let alone an entire World Series.

"Even though the rumors persisted all during the eight games of that Series, I, for one, refused to believe them."[19]

It was in this climate of accusation, rumor, and innuendo that the teams remained in Ohio and prepared to play Game Two. On the mound for the White Sox was the second half of their one-two punch, Lefty Williams. The control specialist was opposed by another control specialist in left-hander Slim Sallee, the veteran of the Reds' staff at 34. The Sox were familiar with Sallee, having beaten him twice in the 1917 World Series when he pitched for the Giants.

This time around, although he gave up 10 hits compared to only four by Williams, Sallee held the Pale Hose to a pair of runs. It was enough. The Reds prevailed, 4–2. Once again the downfall for the White Sox was the fourth inning. Williams, who walked only 58 batters in 297 innings during the season, began the inning by walking Morrie Rath. First baseman Jake Daubert pushed Rath to second with a sacrifice bunt. Now, as White Sox fans and even casual observers scratched their heads, Williams walked Groh. This brought up Edd Roush, who promptly drove Rath home with a single and the first run of game. Reds were now perched on the corners, still one out. Roush then did the Sox a favor by trying to steal second. Schalk's rifle arm threw him out. Duncan then drew a walk, the third of the inning. Kopf followed, hitting the first pitch to the temporary outfield fence for a triple, scoring two runs. The next batter grounded out, but the three runs were all Mr. Sallee needed. His Reds now held a commanding two-game lead. In an almost prophetic statement, sportswriter I.E. Sanborn of the *Tribune* told readers the locals were done in by the "[a]lmost criminal wild pitching" of Lefty Williams.[20]

Although most of the 29,600 in attendance were quite pleased with the outcome, there were a few besides the Woodland Bards who felt sorry for the White Sox. They included 50 fans from Philadelphia, known as the "Famous Fifty" for winning a trip contest sponsored by the *Philadelphia Inquirer*. Their main interest: former A's hero Eddie Collins and former Philadelphia Phillies and Quakers player Kid Gleason. They were particularly disappointed in Eddie's 0-for-3 day.

In his report to the *Daily News* following Game Two, Collins admitted this second loss was a bitter pill to swallow. Once again he told readers the Sox would rebound. The Reds were "lucky" to win a game in which they were so out-hit. And as for Williams, Eddie, in words he no doubt later regretted, told readers the lefty lost Game Two, but "he won't [lose] his next start. I'll bet on that."[21]

After the game Collins packed his typewriter and his bags, prepared to head by train back to Chicago with his teammates, the "Fabulous Fifty" and the rest of the entourage. Was he really so confident his team would bounce back? Were the White Sox really aroused by the two losses as he had tried to convince his readers? Was he really so unconcerned about the obvious instability of Lefty Williams? Again, speaking long after the fact, Collins claimed he was not.

"He [Williams] was famed for his great control. But even good control pitchers have their off-days. What was there to get suspicious about when he suddenly seemed to lose his control in the fourth inning and issued three walks and gave up two hits?"[22]

Collins' team did bounce back in Game Three, never mind his true feelings about the losses in the first two games. Instead of sticking with his one-two punch, Gleason went with a rookie. As the teams lined up at Comiskey Park on October 3, Richard "Dickie" Kerr, according to the *Tribune* "the world's smallest southpaw," shut down the Reds, 3–0. Although it was a beautiful day, the game was not a sellout. Perhaps, the White Sox's fans were starting to believe the rumors, or maybe there was concern over the violence in nearby Gary, Indiana, where a bitter steel strike continued. Still the more than 29,000 fans in attendance were quite vocal in their support. The Reds, of course, were bitterly disappointed, but no more so than a score of big-time gamblers.

Most observers expected the Reds to pitch Hod Eller in Game Three, but manager Pat Moran went with nine-year veteran Ray Fisher, a right-hander. The White Sox were able to touch him early and seal their first victory in the second inning when Joe Jackson singled and Fisher threw wildly on Felsch's weak attempt at a sacrifice. The error placed Jackson on third and Felsch on second. Chick Gandil then drove them in with a single. Risberg was hit by a pitch, placing Gandil at second. Schalk then laid down a bunt, but Gandil was forced out at third. There was some speculation, though far from agreement, that Gandil loafed on his way to third and could have beaten the throw. The play took the Sox out of a big inning, but they had their runs, and behind Kerr's three-hit gem, their victory.

Collins was still not hitting anywhere near his average, nor was he playing the part of the money player Billy Evans had envisioned. He singled and went 1-for-4. In addition, he took a terrific ribbing from the Reds' utility man, Jimmy Smith. In *The 1919 World Series*, author William Cook describes what happened after the game.

"The Reds' taunting of the mighty White Sox even continued after the game. As the players were leaving the field using the same tunnel in Comiskey Park to get to their club houses, Jimmy Smith caught up with Eddie Collins who had spit at him late in the game. Smith had avoided the spit, but was still very angry. Collins attempted to stick out his hand to Smith, but Jimmy hastened that if he had the opportunity tomorrow, he would spit in Collins' eye."[23]

Bill Gleason had his own view of the incident and the events leading up to it.

I like to see that fighting stuff on a ball team. That's the spirit that makes 'em win. But, you know, there were two or three times in that ball game when there was danger of blows being struck. You would hardly believe that Eddie Collins was in a fighting mood but he was. When Eddie gets in a fighting mood something is sure to happen.

He would have mixed with Jimmy Smith, too, if necessary. You see, Smith had been saying some things to him and Eddie got sore, and when he walked across the diamond he took it up with the kid. Well, I was right there and prevented any trouble. It would have been bum stuff for them to mix and get put out of the game. Smith isn't even playing and it wouldn't hurt Cincinnati but would hurt us.[24]

In their respective columns, appearing in the *Daily News* the next day, both Collins and Ray Schalk heaped praise on Kerr, but seemingly went out of their way to praise the individual play of Risberg, Gandil and Weaver. Of course, with the win the betting odds for a Chicago victory improved, as did the interest of their fans. Over 34,000 showed up on October 4 for Game Four. Moran continued to trust in his pitching depth by putting young Jimmy Ring, a 10-game winner, on the mound to face Cicotte. It was a wise choice. Ring was brilliant, flinging a three-hit shutout, while Cicotte was only slightly less so, yielding five hits and but two runs. If Cicotte's opening pitches of Game One are the most analyzed of any World Series pitches, then the top of the fifth inning of Game Four, also pitched by Cicotte, probably qualifies as the most analyzed half-inning. The inning started innocently enough. Edd Roush was out number one. Then left fielder Pat Duncan started the proceedings by hitting hard, but right back to Cicotte, who bobbled the ball, picked it up and threw wildly to first. Duncan ended up on second. Kopf then singled, sending Duncan to third. Kopf's hit might have gone for extra bases but for the excellent fielding of Joe Jackson in left, who then pegged what appeared to many to be an accurate throw toward the plate to hold Duncan on third. Suddenly, Cicotte reached up and deflected the ball. It rolled toward the stands, allowing Duncan to score and Kopf to take second. Cicotte's second error of the inning cost a run and eventually the game. Right fielder Greasy Neale, who later entered the Pro Football Hall of Fame as a coach, then doubled in the second and last run of the game for either team.

Clearly, Cicotte pitched a strong game. It was his sloppy throw and questionable fielding decision that cost him and his team a chance to even the series. The next day Collins, whose own exercise in futility continued — he went 0-for-3 — placed the blame squarely on his pitcher.

"It is most uncommon to see a man like Cicotte commit two errors in one inning, as he did Saturday, but to these alone must be *contributed* [sic] the loss of the game.... Why he interfered with Jackson's throw home, following Kopf's single to left still remains a mystery...."[25]

Years later, armed with a lot more knowledge of Cicotte's possible motivation, and, by then trying to explain his own nonfeasance, Collins was somewhat kinder. He saw nothing all that unusual about Cicotte's wild throw. As far as the cutoff, this was not the first time he saw a player "inadvertently swipe the ball toward the stands."[26]

A rainy day gave the White Sox time to lick their wounds; the Reds, a chance to rest up for the kill. It gave White Sox fans a chance to shudder. Through four games their local heroes had tallied only six times, two on a wild throw in Game Three.

On October 6 the weather improved and the battle renewed at Comiskey Park. Lefty Williams was picked for a second shot at the Reds while once again Moran dug deep, dispatching his fifth different starter by sending Hod Eller to the hill. Hod, who earned his nickname for throwing "bricks" to batters, was a shine-baller much like Cicotte. In Game Five he instead threw a lot of smoke at the Sox, striking out six in a row at one point, including Collins and Schalk. When Eddie, who was 0-for-4, became Eller's sixth straight victim, the normally avid Sox fans cheered the Reds' hurler. For a while Williams matched Eller. He pitched no-hit ball for four innings. The teams were scoreless through five innings. However, much to the chagrin of the Chicagoans, Eller kept his end of the bargain through nine straight innings, yielding but three hits. Williams did not. In the sixth inning, still pitching one-hit baseball, Williams fell victim to some questionable outfield play, including poor positioning. The Reds scored four times. On one play Felsch moved up on Edd Roush, the Reds' best long-ball hitter. Roush made him pay, hitting one over Hap's head for a triple. At the time Rath and Groh were on base. Rath scored easily and Groh headed for paydirt. When Schalk was unable to field Eddie's low relay throw in time to tag out Groh, Schalk reacted to the umpire's call of "safe" by going ballistic.

Schalk's reaction — he threw his mask at the Reds' Jimmy Ring — to what many observers felt was not a close play, may have been a release of pent-up emotion. Collins years later referred to Felsch's play on Roush's fly and the mishandling of Eller's inning-opening hit as "a pair of 'funny' plays."[27] Perhaps Ray Schalk saw it the same way.

What it all amounted to was a 5–0 loss and a 4–1 World Series deficit. The once-invincible Chicago White Sox were a single defeat from a shocking upset. Collins finally conceded that he, too, was impressed with the Reds. "Right now I must admit things look pretty red to us." He did not blame the pitchers. It was the hitters, "wherein we were supposed to be the strongest and about which the experts never questioned, we have fallen down lamentably."[28]

The series returned to Cincinnati and resumed the next day. The White Sox, no room to maneuver, sent out Dickie Kerr, their one bright light to date, to battle a well-rested Dutch Ruether. Kerr was not nearly as sharp as in Game Three, but neither was Ruether. In the early going, however, both pitchers were sharp enough. At the end of two, the teams were scoreless. At that point Kerr's scoreless streak stood at eleven. Then in both the third and fourth innings, the Reds scored twice to lead 4–0. It could have been worse, but then Morrie Rath, who stood on third with still only one out in the fourth, attempted to score on a short fly ball hit by Daubert to Jackson in left. He was out. Some credit a strong throw by Jackson; others say the throw was wide and Schalk saved the run by lunging across to block the plate. The result was the same, no further damage was done, but the Sox still had their work cut out for them, not having scored for twenty-six innings in a row. That was remedied in the fifth when Collins, batting with the bases loaded and only one out, hit a sacrifice fly to Roush, scoring Risberg from third. On the play Dickie Kerr ran toward second base, already occupied by Ray Schalk, and was doubled up to end the inning.

In their next at-bat, the Sox, still trailing by three, tied the game. Key hits to start the rally were made by Weaver, Jackson and Felsch. During the inning Jimmy Ring replaced Ruether on the mound. The game remained tied as it moved into the top of the tenth.

In the tenth Buck Weaver led off the proceedings with a double. Jackson bunted safely, sending Weaver to third. After Felsch struck out, Gandil hit a high infield bounder that scored Weaver with the lead run. When Kerr set down the Reds in order in the bottom of the tenth, the White Sox had a life.

Collins, who despite his sacrifice fly again wore an 0-for-4 horse collar, called the win "sweet," but "mixed."[29] Perhaps he referred to both the Reds' early lead and the Sox's sloppy performance on the base paths, where Jackson was picked off twice and Kerr pulled his gaffe. Years later he pointed out how ironic that the timely bat work of Weaver and Gandil played such a key role in the win.[30]

Following the game, Kid Gleason, who had retired to the bench from his usual spot on the coaching line, remarked that as he sat in the dugout, "I never took my eyes off the batter.... I let some others do the coaching and watched every move the fellow at bat made. I didn't mind it when a fellow failed just as long as I was satisfied that fellow gave his best effort. The best effort of the Sox will beat any ball club in the world."[31]

Gleason was doing what he deemed necessary to straighten out his team's weak hitting. They had responded with ten hits and five runs. Now the manager needed to decide what to do about the pitching. Red Faber's absence made his choice quite difficult. Cicotte was already a two-time loser. His fielding implosions had raised suspicion and ire. Yet during the season his pitching was frequently masterful and overall his pitching in both appearances against the Reds was strong. He was the obvious choice for Game Seven and Gleason went with him. The Reds countered with Sallee.

Game Seven was played in Cincinnati on October 8. Even though the Reds stood a single win from their first championship, the crowd, numbering 13,923, was exceedingly small for reasons still unknown, but subject to continuing speculation by baseball historians. Those that did attend saw a fine performance by Cicotte, as he held the Reds to seven hits and a lone run. Meanwhile, the Sox continued their improved hitting. They scored once in the first and third and twice in the fifth inning. Joe Jackson's singles in both the first and third drove in Shano Collins with all the runs Cicotte needed. Eddie Collins, who went into the game with two hits in 22 trips for a .091 average, finally came alive with a pair of hits in four at-bats. He also sacrificed and scored a run. His error in the first inning did not lead to a run. In the third inning he was called for interference when he went into second trying to break up a double play.

Now both Schalk and Collins were either feeling their Wheaties or putting on a pretty good face. The Sox catcher told readers, "I figured that no club could take three in a row from Eddie Cicotte, and I have exactly the same feeling with regard to Claude Williams." Collins felt the White Sox were "sitting in the golden seat.... I tell you they can not stop us."[32]

And so as the team hurried back to Chicago for Game Eight, there was reason to hope if you lived on Chicago's South Side. The third time was a charm for Cicotte. Certainly Schalk was correct. It would be a charm for Lefty Williams, as well. And 32,930 agreed as they jammed Comiskey with the largest crowd of the series to date.

Pat Moran, of course, had a number of pitchers to choose from for this game. He chose Hod Eller, pitching on two days rest off his Game Five victory. Since the contest was in Chicago and the Sox appeared to be awakening from their slumber, the betting odds increased for another White Sox victory, but there were also reports of large bets placed on the Reds.

It was a particularly windy day in Chicago on October 9 when the teams took the field for what promised to be an intriguing afternoon of baseball. But the suspense did not last long; not much longer than the Reds' second batter, Jake Daubert, who followed Rath's fly out with a single. Not much past Heinie Groh, who did the same, or Edd Roush, who followed that up with a double scoring Daubert. And so it went, to the tune of four runs. Williams pitched as if someone who wanted the Reds to win was holding a gun to his head. Some claim that was exactly what happened.

After the next batter, Pat Duncan, doubled past Jackson in left to drive in both Groh and Roush, Kid Gleason brought out the hook, replacing Lefty with "Big Bill" James. It was a good thing. The two teams might still be playing in the top of the first today. But James was able to limit the damage to one more run. At the end of a half-inning, the Sox were four down.

In the bottom of the first, the White Sox looked as though they might fight back. Nemo Leibold, starting in right and leading off, singled. Collins followed it up with a double to center, his first extra-base hit of the series. However, Eller settled down and retired the side, including strikeouts of Weaver and Felsch.

The Reds scored again in the top of the second and at the end of seven and one-half led 10–1. The lone Sox tally was a Joe Jackson home run. The White Sox did rally in their half of the eighth, scoring four times, but that was it. The final score was 10–5 and this World Series belonged to the Reds.

Game Eight saw Collins' bat finally come alive. He was 3-for-5, scored a run and stole a base, but the 1919 World Series clearly rivaled his 1914 World Series performance as the worst of his career. If, as Billy Evans predicted, the White Sox needed their money player to win the series, he had certainly failed to hold up his end. The Sox had suffered as a result.

Of course, it was not that simple, and, as history shows, it was exceedingly and painfully more complicated, but Collins' flaccid performance cannot be overlooked in any careful analysis of the final outcome. After the series Billy Evans, the umpire behind the plate for several of the games, came to the defense of his "money player."

"To those who did not see the series the hitting of Eddie Collins was a disappointment, yet never did Collins hit the ball harder. In one game he went out on five line drives to the outfield, four of them being brilliant catches. At other times he drove the ball right at someone."

In a separate article Evans decried those such as Johnny Evers who credited the Reds' Jimmy Smith with getting under Collins' skin and causing his subpar performance. Evans, who was stationed behind the plate in Game Two and who said in an American League game he would have stopped play to issue a warning to the Reds for their bench jockeying, said Collins told him during the game that the verbal diatribe was not a bother and asked Evans not to make an issue of it.[33]

For the top hitting performances for the White Sox, one must turn to Joe Jackson (.375, 1 HR, 5 runs, 6 RBIs) and Buck Weaver (.324, 4 runs scored). Ray Schalk batted a respectable .304, while Gandil was at .233, although he batted in five runs. The normally strong-hitting Hap Felsch was at .192 and Risberg a woeful .080, with two hits in 25 at-bats.

Talk of the Reds' great victory lasted less than a day. Instead, the observers turned their attention to a possible reason for the White Sox's demise. On October 10, less than 24 hours after the final out, a report by the *Tribune's* James Crusinberry laid it out there for all to see.

"Stories were out that the Sox had not put forth their best effort. Stories were out the big gamblers had got to them."

He turned to Kid Gleason for an answer. He did not exactly get one, but if he thought the Kid would clear the air, he did not get that either.

"I don't know yet what was the matter. Something was wrong. I didn't like the betting odds. I wish no one had ever bet a dollar on the team."[34]

A syndicated column by Hugh Fullerton that same day in the *Chicago Herald and Examiner* indicated that seven White Sox players would not return the next season.[35]

On the other hand, in his last article on the series, Collins remained on theme, expressing disappointment at the outcome, congratulating the Reds, particularly Edd Roush, for their fine play. He lauded Schalk, who was "fighting and hustling every minute," and even Buck Weaver, who "played true to form," and Joe Jackson, who "maintained his reputation with a stick." He closed by saying "of all the world series in which I have participated I don't think there is one I wanted to win more than this one."[36]

The next day Collins and Eddie Murphy headed for their homes in Philadelphia, each looking forward to their loser's individual share of approximately $3,254.36. When those shares arrived, however, delivery to eight of their teammates would be delayed. Commy, awaiting further developments, planned to hang onto them. The eight were later revealed as Chick Gandil, Eddie Cicotte, Lefty Williams, Happy Felsch, Joe Jackson, Buck Weaver, Swede Risberg and Fred McMullin. Eventually each would receive his portion of the World Series money, but each also now carried an initial blemish that would continue to fester into a permanent scar.

The Reds' individual shares were just over $5,000. The eight-game series was a financial success for both teams. When it came to the revenues, Reds owner August Garry Herrmann was overcome with joy. Even Commy could not kick up a fuss. He congratulated the Reds, thanked the loyal Sox rooters and acted as if all was right with the world. All the while he was fielding or, as many today feel, deflecting rumors of a conspiracy that could doom his high-level ball club, offering a $10,000 (some say $20,000) reward to anyone with information that any such conspiracy took place, and fighting a bar-room brawl with Ban Johnson for control of the American League and Organized Baseball.

In late 1919 as post-war America marched unknowingly toward a decade to be dubbed the "Roaring Twenties," there were major changes coming both on and off the ball field. One major change for the nation was the enactment of the Volstead Act on October 28 to effectuate the recently ratified Eighteenth Amendment, which prohibited the manufacture, sale, transportation or importation of alcoholic beverages.

On the baseball field there were cries for major changes in the game itself as well, most particularly a call for a ban on freak pitches. After years of hemming and hawing, there now seemed a consensus to outlaw the shine ball and several other pitches, including even the cherished spitball. An article in the October 21 *Tribune* indicated a serious movement in that direction, careful to point out of the White Sox, only Eddie Cicotte would be seriously hindered by such a ban.

In November, in addition to changes in the mechanics of the game, the combat between Commy and Ban Johnson loudly surfaced again. Commy made his strongest public statement to date, perhaps emboldened by that ruling in the New York court granting a permanent injunction restraining Johnson from further interference in the Mays case. Shortly thereafter the White Sox's owner, indicating he spoke for owners Frazee of the Red Sox and Ruppert of the Yankees, charged forward. He accused the American League president of "endangering not only the value of those properties [the baseball clubs] but the integrity of baseball, and we therefore intend to do everything possible to rid baseball of the impediment" by removing Johnson from his league presidency.[37]

Of course, Johnson had his loyal following as well. As the year wound down, he continued his attempts to solidify his position with the league. In the end, however, Johnson's power was severely clipped. In this pitched battle Commy was the winner, but he did not fare as well on other fronts. Rumors of that "fixing business" during the World Series persisted with strong opinions emanating from all sides, but little real evidence. On December 15 Commy announced he and Kid Gleason had separately and jointly investigated the rumors and to date found nothing to substantiate them. "[W]e have discovered nothing to indicate any member of my team double crossed me or the public last fall." Still, Commy promised to continue investigating. If any of his players were so involved, he would make sure they were out of baseball.[38]

Commy's quotes appeared in an article written by reporter I.E. Sanborn of the *Tribune*. The remainder of the article reads like an attempt to excuse the reporter and his newspaper from not previously rendering more information to its readers concerning the possibility the World Series was not played on the level, making sure readers knew there was "never any attempt to suppress it [a fix] by Comiskey, Gleason or the newspaper."[39] Clearly shades of "thou do protesteth too much."

The timing of the article is worth noting. It came exactly one month after *Collyer's Eye*, a newspaper devoted to gambling with an interest in making sure bettors shared an even playing field, revealed the names of seven players suspected of involvement. Only Buck Weaver, among those whose players' shares were withheld after the series, was spared mention. The information, it was reported, came from none other than White Sox catcher Ray Schalk, who said those named would not play for the White Sox in 1920. And Commy's quotes, as well as the *Tribune's* self-serving explanation of its reporting of the rumors, appeared the same day as the first in a series of articles by Hugh Fullerton in the *New York Evening World*, challenging baseball to fully investigate gambling in general and the play of the White Sox in the World Series in particular.

Fullerton considered Commy a close friend and praised that friend's investigation of his players. Still, he called for a hearing in front of Chicago Federal Judge Kenesaw Mountain Landis to clear the air. Fullerton's appeal was probably mild compared to what he believed he knew or really wanted to say. He was tethered to some degree by editors who feared charges of libel. He was also conflicted by his loyalty to Comiskey versus his duty to his readers and to himself. Even after presenting this watered-down version of events, Fullerton was branded a muckraker for his trouble. How could anyone believe baseball was not totally above board? F.C. Lane of *Baseball Magazine* blamed Fullerton's charges on simple ignorance. The *Tribune* concluded the White Sox lost because of overconfidence.

Nevertheless, Fullerton's articles had the desired effect. As the year came to a close, the last headline on the matter in the *Tribune* indicated in bold letters, "Investigation of Alleged Series Scandal to be Continued."[40]

CHAPTER 13

Clean Sox

"The honest ball players, or the majority of them, stand before the public as mildly guilty of being accessories after the fact, in that all save a few knew or suspected that crookedness was going forward and failed to protect their own reputation, their business and the sport from the ones who were guilty....

"...They [the dishonest players and the gamblers] proved that the game can be and has been successfully manipulated, provided the honest players on the teams do not 'squeal....

"...Plainly the outsider can not tell to a certainty. An honest player on any team, however, will know within a short time, whether or not his fellows are 'trying' to win...."
— Hugh Fullerton[1]

During the winter of 1919–20, Eddie Collins had more on his mind than battles between team owners and league officials or rumors of scandal. His contract, signed in 1915, expired with the 1919 season. A report in *The Sporting News* in December 1919 hinted that the second sacker was "inclined to be a bit temperamental," particularly when it comes to helping run the team. The article claimed that Pants Rowland was not as understanding as Gleason in that regard, insinuating that Collins might be more receptive to a new contract since Gleason remained his boss. The article hinted that Collins' spirited play on the base paths, as he led his league in stolen bases, was spurred on by the prospects of salary negotiation.[2]

It is difficult to gauge the accuracy of the short piece, but any idea that Collins would be difficult to sign became moot on February 6, 1920, when Eddie signed on Commy's dotted line for three years, salary and terms unspecified. The general consensus — an accurate one — was that Collins was offered the same salary and took it.[3]

Negotiations for new contracts for many of Collins' teammates were more protracted, tinged as they were with the stain of conspiracy. A number of the "suspects" decided this was their year to fight for higher salaries. Weaver, still under contract, even asked for a trade. Many of the contractual negotiations ran right up to and into spring training, even though Commy shortened the training period by deciding to wait until the third week of March to start, at least a couple of weeks later than most other teams.

Comiskey was obviously disgusted at the gall of these holdouts, but eventually capitulated and raised some salaries. Cicotte went up to $10,000; Williams was increased from $2,600 to $6,000 and promised a $1,000 bonus if he won 20 games. Happy Felsch went from $3,750 to $7,000. Weaver's contract was renegotiated to $7,250. Jackson, asking for $10,000, received $8,000 for each of the next three years. The contract contained a ten-day clause, which became a matter of dispute when Jackson, who did not read, claimed Grabiner told him it was not included. Although the owner was disgusted with Risberg's hapless World Series performance, he increased the shortstop's salary to $3,250. Even sub-infielder Fred McMullin received a raise. Yet when Comiskey offered Gandil a small increase and the first baseman announced his retirement and intent to manage a club in Idaho for more money than the Sox had offered him, the owner essentially let the matter drop. Gandil did not play for the White Sox in 1920.

By the time the club finally assembled in their new digs at Waco, Texas, to prepare for another season, the game of baseball as they knew it was dramatically changed. Although many of these changes were in the works for some time, their occurrence, in almost rapid-fire sequence, still left many gasping for air.

On January 5 it was announced that Babe Ruth, the top-notch pitcher turned power hitter, was now a member of the New York Yankees. The deal, actually on paper since December 26 of the previous year, involved $100,000 (some say $125,000) cash and a $300,000 loan to help Red Sox owner Harry Frazee climb out from under the burden of debt. Ruth had come a long way from the minor league pitcher Collins and the A's faced in Baltimore several years before. In 1919 the Babe slammed a record 29 home runs and at age 24 his future still awaited. The purchase price was the largest to date and, of course, worth every penny.

On February 12 Garry Herrmann, the "neutral" member and thereby chairman of the National Commission, submitted his resignation after 16 years in that position. A growing discontent among the owners, as well as problems with the minor leagues, pushed Herrmann to his decision. The fact that his closest ally, Ban Johnson, was in a weakened position did not help. The resignation was actually rumored for some time, but now that it was official, the move to either replace Herrmann, or as some urged, revise the system for governing major league baseball was to begin in earnest.

At the winter meetings in Chicago, the owners addressed issues involving leadership, but they also addressed issues involving the rules of the game. Once again this was not a new topic. For some time the argument persisted that freak pitches gave an unfair advantage to the pitcher at the expense of the hitter and the overall good of the sport. On February 9 the rules committee of the two leagues met in joint session in Chicago and banned the use of all such pitches, including the emery ball, previously banned in the American League, the shine ball, and most significantly, the spitter. As to the spitball, each team was permitted to designate two pitchers who would be permitted to continue to use the pitch. Although this exception was originally limited to the 1920 season, it was extended a year later to last for the careers of each exempt pitcher. In fact, the last "legal" spitball artist to retire was Burleigh Grimes, a Hall of Fame pitcher who last pitched in 1934 for the Yankees. Red Faber flung his wet horsehide until 1933.

This same year saw the introduction of other modifications which favored the hitter. One major change was in the way umpires handled replacement of the game ball. More fans were now permitted to keep foul balls hit into the grandstand. Actually the practice of retrieving the ball was loosened somewhat during the war to permit spectating servicemen to have a prized souvenir. In the past these balls were used over and over until they became quite scuffed and dirty. A dirty ball was much harder to see and hit than a clean one. In order to ensure a clean ball remained in that condition for a longer time, the practice of doctoring the ball by rubbing dirt or tobacco juice on it as it was thrown around the infield, for example after a strikeout, was prohibited. Once again, advantage hitter.

One other change was more subtle, or perhaps as some believe never occurred at all. But beginning after the war in 1919, the American League ball was made with an Australian yarn. Many argue its tighter wrapping resulted in a harder, more elastic "live" ball.

It may have been a new jumpier baseball, or it may have been the much envied and increasingly copied Babe Ruth swing that began producing more offense, particularly with regard to baseball's featured attraction: the home run. Eddie Collins and his contemporaries did not know it, but as they practiced their trade in Waco and other training camps in spring of 1920, they were swiftly moving away from a "dead ball" era and into a "lively ball" era that still exists today.

But all that was for the statisticians and the historians. In March, once Weaver, Risberg and the others resolved their differences with management, the attention of the White Sox was focused on finding a new first baseman.

Not for the first time, Collins was late in arriving to camp, having asked and received permission to remain home in Philadelphia and appear a week late. Even though the White Sox were already encamping later than most, there was little risk in acceding to Eddie's request since he kept himself close to playing condition year around.

One of the early arrivals was Eddie Cicotte, still unsigned but according to Kid Gleason, unfazed by the ban on his beloved shine ball. After watching his ace cut loose with a mix of curves, fastballs and a pitch he called a "sinker," Gleason declared "the new rules will not bother him a bit."[4]

Collins arrived in camp in time to play an exhibition game with a local Waco semipro outfit on March 23. Soon all the regulars save Gandil had reported. But if Eddie thought a few months away from baseball and an adjustment in salaries would mend the fractures on this team, he was wrong. In his biography of Joe Jackson, author David Fleitz describes the atmosphere.

"Even after the holdout players reported to camp, the writers couldn't help but notice a chill in the air. The seven remaining suspected players rarely spoke to anyone but each other. They rode together on the trains, ate together in the restaurants, and went to the movies or the bars together in the evenings. In previous years, the Gandil-Risberg-Weaver group sniped and argued with the Collins-Schalk-Faber group, but now there seemed to be no overt animosity between the seven suspected players and the rest of the team. In its place was a stony silence, an unbreachable wall of quiet."[5]

The early choice for Gandil's replacement was left-handed batter Ted Jourdan. At 24 the New Orleans native's previous big-league experience was a skimpy 46 at-bats, all with the White Sox. The experiment did not last long. In short order John "Shano" Collins, a veteran and a much better hitter, became the regular first baseman. Jourdan's 40 games at first base in 1920 were his last as a major leaguer.

Sometimes in all the fuss that followed 1919, there is a tendency to overlook the 1920 American League season, but in reality it was one of the junior circuit's most exciting campaigns. Even the home opener for the White Sox on April 14 was a nail-biter. It was played over 11 innings before a crowd of some 25,000 Chicagoans, who according to James Crusinberry, "simply forgot all about the nasty rumors, the unexpected series defeats, the bum playing, and all the other things, and went back for more."[6]

What they witnessed was an excellent performance on both sides of the field. The locals prevailed in the bottom of the eleventh when Collins doubled to drive home Buck Weaver for the second time in the game, this time with the game winner. Final score: White Sox 3, Tigers 2. Eddie also contributed a single to the cause in the ninth.

It appeared from his strong performance that Lefty Williams was back in form, as was Eddie Cicotte in the next outing when he shut out the Tigers, 4–0. In fact, the Pale Hose scampered quickly out of the gates in 1920, winning their initial six games and 10 of their first 12. One big factor in the White Sox's quick start was the return of a healthy Red Faber. Over the course of the year, he won 23 against 13 losses. In a year when the hitters ruled, his 2.99 ERA was significant and the best of the White Sox's starters.

The first sign that all might not go the way of the White Sox occurred early on when the Cleveland Indians arrived for a five-game series at Comiskey and left town with four wins. This was a newer, stronger version of the Tribe than most fans were accustomed to seeing. Managed by Tris Speaker, still one of the stars of the game, the regular lineup had few weaknesses in 1920. Only second baseman Bill Wambsganss hit less than .250, and he was far from an easy out. Shortstop Ray Chapman was one of the best at his craft and catcher Steve O'Neill was a standout. On the mound Jim Bagby (31–12, 2.89), Stan Coveleski (24–14, 2.49), and Ray Caldwell (20–10, 3.86) were formidable. In short, coming off a 1919 season in which they finished second, only three and one-half games behind the White Sox, they were legitimate contenders.

The next opponent on the White Sox's schedule was another up-and-comer, the New York Yankees. Sporting their newest acquisition they polished off the White Sox twice at the Polo Grounds, as they too announced their bid to replace the White Sox for league honors. In the first contest Ruth homered twice in a 6–5 Yankee win. The next day all the Yankees got into the act, as they pounded Lefty Williams for a 14–8 victory. Suddenly the White Sox, losers of seven of eight, stood at 11–9 and in third place.

Although the White Sox's fans were seemingly back on the bandwagon and Commy continued to hold his breath, the baseball community was not totally ready to forget what happened in Chicago and Cincinnati the previous October. On May 6 Oscar Reichow, writing in *The Sporting News* under the front page headline, "Why Do Honest Ball Players Stand for Crooks in Ranks?" wondered why players, as well as owners, did not step up "to rid the sport of the men who have no scruples about throwing honesty to the winds."[7]

If anyone on the White Sox's roster read Reichow's article, no one blinked. As the season rolled on, box scores showed that the rule changes instituted during the off-season were having the desired effects. Baseballs were flying all over the field, many out of the park, and batting averages were going way up. The White Sox benefited as well. For the season their .295 team average and .353 OBP stood third. Joe Jackson would lead the team at .382 and also hit 12 home runs, while driving in 121 mates. Hap Felsch enjoyed a great season as well, hitting .338 with a team-leading 14 home runs and 115 RBIs. Weaver was up there, too, hitting .331 and driving in 74. Among the regulars only Nemo Leibold, no longer platooning once Shano Collins took over at first, struggled at .220.

Collins was a beneficiary of the "live" ball as well, hitting a career-high .372. Yet the figure was only fifth-best in the league; George Sisler of the Browns led all hitters at .407. Eddie's 224 hits were also a career high, as was his .493 slugging average.

The White Sox were hitting as the season moved into June, but so was everyone else. By the end of the month, despite a record of 38–26, they remained in third place, four and one-half games from first. On June 30 they raised their 1919 American League championship flag, honored Ray Schalk on his "day" and pasted the Tigers, 14–0, behind Collins' four hits, three runs and two stolen bases. Unlike May when the team struggled at 13–16, in June the Sox were 18–8, and there was still hope for better things to come.

In July the White Sox continued to play good ball, as did Collins, who even hit one into the right field bleachers on July 2 in a loss to the Browns. On July 6 prior to a game with the Indians, Eddie accepted a "loving" cup from his Philadelphia Masonic Lodge. The White Sox won the game which followed, 5–4, behind Red Faber, to complete a three-game sweep of the Tribe. Eddie followed that up with another home run, this time an inside-the-park variety, for the only run for Dickie Kerr in a 1–0 cliffhanger on July 12.

In 1920 at 21–9 with an ERA of 3.37, Kerr was one of four 20-game winners for the Sox, a noteworthy number from one team. The others were Faber, Lefty Williams (22–14, 3.91) and Eddie Cicotte (21–10, 3.26). That the White Sox were still a team of high-caliber, given the depth of their starting pitching and the quality of their every day lineup, could not be argued. Still there were questions about the team involving the remaining "seven."

The question marks of the previous fall remained in 1920, starting with the team's first loss of the season back on April 27. According to Eliot Asinof in his famous book, *Eight Men Out*, the odds clearly favored the White Sox based on their six-game winning streak, yet suddenly shifted to 6–5, with Cleveland favored. Backed by Red Faber's strong arm, the Sox led 2–1 when Joe Jackson retrieved a ball hit over his head and relayed to Risberg. The Swede took the throw, then wheeled and threw so badly to Weaver that neither he nor his backup Faber could touch it. The tying run scored and Cleveland went on in the ninth to win the game.

According to Asinof, "[t]he pattern was repeated periodically throughout the summer" and it was aided in this instance by the gambler's best weapon: "blackmail." If the seven remaining players wanted the lid to remain on the jar, they needed to cooperate.[8]

Perhaps the White Sox–Yankee game on July 17 in New York was another of those games. Eddie Cicotte started for the Sox, who had won a double-bill from the Senators a day earlier. Before it was over, the Yankees scored 20 runs on 21 hits and the White Sox committed seven errors, including four by Buck Weaver and one each by Risberg and Felsch. Two more losses to the Yankees followed.

Interestingly, during spring training when Weaver was still a holdout, a local Chicago paper *The Whip* had compared the third baseman's overall value to that of Eddie Collins. Since Collins was still quite popular in Chicago, his poor World Series performance notwithstanding, the sharp comments were a bit surprising. After calling Weaver the best third baseman in baseball and "the Best Dispositioned Ball Player," the paper went on to praise Weaver as "a Ball Player whose value is more to Comiskey, than a deck of Eddie Collins [*sic*] a player who never caused dissension for any owner, a better hitter [*sic*] in all just as finished a player, and who has made Eddie Collins look better than he really is." Then in an obvious reference to Weaver's resentment: "His refusal to help the Wonderful Eddie Collins to draw his big juicy salary is but natural."[9]

Near the end of July, it looked like the White Sox might find out just how much they would miss Collins when he was beaned by Hooks Dauss of Detroit in the first inning of a game. According to a report of the action, the pitch clobbered Collins on the back of his head and he "dropped as if struck with a sledgehammer and immediately players from both sides rushed to the plate."[10]

Fortunately, Collins opened his eyes and was able to take first. Moments later he scored on a triple by Joe Jackson. Still, Eddie left the game at the end of the inning, a 6–4 Sox win and one of 19 out of 22 over the Tigers. He missed the next game before returning to the lineup. By August 1 the Sox stood at 61–38, in third, four and one-half back of the Indians and tied with the Yankees in the loss column.

On August 17 buoyed by a seven-game winning streak, the White Sox were in second, just a pair behind Cleveland in the standings. They were in Philadelphia with an open date watching the Giants, a potential World Series opponent, when they heard news of another beaning, this time one that left its victim, shortstop Ray Chapman of the Indians, dead. They sadly shook their heads but showed little surprise when told the pitch which eventually took Chapman's life was thrown by Carl Mays, perhaps the game's most notorious bean-ball pitcher.

Although the loss of the valuable Chapman most certainly would affect the Indians' pennant chances, the White Sox's thoughts were on a fallen ball player. The *Tribune's* I.E. Sanborn described their reaction.

"In all the conversation among the players there was not a hint of what the accident means to the White Sox in the pennant race, although unquestionably it will weaken both their contenders for the flag. Only deep sorrow for the loss of a great player was to be heard, varied occasionally with a bit of criticism for American league officials and umpires for not having compelled Carl Mays to break himself of the habit of hitting batsmen by penalizing him more severely for doing it."[11]

Throughout the league there was angry talk of a boycott unless Mays was banned. The newspapers, most notably the *Cleveland Press*, cried out against the Yankees' side-armer. Meanwhile, a dispirited Cleveland team staggered on, losing a pair of games to a Red Sox team they had previously dominated. The scores of 12–0 and 4–0 told the tale. On August 21 a White Sox victory over the Senators at Griffith Stadium pushed them into first place. Since August 8 they had won 11 of 13. One of those games was a forfeit when A's fans swarmed the field thinking a game was over and refused to leave when told by the umpire it was not finished.

As the White Sox arrived in New York for a three-game series with the Yankees, who were thinking about building a huge new ballpark, there was still talk of a boycott. At least two teams besides the Indians, the Browns and Senators, were in agreement. The White Sox and others took the position that Chapman's beaning was an accident. Kid Gleason, a former pitcher, reasoned that if a ball club did not take the field against Mays, it would appear they lacked courage. He recognized that the Yankee pitcher worked inside to any player he thought was crowding the plate, but his boys had never had trouble with Mays. Pitching hitters tight was just part of the game. A team managed by him would never back down.

An important three-game series with the contending Yankees opened on August 26 at the Polo Grounds. The Sox brought their hitting shoes, winning, 16–5. The barrage, which included three hits by Collins and a steal of home as part of a thrilling triple steal, overcame home run number 44 by the Babe. The next day the White Sox could test their manager's theories on the pitching of Carl Mays. The "bone of contention" was scheduled to start.

The contest on Friday, August 27 offered Mays his second opportunity to show his wares since the fatal beaning. By now the Sox led the Indians by two and one-half games and the Yankees by a full three. In the morning the White Sox held an informal meeting. If any of the players urged a boycott, word of it did not leak to the press.

Although Mays had already faced his initial test, passing with flying colors as he shut out the Tigers, he still appeared nervous. He kept the ball to the outside of the plate and low. The White Sox, who probably were a bit nervous themselves, took advantage of May's reluctance to pitch his normal game. They collected eight hits in the first three innings but only turned them into three runs. By the time Mays left the game for a pinch-hitter, it was the tenth inning and the Sox hit total was at 15. Still the score was knotted at five and the Yanks, missing Babe Ruth due to a swollen arm from an insect bite, eventually won it in the bottom of the twelfth. Collins was 3-for-6 during the contest.

As time passed, the boycott effort lost its sizzle. After a disappointing 3–0 loss to the still–Ruthless Yankees, a frustrated White Sox bunch left New York for Boston, hopeful of friendlier confines, still gripping a slim lead. The teams were scheduled for a three-game set, the last series on this road swing. In the opener in Boston on August 30, Lefty Williams was paired off against Sad Sam Jones, a right-hander who won 229 games during an illustrious career. Collins hit well, going 3-for-4 with a double. However, the only other hits were a single by Felsch and a double by Risberg, as the ChiSox fell 4–0 for their third straight loss.

The next day with Eddie Cicotte on the mound versus an old Collins' friend, Bullet Joe Bush, the White Sox were not much better, losing 7–3. Again Collins' bat was hot as he went 3-for-4 with a double, but Cicotte blew up in the seventh inning. *Boston Globe* sportswriter

Jim O'Leary was given to exclaim, "Why, they're playing just like they did in the World Series!"[12]

For the third game played September 1, Gleason juggled his batting order, switching Weaver to the second slot and batting Collins third. Each managed but one hit in four tries, as the White Sox behind Dickie Kerr fell for the fifth straight time. The game and a 2–0 lead vanished in innings four through six when the Red Sox scored one, two and three runs, respectively. During the game errors were made by Eddie, as well as by Kerr and first baseman John Collins. The *Tribune* noted that some of Kerr's problems were his own doing, including walks and a wild heave to Weaver at third base. Yet years later, in 1949, a condensed article from the *Boston Post* appeared in *Baseball Digest* in which Collins discussed the game in a different context. Although by then his memory was a bit shaky, and back in 1920 there was still over a month to go until the season's end, Eddie's remarks about the occurrence bear repeating.

> It was in Boston the incident happened that cost us the 1920 pennant. Some gamblers got panicky that we'd win again and they must have gone to the players they had under the thumb and ordered the rest of the games thrown. We were leading by three games with seven to go. We knew something was wrong but we couldn't put the finger on it. The feeling between the players was very bad. Dickie Kerr was pitching for us and doing well. A Boston player hit a ball that fell between Jackson and Felsch. We thought it should have been caught. The next batter bunted and Kerr made a perfect throw to Weaver for a force out. The ball pops out of Weaver's glove. When the inning was over Kerr scaled his glove across the diamond.
>
> He looks at Weaver and Risberg who are standing together and says, 'If you'd told me you wanted to lose this game, I could have done it a lot easier.' There is almost a riot on the bench. Kid Gleason breaks up two fights. That was the end. We lose three or four more games the same way.[13]

Along those same lines, Collins once told sports columnist Joe Williams he felt members of his 1920 team threw at least a dozen games. They would have thrown more, but the pitching was just too formidable.[14]

Others on the team saw what was happening, too. Schalk's backup, Byrd Lynn, who some say remained close to Joe Jackson, and utility infielder Harvey McClellan were two who spoke out about it. According to Lynn, "We soon noticed how carefully they [the seven playing "suspects"] studied the scoreboard ... and that they always made errors which lost us the game when Cleveland and New York were losing. If Cleveland won — we won. If Cleveland lost — we lost. The idea was to keep up the betting odds, but not to let us win the pennant."

According to McClellan, certain players had deliberately "thrown" the three games just completed in Boston.[15]

Unlike Collins, Lynn and McClellan were speaking just a few weeks after the fact. Their comments as well as the later comments by Collins undoubtedly reflected the overall mood of the team on September 1 as they packed their bags and returned to Chicago for the last month of the season. The very next day, on September 2, an off-day, Eddie Collins, the team's captain and at the very least one of the leaders of the faction of "non-suspects," sought and received an audience with his boss, Charles Comiskey. It was a private meeting. The topic, obviously, concerned the play of certain members of the team. Although it is believed Collins sought the meeting to share his suspicions of the motives behind the play of certain teammates and to report fixed games, Comiskey denied it. Testifying in court in Milwaukee in 1924 in connection with a separate lawsuit brought by Joe Jackson to recover back pay, the White Sox's owner admitted the meeting but claimed Collins was concerned that Eddie Cicotte "wasn't trying" and suggested if the owner talked with Cicotte, the team would win the pennant. According to Commy, Collins told him the pitcher was "nervous and coming to a break," never that Cicotte was crooked.[16]

One thing about the meeting seems clear; Commy did nothing at that point to respond to Collins' report. The season continued and the White Sox, now in second and falling, continued as is. Perhaps one reason the White Sox's owner stood fast was the 21-game homestand his team was about to start. Each game promised to have something to do with the outcome of the pennant, and each would surely produce a tidy sum from the gate. So far, in almost a year, Commy had done nothing substantial to shake the tree and it was working out quite well.

But doing nothing in some cases does not get you very far. In the case of Comiskey and several key White Sox players, it bought only a few more days. None of this was readily apparent, however, when on September 4 it was reported that William Veeck, the president of the Chicago Cubs, was investigating accusations that members of his team plotted to throw a game to the Phillies. The Cubs learned of the plot, tried to avert it, but still lost the game, 3–0. Veeck promised a quick and thorough investigation. He was lauded for his stance, a backhanded slap at the efforts to uncover similar accusations across town.

Three days later on September 7, Chief Justice Charles A. McDonald of the Cook County [Chicago] bench convened a grand jury to look into the rumors surrounding the Cubs-Phillies game. In addition, they were to investigate the overall problems of gambling in baseball. It now seemed certain the broad hand of Ban Johnson was stirring a great deal of the broth here. In the Phils-Cubs game, Johnson saw a way to finally examine the 1919 World Series rumors and, perhaps, trim the sails of his arch-enemy, Charlie Comiskey. Judge McDonald was his man, perhaps even his choice to replace Garry Herrmann on the National Commission. And, sure enough, during the two weeks between the announcement of the grand jury and September 22, when it was to convene, a hue and cry went out not only in Chicago, but also across the land to look into the rumors that the 1919 World Series was fixed.

An example of such pressure locally was verbalized in the September 19 edition of the *Tribune*, where it was stated the Cubs-Phillies "fixed game" had "naturally revived the discussion of last fall's world series." The writer asserted that fans were fed up with repeated delays in getting to the bottom of the matter. In addition the *Tribune* printed a letter which was probably prompted by sportswriter James Crusinberry. The writer, local luminary Fred M. Loomis, "a personal friend of several members of the White Sox club," suggested that the grand jury was the perfect tool to finally determine just what happened and who, if anyone, was to blame.

"There is a perfectly good Grand Jury located in this county....

"Those who have in their possession the evidence of gambling last fall in the world series should come forward with it and present it in a manner that may give assurance to the whole country that justice will be done in this case where the confidence of the people seems to have been so flagrantly violated."[17]

While all this was going on, the White Sox's season continued as well. By now, given all that had passed and all that was ahead, it must have been a conflicted lot, yet overall in September the team was 18–8. And on September 22, the day the grand jury was to convene, the team was in the midst of a seven-game winning streak, in second place, one and one-half games out with eight still to play. There was, therefore, plenty of time for a third pennant in four seasons. And to boot they were back on the road in Cleveland for a three-game season-defining series with the Indians.

On September 22 the White Sox had a day off. By now they were all aware that the Cook County inquiry would encompass their actions in 1919, as well as the Cubs-Phils affair. Although Kid Gleason, who was on the witness list, was excused until he returned from Cleveland, Commy was on the early call list. One question sure to be asked by Assistant State Attorney Hartley L. Replogle was why the club owner delayed distributing World Series shares to eight of his players.

Although the grand jury sessions initiated that same day were supposed to be secret, it did not take long for the press to find out exactly where the inquiry was headed. In fact, the prosecutor Replogle spread the news himself, telling the *Tribune* that the 1919 Series "was not on the square. From five to seven players on the White Sox team are involved."[18]

Exactly what Charles Comiskey said during his testimony on September 22 was not revealed, but the *Tribune* asserted that affidavits to be produced by Cubs infielder Buck Herzog would discuss an even earlier plot to fix a Cubs-Phillies game than the one in question and would implicate the White Sox in a fix scheme during the last World Series as well. The distance between Cleveland and Chicago is about 300 miles. Perhaps in 1920 that was enough to insulate the White Sox from the events beginning to engulf the baseball world. On September 23 as the inquiry continued, the Chicagoans met the Indians needing two of three wins just to stay alive in the pennant race. They took care of part of that equation by winning the series opener in grand style, 10–3. Dickie Kerr got the win. The White Sox were but a slim one-half game from first. The next day they awoke to learn about a statement by Ban Johnson that was startling in both its directness and timing.

"I have evidence, and much of it is now before the Grand Jury, that certain notorious gamblers are threatening to expose the 1919 World Series as a fixed event unless the Chicago White Sox players drop out of the current race intentionally to let the Indians win. These gamblers have made heavy bets on the Cleveland team."[19]

It is possible some of Johnson's information on the White Sox's questionable play in 1920 came directly from Eddie Collins. An uncredited report in *The Sporting News* in February 1921 mentions Collins' September 1920 meeting with Commy, claims that if nothing was changed Eddie threatened to leave the team, and when nothing was changed went to Ban Johnson.[20]

Johnson, of course, was sticking the knife to Commy. When he revealed he had told the grand jury that in late 1919 Chick Gandil, Eddie Cicotte and Fred McMullin asked him for assistance in obtaining their World Series shares from Comiskey, he was just twisting it a little. The White Sox's owner, on the other hand, quickly dismissed Johnson's statements as just another attempt by the American League president to protect his investment in the Indians.

Up until now, the gambling furor seemed to have little effect on the White Sox's ability to win. The 10–3 victory over the Indians the previous night was their seventh victory in a row. One way to show Ban Johnson and everyone else they were playing to win in 1920 was simply to keep on winning. To do that in game two of the series, all they had to do was knock off 25-year-old Walter "Duster" Mails, a lefty with fewer than 10 major-league starts under his belt. In this case, however, looks were deceiving. Mails was enjoying a great season (7–0, 1.85) and he was brimming with confidence. In his book about the fatal pitch that killed Ray Chapman and its effect on the 1920 season, author Mike Sowell described a discussion between Mails and umpire Billy Evans that took place just prior to the game.

"Warming up before the start of play, the brash, southpaw [Mails] turned to umpire Billy Evans and boasted, 'I'm going to shut these bums out.'

"Evans laughed.

"'Have you ever heard of Shoeless Joe Jackson, Buck Weaver, and Eddie Collins?' he asked.

"'Sure,' came the reply, 'but have they ever heard of The Great Mails?'"[21]

That type of bravado could get a young, relatively inexperienced athlete in trouble. In this case the only team in "trouble" was the Chicago White Sox. When the game ended, despite a fine effort by Red Faber, they stood on the short end of a 2–0 count. The game was on the line in the fifth, the bases full of Pale Hose and Speaker about to use the hook, when Mails really went to work. First, he struck out Weaver on three straight pitches. Collins, who went 1-for-3 with a walk on the day, presented a tougher out. He worked the count to 3–2, including three successive fouls, then swung at a ball and missed it by a mile to end the inning and his team's final threat. Mails had, indeed, "shut those bums out."

The next day an article in the *Tribune* attributed Collins' strikeout, as well as Ray Schalk's inability to nail an Indian runner at second, to the reports that reached Cleveland of the grand jury inquiry. If that was so, then one would have thought the White Sox's performance would suffer even more in game three of the Indians series. The newspapers on the morning before that final game were once again filled with reports, now even more detailed, alleging a plot and naming names, including all eight players whose salaries were withheld. In addition, there were reports that Rube Benton, the New York Giants' pitcher, was claiming that a Cincinnati man named Philip Hahn, a betting "commissioner" for a gambling syndicate, told him that the 1919 World Series was fixed for $100,000. According to Benton:

"We discussed various players on the team. Buck Weaver's name was not mentioned, nor were the names of Jackson, Eddie Collins, John Collins or Ray Schalk. Five players were mentioned by Hahn in the course of the conversation. Four are: Eddie Cicotte ... Claude Williams ... Chick Gandil ... and Hap Felsch.... I do not recall the name of the fifth man."[22]

So perhaps even conspiracy theorists could have overlooked the White Sox for offering a shaky performance in that final game on September 25, but this was one mysterious team. Therefore, in keeping with their almost mystic aura, the White Sox won the game, played before 31,000 rabid Indians fans, 5–1. According to the *Tribune*, the game was won by those White Sox on the "doubtful" list.[23] Lefty Williams pitched a five-hitter. Joe Jackson clubbed a home run and added a pair of doubles for good measure. Even Swede Risberg chipped in with a couple of hits. Collins scored a run while singling in four trips. As the White Sox headed home, they trailed the Indians by only a half-game and still had five games to close that narrow gap. In addition, there was good news from the East. The Yankees had split four with the Senators and now faced virtual elimination.

By the time the White Sox arrived in Chicago, the grand jury investigation into their World Series activities was in full swing. The grand jury was using its subpoena power to cast a large net. Subpoenas awaited Eddie and John Collins, Schalk and Eddie Murphy among others, although it was said their appearances could wait until after the pennant race was decided. Their names on a prospective witness list were expected. However, another name on that list, big-time New York gambler Arnold Rothstein, was not. The revelations, emanating from the grand jury sessions, coming at almost a rat-a-tat pace, had everyone on the edge of their seats.

In their first game back home on September 26, the Sox won again, 8–1, over Detroit behind Cicotte. It would be win number 21 for the season and 208 for his 14-year career. It would also be his last.

In the morning, despite their ninth victory in their last 10 games, the White Sox's hopes for a pennant continued to grow dim. James Crusinberry, writing for the *Tribune*, disclosed to readers that Charles Comiskey now admitted that he was convinced after the first game of the World Series "that some one had 'fixed' some of his players." Since Commy was not speaking to Ban Johnson, he voiced his opinions at that time to John A. Heydler, the National League's president. Heydler confirmed that he and Comiskey spoke about the owner's suspicions then and again after Game Two, when Commy was even more convinced. Then after a third discussion, when the teams were back in Chicago for Game Three and Commy told him Kid Gleason was also worried someone had "reached" his players, Heydler stated he went to Johnson, who "replied with a rather curt reply that made me drop the matter."[24]

This sequence of events differs somewhat in manner and considerably in timing from other descriptions, particularly that of Eliot Asinof in *Eight Men Out*. Asinof has Comiskey's visit to Heydler and their joint visit to Johnson occurring in Cincinnati at the Sinton Hotel in the early morning hours, approximately 12 hours after the White Sox's defeat in Game One. Johnson's reply to Comiskey was "a classically vindictive exhalation: 'That is the whelp of a beaten cur!'"[25] Still, the overall effect is the same. Each report served notice that there was serious smoke early on in the 1919 World Series. And where there is smoke, there is often fire. It was also an indication that when it came to the fault in the matter of reporting and investigating the affair, there was plenty of blame to share.

On the afternoon of September 27, the seemingly impervious 1920 White Sox, still intact, got together with the Tigers for yet another game. Behind six-hit pitching from Dickie Kerr, Chicago won the contest, 2–0. Both runs scored on what would be Shoeless Joe Jackson's last major league safety. In fact, as it turned out, even though the win pushed the White Sox's record to 95–56 and kept them a mere six percentage points behind Cleveland, the game would mark a series of lasts.

Although Chicago, with its Cook County Grand Jury, was the lightning rod for the growing investigation into the 1919 World Series, it was the city of Philadelphia that served up the juiciest yarn to date, which in turn served to ignite all that followed. The tale came from former boxer and some-time baseball player Billy Maharg. Now an auto maker, Maharg, presumably motivated by the $10,000 reward still on Comiskey's desk, brought his version of events to sportswriter Jimmy Isaminger of the *Philadelphia North American*. The story broke on September 27 and appeared on September 28 in headlines on page one of newspapers throughout the country. Maharg's tale, startling to even those who were privy to similar bits and pieces over the past several days, was capsulized in the *Chicago Tribune* as follows:

The major points of Maharg's revelations charge:

1. That the first, second and final games of last year's world's series were "thrown" by eight members of the White Sox team to Cincinnati.
2. That the offer to "fix" the series was volunteered by Eddie Cicotte to Bill Burns and Maharg in a hotel in New York.
3. That the White Sox were promised $100,000 to lose the games but actually received only $10,000.
4. That Abe Attell, former feather-weight champion, presented a fake telegram, won a fortune for himself and a clique of New York gamblers, but did not keep his word with the White Sox players in on the deal or with Burns and Maharg.
5. Burns and Maharg lost nearly every dollar they had betting on the third game, which they thought was fixed.[26]

The Maharg story, of course, pushed the temperature in Chicago more than several degrees higher. There was talk that the state's prosecutor Replogle would put Eddie Collins on the stand to answer questions "concerning several plays which occurred during the world series with the Reds." Gleason and Schalk were to testify, as well as a Mrs. Henrietta D. Kelley, a lady who rented to Cicotte and several other ball players and who was a "friend" of Eddie Collins and Ray Schalk.[27]

The focus, of course, was on Eddie Cicotte since according to Maharg, he was the key plotter. The pressure on the Sox's pitching ace so great, it did not take him long to break. Although the exact details of how he came to be in Commy's office on September 28 will probably never be fully known, the fact remains he did appear. Before the day was through, not only Cicotte but Joe Jackson had implicated themselves to Comiskey and his attorney, Alfred Austrian. Furthermore, they had allegedly waived their immunity, testifying before the grand jury that they received money — Cicotte $10,000 and Jackson $5,000 — from gamblers for their play, or lack thereof, in the World Series. Exactly what they said, whom they said it to, when they said it, and what it meant, i.e., was it a confession, and most importantly, what, if anything, did the involved teammates do to earn that money are questions still hotly debated today. What has never been denied is that money was received.

The appearance of Cicotte and then Jackson before the grand jury was followed the next day by both Lefty Williams, who allegedly told a similar story, and through a newspaper interview, Happy Felsch.

As a result of his testimony, as well as the testimony of the prior witnesses, indictments were handed down against Eddie Cicotte, Joe Jackson, Lefty Williams, Fred McMullin, Happy Felsch, Swede Risberg, Buck Weaver and Chick Gandil. Only Gandil was no longer a member of the Sox. The remaining seven active players were suspended by Commy, pending a final resolution of their guilt or innocence. "I [Comiskey] take this action even though it costs Chicago the pennant."[28]

In one fell swoop one-half of the starting pitching staff and infield of the White Sox as well as two-thirds of the outfield were wiped out. In making his announcement, the White Sox's owner attempted to take credit for the disclosures which led to the indictments. The passage of time and a much closer look by baseball historians at the available information on the events and actions of Comiskey, his staff and advisors leads many to draw just the opposite conclusion.[29]

Certainly everyone connected with the White Sox was shaken by the rapid turn of events. However, not everyone was sad. In fact, a number of the White Sox celebrated the indictments. September 28 was an off-day for the team. Aware of developing events, a group of the players, including Eddie Collins, Eddie Murphy, Amos Strunk and Nemo Leibold, drove down to the courthouse around 2 P.M. and parked a block or two away. Sam Pass, a friend of many of the players and a witness during the grand jury proceedings, saw the group on his way into the courthouse. When he arrived inside, he learned of the indictments. Quickly he ran outside, found Collins and the others and told them the news. The *Tribune* reported their reaction.

"Little Nemo Liebold [*sic*] hugged Eddie Collins. Eddie swatted Amos Strunk on the back. Amos swung his left into Mike [*sic*] Murphy's ribs. Then there was a rush to telephones to notify Ray Schalk and Red Faber and John Collins and Dick Kerr and some of the other 'right' fellows who had borne the burden all season."[30]

After the brief celebration, plans were made to meet for dinner at a local downtown eatery. The original group was supplemented by Zeb Terry and Tommy Daly, former White Sox players now with the Cubs. They then headed to captain Collins' apartment on the South Side where they were joined by Ray Schalk. At midnight reports indicated the party was still going strong and someone was sent out for more food. One notable absentee was Kid Gleason. At one point an unidentified player, some believe Eddie Collins, explained to a reporter why everyone felt such a sense of relief.

"No one will ever know what we put up with all this summer. I don't know how we ever got along. I know there were many times when things were about to break into a fight, but it never got that far.

"Hardly any of us have talked with any of those fellows, except on the ball field, since the season opened. Even during the batting practice our gang stood in one group, waiting a turn to hit, and the other gang had their own group. We went along and gritted our teeth and played ball. We had to trail along with those fellows all summer, and all the time felt that they had thrown us down. It was tough. Now the load has been lifted. No wonder we feel like celebrating."[31]

It is not so hard to believe it was Eddie Collins who made that statement. After all, he seemed to be the point man for the divisions on the team. In 1949 he told *Baseball Digest* that during the 1919 season no member of his infield would throw the ball to him and that Gandil never spoke to him the entire time he was with the team.

"Discord was the keynote of the day — everyday."[32] In fact, in 1919, "players would even double cross each other on the field."[33]

It made little difference who made the statement, the *Daily News* now called the group at Eddie's apartment the "Square Sox." Later others would call them the "Clean Sox," in contrast to the eight indicted players who already sported their own particular brand of infamy, forever known as "Black Sox."

But happy or not there was still a pennant on the line and offers of help were coming from unexpected places. Harry Frazee, the Red Sox's president and ardent Ban Johnson foe, suggested each team offer a player to assist a White Sox recovery. The owners of the New York Yankees, also Comiskey's allies, did the same. The offers, which did not involve specific players, were declined.

In the front office and on the field, the remaining White Sox, cautioned by captain Collins to refrain from comment on the indictments, fashioned a positive front. Reports indicated there was no gloom, but in the locker room Kid Gleason was scratching his head as his team prepared to invade Sportsman's Park for its final three games of 1920. As the White Sox yet again sat idle on September 29, they fell another step behind in the pennant chase when Cleveland defeated St. Louis. The Sox now were a game and one-half behind a fast-finishing Tribe. The Indians' victory eliminated the Yankees. Now for the White Sox to even tie for the top, they needed to win all three in St. Louis, while Cleveland split its final four in Detroit. Any less and the race was over. That feat, while certainly not impossible, was nevertheless daunting. In order to accomplish it, Gleason needed to pull more than the normal amount of rabbits from his managerial cap.

First, the Kid took a look at who was left standing. On the mound he still had the effective duo of Faber and Kerr. Then there was Roy Wilkinson, a 27-year-old right-hander who had started 11 games. His 7–9 record and 4.03 ERA were not encouraging, but might do in a pinch, and this was certainly that type of situation. Another possibility was Shovel Hodge. He was also 27 and had only appeared in four games, but was 1–1 and 2.29 in 19 and two-thirds innings.

As to the position players, Schalk and Eddie Collins, of course, were intact. Harvey McClellan, a good young hitting prospect, could play short and old-timer Eddie Murphy could man the hot corner. In the outfield another veteran, Amos Strunk, who saw action in 53 games in 1920, hitting .239, could provide adequate fielding coverage at one position, while Gleason could move John Shano Collins back to the outfield. Ted Jourdan would replace Shano on first. Not exactly picture-perfect, but it would just have to suffice.

Gleason put on his best face, expressing confidence his team would win out. "We will go out and play ball with the honest members we have left."[34]

Those "honest" members left by train for St. Louis in good spirits, still enjoying that esprit de corps that surrounds those who find themselves bound together by special circumstances. Upon their arrival their dreams of a pennant, however, remained intact for less than 24 hours. On October 1 Gleason went with his strong suit, Red Faber, and lost, as the White Sox fell 8–6 in a hard-fought skirmish. They took an encouraging early three-run lead, but

Faber could not make it last. Collins went 1-for-3, walked twice and scored two runs. In a bit of a surprise, Gleason started young outfielder Bibb Falk in right field and the 21-year-old came through with three safeties in five tries, including a double.

The loss essentially dashed any further talk of pennants, but the next day the Clean Sox at least clinched second with a 10–7 win. In that one Dickie Kerr posted his twenty-first victory and Collins continued to swing a strong bat with a triple among three hits. It was his team's final victory for the season. The next day the Browns delivered a crushing 16–7 blow as Gleason sent 21-year-old Joe Kiefer to the mound for only his second appearance. He lasted less than two innings. In the ninth the Browns called upon star first baseman George Sisler to close out the season on the mound. In retiring the side, the former pitcher struck out two.

The two losses in St. Louis left the White Sox at 96–58, in second, a full two games behind the pennant-winning and eventual world champion Cleveland Indians. All was not lost, however, at least from a monetary point of view. By finishing second, the remaining players each received a larger share of the second-place money. In addition, in a belated show of generosity, their boss Charles Comiskey distributed $1,500 apiece to those players still remaining from the 1919 team. The amount represented the difference between the winners' and losers' share in the 1919 World Series, the amount arguably lost by the dishonesty of their teammates.

If it was good publicity Commy sought, he got it. In response to their "newfound" money, the players, which included Faber, the Collinses, Leibold, Kerr, Murphy, Roy Wilkinson, Harvey McClellan and Byrd Lynn, issued a statement to the "Fans of Chicago."

"We, the undersigned, players of the Chicago White Sox, want the world to know the generosity of our employer, who, of his own free will, has reimbursed each and every member of our team the difference between the winning and the losing share of last year's world series, amounting to approximately $1,500."[35]

The White Sox's season was now at long last over, but not the controversy. Not by a long shot. A number of White Sox players were talking — at least about the season just passed. Collins was heard in St. Louis, a day after his team was all but mathematically eliminated from contention. In an Associated Press release the White Sox's captain blamed the team's 1920 disappointments on the lone Black Sox departee, Chick Gandil, blaming him for Collins' belief that two teammates failed to play their best in 1920. These two unnamed players "were under suspicion throughout the season, but were never charged due to lack of proof.

"The White Sox players who remained loyal to the club are satisfied they had the best team in the league, and, while we do not begrudge Cleveland one bit of the honor and prestige that an American league pennant carries with it, we believe that only through the corruption instigated primarily by 'Chick' Gandil was the downfall of the team brought about."[36]

Since he refused to name the two players he accused and offered no more than the accusation as to Gandil, it is difficult to determine just how Collins felt the former first baseman was able to exert such influence on these players in 1920. Perhaps Collins referred to Gandil's part in the 1919 "fix" in a cause-and-effect sequence, i.e., no fix in 1919, no carry-over into 1920. At any rate Eddie's charges were aired about the same time as White Sox reserves Byrd Lynn and Harvey McClellan were leveling their charges that the three games in Boston on that last road trip were in the words of McClellan just plain "thrown."[37]

As to the actual events leading up to and including the play of his teammates in the 1919 World Series, Collins remained silent. Nor did he break that silence on October 22 when the grand jury added former White Sox pitcher and now oilman and professional gambler "Sleepy" Bill Burns, former featherweight boxing champion Abe "the Little Champ" Attell, and baseball's notorious first baseman Hal Chase to an expanding list of indictees. These newest candidates for infamy took their place on the gamblers' side of the room.

Collins, who was listed as a grand jury witness but never actually served with a subpoena, was not called to testify before that august body. It would have been interesting to learn under oath what the second sacker knew and when he knew it since there were few who ever thought he knew nothing at all. Among those who fostered the idea that a testifying Collins would offer valuable information to the inquiry were Tom Shibe and Connie Mack of the Athletics. In a hand-written note delivered to Ban Johnson dated October 31, 1920, Shibe urged Johnson "to insist that the Grand Jury call Eddie Collins as a witness. After reading New York paper comments, Connie and I think it is most essential."[38]

The date of the note is important coming as it did one day after perhaps the most surprising comments of all ever attributed to Collins concerning the Black Sox affair. In its October 30, 1920, edition, *Collyer's Eye*, the small circulation gambler's newspaper which had sounded a lone horn trumpeting the rumors of scandal, reporter Frank O. Klein, who called Collins "probably one of the most intelligent men in the game, and of whose friendship I boast," quoted the White Sox players as follows:

> I felt sure that something was wrong, even before we went to Cincinnati [in 1919]. There was quite some carousing by some of the players. Then I did not quite relish the presence of Joe Gedeon [a St. Louis Browns player] who took my room or rather my bed after we reached Philadelphia. He was hooked up with Risberg and McMullen and came on to Chicago and remained until the end. From what I gleaned it was he who wagered the money of the two above named. I mean the three of them parlayed whatever they "got."
>
> As to the actual playing there wasn't a single doubt in my mind after I went to bat the first time up in Cincinnati. The first man up for us was Leibold. Nemo singled and when I attempted to sacrifice him I forced the lad at second. The next man up was Weaver. On the second ball pitched Weaver gave me the "hit and run" signal and I was caught off second the proverbial mile. When I returned to the bench I immediately accused Weaver of not even attempting to hit the ball. I told all this to Comiskey.

Then in the same article, appearing just weeks after Collins refused to name names regarding his allegations of 1920 skullduggery, Collins pointed an accusatory finger at Buck Weaver and Eddie Cicotte. "If the gamblers didn't have Weaver and Cicotte in their pocket then I don't know a thing about baseball."[39]

It does not appear Collins ever publicly denied the accusations that appeared in *Collyer's Eye* under the heading "Collins Charges 1920 Games 'Fixed.'" Nonetheless they differ, sometimes significantly, from remarks made by Collins over the years during those rare times when he agreed to talk about the scandal and they, perhaps, shed some insight into Collins' persona.

If the *Collyer's Eye* quote attributed to Eddie about Buck Weaver's glaring omission in connection with the hit and run signal is accurate, then it answers a troubling question about Collins' later statements to the effect "we didn't expect anything."[40] Or as he dramatically told writer Jim Leonard, who was writing a five-part series on Collins' life for *The Sporting News* in 1950, "I was to be a witness to the greatest tragedy in baseball's history — and I didn't know it at the time."[41]

Here was a veteran major leaguer, a man many considered the smartest player in the game, one who according to no less an authority than Connie Mack served like a manager on the field, acting as if he knew little more about the actions of several teammates than the fans in the stands. The statement to *Collyer's*, again if taken as true, is the total opposite. It indicates Collins suspected that something was up prior to the series and confirmed it in his team's very first at-bat. He goes further, saying he told "all this" to Commy, although just how much he told and when remains a mystery since Commy denies ever discussing a fix with Collins, insists he knew nothing at all about it until after Game One, and Collins otherwise maintains he knew little about the affair.

Why then, if he knew so much, did Eddie Collins do so little to stem the tide which washed away a World Series and eventually a championship-caliber team? For if Hugh Fullerton's assessment is correct, the silence of Collins and other "honest" players enabled the scandal to proceed.

Gene Carney, a Black Sox expert who placed the scandal under a strong microscope in his book *Burying the Black Sox*, offers one reasonable explanation:

> Once the scandal broke, some of the Clean Sox started telling what they knew. They talked more about thrown games in the stretch run of 1920, which was still fresh in mind, than about the World Series of 1919. They were sure they could have won the pennant again, if everyone had been trying their best to win.
>
> If they had been deaf to the rumors before the Series, their manager Gleason informed them of his and Comiskey's suspicions early-on, perhaps before Game Two. Why did they remain silent? Possibly, they were hoping against hope that what they sensed had taken place was just a bad dream. They were just as uncertain as everyone else about exactly who was involved, and felt that it was not their place to speak up, not if the team management was aware of what was going on. Their job would be to tell their manager, and he had told *them* about the fix.[42]

Hugh Fullerton might have answered some of his own questions on this issue when he voiced his belief that the silent players were acting out of "a false sense of loyalty to fellow players, fear of being called a 'squealer'...."[43]

Fullerton is referring to what might be called "the code of the clubhouse," a sports phenomenon which has always existed and which exists to this day. A more recent example is the silence of non-steroid users when it came to discussing the use of performance-enhancing drugs by some of their teammates. Author Tim Gay discusses the baseball scandals that raked the 1920s in his biography of Tris Speaker. He describes the code thusly:

"The players back then showed amazing solidarity: it's as if they all took a vow of *omerta*— and maybe they did. It is now evident that what went on in the 1919 World Series was just the jagged tip of a lethal iceberg."[44]

If anyone had reason to spill the beans on the "Chick Gandil gang," it was Eddie Collins. Yet Collins was particularly susceptible to the aura of "the code." As team captain he needed to walk a fine line to keep a semblance of unity on a squad which was just one incident or comment away from an all-out civil war. He was certainly aware that the Gandil faction saw him as a "company man," and to a certain extent that was true. Therefore, to run openly to the boss with his "suspicions"—and that was apparently all they were—would not have served him or the team in the long run. It is more likely that his friend and roommate, Ray Schalk, served as the "front man" for the Clean Sox in their efforts to confront their wayward teammates and, by his actions, alert management to their suspicions. It was Schalk who exploded several times at the play of Cicotte and others during the series. It may have been Schalk, although he later denied it, who named the men whose series' shares were withheld. It is hard to believe he did any of this without Collins' knowledge or consent. The pair were on friendly terms and often roomed together when their team was on the road. Only in 1920, when another season appeared to be "thrown" away, did Collins step forward in a more visible way.

There was also the matter of Collins' background and training. Although he was not the product of a particularly well-to-do family, he received the education of a patrician, attending private school with the future captains of industry. In addition to understanding and respecting the authority of ownership and management, he one day aspired to hold such a position himself. Though he denied a present intention, there is no question he one day wanted to manage a team. He might one day want to own all or part of a team. Already he was a part-owner of a minor league franchise. He was also smart enough to know not to bite the hand that feeds you. He was able to read the signs as well, if not better than the next guy. He recalled just how far Christy Mathewson got when he reported his suspicion that Hal Chase was throwing ball games for the Cincinnati Reds in 1918. In what most observers then and today believe was a total whitewash, Chase was cleared and permitted to continue to play. Why should Collins believe the outcome would somehow differ this time around?

Thus, if Commy had been apprised of the situation, perhaps even by him, and both Gleason and Schalk had called out his teammates and still the series continued, business as usual, then it would not be Eddie Collins who pulled the plug. If author Gene Carney and other students of the scandal are correct, and Commy in particular, and team ownership in general, sought to keep a tight leash on gambling in baseball, then Eddie Collins would not lead the charge out of that darkness. Only after the Black Sox began talking did Collins open up. Only after Chick Gandil was no longer active in the majors did Eddie blame him for the corruption of 1920.

In this light a statement once made by Shoeless Joe Jackson about Collins also makes perfect sense. During an interview with Jackson, the preeminent baseball historian Harold Seymour asked the former White Sox outfield star whether he took part in the fix. Jackson vehemently denied it and sarcastically replied, "You ask Mr. Eddie Collins about that."[45]

According to Seymour's widow and research partner, Dorothy Jane Seymour Mills, her husband interpreted Jackson's statement as an allegation that Collins actually knew in advance about the fix, as opposed to merely suspecting something was not right, as Collins allegedly told *Collyer's Eye*. However, in keeping with Collins' character and his standing with the Gandil faction, it seems more likely that Eddie would be the last person to have specific information about the plot. It is more likely that Joe Jackson, who often stated he tried to report the plot to Commy and others, and even attempted to sit out the series, went to team captain Collins during the World Series and told him some or all he knew and that Eddie, already aware that nothing was or would be done about it, declined to act. Instead, he advised Jackson to take the information to Commy. Thus, when Jackson told Harold Seymour to ask "Mr. Eddie Collins," he was referring both to the fact he reported information to his captain and also that Collins was well aware that Jackson was trying to extricate himself from the whole sticky mess. Only then does a remark Shoeless Joe made many years later make real sense. It was in 1949 and Jackson had already told a reporter that the White Sox team was split into "two gangs, [Eddie] Collins and Chick Gandil were the two leaders.... They hadn't spoken to each other off the field in two seasons. Bill Gleason was the manager, but Collins ran the team out on the field." During the interview the reporter had inquired further about Collins, and Jackson replied, "Mr. Eddie Collins" was "as fine a man as ever there was in baseball."[46] Not exactly the type of comment you would make about someone you felt was involved in a conspiracy to throw a World Series.

It then appears likely that Collins suspected a plot and confirmed it early on, but other than perhaps telling Commy and maybe directing others like Jackson, he did nothing further to stop it. In so acting he stayed well within character and he was not alone. There were others who had knowledge, not guilty knowledge, not the kind of knowledge that makes one a co-conspirator, but knowledge just the same.

According to Dickie Kerr, the fact that eight players were trying to throw the series to the Cincinnati Reds was known to four other players on the Chicago team before the second game.

"Manager Kid Gleason, Ray Schalk, Eddie Collins and I knew about what those fellows planned to do, but we had no proof. We wanted to do something, but we couldn't."[47]

In acting as they did, Collins and the others joined Commy, the other owners, and even the accused ball players in one important aspect. They were all conflicted in one way or another. For Eddie and the Clean Sox, the conflict was whether or not to go public with what little they actually did know or suspected, thereby biting the hand that fed them. For Commy the conflict was whether or not to launch a full-fledged investigation to uncover the treachery of some of his players, then go public with it, and thereby lose a World Series and eventually a team. For the other major league owners, it meant deciding between full disclosure of the rapidly spreading infection of gambling both inside and outside the game versus trying to hide or, at the very least, limit knowledge of its insidious hold on the sport so as it keep fans from abandoning baseball. For the Black Sox players, their conflict was whether or not to play to win and, in so doing, continue to perform for an owner who paid them less than their self-determined worth in the face of an opportunity to cash in and earn a tidy sum that might not come their way again. That conflict was exhibited by these players during the World Series by inconsistent play which continues to defy analysis. Even Collins admitted he believed "that at times even the guilty ones played to win."[48]

Of course, all this business about conflict is probably an oversimplification. In the end in each instance, the conflict was resolved in favor of the money, but at least to some extent it is undeniable that the Black Sox scandal and the mystery surrounding it is heavily influenced by the classic elements of conflict.

There was one segment of society, a most important part of the game of baseball, however, that was not conflicted, but yet was seemingly forgotten or cast aside: the fan. To the fan there is no game worth paying to see unless it is an honest one. There are no real heroes to be cheered unless they are honest ones. The fan who would be hurt the most by a scandal of this type and proportion was the young fan, whose innocence once shattered could never be truly restored. One such fan was James T. Farrell, a young Chicagoan of 15, who was a Chicago White Sox fan. As an Irish-American the player he related to the most on his favorite team was Eddie Collins. "He became my model." Farrell, who became a prolific writer, probably best known for his Studs Lonigan trilogy, was one of the observers who perpetrated the much discussed and, perhaps, highly fictionalized "Say it ain't so, Joe [Jackson]" scenario. When the Black Sox scandal broke, Farrell's first thoughts went to his hero. Was Eddie Collins involved as well?

"When I read in the newspaper that one of the accused players had said that he had not even approached Collins with the proposition to throw games, I became very proud. Not only was he a great player: he was incorruptible."[49]

James T. Farrell was one of the lucky ones. He worshipped a player who still inspired pride. He continued to love baseball and return to the ballpark, while for those others still disenchanted, only a new season and a generous dose of time could provide a cure.

CHAPTER 14

Trials and Tribulations

"Charles Comiskey felt like a new man on April 21, 1921. The odious scandal was temporarily forgotten as the brass bands, the banners, a swooping biplane, and, yes, the fans signaled the start of a new season. On a warm spring day the White Sox trimmed the Tigers, 8–3. Kid Gleason forced a smile as he accepted a bouquet of roses and the blessings of a crowd of 25,000. They cheered long and hard when Collins and Schalk were introduced. Baseball had weathered the storm."
— Richard Lindberg, White Sox historian[1]

As the Black Sox Scandal played out, first behind the scenes, then across the nation's front pages, there was another play rehearsing in the wings. In late 1920 this one found its way to the forefront as well. In a selection process which challenged a Vatican election for back-stabbing and spectacular end runs, puffs of smoke finally issued forth signaling the election of a new leader for baseball; one with singular power and an unusual name: Kenesaw Mountain Landis.

Before that final decision was reached, there were numerous alignments and realignments among club owners, and any number of proposed formulas and reformations. The end product left each league totally intact under the umbrella of a single leader with broad and significant power to rule the game. His authority extended not only over the players, but the owners as well. When Judge Landis accepted an offer to be that man at the age of 54, he became the focal point for baseball's future. In large part he molded that future to his vision for the next 24 years.

A great deal of the judge's popularity with the owners stemmed from his handling of the lawsuit filed in Chicago by the Federal League during the Federal League war. As the federal judge handling the case in his U.S. District Court, Landis exercised his judicial discretion — some felt he abused it — and sat on the case until the Federal League had exhausted its funds, essentially forcing it to settle. In this way the judge felt he was able to best preserve the game he loved. In his capacity as commissioner of baseball, he would continue to exercise that judicial "discretion" to obtain the desired results, often at the expense of reaching the correct or even the moral disposition. On November 12, 1920, when the judge accepted the offer of the baseball magnates, baseball justice became a slave to the judge's judgment.

One opportunity for an exercise of discretion by the new chairman of the board would be the handling of the future playing status of the indicted members of the White Sox. Landis took office on January 12, 1921. On that very day the judge gave an early indication of how he might use that discretion. "[I]f they [the indicted Black Sox] are found not guilty by a jury or judge they will not necessarily be allowed to return to organized baseball."[2]

Given that various legal entanglements resulted in postponement of the legal proceedings against the Black Sox, it appeared that no matter the final decision of Landis, at best the White Sox would play most and probably all of 1921 without these players. The team thus faced an enormous rebuilding task. Their manager, Kid Gleason, wore a brave game face, but Collins quickly saw through it.

As soon as the scandal exploded, Collins could see significant changes in his manager and friend. The fight seemed to seep right out of him. Eddie even began to note changes in the Kid's physical appearance.

"His rugged face became drawn and deep seams were etched in his former leathery countenance. He brooded and he became irritated more easily than he had previously. He was at most times morose and sometimes he was even bitter."[3]

Kid Gleason arrived in Waxahachie, Texas, on March 2, 1921, to mold his squad, such as it was, but by that time some of his Clean Sox had already engaged in some mud slinging. The igniter of this fresh fire storm, which targeted Eddie Collins in particular, was arguably Collins himself.

Sometime during the off-season, Collins gave an interview in Philadelphia in which he declared, in no uncertain terms, he no longer planned to play with the White Sox if any of the indicted players were permitted to return. After expressing doubt that any of the indicted players would ever wear a White Sox uniform again, no matter what the court did, Eddie offered the following in response to a question concerning how the "honest" members of the team felt about reinstatement:

> It would be a blow to the team and upset playing. I hardly think it possible for any of the indicted men to mingle with their former mates again. It is almost unthinkable.
>
> You must also regard the effect it would have on the public. You can not whitewash or condone charges of throwing ball games. The fans would never tolerate it. The whole team, honest players and indicted players alike, would be under a cloud.
>
> If one of the players charged with being in the bribery, lost a game by making an error or doing something stupid, then the crowd would yell: "he's sold out again." And, of course, in a season's play all of the players are bound to lose games in this manner at some time.
>
> I read in the papers where one of the indicted players declared that he would be back with the Sox next season, but I don't believe he will, for the reasons I have mentioned. I have talked on this subject to Kid Gleason and he doesn't think that any of them will return, and certainly has eliminated them from all consideration in making plans for the next season.
>
> I feel sorry for some of the players whose careers have been cut short by the scandal, and for others have not the slightest sympathy, for they threw down baseball, the fans and their fellow-players.
>
> It's hard to believe that Weaver would enter into any such conspiracy, yet there is the deadly evidence in the confession. I pity Joe Jackson, for he is a man easily led and could have been swayed by good advice as well as the voice of the tempter. He is a man within a boy's brains and never had the educational advantages of many of the others in the plot. I pity Joe.[4]

When the Black Sox players heard these statements, they were, of course, enraged. Probably encouraged by their attorneys, who saw visions of trial strategies in their heads, they quickly struck back. It was intimated the indicted players had knowledge that some of the Clean Sox, particularly Eddie Collins, bet and encouraged others on the team to bet on the Tigers to beat out the Yankees for third place in the 1919 pennant race. If there was a trial, they planned to disclose the details.[5] The allegation was particularly charged with electricity because the White Sox lost all three games to the Tigers in that last series of the year. It was insinuated that Collins felt the bet was a good one because he and others on the team intended to "throw" these games to the Tigers.

Judge Landis heard the rumors and told the press that over his years on the bench, "I have noticed that when a crook is hooked, he always will try to drag some clean people into the mess if there is a chance.... It generally has been my policy to disregard such things."[6]

Ban Johnson acknowledged hearing the rumors as well. "They [the Black Sox and their attorneys] will try to drag Eddie Collins into it, and he is one of the cleanest and finest men we ever had in baseball."[7]

The accused reacted to the news as one would expect. In a story out of Philadelphia on January 30, the same day that Landis and Johnson were making their statements in Chicago, Collins vehemently called the reports, including statements attributed to Buck Weaver:

> the most ridiculous thing I have ever heard. I never bet a penny on a baseball game, nor did I ever tell any fellow players to do so.
>
> I can not see how they can link my name with such a story, for there is absolutely no foundation for such a statement. I doubt if Weaver ever intimated that he would drag my name into any court investigations, for Buck has nothing on me.
>
> It is the first time that I knew there was any betting among players on other clubs that year on the way the Tigers and Yankees would finish. When we played that final series with the Tigers we did not kill ourselves, for we were resting up for the big series.
>
> I am not a betting man and would not think of laying a penny on a ball game. No doubt the recent scandal is causing all kinds of charges to fly about, and now some of those who went wrong are trying to enmesh innocent players in the mess.[8]

After these initial volleys, the story, for all practical purposes, died. Landis, it appeared, had considered the source, found it wanting, and tossed it in his circular file. However, that was certainly not the case. In addition to the rumors floating around about the 1919 series with Detroit, additional rumors were afloat. These latter rumors revolved around the 1917 Labor Day weekend series between those same White Sox and Tigers in which the White Sox swept the four-game set.

The rumors of the 1917 "fix" of the series with the Tigers were not as fresh as the allegations of wrongdoing in their 1919 series with the Sox. According to Landis biographer, David Pietrusza:

"Rumors of the 1917 fix had long floated about in baseball circles.

"In October 1920 Ban Johnson had informed District Attorney Maclay Hoyne about the fix."[9]

Certainly well aware of the potential harm to baseball if he ignored the allegations and they proved true, Landis decided that despite his public pronouncements to the contrary, he needed to quietly investigate further. Several players, including Eddie Collins and later Detroit pitchers Bill James and George Dauss, were called to Chicago in late February and interviewed by Leslie O'Connor, Landis' secretary and, thereby, top assistant. O'Connor was an attorney. Typewritten transcripts were made of each interview. In addition, Judge Landis personally interviewed Ray Schalk and Red Faber, but no transcripts were made of those conversations. Later O'Connor wrote that the statements of Schalk and Faber did not differ from that of Collins.[10]

In his statement Collins told O'Connor that sometime in late season 1917, "after the pennant had been won," he was approached by Chick Gandil — an interesting concept since both men always claimed they never spoke — who told him, "We are taking up a little collection." Gandil did not mention who the "we" included, but Eddie received the impression that "each member of the Chicago club was supposed to contribute," what figured to be "$45" to be paid either Detroit pitchers or players [Collins was not sure] for "the way they had knocked off Boston either two out of three or three straight in their last series of the 1917 season." Collins claimed he never knew the total amount raised, nor who originated the idea, but it was not him. Also, to his knowledge there was no previous understanding between the White Sox and Detroit that they would receive such a reward, i.e., it was all done after the fact.

Collins admitted taking up the proposal with Ray Schalk and stated they both "looked on it [the idea] askance, but did not think it was sufficiently important to refuse to contribute or to kick up a fuss about it." They decided to contribute.

In Collins' opinion such rewards "were not the common practice." However, "it was not a novel thing for a player to be given a suit of clothes or something like that. So far as players on a club taking up a collection, I never heard of it before. That was the reason Schalk and I looked at it as rather improper, but we let it slide because we thought we would not miss the $45 and we did not want to be instigators of a row." Furthermore, it was the only time while Collins was with the White Sox that he recalled such a fund was collected.

Collins insisted at several points during the interview that to his knowledge the money was not paid Detroit to "lay down" to enable the White Sox to win the pennant. During the Labor Day four-game series, it appeared to Collins that Detroit was playing to win. On that point Collins made an interesting admission in light of his later views on the play of some teammates during the 1919 Series. He told O'Connor, "Of course, it is hard to say whether anybody on a ball field is doing his best."

Collins was then asked if he knew of any other occurrences of "a suspicious nature" while with the White Sox. Collins replied none, "other than possibly in 1919." He then turned to the allegations recently tossed at him about his betting on the Tigers as his team played its year-end three-game series against them.

According to Collins at the time this series was played, the White Sox were already pennant winners. He admitted the team had suffered a letdown, losing a game with St. Louis right before they played the Tigers. The letdown continued into the Detroit series, to the effect "there was ... a considerable lack of interest in the games on the part of the White Sox." He recognized that Detroit still had a mathematical chance for a third-place finish. "Detroit fought hard to win, while the White Sox played loosely, somewhat indifferently." The Sox just wanted to get to the end of their schedule. There was a "general feeling" at least in Eddie's opinion that "we would prefer to have Detroit beat out New York, but there was absolutely no prearranged agreement or understanding that they should win, nor any conference or arrangement between the White Sox players, individually or collectively, or with any Detroit players that we should deliberately permit them to win." In fact, "that was not true of that series or of any game I have ever been in."

As to the allegation that Collins bet on that series, "I want to say I did not bet on it and so far as I know no money was bet on that series by any of the players on the club." However, when asked if it was the practice for players to bet on games in which they participated, O'Connor received the following response from Collins:

A. Not to my knowledge. As far as I am concerned I have rarely bet on a ball game in which I played and I never bet except that I would win.

Q. For any considerable amounts?

A. No. All the bets I have made on ball games including world series games, would not aggregate $50, of which I don't believe I bet half on games in which I participated.[11]

After his meeting with Leslie O'Connor, Collins returned to his home in Lansdowne, Pennsylvania. Less than a week later, on February 24, he wrote Judge Landis, enclosing a sheet with his travel expenses. In the letter he informed the judge of two additional points that came to mind "since my return." One concerned an instance he now recalled where pitcher Fritz Coumbe, perhaps while with Cleveland, received $100 from Boston or some other "leading team" for winning a ball game. His second point was much more startling and revealing, particularly in light of his previous denials to the press and to O'Connor.

Weaver did make a bet for me, how or with whom I never knew of an amount of $40, on the morning of Labor Day 1917 to the effect that we [White Sox] would beat Detroit two games that day. After we had won the morning game, a very close one that Eddie Murphy won with a pinch hit, I made the remark to Weaver that I was sorry I had made the bet or something to that effect, and I did not think I would ever bet on another game that I was in. Gleason as far as I know is the only other player who knew of this bet, and not until I told him about it, and who at my request assumes [sic] half of it. It was the first bet of an amount anywheres near that amount I ever made on a ball game, and I guess it was on my mind more than the game itself. At any rate I have never made one since that time. These two incidents are all that I can recall right now.[12]

Suddenly here was an eyebrow raiser. Collins' letter to Landis is inconsistent with his previous public utterances, as well as his statement to O'Connor regarding his betting on baseball. He continued to deny betting on games during the 1919 series with Detroit. However, by admitting he bet on the 1917 series with that club, as opposed to merely contributing much later to a fund as he disclosed to O'Connor, he completely contradicts his statements to the press in Philadelphia less than a month before on January 31 when he stated, "I never bet a penny on a baseball game." It also casts doubt on his statement to O'Connor less than a week before, claiming he bet less than $50 in the aggregate on ball games. Certainly one bet of $40, a bet, conveniently or otherwise, he did not recall, raises questions about the accuracy of his characterization of his betting habits. Did the trip home to Pennsylvania allow Eddie to sharpen his memory? Or was he overcome by a truth-cleansing pang of conscience? In either event his inconsistent statements in 1921 about the events of 1917 deal a blow to his overall credibility.

Still, it does not follow that Collins also lied when he denied betting on his team to lose to Detroit in 1919. He was consistent in those denials, as well as all statements that he never bet on a game in which he was a participant, except to bet on his team to win. This seems logical, particularly when taken in the context of the times. Although it is no longer the case, it did not violate any rule of baseball in 1917, or in 1919 for that matter, for a baseball player to bet on a baseball game.[13] In fact, at least in Illinois, there was not even a law prohibiting throwing or fixing to throw a ball game.

It is one thing to bet on a game one plays to win, entirely another to bet against one's team as a participant. In the latter instance there is a huge incentive to play less than one's best or even try to lose the game. Collins never admitted to placing himself in that situation and no one ever offered proof to the contrary. Even the Tigers did not profit from their season-ending wins over the White Sox in 1919; they finished one-half game behind the Yankees, thus out of the third-place money.

What did Landis do with his newly acquired information? It seems he did nothing. There is no indication he checked further, for example with Kid Gleason, to confirm Collins' version of his 1917 Labor Day bet and sudden cold feet. Nor did he check with Buck Weaver, who alleged that games were thrown both in 1917 and 1919, and that the Clean Sox were eager participants. Interestingly, Weaver never mentioned the bet Collins claims Weaver made for him in 1917. Perhaps because Weaver claimed, as is perhaps true, that he did not participate in the 1917 "fund," he feared that an admission of this sort could only harm his campaign for reinstatement.[14]

It seems likely that at that early date in February 1921, even before the Black Sox were tried, Kenesaw Mountain Landis had determined to limit the damage to the game by limiting the scope of his public inquiry to only those involved in the 1919 World Series, or others whose conduct was so egregious it could not easily be sidestepped. According to this philosophy, Collins' transgressions were probably the transgressions of many other ball players.

Collins was considered by baseball fans everywhere as a man of honor. To now brand him a liar would not only harm Collins, it also would harm the game. If Eddie Collins, then how many others? If the judge had anything to say about it, and he certainly did, he would sit on Collins' follow-up letter and statement, as well as that of the other interviewees, all consistent on the events of 1917 at least, and react publicly only if he had no other choice.

The matter seemingly at rest, Collins, excused from early training, reported to camp on March 20. By then Commy had made several key personnel changes. On March 4 he traded long-timers John Shano Collins and Nemo Leibold to Boston for left-handed hitting outfielder Harry Hooper. Although he was already 33 by this time, Hooper was a fine hitter and fielder who knew how to lead off and get on base. He did it enough times over 17 seasons to eventually earn a spot in the Baseball Hall of Fame. In 1920 he had engaged the "live" ball to the extent of a .312 average and .411 OBP. It seems in early 1921 Harry Frazee, the Red Sox's owner, was still in a very generous mood.

Other attempts to bolster the lineup were not so successful. Several players were purchased from the minors. One who would work out, at least in the short haul, was first baseman Earl Sheely, purchased from the Salt Lake City club of the Pacific Coast League. He was six feet four inches and hit for power. In 1921 he ended up slugging 11 home runs and driving in 95. He and the others would definitely be needed. On March 13, following reports of new delays in the trial date and facing the start of the new season, Landis ruled the indicted players ineligible. Commy chimed in by saying he was finished with the Black Sox no matter the verdict, a declaration which carried an escape hatch when he said his position remained firm unless the condemned cleared themselves to his satisfaction.

When Collins finally reported for duty, he was ready to play, having worked out with the University of Pennsylvania squad the week prior. By then camp was in full swing and he soon found the new chemistry on the squad to his liking. One evening, for example, Collins and Eddie Murphy took a half dozen of the "recruits" to a Waxahachie music store for an impromptu phonograph party. Collins and the other veterans like Schalk, Faber, Kerr and Murphy were making a real effort to mingle with the newcomers and foster a positive team spirit.[15]

On April 14 the "Darned" Sox, yet another nickname for this patched-up version of the team, tested that new spirit against the Tigers in Detroit.[16] It was Ty Cobb's debut as a manager. The result was a 6–5 loss for the White Sox with Dickie Kerr on the mound. The lineup, Collins back to batting third, sported names like Mostil (Johnny), Falk (Bibb), Mulligan (Eddie), Johnson (Ernie), and the aforementioned Earl Sheely.

It is probably sufficient to sum up the 1921 White Sox by stating that their season highlight was their home opener on April 21 when they defeated these same Tigers, 8–3, before 25,000 highly enthusiastic and, as it turned out, overly optimistic fans. The win fueled by Collins, who went 2-for-4 and drove in two runners, only added to that optimism. Reality, however, soon settled in. By mid–May the team was buried in seventh place at 8–14. It would not get much better. Collins, despite playing without the shackles of discord, was not enjoying a particularly strong year at the plate. Although he was making some fine stops in the field, his average on May 15 stood at .280, well below his career number.

Perhaps his mind was on more than just baseball. It now appeared that the trial of the Chicago "eight" would finally start in June. In addition to the Black Sox players, a number of others, including Bill Burns and Hal Chase as well as several "other" gamblers with names like Zork, Levi and Zelcer, were under indictment. By May these indictments, the latest of several refinements, listed Collins, and at least Schalk if not others, as victims. According to the legalese Eddie and the other victims had been cheated in the scam out of $1,784, the additional share they lost by not winning the 1919 World Series.

In late May as the prosecution readied its case, it appears that Collins and Ray Schalk were contacted by a representative of Ban Johnson and asked why they had been so reticent to date to step forward and provide officials with what they knew about the scandal. Johnson was now the driving force behind the prosecution of the Black Sox. Driven by his hatred for Commy and his desire for self-preservation, as much as a quest for justice, he was essentially putting together the case for the state's attorneys office, now under new administration and leadership. At this point Johnson was lining up witnesses. In that regard his representative, a W.G. Evans (ph.), told the two players how disappointed Johnson was with "the attitude they assumed."

In a letter to Johnson dated May 26, 1921, Evans reported that during a meeting with Evans the previous day, "They both frankly admitted ... they had not talked as freely as they should."

It seems that both Collins and Schalk had at some point, probably recent, been summoned to the state's attorneys office for questioning. When they arrived, they found a stenographer ready to record the conversation and, not knowing the extent or the purpose of the interview, they became extremely cautious in answering the questions. Johnson decided their reluctance was due to pressure from Comiskey to keep quiet. Both Schalk and Collins denied to Evans that "they had discussed the matter with either Comiskey or Gleason."

Evans explained to them that in view of certain statements made by each after the series, their current posture was "all the more foolish." At this:

> Both said now that it [the 1919 World Series] was over a whole lot of things looked wrong, which at the time might be excused. Both claimed they could offer no definite proof of wrongdoing. They said their opinions were merely confined to certain happenings such as Cicotte's steady refusal to pitch spitballs when Schalk called for them. He would shake Schalk off and insist on the fast ball sign, and then come through with a fast one that had nothing on it. Of this happening and some similar ones they of course had definite opinions.
>
> I told them I felt sure it was just such facts that you desired. That you knew they had no definite proofs perhaps to offer, but that they had certain interesting opinions at least on various events of the 1919 Series.
>
> Both said they were very sorry you were not present [at the state's attorneys office]. Had you been they said they would have talked more freely.
>
> I feel positive that the story of both Schalk and Collins if frankly told would prove interesting, and possibly of considerable value. I also feel positive they will tell their story if you request a conference with them. They have absolute confidence in you, but are a bit cautious and careful otherwise.[17]

According to Evans, shortly after their conference with him, both Schalk and Collins made attempts to contact Johnson and talk to him in more detail. There is no telling if or when such a discussion took place, but both Schalk and Collins, along with a long list of other witnesses, received a letter dated July 1, 1921, from the office of the American League, notifying them to hold themselves in readiness to answer a summons from the new state's attorney Judge Robert E. Crowe to appear and testify at the Black Sox trial.

That trial began on June 27 before the Honorable Judge Hugo Friend, although it was immediately set back a day due to the absence of two of the defendants, alleged St. Louis gamblers Ben Franklin and Carl Zork. At the time the trial began, Collins was out of the lineup nursing a dislocated knuckle. He was undoubtedly also listening to the gossip emanating from New York that had the Yankees seeking to acquire him by trade. Experts scoffed and the rumor quickly ran its course.

The Black Sox trial was barely out of first gear and sputtering on June 30 when Frank Navin, the owner of the Detroit Tigers and a Ban Johnson supporter, wrote the league president to tell him of a meeting he had that day at the request of Eddie Cicotte's attorney, Dan Cassidy. The lawyer summoned Navin to his office supposedly to do him a favor. At the meeting Cassidy advised the owner that the indicted players intended to testify at trial that in 1917 each Chicago player contributed to a fund to be given Navin's Detroit players "as a reward for Detroit not playing their best against them in the final games of the season."

It was clear to Navin that Cassidy hoped to use the threat of disclosure of this information as leverage. He told Cassidy that the report was worthless unless "corroborated by some members of the White Sox Club who are at present in good standing." Their meeting concluded, Navin went back to his office and apprised Johnson by letter.[18]

By now the trial was in full swing with jury selection beginning on July 5. The list of defendants was now down to 11, including the Black Sox eight (minus Fred McMullin) and alleged gamblers Carl Zork and the Des Moines trio of Ben and Louis Levi and David Zelcer. They were represented by a high-priced cadre of skilled attorneys. There are those who believe the legal fees of those attorneys were paid by none other than Charles Comiskey.

Ban Johnson was aware the prosecution planned to call several of the "Clean Sox" to the stand. He did not believe Cassidy's tale but decided within the week to go see Eddie Collins, just to make sure.

"I called on Eddie Collins at his hotel the other morning and questioned him on the subject [of the 1917 "fund"]. It was my conviction he would register an unqualified denial, but to my amazement he said it was true that in 1917 a 'pot' was taken up.... Collins said ... the money was to go to the Detroit pitchers as merited compensation in their defeating the Boston club three straight games.

"I gave our attorneys [*sic*] the information and Collins, Schalk and Gleason were all summoned to the office of the State's Attorney yesterday. Each one admitted he had contributed to the fund."[19]

While the discourse between Navin and Johnson offers little in the way of new information about the 1917 Detroit–White Sox series, it offers a great deal of insight into the early relationship between Ban Johnson and Judge Landis. Only a little over a month after his official appointment, the judge was conducting his own investigations and not sharing the results with a league president. Only when an outsider, the attorney for an indicted ball player, attempted to use the information as a form of "blackmail-lite" did Johnson, once major league baseball's dominant force, learn of information which could further scandalize the game and certainly affect the credibility of Collins, Schalk, and other player-witnesses the state was preparing to call. Johnson must have been supremely embarrassed and outraged by the actions of Landis in this regard. It serves as just one more piece of evidence in a Landis-Johnson saga to be played out in installments over the next several years.

Once Johnson obtained the information Judge Landis had possessed for almost five months, the judge turned over the statements he had received from Collins, Jones and Dauss. They were sent on July 15 to the attorney for the American League, George Barrett.[20] Now Barrett and George E. Gorman, the state's lead attorney, had a decision to make. They had requested that Collins, Schalk and the other players be available to testify. This was before they knew of their involvement in the "fund." Could these men be safely placed on the witness stand, or would a skilled cross-examination ruin a carefully conceived policy of containment and spread a grimy stain over the entire game?

Perhaps the decision was already made for them. On July 8 defense attorney Henry Berger stood in front of Judge Friend and asked for the issuance of subpoenas for each member of the 1919 White Sox. He also said he planned to request subpoenas for each of the 1919 Cincinnati Reds.

"We expect to prove by the teammates of these accused players that there was no crooked playing."[21]

On July 12 as the trial progressed, Kid Gleason, Eddie Collins, Dickie Kerr, Red Faber, Ray Schalk and Harvey McClellan entered Judge Friend's courtroom and took a seat. They were present at the request of the defense.

Upon entry "[t]heir companions on trial gave wistful glances toward the new arrivals, but none of the White Sox were seen to proffer a word of greeting. The two groups then carefully avoided looking at each other."[22]

The players were acknowledged and told they would be further apprised of an actual date for testimony, keeping in mind their continuing baseball schedule. It is hard to believe Berger and his defense team would have been so eager to call these players without the potential hammer of the "fund" to hold over their head to keep them in line. It is also not a far stretch to imagine that the hand of Charles Comiskey, who was still walking a tightrope of conflict, was close by reminding these active players who signed their paychecks. No defense attorney worth his salt would consider calling an Eddie Collins or a Ray Schalk, men who carried much weight among the jurors and whose testimony could sink a case, unless they felt confident in advance they knew how each would testify. In fact, if a deal had been cut about the 1917 testimony, it was dealt with early. During his cross-examination on July 18, Commy, who was the first witness for the state, was asked if he and Pants Rowland got into some trouble over the last series with Detroit in 1917. Before he could answer the question, the prosecution, who apparently did not want to enter that territory, objected and the line of questioning was quickly dropped. The defense had shot a warning volley and the ship of state took notice.

On July 28 Eddie Collins and other members of the "Clean Sox" finally appeared and testified at trial — for the defense and briefly. The state had reached its decision. Their appearance on the stand for the prosecution, given the potential for further embarrassment to the game, was too great. By then the state had rested its case. It had introduced its star witness, "Sleepy" Bill Burns, tracked down by Ban Johnson with the help of Bill Maharg and offered immunity in exchange for testimony essentially similar to Maharg's, who also appeared for the state. By then the state had also taken a blow or two on the chin, hindered as they were by the lack of a state law against throwing or fixing sporting events. As a result, the prosecutors were required to prove a conspiracy to defraud the public, as well as to defraud players like Schalk and Collins, and to injure the business of Charles Comiskey.

Prior to the trial the big news was that when the new state's attorney entered office, he found that the original grand jury statements of Cicotte and Jackson, which the state argued amounted to confessions, were missing from the office files. This was now supplanted by the equally startling news that the signed waivers of immunity, obtained from the pair prior to their testimony, were also missing. By then the judge had ruled the statements of Cicotte, Jackson, and also that of Lefty Williams, were admissible, but only as against them. By then the judge had strongly indicated that if the jury were to find certain defendants, namely Weaver and Felsch, guilty, he would not feel the verdict warranted and planned to enter a judgment notwithstanding the verdict, granting each of those defendants a new trial. By then the defense had announced its strategy was to prove the World Series of 1919 was played honestly. To prove such, they would not call their accused clients; instead, they would call a number of their clients' teammates and their manager.

The questions to the players and to Gleason were short and to the point. In the prime the defense sought evidence from the teammates to offset testimony by Bill Burns that the indicted players held a meeting on the morning before the day of Game One to plan the strategy of the conspiracy. The questioning and responses of Kid Gleason were reportedly substantially similar to the questioning and responses of Eddie Collins, Dickie Kerr and Roy Wilkinson. Gleason, Eddie Collins and the others testified, as did Ray Schalk, that all the players practiced on the morning in question at the Cincinnati ballpark beginning at 10:00 for about an hour and one-half. Thus, they would not have been in a room at the Sinton Hotel from 10:00 to noon. Under cross-examination by the prosecution, Gleason testified he could not say when the players left the hotel in order to attend the practice.[23]

In addition, Schalk was asked by Gorman of the prosecution, who announced he was making Schalk his witness for this particular purpose, whether he saw the "defendants" together in a room at the Sinton Hotel on the evening of the second game. Schalk answered, "I did." On cross-examination by an attorney for the defense, Schalk denied that Eddie Collins and other players were there as well.[24]

John Shano Collins, Harry Nemo Leibold and Reds pitcher Dutch Ruether were called to the stand and asked whether they noticed anything suspicious about the play in the World Series games. Before each could answer, the state objected and each time Judge Friend sustained the objection.[25]

The mind can veer in many directions trying to figure out why neither Gleason, Eddie Collins, Schalk, Kerr nor Wilkinson were asked this question. After all, John Collins and Nemo Leibold were no longer members of the White Sox team and Dutch Ruether was never a member. Perhaps the defense was not sure the state would object if the question was put to Eddie Collins and his group or, even if they did, the judge would sustain it. Perhaps they feared the "loyalty" thing with Comiskey would only carry so far. At any rate, this ended the defense of the remaining 11 defendants. They had introduced what is often the best defense: a short one.

On August 2 when the case finally went to the jury, the list of defendants at risk was down to six, including Gandil, Jackson, Cicotte, Williams, Risberg, and a lone gambler-type, David Zelcer. The rest were out: Carl Zork and the Levi brothers by discharge, Weaver and Felsch by reason of Judge Friend's intent to overturn any verdict of guilt rendered against them. In addition, Judge Friend by his charge to the jury had greatly increased the odds — perhaps a poor choice of words in a trial of this sort — that the remaining defendants would prevail. He charged the jury that in order to find the remaining defendants guilty of a conspiracy, it was the burden of the state to prove that the ball players intended to defraud the public and others, not just to throw ball games.[26]

If there was still even a chance of this jury finding the defendants guilty for their actions in October 1919 and the month or so leading up to it, the judge's charge sealed the deal. The jury deliberated for less than three hours, one report said two hours and forty-seven minutes, and on one ballot they voted to free the Black Sox.[27] And as the jurors and the defendants partied "separately" in the same Italian restaurant not far from the courthouse, was there the heart of a White Sox fan which did not beat just a bit faster at the prospect this fractured team, their team, would unite again? Certainly, Commy's pulse quickened at the news. Perhaps there was still time to resuscitate a 43–54 team, already 18 and one-half games behind the leader.

The next day Judge Landis made sure that did not happen. As the *Tribune* editorialized, "Judge Landis took his baseball position to give organized baseball a character bath."[28] He now did just that, although some forever after begged to differ, by issuing the following statement:

> Regardless of the verdict of juries no player who throws a ball game, no player who undertakes or promises to throw a ball game, no player who sits in a conference with a bunch of crooked players and gamblers, where the ways and means of throwing a ball game are planned and discussed and does not promptly tell his club about it, will ever play professional baseball.

Of course, I do not know that any of these men will apply for reinstatement but if they do, these are at least a few of the rules that would be enforced.

Just keep in mind that, regardless of the verdict of juries, baseball is entirely competent to protect itself against crooks, both inside and outside of the game.[29]

The fate of the Chicago "eight" was cemented forever. In time Joe Gedeon, the St. Louis Browns' player mentioned in the Collins' quote in *Collyer's Eye*, was also declared ineligible for having "guilty knowledge" of the Black Sox affair.

The future course of the White Sox franchise was also now cast. They would carry on as is. Unfortunately, "as is" was not very good. They finished the season in seventh place, 30 games below .500 at 62–92. Their fans, so excited and full of hope on opening day, began realizing there was no quick fix. Thus, they took their growing frustration out at the box office. Although there was an overall drop in baseball receipts in 1921, the nearly 300,000 drop in White Sox attendance was particularly alarming. Commy's greatest fear, a significant loss in revenue, was realized. He now had a team which was becoming a financial drain. The White Sox's crown as a front-runner was now worn by the New York Yankees, bolstered by the ever-broadening shadow of Babe Ruth, who hit full stride with 59 home runs and a slugging percentage of .846. The Yankees' pennant, the first of so many, did not bring a world championship — the Giants took care of that in an exciting eight-game all–New York City World Series. The White Sox now joined the Red Sox as a one-time proud franchise required by its own actions to look at things from a different perspective: the bottom up.

There were a few highlights in the otherwise dismal White Sox season, however. One in particular was the stellar pitching of Red Faber, who was a winner in 25 of the 62 White Sox victories. He finished the season with a mark of 25–15 and a "lively-ball" ERA of 2.48. It was a remarkable performance; certainly a primary reason the hurler is now enshrined at Cooperstown. Dickie Kerr won most of the rest of the Sox's games and finished 19–17 and 4.72. No other hurler on the team won more than six.

In addition to the strong showing of newcomer Earl Sheely (11 HRs, 95 RBIs, .304), the Pale Hose were rewarded with strong hitting by Amos Strunk (.332) and Harry Hooper (.327). Outfielder Bibb Falk showed he belonged as well, hitting .285 and driving in 82, second best on the club. Since the league average was .292 that season, the higher batting averages must be examined in the context of an era of rising batting averages, but it is still clear that for the White Sox of 1921 pitching was an Achilles' heel.

After his slow start Collins began to hit stride around mid-season and finished with quite respectable numbers. His .337 batting average ranked tenth in the league, and he walked 66 times. One area where his production dropped off was stolen bases. He finished with 12, his lowest figure since 1908. In the field he continued to excel, leading all second basemen in fielding percentage with a .968 average. His batting average and his OBP of .412 topped the White Sox, as did his bases on balls. He struck out only once per 47.8 at-bats. At age 34 he was still a model of efficiency.

Despite attempts by his former teammates to darken his image, Collins remained a popular figure. If Judge Landis was miffed by Eddie's participation in the 1917 "fund," he did not show it. Both he and now Ban Johnson kept their detailed information about the incident to themselves. In late August, about three weeks after the Black Sox verdict, Collins and Landis met by chance on the golf course at the South Shore Country Club. Landis said he had time for a quick nine holes with the Sox captain. When they were finished, Collins had shot a respectable 44; Landis, an even more respectable 42. According to the club's caddies, the judge normally played better. Collins claimed, "I tried my best to beat him but he was too much for me."[30] Eddie was a competitor, but no one ever said he didn't know on whose head the crown rested.

Earlier in the year there had been that rumor, quickly dismissed, that Collins was on his way to the Yankees via the trade route. In October the rumblings began again, this time to the effect Collins would not only play second base for the Yankees in 1922, but manage them as well.

Miller Huggins, the current Yankees' manager, was not a popular figure with the Yankees' fans, or the New York press, despite directing his club to its first pennant. Although to many the idea of Collins replacing Huggins as the Yankees' manager immediately after that team had snatched an American League flag seemed the wildest of speculations, an old Collins' admirer, Hugh Fullerton, gave it form if not substance in his October 31 column, "On the Screen of Sport" in the *New York Evening Mail.* "There is an insistent and persistent rumor in baseball that Collins is to be with the New York Yankees next season, and that in all probability he will succeed Miller Huggins as manager." As to Huggins, he was "a very sick man during much of the [1921] season ... and his management was handicapped by this fact. Nevertheless his judgment was not good in the crises of the year and there was tremendous criticism of him, not only among the fans but among the players."[31] In this instance, "the players" could just as well have read Babe Ruth, who was on a prohibited barnstorming tour that fall.

By the time Fullerton's article hit the page, Collins had already issued his firm denial, declaring his satisfaction in Chicago and his intent to refrain from managing while still active as a player, but carefully asserting, if not Chicago then the Yankees. "I am serving in Chicago under a three year contract which does not expire until the fall of 1922."[32]

This time around Collins was right and Fullerton wrong. When late December rolled around and a picture appeared in the *New York Evening Journal* of a smiling Eddie Collins sitting on a wagon with five-year-old Eddie Jr. while they were pushed by 10-year-old son Paul, Eddie was still a member of the White Sox. If a trade to the Yankees was on his closely-guarded 1921 Christmas wish-list, that was one item that would remain a dream.

CHAPTER 15

Trade Talk

"Since the fraudulent affair of 1919, all baseball attendance records have been shattered, and a tremendous new interest has manifested itself with each added year. This gigantic success of the game has at times been attributed to the advent of Judge Landis as high commissioner, the lively ball, individual batting records, and home-run hitting generally; yet, without such public confidence..., and the integrity of players like Eddie Collins, and the others who remained after the Judas element was eliminated, the mammoth palace-like structures of concrete and steel, would be permanently deserted, and serve merely as ghosts of a once great and beloved game. For the foundation of the game is the integrity of the player."

— George Moriarty writing in *Baseball Magazine*[1]

By 1922 there were few White Sox fans who labored under the impression that 1921 was an aberration. They understood their team was mired in the second division and might be for some time. As usual, Collins asked for and received permission to report to spring training late — this year it was to Marlin Springs, Texas. By the time he arrived in mid–March, in uniform and in shape, there was already trouble on the personnel front. Dickie Kerr was a holdout, telling everyone he was through with the White Sox. Although his ERA had ballooned to 4.72 in 1921, his 19–17 record and experience on the mound promised to leave a large gap in a floundering pitching rotation. Surely, Commy would see the light and ante-up. After all, it was said that the 27-year-old lefty was willing to accept a three-year contract for $8,500 per year. But Commy stood fast, as did Kerr, who opted for a semipro career rather than accept the White Sox's offer. Later when Kerr played in several games in which the banned Black Sox players also appeared, he was suspended by Judge Landis. By the start of the season, Irving Vaughan of the *Tribune* predicted that only the strong arm of Red Faber stood between the Sox and "an ironclad lease on the cellar position."[2]

Actually, the White Sox were a better team in 1922 than most predicted. Their success was a tribute to the managerial skills of Kid Gleason, assisted by his new sidekick, Johnny Evers. The former Cubs' player and manager was accustomed to the top rung, but he had worked well under John McGraw as a coach in 1921, and it was hoped he could do so again, this time under Gleason.

The local skeptics nodded with understanding when the White Sox opened at home on April 12 by losing to Urban Shocker and his St. Louis Browns, 3–2. Two more losses quickly followed. Their first win of the infant season was secured against Detroit on April 16 in front of a home crowd. In a compressed version of "What have you done for us lately?" Collins erred twice and was booed by the 30,000 in attendance; later, however, he was cheered as he went 2-for-5 and drove in a pair of runs. The final score was 7–6.

By the end of April, the Pale Hose were 8–6. The topper, probably the thrill of the season, came on the last day of the month. On April 30 right-hander Charlie Robertson, at 26 making only his fourth start as a major leaguer, pitched a perfect game, defeating the Tigers, 2–0, at Navin Field. It was the first such feat since 1908 when Addie Joss turned the trick. The only other "modern day" perfect game had been hurled by Cy Young for the Red Sox in 1904. Moreover, no White Sox pitcher has thrown one since. Even on Robertson's "day" the Tigers did not go down easily. At least twice they stopped the game to ask the umpires to check the ball for foreign substances. The protests failed and Robertson and his White Sox prevailed.

Robertson's gem was preserved by some splendid fielding by outfielder Johnny Mostil. Actually, the 1922 outfield, manned primarily by Harry Hooper, who stroked 11 home runs, drove in 80 and batted .304; Bibb Falk (12, 79 and .298); and Mostil (7, 70 and .303), was quite adequate. Mostil, who regularly roamed center field but played left in Robertson's perfect game, was an outstanding glove man; Collins considered him among the best center fielders he ever saw.

"Tris Speaker was the more polished fielder, because he had brains and intuition and uncanny judgment as to where the ball would land. For that reason I'd give him the edge. But for sheer goin' and gettin' 'em as the ball players put it, I consider Mostil the best I've seen."

In fact, Collins awarded Mostil the honor of delivering the greatest catch he ever saw. It was made during "an exhibition game with Birmingham of the Southern Association. Johnny, a center fielder, actually caught a foul fly. He was playing slightly toward the left and when the high foul was hit started to tear for it. Bibb Falk stepped aside to let him make the catch and he got it. Ty Cobb used to say that Chicago had two traffic cops and one outfielder, and all the 'cops' would do would be to wave for Mostil to come on through."[3]

In May ghosts from 1917 and 1919 flitted through the baseball atmosphere yet again when allegations of "sloughing" during the 1917 Detroit series and "throwing" games to these same Tigers in 1919 were tossed around during discovery proceedings in preparation for trial of lawsuits brought by Joe Jackson, Hap Felsch and other Black Sox players against Comiskey and the White Sox. They sought back pay from 1920 and for other damages incurred from their banishment from baseball. In response, Collins, Schalk and Red Faber denied knowledge of a fund to purchase victories. Instead, Schalk publicly alluded to the pool used to reward the Tigers for their 1917 work against Boston.[4] It appeared the battle lines remained firmly demarcated when Buck Weaver stated publicly that the last two series between the White Sox and Tigers were fixed to allow the White Sox to win the pennant and, gate receipts notwithstanding, collect a $5,000 bonus guaranteed to each player by Commy if they won the World Series. According to Weaver, the games he claimed the White Sox threw to the Tigers at the end of 1919 were by way of reciprocation for the Tigers' cooperation in 1917.[5] These allegations were sensational, especially since they came from such a popular figure as Buck Weaver. But just as quickly as they appeared, they disappeared. Apparently, the press and the fans agreed with Landis and Johnson. They considered the sources of the allegations, each one a disgruntled Black Sox player, and quickly cast the charges aside.

The month of June was most kind to the White Sox in 1922. Following a miserable May when the Sox posted an 11–17 mark, the team revived in June to win 17 of 26, including winning streaks of six and eight, which extended into July. The early portion of the 1922 season was not without its highlights for Collins. When the team played in Washington before President Warren G. Harding on May 22, Eddie stroked a pair of triples and scored a run in a 4–3 win for pitcher Red Faber. On May 30 Collins went 4-for-5 in the afternoon portion of a double-bill win over the Indians. His efforts included a double, a bases-loaded triple, a sacrifice and a run scored. At 35 he could still get on base and produce runs.

On July 1, the tail end of their eight-game run, the club stood 37–32 and in third, only four and one-half games from the top. They had bought into Kid Gleason's program, playing aggressive ball and hitting in the clutch. They were succeeding despite a pitching rotation with one shining star, Faber, as well as the rookie Robertson, who despite his shining moment on April 30 had only 48 major league wins left in his arm, and Dixie Leverett, another right-hander who at 28 was enjoying his finest season. The fourth starter was another rookie, Ted Blankenship. At 21 he would perform for the White Sox for eight more seasons, but not at the level of Dickie Kerr.

And, instead of investing in a few hundred more dollars to secure the valuable services of Kerr, what did Commy do? On May 29 he spent $100,000 and sent three players to San Francisco of the Pacific Coast League for infielder Willie Kamm. The future White Sox third baseman did not play for the team until 1923.

The White Sox posted a 17–14 record in July and remained in third place throughout. The Yankees and the Browns were setting the pace; Gleason's boys were still only four and one-half out as the month ended. In mid–July there was a minor distraction. Once again rumors of a Collins-to-the-Yankees deal emerged, as dissension in the Yankees' clubhouse reached a new high. The Yankees still wanted him, and perhaps White Sox management felt they should swing a deal while they could still get something substantial in return, but when names of Yankee stalwarts like Aaron Ward, Carl Mays, Waite Hoyt and, yes, even the increasingly irascible Babe Ruth were bandied about, all Kid Gleason could or would say, "I don't know a thing about it."[6]

Today a Collins-for-Ruth trade seems impossible to imagine. Perhaps even in 1922, given Eddie's advancing "baseball years," it confounded most casual observers. It was not, however, so far-fetched. Ruth's barnstorming venture after the 1921 season resulted in a suspension which cost him the early portion of the 1922 season. Run-ins with umpires caused several ejections and another suspension. At the same time Yankees ownership was involved in financing the construction of a new stadium. Any deal for Collins which included Ruth would have required the White Sox to fork over a significant amount of cash on top of their second sacker. Of course, it was never consummated and baseball fans everywhere could continue to call the new Yankee Stadium "the house that Ruth built."

Instead of trading for Collins, the Yankees continued to mine for gold in Boston, once again utilizing their pipeline to Harry Frazee to lift Joe Dugan and Elmer Smith, a pair of excellent ball players, from a Red Sox team which had traded almost all of its stars — mostly to the Yanks — in exchange for very little. The remaining American League owners screamed and stamped their feet, but did little else.

The White Sox remained in the pennant race into early August, then quickly faded away. From August 2 through August 24 they were 5–16, falling from third to fifth. They now trailed the lead pack by over 13 games. Commy was ill as well, hospitalized with severe gall bladder problems.

To make matters worse, word on the street was that Collins was slowing down as well. Hugh Fullerton wrote that, "[M]uch as we regret it, Eddie is reaching the limit. He is covering ground by thinking now rather than by speed of foot. The old brain is saving him."[7] Even if his skills were diminishing somewhat, Collins continued to show his value as a team captain. On August 16 as the Sox began to wobble and tensions increased in inverse proportion to on-the-field results, Eddie stepped in the middle of a squabble between Ray Schalk and Clarence "Shovel" Hodge, a sometime starter and frequent reliever. Hodge was working in relief in a game in Boston when the Beantowners pulled a double steal. Schalk, who throughout his catching career had no qualms about berating his pitchers, felt Hodge had permitted the steals by failing to properly hold the runners to their bases, trotted to the mound and told him so. Hodge, much taller and also heavier than Schalk, screamed back. Eddie came in from second and quieted the reliever enough to allow him to retire the side. In the dugout between innings, however, no one, including Collins, could hold Hodge back, and the pair slugged it out. Schalk got the best of the pitcher, landing a punch squarely on the taller man's nose before Gleason and Johnny Mostil were able to separate them. Perhaps White Sox management saw what Schalk saw, or rather failed to see, in Hodge. He was traded to the San Francisco Seals as one of the players to be named later in the Willie Kamm deal and never pitched in the major leagues again.

As for Collins, rather than feeling sorry for himself, Fullerton's pointed article seemed to spur him on. Although the words had to hurt, coming as they did from the usually supportive Fullerton, Eddie kept his mouth shut and let his bat do the talking. In the opener of a doubleheader versus Boston on August 17 he went 4-for-4 with a sacrifice. The next day in New York he went 3-for-4, including a two-run home run into the right field seats. It was his only round-tripper of the season. He followed a few days later with 3-for-5 and 3-for-4 outings.

Certainly his fine performance in the series in New York, where he went 7-for-13, scored three times and drove in a pair of runs with his home run blast, only served to enhance his image in the eyes of Yankees management. Even though the New Yorkers were in position for another league flag, Miller Huggins was still feeling the heat and Collins was the leading candidate, at least among most tongue-waggers, to replace him.

In mid–September Collins celebrated his sixteenth anniversary in the major leagues with a single, two walks and one of his 20 stolen bases on the year. That figure was eight more than the previous season, a hint that old Cocky's base running days were not totally behind him.

Eddie Collins of the Chicago White Sox (Photo Collection, Cleveland Public Library).

When the 1922 regular season ended on October 1 in St. Louis with a 2–1 loss to a disappointed Browns team, which finished the season just a single game behind the Yankees, the White Sox stood 17 back in fifth place at 77–77. Given the dire predictions in the spring, these Pale Hose had performed admirably.

So had Collins, the oldest regular on the team, leading his teammates in six categories, including games played (154), hits (194), walks (73), average (.324) and on-base percentage (.401). He also only struck out once every 37 at-bats, again his team's best. His average and OBP were tenth in the league, his number of hits fifth, and walks sixth. Even his 20 stolen bases stood fifth. Finally his team-leading 270 times on base was third in the league. Clearly, he was not ready to hang up his spikes.

In October when the Giants were once again taking the measures of a Yankees team still on the brink of greatness, the Cubs finally won a City Series, besting the White

Sox in seven games. It was the first City Series win for the Cubs since 1909 and a fellow named Frank Chance.

Meanwhile, both during and after the City Series, rumors of Collins to the Yankees persisted, probably fueled by the Yankees' World Series loss, a decided victory by the Giants in five games. On October 9 Yankees co-owner Colonel Jacob Ruppert, in the process of negotiating the purchase of the interest of his partner Captain Tillinghast Huston, refused to firmly deny he wanted Collins. Instead he said, "If Miller [Huggins] wants to manage the Yankees next year the position will be waiting for him. Naturally Collins would be a distinct addition to any club, but I don't know where stories arose about our getting him."[8]

At least one of those "stories" stemmed from a series of reports written by baseball writer Fred Lieb for the *New York Evening Telegram*. The stories appeared in December, some two months after Miller Huggins signed a one-year contract to continue managing the Yankees, thus temporarily derailing the "Collins-for-Manager" express. They coincided with the approach of baseball's annual winter meetings in New York. The articles by Lieb seemed to confirm reports in Chicago papers that the Yankees were still interested in Eddie as a player. On December 12 Lieb announced a trade. The White Sox would send Collins and Dickie Kerr to the Yankees for a pair of good hitting youngsters in outfielder Bob Muesel and second baseman Aaron Ward, plus one of the pennant winner's "regular pitchers." According to Lieb the trade was a certainty, to occur the next day.[9] This report followed a similar but more detailed report in the *Chicago Tribune* two days prior that had the Yankees obtaining shortstop Roger Peckinpaugh from the Washington Senators and including him in the trade with the Sox, as well as young pitching star Waite Hoyt. Others rumored to be involved included outfielder Bibb Falk of the White Sox and even outfielder Sam Rice of the Senators.[10]

Dickie Kerr's availability was, of course, an issue since he was then still barred from baseball for playing semipro ball with a black-listed player, Gene Paulette, the former Philadelphia Phillie. The White Sox were seeking re-instatement, but the uncertainty of a favorable Landis decision was a stumbling block in negotiations. It did seem, however, that Fred Lieb's report was accurate, at least at the time he issued it. A trade was imminent; however, it all fell apart. The apparent reason was the uncertainty of Dickie Kerr's playing status. Judge Landis wanted to reserve judgment on the matter until the 1923 season. A more substantive reason was the insistence by the White Sox on Waite Hoyt as the "regular pitcher" they desired as part of any trade. The Yankees wanted the Sox to take Carl Mays; the White Sox refused. The deal was off for all intents and purposes.

Fred Lieb was one of those who felt the Yankees made the correct decision. Before the trade was officially declared dead, he wrote:

> It has been said that Huggins will make a good deal with Chicago if he gets Collins, even though he must give up Meusel, Ward and Hoyt. We do not agree with such an assertion. Collins is a great player, but such a price would be asinine to pay for an infielder close to thirty-six years of age.
> We believe Huggins would be foolish to include Hoyt in any deal.... [T]he best part of his career still is ahead of him.[11]

As it turned out, Lieb was probably right. Collins would have helped in the short term, perhaps later even successfully managed the Yankees for a number of years. But at 22, Hoyt already owned a pair of 19-win seasons and was well on his way to a Hall of Fame career and a 237–182 career mark.

What was the reaction to the possible loss of Collins in Chicago, where White Sox fans were still not over their withdrawal symptoms from the rapid departure of stars such as Weaver, Jackson and the other Black Sox? Sportswriter Irving Vaughan had an interesting take:

There is more behind the transaction than just the shuffling of talent by which both teams hope to gather strength. It seems that at various times in the last year Collins himself was given to understand that his faithful service to Charles A. Comiskey & Co. before and after and during the trying days of 1919 and '20 would be rewarded. To the greatest second sacker of them all this meant only one thing — a transfer to New York, where he always has wanted to play.[12]

Relocation to New York would have meant more to Collins than just that close hop from Yankee Stadium to his Lansdowne, Pennsylvania, home. Both of Eddie's parents, John and Mary, still lived in nearby Tarrytown, New York, and the relationship between parents and son remained a close one. It was said that whenever Eddie played against the Yankees in New York, his father had a box seat at the stadium. His parents never missed one of his World Series games. Often they came to Philadelphia where John Collins was "on most intimate terms with Ty Cobb and Tris Speaker." He also became friends with his son's good friend, Ray Schalk. Once when John Collins was at Eddie's home at 341 North Owen Avenue to celebrate his birthday, John found he shared the date with Schalk. For years thereafter John and Ray Schalk met at Eddie's home for a joint celebration.[13] There was also the Columbia connection. Clearly a change of venue to the Big Apple would suit the entire Collins family just fine.

That the Yankees' unwillingness to include Waite Hoyt in any deal was the real hang up to obtaining Collins became even more apparent in early 1923. In late January, perhaps inspired by the Yankees' purchase of Collins' former A's pitcher-friend Herb Pennock from the Red Sox, or perhaps due to continued concerns about Miller Huggins' health, there was a renewal of the trade talk involving the White Sox. If Huggins was unable to manage, then Collins' potential value to the Yankees increased considerably. It was Colonel Huston, still involved with the club at this point, who confirmed that Hoyt was the key.

"Sure we have a good chance to get Collins. The minute we are ready to inform Comiskey and Gleason that we will part with Waite Hoyt, Collins will become a Yankee."

Asked if Collins would become the Yankee manager, Huston replied, "It probably would work out that way."[14]

Once again talks progressed to the point that the exchange seemed a certainty. Once again, this time on February 19, it was announced the deal had failed. During the latest negotiations the White Sox upped the ante, which already included Collins and Falk. They offered to include Charlie Robertson if Hoyt joined Ward, Muesel and either Sam Jones or Carl Mays in the deal. The Yanks stood firm, refusing to include Hoyt, with Colonel Ruppert telling the press, "We simply could not afford to meet the Chicago club's demands." Gleason's reaction was earthier. The New Yorkers "must think we're from the country."

In fact, there were those who felt that Gleason never even contemplated parting with Collins, considering his star an untouchable and, thus, continually increased his demands whenever the Yankees adjusted their offer.

Collins, who was nearby since the discussions were held in Philadelphia, admitted he would have been happy to become a Yankee but denied any dissatisfaction with the White Sox.[15] From the inception of the trade talks, he had actually been quite candid about his feelings for New York.

Funny thing, but from the very first day I broke into major league ball I cherished a desire to wear a New York uniform. Perhaps it was because I made my baseball start at Columbia, which is located in that city.

"The financial possibilities in New York also appeal to the player. New York draws the big crowds and can pay the fancy salaries if they want a man. Then there is the World Series to shoot at. New York has won two pennants and despite all the criticism that has been hurled at the Yankee Club because of its poor showing in the series, it still is a mighty tough team to beat over the long route.[16]

The idea persisted through the early spring, probably driven by quotes like this last one, that Collins planned to hold out. His contract had ended, after all, in 1922. When the team arrived in Seguin, Texas, to begin spring training in mid–March, he was absent. Of course, early absences were the custom for Eddie Collins. In addition, Eddie was always first and foremost a team player, no matter how bitterly disappointed he might be that he was still with Chicago. On March 15 he attempted to put holdout rumors to rest.

"It seems whenever a player does not hustle off to training camp at the first whistle in the spring he is called a 'hold out.' I have no differences with the Chicago club and expect to leave for the south in a few days."[17]

A man of his word, Collins announced two days later he had reached an agreement with the boss. "I had a conference with President Comiskey over the phone and we quickly came to terms. I'll leave for training camp ... [early the next week]."[18]

The new contract dated March 19 continued Collins' salary as a player for $15,000 per year through 1924 but added an additional $100 per month for his work as the team captain.[19]

On March 22 Collins was in camp, once again deemed in fine playing condition, ready to go. He was greeted by one new friendly face. During the off-season White Sox pitching great Ed Walsh was named to replace John Evers as assistant manager. Evers' status with the club for 1923 was uncertain. Another change was the insertion of that expensive minor leaguer, Willie Kamm, into the White Sox's lineup. Commy had spent a hundred grand on the youngster, still only 23, and he wanted to start cashing in on the investment. Kamm replaced Eddie Mulligan, a .234 hitter in 1922, as the regular third baseman. Another change was Harvey McClellan taking over for Ernie Johnson at short. The changes shaved at least 10 years off the aggregate age of the White Sox's infield. Management probably deemed this infusion of youth a necessity, given that Schalk and first baseman Earl Sheely were now 30, Hooper 34, and Collins 36.

The replacement of fair to weak hitting everyday players with prospects whose best career days could be ahead of them was a fine idea. If only someone could have done something about the pitching. By now Faber was 34 and only so much could be expected. In addition, the aura of Charlie Robertson's perfect game could only carry over for so long. Young pitchers like Mike Cvengros (23), Ted Blankenship (22), and Dixie Leverett (29) were expected to fill out the rotation and pick up the slack. That they could not was the fault of a management that was inconsistent about when and where they would spend their dollars. Even the addition of Sloppy Thurston, an effective relief pitcher purchased from the Browns in early season, did not help enough.

When the White Sox opened the 1923 season in Cleveland on April 18, they possessed a group of regulars with some hitting punch, a loyal fan base which still remembered the past and thus expected more, and a pitching staff that just could not deliver. Under these circumstances it was difficult to be overly optimistic about where the team might stand in the pennant race.

To make matters even more confusing, there was increasing doubt in the ability of one of the team's remaining stars, Eddie Collins, to keep up the pace. In writing about the White Sox's season prospects in a series of articles for the *Tribune*, Hugh Fullerton, long an avid Collins supporter despite those candid articles about him the previous season, once again expressed serious reservations about Collins' star status, telling readers he "is slowing. He is playing where they hit them now instead of going and getting them wherever they are hit.

His official figures are better than ever — but the sad fact remains that he doesn't get as many as he used to."[20]

As such, at least in Fullerton's opinion, Marty McManus, the 23-year-old St. Louis Browns second baseman, was now the best at that position in the American League. Collins was still Fullerton's pick for second best, although in addition to his diminished play in the field, "he will slowly lose his batting power."[21]

When the Sox opened their season by losing seven of eight and Collins' poor fielding cost them a 1–0 loss to St. Louis in one game and allowed Cleveland to tie the score in another, many were finding a lot to agree with Fullerton's pre-season assessment of Collins and this White Sox team.

In truth, Collins was not fielding all that badly and his bat, as well as his uncanny ability to get on base and score, was as sharp as ever. On May 18 at Comiskey, he went 4-for-4, including two singles in one inning, scored a run, walked and stole a base as the White Sox won, 14–8. But even Eddie Collins in mid-career form could not save these White Sox. A June 2 loss to the Browns at Comiskey Park found the team in last place. An unyielding schedule about to send the Pale Hose on a 27-game road trip promised even more gloom. But with their season on the brink of early extinction, they instead won 18 of 27. When the team returned on July 6, their record was a surprising 33–33 and they rested in fourth place. It appeared this White Sox team had spunk after all and the season was far from over.

On the key road trip, Collins performed brilliantly. His bat was exceedingly hot. For one of the few times in his career, he hit with power, homering in two of the games. Moreover, he was stealing bases with old-time abandon and success. On June 24 the White Sox stole six bases versus the Senators. Eddie contributed one, number 21 on the season, one more than he stole in all of 1922. He was leading the league in that category.

During his career Collins probably never got full credit for his expertise as a base runner. In 11 of the seasons between 1908 and 1928, he stole more bases than Ty Cobb. Of course, by 1923 he no longer stole bases on speed alone. However, he never really had depended solely on his legs for his thievery. Eddie always insisted he stole bases on the pitcher, not the catcher.

"Watch the pitcher's feet and legs! Forget their hands and arms. If you study a pitcher, you can read his feet like they were guidebooks."[22]

He also took as long a lead as anyone else in the sport. According to Miller Huggins, "Nobody ever played baseball who could get back to his base faster than Collins, or who dared to take such a long lead against a southpaw pitcher."[23]

When it came to stealing a base, Collins was not adverse to outright trickery — even if he was competing against a true gentleman like Walter Johnson. Shirley Povich, veteran sportswriter for the *Washington Post*, told of a White Sox-Senators game where Johnson, who due to the great velocity of his pitches detested hitting batters and did his best to avoid it, hit Collins in the leg.

> Collins went down as if his leg was shattered, lay groveling in the dirt for several minutes as players hovered around him. Big Gentle Johnson was most solicitous of all.
>
> Collins insisted on staying in the game and limped to first base. He was accompanied all the way down the line by Johnson who continued to apologize. Finally he patted Collins on the back and returned to his pitching. Collins, the faker, stole second on Johnson's first delivery.[24]

In June 1923 Collins was putting his classroom theories to work on the ball field and giving the entire American League a lesson. He claimed his 28th theft of a base on July 1, but then he was victimized by that old "fly in the ointment." On July 2 Eddie wrenched his knee. Over the next three weeks, he played infrequently or not at all. His replacement, John Happenny, was not up to the task. Although the team's drop-off was not sharp, they seemed to gradually lose their previous momentum. By the end of the season, the final record was 69–85, and they had settled uncomfortably into seventh place, an emphatic 30 games behind another Yankees pennant winner. Kid Gleason would later call the key to the downward slide the injury to Collins. "That fellow's [Collins'] misfortune [knee injury] was what broke us up. The team was never right after that."[25]

That is a gross oversimplification. While Collins was struggling to recover from his injuries, the White Sox did not play badly. A 10-inning win over the Yanks on July 13 even pushed them into third. But there were injuries to others besides Collins. Both Kamm and McClellan were out for periods of time. The pitching staff performed as advertised, meaning it was not up to the task. There was never the pitching consistency to field a winner. Collins' injury was a definite blow, but the collapse of this particular White Sox team did not rest on Collins' injured limb alone. Upon his return, Eddie continued his spirited play. Although he twisted his leg again on one occasion and wrenched his back on another, his performance in 1923 served to postpone further reports of his imminent demise. Despite the injuries, he managed to appear in 145 of the team's 156 contests. He led the White Sox and was fourth in the league in batting average at .360. Harry Heilmann of Detroit led the league at .403, followed by Ruth (.393) and Speaker (.380). Collins' OBP of .455, reinforced by 84 walks (5th in AL) was fifth in the league. He almost always took his pitching opponents deep into the count, striking out only eight times in 505 at-bats. His 48 stolen bases led the league for the third time in his career; teammate Johnny Mostil, quickly becoming a force on the bases, was second with 41. Finally, despite playing for a seventh-place club, Eddie finished second in the voting for the American League's MVP. The honor, which replaced the Chalmers Award, was granted after a tabulation of the votes of one writer from each league city. The award was easily won by Yankee Babe Ruth, who continued his big-swing through baseball history with his career-high batting average, as well as 41 home runs and 131 RBIs.

One reason Collins was eligible for the MVP award was that until 1930, player-managers and previous winners were not eligible. George Sisler had won the first award in 1922. In late 1923 Sisler was named manager of the St. Louis Browns, joining a list of active players who were also managers, such as Cobb and Speaker. In 1923 there was once again talk of Collins becoming a manager. This time, however, it involved his very own White Sox club.

As early as August there was talk that Kid Gleason might not return to the White Sox in 1924. By then the current season was lost. If this were to occur, the early betting was on Collins as Gleason's successor. Even though Eddie repeatedly denied interest in the job, it is safe to say his stance was taken out of respect for Gleason. Little more was said about Gleason's status as the season wound down. In mid–October the Cubs, a fourth-place finisher and for now the main baseball attraction in the Windy City, and the White Sox waged their annual war. Interest was keen; a record 41,325 stormed Comiskey on October 14 to witness a Sox victory. Two days later the city's American League entry won the series, four games to two. But the real news the following day was not the White Sox's victory, but the announcement that, in fact, Kid Gleason was calling it quits after five years at the helm. It appears the Kid's decision to leave was his own; his health was a factor. Thirty pounds underweight due to illness, he was a thoroughly beaten-down man. Collins knew his manager well and felt he also knew exactly where to place the blame for the man's decline: the Black Sox.[26]

Now the search was on. Collins had been deemed a candidate even before there was an opening. The veteran Ray Schalk was now certainly another, with some speculation the two friends might cancel one another out for fear they might not take kindly to direction from the other. Other internal candidates were assistant manager Ed Walsh and veteran outfielder Harry Hooper. One outsider whose name was mentioned was Frank Chance, the former Cubs' player and manager who had just finished piloting the now Ruth-less and toothless Red Sox to a last-place finish. The Red Sox were now under new management, purchased from the beleaguered Harry Frazee by a group headed by Bob Quinn, a former executive with the Browns. Caught up in a season of change in Boston, it seemed certain Chance would quickly re-enter the managerial market. In Chicago where he was known as "The Peerless Leader," he was quite popular, at least among Cubs fans.

The issue for Commy of whether to choose an insider or go outside the White Sox family for his new manager engendered a lively discussion around town about the qualifications and drawbacks of Collins and Schalk. One member of the local media who went public on this subject was Irving Vaughan of the *Tribune*. After cautioning readers that Collins was on record that if offered he would not accept, he discussed the merits of his selection.

> Collins qualifies for the post principally because he ranks with the smartest ball players of all time. None can dispute this. Further, the great second sacker has the disposition to lead. He is the kind of a fellow who can keep his head in a pinch and give orders without rankling the man receiving them, the temperament of the receiver notwithstanding.
>
> And "Cocky," as his mates call him because he is just the reverse, is ambitious to top off his playing days with a managerial career. At least, such was his ambition last winter when there were prospects of him being traded to the Yanks to supplant Miller Huggins.

Vaughan was even more candid in discussing the White Sox's catcher.

> Schalk qualifies by the fact that he has long been a faithful employe [*sic*] — probably more so than any other man ever on Comiskey's payroll. He is a fighter, in the sense that he doesn't know what it is to quit....
>
> The one thing that might stand in the way of Schalk's promotion is that he never has minced words when dealing with pitchers.... Two of them even went so far during the last season as to say they couldn't pitch to him.

Then Vaughan hit the issue of compatibility. Would these players cooperate if one was Commy's choice over the other?

"In weighing Collins against Schalk, and vice versa, there is the question of whether one would play under the other without feeling resentment. Knowing the men, one can say that both will play to win and nothing can submerge that trait in either. But it is such little details as this that Comiskey must consider."[27]

It never came down to Schalk or Collins. On October 27 White Sox club secretary Harry Grabiner verified that Frank Chance was selected to manage the club and planned to sign a one-year contract. One day later it was reported Chance had told reporters he would do nothing to deny Eddie Collins the opportunity to manage a ball club.[28] The Peerless Leader had spotted a source of trouble and hoped to steer it away. Washington seemed interested, their immediate denials notwithstanding.

This was all news to Collins, every bit of it. Some two weeks after the news about Chance was released, Eddie pulled into his garage in Lansdowne, a good-sized buck deer strapped to his auto, and learned the identity of his new manager. Fresh from a hunting expedition which saw him trampling the brush around Moosehead Lake, Maine, with pitchers Bob Shawkey and Joe Bush and catcher Fred Hofmann of the Yankees and a few of their friends, the second sacker was in no mood to cast stones. He claimed he did not apply for the job, intending instead to concentrate on his play. Frank Chance was "the logical selection," given his popularity in Chicago.

"All these reports about me being dissatisfied over Chance's appointment was news to me. I left Chicago one hour after the final game of the series with the Cubs....

"I'll be back playing second base for the White Sox next spring with bells on."[29]

One place it appeared Collins would not play was second base for the New York Yankees. On the third try the American Leaguers had finally beaten their cross-town rivals for a World Series title. One of the solid contributors to their lofty status was second baseman Aaron Ward. Shortly after vanquishing the Giants in six games, Yankees owner Colonel Jacob Ruppert confirmed as much.

"I was disappointed last winter when we did not get Collins, but I wouldn't trade Ward for Collins even. Eddie is now in his late thirties, and Ward today is the best second baseman in our league. What a game he played in the series. Collins, in his prime, never played any better."[30]

But where Collins was concerned, the trade speculation never ended. A few weeks after the Colonel's rather definitive statement about Ward versus Collins, Yankees manager Miller Huggins, who by now had quieted his critics by directing his club to a world title, hinted that Ward might be switched to shortstop if it would strengthen the infield. Perhaps the Yankees were hoping to head off a move that would find Collins playing second for the Senators and managing them as well.

In retrospect, this all seemed a precursor for Frank Chance's announcement on December 10 at the winter meetings in Chicago that Eddie Collins was on the trading block. Apparently, Eddie's loyalty to Comiskey and the White Sox counted for little. He was not even told about their decision.

"This is rather a shock to me. I did not expect to be placed in the open market," he told reporters in a telephone conversation from his home in Pennsylvania. He had no idea where he might land, but the move had made him reconsider his stance on one point. He was now willing to manage a big league club.

As for Chicago, he mentioned he would still be "delighted" to play for Frank Chance, "but as he is the boss and wants to get rid of me — O, well, that is all in the game. What else can I say?"[31]

Actually, in a back-handed way, the White Sox were trying to do Collins a favor. Chance felt Eddie would be uncomfortable under his tutelage in Chicago. If he could move Collins into a managerial position, it would actually serve as a promotion, as well as a smooth entry into Eddie's retirement as an active performer.

Perhaps Washington owner Clark Griffith was seriously interested in Collins, perhaps not. It is said the White Sox wanted the fiery infielder Stanley "Bucky" Harris in return. In any event, the owners left the winter meetings in Chicago and the White Sox still owned their aging, but still highly productive star. Nothing came of separate talks between Chance and Ed Barrow, the Yankees' business manager, either.

Still, given all this publicity, the city of Chicago was both convinced and resigned to the fact the stay of Collins in Chicago was coming to an end. A poem of tribute by the anonymous "Hoosier Pat" appeared in the *Tribune* in the column, "In the Wake of the News" on December 13. The author bemoaned the loss of one so "(r)espected and feared by the hostile clan," at the same time recognizing "(w)e need the strength a deal may bring...."[32]

A few days later the same column paid tribute again. Extolling Collins' virtues as a "gentleman of baseball," the columnist reminded readers that the star

> has given many of the best years of his baseball career to Chicago, playing the game for all that was in him....
>
> To his intimates it was no secret that Collins would have preferred to play in a city near his home in a Philadelphia suburb — on one of the New York teams for instance. Yet never a whimper came from him, never a question of his loyalty. He was one of the outstanding figures of the

White Sox in the black days of the 1919 world's series [*sic*]. He always has given his best to the city which he represented.

From what we know of Collins we think his pride will be hurt by the present willingness to trade him for other material. For his sake and the past services he has rendered The Wake, although a most ardent admirer is reconciled to his departure — provided a change brings a connection as good or better than he has here.[33]

Over time Collins became more wistful about his days with Gleason, recalling that unlike many team captains, Gleason "sought my advice and took my judgment very often in preference to his own."[34]

Collins realized and was reconciled that under Chance his authority would diminish. He had a real concern, however, about the reception the new manager might receive from White Sox fans given Chance's ties to the Cubs as a former player, captain and manager of the cross-town rivals.

"[A] Cub running the White Sox! I assure you I was not disturbed in the least, but along that eccentric frontier of baseball partisanship in Chicago, as you may suppose, there ran a current of dissatisfaction."[35]

Yet despite Collins' misgivings, in early 1924 the White Sox's management story was by no means the top story in baseball or, for that matter, the top story in Chicago. Once again the Black Sox scandal took top billing. This time it was the sideshow unfolding in Milwaukee in the person of Joe Jackson and the trial of his lawsuit against Commy and the White Sox for back pay. Although it revealed many new tidbits of information, including the reappearance of missing materials from the grand jury proceeding, and served to tantalize and further confuse or enlighten conspiracy theorists, depending on the flavor, Collins was only mentioned in passing. Comiskey was asked to testify about whether Eddie went to him at any time about the fix. Commy replied that he had, but only once, the previously disclosed meeting a week prior to Cicotte's confession. In the end Joe Jackson would win his lawsuit but incur charges for perjury for changed testimony in the eyes of a judge who overturned the former player's favorable verdict. Commy and Jackson later settled for a small sum.

In early February the Yankees took one more shot at Collins, offering to substitute shortstop Everett Scott and utility infielder Mike McNally for Aaron Ward. When the White Sox stuck to their guns, demanding Ward, the deal was officially declared dead by both Colonel Ruppert and Ed Barrow, who days later turned down an offer to manage the Senators. That job, once considered the logical move for Collins, was eventually filled by Bucky Harris, at age 27 the youngest big league manager.

One of Frank Chance's first moves as manager was to bring back his old teammate, Johnny Evers, to coach. On February 16 the move seemed fortuitous as Chance announced he was battling a bronchial infection stemming from the flu and had sent Commy his resignation, but at the owner's insistence he planned to try to recover in time to manage the team. In his absence Evers and Ed Walsh would handle the squad. If Chance's recovery was quick, he could join the team at its new spring environs in Winter Haven, Florida.

The announcement of Chance's illness sparked a rash of new speculation that Collins would now become the manager. One rumor even had Chance giving up the job because he could not get rid of Collins and was stuck with this potential thorn in his side. On February 19 it was reported that Collins arrived in Chicago from the East in order to accept Commy's offer for the managerial reins and begin immediate preparations for spring training. One day later Eddie reported from Lansdowne that he had barely left his home in three days. Finally, Collins had heard enough. Speaking from Philadelphia, he blasted the reports, including those saying he planned to hold out this season.

I cannot understand why so many liberties have been taken with my name and so many wrong conclusions put in the newspapers about my future in baseball.

What am I expected to say? I wish I knew. All I know is that I was very sorry to hear that Frank Chance is in ill health. I was glad to hear that President Comiskey induced him to withdraw his resignation....

I didn't sign a contract this year with the Sox because I didn't have to. Last year I signed a two year contract that does not expire until next October.[36]

A few days later Chance told reporters from his Los Angeles, California, home that his condition was asthmatic. He planned to recuperate in nearby Palm Springs and then head east. At least to his way of thinking, he and Eddie Collins were friends. Collins would play for the White Sox in 1924 unless he told Chance he preferred to play elsewhere.

Of course, Collins would not so state. For Eddie the new year represented his eighteenth in the majors. Unlike the previous season, when Hugh Fullerton expressed strong doubt, this season Irving Vaughan, after conceding Collins had "slipped" a bit, quickly placed it in context.

"He [Collins] may be a fraction slower getting to first and maybe he's not covering the ground as he did of yore, but to the average fan these slight changes are not visible. What is visible to the fan is that Collins still ranks with the top notch hitters, leads his league in base burglaries, is one of the best bunters in the game, one of the hardest men to pitch to and probably without a superior in directing defensive play."[37]

Collins had not yet arrived in the White Sox's training camp, however, before he received some criticism from other quarters. Some members of team management, as well as a number of veterans, left for the Winter Haven spring headquarters on the last day of February. Although Collins was usually a late arrival for spring drills, there was a school of thought that as captain he would want to pitch in and assist Evers and the other coaches and veterans in schooling the youngsters for the upcoming season. For a second year the club planned to play a series of games with the top-flight New York Giants. Collins' steadying influence could be a big help. Therefore, when Eddie still had not arrived by mid–March, one reporter, Frank Smith of the *Tribune*, wrote that "[t]here has been some criticism of Capt. Collins on and off the field for his dilatory method of reporting when the squad was handicapped by the absence of Chance. Some insist he would have shown a more loyal spirit if, when he learned that Chance could not report on account of illness, he had turned in early and given Evers and Ed Walsh assistance in sizing up the recruits."[38]

It is not clear exactly when Collins did arrive in Florida in 1924. He was not in the lineup for the first contest with the Giants, played in Sarasota on March 17. It was reported that on that date he was in New York ready to depart for Chicago, set to arrive in that city on the 19th. The purpose of the visits to both New York and Chicago was unknown. By March 21 he was in the Sox's lineup, stroking a trio of hits as his team topped the Giants in 10 innings at Winter Haven.

The discussion of his absence did spark his most candid comments to date on his feelings about his status with the White Sox and the failed efforts to place him in New York. In the March 27 edition of "Scribbled by Scribes," a weekly column which appeared in *The Sporting News* and related excerpts of the writings of various sportswriters around the country, he was quoted by Warren K. Brown in the *Chicago Herald-Examiner* as saying that he had only talked with the White Sox one time about a possible trade and that to Kid Gleason. After telling Kid he had enjoyed his stay in Chicago and would continue to do so, Collins confided his long-time desire to play in New York. He then asked for Gleason's help in realizing that dream. In addition, he went to Comiskey on one occasion for a general discussion of his future with the team and was told the owner would trade any player, no matter when, if it would help the club. Collins claimed he reiterated to Commy his willingness to play his best ball for Frank Chance.

"Was I disappointed because I had not been named manager? Perhaps, but I learned from the New York incident a few seasons ago that it does not do to build air castles when one is a baseball player.

"I have my opinion why that deal with New York did not go through, but it is my opinion, and I will not state it; at the time I was bitterly disappointed."[39]

Now the players, including Collins, and the coaches were in place. Where was the White Sox's manager? Throughout the spring there were numerous reports of Frank Chance's improving medical status and predictions he would join the team, first in Florida and then, when that did not happen, on the way north. Nevertheless, it was in Chicago and at the tail end of the exhibition season before Chance finally took his seat on the bench. The opponent was the Giants, in Chicago for a two-game wind-up series. It was a frigid day, yet 8,500 fans braved the low temperatures to see the Peerless Leader. The White Sox played well and won, 2–1. Collins was in the lineup. The next day the teams played again, but Chance was not there. It was reported he stayed at the hotel and later met with Comiskey, himself recuperating from his battles with gall stones.

On April 15 the season opened at Comiskey Park. The White Sox, with John Evers managing, lost to the Browns, 7–3. The manager for the visitors was George Sisler, their batting and fielding star, making both his return to the field and his managerial debut after a year's absence due to complications from sinusitis. One day later it was reported that Frank Chance had a sinus problem of his own. One day after the season opener he was in Mercy Hospital for an operation to relieve the problem. Apparently, the night before the home opener, Chance had gone to the hospital for treatment of a cold, probably the result of his return to the colder Midwest climate and perhaps exacerbated by an afternoon spent managing the White Sox in a damp dugout in Comiskey Park. He was expected to remain in the hospital for an additional two days. Less than a week later, he returned to California, ruled out of baseball for the season. Although Chance still carried the title of White Sox manager, John Evers was now in full charge.

It actually was not the first time Evers had taken over for Chance. He had replaced the Peerless Leader as the Cubs' manager in the fall of 1912, managing that team in 1913. Then, solely as a player, he headed to the Boston Braves and their World Series triumph over Collins' A's in 1914.

The team Evers inherited from Frank Chance this time around, the Chicago White Sox, was much the same team fielded in 1923. There was one bright spot, however. Ted Lyons, a 23-year-old right-handed pitcher out of Baylor University, was ready to take his first step as a regular part of the starting rotation; this would prove to be one of many steps on his road to the Hall of Fame. Actually Lyons had appeared in nine games in 1923. The first game was on July 2, the same day Collins suffered the injury that Kid Gleason tabbed as the turning point in his swan song as a manager.

According to Lyons' recall, Collins was filling in for Gleason that day in 1923 as manager. The point is debatable, but the story is worth repeating, nonetheless. The rookie had pitched one inning, retiring all three batters he faced. It was now his turn to hit, so he reached for his bat and started toward the plate.

"'Where do you think you are going?' barked Collins.

"'I am going to hit,' replied young Lyons.

"'Somebody is going to hit for you,' came the reply.

"'All right,' said Lyons, 'but they never used pinch-hitters in college.'"[40]

It was the first major league game Lyons had seen, but playing for a team with a pitching staff like the White Sox, he would soon become a wily veteran. In 1924 his 12–11 record earned through 41 appearances, along with a first-rate campaign by Sloppy Thurston, now a starter and at 20–14, 3.80 the team's ace, gave hope for the future.

The White Sox, out of necessity, continued their youth movement. In April Amos Strunk, by now 35 and one of the few Mackmen still playing, was given an unconditional release. Eddie Murphy, another of Collins' A's cronies, had been traded by the White Sox a year or so earlier. Only Collins and Stuffy McInnis were still active from that old Athletics gang.

Evers' assignment in Chicago in 1924 was simple. He must improve a seventh-place club that went 69–85 in 1923. It was not a particularly daunting task, and by mid–May he seemed on his way to accomplishing it; Chicago was in fifth at 11–11. Then he suffered appendicitis. On May 18 he underwent surgery to remove his appendix. While he "rested comfortably," Ed Walsh managed the team to a pair of losses to the Red Sox. Then on May 19 they lost again, this one to the Athletics. This time, though, something was different: there was a new man at the helm. The acting manager was now Eddie Collins. It had taken a number of unfortunate illnesses for White Sox management to finally reach inside the team and appoint a player-manager. Collins' assistants would be Ed Walsh and Tom Needham.

In a description that would have been a lot funnier for the individuals involved under less trying circumstances, James Crusinberry wrapped up his description of that first game by noting Eddie "was in command of the Chicago forces and got through the entire game without developing an apparent illness."[41] That is unless you count the 0-for-4 horse collar the newly crowned interim manager wore at the end of the contest.

It did not take long, however, even under this new regime for another problem to arise. This time it was the injury bug. On May 25 in one of those ironic events that frequently stamp any sport, Ray Schalk, the steady rugged backbone of the team, celebrated his 1,500th game caught in the major leagues on the same day he injured his finger when it was struck by a foul tip. It was the team's twenty-eighth game. As a result, Schalk was out of the lineup for most of the remainder of the season, appearing all told in only 57 games in 1924 and batting a meager .196. His place was taken by Bucky Crouse, who did a credible job, but not on Schalk's Hall-of-Fame level.

Still in late June when Evers resumed his position, the team was only one loss below .500. Their record of 29–30 enabled them to cling to sixth. Eddie had shown that he could continue to hit, run and field at a high level, while also offering strong direction to the club. In a game with the A's in Chicago on June 11, he even shuffled the lineup by moving himself from the number three slot to the number two position. This was no minor decision for the acting skipper. Throughout most of his career, Collins hit third, and there were those who thought superstition would rule the day to the extent he would never voluntarily change spots; however, that was not the case. Collins thought it might help spark the team if he switched places with Johnny Mostil. The move worked, at least for a while. Eddie went 2-for-5 and scored three times in his first outing after the move. One problem occurred, however, when Schalk, who had returned to the lineup, suffered yet another finger injury in that game. The Sox won, 10–2, as Ted Lyons fashioned a six-hitter, but Schalk's loss served to moot any gains from the revised lineup.

Collins remained in the second slot throughout his remaining tenure, but when Evers returned on June 26, he reset the lineup with Eddie batting third. When Evers resumed command, the team continued its habit of winning a couple, losing a couple and remaining in fifth place. Then in early August the Pale Hose made a wrong turn. Beginning on August 9

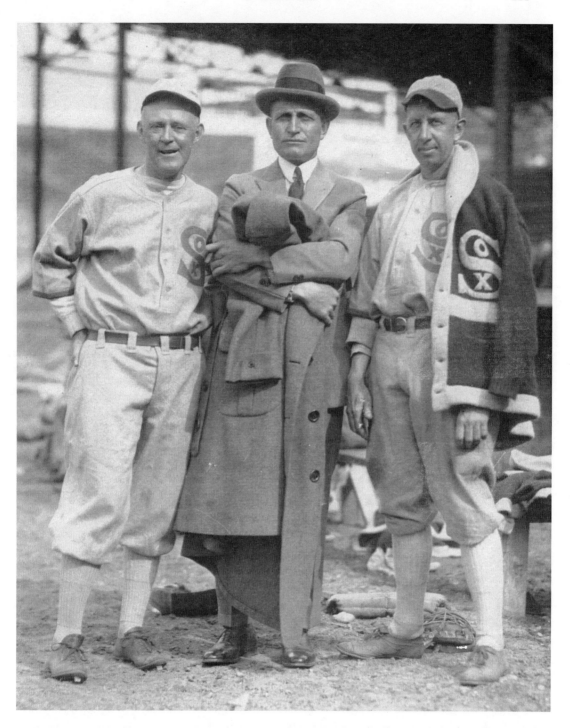

Johnny Evers, for many years a star National League second baseman, managed the White Sox for 124 games in 1924. Here he is shown (left) in Atlanta with Eddie Collins (right), his successor as manager in 1925–26. According to a caption which accompanied this photograph, the gentleman in the middle is Bert Niehoff, a former infielder for the Philadelphia Phillies. The White Sox were in Atlanta for an exhibition clash with the local club that Niehoff managed (Transcendental Graphics).

with a loss to the Senators at Comiskey in the second half of a double bill, the team lost 13 games in a row, a single-season White Sox record. The long dry spell dropped them into last place, their position on September 29 when yet another loss left them at 66–87 and over 25 games behind the soon-to-be world champion Washington Senators. Their manager was the same Bucky Harris who seemed such an afterthought when Clark Griffith was looking at Collins, Barrow and any number of others to lead his club.

A season already in disarray due to injury and illness became tragically marred on September 15 in Los Angeles when Frank Chance experienced another attack of bronchial asthma that resulted in heart failure and his death. He had managed but one game for the White Sox, an exhibition contest that might well have cost him his life.

All that was left to the White Sox was the City Series against a fifth-place Cubs finisher. Once again the White Sox found some solace in their own backyard, winning their ninth City Series in 12 tries, four games to two. A fine relief effort by Ted Lyons and a sparkling fielding play by Collins, when he raced into short right to field a grounder and fired to first for the out, brought victory and a now rare smile to Charles Comiskey. The fact Collins was acting manager in that last game did not go unnoticed. The White Sox players shared over $19,000 for their efforts, just over $707 per player.

It is often said one man's loss is another's gain. Such was the case on the south side of Chicago in the fall of 1924. The pitiful performance of the White Sox, especially in August when they were 7–20, could not be ignored. Yet the 37-year-old Collins' numbers could not be easily ignored either. In leading the team in most essential categories, except average, where Bibb Falk had a terrific year hitting .352, and in home runs, where Hooper had 10 to Collins' career-best six, Eddie once again held his own. His 42 stolen bases led the league for a second consecutive season. His batting average of .349 was fourth in the league and his OBP of .441 was second. As usual he was up among the leaders in walks, finishing fourth with 89. Only two players reached base more often. He also had a career-best 86 RBIs. And although he was now the sixth-oldest player in the American League, he finished behind only Walter Johnson, the pitching star of the league and world champions, in the voting for the American League's MVP.

Although originally announced as a member of the White Sox's tour to Europe for a set of exhibition games with the Giants, Collins did not make the trip. Globetrotting, even when it involved baseball, was not to his liking.

"Some people want to trot around the globe to see Japan and China or India and Australia. Not me, I've been riding around this country for a good many years and when I have time off, I prefer this quiet house [his Lansdowne, Pennsylvania, home] or a hunting trip in the woods."[42]

After the 1924 season ended, Collins went on one of those hunting trips, once again heading to Canada with his Yankee friends Meusel, Bush and Hoffman. The group departed for Cronin's Camp, located at Bathurst Lake near Fredericton, New Brunswick, in mid–October.

While Collins was in Canada and the White Sox in Europe, Charles Comiskey used the time to mull over the leadership of his team. John Evers' task in early 1924 when he picked up from Frank Chance was simple: get better, not worse. It did not happen and it cost him dearly. Although Evers managed the White Sox throughout their European tour, on December 11, instead of taking another shot at trading Eddie Collins, Charles Comiskey decided to make the veteran his new manager. Eddie traveled from Philadelphia to New York to discuss the position. The negotiations were handled by club secretary Harry Grabiner. He met Eddie at the Biltmore Hotel. Comiskey remained in his room at the Belmont Hotel, a block or so away.

Once again New York was the scene for an important occasion in the Collins' saga. It would, of course, be unlike Eddie to simply roll over and sign on the dotted line. He had not done so for Connie Mack and he would not do so for Charles Comiskey.

"'I like being a player' I told him [Grabiner]. 'Running a ball club isn't something I particularly want to do, but —....'" Then Eddie stated his price. "The amount was audacious!" Nevertheless, by the end of the day he was the new skipper of the Chicago White Sox.[43]

Collins, indeed, had cut himself a fine deal — as usual. His new salary as player and manager was $30,000, double his previous base.[44] The new contract only served to sharpen Collins' image as a shrewd businessman. Irving Vaughan, writing for the *Tribune*, estimated that by 1925, including his pay as captain and his World Series and City Series playoff share, Collins had earned close to $175,000 in his ten years as a White Sox player.[45]

Collins was a popular choice with the local media. John Hoffman of the *Chicago Daily News* wrote that the selection found "unanimous approval.... It was not only a Christmas gift to Eddie, but one to Chicago as well. Collins is exceptionally popular with followers of the game here."[46]

James Crusinberry of the *Tribune*, who had noted in an earlier report that Collins as manager excited South Siders to an extent not seen in years, wrote that Collins was selected neither for politics nor favoritism, but "for the simple reason that he deserved the job."

> Collins is not the type of man to impress the public in places where men gather to be good fellows. Eddie knows nothing of that sort of life. He's a bashful boy in social life and a man among ball players. Off the ball field he's retiring and demure. On the diamond he's a fiery leader....
>
> Collins has done well in baseball, not only as a player but as a financier. He has drawn a big salary since 1915, but no one will say he hasn't earned it. He has been thrifty and possesses more of the world's goods than ninety percent of the ball players have when they are through. But no one will say he hasn't deserved it all and anything more he can get out the game.
>
> Bad luck and bad breaks may prevent his rise to fame as a manager, but he never will fail by lack of effort. America's fans will be pulling for him. For several years he has received more applause from fans in hostile territory than any player in the league. Babe Ruth may get more glory, but Eddie gets more praise.[47]

So it was clear that Collins was happy, the media was happy, and the club's fans were ecstatic. What then about Charles Comiskey? On the surface, the White Sox's owner acted pleased, telling reporters he had seen something he liked about Eddie's management skills when he took over for Evers in mid-season for a spell and performed well in the interim post. Like any new marriage, the bride and groom forecast a long, rosy future. But underneath the fancy trappings, the seemingly happy couple may have harbored deep-rooted animosities that in retrospect carried all the elements for an early divorce.

Less than a month after Collins took the rudder for the White Sox, *The Sporting News* in its column, "Scribbled by Scribes," carried a report from Manning Vaughn of the *Milwaukee Journal* which would have done the *National Enquirer* proud as he told readers that the Collins hiring could be troublesome.

> [His] appointment ... presents a peculiar situation.... Collins and Charles Comiskey have never been friends. Those in the know, claim that Eddie and the Old Roman have not spoken ten words to each other in the last year. Collins, it is said, was disgusted the way his employers handled the World's Series scandal of 1919, and on one occasion took ten minutes of Comiskey's time to tell him what he thought of him. Since then there has been little love lost between them, and Collins did all his business with the club through Harry Grabiner, secretary of the Sox Corporation. Commy, it is said, did not even see Collins when he was signed to manage the club. Eddie was called to New York by Grabiner, offered the management and accepted without one word from the Old Roman.[48]

Were the statements true? Years later Collins termed Commy a "grand man and a fair one," but in the same article he called Harry Grabiner "my good friend."[49] There is every indication that at one point in his career Collins admired Charles Comiskey, but unlike Connie Mack, Kid Gleason, and several other authority figures in his life, Collins never considered Comiskey a friend. Still this was not the first strained relationship between a boss and his prime spear-chucker and it would not be the last. In baseball, unlike many other businesses, the success or failure of a new venture is revealed in the team's standings that appear almost daily each spring and summer in newspapers across the country. Taking over as manager of a last-place club, Collins had scant time to worry about the rumors of bad feelings with his boss. Instead, he needed to turn all his attention to the task of proving that the boss man had made the right decision.

CHAPTER 16

Leader at Last

"Some might have been better at this or that ... but nobody was so good all-around! He was second to none in versatility."

— Sportswriter Dan Desmond[1]

After enjoying the initial rush which resulted from his managerial appointment, Eddie Collins settled down to face the task at hand, improving the performance and, in turn, the win-loss record and standing of his White Sox team. His philosophy was simple. He took his cue from Mr. Mack, only exercising authority "when the situation called for it."[2]

There was little question he had inherited a group of regulars who could hit, including Sheely, Kamm, Mostil and, if healthy, Hooper and Schalk, not to mention his new hitting star, Bibb Falk. On the mound in addition to Sloppy Thurston, he had emerging pitching stars in Ted Lyons and Ted Blankenship. Like any manager, Collins loved to talk about his players. He particularly sang the praises of Thurston, a 20-game winner in 1924 for a last-place club. Sloppy was slender in build and Collins always "wondered ... where the power came from with which he zipped balls past the batters who faced him."[3]

Before he did much of anything else, Collins selected a coach. In this case Eddie turned back the clock, choosing his old college coach, Billy Lauder, the man who "taught me the way to field a ground ball and swing at a curve."[4]

If Lauder's teaching skills rubbed off on Collins, why not the young White Sox? Lauder's career, post–Collins, included coaching stints at Williams and Yale. In addition, at the time of his hiring, the Thomas E. Wilson Sporting Goods Company was outfitting college and professional teams throughout the country with a Lauder invention. The new White Sox's coach had tackled the problem many ball players experienced with constantly flopping shirt tails and sagging trousers by designing a suit of baseball duds which used inter-locking tabs to fasten the shirt and pants together. Once fastened, the player's belt was looped through this new configuration.

A few months later in mid–June, Collins reached into his Philadelphia Athletics' scrapbook for a pitching coach, selecting his old pal, Albert Chief Bender. It was obvious that Eddie still held his former teammate in high regard, despite his pitching woes in the 1914 World Series. During the course of the year, the Chief would receive plaudits for his development of the youngsters on the White Sox's staff, particularly Ted Blankenship, who developed a fine changeup, won 10-straight games at one point, and finished the year with a fine 17–8 record and ERA of 3.03, the lowest among the pitching regulars.

One staff member Collins retained was the team's black trainer, William "Doc" Buckner, another interesting decision given unsubstantiated rumors years later that some time before Collins had sought the trainer's dismissal.

Early on under Collins there were changes in the White Sox's spring training plan. For one, the inter-league match-up with the Giants, a spring staple for several years, was scrapped for a 20-game schedule against minor league opponents. In addition, the White Sox's camp was now in Shreveport, Louisiana. Finally, on a more

Right: When Collins was named manager of the Chicago White Sox in 1925 he soon appointed Billy Lauder as a coach. Lauder (left) coached Collins when he played baseball at Columbia University (Photo Collection, Cleveland Public Library). *Below:* When Collins became the manager of the Chicago White Sox in 1925, he hired former A's teammate Albert "Chief" Bender to coach the White Sox pitchers. Here the pair, in White Sox road uniforms, stand at the edge of the dugout to observe their team (National Baseball Hall of Fame Library, Cooperstown, New York).

personal note, Collins would no longer enjoy the luxury of a late arrival. He was now in the first wave, set to arrive in Shreveport with the young pitchers and catchers to begin practice on March 2.

In late February just a few days before the team traveled south, Collins arrived in Chicago to make last-minute preparations for the season and, more significantly, to meet with Charles Comiskey. The two had also met in Chicago in January. If the pair really were not getting along, these were probably the shortest meetings on record. One possible topic, the issue of how Ray Schalk would react to Collins' appointment, was averted in mid–February when the catcher, now recovered from his injury travails of the preceding season, pledged his support to his long-time teammate.

"I am willing to do all I can to help Eddie get a start as a manager. He's a great fellow and I know every player on the team thinks the world of him and will hustle his head off to win. I think the spirit on the club this season will be great."[5]

Given Collins' feelings that his everyday lineup was essentially solid and the pitching staff satisfactory, he saw his job as one of plugging in the holes. One area which needed work was shortstop. The previous year's regular, Bill Barrett, posted a paltry .904 fielding average. In an effort to arrive at a suitable choice, six shortstop candidates were invited to spring training. Although Barrett was six years younger than 30-year-old Harvey McClellan and a better hitter, Collins decided to go with the better-fielding McClellan entering the training period. Barrett could play second base and the outfield, so he remained on the squad as a utility player.

McClellan, on the other hand, never saw the field during the regular season in 1925 or thereafter. The popular Little Mac, who had previously lost considerable playing time for an operation to treat stomach ulcers, would now fight gall stones. Once again he required surgery. By early June he was fighting for his life; he died tragically on November 6.

As a result of McClellan's medical woes, the shortstop job went to Ike Davis, a 30-year-old infielder from Colorado who broke into the majors with the Senators in 1919, played eight games, then did not reappear in a major league uniform until 1924 with the White Sox. His total big-league experience entering this new season was 18 games, but he did his best by batting .240 with 61 RBIs in 146 games. He also stole 19 bases. His 53 errors, however, probably explained why he never played in the majors again after the season closed.

Collins' first spring training as the leader was a good one, despite the loss of McClellan; the team went undefeated. Although the wins came against weak opponents, the victories were still important confidence builders for a team accustomed to losing often. The players seemed relaxed as they played one minor league club after another. During off-days many baseball players often sat around playing cards, but not these White Sox. The Roaring Twenties were in full swing and the current fad was crossword puzzles. Collins was a busy man, but when he caught a spare moment, he invariably could be found hunched over a newspaper, pencil in hand, working the latest brain teaser. His players followed suit. Then there were the visitors, eager to see what the new "Collins' Sox" had to offer. One in particular, Judge Kenesaw Mountain Landis, stopped by in early March on his tour of spring training camps. Of course, each stop also involved a visit to the local country club for a round of golf. In this instance, Collins and Schalk were happy to oblige. As soon as the morning practice was over, the threesome headed out for a spot of golf.

Collins' off-the-field moments were not always as pleasant. He now had roster decisions to make. In 1922 Dixie Leverett won 13 games for the Sox and was in the starting rotation. By 1924 his production was way down. He was 2–3 with a 5.82 ERA and now 30 years old. On April 4 he was released to Columbus of the American Association. He resurfaced briefly with Chicago in 1926 and later with the Boston Braves, but it appears Eddie made the right decision. Leverett won only four more games in the major leagues. Still, only a few months before, Leverett and Collins had been teammates. Now a Collins' decision cost this former mate his job. Perhaps this was what Eddie meant when he told anyone who listened that he would prefer to finish his career before he became a manager.

At any rate, Collins was now the manager, and when the team arrived in Detroit for his managerial debut, everyone wanted to know what he thought of his team. "I am pleased," he told reporters, "because we went [won] nineteen straight games, but I am more pleased with the spirit in which they were won than over the number of victories. I would not say what the White Sox may do in the American league race. I have not seen any of the other teams this spring. Possibly the pitching staff is yet a bit doubtful. If we can get good pitching I see no reason why we should not have a winning team. At least I feel sure all of the fellows will be hustling all of the time."[6]

If they were "hustling," they would do it in brand new uniforms. For the start of the Collins' era, at least on the road, the team would wear blue uniforms with white pinstripes and white stockings.

The start came on April 14 in Detroit. A crowd of 40,000 watched as Ty Cobb's Tigers started their own season with a 4–3 win. Cobb, who had the flu, was not in the lineup. The White Sox rallied with two out in the top of the ninth and would have tied the game on a Collins' hit, but when it was ruled a ground-rule double, only one run was permitted to score. The rally fell short when the next batter was out. Collins, hitting in his familiar third slot, behind center fielder Johnny Mostil and Ike Davis, went 1-for-4 and stole a base. His first win as a full-fledged manager came the next day in a 9–6 victory over the Detroiters.

The White Sox left Detroit having split four and continued their road trip in St. Louis, where on April 18 they thrashed the Browns, 14–5, and saw a strange site. A surly group of fans, angry at Browns owner Phil Ball for failing to sign "Baby Doll" Jacobson, a hard-hitting fan favorite, mobbed the owner's box. Ban Johnson, who was seated in the box at the time, watched silently as the crowd swelled to over 2,000. He left the area when a few of the unruly fans picked up dirt and threw it at Ball. The police were called in to quell what had all the earmarks of a full-fledged riot. They were able to settle things down by escorting the Browns' owner from Sportsman's Park.

By the time the White Sox reached home for their much anticipated home opener against the Tigers on April 22, their record stood at 4–4. The game had been loosely designated as an "Eddie Collins Day" with 1,500 of his fellow Elks promising to participate in a pre-game parade, then take to the stands to watch fellow members present Eddie with a chest of silver, as well as to loudly cheer him and his team to victory.

On a day when his star player of the last 10 seasons was introduced to over 25,000 home fans as their new manager, Charles Comiskey stayed home due to "threatening weather." By so doing he took the opportunity to miss a great deal of fuss over Collins, who just before the start of the game received a large horseshoe floral arrangement in addition to his other gifts. Cobb was in the dugout, still not playing as he continued his recovery from the flu. Unlike Comiskey, he watched as the White Sox used three unearned runs to carve out a 3–1 win behind Sloppy Thurston. Collins was 1-for-3 with a double, a sacrifice and an RBI. In all it was a day to remember. Apparently, many White Sox fans liked what they saw; they began coming to Comiskey Park in ever-increasing numbers. In fact, 832,231 fans watched the White Sox in 1925, an increase of almost 225,000 over 1924. Only the rejuvenated Philadelphia Athletics drew more fans that year in the American League. In recalling the season,

Collins remarked, "Financially we were a great success…. The White Sox of 1925 enjoyed the greatest year of prosperity in their history, including the years we were champions."[7]

One throng of White Sox rooters saw an unusual conclusion to a game with the Indians in Chicago on April 26. A crowd of 44,000, thought at that time to be the largest ever to see a ballgame in Chicago, watched as their warriors trailed the Tribe, 7–2, with two outs in the bottom of the ninth. When Willie Kamm, the Sox third sacker, sent a routine grounder to the dependable Indians shortstop Joe Sewell, it appeared to most the game was over. But the first baseman for the Indians was a collegian out of the University of Michigan named Ray Knode. In the excitement of the moment, the young man failed to touch first, keeping the game alive. The crowd, which included about 8,000 who were encamped around the outfield banks and just off third base, thought that Kamm was out. They, along with a couple thousand more fans who thought the game was over, massed onto the field. Clarence Rowland, he of the nickname Pants, was now an umpire and assigned to this game. Sensing the futility of clearing the field to try to resume play, he called the game a forfeit in favor of the Indians.

Two days later Rowland and Collins, perhaps upset at Rowland's decision to call that recent contest, went at it over a call. The former manager, who had earned Collins' respect in 1915, refused to call Joe Sewell out for what Collins deemed a base-path violation. The current Sox manager stormed over to the former manager and spoke his mind, but to no avail. Whatever Collins might have said, Rowland held no grudge. Years later he had only the highest praise for his old second baseman.

Through May the White Sox played well for Collins. At the end of that month, they stood 23–18, in third, some six games from first. Their play on and off the field continued to hold their fans' interest. On May 11 Ray Schalk took his catching skills to the Tribune Tower on North Michigan Avenue to attempt to catch a ball thrown from the top of the structure, some 460 feet in height. It took three tries, but the third was the charm. Someone dug into the record books and found that the feat, while worth mentioning, was not record breaking. Apparently Washington Senators catcher Gabby Street and an old White Sox catcher, Billy Sullivan, both caught balls dropped from the Washington Monument, a distance of 550 feet.

On May 17 the White Sox faced off in a three-game series with the A's. It was the first formal meeting as managers between former pupil Collins and his mentor Connie Mack. The White Sox won two of the three.

In early June Collins showed once again that he had no qualms about stretching the rules of the game to their limit to gain an advantage. One pitcher he respected as much as any was Walter Johnson. Collins always felt a particular need to gain some extra leverage when Johnson was on the mound, having proved as much with his shenanigans on the occasion when he was felled by a Johnson pitch. On June 6 in Washington, Collins and his Sox faced Johnson's defending-champion Senators. By now, Walter was 37, although one could not prove it by his 20–7 record and 3.07 ERA. Collins decided a little extra time on the base paths in the hot sun might be in order. When Johnson came to the plate with a man on first and popped one toward second, Eddie let the ball drop instead of fielding it, then threw to second to force the runner. Johnson was now on first and had to remain standing in the hot sun until the inning was over. An astute Senators crowd was not fooled. They booed Collins for the rest of the game and then joined Johnson in a last laugh as the wily pitcher stopped the White Sox, 4–1. Collins made up a little bit for the booing by doubling twice in four trips off the "Big Train."

In June and July the White Sox remained the picture of consistency. Their 14–12 mark in June matched their May results. A 17–16 mark in July kept the team in third at 54–46, although they were now a full 11 games off the pace.

In addition to the modicum of success, Collins and each of his coaches enjoyed a pleasant memory or two as the season continued to unfold. In New York on June 19, Collins received a traveling bag from friends in Tarrytown who traveled to the park for that purpose. These suburban New Yorkers then undoubtedly joined Eddie's parents to watch a disappointing Yankee team, on its way to a seventh-place finish, gain an extra-inning win over the White Sox. Billy Lauder received a gift the same day from some of his hometown folks as well. On July 21 in the first game of a twin bill with the last-place Red Sox, Chief Bender received his own gift, by way of an opportunity to enter a ballgame and pitch in the majors for the first time in some seven years. In the ninth with his team trailing 4–3, Collins inserted Bender, who had only recently been activated. The old pitching star, working amidst loud cheering, walked the first batter before retiring the next two. Left fielder Roy Carlyle then planted one of the Chief's next offerings into the right field bleachers; Bender then retired the side. So ended the Chief's comeback and his major league pitching career, although the next day he pitched three innings in an exhibition game the Pale Hose played in Battle Creek, Michigan.

By now Collins had a few games under his belt as a manager. What were the early impressions? According to E.W. Smith of the *Chicago American*, Collins the manager was much like Collins the player.

"Eddie Collins sets a pace that is tremendous. There isn't a thing that he won't do to make his team. That is what makes him the most effective manager in the game. He is one of those playing fellows who sets a good example."[8]

On June 3 the "playing fellow" quietly passed what is today deemed a mark of greatness. On that date playing in Detroit, Collins singled for his 3,000th major league hit.[9] A single off Rip Collins, one of three singles in a 12–7 win over the Tigers, made Eddie the sixth major leaguer to reach that mark. From his perch in center field, Ty Cobb, one of the others in the select club, just happened to view Collins' achievement. A little over two weeks earlier on May 17, Tris Speaker had struck his 3,000th hit. Others who had reached the mark were Cap Anson, Honus Wagner and Nap Lajoie. The next to reach that height was Paul Waner, more than 17 years later. It was and remains a select club, an important credential when one presents his career profile to Hall of Fame voters.

In 1925, hit number 3,000 was just another in Collins' quest to improve his team and prove his worth as a player-manager. One problem with accomplishing that goal was his team's lack of quality left-handed pitchers. The only lefty getting any starts was Mike Cvengros, a 23-year-old pitcher whose 3–12 record and 5.88 ERA in 1924 offered little hope. In 1925 he was not much better. In 11 starts and 22 appearances, he went 3–9 and 4.30. In July Collins tried to plug the gap by purchasing Jim Edwards from the Indians. He started four games and went 1–2 and 3.97. Clearly more was needed. In early August Eddie thought he had it when Dickie Kerr was reinstated to baseball and once again became a member of the White Sox. His addition caused quite a stir, but little else. Kerr's screwball curve no longer was effective; the years of semipro ball had taken their toll. In 12 appearances, including only a pair of starts, the former World Series hero went 0–1 with a 5.15 ERA. At 32, Kerr's big-league career was finished. His 53 career wins were bunched together in just three seasons.

By August 22 the White Sox's record of 65–53 and third-place standing were admirable given their limited pitching. Collins, the player, was having a commendable year as well. He was hitting .346 and getting on base at a .461 pace, both top-ten American League figures. His 87 walks had him in the third position. He had already amassed 147 hits and stolen 19 bases, fourth among American League runners. And although there were now only seven players in the league who were older, he had fought off a series of ankle and leg injuries to appear in all 118 games to date.

That all changed, however, on August 22 in Chicago as the White Sox faced off against Philadelphia and lost the game, 6–1, as well as their second baseman. It all happened in the first inning before most fans were settled into their seats. The starter for the Sox was Sloppy Thurston. The righty was now showing little of the brilliance of 1924. In this one he issued a walk and four hits right off the bat. Eddie had seen enough and, even though it was still the first inning, called on Jim Edwards for long relief. The Athletics reached him as well. On a scratch hit by the A's first baseman, Jim Poole, Eddie went down.

The play was not all that unusual for Collins. He threw himself at a liner shooting toward the gap between first and second. He was able to reach the ball and knock it down, but as he did so he stepped on the ball.

"The baseball was right under the ball of my foot, between the spikes and the heel, so that as I fell I was pivoting on it. I knew I had done plenty of damage to a high-priced baseball mechanism; the physical pain of it was terrific, but even worse than the feeling of nausea was the depressing thought that I had torn more than big muscles in that left low leg of mine."[10]

Years later Collins described the scene metaphorically for those fans not present.

"The ball rotated in a peculiar motion and I must have looked like a ballet dancer as I wavered and pirouetted and finally crashed to Earth after stepping on it."[11]

Trainer Bill Buckner and A's pitcher Eddie Rommel helped Collins from the field. In the clubhouse Dr. Phillip Kreuscher, the team physician, examined Eddie and ordered him to Mercy Hospital for X-rays. The diagnosis was a pulled tendon in the left hip. Perhaps, the media speculated, he could return to the field in a few days; however, the patient knew better.

"I had, I feared, come to a crisis in my career. Nine times out of ten, what makes an old man out of a ball player is bad legs. As they helped me off the field to be taken to a hospital, I was, mentally, seeing the ugly scenery of old age — me, aged thirty-eight. Well, it was an appropriate accident; my whole life has turned on a baseball."

For the next three nights Collins slept in the hospital with ice packs on his injured leg, but each afternoon he brought those ice packs and his nurses to the stadium so he could manage his team. All told he was on crutches for 10 days. He did not need to be told that he was finished for that season.

"As a manager, I knew I had lost a second baseman."[12]

Over the next few days, the White Sox fought gamely as Bill Barrett took over at second and their field leader called the shots from his new spot on the bench. In fact, they won three of the next five games. When, however, it became apparent Collins was lost for the season, the losses began piling up. When the Pale Hose beat the Indians, 10–8, on October 4 in Chicago, their final record was 79–75. They finished in fifth place, 18 and one-half games behind the Senators. Instead of continuing to improve, they went downhill. Only a five-game win streak kept it from being worse. Their record in September was 8–17; overall, without Collins they were 14–22. The skipper thought he knew the answer.

"Out at second I had been able to direct the team wonderfully well....When I was behind the pitcher I could sense it subtly if he began to fail.... It is the perfect position, to my mind, from which to command shifts designed to take advantage of the other fellows' weaknesses or strengths....

"It is a perennial argument, this one as to whether a manager is more effective on the bench or in the field. I know that when my injury made me sit on the bench I felt as if I had to learn all over again to watch a ball game."[13]

The team's woes continued into the City Series played against a Cubs' team which finished dead last in the National League race. That mattered little to the northenders. They took the series in five games while their league counterparts, the Pittsburgh Pirates, were trimming the Senators in the World Series. In the White Sox's second game with the Cubs, Collins made an appearance, batting for Ted Lyons in the eighth inning. Perhaps Eddie's appearance on the field was an effort to show Comiskey he could still play. If so, the showing was a failure. He bounced a ball toward the shortstop and almost fell down as he ran to first, finishing the jaunt on one leg. Obviously, there was a lot more rehab work to complete.

The condition of Collins' leg did not keep him from his off-season expedition. Immediately after the City Series, Eddie returned home to Philadelphia. Then just a few days later he joined Babe Ruth, Yankee back-up catcher Benny Bengough, Senators catcher Muddy Ruel, and regular hunting buddies Shawkey and Bush for a three-week hunting trip into New Brunswick. The Babe needed the break as much as anyone, having finished a season that saw him continue to enhance his image as the bad boy of baseball, tangling with his manager Miller Huggins to the point the Babe had issued a "him or me" edict after Huggins suspended him and fined him $5,000. Colonel Ruppert and Ed Barrow backed Huggins to the hilt, forcing Ruth to make peace with his manager. The fact that only a miserable Red Sox team kept his Yankees out of the basement while the Babe played but 98 games and hit but 25 homers added spice to the ruckus. The trip reportedly helped Ruth improve his physical conditioning and it seemed to serve Collins in his recovery, as well.

Once the hunting trip was over it was time for Collins to report to White Sox management, who were anxiously awaiting an update on his condition. Club secretary Harry Grabiner, accompanied by Commy's son J. Louis Comiskey, attended the winter meetings in New York in December. As his father declined in health, Lou, who was a team vice president and its treasurer, assumed an expanded role. He and Grabiner sought and received Collins' assurance that he was recovered and ready to resume his second base position in 1926, leaving shortstop and, of course, pitching as areas of need for the forthcoming season. The shortstop position was up for grabs, given the weak hitting and erroneous fielding of Ike Davis, as well as the additional fact that he broke a knee cap in the City Series, leaving his playing status in doubt. As a result, the White Sox planned to take a long look at Moe Berg, the collegiate star from Princeton, picked up from minor league Reading in the hope he might be ready to step into the regular lineup.

As for 1925, Collins had earned passing marks. In early September while Eddie managed from the bench, a columnist for *The Sporting News* ventured that the fledgling manager "has done wonders with a team that got nothing under other managers, and the fate of which this year was admitted to hinge altogether on such inspiration as Eddie could put it into it."[14]

That said, in 1926 Collins would no longer have the tag "newcomer" to lean on when his managerial skills were assayed. If 1925 was a mid-term quiz, then 1926 was a test. Eddie's fervent hope was that it was not to be a final exam.

Collins would continue to be paid well for his work. The White Sox recognized his achievements in 1925 by giving him a $5,000 raise. He was now earning $35,000.[15]

In February Collins stepped into the fray caused by changes in the rules involving the use of resin, more popularly known as rosin, by pitchers to enhance their grip on the ball. The use of the substance was banned in 1920 when, in general, the rules on the use of substances were tightened. There were, however, ways to get around the rule as to rosin. Nothing much was said about it until late 1925 when a formal move was instigated to permit it once again in the form of a rosin bag. In February the issue turned into another Landis-Johnson tussle when the American League voted not to permit it. Collins, given a team who drew its strength from hitting and not pitching, supported the ban.

"I don't want to see the pitchers given the slightest opening. We have enough trouble now keeping pace with the fellows who are able to get around the rules. With the help of resin there'll be no stopping them."[16]

Many, if not most, experts felt the use of rosin did not really make much difference, but in the end Landis ruled in favor of the rosin bag. Johnson countered by permitting the bag to be placed behind the American League pitching mounds, but forbidding its use. Thus, the tug of war continued.

During the off-season Collins tinkered with his coaching staff as well as his roster. He named retired big-league catcher Ben Egan, his former Athletics' teammate, as his coach and assistant. Bender would return as well, but not until late spring. Dickie Kerr was released. The move must have hurt since Collins and Kerr shared many memories, but the experiment was over. So was the White Sox tenure of Charlie Robertson, never able to overcome the bloated expectations stemming from that perfect game. Collins also released Harry Hooper, like Eddie now approaching 38, but not hitting nearly as well as his manager. In an effort to overcome the loss of the injured Ike Davis, the White Sox purchased veteran Everett Scott from the Senators. Scott, one of baseball's early iron men, whose best years were spent with the Red Sox where he perennially led American League shortstops in fielding, was 33, not really much of a hitter, and declining as a fielder. He was not Collins' first choice but was present as insurance if other prospects failed to pan out.

One of those prospects was Princeton ace Moe Berg. Collins eagerly anticipated his arrival in Shreveport. After joining Judge Landis and Ray Schalk, along with *Tribune* writer James Crusinberry, for a round of golf—a match played out before a large gallery in which the White Sox stars came out on the short end—Eddie learned Berg had decided to delay his arrival to finish law school. It appeared at the time the job would go to either Scott or the eventual winner, 27-year-old Bill Hunnefield, but Collins was non-plussed. Berg was a student at Columbia Law; Collins knew a little something about the place. He went to see the youngster in order to talk some sense into him. He came back empty-handed. Berg would later join the team, play a little infield and end up a catcher more famous for his eccentricities, his great intellect, and his work during World War II for Collins' former football teammate, William Donovon, who was by then the head of the OSS, the forerunner of the CIA, than for anything he did on a ball field.

Normally a serious guy, Collins, nevertheless, did have a sense of humor. He enjoyed a good time and could laugh at himself. These facets of his personality were often displayed best during spring training. In 1926 the White Sox were scheduled for a game in Fort Worth, Texas, where a number of prominent Fort Worth businessmen wanted to meet the Chicago star. They called at the local hotel where the team was lodged and were granted an audience in Collins' room. The men were each wearing the customary broad-brimmed Stetsons for which Texas is famous. One of the men dared Eddie to wear one, offering to buy one for him and writer Crusinberry, who was present at the time. The pair agreed, and each was promptly fitted with the $40 models.

"I'll [Crusinberry] admit that I was rather timid and self-conscious in wearing the big hat around the streets of Fort Worth and out to the game the next day, but Collins enjoyed it like a small boy with a toy."[17]

Crusinberry had worked the White Sox beat for a significant number of years by 1926. As a result, he knew Collins about as well as anyone. "Collins didn't begin to slip as a player until 1926 ... and like almost all players it was his legs that began to fail as he advanced in years."[18]

At least in the early going that season, Collins did not agree.

"We went back to Shreveport for the season of 1926, and once more I was back on second base, running the team from the field, now and then taking a pat at my good old left leg as if it were a pet horse. Boy, it was holding up!"[19]

This part was true. Collins was playing—some—and the leg was holding up for him because during the spring Eddie took no chances. If he thought the infield footing was bad, he did not play; if a ball was on the edge of his fielding range, he let it go. But when he did play, he showed a quick bat.

On April 13, a warm spring day and that ever-present dose of early-season hope brought 37,000 fans to Comiskey Park to watch Ted Lyons pitch and Eddie Collins play second in the opener. The White Sox initiated combat 1926-style with a 5–1 win over the St. Louis Browns. Lyons did not permit a run until the seventh, Collins went 1-for-4, walked once and scored a run. The White Sox went on to sweep the three-game series and gave the impression they planned to pick up where they left off before Eddie was injured in August of the previous year. Collins liked this team a lot.

> We were such a congenial crowd, the White Sox of 1926, that I suppose I failed to experience a lot of the grief that is likely to afflict a manager of a big-league team. I never had to fine anybody. There was only once when I had to reprimand a player, and that was not a serious matter. We came north that year as confident, I think, as that crowd of youngsters Connie Mack brought up from New Orleans in 1909. If you want to know, that was when I began to learn what I regard as the whole trick of managing....
>
> What it amounts to is this: You must remember that baseball is a game and that, if it is to be played superlatively, your players must get real delight out of playing. You can't hire the kind of enthusiasm you need to win ball games. You have to generate it out of Cobblike self-confidence, out of sound strength and developed skill. To my way of thinking, the poorest way to achieve it is by bull-dozing.[20]

The philosophy seemed to work. As late as July 6, the White Sox were in second place. Their hitters, in particular Bibb Falk and Johnny Mostil, were strong. Falk hit .345 for the year with eight home runs and 108 RBIs, while Mostil hit .328 with a league-leading 35 stolen bases. Hunnefield, who got most of the turns at shortstop, particularly after Scott was released mid-season, hit .274. The pitchers were led by Lyons, who finished the season 18–16 and 3.01. Ted Blankenship (13–10, 3.61), Red Faber, still perking along at 15–9 and 3.56, and newcomer Tommy Thomas (15–12 and 3.80) filled out an above-average starting rotation on a staff whose ERA ranked third in the league.

If Collins liked this team, most of his players liked him as well. Reserve catcher Buck Crouse considered Collins the best manager he ever played for, and he also played for Kid Gleason and later Ray Schalk, Lena Blackburne and Donie Bush.[21]

Collins particularly caught the fancy of Ted Lyons.

> [Eddie] was as great a manager as he was a ballplayer, [and] did more to make me a winning pitcher than anyone else....
>
> He was a great manager because he had the respect of his men and because he was one of the most fiery competitors the game has ever known.
>
> He wanted to win. Defeat hurt him deeply. You couldn't be associated with him very long without becoming infected by his winning spirit. It was contagious....
>
> He wasn't a hand-shaker but the friends he made he kept. He gave the impression of being hard-boiled during his playing days, but I never knew a man with a bigger or softer heart.[22]

A great deal of the respect of Lyons and others flowed freely toward Collins on June 19 in Chicago as 27,000 joined Cardinal Patrick O'Donnell of Ireland and Chicago Mayor William Dever for another "Eddie Collins Day" at Comiskey. The fans were particularly fortunate in seeing Collins play on his "day" since he had missed several of the previous games due to a right thumb injury. Eddie, who often played his best when he was the center of attention, went 3-for-3 with a double, but his team lost to a rejuvenated Yankees team boasting a renewed Babe Ruth. The next day 43,000, boasted as the largest ever at Comiskey, crammed the ballpark to watch this "new" Babe but instead saw the Sox regain second place with a 4–3 win. It was noted, however, that at least two of the Yankees' hits were the type Collins would have easily snuffed out "in his palmier" days.[23]

It was apparent that Collins was playing on borrowed time or, perhaps it is better to say, a "borrowed leg." On July 27 it was reported that Collins was not sleeping well, perhaps a referral to the fact his team was in the midst of a six-game slide which saw their record fall to 49–48, pushing them back to sixth place in the tightly-packed standings.[24] He missed a pair of games before returning to the lineup on July 28 to help end the losing streak, only to soon learn one of his better pitchers, Blankenship, was lost for the next month with a fractured thumb.

Then on August 2 as his boys took a 2–1 win from New York, snapping an 11-game Yankees' win streak, there was a report that Collins had scored a run, "although bothered considerably by his bum leg."[25] Three days later when the White Sox's manager walked, he inserted his backup, Ray Morehart, to run for him, even though earlier in the game he had successfully participated in a double steal. A day later on August 6 the *Tribune* reported Collins, who helped his team top the Red Sox with three hits including a triple, and three runs scored, was operating on a "trick leg."[26] The next day the wheels, almost literally, came off. Batting against the A's on August 8 in Chicago, Collins stepped to the plate in the first inning.

"At bat, I hit a ball I thought was going into the bleachers. I was off for first, but it bounded back and I turned quickly. It was a wet day, and turning I slipped. I knew it was serious; it was that left leg, of course. I was out of the game. I was a bench manager."[27]

Collins made it to third that day, his "bum leg dragging." Morehart went in to run. The White Sox lost in the tenth, 6–5. The defeat left their record at 56–54, in fifth place. During the remainder of the regular season, Collins appeared in only three more games. In two of these he walked, once was intentional, and in both of these cases he inserted a base runner for himself. In mid–August the *Tribune*, calling Eddie a "baseball marvel," attributed Collins' 1926 demise to his 1925 injury, stating that "[t]oday Collins plays only because he knows his team needs him."[28]

This was not totally true. Collins played on because he still had a competitive fire, the type driven and fueled by that combination of skills, intellect and desire that set him apart as one of the truly great ones. His desire to continue to perform was bolstered by his continuing ability to hit a baseball better than anyone else who was then available to replace him. And, perhaps, he played on because he knew there was no other way Commy would have him.

For all these reasons, as well as the additional fact his team still had a shot to finish in the first division, Collins played through an entire game on September 21 as the White Sox experienced a 14–0 clubbing by the Yankees. Like his similar attempt to play in late 1925, this trial balloon sank as well. Collins went 1-for-4 with a single but committed a pair of errors as the White Sox practically ensured themselves a spot in the second division. Collins' appearance also drew a sad salute from the *Tribune*'s Crusinberry.

"Boss Collins limped through the combat at second base with deep furrows forming in his brow, and in the ninth inning when he hobbled to the plate for his final attempt at bat more than half of the 8,000 or more fants [*sic*] present gave him a hand, not, perhaps, for what he had accomplished in this game, but for his spirit and for the heroic deeds of days gone by."[29]

When they closed the book on 1926, "Boss" Collins had played in 106 games and ended his season hitting .344, eighth in a league that averaged .282. He scored 66 times, walked 62 times and drove in 62 runs. As usual his OBP (.441) led the team and was third in the league. On a bad leg his 13 stolen bases were tenth best in the American League, even though by now he was its fifth-oldest player.

In fairness to Collins the bench manager, his team actually fared well in his absence from the field. His substitutes Ray Morehart, who did not field too well, and later Bill Hunnefield hit the ball well enough to make things competitive. By the end of the year, the White Sox had climbed back to fifth place with a record of 81–72. They were continuing to move in the right direction as they finished only nine and one-half games behind the pennant-winning Yankees. Attendance had dropped to 710,000, but that figure still stood third in the league. When they polished off the Cubs, a fourth-place finisher in their league, by a 4–3 count to recapture the City Series crown, it appeared Collins' future with the White Sox should be secure.

By mid–October the managerial hatchet, seldom dormant, had already fallen on Ty Cobb, George Sisler, and Lee Fohl of the Red Sox. These moves did raise speculation that since Collins' presence in the regular lineup was no longer a certainty, his position was in jeopardy, as well. Cobb was used as an example. In 1926, like Eddie, he spent more and more time on the bench.

Still, on November 11, it came as a surprise to many, certainly to Eddie himself, when Charles Comiskey named Ray Schalk to succeed him as manager of the White Sox. At the same time the club asked waivers on the second baseman. Eddie's days as a White Sox player and manager were over. Several years later Collins told how he first learned of his dismissal.

As in 1925, we finished in fifth place, but we won the city series and the club had made enough money to rebuild its plant. I was pretty well satisfied.

I went north into the woods to hunt, because after baseball I think hunting is the next best dish. I got home on Armistice Day, 1926, and was putting away my guns and duffel when I was called to the telephone. A newspaper man was on the other end of the wire.

"What," he asked me tactfully, "would you have to say about the appointment of Ray Schalk to be manager of the Chicago White Sox?"

"What are you talking about?"

"Don't you know he has been appointed to your place?"

I hung up the receiver very gently.[30]

When contacted in Philadelphia by the press and asked about the change, Collins issued a terse statement.

"I have not received any word from Comiskey and have not talked to him since the close of the baseball season. I have nothing to say and will not talk until I am officially notified by the club."[31]

It did not take long for the official notice to arrive. The next day Eddie told sportswriter Jimmy Isaminger of the *Philadelphia Inquirer* all about it.

I was notified officially this afternoon that I had been removed as manager of the White Sox. The letter from Mr. Comiskey also said he had asked waivers on me and if the clubs would agree to this waiver that they would make me a free agent....

Of course, I was amazed when I received the news. I hadn't an inkling that I was to be displaced. I parted company with Mr. Comiskey after the Sox-Cub series in October on the best of terms. I had no idea but that I would manage the Sox again next season.

Please get this straight. I will not say one word against Mr. Comiskey for removing me. That is his business. It has hurt Mrs. Collins more than it has me. I will only say that I was treated fine by Comiskey and that I leave with no malice.[32]

The news of Collins' dismissal as manager and release as a player brought both tributes and critical analysis. In their editorials, newspapers in Chicago were careful not to offend Schalk when issuing praise for Collins who was "more than a brilliant second baseman and a conscientious manager; he is a gentleman with a fighting heart."[33]

"Seldom has a city, in successive managers, been favored with two men of such inherent honesty and worth as Collins and Schalk."[34]

The praise was not confined to Chicago. Isaminger wrote from Philadelphia that Collins "meant as much to the American League in character and fame as Christy Mathewson did to the National League." The Philadelphia writer shared his anger at what he deemed Collins' mistreatment in Chicago.

"Yet the fault is not with baseball or the American League, but solely with the man in control of the White Sox, who overlooking the sterling worth of a man who has delivered $2 in service to $1 in salary ever since joining the team in 1915, sacrificed him the first instant he believed he might not be able to play 154 games at second base next season."[35]

Joe Vila, writing in his syndicated column, praised Collins as a player. "[W]ith the possible exception of Dave Bancroft, he has a keener 'sixth sense' than any infielder in baseball.... No team in either league was as well drilled as the Sox with Collins in command, and even in defeat they seldom made a poor showing."[36]

The Sporting News editorialized that there were rumors that White Sox management at times ordered Collins to change his pitching rotation to start his best hurlers on the weekend in order to draw better crowds.

"If Collins had to labor under anything of that sort he had as much chance to win a pennant as a coolie would have against a Chinese mob."[37]

Collins' managerial numbers, however, were not overwhelming. In his time at the White Sox's helm, the record was 174–160, including those 27 games in 1924, with a winning percentage of .521 and two fifth-place finishes for his trouble as the full-time leader. There would be those who said his release was deserved. Columnist Don Maxwell of the *Tribune* was apparently one, blaming Collins' aloofness, rather than the general respect enjoyed by Ray Schalk, as a reason there was not a louder uproar over Eddie's abrupt dismissal.

"They say that with Collins, baseball was a business based on dollars and cents. Babe Ruth is a showman. Ty Cobb, whose resignation as the leader of the Detroit team got nationwide attention, was a showman. Romance was built around his name.

"There was none woven around Eddie Collins because Collins didn't want it. Newspaper men can't ballyhoo a player who won't let them know him. And Collins didn't want reporters as close friends."

Maxwell, who questioned why Collins had to be fired rather than be permitted to resign like Cobb, then discussed why the change was made.

> Baseball men admit the club was justified in making the change in managers. Collins was an aggressive leader when he was playing. As a bench boss he seemed to lose his hold on the men. The experts think Eddie failed to get the most out of his team when he wasn't in the lineup. And the experts probably are right....
>
> "Whether the White Sox will let Schalk get the men he wants is the principal point. The reporters say Comiskey didn't do it for Collins. They think Collins' ouster partly may have been due to his talk on this score. Last season he didn't make any attempt to hide his disgust at the material given him. He told club officials to stop giving him rookies who had no chance in a high class minor league.

Then Maxwell got to the chief reason Collins was "fired." In this he agreed with just about everyone else.

"Naturally the chief reason for the banishment of Collins was the disinclination of the White Sox to pay a high salary for a non-playing manager."[38]

And what about Ray Schalk, who was about to be a player-manager, too? How much longer do 33-year-old catchers last? Even if Schalk was somewhat successful, how long would he last once he could no longer crouch behind the plate? Actually, not too long at all, as in 1927 the Schalk-managed White Sox went 70–83, again finishing fifth. The next year, a 72–82 mark brought another fifth-place finish. But Schalk can't be blamed for everything in 1928. He resigned in mid-season, a year in which he appeared in only two games.

In late November 1926 Collins announced he had cleared waivers. He had just come from Tarrytown and a Thanksgiving holiday with his parents. Already there were rumors he was the next manager in Cleveland. The Red Sox, looking for a manager of their own, was another potential suitor. Given the abundant opportunities, it was really up to Collins to determine his baseball fate. In that case the answer was simple. Ask Eddie and he would tell you. "I believe I have several more good years of good playing left in me...."[39]

CHAPTER 17

Hot Seat

"You never thought you would live to see the day that Eddie Collins, as game a fighter
as ever lived, would break."

— Will Rogers[1]

It did not take Eddie Collins long to reveal to the public his wish for future baseball
employment. On December 19, 1926, he spoke with a reporter from the *Philadelphia Inquirer*.

"If Connie Mack desires my services, all other things being equal, he is the man who has
his first call."

Collins claimed he was not angry at the White Sox or any other major league club.

"At the same time I do lean toward the man and the club that gave me my first impetus
in the game....

"My one ambition now is to have another great year. My legs are as good as ever and
nothing could please me more than to end up my major league playing career in a blaze of
glory and in an Athletic uniform if possible."[2]

What about Connie Mack? Did he still hold Collins and other 1914 Mackmen in low
regard for holding him for ransom and forcing him to sell his team into the baseball cellar?
Apparently not. Speaking some time later, the Tall Tactician spoke about those Mackmen
and his feelings about them as the years passed.

"I was pretty sore at the time — awfully sore.... Today over the perspective of years, I feel
a little differently. The players were taking advantage of a baseball war to get all they could,
just as I took advantage of a baseball war to raid the National League when we first put a club
in Philadelphia. I long have forgiven the players who gave me those 1914 headaches, and most
of them have been back with me in some capacity."[3]

In 1926 the player he was about to forgive was Collins. Mack wanted to make sure Eddie
had a shot at managing, but "if he [Collins] doesn't sign up somewhere else pretty soon he
will sign up with us."[4] A meeting between Collins and Mack was scheduled for the next few
days.

Despite Mack's sale of Collins in 1914, the pair had remained friends. It was probably
no coincidence then that on Sunday, August 22, 1926, when Mack and his A's decided to test
Philadelphia's "Sunday Blue Law," it was Collins' White Sox team who played opposite. That
game, a 3–2 A's win, was played before 12,000 fans. Mack, tongue-in-cheek, expressed relief
at the time that "nothing happened that could be construed as a breach of the peace," but
scheduled no further Sunday games when a local minister decried "the disgusting noise," and
adjacent property owners signed a petition against the practice. In September the A's were
taken to court and lost, the judge deciding Sunday baseball was an "unlawful worldly employment."[5]

In December, before Collins and Mack could get together to discuss a new partnership, the baseball world was racked by news of another potential scandal. This one involved a pair of the game's giants — Ty Cobb and Tris Speaker. In the fall two seemingly unconnected, but most startling, personnel changes had occurred in baseball. On November 3 Ty Cobb resigned as player-manager of the Detroit Tigers and announced his retirement from baseball. Less than a month later on November 29, Tris Speaker of the Indians followed suit. Although Cobb, the manager, had not succeeded all that well, he could still hold his own on the ball field. The same was true of Speaker, whose managerial résumé also remained strong, his Indians having finished a close second to the Yankees in the season just completed. Thus, the moves made little sense, and there was much speculation.

On December 21 Judge Landis, who had only a few days before received a huge vote of confidence and a seven-year contract from major-league owners, under pressure from Cobb and Speaker and faced with rampant speculation, announced the reason the two men had resigned. They, along with former Red Sox pitcher and Indians outfielder Smoky Joe Wood, were accused of throwing a rather meaningless ball game between Cleveland and Detroit in 1919. Their accuser was former Tigers hurler Dutch Leonard, disgruntled with Cobb over his release from the team, and with Speaker over not picking him up and preventing him from a trip to the minor leagues. Leonard produced two letters, one from Cobb and one from Wood, which detailed a plan to bet on the game. Ban Johnson, the American League president who also had recently received a vote of confidence from his league's owners, determined to bury the incident in exchange for the resignations of the two players. Now Cobb and Speaker were demanding an opportunity to clear their names rather than adhere to Johnson's plan. The decision of Landis to release the information went over Johnson's head and both embarrassed and incensed him. Landis, perhaps wanting to let some of the shards of shattered glass settle, and no doubt taking joy in watching Johnson stew, announced he would defer a decision until sometime later in the winter.

In the meantime a number of baseball's elite weighed in on the controversy. One of the first to come to the defense of Cobb and Speaker was their long-time adversary Collins, telling reporters, "I don't believe it of Ty and Tris. Anybody who is acquainted with Cobb and Speaker know they are thoroughly honest men and above suspicion. I have known Ty and Tris for many years and will believe nothing that I read or hear that these men have been linked with a crooked angle of the game. These two men have been great assets to baseball. They have played the game fair and square, and this slush which is now being cast at them looks contemptible."[6]

Little did Collins know that in a matter of days he would be defending his own honor from a similar attack. For the Cobb-Speaker affair had stirred the juices of a dairy farmer living outside of Rochester, Minnesota, with a familiar name: Swede Risberg. He had heard the allegation against Cobb and Speaker and announced he could go that one better. A day or so before the end of the year, he told a *Chicago Tribune* reporter that he had "information that will implicate twenty big leaguers who never before have been mentioned in connection with crookedness."[7]

As it turned out, Risberg was referring to that Labor Day weekend 1917 White Sox–Detroit series and the White Sox–Detroit series of 1919. He was making those same allegations that Landis and later Johnson had fully explored with Schalk, Collins, Detroit's Bill James and Hooks Dauss, and others in the early 1920s. These were the same dealings the attorneys for the Black Sox players threatened to expose at their trial in 1921.

Landis heard Risberg's comments, suggested he come to Chicago to report them, and then wired him an invitation. The judge had heard this before. Why rehash the events yet again, this time, perhaps, in public?

During his long reign Judge Kenesaw Mountain Landis was all about image. Although the 1917 White Sox–Detroit affair had lingered under the surface for years, the statements of the players probably drawing dust in some corner of the commissioner's office, this time around Risberg's words touched a nerve.

"Judge Landis never will ask me [Risberg] to tell him what I know. The facts are there, but they don't want to know them. Neither do they want to know the facts of this Cobb-Speaker affair."[8]

By this pronouncement Risberg had challenged Landis, Organized Baseball for that matter, and as a direct result Landis decided to rise to the occasion. He decided to clean the decks once and for all. Perhaps he thought, granted an invitation, Risberg would back down. Some believe the Swede did hesitate; then, he took a deep breath and hopped a train for Chicago.

By the time Risberg's remarks hit the press, Collins was the newest member of the Philadelphia Athletics. On December 23 Eddie met with Connie Mack, as well as A's president Tom Shibe and vice president John Shibe. The meeting took place at Mack's office at Shibe Park. After invoking the usual pleasantries, Mack pulled a contract out of his desk. Collins quickly reviewed it, probably realized that this time around he lacked any real leverage, and within five minutes was once again an Athletic. Mack declared the signing was his best move yet in ensuring a pennant for 1927. The manager was asked what he would do about Max Bishop, the promising young second baseman who had appeared in 122 games the previous season. After stating that Collins "should help the younger players on the team considerably," Mack added, "I couldn't put Max on second and keep Collins off. Bishop is a good player and I intend to make him Eddie's under-study."

For his part Collins was ecstatic. "It sure is a great feeling to think I am back in Philadelphia after being away for twelve years."[9]

In penning the deal, Collins' salary was $15,000.[10] Reports had him turning down four offers, including one from the Yankees for $18,000.

The Athletics' new second sacker hardly had time to enjoy his new status or his New Year's holiday, when he found himself under the microscope. On December 31 Swede Risberg arrived in Chicago and appeared the next day in Judge Landis' office, testifying under oath in a statement to the judge that the White Sox–Tigers series in 1917 was fixed to allow the Chicagoans to win all four games and help them take a big step toward the pennant. By Risberg's version, the "fix" was engineered by White Sox manager Pants Rowland. Eddie Collins and Ray Schalk, along with almost all the other White Sox players, were involved. As an example of Collins' participation, Swede cited a statement Collins made after an error by the Tigers' shortstop Ben Dyer. According to Risberg, Collins remarked, "Isn't that terrible." Risberg claimed that when it came time to contribute his share, Collins told him, "I don't like to do this. I'll never do it again."

The Swede denied the money he and Chick Gandil collected from their teammates was a fund to reward Detroit for beating Boston in a later series near the end of the 1917 season. Furthermore, Risberg claimed his club repaid Detroit's "favor" by what he termed "sloughing" off in a late season 1919 series between the clubs so that Detroit would earn third-place money. He later added that it was not his purpose to get back at his teammates, but rather to make sure they did not get away clean while Cobb and Speaker paid a price for a similar deed.

"I [Risberg] think it's only fair that the 'white lilies' get the same treatment."[11]

Buck Weaver was present when Risberg gave his statement, nodding agreement throughout, but not providing details. He particularly agreed when Risberg told Landis that Buck had not contributed money to the affair, planning instead to later give a handbag to Detroiter Oscar Vitt, an act Weaver later told reporters was simply a gift.

From the time Risberg's charges were brought to light, Collins had maintained silence. But when the Swede's testimony to Landis on New Year's Day directly implicated him in a fix, he scratched back. In a story which appeared on page one of the *Philadelphia Inquirer* on January 2, 1927, he admitted a fund was raised but vehemently denied the money was a bribe for the Tigers to throw the four-game series, claiming all along that it was a reward to them for their work against Boston.

> At the outset let me say that the fund which was raised, and the purpose for which it was used is known to Judge Landis to Ban Johnson and to the officials of the Chicago White Sox. Also ... rehashing the thing now is simply an attempt on the part of Risberg, Buck Weaver and the other members who threw the World Series of 1919 to cast discredit on the other players....
>
> When I gave my contribution to Chick Gandil it was during the last week of the season, and after we had clinched the pennant. This would make it the last week in September, as the season did not close that year until the first of October.

Then differing from his statement in February 1921 to the commissioner's emissary Leslie O'Connor, when he said he was aware of instances of rewards but not a similar collection in baseball, Collins told reporters he knew of "hundreds" of times "when this has been done." And further that, "I reached down in my pocket and found that all I had at the time was $45 and I handed that over to Chick [Gandil]."[12]

Collins' portrayal of rewards as nothing out of the ordinary was supported by a number of fellow players, as well as by several club officials, including Charles Comiskey and the Tigers' Frank J. Navin.

When asked about whether he intended to go to Chicago to face off against Risberg and Weaver, as well as Chick Gandil, who had now entered the fray, Collins said, "No." He would not dignify the charges by his attendance. He had already told his story.

Then on the morning of January 3, when Eddie received a wire from the commissioner asking him to appear in Chicago as one of 38 active and former players, including amusingly one deceased player, Jack Lapp, all summoned to attend a formal hearing, he changed his mind and readily agreed to make the trip. As he made final preparations for the train ride to Illinois, he received telegrams, presumably in support, from all over the country. He traveled with Kid Gleason and former Tiger George Burns, arriving in Chicago in plenty of time for the hearing scheduled in the judge's office on January 5.

On the eve of the hearing, the *Tribune* editorialized in its sports section column, "In the Wake of the News."

> On the ethics of the question there is no doubt. The Wake feels strongly that no such purse should have been collected. This does not mean we imply wrongdoing. It simply was a bad and dangerous precedent.
>
> Now as to those who contributed to this pool. We can conceive a perfectly innocent player doing so. If several leading spirits thought Tiger pitchers should be rewarded for work against Boston ... the chap who did not contribute would be labeled among his mates as a "cheap skate" or a "mucker" no matter how repugnant the action might be to him personally. We can understand Eddie Collins' reported saying of "I'll never do this again."[13]

In one fell swoop the columnist had captured the essence of Collins. Setting aside for the moment the most important issue, i.e., what the contribution was for, the columnist had reached back and peeled off the Collins' veil as it related to his relationship with his teammates. The same restraint Eddie exercised in 1919 in not taking an active role in exposing his teammates' activities during the World Series was at play even earlier in 1917. In order to be a good teammate, he would contribute to a fund even though it went contrary to his better judgment. He did not want to be labeled what the columnists called a "mucker," even if it involved dealing with players he despised like Risberg or Gandil.

Now these former teammates, whose actions he had viewed with disdain, but cloaked in silence, had accused him and his other teammates, as well as his manager, of throwing baseball games. If this was his habit, known to his White Sox teammates in 1917, why was he the last player on the team the Black Sox would think to approach to throw the 1919 World Series? Why didn't he and Gandil speak for two years after 1917? Perhaps it was simply his statement that he would never do something like that again, the "that" still at issue some 10 years later. And in that regard, the gloves were now off, Collins prepared to come out fighting mad to defend his honor and that of his fellow "white lilies."

The hearing was set for 10 A.M. on January 5 at the office of Judge Landis, located in the People's Gas Building, a skyscraper on Michigan Avenue. The office was small, providing nowhere near enough room for a hearing of this sort. Nevertheless, the commissioner as well as a reported 200 newspaper people and ball players tried to stuff themselves inside it to hear the first scheduled witness, Swede Risberg. Unfortunately, the Swede was a no-show. Fifteen minutes prior to the start, he called Landis and told him he would not appear until 1:30 that afternoon. No explanation was provided.

In the afternoon the hearing began, but even then Risberg was late. The scene in the judge's office was a classic. At one end of the long, narrow office, the judge positioned himself. He wore a winged collar deemed "even starchier and higher than his wont to wear." During the hearing he frequently leaned forward as he examined a player, close enough to them to wag a forefinger "menacingly under their nose." Then from time to time he "barked questions" as he stood and paced to and fro from behind his desk. To his left sat his secretary Leslie O'Connor. Immediately to O'Connor's left was a makeshift witness box, a chair which sat up against the wall. Risberg, the accuser, sat in a separate chair on a direct line with the judge.

Similar to the aborted morning session, the room was once again packed and it was smoke-filled. At least 40 news people crowded around a long table and ball players stood in the aisles. At long last Risberg arrived to take his seat and the hearing finally began.[14] Over the next hour Risberg told his story, varying little from earlier versions, but clearly laying the affair at the feet of Pants Rowland.

"I was informed by Mr. Clarence Rowland before the series that everything was all fixed, and we won four ball games from Detroit."

About two weeks later while the team was in New York at the Ansonia Hotel, Risberg claimed he and Gandil collected $45 each from their teammates to pay Detroit, mainly its pitchers, for "sloughing" the series. This was the first time Risberg said he really knew the fix was for real. Later he and Gandil were given permission by Rowland to go to Philadelphia, where they met Detroit pitcher Bill James and gave him the money they had collected.

When Risberg was finished with his version, Landis, by way of a loose cross-examination, attempted to pin Risberg down to detail, but the Swede remained vague. As to how Detroit helped the Sox to their victories, Risberg maintained he felt the Detroit pitchers were not bearing down, but gave no specific instances. He did point to the high number of stolen bases. He also pointed to the remark Collins made about the "terrible" play of Detroit shortstop Dyer. From this Risberg inferred Collins knew all about the fix. When asked if the Detroit games were a subject for discussion in the ensuing weeks, Risberg stated "frankly they were not." He did tell Landis that in 1920 he ran into Rowland, who asked him not to get into the 1917 Detroit series, presumably while Risberg was mounting his defense from the allegations of a thrown World Series. At the end Risberg reminded Landis that the White Sox needed these wins from Detroit at the time and again referred to their late-season losses to these same Tigers in 1919 as a payback.[15]

When Risberg's testimony concluded, Landis asked if any of the players had questions of their own for the former player. When they did not, he then called Pants Rowland for questioning. Over the next four hours, Rowland and the involved White Sox and Tiger players offered their rebuttal to Risberg's charges. After being cautioned early on by Judge Landis for branding the allegation that prior to the 1917 Labor Day series he told Risberg to count on four wins "a damn lie," Rowland continued in only a slightly more restrained tone. According to the former manager, he heard nothing about any money transfers until the team arrived at the Ansonia Hotel in New York later in September and Red Faber told him about giving Chick Gandil a check. [Author's Note: Risberg had testified Faber's check was given to him to cover the shares of Faber and several other White Sox players.] Faber told him it was a loan to Gandil, nothing about the purpose as a fund. Later, while still at the Ansonia, Pants recalled he heard talk about a fund to reward Detroit for its efforts in defeating Boston. [Author's Note: The White Sox closed their season with the Yankees in New York with games on September 27, 29 (two) and October 1. Detroit's three victories over the Red Sox in Boston occurred on September 19 and 20.] Rowland was neither solicited to contribute to the fund, nor did he contribute. He saw nothing to indicate and did not believe Detroit threw the four-game series to his club.

During Rowland's testimony Landis failed to flesh out one interesting statement. Rowland claimed that at the time of the series, his club was satisfied with a three and one-half game lead over Boston, thus, not motivated to pay Detroit to help them increase that lead. Yet by the time the Tigers played Boston and the players, at least according to Collins and his group, saw fit to reward them for beating their adversary, the White Sox's lead over those same Red Sox was up to eight games. On the other hand, perhaps since the White Sox had not yet clinched the pennant when Detroit played the Red Sox, Landis did not consider the standings an important factor.

Another interesting point was brought up by Rowland in a newspaper interview prior to the hearing, but apparently not developed during it. This one involved Rowland's use of pitchers and weighed toward Pants and the "White Lilies." Why, Rowland asked, if he knew he was about to win four games from the Tigers, did he use his best pitchers against them during the series? In the first game of the two on September 2, Rowland pitched Eddie Cicotte. In the second game he started Reb Russell, and when the game later was tied, sending it into extra innings, he inserted Lefty Williams, "one of the best left handers in the league, to keep the Tigers in check...." The next day it was Faber. When he lasted only five innings, Danforth, who had appeared briefly the day before, went in again, followed by Williams. Rowland came back in game two with Faber yet again, followed in relief by Danforth, Williams and Cicotte.

"Nobody seems to have given thought to the fact that if I was in on any kind of a deal as Risberg declares I certainly would not have used about every good pitcher I possessed. If the games were fixed and I had knowledge of it I could very easily have bluffed my way through by working some of the second raters."[16]

Next in the box was an emotional Eddie Collins. At the outset he told Landis he did not believe Risberg's testimony. "[T]here was nothing irregular, as I remember it, about those games." Collins did not recall making a statement to Risberg after Dyer's "booted" ball and, further, if the inference was that it was a fixed game, "then I know I didn't make it." He did, however, contribute to a pool. When the team was in New York, he often stayed with his parents in nearby Tarrytown. In late September 1917 while the team was in New York, he followed his usual pattern while the rest of the team lodged at the Ansonia Hotel. After the trip he and Cicotte remained in the East, traveling to Philadelphia to watch the play of the Giants, their upcoming National League opponent. They then returned to Chicago to prepare for the Giants and the World Series. [Author's Note: The Giants and Phillies played in Philadelphia on October 2 and 3.]

> When I got back to Chicago in the club house was the first intimation I ever had that there was any money being raised to give Detroit. I think Gandil approached me on the subject and said he was collecting a pool to pay, or to remunerate, the Detroit pitchers for Boston, and I hesitated. I didn't give him anything then. In fact I wanted to satisfy myself that such a thing was being done, and before I did anything I asked several players whether they had contributed, and it was not until we went back to New York and finished the season there that I paid Gandil the money, and I have got a check book here which shows the check I cashed in the Ansonia hotel with the notation on it that I gave Gandil $45. That was after the world's series was over. If he said that I gave any money before that time he is a — damn liar. I will find it for you. The date of the check is Oct. 16.
>   Q. [Landis] — "Check stub 3.230, October 16, 1917, Ansonia hotel, cash for use $45 Gandil; check $100. And you gave $45 to Gandil?"
>   A. [Collins] — "Yes, sir."
>   Q. — "And where were you and he when you gave him that money?"
>   A. — "In the lobby of the Ansonia hotel."
>   Q. — "This was on October 16?"
>   A. — "Yes, sir."[17]

The nation's favorite humorist Will Rogers was in Chicago at the time and gave a more dramatic description of Collins' testimony regarding his check.

> You never thought you would live to see the day that Eddie Collins, as game a fighter as ever lived, would break. But I want to tell you the most dramatic moment I ever saw in either court room or stage was when he even produced his check book to show the stub where he had given Gandil the money. He threw it on Landis' desk and said, "There is where I paid the money, and any man that says I did it for a thrown ball game, or that I ever knowingly participated in a crooked game in my life is a blank blank blank!" and he broke so that if they hadent [sic] been swear words, they were the only ones that would have come out. It was from the heart, so the judge dident [sic] even admonish him for it.[18]

The production of Collins' check was a surprise. He had not mentioned it in 1921 in his statement to O'Connor nor to the reporters he spoke with shortly after Risberg raised the matter in late 1926. In both instances one is given to understand that Gandil approached Collins and he reluctantly paid him the sum requested at that very time.

The testimony about the check was important, if accurate, because it offered a date of payment that was well after the regular season ended and the pennant was secure. In fact, it was the day after the White Sox won the World Series. It did not prove a whole lot more. Since the check was made out to cash, only the notation written in by Collins indicated its purpose and use. If one believed Collins was telling the truth, then that was that, but if he did not otherwise find Collins credible, the notation, in the form of a memo to the check writer, which could have been made at any time, really proved nothing.

And, what about the production of the check at this late date? In fairness to Collins, he may have forgotten all about it when he spoke to O'Connor, but it seems the availability of the check, although maybe not its corroborative value, was known to Collins at the time he spoke with reporters shortly after Risberg's latest allegations. Mabel Collins added insight in that regard.

"I wanted to throw them [the check stubs] away last spring when we cleaned house, but he [Collins] looked them over and said we might as well keep them a little longer. I am glad now that he saved that book."[19]

Assuming the judge already had a good idea where he was headed in deciding the case, Collins' testimony concerning the timing of his payment to Gandil only served to complicate matters. It differed from his transcribed statement to O'Connor, where he said, albeit vaguely, that the payment was probably made in Chicago after the last trip east. Also, by claiming he delayed making the payment to Gandil until he checked with others, it again differed with his statement to O'Connor, as well as his more recent newspaper quotes. In his statement to O'Connor, the only person Eddie mentioned talking to after his first contact with Gandil was Ray Schalk, implying that discussion occurred after he had reluctantly proffered his $45. Finally the testimony about the check differed with the recollections of his White Sox's teammates, friend and foe, and that of the Tigers' players, who all concurred that the promised reward was satisfied in late September.

Certainly when Eddie met with O'Connor, he did not have the 1917 season schedule in front of him. He even mentioned this as a caveat when he gave O'Connor his statement. Nonetheless, only if one determines that Gandil allowed Eddie's share to ride at least for the time being, highly unlikely in view of their distrust for one another, can one believe that the Collins' check in mid–October 1917 was the date Eddie gave Gandil his portion of the fund.

But in the final analysis the weight of any evidence offered in the Risberg-Gandil hearing would come down to a determination of credibility. And, like it or not, when it came to Judge Landis, Eddie Collins and the other "White Lilies" carried plenty of that credit on their side, no matter whether their testimony totally meshed or not. Thus, when Collins concluded his testimony by denying Risberg's assertions for not only the 1917 series with Detroit but also his allegations of "sloughing" games to Detroit in 1919, the judge felt justified in over-looking the discrepancies in Eddie's testimony, including that Eddie had never before heard the allegations about the "sloughing" of 1919, as just that — discrepancies and not untruths. It is likely the experienced arbiter saw Collins' version of events as merely an effort to over-state his case, culpable of nothing more than a case of overzealousness. As such, he did not cross-examine the star second sacker, nor did he bring up Collins' letter to him describing how he bet on the first two games of that 1917 series with Detroit, matters which would not have escaped unmentioned in the hands of a skilled cross-examiner, such as a lawyer with a client to represent. In this case the commissioner's client was Organized Baseball and his mission was its preservation. And with that in mind, Collins, unscathed, was dismissed and the parade of witnesses resumed.

Ray Schalk was next in the box and his testimony differed from Collins' only in placing the time of payment at an earlier date. He was not asked to explain any discrepancies in Collins' testimony. Ty Cobb took the stand and denied knowledge of the matters in both 1917 and 1919, taking the opportunity to remind the judge and his newspaper audience, perhaps with a twinkle in his eye, "There have been a lot of charges in the last six or eight months that are untrue. Do you get just what I mean?"[20]

As the parade of witnesses continued, the scribes in attendance watched Risberg as he listened to one after another player sit down in front of Landis and in one form or another call the Swede a liar. All the while the accuser, who now seemed more like the accused, sat in his chair, grinned and exhibited nervousness only in the high number of cigarettes smoked.

As often occurs when one dissects a large body of testimony in a contested matter, there were some victories for each side. For example, Detroit pitchers Bernie Boland and George Cunningham testified they each received $50 but did not pitch against Boston. Score one for Risberg-Gandil. On the other hand, this duo claimed that the pitchers and catchers were recipients of payments for throwing games to the White Sox. Thus, why give $180 to George "Hooks" Dauss, a Detroit pitcher who was not even with the team for the Chicago-Detroit series that Labor Day weekend? On the other hand, he started the second game of the 1917 Detroit-Boston series, a game in which his team was victorious, thus perhaps earning a reward. Score one for the "White Lilies." And that was the way it went throughout the total of four hours of testimony from those witnesses who followed Risberg to the stand.

There was some fear the day's events would end in fisticuffs. There were none, even though at one point Risberg accused Detroit's Donie Bush of nodding his head to direct Bernie Boland's testimony. Boland then turned to Risberg and told him, "You're still a pig." Risberg retorted and Bush rose to join in but was quickly quieted by Landis.

The hearing did have its funny moments. One occurred during the testimony of Detroit's Oscar Stanage. Asked about the unusually high number of stolen bases which occurred on his watch, the catcher brought down the house when he replied that it was certainly not the first time that had happened.

One witness who most predicted would side with Risberg-Gandil, perhaps who even instigated the whole matter, was Buck Weaver, but he did not. Instead, he told Landis how he was injured, did not play in the Labor Day series due to that injury, and claimed to his knowledge the games were honestly played. The same for the Detroit-Chicago series in 1919 as he stated the games were above board, despite prior statements to the contrary. By this time Buck knew exactly which way the wind was blowing. He tried to use what he deemed his favorable testimony to his advantage, asking Judge Landis for reinstatement. The move surprised Landis, who asked Buck to write him about it. In a less inflammatory moment, the judge would deny his request.

The hearing was adjourned, but it was not over. The next afternoon Chick Gandil appeared at Landis' office to take his turn at corroborating the testimony of his former teammate Risberg. As was quickly apparent, it was Gandil and not Risberg who was at the center of the affair, telling Landis that Bill James approached him on the first day of the series with the Tigers to assure him Detroit would not play hard. They did not talk again until after the games were completed, when Gandil assured James he would be "fixed up."

The next time Gandil said he saw James was in Philadelphia in late September 1917, about the 29th or 30th. By then he had told Rowland it would be a "good time to collect that money and I can go over to Philadelphia and give it to James." Pants gave his consent to the trip, as well as to Gandil's request that Risberg go along to act as a witness to the payment. The trip was made and the money, between $900 and $1100, transferred to James at the Aldine Hotel. The money was paid for Detroit's "friendship" during the series with the White Sox. It had nothing to do with Detroit versus Boston.

The amount to be given Detroit was, according to Gandil, decided by the players during a clubhouse meeting attended by Collins, Schalk and most of the other players. Only Buck Weaver dissented from the decision to pay the Tigers. The distribution to Detroit was left up to James.

Gandil specifically recalled he got the money from Collins in New York on "the day I asked him." It was cash, not a check. It was "[a]t the Ansonia hotel. When I first asked Collins for the money he hesitated and said he didn't know whether he wanted to do it; he would have to have time to think it over." Then he gave him the $45 in "about an hour, maybe a little longer."

Gandil pointed to the number of walks as an irregularity during the series. He also claimed that during the 1919 series with Detroit, he had played "out of position," and noticed Risberg was playing out of position, too, a point confirmed by Risberg during his time on the stand.[21]

During his testimony Gandil protested his "blacklisting" from baseball. Unlike his reaction to the request from Buck Weaver, Landis hopped on this one, pointing to Gandil's statement about deliberately playing out of position in 1919, telling the former first baseman that this alone rendered him ineligible.

In exchange for $500 in travel expenses from the *Chicago Tribune*, Gandil had provided a sworn affidavit in that newspaper's offices prior to his testimony, sometime after the first day of testimony and prior to his own appearance. As to Collins' production of a check written on October 16, affiant Gandil stated, "I can't explain this," claiming that Risberg was with him, that it was the same day they approached all the other players, and that in about an hour Collins returned with the money, telling Gandil, "I hate to do this — I will never do it again."

In this same affidavit, in a statement that may have come the closest to the truth of the matter, Gandil offered his former teammates an out. "I don't claim that every single one of the fellows who contributed to this pool, which to my recollection seemed between $900.00 and $1,100.00, did so thinking we were paying Detroit for throwing four games. I only know that it was the general talk among the fellows that Detroit had been pretty friendly with us in September when we needed it, and we ought to do something for them."

Finally, after reminding whoever might read the affidavit that no one offered to help him when he was tried and convicted, Gandil offered a bit of sardonic humor of his own. "I haven't any grudge against any ball players on the White Sox or Detroit team."[22]

Landis had one more witness to call. Big Bill James, now better known as the "payoff man," sat down and faced the judge. In 1919 as a late-season acquisition, he had pitched for the White Sox, relieving Williams in that controversial last game of the World Series. In 1917 he was a Tiger with a 13–10 record and 2.09 ERA.

Now in 1927 he immediately denied meeting Chick Gandil before the first day of their Labor Day weekend series to discuss throwing the games, calling it "an absolute lie" and saying that between innings of one game, Gandil asked him if he thought the Tigers would fare well against the Red Sox when they met them later that year. James told him the Tigers would do just fine, particularly himself and pitcher George Dauss. Gandil then told James there was $200 for Dauss or any other Tiger pitcher who beat the Red Sox. Risberg later asked James if Gandil's proposal would work. James told him it was "fine." His conversation with Risberg was after the fourth game. Risberg was quite specific in telling James to let Dauss, who was not in Chicago for the just-completed series, know of their offer.

James testified that sometime after the Chicago series, but before the Boston series, he told several Tigers pitchers about Gandil's offer. There was no further talk about the offer when the White Sox and Tigers met after Labor Day for another series, which occurred prior to the Tigers-Boston contest. Then a day or two before the end of the season, Gandil and Risberg came to the bar in the Aldine Hotel in Philadelphia where James and several Tigers players were having a beer. James described the meeting as well as the transfer and distribution of the money.

> There was a little lobby there attached to the bar in the Aldine, and they called me out there, and I believe it was Chick that said, "Well, here is that money." I said, "Good, how much?" And he game [*sic*] me $870.
>   I said, "Well," I said, "what will I do with the extra money?" "Well," he says, "who did the most work up in Boston?" "Well," I said, "that is hard to tell; but there isn't enough money to go all around, if Mitchell, Dauss and I get $200." And he says, "Well, give it to the one or two that did the best work up there." I says, "Well, there was only one player up there that did any work." He says, "Who?" And I said, "And that was Stanage." And he says, "Well, use your own judgment, what you want to do with the money."

So he gave me the money, and we went out then and had a couple of drinks, and they left. I went into the dining room with George Dauss, I believe, and Oscar Stanage and Willie Mitchell — no. George Dauss wasn't in there then. He had gone. It was Oscar Stanage and Willie Mitchell that went over and took Dauss away from the table; and we went off in a corner, that is, in the dining room, and I took and I put $200 in my own pocket, and I gave Willie Mitchell $200, and I gave George Dauss $200; and I gave Stanage, I think, $75 or $100. We sat down there and we ordered, and I believe I made the remark, "Stan ought to share even with us." I said, "We ought to give Stan enough of it to make pretty nearly even." And if I remember correctly, Dauss and Mitchell and I gave Stanage $20 apiece to buy a new suit of clothes; and I still had $150.

I remember, distinctly remember, of giving George Cunningham $50; and he wanted to know what it was for. I gave it to him because he was in the bull pen most of the time and had no chance to pitch; and I gave Bernie Boland $50. I did not leave it there, but I kept it in an envelope and left it at the club. [Bernie] wasn't with the team at that time.

I don't remember whether I gave Howard Ehmke anything or not....

In closing, James admitted his Tigers played "rotten" against Chicago, but "that was customary for our ball club at that time. We were in and outers."[23]

Clearly, there was a difference between the amount of money James testified he received and the amount Gandil claimed the White Sox contributed. In the end, however, the amount involved was never really the issue.

After James finished, Judge Landis recalled several player-witnesses, including Collins, for further questioning. Eddie reiterated that he paid Gandil in New York at the Ansonia Hotel one day after the World Series, after first learning about the fund from Gandil in the Chicago clubhouse just prior to their first journey to New York for the 1917 Series. When Gandil was permitted to ask Collins what time of day Collins gave him the money, Eddie did not look at Gandil as Eddie recalled "it was around noon, just before we left for Mineola to play an exhibition."[24]

By now it was quite late on a Friday night and Landis had heard enough. He told his audience he would consider the case and issue his opinion the following Wednesday. The stakes were quite high. Based upon the position Landis had taken in the Black Sox scandal, a finding against Collins and his fellow players meant banishment from the game.

The judge, however, had already hinted the direction he was headed. When he ended his questioning of Gandil, he showed him records indicating that the White Sox received paychecks right before the Labor Day series with the Tigers, as well as before their next series with the Tigers in Detroit. Both of these series took place before the Tigers-Boston series, yet the Tigers did not receive money from the White Sox until after the Boston series. The pay records begged the question: Why did the White Sox not pay off their debt right away, instead of waiting, especially when the team was with the Tigers for several days in Detroit? Obviously, Landis thought their failure to so act was important.

While the judge pondered the evidence, the baseball world sat back and waited, holding its collective breath. In Philadelphia that intrepid *Inquirer* columnist, the Old Sport, offered an alternative theory. Taking a page from Gandil's affidavit, he ventured that both Collins and Gandil "may be right. Gandil may have told such honorable chaps as Collins and Schalk that the pool was a bonus to reward the Tiger pitchers for thwarting the Red Sox. Then Gandil may be telling the truth when he says that he conspired with certain players to throw the series, and that the slush fund was an out-and-out bribe, used for that despicable purpose....

"But the question which obtrudes itself into any consideration of this alleged scandal is quite a simple one. Just why should it be the custom to pay a bonus to any player, or any coterie of players for playing winning baseball?"[25]

On January 12 Commissioner Landis issued his ruling, answering the Old Sport's question, as well as others. Appearing in the morning outside his office, he handed out written copies of a five-page, 3,000-word opinion that exonerated Collins and his fellow "White Lilies." It was no surprise, given the judge's comments years earlier, that he reached his decision by heavily discounting the testimony of Gandil and Risberg, while resting a good part of his ultimate reasoning process, interspersed with several detailed discussions of the facts, on their motive for raising the affair in the first place.

"To some it may seem inexplicable that Risberg and Gandil should implicate themselves in these alleged corrupt practices. Obviously that self-implication may have been conceived upon the theory that 'they have been incriminating themselves, so it must be true.' However, being already on the ineligible list, it would not affect them, and it might blacken the 'lilly whites.'"[26]

When discussing the evidence, specifically Collins' remark that Dyer's shortstop play was "terrible" and Risberg's inference that it showed Collins knew that the games were fixed, Landis took pains to point out that Dyer was a substitute, played only three innings in the series, and thus was not someone anyone would purposely select to help throw a baseball game.

As the trier of fact, Judge Landis found the statistic that the White Sox led the league in stolen bases in 1917 more impressive than the Risberg-Gandil assertions that the steals were due to "sloughing" by Detroit. In that view he noted two White Sox runners were thrown out in the third game of the series, while ignoring the fact the White Sox of 1917 stole less than two bases per game and that there were allegations that during the series the Detroit pitchers were particularly guilty of failing to hold runners, thereby making it easier to steal bases.

Landis also noted that the White Sox were a hot team entering their Labor Day series with Detroit, an opponent they had played well against all year. Finally, Landis reached the crux of his argument: the timing of the collection of money, factual evidence he introduced at the hearing himself during his questioning of Gandil.

"The Chicago players' salaries were paid August 31 [1917]; they had funds, yet there was no discussion about raising money to pay Detroit for 'sloughing' that Risberg claimed was 'common talk' on the Chicago team. Again, on September 12, Chicago players received checks and two days later they played 3 games in Detroit. Although Gandil and Risberg and [Bill] James and the other pitchers were all there, and that was the last time these teams would meet all year, still not a word [was said] about the 'bribe' money, and no inquiry or promise as to when payments would be made."

Earlier in his opinion Landis had addressed his strongest remarks about the conduct of the "White Lilies."

"If the Risberg-Gandil version be correct, it was an act of criminality. If the other versions are true, it was an act of impropriety, reprehensible and censurable, but not corrupt."[27]

Then Judge Landis, perhaps finally disclosing his real agenda in holding the hearing in the first place, issued a proposal to close the books on any scandals occurring prior to his ascendancy. At the same time he set the bar high for any player conduct occurring thereafter. It was a four-prong proposal. Coming from Landis it carried the force of law and asked for:

One — A statute of limitations with respect to alleged baseball offenses, as in our state and national statutes with regard to criminal offenses.

Two — Ineligibility for one year for offering or giving any gift or reward by the players or management of one club to the players or management of another club for services rendered or supposed to be, or have been rendered, in defeating a competing club.

Three — Ineligibility for one year for betting any sum whatsoever upon any ball game in connection with which the bettor had no duty to perform.

Four — Permanent ineligibility for betting any sum whatsoever upon any ball game in connection with which the bettor has any duty to perform.[28]

Reactions to the judge's decision were fairly predictable. Collins was ecstatic, expressing joy at vindication and relief the ordeal was over, even if the judge's ruling ignored his testimony about the check. Certainly the allegations had caused Collins considerable anguish and embarrassment, even if it did little to tarnish his reputation. Gandil had done him one favor. If Gandil's testimony at the hearing was truthful that he hatched his plan with Detroit's Bill James on the morning of the first two games of the Detroit series, it seems clear that at the very least Collins had bet on these games with no foreknowledge they were to be fixed.

After the decision Risberg remained adamant he had told the truth but expressed no surprise at the decision. The media offered mixed reviews, Will Rogers noting the decision as "just and fair,"[29] while the editorial page of the *New York Herald-Tribune* told its readers, "Professional baseball has been whitewashed once more."[30]

There were a few who felt left out in the cold by the judge's ruling. There was no mention of Buck Weaver and his plea. And, of more immediate concern, nothing was said as to the Cobb-Speaker matter, the spark which ignited the Risberg-Gandil affair in the first place. For his part as he handed out copies of his ruling, the judge mentioned he had plans for a much-needed vacation.

Any chance for Landis to relax for any length of time, however, was shattered on January 17 when the *Chicago Tribune* printed an article in which Ban Johnson charged the judge with smearing the reputations of Ty Cobb and Tris Speaker by revealing that the American League had barred them from managing or playing. In the article Johnson stated paradoxically, since he was the one who banned the player in the first place, that he did not believe "Cobb ever played a dishonest game in his life, but that Speaker was 'cute.' He knows why he was forced out of the managership of the Cleveland club." Then, "As long as I'm president of the American league neither one of them will manage or play on our teams." In addition, Johnson threatened to tell all, including the reasons for his falling out with Landis, when he appeared at an American League meeting called by Landis for early the next week at Chicago's Congress Hotel in order to discuss the status of the two players. "When I take the stand Monday I may tell the whole story of my relationship with the Judge."[31]

Some believe Johnson, who by this time was in ill health, was baited by Landis into making these comments. The latter pounced on reports of quotes printed by the *Tribune* from an unidentified "leader in baseball" to the effect that Cobb and Speaker would never play in the American League again. The quotes were obviously from Johnson. Landis retorted by summoning Johnson and his league's ownership to the meeting in Chicago.

If Landis was not angry before, he certainly was now, after reading these additional inflammatory quotes clearly attributed, this time, to his adversary. And angry as well was an embarrassed group of American League owners who had just joined their colleagues in the senior circuit in extending the judge's contract, and who had over recent weeks listened to Johnson make a series of other inflammatory charges, then deny making them, including that the 1922 World Series was fixed. Therefore on January 23, one day prior to the meeting called by Landis, the American League owners held their own meeting and wrote a resolution of support for Landis, which repudiated the criticism of him leveled by Johnson. Further, instead of censuring Johnson as most surely intended to do, they advised Landis that Johnson's personal physician had recommended that he take a much-needed rest due to his failing health. In his absence Frank Navin of Detroit would take over. Landis was called to the hotel where the meeting had taken place and handed a written form of the resolution. Over the weekend he had remained silent by design. The strategy worked. The wily white-haired courtroom veteran knew when a victory was achieved. He refused to stomp on Johnson's flattened prestige. After he was handed the resolution, instead of trumpeting his victory with a verbal assault on Johnson, he merely issued regrets about the condition of the league president's health and indicated he never sought his long-time adversary's resignation.

The widespread feeling was that Ban Johnson had reached the end of his road. However, he had a few ticks left on his clock. He rehabilitated at Hot Springs, Arkansas, and returned to his position for a short while, but later disputes with Connie Mack over minor issues made Johnson's resignation imminent.

All this was a major opening act for the show everyone originally came to see. What would the now even more powerful commissioner decide in the matter of Cobb-Speaker? On January 27 he issued his decision. The ruling contained none of the detailed recitation of facts contained in his Risberg-Gandil opinion. In fact, just the opposite, as Landis rested his decision on the absence of a definitive hearing to develop the facts. After first establishing that the accused players had requested a full hearing before their accuser Dutch Leonard, which Leonard declined to attend, the judge related how Cobb and Speaker decided they would prefer to retire from baseball than go forward with a one-sided hearing, which would prove nothing. It was decided they would quietly leave baseball, the matter dropped unless circumstances required it to be revived. Thereafter, reports surfaced containing gossip and innuendo "infinitely more harmful to the individuals concerned than the truth could possibly be." Thus, Landis claimed he made another effort to secure Leonard's appearance for a hearing. When that proved unsuccessful, a hearing was held without him. As a result, the judge did not uncover evidence to find Cobb, Speaker, or the retired Wood guilty of fixing the game in question. Cobb and Speaker were, therefore, restored to the reserve list.[32]

Then, this same judge who had shown such grace in refusing to force Ban Johnson to resign just days before took that smashing step previously avoided and required that Cobb and Speaker play their baseball in the American League, the very act Johnson insisted would never occur under his presidency.

Now Cobb and Speaker were on the market. Would Mack be interested in adding even more veteran star talent to his roster? Already he had taken one step beyond Collins on that road. On January 12 he signed 38-year-old Zack Wheat, the former Brooklyn Dodger outfielder who would one day take his place in the Baseball Hall of Fame. Indeed Mack had big plans for his A's. He had been rebuilding for a number of years now, intent on turning his franchise into a blue chip stock once again. Although the youngsters were developing, Mack's plan still had room for aging veteran superstars. Just how much of the plan really included Eddie Collins remained to be seen.

CHAPTER 18

A's Redux

"When baseball has meant as much as it has to me, fun everyday and a grand living to boot, it is just undiluted hell to discover that you are about through. Well, Ty Cobb and I went through it on the same bench....

"It seems to me that before my ego would permit me to see that anything was wrong with Collins, I could see plainly that Ty Cobb was slipping. That is the way we humans are made."

— Eddie Collins[1]

When Eddie Collins was given his release by Comiskey in Chicago in 1926, there were obviously some who felt the move signaled the end of the second baseman's career. Perhaps that was why the North American Newspaper Alliance, a news syndication, contracted with him to write a 21-part autobiography of his life in the big leagues. The series entitled "Twenty One Years of Base Ball" appeared in newspapers throughout the country as early as January 1927. The series ran the gamut of baseball topics, including the writer's career, teammates, opponents and managers, as well as his take on baseball strategy. There was even a section on baseball superstitions. In describing the greatest teams he played on, Collins named the 1919 White Sox as the one having "the greatest possibilities of any baseball combination ever assembled." Alas, "the great defect of this team, which made its disruption, was the character of some of the men and the consequent lack of morale and proper spirit."[2]

In writing the series Collins was asked to name his "All-American League Champions." Unlike Babe Ruth, who often named himself when asked to list an all-star team, Collins placed Napoleon Lajoie on second base. In right field he named Ty Cobb and in center Tris Speaker. Neither outfield choice was a surprise to anyone.[3] What was a surprise was that both men were now available in early 1927 and Eddie Collins, the newest member of the Athletics, was working hard to make them his teammates.

In pursuing these former opponents and friends, Collins was acting as more than a potential new teammate. He was now cloaked with an additional title. For shortly after Connie Mack made one of Eddie's dreams come true by bringing him home to Philadelphia to finish his career, he fulfilled another long-time Collins' dream by naming him the new captain of the Athletics.

The pursuit of Cobb and Speaker by Collins and his A's began in earnest on January 27 when Connie Mack announced he was "willing" to discuss adding each star to his roster, careful, however, not to appear overly anxious, given each player's aspiration for a large salary.

"At this particular moment I'm not entertaining any fixed plans to bring Speaker to this city to join the Athletics. The same thing applies to Ty Cobb. Of course, Speaker, as I understand it, is to be the guest of Eddie Collins, who is captain of our club."[4]

When Speaker arrived in town, Collins, who shared an avid interest with Speaker in hunting, made sure the welcome mat was spread wide. On January 29 Eddie took the former Indians' manager to see Mack and then hosted an informal luncheon for Speaker and several local baseball writers at the Penn Athletic Club. While the men were keeping busy in downtown Philadelphia, Mrs. Speaker drove out to Lansdowne to spend the day with Mabel Collins. Later that evening Collins was asked to say a few words at the banquet of the Veteran Athletes of Philadelphia held at the Club. Collins made no secret of his desires when it came to Speaker nor of his efforts to entice his friend to join up with Connie Mack's forces.

"I have told Tris here, not once but many times, that if he wants to come to a town where business can be combined with pleasure, he would do well to come to Philadelphia."[5]

In the end, however, the sales pitch did not work. Two days after his trip to Philadelphia, Speaker signed a one-year contract with the Washington Senators. It was a matter of money. Clark Griffith, the Senators' president, outbid the Yankees, Tigers and Chicago, as well as the A's, to get him. It is reasonable to assume that in attempting to attract both Speaker and Cobb to Philadelphia, Mack was forced to temper the amount of money offered to each. Now the Tall Tactician no longer had to hedge his bets. Ty Cobb firmly in his sights, he traveled to Augusta to see the Georgia Peach and make his bid. And a very large bid it was. Although the exact figure varies, depending on the source, the amount was in the $75,000 range, enough to make Cobb once again the best-paid player in baseball. The *Philadelphia Inquirer* reported on February 9 that Cobb liked the deal enough to sign.

Collins was ecstatic. He considered Cobb the best player ever and had always wanted to be his teammate. Now that dream was about to become reality.[6]

Cobb probably would have been well paid wherever he went. Why then did he choose the A's? The answer lay in their more recent performances and current reviews. For after Collins and many of the other key Mackmen were sold, traded, or merely left the team in late 1914, the proud Athletics quickly became a regular inhabitant of the American League's second division.

The A's followed their elevator ride to the basement in 1915 with six more last-place finishes. Then in 1922 they climbed to seventh and followed that a year later with a sixth-place finish. By 1924, however, the A's were knocking once again on the door of the first division. They finished fifth

Collins in August 1929 conferring with his manager, mentor and friend Connie Mack (National Baseball Hall of Fame Library, Cooperstown, New York).

with a 71–81 mark. In 1925 their 88–64 second-place finish gave strong indication their stock was on the rise. An 83–67 mark in 1926, good for third place, did little to dissuade that thinking, particularly when they trailed the pennant-winning Yankees by only six games. As the fortunes of the team improved, so did attendance. In 1919 a league-worst 225,209 favored Shibe Park with their presence. By 1925 the club led the league in attendance with 869,703.

As the A's progressed through the early twenties, Connie Mack began to carefully assemble a powerhouse to rival his dynasty of the early teens. In 1922 the death of Benjamin Shibe, the original majority owner and president of the club, led to his son, Thomas, assuming the presidency. By now Mack was a half-owner of the club, and the younger Shibe showed sense in letting the more experienced man make the player moves necessary to once again make the club into a consistent winner. One thing Mack seemed to have in abundance was patience. He knew his task could not be completed overnight and, therefore, did not hurry the process.

In 1918 Mr. Mack picked up a feisty infielder from the Eastern League named Jimmy Dykes, who would reward his selection by staying on board for 13 productive seasons. A couple of years later in 1920, Mack plucked a 23-year-old pitcher from the International League. Right-hander Eddie Rommel would also stay with the A's for 13 years and win 171 games in the process. Although he peaked in 1922 when he went 27–13, he was still a steady force heading into 1927. Sammy Hale was added in late 1922 when he was purchased from Portland of the Pacific Coast League. In 1925 he hit .345 in 110 games. Six months after the Hale deal, in another transaction with Portland, George Elvin "Rube" Walberg came to Philadelphia. By 1927 he was 30 and just reaching his stride in a career that would produce 155 victories.

These acquisitions were just the beginning. In late 1923 Mack obtained a young boy of Polish ancestry, Al Simmons, from Milwaukee of the American Association. Although he showed he could hit the cover off the ball in the minors, many thought the Tall Tactician had made a mistake. Simmons had a habit of stepping into the "bucket," moving his left foot toward the dugout and away from the pitch with each swing. The writers were not enamored, but the pitchers who had to face him were most impressed. By 1927 "Bucketfoot Al" was a consistent top-ten hitter with power, well on his way to the Baseball Hall of Fame.

Mack knew that to return the A's to previous glory he needed an exceptional pitching staff. He took a major step in that regard in the fall of 1924 when he dug deep into his strong box and paid his old friend Jack Dunn of Baltimore just over $100,000 for Robert Moses Grove, better known as "Lefty." After a couple of years of seasoning, the strike-out specialist, who would finish his career with 2,266 whiffs, was ready for a breakout year in 1927. Another purchase from Jack Dunn's Orioles was Collins' competition at second base, Max Bishop, a fine fielder with a knack for getting a pass to first base.

Behind the plate was Mickey Cochrane, another acquisition by way of Portland in late 1924. Cochrane, a former football player for Boston University who brought a tough mentality with him to the ball diamond, immediately proved he could hit with a .331 average in 1925. Like many of the other newcomers, he was still in his early twenties and just coming into his own by the time Collins and Cobb arrived on the scene.

The greenest Mack find, but perhaps the one with the most potential, was 19-year-old Jimmie Foxx. Years of hard work on his father's Maryland dairy farm put him several steps ahead on the maturity curve. He would play sparingly in 1927 — much like Collins in 1908, a hitter still in search of a fielding position — but the talent and raw power were there. Frank "Home Run" Baker, who managed Foxx in the minors, had eventually recommended him to Mack but, perhaps because of their past differences, not before he offered him to the Yankees. Nonetheless, Miller Huggins passed and Mack added yet another important brick to his growing fortress.

To some degree each of the new players provided the spark that propelled the "new" A's up the ladder toward the top. Now with the addition of veterans Collins, Wheat and Cobb, Mack thought he had a chance to complete the climb to the top rung. Along for the ride were Eddie's old friend Kid Gleason, added to the A's coaching staff in 1926, as well as former team-mate Ira Thomas. If there was trouble still brewing between Collins and Thomas, it now remained buried well under the surface.

While Mack waxed poetic about his veteran superstars, there were others, including members of the press outside Philadelphia, who were skeptical. Jim Kaplan put the signing of Collins, Wheat and Cobb into perspective in his biography of Lefty Grove. "Violating his policy of building with youth, Mack signed ... a six-legged, one-hundred-and-sixteen-year old veteran with sixty-one years of experience."[7]

Of course, Mack knew Collins the best of the new crop. He realized that the veteran would report in good condition, and once even described his former star as a "young old man."[8] Collins made sure he could live up to his mentor's faith in his ability to hold down a regular spot by filling his off-season days at the Penn Athletic Club playing squash. It seemed to pay off. In early spring umpire-scribe Billy Evans noted he was "agreeably surprised" by Collins' conditioning. "He is cavorting around second base like a youngster.... He shows no ill effects of the leg injury that has troubled him for several years."[9]

Collins was in shape and scheduled to arrive at the A's camp in Fort Myers, Florida, on the last day of February. Even before his arrival Eddie had made at least one new friend on the A's team, joining Al Simmons for some squash before they departed south.

Ty Cobb was a different story. A notorious avoider of all things spring when it came to baseball — usually arriving in camp even later than Collins — the former Detroit star did not show up in Florida for another week. When he did put in an appearance, he joined Thomas Shibe, Mack, Collins and others for a drive to Venice, some 40 miles north, to celebrate John McGraw's twenty-fifth anniversary as the skipper of the Giants. One of the speakers at the banquet was John Ringling of circus fame. Connie Mack said a few words as well.

Once he arrived in camp, it did not take Ty Cobb long to stir up a fuss. On March 17, St. Patrick's Day, the A's were in St. Petersburg for a game with the National League's Boston Braves. The stands were packed. The largest crowd of the season was there to see Cobb play. In the fourth inning with the Athletics in front, Collins, who had been fielding well but hitting lightly all spring, stepped to the plate. Cobb was in the on-deck circle. There are several versions of the story, but the noted Yankee scout Paul Krichell was in attendance and provided his description.

When "Collins started up to the plate Cobb stopped him. 'Say, Eddie,' Cobb asked him, 'do you smell anything around here?' Ty looked at the plate umpire, a man by the name of [Franklin] Wilson. He hated Wilson.

"Well I guess Wilson hated Cobb, too, because he forfeited the game to the Braves."[10]

Collins was surprised, later telling reporters that Cobb had not used the type of language which usually results in an ejection. Apparently Ty's words, his look, and his reputation were enough justification for Wilson. A second game was immediately scheduled and played without Cobb.

In late March the A's first-liners began playing their way north. In a precursor of things to come, Mack put Collins in charge of the venture and traveled separately to Philadelphia.

After besting the Phillies, a last-place finisher in 1926, in their City Series by taking four out of five, the A's prepared to open on the road in New York. One surprise during the local face-off was the appearance of Collins in the lead-off position in the lineup. It was a major league first for the veteran but made good sense given his penchant for getting on base. He took the change in stride, slashing a home run and single in one game to break from his spring doldrums.

As the April 12 opener approached, optimism for the Athletics' pennant chances remained high. Veteran sports writer Jimmy Isaminger liked what he saw from Collins, particularly in the field. "If he has slipped, he slipped on a banana peel, his keystone chores don't show it."[11]

Unfortunately, as the season opened, someone forgot to tell the Yankees that the A's were the league's new powerhouse. Over four games the Yankees, whose 1927 club is generally considered the greatest in baseball history, won three, with one game ending in a 9–9 tie. Collins went hitless against the Yanks, finally getting a hit, his first as an A's player since 1914, when he doubled in an 8–7 win over the Senators on April 16. The A's returned home with a record of 3–4, ready to again meet the Yankees, this time in front of a home crowd on April 20. It turned out to be a fitting homecoming for Collins, and the 35,000 in attendance enjoyed it. Eddie hit the ball hard all four times at the plate, a pair of singles his reward. In addition, he combined with shortstop Joe Boley, a 30-year-old rookie, to record a strong day in the field. Between them they handled 16 chances flawlessly and turned a trio of double plays. The A's won, 8–5, one of their eight victories over the team now better known as "Murderer's Row."

By late April Collins sustained what was the first of several nagging injuries, pulling a leg muscle that required him to miss several games and to limit his appearances to pinch hitting. When he did reach base, he required a pinch runner. By the time Eddie celebrated his fortieth birthday on May 2 with a dinner in his honor in Lansdowne, he was living on borrowed time as an A's regular.

When Collins did play, he was swinging a good bat. He was in the lineup on May 5, stroking a single and double, as the A's fell to the Red Sox, 3–2, in a game loaded with controversy. In the eighth inning the Red Sox took a 3–2 lead on a two-run home run by Ira Flagstead, their center fielder. The A's thought they had countered in the bottom half of that inning when Ty Cobb lifted a long drive over the right field wall onto Twentieth Street. When the ball cleared the fence, it was fair, but umpire Emmett Ormsby declared that after it cleared the fence, the ball veered foul. Under a rule in effect until 1931, the ball was foul. The A's argued long and loud, but to no avail. When the smoke cleared Cobb and Al Simmons were ejected. Mack argued that the ball was fair and stayed fair, also to no avail. The game proved even more costly when Ban Johnson, back in office after his rehabilitation effort, suspended Cobb and Simmons for three days each. Simmons' loss was the more crucial as Cobb, like Collins, was fighting leg problems of his own.

Normally one to take the high road and avoid ugly confrontations, this time around Connie Mack refused to back down. Believing Cobb's ejection was due to a misunderstanding (Cobb claimed he accidentally bumped into Ormsby when he resumed his stance at the plate) and wanting the star reinstated in time for a special celebration in his honor on his first trip back to Detroit, Mack asked Ban Johnson for an open meeting. He wanted umpire Ormsby, Simmons and Cobb to tell their versions of the matter to the American League president. Johnson declined to meet, but in the end lifted the suspension. He did, however, fine each player $200 and took a verbal swing at Mack, one which the Tall Tactician would remember down the road.

On May 10 Cobb received his recognition from the Tigers' fans and contributed a double in a 6–3 A's win. The game saw another strong performance from Lefty Grove on his way to a 20–13 record and a 3.19 ERA.

When the A's reached Chicago on May 18, Collins was honored with a day of his own. At this point Eddie was back in the lineup and hitting the ball well. In an 8–6 loss to the Browns in St. Louis, he stroked a pair of hits, including a home run into the right field stands.

It was his only round-tripper of the season. He followed a day later with three hits, including a double, in a victory over the Browns. Eddie's fielding, on the other hand, was another story. In the victory he had been late to cover second base, allowing a run to score and narrowing the A's lead. An error in Cleveland a week or so earlier had been much more costly, allowing the winning runs to score in a 4–2 loss to the Tribe.

Once the team reached the Windy City, Collins' fielding woes were, at least temporarily, forgotten. Although a cold rain dampened the spirits of 12,000 fans, they still got to see what they came for in the first place. Prior to the contest, called off at the end of one inning, Eddie received a wristwatch and a Shriner's stickpin, studded in diamonds. These were gifts from the White Sox's players. One clever scribe offered that, given the weather, the former Pale Hose captain would have preferred a fur coat.

On May 30 the A's and Yankees met at Shibe Park for a pair of contests, one set for the morning and one for the afternoon. It was the Memorial Day weekend and two more games were scheduled with the Yankees for the next day, plus a single game for June 1. In 1925 Shibe Park was renovated to add upper decks to the bleacher sections. This added some 10,000 seats, raising the facility's capacity to 33,500. On May 30 approximately 40,000 fans jammed Shibe for each contest, sensing the importance of this early-season confrontation and yearning for a chance to see Babe Ruth, on pace to break his home run record of 59. In the first game the A's did not disappoint, winning, 9–8. In the second game the Babe did not disappoint either, breaking a tie in the eleventh with home run number 14.

The Babe may never have had a chance for his late-game heroics, but for a strange play that occurred in the fourth inning and later served as a final push in Ban Johnson's exit from baseball. At the time the A's trailed in the game 2–0, but with one out they threatened with Cobb at first and Collins on second. Then Al Simmons lofted a foul pop-up in the direction of the A's dugout. Yankee catcher Johnny Grabowski gave chase, catching the ball as he fell over the railing and into the dugout. Meanwhile, as Grabowski tried to regain his feet, both Collins and Cobb scored to tie the game. Miller Huggins, the Yankees' manager, ran out to protest, but chief umpire Roy Van Graflan ruled it a sacrifice fly and allowed both runs. When Huggins appealed to the other umpires Connelly and Rowland, a long meeting ensued. At the end the crew decided Collins could score but Cobb must return to third base, where he was eventually stranded. That run would have given the A's a one-run margin and might have led to a victory. Instead, the A's lost that game and the next three. The scores of the two losses on May 31 were 10–3 and 18–5. When the Yankees left town, the A's appeared a beaten team while the Yankees were well on their way to the pennant.

Once more the actions of an umpire crew raised the ire of Connie Mack. He was not the only one upset by umpire decisions that season. Thus, when he took his protest of the May 30 game to Ban Johnson for resolution, he found a receptive audience with the American League owners. They asked the league's board of directors to investigate the competency of the crew. A few days later the umpire's decision to send Cobb back to third base was upheld, but the real significance of this latest fracas was the decision by the board to decide the matter, not Ban Johnson. His power was once again diminished; the end was near.

The devastating losses to the Yankees over the Memorial Day weekend were not only collectively damaging to the Athletics as a team, but they also indirectly served to hasten the end of Eddie Collins' career as a regular. The defeats signaled to Connie Mack that this team was not capable of keeping pace with the pennant-bound Yankees. Under these circumstances it made little sense to continue to play Collins at second base. His back-up, Max Bishop, had proven his ability to get on base, as well as to run and field with some aplomb. Perhaps Collins would still out-hit Bishop, but on June 13 when Eddie suffered a finger injury and began missing games, the Tall Tactician took advantage and started easing Bishop into the lineup on a more regular basis. On June 21 Eddie started the second game of a double-bill versus Washington, but by July his appearances were few; his days as a regular were over.

"I went through the greater part of the [1927] season as second baseman, but I know now in early July Connie Mack had been forced to admit to himself that my days as a regular player were nearly over."[12]

Mack broke the news to Collins late in the season when he asked the veteran to step into his office. He began what was certainly a difficult task by extolling the virtues of third base coaching and bemoaning his lack of solid candidates for the position. As Connie stumbled along, looking for just the right words and not finding them, Eddie interrupted. He acknowledged he was slowing up and Max Bishop was more than ready at second base, informing his boss he would "gladly" step aside and "go on the line." Mack had been able to make his point without ever directly broaching the subject.

"We both laughed and the tension was snapped. It was Connie's way of not hurting my feelings."[13]

Although the occasion was probably not related to Mack's decision to go with Max Bishop, it still seemed timely and not a little appropriate that on July 13, 15,000 White Sox fans turned out at Comiskey Park to view yet another "Eddie Collins Day." This time the honoree's gift was too big to wrap. The band played "For He's a Jolly Good Fellow" as Eddie was presented with a brand new automobile. Collins, who started the game for the A's, went 2-for-4 with a walk before giving way to Bishop in the late going. The next day Mabel Collins arrived from Lansdowne by train, prepared to drive this latest prize home.

Collins was not the only old-timer facing reduced playing time. On July 8 Ban Johnson had announced his resignation as league president, effective November 1.

When the Tall Tactician decided mid-season that his team could not catch the Yankees, he was quite correct. Indeed, even though the A's finished the year in second with a sparkling 91–63 record, they still trailed the Yankees, who would sweep the Pittsburgh Pirates in the World Series in four straight, by a full 19 games.

By winning 91 games, Mack, at least, proved to many that he was on the right track. His young catcher, Mickey Cochrane, still learning behind the plate, had no problems standing next to it and swinging the lumber. He hit .338 with 12 homers, 80 RBIs and a .409 OBP. Dykes, who played first base for the most part, was not far behind at .324. The top batter on the team was Al Simmons, second in the league at .392, trailing only Detroiter Harry Heilmann's .398. Simmons' 15 home runs and 108 RBIs also topped the A's. Jimmie Foxx, who appeared in just 61 games, made a strong bid for more playing time by hitting .323. At second Max Bishop showed he would remain, appearing in 117 games, walking 105 times (third in the league) and batting .277.

The A's veterans gave a strong accounting, as well. Zack Wheat appeared in 88 games and batted .324 in what turned out to be his final season. Ty Cobb was much more. At age 40 he played in 134 games, batted 490 times, over twice as many as Collins, and hit .357 with an OBP of .440—both fifth-place league marks. And, despite his age, Cobb remained the same irascible soul he had always been. On September 21 he packed his bags and left for a hunting trip in Wyoming, even though nine games remained on the schedule. Mack could not have been happy. Speculation ran rampant that Cobb was through in baseball, certainly with the A's.

As for Collins, a quick look at the statistics did not show much of a downslide. In his 95 games he batted .336, and by walking 56 times, he boasted an OBP of .468. A telling sign, however, was his six stolen bases and his .965 fielding average (10 errors), his lowest since a similar mark in 1913.

Clearly, the 1927 Athletics, particularly veterans like Wheat, Cobb and Collins, were aided by the lively ball. The league average was .285, the Yankees leading with a .307 team average, the A's close behind at .303. At the same time the stolen base, on its way to designation as a "dead ball" anachronism, was becoming a rare phenomenon; George Sisler led the league with but 27.

Since everyone had players who could hit, for the A's to take that next step, they would need to do it through strengthened pitching. In 1927 Lefty Grove, who led the league in strikeouts at 174, pointed the way. Rube Walberg (16–12, 3.93) and at age 43 the remarkably well-preserved Jack Quinn (15–10, 3.26) were solid, but everyone wondered how much longer Quinn could last. This meant help was needed from 33-year-old righty Howard Ehmke (12–10, 4.22) and Eddie Rommel (11–3, 4.36).

Given Collins' lack of playing time near the end of the year, there was some speculation by those not privy to Mack's plan for his new third base coach that Collins would not return to the A's in 1928, at least as a player. Nonetheless, Mack started Collins in the last home game of the 1927 season. It was against the Red Sox, the second game of a double-header. Collins responded with a perfect 4-for-4 day, including a double in a 3–2 win. Eddie recognized he might not find the field too often anymore, but according to his boss he would get his chance as a pinch-hitter.[14]

Again a hunting trip to New Brunswick was the order of business in the fall for Collins and a number of his baseball buddies. The group included the usual suspects Shawkey and Bush, as well as Yankee shortstop Mark Koenig, Red Sox catcher Fred Hofmann, Sad Sam Jones of Washington and Yankee Benny Bengough. This year Collins, Bush and a pair of non-players received more excitement than they bargained for when their vehicle rolled over in New Brunswick. No one was injured, but the vehicle was so badly damaged it had to be shipped back to Philadelphia for repair. The mishap was soon forgotten, at least by Collins, who would not let a mere accident or even unusually heavy rains keep him from enjoying the thrill of downing a monster bull moose in those Canadian wilds.

For Collins 1927 ended much the same as 1926, his exact playing status muddled, at least to the public, and a number of teams eyeing him as a manager. This time around there were rumors of interest by the Boston Braves and Cleveland, where long-time Collins' admirer Billy Evans was the new business manager. But as he did before, and as he would do again in the future, Collins turned the efforts away. He was in Philadelphia to stay.

During the off-season one big-name player joined him. On February 5, 1928, Tris Speaker advised Connie Mack he would accept the A's offer and play in their outfield in 1928. Speaker had enjoyed a fine season at the plate in Washington the previous year, batting .327 and driving in 73 runs in 141 games. When Speaker's acquisition was announced, he and Collins were in New York attending the local sportswriters' banquet, joining others in attendance in a moment of silence for the death of former player and longstanding Tigers manager Hughie Jennings.

It was thought that Speaker's signing meant the certain end for Ty Cobb's association with the Athletics. However, on March 1 Mack announced the Peach would return to the fold and report to camp the following week. It was reported that Cobb and Speaker each received $30,000 in 1928. If so, the figure represented a large reduction for Cobb, but he was still making twice as much as Collins, who re-signed in early February, once again for $15,000—a figure he would continue to make until the end of his playing and coaching career.[15]

Despite this stable of star power, Mack's best off-season move probably was the acquisition of Edmund Bing Miller, the smooth-fielding outfielder the A's traded to the Browns in 1926, then reacquired in December 1927 for pitcher Sam Grey. Miller was a highly successful hitter who averaged .311 in a 16-year career. In 1928 he became a fixture in the A's outfield.

There were additional changes. Joe Hauser, a 29-year-old left-handed batter who last played for the A's in 1926, returned and was penciled in at first. George "Mule" Haas at 24 was added to the outfield. As the season progressed, he would play a greater role. And George Earnshaw, a right-hander, was added to the pitching rotation.

In late February Miller, Haas and several other players joined Collins for the train ride to Fort Myers for spring training. Collins, along with Gleason, Thomas and Mack's son, Earle, comprised the A's brain trust. As such, for the first time in his career, Collins would spend more time conditioning and training others than he would spend getting himself ready to play. He had already done a little bit of coaching the previous spring. Jimmie Foxx, about to enjoy a break-out season in 1928 because he learned out how to play the infield, credited Collins with making it all happen in 1927.

"Collins really developed me as an infielder!"[16]

In spring 1928 Collins did more of the same, playing sparingly when he managed the team in Mack's absences, as well as when the Tall Tactician preferred to play his younger play-ers.

Not training so intently meant Eddie had more time for recreation and he took advantage, joining Miller, Speaker and A's trainer Doc Ebling on an off-day for some fishing on the Caloosapatchee River. In mid–March, Mabel and Eddie Jr., now 11 and a fourth-grader at the Episcopal Academy, joined him. One day the Collins family accompanied Speaker and his wife, as well as Cobb, for a trip to an alligator farm. The Speakers were by now fast friends with Eddie and Mabel. On one occasion when the team headed by bus, the two couples hopped into Speaker's slick coupe and drove to the game separately.

At the end of March, Mack, as well as most of the wives and family members, traveled to Philadelphia ahead of the team. The Tall Tactician left Collins in charge of a group of players who would play their way north. Cobb, whose wife required surgery, did not travel north with the team, instead arriving in town as the City Series was in swing. The A's showed their obvious superiority by winning six of seven.

For the first time since 1909, Eddie Collins was not in a starting lineup when the A's opened their sea-

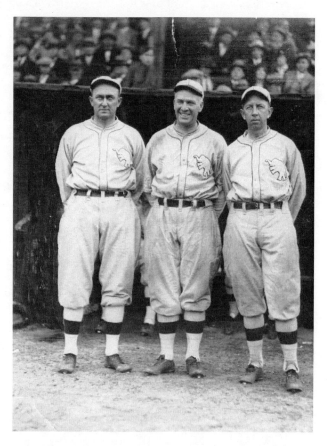

After years of fierce competition against each other, Collins (right), Tris Speaker (center), and Ty Cobb (left) played together for the 1928 Philadelphia A's. It was the last season for both Speaker and Cobb (Boston Public Library, Print Department).

son at home with an 8–3 loss to the Yankees on April 11. He made his first appearance in the second game, played April 13, also with the Yankees, and walked while pinch-hitting for short-stop Joe Boley in the eighth inning. This was now Eddie's role. He was a coach first, a pinch-hitter second, and only rarely [two late-inning appearances at second and one at shortstop] did he take the field. Notably, on May 17 against the White Sox, Collins was a late-inning substitute for Jimmy Dykes at shortstop. Ironically, while playing the position which almost prematurely ran him out of baseball, he recorded the final assist of his career. Now that the end of his regular playing days was near, Collins discussed the evolution of his new role in some detail.

In the first instance he was just happy to continue his association with his former manager and mentor. Over time he realized he was more than just a line coach. "I had become the adjutant of Connie Mack." On the morning of a game the pair met in Mack's office to confer, taking time to review the previous day's events. Then Eddie obtained the lineup for that afternoon's contest. Afterward he headed to the clubhouse to deliver the news to the players. "I had plenty to do; I was completely absorbed in my job."[17]

If down deep the constantly energized Collins found his new life dull, one could not tell it by public pronouncements like these.

"Coaching at third base was fun. Next to playing second it was just about the most exciting place in the world for me.... [A]s coach all my muscles were twitching and I had hard work to stay on the ground. If a runner was a tenth of a second slow in starting to steal, I swear I would ache from the mental effort of trying to get him under way with will power."[18]

All was not fun and games coaching for the A's, however. Even coaches came in for their share of criticism from a picky Philadelphia press, especially when the team was off to a relatively slow start as in 1928. By May 20 the club was 17–8, but the Yankees were much better. One of the losses on the A's ledger occurred on May 12 when the team lost a 3–1 decision to the Indians with Collins coaching at first base. Another was a loss to the White Sox. Collins' coaching was widely blamed for the loss. A few days later Isaminger of the *Inquirer* came to his defense in both instances.

> There has been a disposition lately to chide Eddie Collins for alleged faults in coaching runners while he was stationed at first base. In the Saturday game with Cleveland he was apparently made responsible for the defeat.
>
> Spectators also were inclined to blame him for the defeat at the hands of the White Sox Wednesday when he sent [Ossie] Orwoll to the plate. These are two concrete instances and are perhaps the only time Eddie has been adversely criticized for his coaching.
>
> But are the critics fair? This writer plainly says no. In neither case can Eddie be censured. The ball on which [Bing] Miller was sent home was a loose ball partly stopped by [Johnny] Hodapp that caromed foul. This kind of a hit is particularly hard to retrieve clean. It just happened that [Charlie] Jamieson, the Cleveland leftfielder, picked it up without a wobble and then unloosed one of the greatest throws of his career.
>
> Yet critics of Collins did not see the finish of Miller's run. Bing would have scored had he slid in time, but he was too late hook sliding into the plate. He was almost on top of the pentagon before he slid. Collins was right and Miller would have scored had he slid in time.[19]

Collins recaptured some of his luster on May 22 in a 7–6 win over the Senators when he batted for pitcher Howard Ehmke in the ninth and doubled to tie the game. He then stayed in the game at second and singled Sammy Hale home in the eleventh for the game winner. Two days later he participated in a bit of baseball history when he pinch-hit in the opener of a double-header with the Yankees at Shibe Park. A crowd of 42,000 packed every nook and cranny of the stadium to watch the two American League front runners in action. They saw each team win a game, but although they did not know it, they also saw a record 17 future members of the Baseball Hall of Fame take the field.[20]

A victory by the A's in game two of that May 24 double-bill with New York was one of the few highlights of the early portion of the A's season. The A's were expected to give the Yankees stiff competition, but an early-season scheduling quirk which saw the teams play 18 games before July 4, and the Yankees take 13 of them, was all the explanation needed for the A's 13-game deficit as they readied themselves for the July 4th holiday. The A's won both games against the Red Sox that day and stayed hot.

On September 7 they caught the Yanks. Their run to the top was fueled by great pitching from Lefty Grove, 24–8 on the season with an ERA of 2.58, as well as Rube Walberg (17–12, 3.55), Jack Quinn (18–7, 2.90) and reliever Eddie Rommel (13–5, 3.06). Sporting a five-game winning streak the team headed to New York for a crucial four-game series. By the time they reached the Big Apple, they actually led the defending world champions by one-half game.

Then, as so many times for the A's over the past two years, it all unraveled. Even a split of the series would preserve their lead, but it did not happen. They proceeded to lose both ends of the doubleheader played before a record 85,000 fans, then the single game two days later, before Howard Ehmke stopped the bleeding by besting Waite Hoyt by a 4–3 count on September 12. When the A's left town, they were one and one-half games behind, in second, a position they maintained the remainder of the year. Their 98–55 record sparkled, but not quite enough as they finished two and one-half games out of first to a Yankee team that dominated them in 16 of 22 games over the course of the season on their way to yet another world championship and four-game sweep — this time versus the St. Louis Cardinals.

Even as a coach, Collins competed until the end. In a game against the Browns, Al Simmons hit a long drive. The outfielder went after it, crashed into the wall, and fell in a heap. Players from both teams ran onto the field to help the injured player, but not Collins. He stayed in his coaching box at third, making sure Simmons stayed on target and scored. Later, rather coldly, he explained why.

"If that guy felt like being carried off the field that was his business. We had a ball game to win."[21]

Collins was still able to apply some of that same intensity to his plate appearances in 1928. In 36 games he batted 33 times. His 10 hits calculated into a .303 average. An additional four walks gave him an OBP of .378.

A number of A's batters had great years. The team's overall average was .295, second in the league. Al Simmons had another great year, hammering 15 homers, knocking in 107 runners and hitting .351. Bing Miller proved a good acquisition, driving in 85 runners and batting .329. Max Bishop, at second, had a terrific year hitting .316 and walking 97 times, third best in the league. Mickey Cochrane's numbers were down a bit (.293, 10, 57), but not the respect for his game. Named the league's Most Valuable Player in October, he learned about the award while on a two-week hunting trip with Collins and his hunting companions.

As for the A's other veteran stars, Speaker ended his career by appearing in only 64 games, batting .267 and driving home 30 runs. Cobb, on the other hand, played in more games (95) and batted .323, while still driving in 40. Even though it appeared he still had something to offer, he too ended his career, announcing on September 17 that after 24 illustrious seasons, he planned to retire at season's end.

Given the retirement of Speaker and Cobb, as well as Collins' continuing transition into a full-time coach, Connie Mack was about to turn his team's fortunes over almost entirely to his "young pups," including the ever more impressive Jimmie Foxx (.327, 13, 79).

In 1928 the A's had dominated every team in the American League, save the Yankees. The cast of characters and opponents might be different, but Mack had been here before. In 1909 his young but improving team was 95–58 and finished second, just over three games from the top. Even attendance figures during those two years, in each case just under 700,000 fans, were remarkably similar. Over the next five years, his 1909 team had dominated the league and for three of those years, all of baseball. Could lightning strike twice?

CHAPTER 19

On the Line

"[Collins] is a sort of assistant manager, although he will tell you himself that the A's
have only one boss, Connie Mack, and no secondary managers....
"He [Collins] is a steadying character like an old sergeant, neither hysterical nor bored."
— Writer Westbrook Pegler[1]

Illness and loss struck Eddie Collins at the same time in early 1929. As he battled the flu
in mid–January, he learned of the death of his father John. At age 90 the elder Collins died
of pneumonia, which affected a heart condition. He had been ill for 10 days, but perhaps owing
to his own illness, Eddie was still in Philadelphia when his father died, arriving grief stricken
late the same day.

At the time of his death, John Collins was the oldest man in point of service in Tarrytown, still employed in his thirtieth year as registrar of the village's Board of Water Commissioners. There were those who blamed his death on his devotion to duty since the elder Collins
refused to miss work despite suffering from the severe cold or flu, which ultimately led to his
death. Only two years earlier there was an attempt to remove him from his registrar's position, but the community rallied to his side. At his death the local newspaper claimed Tarrytown had lost "its grand old man."[2]

The loss of Collins' father seemed only to strengthen Eddie's bond with Connie Mack,
a man who had served as a second father ever since the pair first met almost a quarter of a
century before. As the 1929 season progressed from spring training to regular season, it became
more and more apparent that Eddie was Mack's right-hand man and choice for his successor
as manager of the A's. Of course, it was a job without an opening. And, for the time being,
Eddie still had plans for a few more home plate appearances.

For a few days in early spring 1929, while Max Bishop staged a brief holdout, it looked
like Collins might even still play some second base. But Bishop arrived and Collins resumed
his role of easing Mack's managerial burdens in Fort Myers, allowing the Tall Tactician to
work with the youngsters and plan the strategies necessary to bring the Athletics their first
pennant in 15 years. During the off-season Mack had decided that his baseball machine needed
few parts, requiring only minor adjustments to the engine he already owned. He did purchase
outfielder Homer Summa from the Indians and later, in early season, let first baseman Joe
Hauser, who hit .260 in 1928 including 16 homers in 95 games, go to the Tribe on waivers.
That move permitted Mack to insert Jimmie Foxx at first base — in 1928 he played 30 games
at first and 60 at third — and use Jimmy Dykes more frequently at third and short. Both players enjoyed fine, and in Foxx's case spectacular, seasons.

In the spring Collins, now the veritable "old man" of active players with the retirement
of Cobb and Speaker, prepared for essentially the same role he had played for the A's in 1928.

255

"I'll be an active player this year, ready to swing a bat in a pinch and fill in on the infield if Connie needs me for an occasional inning or two. I want to do enough playing this year to get my name in the records."[3]

Collins did not consider the role of a pinch-hitter a particularly easy one, once telling a reporter he found it "harder than playing every day" and reminding his listener that the pinch-hitter is used "in an emergency and it usually is a very important part of the game."[4] However, in spring training 1929, he shredded his own theory and made it look easy, at one point stroking hits in five consecutive at-bats, several as a pinch-hitter. Indeed, by early April it looked like the A's and Collins were both ready for another fine season.

It was that and more. The key was team chemistry. By keeping the bulk of his roster intact, as well as his veteran coaching staff, the Athletics of 1929 came out of the starting gate strong and only got better. On April 17 the A's opened in Washington, winning 13–4, before a crowd that included presidential ball-tosser Herbert Hoover. Foxx hit the first of his 33 home runs. The Senators turned the tables when the A's opened at Shibe, its grandstand capacity expanded by 3,500. The Senators won, 4–3, but it made little difference in the overall picture. During April and early May, the A's flitted in and out of first, then beginning May 17 with a 4–1 win in Washington, won 11 straight, took a firm grasp of first place, and never looked back. Unlike the previous season, when the Yankees dominated almost every meeting, this time around the Athletics took the season series 14–8. The closest any league opponent came to playing the A's even was St. Louis, which won 10 of 21 decisions with one tie.

The success of the team probably limited Collins' opportunities. During the year he turned 42; he simply was not needed all that much. He appeared in but nine games, with seven official at-bats and no hits for his efforts. He did reach base twice on passes. He did, however, prove his worth in the coaching box and in the clubhouse, where he remained team captain. One of Collins' jobs was to keep the troops loose. Jimmy Dykes, a great storyteller, liked to tell a tale on Collins and his pal Kid Gleason.

> There was an air of dignity and propriety about Collins which was often mistaken for aloofness. To many it seemed that one of his closest friends was ... Kid Gleason, one of baseball's fabulous characters and as rough, tough and kind-hearted a man as ever came into the game.
>
> Oh, that Gleason was tough.... Everybody was afraid of him. He'd do anything to you that came into his mind if you got fresh with him. I remember one day in the A's clubhouse Collins threw something at him and hit him and then he hid in his locker and pulled the door closed. Gleason saw who threw it, walked up to the locker, turned the key, took it out and put it in his pocket.
>
> It must have been two minutes later, when we were on the bench almost at game time, Connie looked down the dugout and said, "Where's Eddie? We're ready to go." Collins was the captain and had to take out the lineup to the umpires.
>
> Gleason almost fell off the bench. He'd forgotten about locking Collins in the locker. He rushed to the clubhouse and let him out.[5]

There was good reason for a relaxed atmosphere. Near the end of July, the A's held an eight-game lead over the Yankees in the loss column and another 10 over the third-place Browns. In mid–August the A's left Philadelphia on a 17-game road trip, the last extended one of the season. One player who did not make the trip was A's hurler Howard Ehmke. There was much speculation that the veteran right-hander, who would finish the year with eight starts, the lowest of the regular starters, was in Mack's doghouse and, perhaps, finished as a pitcher. Other rumors floated around that a number of the players on the team were bothered by Ehmke's presence and did not want him around. If the latter were actually the case, these and other observers asked who was running the team, Mack or his players?

According to Connie Mack's biographer Fred Lieb, the Tall Tactician had something else in mind, but only after some convincing fast talk on Ehmke's part. Mack had indeed intended to let the veteran go, but after conferring with his pitcher he was convinced Ehmke had the proper mental framework, as well as enough life left in his arm, to win a big game. Realizing that his team was headed for a pennant, even though he continued to publicly state otherwise, Mack told Ehmke to stay home, study the potential National League opponents New York and Chicago, and make ready to pitch the first game of the World Series.[6]

Ehmke started but one more game, a 5–2 win over the White Sox at Shibe on September 13. Meanwhile the rest of the A's continued to win, clinching the American League pennant one day later on September 14, behind a 5–0 shutout by George Earnshaw.

On September 18 Collins was honored at Shibe in celebration of the anniversary of his twenty-third year in the major leagues. A week later on September 25, just a few days before the season ended, the baseball world was saddened by the death of Yankee manager Miller Huggins at age 49. Even Babe Ruth, a frequent thorn in the side of this highly successful skipper, was overcome with grief.

Fittingly, the A's ended their 1929 season in New York with a pair of games against the Yankees. The A's won both contests to end their season at 104–46, breaking the previous franchise record held by the 1910 A's, who won 102. These last wins left the Yankees in second, a full 18 games off the pace.

One need not look too far to find the players responsible for the A's record-setting success. Of particular note were the hitting performances of Jimmie Foxx and Al Simmons. At age 21 Foxx finished the season batting .354, with 33 home runs and 118 RBIs. Simmons did even better, hitting .365 with 34 homers and a league-leading 157 RBIs. Cochrane (.331, 7, 95), Miller (.331, 8, 93), outfielder Mule Haas (.313, 16, 82) and Dykes (.327, 13, 79) were splendid as well. Max Bishop fell off, batting only .232, but he walked 128 times, a league high.

On the mound Lefty Grove dominated. He won 20, lost but six and maintained a sparkling 2.81 ERA. He also led the league in strikeouts for the fifth consecutive year. Walberg was solid as well (18–11, 3.60) and, working for the most part out of the bullpen, Eddie Rommel was once again impressive (12–2, 2.85). The most pleasant surprise, however, was George Earnshaw. The righty led the league in wins, finishing 24–8, while holding opponents to 3.29 earned runs per game.

By mid–September it was obvious the A's opponent in the World Series would be the Chicago Cubs, led by crafty manager Joe McCarthy and their big guns, second baseman Rogers Hornsby and a power-laden outfield of Hack Wilson, Riggs Stephenson and Kiki Cuyler. Their top pitchers were Charley Root, Pat Malone and Guy Bush.

As the date approached for the opener in Chicago on October 8, most knowledgeable observers expected Mack to choose from Grove or Earnshaw to open the post-season festivities. Even when word leaked that the well-rested Howard Ehmke was the Tall Tactician's choice, most everyone thought it was merely a weak effort to conceal the more obvious choices. Nevertheless, Mack held his cards close to his vest and stuck with the choice he had quietly made almost two months prior. Only one other person knew for sure — Eddie Collins. Mack told Eddie that by starting Ehmke instead of one of his regular trio of starters, they gained "a psychological advantage."[7] Just think how the Cubs would feel if they could not even best the A's number four starter.

By going with Ehmke, Mack risked a lot. When the veteran began warming up, the natives, in this case the A's players, were restless. Some thought the aging Tall Tactician had completely lost his mind. By game's end, however, there were few on his team, or anywhere else for that matter, who doubted his genius. Ehmke not only pitched a complete game eight-hitter and was the winning pitcher in a 3–1 victory, which also featured a Jimmie Foxx homer, but he also set a new World Series record by striking out 13 Cubs. In so doing, he gave Mack his greatest day in baseball and set the tone for the A's, who went on to take the World Series in five games, including a dramatic 10–8 win in Game Four when they scored all 10 runs in the seventh inning to erase an 8–0 deficit.

Now the A's of Connie Mack were once again the bluest of blue-chip stocks and the toast of Philadelphia and the baseball world. As Mack knew they would, the fans responded. Over 839,000 jammed Shibe Park in 1929, 150,000 more than in 1928.

As this great team, who some believe rivals the 1927 Yankees as baseball's all-time best, and their legions of fans celebrated the A's return to glory, few, if any, were aware that the nation was teetering on the brink of economic chaos. On October 24, just 10 days after a large Philadelphia crowd, which included President Herbert Hoover, watched Bing Miller drive in Al Simmons for the ninth-inning game-winner in a 3–2 final victory, the stock market experienced what is now known as "Black Tuesday" and crashed, sending the country into the Great Depression.

But now, as the year ended, there was widespread speculation the A's were about to lose a third-base coach. After Miller Huggins' death, his place was taken by interim manager Art Fletcher, the long-time Giants shortstop, unsuccessful Phillies manager, and Huggins' assistant manager and Yankees coach since 1927. There was little doubt Fletcher would be a serious candidate to replace Huggins. Others in the mix might be Babe Ruth or even Donie Bush, the preferred choice of the Yanks' business manager Ed Barrow. To Barrow's chagrin, Bush had just inked a two-year deal to manage the White Sox.

Under these circumstances then, there is little doubt that the leading candidate for the Yankees' post became Eddie Collins. Only in later years would he confirm it since at the time he agreed with the Yankees' ownership to keep it quiet. When he finally spoke about it, Collins admitted that, indeed, an offer was made by Colonel Ruppert during the winter of 1929. The Colonel wanted Eddie to visit him at his New York City apartment, telling the A's coach he had a business proposition that might be of interest.

To say there "might be interest" was an understatement. Certainly the managerial post of the Yankees had been a dream of Collins for many years. While there is some question whether or not Eddie ever made the trip to Ruppert's apartment, there is no doubt he received a lucrative offer from the Yankees, which he surprisingly turned down.

"I declined because I had been assured by both Connie Mack and the Shibes, John, then president of the A's, and Tom, the secretary of the club, that I would become the manager of the Athletics when Connie Mack decided to call it a day."[8]

In late 1929, however, Connie Mack, even at 67, was not ready to "call it a day." His latest edition of the Mackmen had only just arrived. Furthermore, Mack, along with others like Mickey Cochrane, had invested heavily in the stock market and he was taking a bath. If Collins seriously thought his friend and mentor was about to turn over the reins to him anytime soon, he was sorely mistaken. Unlike Collins, who apparently felt financially secure enough to reject Ruppert's offer of big money, Mr. Mack still needed to work.

In truth, the marriage between Mack and Collins was a good one. Eddie was in his glory, part of a highly successful baseball franchise and working close to home, near family, friends and church. His time would surely come, but it need not be anytime soon.

By November Collins literally had bigger game on his mind, in the form of a 500-pound bear. As his hunting group looked on, swelled by teammates Bing Miller and George Earnshaw but minus Bob Shawkey, who had recently accepted an offer to manage the Yankees, Eddie's shot brought the animal down, believed the largest kill in that area in years.

Given his team's success in 1929, there was not much for the Tall Tactician to do per-sonnel-wise to prepare for a 1930 season in which most experts predicted a return to the World Series. One change of note occurred on December 11, 1929, when Sammy Hale, certainly a respectable player that year in hitting .277 in 101 games, was traded to the Browns for catcher Wally Schang. The former A's catcher was now at the tail end of a fine career, but he still wielded a decent bat and would provide Mack with some back-up insurance behind the plate. Jimmy Dykes was now the A's regular third sacker; Foxx, entrenched at first. Another addi-tion was Dib Williams, a 20-year-old infield prospect brought in to back up Max Bishop.

When the A's arrived in Fort Myers in spring 1930 to begin preparations for the new year, they did not play at all like the group that ended the previous season on such a high note. They lost frequently in the early going; then in late March they lost six in a row. Their record against major-league competition was a disturbing 6–9. One reason for the poor start was the absence of Al Simmons. Although early reports indicated he was a hold-out, he was actually in Hot Springs, Arkansas, taking treatment for rheumatism in his ankles.

Confirming his diminishing status as an active player, Collins did not appear in any of that year's spring games. Eddie's playing status for the upcoming year was on Mack's mind and still up in the air in late March. Mack's plan at that point was to list Collins "as a player and in a pinch I can take his name off [the roster] to keep another youngster, but that is just a thought and nothing definite has been done about that."[9]

Collins was still available in April when the A's met the Phillies for another chapter in their now lengthy City Series. Although the A's won the opener in convincing fashion, 13–1, they ended up losing the series by a 5–3 count, raising further questions about their chances to repeat.

By 1930 money was becoming an increasingly important issue. People across the board were feeling the pinch from shrinking investment accounts, as well as losing saving accounts that were lodged in failed banks. Suddenly the gate receipts from exhibition games the big league teams played on off-days took on added significance. Collins' quick thinking saved one such gate receipt, a significant one at that for the A's ownership.

On Sunday April 6, while the A's and Phillies delayed their series in order to comply with the continuing restrictions on Sunday baseball, the A's traveled to Newark, New Jersey, for an exhibition game with the city's local minor league club. During batting practice the A's lost some three dozen baseballs as customers, particularly those in the bleachers, ran onto the field and grabbed them. Collins was conducting batting practice. He looked into his bag, saw he was down to one ball and immediately ended the drill. As a result, the game started ten minutes earlier than scheduled. A crowd of 12,000 was in attendance, despite threaten-ing weather. Because of the early start, by the time the bad weather necessitated calling the game, the teams were already through six innings. Since it was an official game, no refunds were necessary. Had the game started at the usual time, the fans were due a refund, one the A's could ill afford.[10]

The Athletics opened at home on April 15 with a 6–2 win over the Yankees. Lefty Grove gave notice that he and his team were ready to defend their title, although they did continue to exhibit less than championship form at times during the early portion of the season.

On May 11 in Cleveland in one of those lackluster performances, Mack inserted Collins to bat for Wally Schang in the late innings of a 25–7 pasting at the hands of the Indians. The game was out of reach and the veteran's appearance meant nothing to the outcome of the game, but it did bear significance for Eddie. The at-bat, which resulted in a ninth-inning out, marked the twenty-fifth consecutive year Collins had appeared in a major-league game, breaking Ty Cobb's American League and "modern-day" record of 24 and tying Bobby Wallace's record of 25, set from 1894–1918 with Cleveland of the National League as well as with the St. Louis teams in both the National and American leagues. Still Cap Anson, who played 22 consecutive years with the Cubs from 1876–1897, could claim the overall record of 27 if one added in his five seasons from 1871–1875 in the National Association. Nonetheless, it was a significant accomplishment for Collins.

In late May Mack became sick. Although Gleason held more seniority, Collins took over the team. Under his tutelage the A's endured a double defeat right out of the box at the hands of the Yankees in New York on May 24, then won the next four in a row and were in the midst of a season-high 10-game winning streak when a healthy Mack returned on May 30.

By the July 4 mid-season marker, the A's were alive and well in first place with a record of 49–26. For Collins the renewed success meant he was still on the active roster, a survivor of the annual June 15 reduction required for teams to meet the 25-player restriction. On August 2 in the seventh inning of the second game of two with the Red Sox at Shibe, Mack scanned the bench and found it wanting, then called Collins in from third to bat for the age-less pitcher Jack Quinn. It had been over a year since Eddie had hit safely in a game that counted. This time he was up to the task, bouncing a single off the leg of Red Sox starter Danny MacFayden. Dykes was on first at the time. Instead of sending in a runner, Eddie remained in the game. Mule Haas, in the midst of another solid season as an A's outfielder, followed a foul ball out with a double, scoring Dykes, and sending Collins, on unfamiliar legs, to third. Then the ever-reliable Mickey Cochrane stepped to the plate and sliced a sin-gle to center, scoring Collins and Haas. The runs aided an 8–7 win and gave the A's a sweep. It was for Eddie Collins the final hit and last run scored of his major-league career.

Three days later Mack went to the well one more time, calling Collins in to bat for short-stop Joe Boley in the bottom of the ninth at Shibe as the A's trailed the Red Sox, 4–3. This time Eddie did not come through. The ninth-inning appearance and out represented the final trip to the plate of his lengthy record-setting baseball career. His numbers for 1930 were three games, three at-bats, one hit and one run.[11]

In 1930 in a reversal of form, the Yankees were not the A's chief rivals. They were still a strong team, finishing the season at 86–68, but the Washington Senators played much bet-ter, actually taking the season series from the A's by winning 12 of their 22 contests.

One of the A's wins that season was at Griffith Stadium on July 31. Collins, however, was not on hand to direct traffic at third base. For only the third time since 1907, he was nei-ther in uniform nor on his team's bench. The first time was in 1908 when he was ill and arrived in Philadelphia after the season was well under way. The next time was in 1911 when Mack excused several of his starters from a road trip to Washington to rest them for the World Series. Now he was absent due to the death of his mother-in-law, Mrs. Charles P. Doane. Mabel's mother became ill several days earlier while Mabel was traveling with her husband and the team on their current road trip. Mabel, an only child, returned to Philadelphia immediately and was with her mother at the time of death. Now Collins traveled back to Philadelphia to attend the funeral.

Collins rejoined the team shortly, but on August 21, just three weeks later, he was miss-ing in action once again. This time it was reported he was confined at home due to a bout with the "grippe." In his absence pitcher Eddie Rommel, who sometimes coached at first, took over at third.

Initial reports concerning Collins' illness indicated he was running a high temperature. He planned to rest and return in short order. The prescription seemed to work. By August 25 he was in the stands in Shibe Park as the team lost a 3–2 bout with the Senators. The plan was for Eddie to remain off the field a couple more days, returning to the coaching box when the team arrived in Boston three days hence. But true to form, he could not wait. On August 26 he was back on the field as the A's returned a favor, topping the Senators in an exciting brawl, 10–9. The change of plans backfired. The excitement of all those A's runners passing by on their way to the plate may have proven too much. On August 29 the *Inquirer* reported that Collins was in Boston and quite ill again with a temperature of 101 and a physician arranged by Connie Mack in attendance. The A's captain and coach had arrived in Boston in advance of the team, accompanied by Mabel. He was now in bed at the Brunswick Hotel.[12]

As soon as Eddie was better, Mabel, still grieving the loss of her mother, wanted to take her sick husband to her parent's summer cottage in New London, Connecticut. After the season he would have his tonsils, the suspected culprit, removed. Fortunately for the Collins' family, Paul and Eddie Jr. were in school and Mabel was able to stay and care for Eddie. By this time oldest son Paul was a student at Dartmouth College and young Eddie Jr. a student at the Episcopal Academy in Philadelphia. On the last day of August, Collins felt well enough to travel and the couple left for New London. Several days in Connecticut did the trick. On September 7 the A's had their third-base coach back, although it did not change their fortunes as they went down to the Senators and Sad Sam Jones, 7–6.

Right after the game Collins headed for Boston to participate in one of the first of many all-star games he would attend over the coming years. This one was particularly special. Played on September 8 before 30,000 fans at Braves Field, this benefit for the local Children's Hospital saw the reunion of the "$100,000 infield." Collins did not miss a step, however. The next day he was in the coaching box in Detroit as Lefty Grove won another of his 28 victories, 3–1.

Although the 1930 A's did not soar quite as high as their 1929 version, they still won frequently enough to secure another American League pennant. The clincher came in Chicago on September 18 when a five-run comeback in the seventh inning gave them an eight and one-half game lead over the Senators with seven games to play. When the season ended with a 9–4 loss to those same Senators on September 28, the A's record stood at 102–52, only two fewer than the previous season. Washington was eight games back while the Yankees were a full 16 rungs off the pace.

Remarkably, although the economy was shrinking, attendance at baseball games was not. A record number of fans attended games in 1930. The A's continued to draw well by attracting 721,663 to Shibe Park. Nevertheless, the number was over 100,000 shy of the 1929 total, giving new support to Mack's theory that the team's fans quickly became bored with a winner.

While the A's salted away their second straight pennant in convincing fashion, across the aisle the National League race was much tighter. When the dust settled, the surprising St. Louis Cardinals, fourth-place finishers the previous season, were the winners with a 92–62 mark. Chicago played well in defense of their title in finishing only two back while the Giants were five in arrears. Even Brooklyn was in the hunt, just one game back of the Giants, thus only six behind the winners.

The Cardinals, clearly a franchise on the upswing, were powered by their flashy second baseman Frankie Frisch. The Fordham Flash, who cut his teeth for McGraw's Giants, was in the prime of his Hall-of-Fame career, batting .346 and knocking in 114 runs. The team's power hitter was outfielder Chick Hafey. The 27-year-old right-handed hitter fashioned 26 homers, drove in 107 runs and batted .336. In fact, the entire Cardinals' lineup hit above .300 in 1930, only good enough for third in the league in a season where the lively ball became even livelier. The National League average for the season was .304, while the American League, normally more hit-happy, was still high enough at .288.

On paper, as well as on the field, the Cardinals presented a worthy opponent, but the defending world champions were no slouches themselves. Al Simmons was still improving. He led the league in batting at .381, hit 36 homers and finished with 165 RBIs. Jimmie Foxx, playing 153 games at first base, had another remarkable season. Still only 22, he hit .335, clobbered 37 homers and pushed Simmons for team RBI honors with 156. Cochrane followed up his MVP season by hitting .357 and driving in 85. Even Bing Miller drove in 100 runners. And Max Bishop, whose average increased from .232 to .252, once again worked pitchers for 128 walks, second in the league. His .426 OBP, fourth in the league, showed he was doing the job at lead-off.

On the mound Lefty Grove was almost unstoppable, winning pitching's triple crown by leading the league in wins (28–5), won-loss percentage (.848), ERA (2.54), and strikeouts (209). Although statistics for saves were not kept at the time, later research showed he had nine to also lead the league. Still he was not the A's only option. George Earnshaw (22–13, 4.44) showed he was one of the league's best, and 26-year-old Bill Shores (12–4, 4.19) and veteran Rube Walberg (13–12, 4.69) filled out the starting rotation. Jack Quinn, now 46, was becoming increasingly vulnerable but still fashioned a 9–7 season, working more and more in relief. Rommel again was strong out of the bullpen and was 9–4, 4.28.

On October 1 President Hoover, his popularity dwindling even faster than people's bank accounts, joined 32,000 others at Shibe Park for the opening round of the 1930 World Series. This time Howard Ehmke did not make a surprise start. He had pitched only three games during the season. Instead Grove, who was used in relief in the 1929 series, was Mack's logical choice to initiate the proceedings. Although the A's had difficulties solving the offerings of the last of the spitballers Burleigh Grimes, they scored five times on five hits. Grove gave up more hits (9) but less runs [2] and the A's were a winner, 5–2. As he had all year, George Earnshaw gave the A's the second half of their one-two punch and the A's won Game Two, 6–1. For the second day in a row, Cochrane homered.

If the A's and their fans thought the Cardinals, down two, would now fold, they were wrong. The next two games were played in St. Louis where the Cardinals won both. In Game Three left-hander Wild Bill Hallahan shut out the A's, 5–0, beating Rube Walberg. In Game Four Mack came back with Grove, who pitched a five-hitter, but it was not enough. Veteran Jess Haines pitched a four-hitter and the A's succumbed, 3–1. In analyzing the series through four games, it was clear the Athletics' pitching staff was doing its job, but the A's hitters were struggling.

On October 6 the two teams, now viewed as well-matched, met again in St. Louis for a pivotal Game Five. Once again the pitching on both sides was superb. Earnshaw threw two-hit baseball through seven innings when he was lifted for a pinch-hitter. Against the equally brilliant Grimes, the A's, however, could not score and the game remained scoreless. Then in the A's ninth, lightning struck in the form of a two-run home run into the left field bleachers by Jimmie Foxx. Grove, who had come back in relief in the eighth, shut the door. The A's were now up three games to two.

The dramatic Foxx home run broke the Cardinals' back. The A's, behind Earnshaw's third start, won 7–1 on October 8 to the delight of a large hometown crowd. Once again the A's were winners of back-to-back world titles.

In the aftermath Connie Mack waxed poetic about his many star players, but he also took a moment to pay tribute to his team captain and "able lieutenant, who has been a source of encouragement and inspiration to my players, throughout the playing season and the World's Series and who was a big factor in our double success of the year."[13]

The A's victory earned each eligible player, including Collins, a check for $5,037. It was

Collins and his hunting group pose for a picture with the Canadian Legion softball team of Fredericton, New Brunswick (back row). In front (left to right) are Tris Speaker, Mickey Cochrane, Cy Perkins (A's), Bob Shawkey (Yankees), Doug Black (New Brunswick official in charge of the trip), Collins, John Kracke (New Yorker, affiliation unknown), Harry Rice (Tigers), and Benny Bengough (Yankees). The photograph was taken in November 1930, shortly after a softball game won by the major leaguers, 9–6 (Photo Collection, Cleveland Public Library).

big money in a Depression year, though less than their 1929 share of $5,620. In the case of Collins, it was particularly good money inasmuch as he did not appear as a player in either series. But he probably picked up a few additional dollars from the 1930 World Series, as the post-season event marked his return as a sports scribe, this time covering the event for the *Philadelphia Evening Bulletin*. The extra money from the series and the newspaper came in handy since Collins, Cochrane, catcher Cy Perkins and Tris Speaker took their wives with them on their annual Canadian hunting expedition, a venture marred by poor weather and meager results. The highlight was the celebration of the twentieth wedding anniversary of Mr. and Mrs. Eddie Collins.

The onset of the 1931 season once again saw few changes in the makeup of the A's. Wally Schang and Cy Perkins were gone from the catching corps. Johnnie Heving, age 35, was picked up from the Red Sox on waivers to replace them. Back-up first baseman Phil Todt came over from the Red Sox as well. Later in the year Waite Hoyt, now with the Tigers and still sailing along at 31, was purchased to fill the slot of the departed Jack Quinn. The core, however, remained intact.

The same could not be said for the baseball. During the off-season it was decided by major league moguls that the hitting spree by players from both leagues in 1930 was not in the best interests of the game. In preparation for the 1931 season, a less lively ball was introduced. Collins was aware of the changes to the sphere, but in an interview with *Baseball Magazine*, expressed doubts about the ultimate result, taking the opportunity to air his feelings about the advent of the hitter's game.

> As for the new ball, I have examined it very carefully and can detect a definite change. The seams do stand out more prominently and the cover is no doubt thicker, as the manufacturers declare. The raised seams may increase the break of the ball as the pitcher delivers it to the batter, and the heavier cover may, quite likely, prolong the life of the ball and thus avoid the too frequent introduction of a brand new ball into play, always an irritation to a pitcher.
>
> But admitting these things, it is my opinion that the influence of the new ball will be more psychological than otherwise....
>
> I might go further and say that to my way of thinking the much condemned lively ball never played quite the prominent role it was accused of playing in the upset balance of power between pitching and batting. At best it was only one of a number of factors that served to usher in the so-called slugging era.
>
> The bat as much as the ball, was responsible for this era....
>
> A livelier ball, a lighter bat and a hardier swing have all combined to change the game as a whole and to change it decidedly at various positions....
>
> No doubt I was fortunate in entering baseball when I did. The old style was better suited to my talents, such as they were and my limitations. The lively ball would not have helped me much, if any, for I was never a slugger. But with all my prejudices of a former day, I'll bow to the general consensus of opinion and admit that the modern game is the greatest ever.[14]

In 1931 the A's played spring ball without the services of Al Simmons and George Earnshaw, who were both at Hot Springs and unsigned, until April 9. By then the baseball world, in particular the American League, reeled from the deaths of both Ban Johnson and his replacement, former Cleveland executive E.S. Barnard. The advent of Barnard had introduced much smoother sailing between the American League and the Office of the Commissioner. By an almost eerie coincidence, Johnson and Barnard died in late March within a 24-hour period. Barnard was eventually replaced by William Harridge, a former ticket agent for the railroads who served as the long-time private secretary to Ban Johnson and then as the official league secretary under Barnard.

On April 14 the A's opened their regular season right where they finished the previous one — at Griffith Stadium. The final score this time was different, however, as the A's bested another fine Senators team, 5–3. Prior to the game Eddie Collins, dressed in his new grey A's uniform and oxford blue cap, performed his usual function, carrying Mack's lineup to the plate and discussing the ground rules with the three-man umpire crew and, in this case, Washington's fine first baseman, Joe Judge. Nevertheless, something was different. For the first time in his baseball career, a number appeared on Eddie's uniform, as well as on the uniform of each A's player. Captain Collins wore number 31. The number "1" was reserved for the Tall Tactician but not used since he still dressed in business attire.

The idea of a numbering system, long advocated and long resisted, was briefly used by the St. Louis Cardinals in 1924 and 1925. Previously, on June 26, 1916, the Cleveland Indians wore numbers on their sleeves in a game, but they proved too small to read and the practice was soon abandoned. In 1929 the Yankees announced that their players would wear numbers on the backs of both their home and road uniforms, but the Indians beat them to the punch that year by affixing numbers to their home uniforms and playing a game on April 6, prior to the Yankees, whose own first game was rained out.[15] In 1931 the league required all teams to place numbers on players' uniforms. The A's plans for 1931, nevertheless, called for numbers on road uniforms only.

The A's home opener was a success as Lefty Grove stopped the Senators, 5–1. Grove at 31 was the real story in 1931, both on and off the field, winning eight in a row in the early going, only to see the streak stopped by a relief appearance in early June when he allowed a run in the eleventh inning and took a loss. After the game an enraged Grove drove home to Maryland and stayed for five days. Then he returned and picked up where he left off before the unsuccessful relief appearance.

In the meantime on June 10, an off-day, with the A's having overcome a relatively slow start to now rest comfortably in first place at 35–11, it was announced that Captain Eddie Collins was removed from the team's active roster. Although still a third base coach and the team captain, his long and illustrious career was over. The decision made total sense. Eddie had yet to appear in a game almost two months into the season and the move allowed the A's to meet the June 15 25-player limit. As the *Inquirer* aptly put it, "to all intents and purposes Collins has been retired as a player since 1929."[16]

Although a great deal of the true legacy of a baseball player ends with the deaths of those who had the good fortune to see him play, a player's career in another sense is set in stone by his statistical standing. As such, it can be measured to some degree against that of others in his craft. In that regard Collins certainly still holds his own. At the close of the 2006 season, Collins remained in the top 100 players all-time in the following batting categories:

Category	Rank	Career Total
Sacrifice Hits	1	512
Singles	3	2,643
SB's	7	744
Hits	10	3,315
Times on Base	10	4,891
Triples	12	187
Runs	14	1,821
OBP	13	.424
Walks	17	1,499
Games	18	2,826
At-bats	25	9,949*
Batting Average	26 [Tie, Paul Waner]	.333
Total Bases	48	4,268
RBIs	95	1,300
Doubles	96	438

Author's revised number — 9,950

One statistic Collins does not stand out in is home runs. Over his career he hit but 47. However, at least in the mind of Bill James, perhaps baseball's premiere interpreter of the elusive field of statistical analysis, based "100% on the statistical record" Collins ranks second behind only Joe Morgan and ahead of Rogers Hornsby, both of whom possessed significantly more power than Eddie, as the second-best second baseman of all time. These three in James' opinion "rank almost even with one another, and far, far ahead of any other second baseman in history."[17]

In his six post-season classics, Collins batted .328. His OBP was .376 and he stole 14 bases, a World Series' record he shares with the great theft artist of the Cardinals, Lou Brock.

Of course, batting statistics are not the only gauge of a ballplayer's prowess. Collins played 2,650 games at second base. He handled 14,156 chances (1st all-time), and finished with 6,526 put-outs (1st) and 7,630 assists (1st). Because of the high number of games played, he committed 435 errors (1st in AL) but still maintained a fielding percentage of .970. Overall, he played in 2,701 games, fielding at .969 and participating in 1,223 double plays.

Nonetheless, in mid–June despite awe-inspiring career numbers, Collins' departure did not even cause a minor ripple in the baseball stream. The big news was Lefty Grove's second consecutive-game win skein. Collins once described the early Grove as a "touchy, irritable fellow with just about everything to learn, but he had all the undirected explosive power of a handful of cartridge shells tossed into a bonfire."[18]

By 1931 all that undirected explosive power was directed, but Grove was as touchy and irritable as ever. On August 23 he, not his A's who held a comfortable lead and an 84–32 record, was the talk of baseball. As he headed to the mound to face the Browns' Dick Coffman, Grove, the left-hander many called "Mose," had won 16 consecutive games and held a piece of the American League record, along with Smoky Joe Wood and Walter Johnson. Only a victory over the hapless Browns stood between him and the new mark.

This was a game Lefty Grove wanted to win in the worst way. The fact the Browns sent Coffman to the mound, a pitcher with a bus ticket back to the minors in his hip pocket, made victory a distinct possibility. Thus it was becoming increasingly tense when the combatants were still scoreless into the St. Louis half of the seventh. Still there were two out when the third Brownie reached base on a hit. Then the next man up hit a line drive to left, normally that portion of real estate protected by Al Simmons, but this day manned by a substitute named Jimmy Moore. He misjudged the ball and the runner on first came all the way around to score what proved to be the winning run.

In the clubhouse after the game, Collins recalled that "Grove, raging, said things to Moore that were terrible." Eddie felt bad for both Grove and Moore, but noted Connie Mack said nothing until later that evening after dinner. By then Grove was somewhat less electrically charged. Still, Mack did not address Grove's actions toward Moore, merely commented on what a splendid game the Browns' Coffman had hurled; a point they all realized they had "overlooked." In looking back Eddie felt "(t)he lecture had its effect on all of us, but on Grove it worked like a strong powder."[19]

According to Collins, after Mack's message sunk in, Grove seemed to quit worrying about getting credit for the win and began concentrating on just doing his best no matter the outcome. When he did that, he set a course to become one of the all-time greatest. In 1931 it meant a record of 31–4, a league-best ERA of 2.06, a league-leading 175 strikeouts and recognition as the league's first MVP under the "modern" voting procedures. When melded with still another terrific year from George Earnshaw (21–7, 3.67), a much-improved Rube Walberg (20–12, 3.74) and help from relative newcomer Ray Mahaffey (15–4, 4.21) and Waite Hoyt (10–5, 4.22), it was no surprise the A's final tally was an all-time team best 107 wins versus only 45 defeats. It also represented the first time a franchise won 100 games in three consecutive seasons. The effort gained them a pennant by a margin of 13 and one-half games over the Yankees and 16 over the third-place Senators, as well as another berth in the Fall Classic. Once again their opponent was the St. Louis Cardinals, themselves winners of a franchise-record 101 games.

The Cardinals for the most part fielded the same team as the previous season. One change was in the outfield where John "Pepper" Martin, a 27-year-old Oklahoman, replaced Taylor Douthit. Martin, 5 feet 8 inches, 170 pounds, made up for his size by playing an aggressive brand of ball. His experience prior to 1931 was limited to 14 trips to the plate, but his greatly increased playing time produced a .300 average and 75 RBIs. In addition, he finished third in the National League with 16 stolen bases, many of the head-first, belly-slide variety. Teammate Frankie Frisch led the league with 28. Certainly Martin was a valued newcomer but would be only a role player in a World Series that featured so many bona-fide stars — or so it was thought.

The A's certainly had their share of that caliber everyday player on their 1931 squad. Once again Simmons (.390, 22, 128) and Foxx (.291, 30, 120) deserved special mention. Mickey Cochrane continued to set a pace both at and behind the plate, batting .349, hitting 17 homers and driving in 89 runs.

Given the cast of characters, there was little doubt the 1931 World Series would be closely fought, but most observers felt the powerful A's would once again prevail. Nothing that occurred in Game One in St. Louis on October 1 altered that opinion. The A's, behind a strong effort by Lefty Grove, won over the Cardinals and 18-game winning rookie Paul Derringer, 6–2. Game Two, however, was a different story. Mack went with Earnshaw and the Cards countered with their ace, Wild Bill Hallahan [19–9, 3.29]. Earnshaw pitched well; Wild Bill, better. But the star of the game was Pepper Martin, particularly his running exploits, stealing a pair of bases, taking chances to secure an extra base and generally shaking things up. The final score was 2–0.

The A's, however, did have a great chance to score in the top of the ninth, in large part due to the keen eyes and cool savvy of their third base coach. The opportunity for Collins to earn his keep was set when Jimmie Foxx led off the inning with a walk. After Bing Miller flied out to left, Dykes worked Hallahan for a walk. Then Dib Williams, playing shortstop, took a called third strike. Now two were out and Earnshaw was due up. Mack then sent Jimmy Moore to the plate to pinch hit. The count on Moore went to two balls and two strikes. On the next pitch Moore swung at a low curve and missed, apparently ending the game, but from his vantage point Collins "saw the ball knock up dirt."

Under the rules of the game the catcher must catch the third strike, thus Moore was not yet out. However, all St. Louis catcher Jimmy Wilson needed to do to register the out and end the game was throw Moore out at first base. He did not. At the pitch the A's base runners Foxx and Dykes were running. In the confusion Moore threw the ball to third.

It seemed to make no difference. Apparently no one, except Collins that is, realized the ball was still in play. They all, players and fans alike, thought the game was over. The St. Louis players headed off the field and their fans stormed it. Even Jimmy Moore, head bowed in dejection, began making his way to the A's dugout.

Collins was beside himself. "In that situation there was stuff for future nightmares of futility for Eddie Collins. Out there on the coaching line I thought I never would make Moore hear me, or understand me."[20] He screamed at Moore, urging him to run to first, but the player was not getting the message. Then Moore suddenly realized what his third base coach was trying to tell him. He raced to first. The St. Louis third baseman had figured out the message as well by now, but his first baseman, Jim Bottomley, was clear across the diamond by then. There was no Cardinal at first to accept the throw. Moore was safe and the A's had the bases loaded. A hit by the next batter, Max Bishop, might have tied or won the game, but it did not happen. Bishop popped a foul ball toward the first base side. Jim Bottomley ran into the box seats to get it and the series was tied at a game apiece.

The next day Mack, who must have veered dangerously close to a heart attack as he watched Moore walking toward the bench, described events from his vantage point, noting that "Collins saved the situation by dusting home like a greyhound and ordering Moore to run to first."[21]

The loss of Game Two really hurt, for with a two-game lead and a return home to Philadelphia for the next games, the A's would have been practically unstoppable. As it turned out, the Cards continued to run free. The main culprit was Martin, or as some began calling him "the Wild Horse of the Osage." He had five of the Cardinals' eight stolen bases.

Game Three went to the Cardinals in Philadelphia, 5–2, as Burleigh Grimes bested Grove. The next day Earnshaw pitched a two-hit gem and breathed hope into the hometowners as the Athletics won, 3–0. The series continued to see-saw, however. The Cards and Hallahan were 5–1 victors on October 7 as Martin added a home run to his other heroics, then 8–1 losers to Grove and the A's in St. Louis in Game Six to set up a dramatic Game Seven. In that one, played in St. Louis before a disappointing crowd of 20,805 on October 10, Earnshaw and Grimes hooked up in another pitching duel. The Cardinals took an early four-run lead and Grimes made it stand until the ninth, when the A's scored twice and Wild Bill Hallahan rode to the rescue. The game ended with the tying runs on base and Pepper Martin continuing his one-man show by making a spectacular one-hand snare of Max Bishop's line drive. The final score was 4–2. The closeness of the series hid the reality. The A's did not then know it, but the second coming of Connie Mack's baseball dynasty was at an end. The Athletics never returned to a World Series again while in Philadelphia.

In defeat, Mickey Cochrane, long a fan favorite, came in for a major chunk of the blame due to the thieving antics of Pepper Martin. Amidst all the criticism it was forgotten that it was the A's pitchers who put Martin on base to begin with — he went 12-for-24 and walked two times — and held responsibility to hold him close to the bag as they delivered the ball. Collins defended his friend and former teammate in the syndicated column he prepared on the series, pointing out that after the Game Four shutout victory, Cochrane was playing with an injured leg.

"Please don't overlook the manner in which Mickey Cochrane handled the delivery of Earnshaw and few know of the physical handicap under which Mike is working."[22]

Cochrane was not the only member of the Athletics' organization to receive his share of criticism. The Tall Tactician was criticized for his pitching selections, particularly Waite Hoyt, who was unable to go the route in Game Five. Even Collins came under fire in that one when he permitted Al Simmons to try to score from second base on Bing Miller's grounder, which was bobbled by the shortstop who recovered in time to get Miller at first. As soon as the out was recorded, Jim Bottomley turned and fired home. Simmons was out by a mile.

According to John McCullough of the *Inquirer*, who analyzed the play in colorful language, "There are some as call Edward Trowbridge Collins, who was coaching at third, a lot of uncomplimentary things, the least baleful of which is chump...."[23]

Given those events which occurred in the aftermath of the A's upset loss to the Braves in 1914, there was some speculation that once again Connie Mack would seek to unload his catalog of high-priced talent. Attendance figures in 1931 did not argue against it. The 627,464 fans passing through the gates at Shibe Park represented a drop-off of almost 100,000 paying customers in the face of a record-breaking season. However, unlike 1914, there were other factors at work, not the least of which was the continuing and worsening depression. Unlike 1930 when overall major league attendance climbed, in 1931 the big leagues felt the crush just like everyone else. The 8,467,107 combined attendance figure represented the lowest since 1919. In addition, unlike 1914, there was no Federal League around determined to run off with the A's stars. If Mack was preparing to dismantle, it would be piece by piece, not wholesale as before.

On the other hand, in October there were enough rumors that Mack was planning to retire and hand the team over to Eddie Collins that Connie's son Earle saw fit to firmly deny it. "Why, he [Connie] looks as young as I do."[24]

Whether rumors of Mack's imminent retirement and his own promotion reached Collins is not known since he was once again off hunting, this time with a group that included Bing Miller and the A's club trainer, Doc Ebling. Then in February Eddie joined a larger group at the farm of ex–Yankee Whitey Witt near Woodstown, New Jersey. The group included A's players Cochrane, Walberg, Miller and Foxx, as well as Goose Goslin and a number of others.

The next spring another of Collins' old pals was missing in action when the team went south to Fort Myers. Shortly after the first of the year, Kid Gleason, now 66, injured his chest in an automobile accident and developed heart problems. It was thought he would join the team in short order, but on January 2, 1933, he died. In Gleason's passing, Collins lost not only a former manager and valued colleague, but also a close friend.

In the spring of 1932, while Gleason was still alive and home recuperating, Collins picked up the slack by not only hitting to the outfield as he normally did, but also handling infield practice, which was Gleason's regular task. In time, when it appeared Gleason's absence would be lengthy, pitcher Ed Rommel, the team's maestro of relief, took over many of the Kid's coaching responsibilities.

There are those who take a quick look at the Athletics and assume that their decline following the 1931 World Series was sudden and brutal. That is not the case. One must remember that the 1931 Series was a seven-game affair. A bounce here or there and the A's might have won their third consecutive title.

The team that returned in 1932 was much the same squad as had come so close to performing that then-unprecedented feat. In 1932 their final record was still quite good. Nevertheless, their fate, a second-place finish to the resurgent New York Yankees, was sealed by a slow start. On May 12 one month into the season, they stood in fifth place at 9–12. Even though they righted the ship later that month, winning 19 versus eight defeats and posting a winning record each month thereafter, they were unable to overcome their 4–10 record in April. In the end a fine 94–60 record left them 13 games off the pace as the Yankees, now managed by Joe McCarthy, equaled the A's 1931 win total of 107 games. This was one of the greatest of many great Yankees teams, powered by Lou Gehrig, catcher Bill Dickey, second baseman Tony Lazzeri, outfielder Earle Combs, and the still quite productive Babe Ruth (.341, 41, 137). Add a fine group of moundsmen, including young Lefty Gomez (24–7, 4.21), and there should have been little shame in Philadelphia over the A's performance.

A major story in Philadelphia in 1932 was the performance of Jimmie Foxx, who had Babe Ruth's home run record directly in his sights before he finished with 58 round-trippers of his own, two short of the record. Add in 169 RBIs and a .364 batting average and it was clear why Foxx was voted the league's MVP.

There were other A's who enjoyed fine years as well. Al Simmons (.322, 35, 151) and Mickey Cochrane (.293, 23, 112) excelled. Grove was still at the top of his game with a 25–10 record and a 2.84 ERA. In the coaching box Collins continued to draw raves, his World Series' faux pas forgotten, particularly by the *Inquirer's* Jimmy Isaminger.

"Ask any umpire and he will tell you that Captain Eddie Collins is one of the quickest witted coaches in the major leagues....

"[O]n playing rules he is perhaps the smartest man in the American League....

"Umpires will tell you he knows the rules better than anybody else in the circuit."[25]

As the season ended, Mack promised "no revolutionary shake-up of my team next winter. As a matter of fact, neither my fellow owners nor myself have any serious thoughts at the present time of letting any players go in trade."[26]

In light of a high payroll, some said the highest in baseball, unpaid debts incurred in remodeling Shibe Park, losses in the stock market, and over 200,000 fewer fans in the stands (405,500 versus 627,464 in 1931), it was hard for anyone to believe the Tall Tactician could or would back up such a statement.

CHAPTER 20

Junior Executive

"Do you wonder that even the chance to be a part owner of a club like Boston would leave me wavering? I tell you, the day I really said good-bye to him [Connie Mack] as I was starting for Boston, I had something in my throat that felt like a baseball."
— Eddie Collins[1]

In early 1933 it seemed that not much had changed for Eddie Collins. As he prepared for yet another season with the A's, he and Mabel continued to keep house at 341 N. Owen in Lansdowne. By now son Paul was an upperclassman at Dartmouth, preparing for the ministry. An excellent swimmer and skater, the elder Collins' offspring had no interest whatsoever in playing baseball. His younger brother Eddie Jr., however, was a different story. One year remained for him at the Episcopal Academy where he excelled at all sports, particularly football and baseball. Eddie Jr. further mirrored his famous father by playing quarterback and second base, respectively, and captaining the baseballers.

In addition to concentrating on his family, the elder Collins continued to spend his time away from baseball hunting and golfing, although he now supplemented his social life with a round or two of "non-competitive" bridge. He was also frequently found reading a mystery or bent over a crossword puzzle.[2]

On the whole as winter faded to spring, Collins' road in life ran flat and straight, no elevations or curves in sight. But all that changed in a significant way on February 25 when Robert A. Quinn, a financially troubled owner of the Boston Red Sox, announced the sale of the club to a 30-year-old millionaire named Thomas A. Yawkey.

"I have been carrying for many years a load that would make most men jump out of a 14th-story window. I tried and spent plenty of money to build up the Red Sox," Quinn admitted to a gallery of scribes and others, including American League president William Harridge, during a luncheon at Boston's Copley Plaza Hotel.[3] Quinn, a former minor league executive in Columbus, Ohio, and later business manager of the St. Louis Browns, had formed an ownership group consisting of several wealthy Columbus businessmen to purchase the struggling Red Sox from Harry Frazee in 1923 for a price reported as anywhere from $1,200,000 to $1,500,000. Since that time the franchise continued to struggle on the field, hitting rock bottom in 1932 with a major-league and franchise-worst record of 43–111, 64 games behind the pennant-winning Yankees. As a result, attendance, already affected throughout baseball by the Depression, dipped to a franchise-low 182,150. Quinn was well liked in Boston with his ownership group well intentioned, but the club needed an infusion of money to survive. An owner with wealth was needed.

Although in Boston he was a totally unknown quantity, Tom Yawkey had money. The future majority owner of the Red Sox was born Thomas Austin on February 21, 1903, the son

270

of Thomas Austin, an insurance executive. His mother Augusta was the daughter of William Yawkey, who made a fortune in the lumber and mining industries and was generally considered by 1900 as Detroit's wealthiest man. His son and young Tom's uncle was Bill Yawkey, a fun-loving type who used his share of the family treasure to enjoy himself at the race track, the hunting lodge and the baseball park. He eventually satisfied this latter craving in a way afforded only the rich; he convinced his father to purchase the Detroit Tigers.

Only seven months after his birth, baby Thomas lost his father to pneumonia. His mother Augusta attempted to raise him on her own, but when Thomas was three, she turned his care over to Uncle Bill, by then living mainly in New York, who raised the boy as his own. As young Thomas grew, he came to know and love baseball as much or even more than his uncle. However, unlike most boys his age, Thomas not only went to the ball park to see the games, but he also was surrounded by and became familiar with the ball players, including his uncle's most famous prize and Thomas's personal favorite, Ty Cobb.

Collins' youngest son, Eddie, Jr., followed in his father's footsteps by playing both football and baseball as a youth. Shown here in late 1928, the older Collins furnishes some gridiron pointers to Eddie, Jr., at the time a star performer for the football team of Episcopal Academy in the Philadelphia area (Urban Archives, Temple University, Philadelphia, Pennsylvania).

In 1918 when his mother died, Thomas Austin became a multi-millionaire, inheriting an estate estimated at four million dollars, to be held in trust until age 30. Soon thereafter Bill Yawkey adopted both Thomas and his sister. Then tragedy struck again. In March 1919 Bill Yawkey died, also of pneumonia. The bulk of his estate, then valued at around twenty million dollars, was equally divided between his wife and his adopted son, who was now known as Tom Yawkey. When the estate was finally audited, it turned out its true value was less, but nevertheless at age 16 Thomas Austin Yawkey was an affluent young man with an extremely keen interest in baseball. He would turn 30 years old and take control of his vast wealth on February 21, 1933.

Given the young man's background, there was no question why Bob Quinn found Tom Yawkey "well-equipped to build up the Red Sox."[4] Indeed, Yawkey planned to purchase almost all of the franchise. But Yawkey had a minor partner, and it was that partner and his stature in the baseball community that created the real surprise and quickly energized the Red Sox faithful. For Yawkey's new partner, vice president, and business/general manager was none other than Eddie Collins, late of the Philadelphia Athletics.

Over the years Collins told at least two different versions of the unfolding events that led to his remarkable ascent to a leadership role in the operative management of a major-league franchise. The main players in each version are essentially the same. It all began with an introduction by Ty Cobb when he and Collins were teammates.

During the 1928 season on an occasion when the pair were together in New York, Ty took his friend Eddie to a restaurant at the Alamac Hotel to "meet a good friend of mine [Cobb's], a young fellow who is keenly interested in baseball." The young friend was Tom Yawkey, and the meeting took place before Yawkey and Cobb had a falling out and parted company. On the other hand Collins and Yawkey "got along famously." Eddie recalled talking to Yawkey for over two hours. During that conversation he learned they were bound by an "old school tie." They were both graduates of the Irving School, although Collins preceded Yawkey by a number of years.

Actually, the Irving connection went deeper than just a pairing of fellow alums. Yawkey began attending Irving at age nine in 1912. By then Eddie Collins was not just another graduate of the school. He was, perhaps, the school's most famous graduate, a major league baseball star. In his honor the school had established a medal, awarding it annually to the school's best student-athlete. Every boy who played sports at Irving aspired to attain the Collins award, no one more than a boy like Tom Yawkey, who fashioned himself a nifty second baseman just like his new idol Collins, and not once, but twice finished second in the award competition. Thus, when Cobb introduced Eddie and Tom, it was much like bringing a flame to a wick.

"I met Yawkey many times after that initial meeting.... I discerned from his talk ... that he wanted to be more closely associated with the game than he could possibly be as an ordinary fan."[5]

It is here that Collins' tales diverge. About a year after the Red Sox deal, he tells of Connie Mack's concern that the financial burdens created by dwindling attendance in the early 1930s were seriously affecting competitiveness in his league. One team in particular that needed help was the Red Sox and Mack was worried about them. On one occasion when the A's were in New York, Collins took Mack to Yawkey's home. The A's had lost their game that day and Yawkey was complaining on their behalf. Eddie claimed he no longer remembered exactly what Yawkey said, but he never forgot a comment made by Mrs. Yawkey, who was present at the time.

"Well, Tom," she said, "get a club for yourself someday, and then you can make it do as you like."
When we left, Connie had no more than adjusted his hat to his grey head before he asked me:
"Do you think she was in earnest?"
"About what?"
"Yawkey buying a ball club."
"Hey, is that what wives generally tell the men to buy when they are feeling extravagant?"
"You can't tell, but if he's got such a notion in his mind there's one club in the American League I think he could buy. I know the owners want to sell."
"What club is that?"
"Boston."
"I don't think she was serious, but I'll ask Tom next time I see him."

Collins remembered to ask Yawkey the next time they were together and young Tom agreed to meet with Red Sox owner Bob Quinn. Shortly thereafter, sometime in mid-season 1932, Eddie arranged for the pair to meet for lunch, but he did not immediately learn the outcome.

During the winter of 1932–33, Mack took Collins with him to the American League meetings. Normally as a coach Eddie would not attend, but while there he was approached by William Harridge, the president of the American League.

"Has your friend Tom Yawkey said anything to you about buying Boston?" he asked. Mr. Harridge has to think about turnstiles too.

"Not a word," I said. "He's down South now, but I'll write and ask him."

After some communicating another meeting with Red Sox owner Bob Quinn was set up for mid–January. Collins was present but after the introductions he prepared to leave. Then Yawkey, who was accompanied by business partner and attorney Frederick W. DeFoe, asked him to stay. Quinn made his proposition and Yawkey and DeFoe decided to look into it further.

Later that winter Collins and Tom Yawkey met while attending the funeral of Dr. John M. Furman, their headmaster at the Irving School. After the service they returned together by train and engaged in another conversation regarding the Red Sox situation.

"What are your connections with the Philadelphia club?"

"You know. Coach and assistant to Connie."

"Yes, but could you be released? Would you come to Boston if I bought the club and took you in for a piece of it?"

"Say that again, will you?"

Still flabbergasted, I went to Connie Mack the next morning.

"Something funny has come up about this Boston deal," I said.

Connie began to laugh.

"This is no laughing matter," I protested.

"I know," said Connie. "Yawkey wants you to go to Boston. I've seen it coming for months. It's a grand opportunity."

The next one I talked with was President Harridge.

"Look," he said, "if you go along with Yawkey, the deal will go through. That Boston club ought to be built up."

"Well, between Tom Yawkey, Mr. DeFoe, Mr. Shibe and Connie Mack, I finally decided what I would rather be than anyone else in the world was Tom Yawkey's partner in the ownership of the Boston club, me that used to think that the whole world was just something that extended out in all directions under second base.[6]

That was one version. Some 20 years later Collins offered a slightly different version, recalling that by chance in 1931 he overheard Bob Quinn tell Will Harridge he might be willing to sell the Red Sox "to the right party." Collins immediately thought of Yawkey and set up a meeting between the principals and Harridge. The deal went on from there.[7]

Under either version Collins' decision to leave Mack and the A's was a difficult one. After all, he had turned down several offers, including one to manage the Yankees, each time because the A's ownership (Mack and the Shibes) had consistently promised he would eventually manage their club.

"[B]ut the Red Sox proposition was decided for me by Mack and Shibe. They knew about Tom Yawkey, both had been friendly with his dad and had great respect for him.

"'By all means,' said Mr. Mack, 'accept this offer. It's much better than we can offer you and you'll be associated with a man who is destined to become one of the leading baseball figures of the present generation. We don't like to lose you. You figured prominently in our future plans, but this is an opportunity you can not afford to pass up.'"[8]

And Collins did not. At age 45 he was now on board as a baseball executive, a position for which he was well suited by both intellect and mental framework. Eddie had always been more acutely aware of the management side of the corporate ledger than the average ball player, even owning a piece of Baltimore's minor league team until he sold his shares to his friend and fellow shareholder Jack Dunn in late 1920. It had just taken him a little extra time to step across the hallway and find an office there, due to his lengthy playing career.

Collins' new partnership with Yawkey, however, did not come without a price. Here is yet a third version of the purchase, this one from Tom Yawkey, as he discusses the financial outlay.

I had known Eddie Collins from our school days. We went to the same school, in Tarrytown, the Irving, though at different periods. Later I went to Yale and he went to Columbia. However, as a result of that association, we became fast friends.

The years passed and ... [the] idea of getting a ball club sort of grew on me. I talked it over with Collins from time to time, and asked what he figured to be the best spot. He finally suggested Boston. He lauded the city as a baseball center, he said the fans were intensely loyal and enthusiastic, and knew a lot about baseball, and he figured the chances of developing a good team were bright in that particular spot.

So we got in touch with Bob Quinn, and discovered a none too edifying picture. It really should have scared me off. The club was in very bad shape. Lack of funds had hampered Quinn terribly. He had taken over the club with the backing of Palmer Winslow of Columbus, O. Winslow had assured Quinn of big support — half a million for players. But three months after Quinn had taken over the Red Sox, Winslow died, without having made any provision for Quinn's backing. Bob was left high

In 1933 Collins took a permanent seat in the grandstand, leaving the Philadelphia A's to become a minority-owner and the business (general) manager of the Boston Red Sox. He remained with the Red Sox in some capacity until his death in 1951 (courtesy of the Boston Red Sox).

and dry, and after trying to surmount one obstacle after another was ready for a proposition to release him from his load. Then we stepped in.

Well, we examined the proposition and decided to go in. Maybe it was something like a million we had to pay for the club. Then we examined the park and we looked over the roster. I was fortunate in being able to get Collins to step in and become the general manager of the works. He knew the league and the players, and he knew Boston.[9]

It was said Collins' stock interest in his new club was in the neighborhood of 10 percent, in other words approximately $100,000.[10] Years later one scribe had Collins coming up with $50,000 in cash at the time of the purchase to solidify his participation.[11] It had been long rumored that Eddie was carefully salting away his paychecks even though he lived comfortably in a fine home and moved in the upper levels of Philadelphia society. He had apparently also survived the Great Depression, for while many were dropping out, Eddie Collins was buying in.

What did Mabel Collins think about her husband's latest venture? A day or two after the news broke, the Collins' home in Lansdowne was a madhouse. Flowers and telegrams arrived by messenger. Visitors stopped by to see Mabel and plumb her reaction. In fact, the mistress of the house was in conflict, a handkerchief in one hand to wipe away the tears of joy, one in the other to dab at droplets of sorrow.

"It all seems so wonderful.... You know all his life he's [Eddie] wanted to own a baseball club...." Nevertheless, "[T]here was lots to discuss about it. You know when you have two boys in school and have lived in one place for 22 years; you don't just pick up and leave in a hurry." Then again for an old New Englander whose family is from Webster, Massachusetts,

"I'm going to feel very much at home returning to Boston." For the present, however, "I will probably spend most of my time from now on commuting from Philadelphia to Boston, but do you know I think I will rather like it."[12]

That is where her husband was, in Boston facing the press along with Tom Yawkey, whose business offices were in New York and his heart in his South Carolina estate. The new owners were telling the media that although they tried to convince Bob Quinn to stay he had refused, making sure they knew that Collins had no plans to manage the team now or ever, and that Marty McManus, the former Brown and Tiger infielder who took over the Red Sox in 1932 mid-season from Collins' former teammate John Shano Collins, would remain as player-manager.

Yawkey, Collins, McManus and Frederick DeFoe, named team secretary, had their work cut out for them. They were optimistic but still quite frank from the outset about their difficult situation.

"It's going to take a lot of money and a lot of time to rebuild the Red Sox," Yawkey told the *Boston Daily Record.* "It will not be accomplished in a day, a month, or a year."

Collins described the arduous task in the most simple of terms, "There's no doubt that the [Red] Sox need plenty of new strength. And it's our business to dig up this strength. We

In early 1933 Eddie Collins joined young millionaire Thomas Austin Yawkey as a minor partner in the purchase of the struggling Boston Red Sox. Pictured here are (standing, left to right) Yawkey's attorney Frederick DeFoe and Collins; (seated) former business manager and owner Bob Quinn, Yawkey and American League President Will Harridge (National Baseball Hall of Fame Library, Cooperstown, New York).

will have to use both players and money. And Mr. Yawkey is prepared to invest plenty of money in new players."[13]

Collins knew what he was talking about. In 1932 his A's had faced the Red Sox pitching staff, arguably the league's worst, and had only a little more trouble with Boston's batters, all save first baseman Dale Alexander, who led the league in batting at .367 after arriving from Detroit.

According to Glenn Stout and Richard Johnson, the authors of *Red Sox Century*, "Rebuilding was a misnomer. The Sox would have to start from scratch."[14]

In so doing, it would not take too much at the outset to improve on the product. Since the last Red Sox World Series title in 1918, when they vanquished the Cubs in six games, they had finished in fifth place twice, sixth twice [once in 1919, the last year Babe Ruth played for the team], seventh once, and dead last nine times. Thus in 1933, the first season for "Yawkey and Company," when they finished seventh with a record of 63–86, 34 and one-half games behind the winning Senators, but a mere three and one-half behind sixth-place Chicago, it was seen as an encouraging sign.

Even more important in 1933 than the standings was what was going on in the backrooms of baseball, where the dreams of pennants and world titles are bought and sold. The story is told that in May of that year, Yawkey and Collins attended their first owners' meeting. Following the announcement of the purchase of the Red Sox, it had taken some time to complete the paper work, but now Eddie and his boss were the legitimate owners of their own big-league franchise.

The owners' meeting was held in Cleveland on May 9. Before the meeting had progressed very far, Yawkey stood up and announced he was present to purchase ball players and "the money is on the table."[15] Rumors were already floating around that Yawkey had given Collins some $250,000 to spend on the purchase of ball players. Thus, Yawkey's open-ended offer to buy hit this group of financially-strapped owners like a wave of sailors landing on a South Seas island on a weekend pass. Within moments Phil Ball of the Browns cornered Yawkey and they struck a deal to send catcher Rick Ferrell and pitcher Lloyd Brown to the Red Sox for back-up catcher Merv Shea and a sum generally believed to be $25,000, although some say the amount went as high as $50,000. Even the lower figure was an astronomical price given that Ferrell was a top-notch catcher, but not a star, and Brown was at best mediocre. Even Collins had to admit the expenditure of his majority partner's money was "a whale of a lot of the coin of the realm" and "a sum so vast as to shock the baseball world in these parious [*sic*] times."[16]

Collins, of course, later put a different spin on the affair; one in which the road runner out-foxed the wiley coyote.

"Tom Yawkey and I had gone to the meeting glad of the chance to be sociable ... but we were worried over our need of a catcher....

"The first and really great step in rebuilding a run-down ball club is to get yourself a catcher.... It is the catcher who stabilizes the play of a ball team."

Collins' preference was his old friend Mickey Cochrane of the A's, but he realized "Connie Mack would have to go stark raving mad" to part with him. Then Collins overheard Colonel Ruppert of the Yankees talking with Ball of the Browns. During the course of the conversation, Ball complained of his problems in signing catcher Rick Ferrell. Collins' heart skipped a beat. He went directly to Yawkey, who opened his purse, and they "closed the deal in an hour.... When Rick Ferrell joined the Boston Red Sox, I felt that we had our ball club heading for a rise."[17]

Just three days later the dynamic duo struck again, this time purchasing Yankee pitcher

George Pipgras and infielder Bill Werber for the sum of $100,000. Once again the baseball world was set on its ear. This was an astronomical sum, particularly considering the players involved were both quite good, but neither a major star.

What was the impact of these player transactions? In less than a week, the new Red Sox's owners had announced they were now a major player in the American League and backed it up. For the first time in ages, the flow of baseball talent ran into, not out of Boston. At the same time they established a more dubious mark. As these deals and others developed over the years, the Red Sox showed a penchant for pulling the trigger too often and too quickly, spending an awful lot of money for what they received in return. But at least in 1933, Yawkey's great adventure stood before him. Some may criticize, but Yawkey saw it much differently. "Baseball is my fun, my hobby. Others run stables of racehorses at tremendous financial loss, yet nobody calls them suckers.... Others collect stamps....

"Those other hobbies are all going out nothing coming in. I have a chance to cash in on my investment."[18]

Lest one forget, when Collins and Yawkey were conducting all this heady business in Cleveland in May, Collins was only a few months shorn of his baseball uniform. Less than two months later, he was back in uniform, once again through the good graces of old friend Connie Mack.

In the summer of 1933 despite the stormy financial climate, the city of Chicago was the host for the Century of Progress Exposition. As the time for the Exposition neared, the sports editor of the *Chicago Tribune*, Arch Ward, approached baseball's leaders with an idea for a charity game pitting the stars of each league. The players involved would only receive expenses, the proceeds to benefit indigent old baseball players. When the idea was approved, the game was set for July 6 at Comiskey Park. Connie Mack was named to manage the American Leaguers; John McGraw, the Nationals. According to Collins it afforded him yet another opportunity to don a baseball uniform.

"That was in the summer of 1933, when Mack did me the great honor of selecting me as a coach for the first All-Star Game. The American League team won it. It marked the first time that I played, or rather appeared, in uniform with such greats as Babe Ruth, Lou Gehrig and Charley Gehringer. It was one of the greatest thrills of my life. I was teamed with men I had long admired and enjoyed myself immensely that afternoon in Chicago."[19]

Collins had a bird's-eye view of the historic proceedings in what is now an annual rite of summer. From his third base coaching box, he saw an aging Babe Ruth excite fans at least one more time with a two-run homer into the right-field upper deck and make a late-inning run-saving catch that preserved an American League victory. He also had time to take yet another close peek at Lefty Grove, who took the mound and pitched well for the winners.

By the time of the All-Star Game, the Red Sox were mired in seventh place. Already, rumors were rampant that all was not well between on-the-field management and the front office. It seemed that Collins was not totally pleased with the managerial work of Marty McManus and said manager not too pleased with his immediate boss, either. According to J. G. Taylor Spink of *The Sporting News*, McManus was telling friends he would not return in 1934, no matter where the team finished.

"McManus is not getting along with Eddie Collins. Marty's pals insist that Eddie is pulling a Connie Mack from the grandstand, and wigwagging to the outfielders. McManus resents this poaching on his preserves. Collins' supporters insist that Eddie is a master, and that McManus should welcome aid from so high and able a source."[20]

The situation had ripened, Spinks reported, to the point Collins asked McManus to step down and stay with the club as a player only. Spinks' sources had Roger Peckinpaugh of

New Boston Red Sox owners Tom Yawkey (left) and Collins join the club's manager Marty McManus (center) to look over their 1933 club as the team trains in Sarasota, Florida. At the end of the season, McManus was replaced by Bucky Harris (courtesy of the Boston Red Sox).

Cleveland taking over, but McManus demanded to be fired or else he planned to finish out the season. He might have gotten his wish, but a few wins over the Yankees and the support of Boston's large Irish community for a fellow of similar blood kept Collins at bay. McManus finished the season.

In early October, that season completed, Collins was telling those in attendance at a dinner gathering for the Boston Parke Department that McManus had done a fine job handling the club. Apparently not nearly fine enough though, for on October 29 Stanley Raymond "Bucky" Harris, the boy wonder of the Washington Senators' 1924–25 heroics and most recently at age 36 the manager of the Detroit Tigers, was named new manager of the Red Sox.

The choice of Harris was an interesting one. Since his early exploits in the nation's capital, his results as a manager were unspectacular. In addition, his playing days had ended. In view of Yawkey's spending policies, any number of suitable candidates would have eagerly stepped forward. Yet Harris quickly filled the slot. Perhaps, as the authors of *Red Sox Century* relate, Harris was selected by Tom Yawkey without consulting with Collins, and chiefly because of ties between Bucky's wife and the current Mrs. Yawkey.[21] Or, perhaps as Collins insisted, he was chosen from a long list of candidates and only because "he was the best man we could get."[22] At any rate there was no love lost between Collins and Harris. These two had not liked each other since their playing days. It appeared certain when it came to managers, Collins was about to experience a called-strike two, and it seemed only Tom Yawkey was out of the loop. Paul Gallico of the *New York Daily News* was but one of many who sensed the chemistry for a soap-opera scenario.

"Bucky is a very high-spirited young man who always manages his own ball club. In fact, when he was with the Athletics, Master Collins was marked Number 1 on Bucky's you-know list. There will no doubt be what we boys on the Bowery call some charming contretemps when these two lads begin to work together."[23]

One would think, given the purchase of the club, the management maneuvers, and the influx of new players at significant cost, that on the Biblical "seventh day," Yawkey and Collins would rest, but not so.

In late September the Red Sox were in Philadelphia for a double-bill with the A's. According to Collins, "Nothing much hinged on these two games for either team, and so Connie Mack abandoned his habitual place on the bench to come and sit with me in the grandstand."

Collins saw Lefty Grove standing near the dugout and remarked that the great hurler must be about done pitching for the year. Mack agreed. Then he about knocked Eddie off his seat when he said, "Will I have Bob next year, I wonder?"

Collins tried not to think of the impossible. Surely, Mack was joking for "that fellow Grove, who is 'Mose' to me and 'Bob' to Connie, was to each of us a synonym for superlative pitching." Still, Collins could not remove Mack's remark totally from his mind. A few days later the pair were together again. This time Mack got to the point. He and his partners had decided they needed to unload some high-priced timber. Despite the previous remarks about Grove, Collins asked about the still-youthful Jimmie Foxx and was told he was not for sale. Then Mack laid it on the table.

"Would you and Yawkey consider Grove?"

They did, and on December 12 a deal was completed. Although there were rumors that the price was as low as $100,000 and as high as $150,000, Collins always insisted that Mack named his price and the Red Sox paid it. As to the amount, the most Eddie would say was that "for my two cents' worth ... we paid plenty."[24]

Most observers feel the actual amount paid for Grove was $125,000. To complete the deal, the A's added the veteran pitcher Rube Walberg and Eddie's successor at second base, Max Bishop. The Red Sox threw in pitchers Bob Kline and Rabbit Warstler. Neither was a loss.

The Red Sox now owned what many considered baseball's best pitcher. In 1933 the 33-year-old craftsman's record with the Athletics was 24–8, although his strikeouts were down (114) and ERA (3.20) up a bit from their norm. Needless to say, the Red Sox's faithful were excited. In 1933 the 268,715 fans who came to see this new edition represented an increase of about 85,000. In 1934 a lot more were expected to visit Fenway and the new ownership wanted to offer its team and its increasing fan base more to cheer about.

Few would argue in 1933 that Fenway Park, the ballpark that came along with the purchase of the Red Sox, was much better than its team. Bob Quinn and his associates simply had not possessed the cash to properly improve the aging facility. Tom Yawkey had the magic green elixir, and after initially discussing mainly minor changes, he also had the wherewithal to undertake a major renovation which, when finished just prior to the 1934 season, increased capacity, but more importantly replaced the wooden grandstands with concrete and steel. Many other changes were included. One — perhaps an idea Collins borrowed from Charles Comiskey — was the addition of a new press box and press room. Here the men with the typewriters, those who would report on the ball club and its players, hopefully quite favorably, were treated like kings, the liquor flowing freely and the food on the house as well.

In addition to the steel and concrete, there was one feature of particular import. In left field a huge new scoreboard was installed, accompanied by a high, wide fence, actually a wall an inviting distance from home plate. One day the fence, originally covered with advertisements and standing some 37 feet high, making it easily the most distinctive part of the ball park, would be painted and aptly described "the Green Monster."

The Fenway project was quite costly; nevertheless, it was of benefit not just to the Red Sox but to the city and region as well. According to Yawkey, he originally planned to spend $200,000 on the renovation. Then the architects got to work, suggesting a whole host of additional improvements. In addition to helping themselves, the Red Sox's owners saw a chance to help others.

In 1934 after the project was completed, Yawkey told *Baseball Magazine*, "Unemployment was rife and Mayor Curley of Boston urged us, if possible, to elaborate our plans so as to give employment to more men. This, I may say, had a considerable influence on our plans.... During the months of January, February and March there were over a thousand laborers on our payroll. The net result was that instead of two hundred thousand dollars we planned to spend, we have already spent well over a million."[25]

Part of that expenditure, on what certainly was one of the largest building projects in Boston during the Depression, was not in the original plans. On January 5, 1934, a five-alarm fire broke out, destroying the new bleachers. The loss was significant, but Yawkey and Collins pledged to finish the project on time.

"[T]here was a loss of one hundred and fifty thousand dollars," Collins said later, "and it cost rather more than that to tear out the ruined construction and rebuild anew."

But they did complete the project in time for the season opener, as even another similar fire in February and the belief that the two fires were the work of arsonists, did not stop it. Collins proudly remarked, "[W]e now have a stand that is worthy of the club we hope to have, and I hope, worthy of the city of Boston."[26]

It was the aim of the new ownership of the Red Sox to completely revamp the organization. In so doing, Collins released — a gentler term than "fired" — many long-time groundskeepers and concession workers. One disgruntled employee, Bill Gavin, reportedly claimed that religion was the reason for the dismissals, pointing out that Collins was Episcopalian and many of the workers Catholic.[27] Since the goal of the Yawkey-Collins team was a complete overhaul of a broken machine, it is hard to ascribe such a nefarious purpose to Collins who carried plenty of his own Irish blood.

By now the new ownership had spent a ton of money. If hard cash could buy a pennant, the Boston Americans were well on their way. But while they recorded good progress with facilities and the organization, it was on the field where the going proved the toughest.

The main reason for optimism in Boston in 1934 was the presence of one Lefty Grove on the Red Sox's roster. By now the team was clearly leading the cross-town Braves in fan interest. That the 1934 Sox finished the season at 76–76, in fourth place in the league, and drew some 610,000 fans (third in the league) is noteworthy for one reason: Grove that season was nowhere near the Lefty of old.

In plain fact, Lefty Grove arrived to pitch for the Boston Red Sox in the spring of 1934 with a sore arm. According to his biographer Jim Kaplan, "Within two days Grove's arm had become a major concern."[28] As the problems persisted, Collins spent the spring defending Connie Mack and denying claims his mentor had sold him a "pig in a poke." There were even rumors Mack at one point offered to give the Red Sox their money back. If true, the Red Sox weren't buying it. They did try everything else, including extensive dental treatment when an examination uncovered several abscessed teeth, and later a tonsillectomy when there was evidence of swollen tonsils. In the short term nothing helped. Grove finished the season at 8–8 with a sky-high 6.50 ERA.

Yawkey must have been devastated. He had quickly become infatuated with Grove, three years his elder, and had given him the run of the shop. Ever temperamental, Grove soon began ignoring whoever managed him, instead taking his problems directly to the top.

When it came to Grove, Collins was more philosophical, perhaps rationalizing his first big mistake as a wheeler-dealer, saying that Grove's arm trouble "was something entirely new, and for a time it made him a little panicky.... But in Lefty's case I think it was largely psychological. He was so bent on making good in his surroundings and justifying Mr. Yawkey's estimate of his abilities, that a sore arm in spring training struck him like a blow between the eyes."[29] Later he admitted, however, that "Grove has been a big gamble from a financial standpoint."[30]

Collins enjoyed better initial success with another multi-player transaction. This one in late May brought temperamental pitcher Wes Ferrell, then 26, to the Red Sox. The brother of Rick Ferrell was a multiple 20-game winner in Cleveland, but an off season in 1933 made him available. In Boston the right-hander did not disappoint, finishing the season with a team best 14–5 record and posting a 3.63 ERA.

Given past performances, the fourth-place finish of the Red Sox should, at the very least, have earned team manager Bucky Harris a return engagement. That it did not said more about his rocky relationship with Collins than it did his managerial abilities. By November Harris was out and his replacement stunned the baseball world.

As the 1934 season passed by, Tom Yawkey began to fully realize that his impetuous action in hiring Bucky Harris without consulting with his general manager had created a difficult situation. At one point late in the season, he sat down with Collins and asked him if he could have anyone as his manager for 1935, who would he choose? Collins told him Mickey Cochrane would be that choice. Of course, Cochrane was now with the Detroit Tigers and in the process of winning a World Series. He was out of the question. Exploring further, Yawkey learned that it would be just as difficult for the Red Sox to lure Collins' second choice.

"'Who is it?' Yawkey wanted to know.

"'Joe Cronin, but Clark Griffith would never let him go.'"[31]

When he said it, Collins was speaking from the heart. He could not in his wildest dreams imagine Griffith and his Washington Senators parting with young Mr. Cronin. Born in 1906 in San Francisco just a short time after the famous earthquake and resulting fire devastated the city, Joseph Edward Cronin was the offspring of Irish laboring parents. As he grew, it was apparent that Cronin was a tough kid who excelled at baseball, particularly with a bat in his hand. By July 1928 after a couple of indistinct years in Pittsburgh playing behind the Pirates' great Arky Vaughan, Cronin was purchased by Washington. In 1930 he had a break-out year, batting .346 and driving in 126 runs. The fine hitting continued and in 1933 Washington owner Clark Griffith named Cronin his player-manager. The choice proved a wise one as the Senators won the American League pennant before succumbing to the Giants in the World Series.

The next year Griffith solidified his hold on Cronin, who was still only 27 — and likewise Cronin his hold on Griffith — when the young infielder married Mildred, Griffith's niece and daughter-by-marriage. In 1934 Cronin's hitting and his fielding, never a strong suit, dropped off a bit, but not nearly as much as the fortunes of his team. The Senators fell to seventh with a disappointing 66–86 record. Still Cronin was young, one of baseball's biggest stars, wildly popular in the nation's capital, and a solid member of the Griffith family. Only a feverish colt of the Yawkey mold would even consider throwing a slender fishing line in the drink to try to haul in a big fish like Joe Cronin. But that is exactly what he did. On October 26, 1934, he was named the new manager and shortstop of the Boston Red Sox.

There are many versions of the Cronin deal. Since Clark Griffith was on the giving and not the receiving end, his version is worth repeating here, particularly since he accused Collins of instigating the whole affair.

"In August 1934 a Boston newspaper ran an interview with Eddie Collins ... in which Eddie, normally a conservative, non-tampering, non-popoff gentleman, was quoted as having said 1935 would find Cronin managing his club.

"I wrote a hot letter to Collins and he came back with an apology. Tom Yawkey ... also wrote, disclaiming the interview."

From subsequent events the letter exchange did not end the matter. According to Griffith during the 1934 World Series, he was resting in his hotel room in Detroit when Yawkey paid him a visit. Suspecting Yawkey had come to talk about Cronin, he waved him away. But Yawkey lingered and eventually the pair sat together in Griffith's room and talked about everything except his son-in-law.

"Finally, Tom said, 'Let Cronin come to Boston, and I will give you a check for $250,000.'"

At this point Griffith asked Yawkey to leave, the matter dropped, in his mind at least. A few weeks later Yawkey telephoned and asked about the proposed deal.

"I [Griffith] shouted, 'To Hell with you,' and hung up on him."

Then Griffith began to ponder. He realized the burden Cronin carried as the owner's son-in-law. Even more he knew that his club was in bad financial shape. The 1934 season had been a big loser at the bank as well as on the field. Yawkey could offer Cronin, and therefore his own beloved Mildred, more financial security than he could presently provide. He bought a train ticket to New York and walked into Yawkey's office.

"'I have decided to let you have Cronin,' I told Tom. 'You give me a check for $250,000, and shortstop Lyn Lary.'

"Yawkey shouted, 'Lary, too?' I replied, 'Yes, Lary too, because I need someone to replace Joe.'"[32] Yawkey agreed and Cronin was a member of the Red Sox for what was then by far the largest cash amount ever paid for a baseball player. And in the bargain Griffith purchased financial independence for his adopted daughter and son-in-law, too. It was reported Cronin was signed to a five-year contract at $30,000 per year.

Once again Boston had an Irish star, one who played shortstop and managed, who boldly predicted victory over the Yankees and immediately received Eddie Collins' endorsement and promise of no interference.[33] Yes, indeed, Collins and Yawkey had gotten their man. In the end, however, getting Joe Cronin proved to be the easy part. Winning a World Series, or even an American League pennant, was another thing entirely.

CHAPTER 21

Building Blocks

In early 1936 Red Sox fans "leaped to the conclusion that the pennant was in the mail. When it was not delivered, their disappointment was as bitter as that of a boy who has not received the promised atomic peashooter for 1,000 cereal labels."
— Harold Kaese, sportswriter for the *Boston Globe*[1]

When Eddie Collins decided to leave the comforts of Philadelphia and accept the challenge of restoring respectability to the Red Sox franchise, the change meant more than merely acquiring a new office address and job description. The entire Collins' family was affected. As planned, Mabel and Eddie Jr. remained in Lansdowne while the junior Collins finished high school. Meanwhile, his older brother Paul graduated from Dartmouth. By the fall of 1935, Paul was in New York City, a student at the General Theological Seminary, in preparation for an Episcopalian ministry. In the spring of 1935, Eddie Jr. finished high school and headed to Yale, where like his father years before at Columbia, he would play football and star in baseball.

Now that both sons were essentially out of the nest, it was time for Mabel and Eddie Sr. to sever ties in Pennsylvania and create new ones in Boston, where the couple had maintained an apartment the past two-plus years. In late 1935 the family acquired a country estate in Weston, Massachusetts, a community some 20 miles from their previous location.

By the time the Collins' family was settled into their new home, the results were also in on the 1935 Red Sox campaign. The team improved its record a bit to 78–75, but once again finished fourth. The Detroit Tigers finished 16 games ahead of the Red Sox, then won the World Series over the Chicago Cubs in six games. The season was especially noteworthy in Boston for the strong pitching comebacks of both Lefty Grove (20–12, 2.70) and Wes Ferrell (25–14, 3.52).

Attendance at Fenway dropped off a bit in 1935. While the fans recognized and, to an extent, appreciated the improved brand of baseball the Yawkey regime had introduced, neither the Red Sox's fan base nor ownership were close to feeling satisfied with the current product.

Following the Grove deal with the Athletics in late 1933, the A's–Red Sox pipeline remained open. In January 1935 the Red Sox purchased Bing Miller, then added infielder Dib Williams in May and pitcher Joe Cascarella in June. All were A's. It was now obvious Connie Mack was in a major sell-off phase. It was also obvious that given their cash infusion, the Red Sox were the A's best customers. And, of course, there was the speculation that Mack had permitted, even encouraged Collins to head to Boston in order to act as his agent of transfer in that process, much as the old Red Sox–Yankee thoroughfare. Nothing that happened in late 1935 did anything to dissuade anyone from peddling that notion, although the primary participants denied it to the last.

In 1933 Jimmie Foxx had a second-straight MVP season, winning the American League triple crown as his A's enjoyed an otherwise unspectacular year. He continued his pace as the American League's premier long-ball threat by clearing the bases 44 times in 1934 and 36 in 1935, all before he was 30. Nonetheless, at the Philadelphia Athletics' "supermarket," he was for sale as the 1935 season closed. By no mean coincidence the Red Sox were pushing a shopping cart in search of power.

In early October it was reported that a week earlier Red Sox officials, including Yawkey, Collins and Cronin, met at a Boston hotel with Connie Mack and spent a night in talks.[2] Although Collins claimed that nothing was accomplished and no names were mentioned, it is hard to believe that Foxx's name was omitted from the discussions. The fact that Mack was also talking with the Yankees about a number of his players, including outfielder Doc Cramer, only served to raise the anxiety and the stakes.

On December 10, 1935, a deal was cut. In exchange for a couple of lesser lights and a reported $150,000, the Red Sox obtained Jimmie Foxx and 26-year-old right-handed pitcher Johnny Marcum. Once again Tom Yawkey's money had spoken volumes and another high-priced all-star talent had been added to the roster. No longer was the term Yawkey's "millionaires" a casual reference. On payday young Mr. Yawkey must now dig deep.

When a baseball club shells out a lot of money for a highly paid player, the level of expectation for that player increases. Such was the case with a number of the Red Sox's new acquisitions, no one more than Joe Cronin. Despite his popularity, his batting production (.295, 9, 95) was disappointing and his low fielding percentage (.949), on the heels of 37 errors at shortstop, eyebrow-raising. It appeared Cronin was heavier and slower and that Collins was off in his lofty assessment of the shortstop. Not to be put off, however, the Red Sox had quickly corrected the oversight with the purchase of Foxx.

There is no question that by now the Boston Americans were wheeling and dealing in an effort to make 1936 their year. The trades they consummated are almost too numerous to mention, but one additional one with the A's involved a couple more part-time players and another chunk of cash. This time it was $75,000 for a perennial .300 hitter with little power in outfielder Doc Cramer and a 26-year-old shortstop Eric "Boob" McNair, who did not add any heft with the bat but was better in the field, though not enough to totally erase the problem at short.

Heading into the 1936 season, the Red Sox were stocked with front-line players. A question arose, however, given the high price tags which accompanied them, whether or not Yawkey and Collins paid too much to acquire them. In *Paths to Glory*, a book which analyzes how great baseball teams came to be, authors Mark Armour and Dan Levitt conclude that in this case the answer is a difficult one "[s]ince Yawkey was the only one buying players in the 1930s...."[3]

Actually by 1936 even Tom Yawkey was beginning to tire of trying to purchase his way to a pennant. Estimates had his investment in new players at about a $1 million and his total investment at over $3 million.[4] All this and no profits, nor was there even a sniff of pennant fever.

In an effort to stem a rapidly flowing tide and at the same time build a firmer foundation for the future, the Red Sox were undergoing a change of philosophy. Since the early 1930s teams like the St. Louis Cardinals, under the auspices of Branch Rickey, and the New York Yankees with George Weiss were developing talent for their clubs through the formation of extensive farm systems. Like many of the other clubs, the Red Sox under Yawkey and Collins dabbled in the art, but beginning in 1936 they really began to buy into the idea by hiring Billy Evans, the noted umpire, baseball writer and analyst, and most recently the general manager of the Cleveland Indians, to develop a farm system that would pay dividends down the road.

In 1936, though, the talent was already in town, and with Foxx now on board, pennant talk was in the air over Boston Harbor. For a while, it seemed the Sox were on their way. In the early going they were in second place, for the most part. On June 26 they were still there, five and one-half out. Then an 8–7 loss to the Indians in Old League Park sent them on a seven-game skid that included four straight losses in New York; the team never recovered. By August 8 another seven-game skid left them in fifth place and 17 behind. The final tally left them in sixth with a bleak record of 74–80, 28 and one-half games out of first. The front-running Yankees took it all, besting the Giants in an all–New York series that went six games.

This time around, given the high expectation level and a record of continuing improvement under the current ownership, all the plush press boxes and free booze and meals in the world could not keep the sports scribes from frantically searching for hides to tan. And this time around Collins was a prime target, although not all agreed.

According to sportswriter Paul Shannon, writing in an article published in *The Sporting News* during the team's struggles in early July, there were rumors of impending changes in the Red Sox's organization and "a few of the more caustic critics seemed to have singled out Eddie Collins as the target for blame." Nevertheless, Shannon was not certain Collins should bear the brunt of blame for baseball stars who leave some of their luster when they shift scenery. Thus in Collins' defense, he "has all that he could be expected to handle in running Fenway Park and looking out for the business administration.

"Eddie has done his part splendidly, but as far as the operation of the team itself is concerned, he has had no hand in it. And the suggestion he has interfered with the management of the Sox in any way is ridiculous."[5]

But that is just the crime Collins was charged with, as the Red Sox's hopes for a banner year, or even a decent one, drifted away. Yet Shannon was not alone in his defense of Collins. A week later the editorial staff of *The Sporting News* reviewed the situation in Boston and defended Collins as a man in the middle.

"Through warped judgments and twisted stories whose authenticity becomes steadily lessened in traveling from mouth to mouth, General Manager Edward Trowbridge Collins of the Boston Red Sox has been put in the middle of a storm that has risen like a tide and is pounding against the gates of Fenway Park. Eddie has been accused of every mistake inside and outside of the catalog, because of the failure of the so-called gold-plated Red Sox to make a stronger bid in the 1936 American League pennant race."

Telling readers that Collins was blamed for spending Yawkey's money on "worn-out players" and agreeing that some of the new arrivals had not lived up to expectations, the newspaper reminded readers that this was the fun in baseball, and that if all it took was money to win, then the game would be the lesser for it. And as for Collins, perhaps, the players should share some blame if indeed he even did all the recommending.

As for interference on Collins' part, the newspaper pointed out the charges "are not supported by those in the best position to know the facts," mainly, the scribes who have followed the fortunes of the Red Sox since Collins arrived. "Even Bucky Harris, ... never accused Eddie of meddling with the team. Bucky was permitted to make many changes, some of questionable value....

"Even if he [Collins] had meddled, that wouldn't account for the sour pitching, failure to hit and slumberous work on defense that the team has shown as it has stumbled away from, instead of toward a pennant."[6]

Of course, there were those who pointed the finger not at Collins, but at Joe Cronin. It was not long before there was talk of a Collins-Cronin feud. Gene Desautels, a catcher with the Red Sox in the late 1930s, addressed it. "It wasn't only the players who didn't like Cronin. The general manager didn't like Cronin. That's the truth, because Eddie Collins used to ask me a lot of very personal questions about Cronin on the road. I was afraid to say too much. Eddie would say, 'Did he get to the ballpark on time?' Things like that. I'd say, 'Yeah, oh yeah, he's always there.' I could tell that they didn't like each other."[7]

Perhaps Collins was sorry he had ever recommended that the Red Sox bring Cronin to Boston, perhaps not. Collins publicly never uttered a mean word about the manager. And in the end it made little difference. The reason: Tom Yawkey. If Eddie Collins was Tom's favorite "uncle," Cronin was his favorite "nephew." And prima donnas like Grove, Ferrell and the rest were his best buddies. They would all stay, whether they got along together or not because Yawkey wanted it that way. Some were his drinking buddies — word had it the Red Sox were a hard-drinking bunch — and some like Collins frequently went hunting with him on his 32,000-acre shoreline estate in South Carolina.

The hunting was not all confined to South Carolina. In October 1936, apparently oblivious to all the criticism, Collins joined Yawkey, Bing Miller — now a Red Sox coach — Rube Walberg, Mickey Cochrane, Tris Speaker and several others in Wyoming. Miller bagged a 500-pound brown bear, a moose, an elk and a big buck deer. Collins supplied Yawkey with the laughs.

"Agile did you say? On a baseball diamond maybe, but not out hunting. Why, all Bing Miller and I [Yawkey] did was pick that guy [Collins] up.... He fell over rocks and when he couldn't find anything else to fall over, he'd trip over his own feet. He practically wore us out."[8]

All this camaraderie was great fun for Tom Yawkey; after all, baseball was his hobby. What it did for his team was create a leadership vacuum, which allowed key players to bypass middle management and take their problems directly to the top, where important decisions were made in the interest of maintaining friendship as opposed to making sound baseball or business sense. It was a situation which existed in 1936 and would continue essentially unabated for many years.

While his team was struggling with its veteran players, Collins was out of the office looking for young talent to supplement or replace them. Although these road trips were infrequent, the one he took to the West in August 1936 was his most fruitful. There are several versions of what occurred. Collins recalled it in 1950 for *The Sporting News* in their five-part series on his life. It began when Yawkey asked Eddie to check out a pair of players at San Diego named George Myatt and Bobby Doerr. The boss of the San Diego club was Bill Lane, a good friend of Collins and according to Eddie "one of the grand characters of the game." Collins claimed the Sox held options on all of San Diego's players. He traveled west, checked out Myatt, the higher rated of the two, but liked what he saw in Doerr much more. He immediately exercised the option, considering Bobby a potential great.

Collins saw the San Diego team take batting practice and play several times while he was on the coast. It was during this time he caught his first glimpse of Ted Williams.

"He was then a tall, gangling kid, just out of a San Diego high school. He comported himself in an easy, confident manner and I was impressed the minute I saw him."

Doerr's option in hand, it was time for Collins to return east. But he could not get Williams out of his mind. He mentioned him to Lane and was surprised at his friend's "brusque" reaction. The San Diego owner said that since Williams was barely out of high school he had promised the boy's mother that Ted would remain in San Diego with the local club. Nonetheless, he assured the Red Sox official he would have the first opportunity to purchase the kid's contract.

"We shook hands on the deal. That's all the assurance I ever had.... A man's word meant something then — would that there were more of it in the world today."[9]

Collins' tale covers the generalities. It is up to others to fill in the details, which do not always match up. According to Bobby Doerr, he and George Myatt, his teammate at short, heard in July that Collins planned to travel west to see them play. Unbeknownst to the pair, Collins was in the stands to see them during a series with Pacific Coast League rival Seattle. When the team left Seattle and arrived in Portland, they first learned Collins was there to watch them. In the first game of two on Saturday, August 8, Doerr became nervous, committing four errors, while Myatt committed a pair himself. San Diego lost, 9–6.

Doerr recalled that in between games Collins came to the clubhouse door and told the awestruck young man that he planned to exercise his option on him, but not on Myatt.[10] It was clear that despite the four errors, Eddie Collins knew a good second baseman when he saw one.

Doerr believed that it was at this time Collins got to see Ted Williams in batting practice and liked what he saw. Over the years Williams himself concurred. But it also seems Collins may have actually seen Williams perform in game action, rather than just batting practice, although how many games and which ones may never be known for certain.

Collins said he first saw the left-handed Williams bat in a seventh-inning pinch-hit role in Portland. Since Williams did not play in Seattle and played in Portland only through a series of personnel changes and mishaps to other players, that part of the story can be confirmed. It is not as clear that Collins is accurate in his description of the pinch-hit appearance, but his reaction to Williams is what is worth noting.

> The announcer yelled, "Williams hitting for San Diego." I looked down on the field and nearly broke out laughing when I got a peak at a gawky bean-pole who was striding toward the plate. But I didn't laugh when I saw him swing at the ball and line a double over the first sacker's head.
>
> There was nothing remarkable about the hit. There certainly was nothing impressive about the appearance of the hitter. But there was something about the way he tied into that ball which all but knocked me out of my seat.
>
> It was as though a shock of electricity had just passed through my body. In that fleeting moment, as he swung at that ball, I became so convinced that here was one of the most natural hitters in baseball history, I'd have staked my life on it.[11]

In his biography of Ted Williams, author Ed Linn has Collins most likely watching Williams play on Saturday the 8th, as Doerr and Myatt performed their comedy of errors. If so, he saw Ted get two hits in three at-bats in the first contest and go hitless in the second game. If he remained to watch the doubleheader on Sunday, Collins saw his new find get a pair of hits in the first game, knocking in two key runs, and hit a double in the second contest. But if Collins followed the San Diego team from Seattle to Portland, then he was probably in the stands earlier than Linn states, watching Williams run for the injured Cedric Durst in the tenth inning of the first game of yet another double-bill. In the second contest of the August 7 meeting, he then saw Ted bat for the first time, singling in three trips and driving in a run in a 10–0 win for his team.[12] But no matter how little or how much Collins saw of this sweet-swinging wonder that weekend in August, the fact is he came, he saw, and he optioned. He then left, excited to report his discoveries to Yawkey and Cronin.

One wonders in later years if Eddie Collins believed it was fate that brought him to that Portland grandstand in August 1936. For throughout the years it was frequently noted that Collins was a religious man who regularly taught Sunday school. Just four months later he was bursting with pride as he joined Mabel and Eddie Jr. in Hays, Kansas, to watch the ordination of son Paul as a priest in the Episcopal Church.

"'That's my son, Paul,' Collins would later tell others. 'He was never interested in athletics. His thoughts were on a higher plane....'

"He realized his first ambition and we're very proud of him."[13]

Eddie Jr., now a sophomore second baseman at Yale, was making a name for himself as well. Whenever he could, the proud father was in the stands to watch. He liked what he saw. According to Eddie Jr.'s baseball coach Smoky Joe Wood, a man who knew a thing or two about baseball players, "The Kid handles himself with an ease which more seasoned players don't show. He has many of the characteristics which stamped the play of his father...."[14]

Collins may have been on the hot seat in Beantown, but at least the pay was good. By the mid-thirties he was earning $24,000 for his troubles.[15] And his efforts did pay off to some extent as the 1937 edition of the Red Sox improved their record to 80–72, although it only lifted them one notch to fifth place. The continued failure to contend seriously was hitting the club in the pocket book, too, as attendance dropped over 65,000 from 1936. Most of those fans poured into Fenway when the club made a brief surge in late July and August and won 12 in a row (with one tie) before fading.

Unlike 1936 the problem with the current edition of the Red Sox was not their hitting, although Jimmie Foxx, a bright spot in that first year with the Red Sox when he batted .338, hit 41 homers and drove in 143 RBIs, fell off a bit (.285, 36, 127). Joe Cronin, who had broken his wrist in 1936 and reinserted himself at shortstop after moving Eric McNair to second and recently acquired Pinky Higgins to third, had a fine year — at least at bat — hitting .307 and driving in 110 runners. The problem it seems was with the pitching, although Grove still found enough to finish 17–9 and 3.02. Wes Ferrell, however, was ineffective and a problem child. In June both Ferrells were traded to the Senators, along with part-timer Mel Almada. The Red Sox received Bobo Newsom and outfielder Ben Chapman, a decent hitter who became infamous years later for his resistance to the introduction of African-American ball players. Newsom helped and so did 25-year-old Jack Wilson, who surprised with 16 wins, but it still was not enough.

Once again during the year, rumors surfaced of unrest between Collins and his manager. Collins denied it, at one point saying he admired and loved Cronin.[16] Yawkey backed him up, telling writer Dan Daniel that Collins was upset with the rumors and "when Joe Cronin comes to me and says he is being interfered with, and wants to go, then I believe that yarn."[17]

Collins had more trouble garnering Yawkey's support on another matter — the purchase of Ted Williams. During the 1936–37 off-season, Collins had kept tabs on his new find through catcher Gene Desautels, another player Collins had scouted and then signed. At the time Desautels was catching with the same San Diego Padres, who employed Williams. In 1937 Desautels would play in 96 games for the Red Sox, but prior to spring training Eddie asked the catcher to work out with Williams and let him know what he thought. Desautels gave a thumbs-up, and nothing Williams did in his first full minor-league season in 1937 changed that verdict.[18]

By winter 1937–38 Collins was ready to exercise his option on the young Padre. The only problem was that interest by other clubs in Williams, present even before Collins saw him, had now intensified. At the same time Yawkey had decided he wanted to develop from within, through a farm system. He was no longer interested in buying players from other teams. In his mind the purchase of a youngster who was property of another team, even a minor league team, fit that mold. Collins had to work hard to convince him otherwise. In this he had Cronin's support. Collins told Yawkey that "this happens to be the one time in 100 that we should break our rule."[19]

It all came together in December 1937 at baseball's winter meetings in Chicago. Collins entered the meetings well aware that Casey Stengel of the Boston Braves and Bill Terry of the Giants were particularly interested in his quarry. Eddie, however, had Bill Lane's verbal assurances, confirmed on more than one occasion. Once he had Yawkey's assent, he felt good; still, it was a close call. Lane wanted an answer and it took Collins time to get it. When he did, he almost missed Lane, who had a firm offer from Stengel's club and was about to take it. Collins located Lane and said he was ready to deal. In minutes they had one, involving options on two minor-league players and the eventual rights to two more, all in exchange for Ted Williams. The reported out-of-pocket cost to the Red Sox for the entire deal was $35,000, the cost of the options on two of the players sent to San Diego.

Williams heard about the deal second-hand and reports are mixed on whether or not he was pleased. If their son was conflicted, his parents were not. They were upset. May Williams, Ted's mother, had received a promise from Lane to keep her son, 19 and thus still a minor, at home in San Diego. In addition, she said Lane promised her a cut of any sale price the owner obtained for the boy. May and Sam Williams, Ted's father, did not agree on much, their marriage was badly strained, but they agreed that they should have some of what they felt was a $35,000 sale price.

No sooner did Collins return home from the winter meetings and report his purchase of Williams than a letter dated January 1, 1938, was sitting on his desk from Sam Williams, reminding the Red Sox that Ted was a minor and threatening to withhold consent on a contract if certain demands were not met.

"It is my [Sam William's] understanding that Ted was sold to the Boston Red Socks [*sic*] for a sum of $35,000 and two players and in fairness to this boy I believe that he should receive half of the selling price; which I believe is not only good sportsmanship but would be fair to him...."[20]

Collins dutifully turned over the letter to President Harridge of the American League. He wanted to write Sam Williams and explain that the Red Sox had nothing to do with giving the Williams' family any part of the purchase price but hesitated to do so in view of issues, particularly the precarious legality of baseball's reserve clause, as related to the handling of contracts of minors.[21] At the time Organized Baseball had no definite instruction as to handling the contracts of minors, but the accepted practice was to have the parent approve the contract initially and each time it was renewed until the player reached the age of 21.

On Harridge's advice, Collins sent the Red Sox contract to the elder Williams on January 7, politely advising him he was misinformed as to the purchase price, as well as explaining that the Red Sox were "in no position to give any part of the purchase price to other than the San Diego Club, because the Boston club is the donor and not the receiver of the amount involved for your son's contract."[22]

Sam Williams was not done. He replied to Collins' letter of explanation by stating he never intended the money to come from the Red Sox, insisting he had a deal with the Padres and Collins was well advised to move cautiously with San Diego ownership because he planned to stand on his deal.[23]

For his part, Bill Lane in San Diego was, of course, aware of what was transpiring. In early January he wrote a personal letter to young Ted encouraging him to take advantage of the financial reward the Red Sox would offer for his signing, then in late January advising Collins that Ted's father, a jail inspector, and mother, a Salvation Army worker, were "money hungry.... There was never any agreement in the original contract and there is not [*sic*] way that I can pay them." In his opinion the family is "going to bluff around a little," but eventually will sign.[24]

Given all that transpired and what was at stake, it should come as no surprise that in short order Collins packed his bags and in February 1938 made the three-day train trip to San Diego. Upon arrival he visited the Williams family at their home on Utah Street. It was the first time in the entire process that Eddie had actually met his prime target. Ted liked the former big league star and felt comfortable at once. He recalled that "the only decent chair we had was an old mohair thing that had a big hole you could see the springs through. We covered the hole with a five-cent towel and that's where Collins sat."[25] And that is exactly where the deal was struck. Somewhere along the line the Red Sox had decided it was not worth the risk to deny Ted's parents some penance. Collins offered them what some say was $1,000, others $2,500, and their son a two-year contract for a reported $7,500.[26]

On February 18 Collins wired Will Harridge from Los Angeles. "Williams matter all settled. I have his signed contract."[27]

It was probably the best money Collins and Yawkey ever spent. Yet Eddie never took much credit, once telling a writer, "Your Aunt Susan could have picked Teddy out of 1,000 players."[28]

If the Red Sox's acquisition of Doerr and Williams favored brilliance, that light dimmed when one considers the handling of another prospect: one Harold "Pee Wee" Reese. In 1938

Although his days in Boston with the Red Sox were frequently stormy ones, Ted Williams enjoyed a particularly cordial relationship with Collins, the man who signed him to his first major league contract. Here a smiling Williams (left) joins Eddie to ink another one in 1947 (courtesy of the Boston Red Sox).

Reese was playing shortstop for the Louisville Colonels of the American Association. The young man was then just approaching 20. He was a very fine fielder who showed he could hit well enough that he caught the eye of the Red Sox's farm director Billy Evans. Enough so, Evans convinced Red Sox management, Tom Yawkey in particular, to do something Yawkey did not like, that is join hands with outside ownership, in this case former player-manager Donie Bush, to own a minor league club. In order to bring Reese into the Red Sox's fold, that is just what the Red Sox did, becoming part owners of the Colonels.

The Reese move seemed like a good one. In 1938 Cronin was still the shortstop and, one might add, playing quite well (.325, 17, 94). But at 31 Joe was old for his age and his liabilities in the field detracted from the respectability needed to command. Of course, the viability of Reese as Cronin's replacement depended to some extent on the cooperation of Cronin, who apparently did not recognize his faults and was not ready to step down. Eventually, in 1939 Cronin overrode a furious and frustrated Evans. On July 18, just months after the Louisville franchise was purchased primarily to obtain him, Reese was traded to the Brooklyn Dodgers for money and four nondescript players. A 10-time National League All-Star, Reese is now enshrined in the Baseball Hall of Fame.

By comparison with their previous five years in Boston, 1938 was a quiet one in the Red Sox's front office. Perhaps that is one reason they turned in a much more successful, if still pennant-less season. Another major reason was the great campaign turned in by Jimmie Foxx (.349, 50, 175), who won the league's MVP award for the third time. In late 1937 Collins gave up recently acquired pitcher Bobo Newsom and two others to obtain a fine right-handed hitting outfielder from Cleveland, Joe Vosmik. The career .307 hitter, a discovery of Billy Evans while in Cleveland, hit .324 in his first year with the Red Sox. Former A's outfielder Doc Cramer hit well, too.

On the mound the Bostonians squeezed yet another good year from Mose Grove (14–4, 3.08) and enjoyed the rookie season of Jim Bagby, Jr. (15–11, 4.21), a 21-year-old righty.

The result was a team which won eight more games than its predecessor and moved from fifth to second, nine and one-half games behind the Yankees. New York then swept the Cubs to claim another world championship. The fans, an additional 85,000 over 1937, bought into it, as they saw the club post a sterling 52–23 record in Fenway. If the club had come close to duplicating that record on the road, instead of their weak 36–38 mark, they just might have claimed the championship for themselves.

One player who did not help the club improve in 1938 was Ted Williams. After an interesting spring in which he exhibited unusual cockiness for a newcomer, to the consternation of his new teammates and the delight of a bored media, he was sent to Minneapolis for more seasoning. Already, however, the media focus was shifting away from Collins and Cronin and onto this tall, awkward-looking youngster who would become known in his early days as "the Kid." His arrival in Boston in 1939 was eagerly awaited.

Shortly after Collins dealt so deftly with the Williams family, he faced a sad detail within his own family. Following the death of Eddie's father in 1929, Mary Collins spent the majority of her time with Eddie and his family. On May 23, 1938, following a lengthy illness, she died at Eddie's home. Two days later Mary was buried in Sleepy Hollow Cemetery in New York state, next to her husband John.

In the standings at least, 1939 was almost a carbon copy of 1938. The Red Sox won one more game and finished in second place once again, behind those same New York Yankees. Although the Bostonians ran second almost the entire season, the team did create a real wave of excitement in early July by sweeping the Yankees in five games at Yankee Stadium. At the end, nonetheless, the Sox were 17 behind the boys from the Bronx, who featured a young man of their own: Joe DiMaggio. He and his teammates swept the Reds to win their fourth title in a row with a combined record of 16–3 in post-season play. The fact their Red Sox were essentially out of the race early cost the franchise some fans, as attendance dropped, but what they did see was a fine hitting club which continued to lack pitching in sufficient numbers and cost themselves additional games by poor fielding. Among the starters, only Lefty Grove was effective (15–4, 2.54). The staff's ERA was fifth in the league.

At the plate, however, the 1939 Red Sox were quite capable. Foxx had another strong year (.360, 35, 105), as did Cronin (.308, 19, 107). Bobby Doerr, at 21 now the regular second baseman, hit .318 and drove in 73 runs, but the real sensation and talk of the town was Ted Williams. Although the rookie outfielder's fielding left quite a bit to be desired, (19 errors), his .327 average, 31 round-trippers and league-leading 145 RBIs captured everyone's attention. In fact, the entire everyday lineup came through for the club; Boston led the league with a .291 team batting average.

For the Collins' family, on the other hand, 1939 was more notable for personal achievements than anything else. On July 4 Eddie Jr., only recently graduated from Yale following another fine season in which he captained the baseball team, made his major league debut in a pinch-hitting role in the first game of a double-header. He fouled out and then went 1-for-3 playing left field in the second contest. Naturally, the opponent was his father's own Boston Red Sox. His new team, even more naturally, was the Philadelphia A's and its manager Connie Mack.

Only months before, the senior Collins had remarked that given his own love for the game, "nothing would make me prouder than to have my young son, Eddie, follow my steps in baseball and become a success therein."[29] The first part of that equation had been achieved. At age 22 Eddie Jr. was a major leaguer, but career success would be more difficult to attain. In his rookie season the fleet left-hand hitting outfielder, now 5 feet 10 inches and a solid 175 pounds, played in but 32 games. In limited plate appearances (21), he batted .238. His next appearance with the A's in a career seriously affected by World War II was in 1941 when he appeared in 80 games and batted .242. His brief big-league career ended the next season as he appeared in 20 games and batted .235. All told Eddie Jr. played in 132 games and left the majors with a .241 career average.

In mid–January 1939, while Eddie Jr. still wore Yale blue and awaited the honor of a Yale degree, his father received a most coveted honor of his own. By receiving 213 votes of a record 274 cast by the Baseball Writer's Association of America, the senior Collins was voted into the still rather infant Baseball Hall of Fame. Also elected as new members in this class were George Sisler, who received 235 votes, and Wee Willie Keeler, who received 207, just one vote over the necessary 75 percent of all votes cast, required for selection. The addition of these three brought to 26 the total number of members, including the first set of five, elected in 1936 — Ty Cobb, Christy Mathewson, Walter Johnson, Honus Wagner and Babe Ruth. Collins was particularly pleased to join this special group of players, managers, pioneers and executives, which also included his mentor, Connie Mack, named along with several others in 1937 by a special committee.

Eddie responded to the election with his usual grace. "Frankly, I know of hardly anything that causes me more satisfaction than to be enrolled among those great players who have been named for the Hall of Fame."[30]

It was a particularly good year to become a member of the Hall. Baseball was celebrating its centennial and, accuracy of its historical ties aside, Cooperstown, New York, was the site chosen for a building in which to enshrine the members of its Hall of Fame, as well as to house the nation's preeminent baseball museum. A gala celebration was set for mid–June in that small town which sits on the banks of Otsego Lake, the body of water memorialized as "Glimmerglass" in James Fenimore Cooper's *Leatherstocking Tales*.

On June 12 some 15,000 spectators were on hand for the dedication of the National Baseball Museum and Hall of Fame and the first official induction ceremonies. When it was his turn, Collins strode to the podium. After thanking the crowd, his specific remarks were brief.

"This is about the proudest day of my life. To be able to rub elbows with the players that are here today I feel that's why I'd be glad to be the bat boy for such a team as this. Certainly a happy moment for me and I am most grateful to the baseball writers who have made it possible for me to be in this Hall of Fame. Thank you very much."[31]

In describing the ceremonies in his book *A Great Day in Cooperstown*, author Jim Reisler deems Collins acceptance speech "apt." He "*did* resemble a bat boy. That he was dressed in a slick double-breasted suit and white-tinged shoes — the nattiest of those honored — didn't hide what dominated his features, his sleepy eyes, prominent jug-ears, and only 5' 9" in height, which made him appear far younger than his fifty-two years. He looked more like an aging stock boy than one of baseball's greatest stars...."[32]

Later in the day Collins and National League shortstop great Honus Wagner each took a handful of current players and faced off in an all-star game won by the Wagner team, 4–2, at nearby Doubleday Field. Amazingly, it was the first time Collins and Wagner ever met.

Collins' induction into the Baseball Hall of Fame firmly planted his tree in the forest of the game's history. However, as another decade came to a close, unlike some of those enshrined that warm June day in upstate New York, there was a lot of baseball and a lot of life left for Collins to sort through before his career was complete. The days ahead would bring sadness and joy. Events, some within Collins' control and some not, would occur and shape his legacy. Eddie Collins was enshrined in Cooperstown, but his life was far from over.

CHAPTER 22

Missed Opportunities

"Unspoken, but underlying all the stated objections [to integrating baseball], was the most compelling reason of all: baseball tradition.... Tradition is the father of inertia and the balm of the don't rock-the-boat school."
— Robert Peterson, author, *Only the Ball Was White*[1]

In 1940 there were rumors the Yankees were for sale. Colonel Ruppert had died in 1939. One of the few men in America with the interest in baseball and the money to meet the steep sale price was Tom Yawkey. But it was neither lack of interest in the Yankees — after all, Yawkey ran his business from New York City — nor the amount of money involved that kept the maturing Red Sox owner from making the deal. The reason was Eddie Collins, who had roots in New York, but by now had developed much deeper ties to his adopted Boston.

"I [Yawkey] would like to buy the New York club, but that would mean breaking away from Eddie Collins who got me into the Red Sox deal and has a lot of his own money invested in the club. I can't do that to Cocky."[2]

So Yawkey and Collins would stay in Beantown and the arrival of a George Steinbrenner–type owner would have to await the man himself. By 1940, however, there were other changes occurring in baseball and in Boston. One in particular, the transition to regularly scheduled night baseball games, had been going on since May 1935 when the Reds and Phillies played under lights in Cincinnati. Nonetheless, the Red Sox had no interest at all in playing at night in Fenway. They did modify the ballpark during the 1939–40 off-season by installing bullpens with low fences in front of the right field bleachers. This significantly reduced the distance from home plate to right, an aid to left-handed hitters, particularly Ted Williams.

The 1940 season was a bizarre one, at least record-wise. The club ended in a tie for fourth place with an 82–72 record. That meant they won seven fewer games than in 1939. Despite the small dip, they benefited from a close race, finishing only eight games behind a Detroit team that went the distance with the Reds before losing the World Series. The Boston fans, encouraged by a team which was in first place through mid–June and still only four behind the leader on September 10, set a franchise record of 716,234 admissions.

It was a strange season for Ted Williams as well. The young slugger, by now installed in left field, had another season most would covet (.344, 23, 113). But he was not happy, complaining about his place in the lineup among other matters. He was still popular with the fans, but his brashness was wearing thin with reporters. He began to receive some critical press, did not wear it well and, in turn, received more. Instead of stepping in to treat a festering sore, team management did little or nothing. According to the authors of *Red Sox Century*, instead of bristling at the criticism of its newest star, management savored it.

"For they knew every story about Williams meant fewer stories about Cronin's managing, Collins's deals, or Yawkey's record of ownership. As long as Williams played for the Red Sox, there was little scrutiny of the organization as a whole."[3]

Perhaps that was the case when it came to management's attitude about Williams and the press, but it also could have been because Collins and his colleagues felt that Williams needed to be taken down a peg. However, when the Kid took his anger out on the Fenway fans, eventually deciding he would never again tip his cap to them, Collins fretted, one time saying, "If he'd tip his cap just once he could be elected Mayor of Boston in five minutes."[4]

And Williams, himself, credited Collins for trying to help him, saying that from the start "he was always with me and for me.... When I'd step out of line, he'd gave [sic] me fatherly advice and straighten me out."[5]

Once again the Red Sox owned the league's top team batting average. Cronin, Foxx and Doerr each had productive years at the plate. Doc Cramer hit over .300 again and the club's newest acquisition, outfielder Dom DiMaggio, younger brother of Joe, showed great promise by hitting .301 in 108 games. As usual, it was pitching that let the air out of the Red Sox's tires. It was now clear Lefty Grove at 40 was nearing the end. He finished the season 7–6, although at least his ERA was a team-best 3.99.

As the 1941 season approached, Collins earned his paycheck as he tried to sign his young stars, particularly Doerr and Williams, who were holding out. They both signed, but Doerr recalled that Collins could be tough. He did not see him in the clubhouse, recalling that Eddie was not a particularly approachable person. This notion was seconded by Billy Werber, by then no longer on the club. On the occasions when Collins invited Bobby to lunch, he was reserved and kept the discussion to the business at hand. On one occasion Doerr sought a $5,000 contract after Collins offered $3,000. During the negotiations Bobby received a rather sarcastic letter from the general manager, telling him he would receive a higher salary when he "became more established." Inside was a contract for $3,300, the amount the second sacker signed for that season.[6]

It was clear that General Manager Collins was in Boston to run a business, not win friends. That did not keep him from a cordial relationship with his biggest star, Williams, when it came to new contract time. The pair negotiated tough with one another and regularly reached an agreement in an era before agents were standard fare.

By 1941 the nation was in transition as Franklin Roosevelt's New Deal continued to attack the Great Depression while the country began getting used to a world rearming for war. What became a signature year for Ted Williams, if not the Red Sox, began during the spring with the Boston star nursing a bone chip in his ankle. By year's end he had healed to such an extent that he became the first player to reach .400 since the Giants' Bill Terry in 1930, hitting a sparkling .406. He finished boldly, by playing both ends of a doubleheader when he could have easily taken a seat on the bench to protect the mark. To add to the significance of his feat, no one has hit .400 again through the remainder of the twentieth century and beyond. Nor has anyone bettered the 56-game hitting streak, also recorded in 1941, established by Joe DiMaggio, who walked off with the league's MVP award.

The Red Sox as a team won only two more games than the previous season, finishing at 84–70, but the final count was good for a second-place finish. Still the club spent a good portion of the year in third place, well out of the pennant picture. A 17-game gap between the Sox and a Yankee squad, which also took care of their cross-town rivals, the Dodgers, in five games to capture the World Series, left Red Sox supporters wanting a lot more. A major problem, now a chronic one, was the team's inability to win on the road. In 1940 they were 37–38 and in 1941, 37–40, despite overall winning records.

Nonetheless, for fans both inside and outside Boston, there was the thrill of watching Ted Williams reach his hitting plateau in a season which also saw him lead the league in home runs (37) and finish fourth in RBIs (120). Foxx, who was slowly fading, still had 19 homers, 105 RBIs and hit .300. The other starters were solid as well, including Cronin (.311, 16, 95).

In the All-Star Game in Detroit, Williams put the icing on his cake and thrilled fans everywhere, including Eddie Collins, by hitting the game-winning home run as the American League won, 7–5.

"Brother what a beating I [Williams] took after I touched the plate! I got pounded from all sides and my own boss gave it to me the worst. Eddie Collins had come out of the stands and he gave me a belt...."[7]

Then there was Lefty Grove. His best years were behind him, but he still had one highlight left. Overall, the pitching in 1941 was weak. One bright spot was Dick Newsome, a 31-year-old rookie right-hander who went 19–10, although his 4.13 ERA was telling. On the other hand, Grove at 41 could muster but a 7–7 record. In addition, his ERA had climbed to 4.37, while his strikeouts dipped to 54 in 134 innings. It was obvious the veteran was hanging on to win a milestone 300 games. His opportunity finally came on July 25 against the Cleveland Indians in a game his manager told him was his to win or lose all the way. The game see-sawed back and forth and was tied 6–6 in the bottom of the eighth when the Red Sox tallied four times, two on Foxx's triple. Somehow an exhausted Grove made it stick and was awarded win number 300, the twelfth pitcher to do so. He never won another one, finishing his Hall-of-Fame career at 300–141 with 2,266 strikeouts.

In late 1941 the denizens of the top floor of BoSox management were at it again. During the season, apparently without consulting Cronin or Collins, Tom Yawkey convinced Billy Evans to relocate his home from Cleveland to Louisville, still the home of an upper-tier Boston minor-league franchise. Evans was led to believe the move included a free rein on player development. Evans, never completely over Cronin's interference in his handling of Pee Wee Reese, saw Yawkey's suggestion as an encouraging sign and accepted it. Then in September, Yawkey suddenly changed horses. Reports have it that after a night of heavy drinking, a frequent occurrence, the owner called Evans and relieved him of his duties. At some point between Evans' move to Louisville and the season's end, Cronin had gained the upper hand once again. Even Collins, who liked and trusted Evans, came in for some rare criticism from Yawkey. When it was over, Herb Pennock, who had returned to the Red Sox briefly as a player before becoming involved in coaching and later in minor league operations, was named head of Red Sox farm operations.

Pennock was one of Collins' best friends, if not his best. That relationship became even more solidified on October 25 when Eddie Jr. and Pennock's daughter, Jane, became engaged. The pair had known each other since 1927, but it was in the mid–thirties at an All-Star Game at Braves Field in Boston that it became something more.

According to Eddie Jr., "We immediately took a liking to each other, but nothing happened until 1939 when I signed with the A's. We played a lot of day games back then, so I'd go out to Kennett [where the Pennock family lived] in the evenings."[8] The pair married on January 3, 1942. The wedding, which took place at the Episcopal Church of the Advent in Kennett Square, was officiated, in part, by the Reverend Paul Collins, the brother of the groom. Guests included the Connie Macks, the Tom Yawkeys, and the widow of former A's president Tom Shibe.

The Collins-Pennock union came less than a month after the Japanese aerial attack on Pearl Harbor. The sneak attack on December 7, 1941, changed many lives. Baseball players, even baseball-playing sons of Hall of Famers, were not immune. A few short months after his marriage, Eddie Jr.'s baseball career was on hold when he enlisted in the navy. When he returned in 1946, a lot was changed. Like many fellow ball players, his skills had diminished. He took his shot, playing minor league ball, but his major league baseball career was over. Aided by his father-in-law Herb Pennock, who by then was the general manager of the Philadelphia Phillies, Eddie became an assistant director in their farm system. After a few years he left to go into education.

Not long after the country went to war, President Roosevelt declared that baseball should continue, noting that it was good for the country's psyche. That did not mean, however, that the players were immune from armed service nor from inspection by the "court of public opinion" under a magnifying glass like the one which examined Joe Jackson and others in World War I.

One large target brought face to face with that court was Ted Williams. Even before Pearl Harbor, the country prepared for the inevitability of war by instituting a draft system. Williams, as sole support for his mother Mae, was classified 3-A, meaning a call-up anytime soon was unlikely. Then in Janu-

Like father, like son. Eddie Collins, Jr., threw right-handed and, as shown here, batted from the left side. His brief major league career was interrupted by military service in World War II. He played with the Philadelphia A's in 1939 and again in 1941–42 (National Baseball Hall of Fame Library, Cooperstown, N. Y.).

ary 1941 he was ordered for a physical examination and reclassified 1-A. On hearing this, a patriotic Collins, who in February appeared on sportscaster Bill Stern's radio show to extol the virtues of baseball and its ability to outlast the Hitlers and Mussolinis of the world, commented on his star's reclassification. "I can tell you baseball ought to be proud to have men like Ted Williams in the service. That's the way we feel about it. And he'll make a fine soldier."[9]

Seemingly unbeknownst to Collins or anyone else, however, Williams had appealed his reclassification. Although the initial appeals were unsuccessful, eventually, by order issued from the desk of President Roosevelt, the decision was reversed. Ted Williams was again 3-A and preparing for spring training. No surprise—the appeals and the eventual reversal did not sit well with the press or the public. Although they hated to even consider the possibility of losing baseball's newest member of its ".400 Club," even the Red Sox's brass could not have been pleased with the negative publicity surrounding Ted's reclassification battle. On May 22 after enduring a storm of protests, Williams enlisted in the Naval Aviation Service, a decision which essentially guaranteed he could complete the 1942 season.

Williams' bat, if not the bad press, was certainly welcome. He ended the season winning the Triple Crown (.356, 36, 137), but apparently Ted had enlisted too late. The league's

MVP award went to the more popular choice, Yankees' second baseman Joe Gordon. Perhaps that was also because Gordon's team once again bested the Red Sox in the pennant chase. Despite a fine 93–59 record, the best Red Sox record since 1915, the Bostonians trailed the New Yorkers by nine at the end. Nevertheless, the Red Sox were much improved and certainly a competitive force. They even showed a winning record on the road (40–35), although not nearly as good as at home (53–24).

Even though the Red Sox still fielded a lineup featuring right-handed hitters, a design intended to take advantage of the friendly confines of Fenway Park, the lineup showed several significant changes in 1942. A pair of new regulars batted from the left side. At shortstop Johnny Pesky, at age 22 a speedy guy with a good glove, now stood in place of manager Joe Cronin. Collins scouted Pesky as he prepped in Louisville in 1941, liked what he saw, and signed him up. Now he was a regular. Although Cronin was still a part-time player, many thought the move was long overdue. The right side of the infield was no longer anchored by right-hand hitting Jimmie Foxx. Now 34 and the victim of an off-season beaning incident while barnstorming, Foxx was placed on waivers and picked up by the Chicago Cubs on June 1 for $10,000, an amount $2,500 over the minimum waiver price. His place was taken by 20-year-old Tony Lupien, a left-handed hitter.

There are those who criticize Collins for purchasing so many established players for so much money when he first arrived in Boston. Certainly some of those players fell below expectations, but Foxx was not one of them. From 1936 through 1940 he averaged over 39 home runs and 133 RBIs and carried a .325 batting average. Foxx was a popular player in Boston, some say the franchise's all-time best right-handed hitter. His departure was met with disappointment and criticism, reports surfacing of team dissension between Foxx and others on one side, Cronin on the other. Nonetheless, the decision was made and Foxx was gone.

The big news on the mound, where Lefty Grove no longer stood, was 26-year-old Tex Hughson. The right-hander, a Texan, used a sinking fastball and a hard curve, even mixed in an occasional knuckler, leading the league in a number of categories, including wins, as he finished his first full season at 22–6.

In spite of his team's improvement, 1942 was a difficult year for Collins. Not only did he send a son to war, he also dealt with the Williams' deferment issue, the departure of Foxx, and the certainty that a number of his younger players would not be in uniform by the next season. Even Eddie's own health was suffering. But all these difficulties paled in comparison to what Collins would face in the next few months. By the early 1940s Eddie and Mabel Collins were confirmed suburbanites, firmly entrenched in their country estate in Weston. The home at 455 Concord Road was built circa 1850 on 74 acres of farm property. When the Collins family arrived in the area, they were immediately accepted, especially with the neighborhood kids who recognized familiar faces in Williams, Doerr and Foxx when they stopped by to see their boss. Eddie repaid their interest by frequently giving the youngsters tickets to Red Sox games. One of those youngsters is now grown but recalled the Collins family to a reporter.

> He was a great guy. He was very generous giving tickets to ball games. We went to quite a few and sat in his private box besides the Red Sox dugout. He even got me tickets to the 1946 World Series.
> He was kind to my parents, too. Every holiday, he and his wife always remembered us with something. They were just great neighbors.
> When he was out in his yard, he'd say hello. And he did a lot of work on the house. He painted everything in Red Sox colors. He painted the serpentine wall white with a green top, like the green monster [at Fenway Park]. And the weathervane on the top of the barn is in the shape of a baseball bat.

He also held barbecues that Red Sox players, like Ted Williams and Bobby Doerr, attended.

His wife, Mabel, was especially nice to me. She wrote me many, many letters when I was in the Navy during World War II. She kept me up-to-date on how the Red Sox were doing."[10]

That good life ended, at least for Mabel Collins, in early 1943. She died of cancer of the colon on February 24 at age 54, following several months of illness. In writing of her death, *The Sporting News* recognized Mabel as the ultimate baseball wife, torn in recent years between rooting for her husband's team, the Red Sox, or her son's, the A's. Declaring Eddie and Mabel as "a devoted couple," they noted that "[f]ew women ... had a finer knowledge of baseball and its component parts...."[11]

Reeling from the loss of his wife of 32 years, Collins now also faced the loss of many of the players the organization had brought together for what appeared, only a year before, to be a roster ready to make a serious challenge for the pennant. They were not alone. Almost every team faced serious challenges, but the Red Sox were certainly one of those to lose the most. According to the authors of *Red Sox Century*, "No team was hit harder by the draft and rash of enlistments than the Red Sox....

"Between the end of the 1942 season and opening day of 1943, Boston lost virtually its entire starting team."[12]

Eddie and his first wife, Mabel, enjoy an afternoon at the ballpark. The couple married in 1910 and remained together until Mabel's death in 1943 (National Baseball Hall of Fame Library, Cooperstown, N. Y.).

Local sports columnist Dave Egan, a hard-drinking, hard-driving writer who delivered his views as "the Colonel" and for years carried on a running feud with Ted Williams, had a solution for the manpower shortage and quality of play. He suggested, "It might be advisable to invite the best players regardless of complexion, to the training camps."

Statements by Judge Landis and baseball ownership to the contrary, baseball in twentieth century America into the mid–1940s was a white man's game. The company line was that there was no rule agreement to discriminate against the hiring of black men to play baseball, but the lack of any African-American ball players was simple proof of the lie. One of the many excuses was that major league teams traditionally trained in the South where segregation was a way of life. In 1943 Judge Landis in a war conservation move ordered teams to train near their home base. Collins and the Red Sox scheduled their spring training at nearby Tufts College. Thus in Egan's mind the Red Sox, and for that matter the hometown Braves, no longer had "a territorial problem, no housing problem, and no travel problem, and nothing except dark and ancient prejudice will keep them from giving the black man an equal opportunity with the white." But Egan knew nothing would be done because, "Neither Eddie Collins ... or Bob Quinn [now] of the Braves ever has opened his mouth on the subject, for the very good reason that baseball has no defense."[13]

Egan was correct on both counts. Nothing was done in 1943 by the Red Sox or anyone else to change the existing system, and the Red Sox, as well as all of baseball, would have benefited from an infusion of African-American baseball talent. When the season ended, the Red Sox had fallen to seventh place. Their 68–84 record left them 29 games behind the Yankees, once again World Series winners, this time in five games over the Cardinals of Billy Southworth. Just as distressing was the drop in attendance of almost 400,000 patrons.

For Eddie Collins it was, indeed, lonely at the top. Living the life of a widower, he kept busy attempting to plug holes in a leaking tub, as one after another his remaining regular players went off to war. In September he found some solace, joining a vast array of former star players on August 26 at the Polo Grounds for a War Bonds game, where the only way to gain admittance was to purchase a war bond. Connie Mack was there as was the Babe, old friend Tris Speaker, George Sisler, Walter Johnson, and many others who donned uniforms for an old-timers' game. The crowd roared with laughter when first outfielder Red Murray, then Collins and finally Speaker all muffed routine pop flies off the bat of Ruth. The old timers were "terrible," said *Time* magazine, "but the galleries loved them."[14]

One positive in 1943 for Collins and family occurred in late November when the junior Collins and wife Jane gave birth to a boy, Eddie Collins III. A photo of mother and child, with proud grandfathers Herb Pennock and Eddie looking on, is a unique one, as Eddie III and younger brother Pete are the only grandsons whose grandfathers are both members of the Hall of Fame.

The granddads were friends — that is well known — but on this occasion they were not in total agreement. General Manager Pennock of the Phillies saw the newest member of the family as "a left-handed pitcher" while General Manager Collins of the Red Sox insisted "he will throw with his right arm and play second base."[15]

In 1944 a strange thing happened: The Yankees did not win the pennant. It was the St. Louis Browns, usually not even a suitor, who captured the flag. The patched-together Red Sox showed improvement, finishing in fourth, 12 behind the winning Browns, who eventually lost the World Series in six games to their cross-town rivals the Cards. In August the Red Sox had been very much in the thick of it, in second only three and one-half games out, but a dismal record in September proved their undoing. Their final record was 77–77. The best performances in 1944 were turned in by the soon-to-be drafted Bobby Doerr (.325, 15, 81) and Tex Hughson (18–5, 2.26).

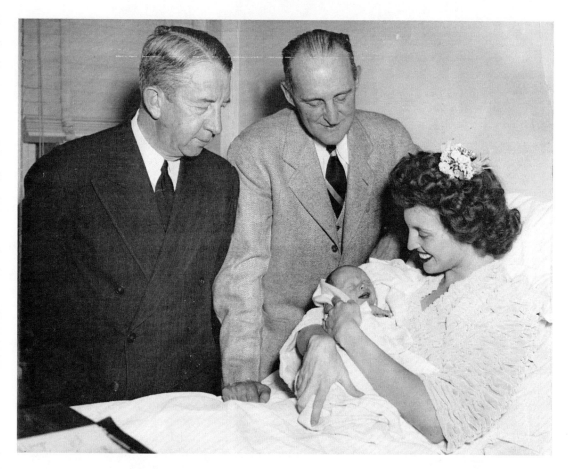

In November 1943 Collins and former teammate and close friend Herb Pennock (right) took a first look at new grandchild Eddie Collins III. The eight-day-old baby was the son of Eddie Collins, Jr., and Pennock's daughter, Jane. Eddie, Jr., served in the armed forces at the time (Urban Archives, Temple University, Philadelphia, Pennsylvania).

If nothing else, more fans showed up in 1944 (506,975), but the final figure stood only seventh in the league when team attendance figures were compared. For Collins better attendance made for better pay. His $24,000 salary was reportedly increased by a bonus in the neighborhood of $6,000, a figure calculated on team attendance.[16]

The new year started off in more encouraging fashion for Collins and his family. On February 13, 1945, Reverend Paul Collins, now of Poultney, Vermont, proudly officiated at the wedding of his father at St. Peter's Episcopal Church in Weston. Eddie's bride was Emily Jane Mann Hall of Brookline, Massachusetts. It was a second marriage for Emily. Her first husband, an army colonel, was killed in a plane crash in California the previous year. The new Mrs. Collins and Mabel Collins had been close friends and the two couples spent time together, as well.

Collins' honeymoon, however, was a short one. By March he was feeling heat from several sides on the question of baseball integration. This time it was a lot more intense than a mere volley of rhetoric from the Colonel, and at least some of it was the result of his own doing.

Much of baseball's record on integration is unclear, the result of maneuverings and machinations that took place behind closed doors. There are some things, however, that are crystal clear. One is that no black had taken the field in Organized Baseball in the twentieth century and only a handful before it. Second, that in contradiction of the obvious, Judge Kenesaw Mountain Landis, the granite face of baseball and its ruler for over two decades, publicly maintained in 1942 that, "Negroes are not barred from Organized Baseball by the commissioner [Landis] and never have been in the 21 years I have served...! That is the business of the managers and the club owners."[17]

In the meantime Larry MacPhail, then president of the Brooklyn Dodgers, challenged the judge's assertion and set the record straight, admitting there was a barrier. "[T]here has been an unwritten law tantamount to an agreement between major league clubs on the subject of the racial issue."[18]

That was the status quo in 1942 and it remained so in early 1945, although by now a number of actors were combining to bring matters to a head when it came to the issue of allowing African-Americans into Organized Baseball. Over the years white owners and team management had maintained that black ball players did not possess the skill level required of major league ball players. This issue was broached in 1943 by Dave Egan as "the Colonel" when he questioned Collins and the Red Sox, as well as the Braves, for not addressing wartime manpower issues by signing black ball players. Implicit in his argument was the general feeling, often borne out in exhibition games involving the two races or when one attended games involving teams from the professional Negro leagues, that many black ball players possessed major league skills. Then there was the growing notion of moral fairness. During the war black men fought side by side with white men, soldiers all, much too often shedding blood. That blood was always red–American and not black or white. This commonality called for an equal opportunity on the ball field. The cause was trumpeted by an ever-increasing outcry from not only a vocal black press, but even some members of the white press. In Boston, for example, there was Mabrey "Doc" Kountze, a black journalist for the *Boston Chronicle* and the *Boston Guardian*. In addition to Dave Egan, there was Bill Cunningham of the *Post*, as well as other white newsmen. In the face of the heat emanating from their typewriters and pens, many old unspoken barriers were slowly fading or dying off all together. And on November 25, 1944, there was the passing of Judge Landis, dead of a heart attack at 78.

While it is unfair to place all the blame on the judge for baseball's whites-only policy, it can be argued that if instead of inaction Landis had taken action to integrate, the face of the game literally would have changed much earlier. His position as baseball's leader was taken on April 24, 1945, by Albert Benjamin "Happy" Chandler, a former U.S. Senator from segregated Kentucky, whose philosophy on the race issue was untested, but who acted as if he meant it when he said if blacks can make it in war, they can make it in baseball.

Against this backdrop came an effort in Boston in 1945 to gain a tryout for several black baseball players. Pressure for the tryout came from a liberal Jewish city councilman named Isadore Muchnick, who was threatening both the Braves and Red Sox with denial of their permit to play Sunday baseball if they did not employ black ball players. Collins, who was acutely aware of the negative financial impact of the lack of Sunday baseball from his days in Philadelphia, wanted to head this matter off at the pass. Never one to stray far from the company — and in this case the Organized Baseball line — Eddie wrote back to Muchnick sounding very much like Judge Landis in 1942.

"As I wrote to one of your fellow councillors last April [1944], I have been connected with the Red Sox for twelve years and during that time we have never had a single request for a try-out by a colored applicant.... It is beyond my understanding how anyone can insinuate or believe that 'all ball players regardless of race, color, or creed, have not been treated in the American way' so far as having an equal opportunity to play for the Red Sox."[19]

At some time in the recent past, perhaps just a few years prior to 1945, Collins' letter to Muchnick might have sufficed to postpone the matter for some other day. Similar responses to similar efforts had obviously done the trick in the past. But the times were different, and apparently so was Isadore Muchnick.

Wendell Smith, a writer for the *Pittsburgh Courier*, a black weekly newspaper, takes credit for giving Muchnick the idea for his cause. Later Muchnick advised Smith of Collins' response to his plea. "So I [Smith] called him [Muchnick] back and said I was prepared to bring some Negro ball players for a tryout" with both Boston clubs. While Muchnick made the arrangements, Smith chose the players.

I picked Jackie Robinson, Marvin Williams who was a second baseman for the Philadelphia Stars and Sam Jethroe of the Cleveland Buckeyes. Jethroe was an outstanding outfielder, great speed, a good hitter. He wasn't a power hitter. He was more of a slap hitter. In the Negro leagues he was a .350 hitter. Williams was what I could call a a [*sic*] steady, dependable hitter.

I picked Jackie because he had played on integrated teams. He was a college man, UCLA, great collegiate athlete, a natural. He played all the major sports — football, basketball and baseball. He had just come out of the Army and had signed with the Kansas City Monarchs. He wasn't necessarily the best player but he was the best player at that time for this particular situation.[20]

In the midst of Isadore Muchnick's push for a tryout, Collins was approached about integration from another direction. Again a writer for a black newspaper, this time Sam Lacy, sports editor of the *Boston Afro-American*, was the source. In a letter dated March 3, 1945, Lacy wrote identical letters to Collins, Larry MacPhail, by now the president of the Yankees, and Bob Quinn of the Braves. The thrust of the letter was toward Collins, due to his recent remarks. Word traveled fast. In the letter Lacy proposed the "appointment of a colored man to make a survey of Negro baseball to the end of ... finding the best way" to employ a black ball player, "if and when that occurs."[21]

Unlike MacPhail and Quinn, Collins replied to Lacy by letter dated April 11, 1945, telling him he thought the idea "contains a lot of merit," but is better left to the league president to decide. He therefore was passing it on to current league president Will Harridge. In his letter Collins claimed Lacy's letter had only arrived the week before, therefore questioning the March 3 date as, perhaps, a typo.[22]

On its face the letter was quite positive and encouraging. In his book *Shut Out: A Story of Race and Baseball in Boston*, author Howard Bryant attributes both the timing and the cordiality of Collins' letter to Lacy to the pressure the Boston general manager was feeling from Muchnick and others. For by early April, although the Braves did nothing, the Red Sox had agreed to give a tryout to the black ball players selected by Wendell Smith. In Bryant's opinion, "While Lacy's letter sat on Collins' desk he succumbed to Muchnick and hastily agreed to a tryout. Cornered, he then replied to Lacy...."[23]

It is difficult to determine the accuracy of Bryant's assertion. Certainly Collins was feeling pressure. In his cover letter to Harridge, enclosing Lacy's letter and his reply to it, Collins tells the league's chief official, "I personally feel that it is an issue that we are going to be faced with in the future, possibly the immediate future."[24] It was not the first time Collins had corresponded with Harridge on the subject. In January 1943 he sent the league president a copy of Dave Egan's column criticizing Collins and the Red Sox for not filling their manpower shortage with black players. Apparently, this was not the first such clipping sent by Collins, and they were finding their way to Judge Landis, who had called Collins about Egan, as Collins closed by saying, "Maybe he [Landis] will 'enjoy' reading this one."[25]

Perhaps between 1943 and 1945 Collins' feelings about the issue had changed, perhaps not. At any rate, the Lacy letters dutifully forwarded, it was out of his hands. A committee of two, one from each league, was appointed to join Lacy and at least one other individual to do the proposed survey. Branch Rickey represented the National League. Larry MacPhail, either a calculated choice or a spectacularly poor one, based on his previously stated sentiments, was selected for the American League. MacPhail protested his selection and expressed doubts the proposal would accomplish anything. And, perhaps in a self-fulfilling prophecy, little or nothing was accomplished.

As for the Red Sox's tryout, it went forward on April 16, although not before some delay. And despite indications this was the first tryout of African-American ball players by a major league club, it was not. On April 6, only a few days prior to the scheduled Red Sox's tryout, Branch Rickey, now in the Dodgers' front office, under pressure himself and enraged because of its timing, held a tryout for two aging black players at his club's wartime camp at Bear Mountain, N.Y. A reporter and photographer from the *Daily Worker*, a Communist newspaper, only added to Rickey's frustration. The tryout left Joe Bostic, the black sportswriter who pushed for it, with the feeling Rickey would be the last person to support bringing an end to the color line in baseball.[26]

On the whole the Red Sox's tryout, not the Dodgers' tryout, is the best remembered. Not for a different outcome, but because there was no Communist stigma attached, the tryout was at Fenway Park instead of an out-of-the-way baseball camp, it involved younger players — particularly Jackie Robinson, the man who eventually broke the color barrier — and finally because of the overriding fact that the Red Sox, given a grand opportunity to be the first, were instead the very last team to employ a black player. Not until Pumpsie Green in 1959 did an African-American play for the Red Sox. To be sure, the Red Sox's tryout is of particular importance to any study of the baseball career of Eddie Collins, for he was the general manager of the Boston Red Sox. Although it did not take place at any time during his 25-year playing career, the Red Sox's tryout and its result form a large chunk of his baseball legacy as it stands today.

In April 1945, Wendell Smith met his three players in New York and they took a train to Boston, where they cooled their heels before the Red Sox finally said the tryout would go forward on Monday, April 16, one day before the club opened the 1945 season in New York. How much a newspaper piece by the Colonel played in that scheduling will never be known. Since the column did not appear in the *Boston Daily Record* until the same day as the tryout, perhaps it made no difference at all, but maybe advance knowledge of Dave Egan's intent to write it had an energizing effect. Just the same, the column once again placed Collins flatly on a hot griddle. And just in case the Red Sox were using the death of Franklin Delano Roosevelt as an excuse — he died on April 12, one day after Smith's players arrived in town — it addressed that as well.

> He [Collins] is living in *Anno Domini* 1945, and not in the dust-covered year 1865.
> He is residing in the city of Boston, Massachusetts, and not in the city of Mobile, Alabama.
> ... [I]t is not Abraham Lincoln for whom his flags flutter at half-staff...; it is Franklin Roosevelt for whom the bells toll, almost 80 years later to the day....
> There! We thought that somebody should help Mr. Collins straighten himself out on these little matters.... [W]e feel obliged to inform you that since Wednesday last three citizens of the United States have been trying vainly to get a tryout with his ball team....
> But Eddie Collins has slammed the door shut and placed his back against it.[27]

If, indeed, as the Colonel alleged, it was Collins who slammed the door shut, it was then also Collins who opened it on April 16. After reporting to the Fenway Park clubhouse, Robinson, Williams and Jethroe dressed in their uniforms and joined in progress a tryout of several young white boys. As Muchnick and Smith looked on, their three stalwarts went to the outfield to shag some fly balls. Although reports differed as to their presence, it seems Joe Cronin was there to watch and Collins, too. Several reports place Collins by himself high in the stands near the club offices on top of the park itself. The presence of Cronin and Collins notwithstanding, the black ball players were skeptical from the start.

"I remember it clearly," Jackie Robinson later said. "I sort of laughed within myself at what I felt was the uselessness of the venture. I didn't feel anything would come of it, especially after the run-around that we thought we had been given for the three or four days we were in Boston." Nevertheless, Jackie and the others felt when it came to hitting they put on a good show. Robinson in particular felt good, saying, "I don't believe I ever hit the ball better than I did that day. I hit the fence several times with good, hard line drives."

Hugh Duffy, a Red Sox coach and former star with the club in the 1890s, conducted the tryout and impressed the black stars when he brought out a new box of baseballs.

"They gave us all the chance in the world to display our potentialities," Robinson said. "They gave us the equipment to bring out the best in us, and we sensed there was an extra effort on the part of the men who were running the tryout. If it hadn't been for the fact there were no Negroes in Organized Baseball — and at the time we didn't have any idea that Brooklyn was planning to bring them in — we would have felt that we had a wonderful chance."[28]

At the end of the tryout, Duffy congratulated the players on a fine showing and had each fill out an application card, saying the Red Sox would contact them. They did not.

Instead a few days later, in response to a letter from Wendell Smith requesting further information, Collins responded that an injury to Cronin "threw everything out of gear." He also expressed concern about tampering with players under contract with the Negro leagues.[29] A little over six months later, however, Branch Rickey and his Dodgers stunned the sports world, in particular, and the country, in general, by signing the same Jackie Robinson to a minor league contract. On April 15, 1947, about two years to the day of the Red Sox's tryout, Robinson took the field against the Boston Braves. The color line had been crossed forever.

On Robinson's initial signing Collins was quoted thusly: "Robinson worked out for us last spring. Very few players can step into the majors from college and sandlot ball. Of course, they always have the chance to prove themselves in the minors. More power to Robinson if he can make the grade."[30]

Of course, Collins' reaction to Robinson's signing avoids the main issue and also begs the question: Why did Rickey seize the moment and not Collins? Both men had keen eyes for baseball talent, perhaps as good as any in the game. Each had a firm grasp on the economics of baseball, as well. A black baseball star meant a larger demographic to draw upon and the prospect for increased revenue. Rickey was able to grasp that concept, but so was Collins and just about every other baseball executive. Was the difference simply that Collins carried a deep-seated prejudice and Rickey did not? Author Howard Bryant thinks so, calling Collins "a known insider and a bigot. He played his entire career in a segregated game and saw no reason to change it. If change was inevitable he wasn't going to help it along. For Collins, it wasn't just blacks, either. During his time with the Red Sox the club suffered from the ironic reputation of being horribly anti–Catholic and anti–Semitic as well."[31]

That Collins was a baseball insider few can argue. If baseball was inclined to follow an unwritten rule which barred blacks, not only would Collins follow it, he would find reasons to publicly support it, such as when he claimed blacks would not want to play in the major leagues since "they were doing better financially in their own leagues."[32] Eddie had stayed well within the lines during his entire career, particularly during the Black Sox scandal. Back then he could have spoken out and, perhaps, damaged the baseball establishment. He did not do so then and he would not veer off the playing field now.

Rickey, on the other hand, was a baseball maverick. He clashed often with his baseball bosses; owner Phil Ball of the Browns was just one example. He had also clashed from time to time with Judge Landis, one of the few to do so. The pair had a well-documented feud over the development and use of minor league farm systems and the signing and retention of minor league players. If Rickey decided integration was a good thing, on humanitarian terms or economic, he would move forward, baseball tradition and convention be damned.

But was Collins a bigot as Howard Bryant contends? Did his actions over the years indicate a person who regarded or treated African-Americans, Catholics and Jews with hatred and intolerance? Setting aside for the moment the issue of baseball integration, there is scant evidence. In his early semiprofessional days in the Northern League in New England, Collins had been a member of Billy Lush's team that refused to play a game against a black pitcher. Since Lush was in charge and had played against blacks before in his career, it seems the maneuver was a sick ploy by a manager to win a game. Collins played no significant part in it.

Later in 1918 there were rumors that Collins demanded the dismissal of long-time White Sox trainer Bill Buckner, a black. Since Collins was still with the team when Buckner was rehired in 1922, the charges against him seem groundless. In fact, Buckner served as trainer while Collins managed the White Sox in 1925–26, and when Eddie was seriously injured during a game in 1925, he draped his arm around Buckner for support as he was helped off the field.[33]

On a more personal note is the unsolicited sentiment of a black Pullman attendant, interviewed in 1931 about his experiences with traveling ball players, all presumably white. According to the porter, H.N. Hall, who had been at it for 18 years, "Baseball players are the limit; most of them are vulgar and uncouth....

"Yet one of the finest passengers I ever had the privilege to wait on was a ball player. Mr. Eddie Collins; very quiet, and dignified."[34]

Such actions and statements, as well as Collins' entire demeanor, argue against one totally unsubstantiated charge that came out of the Red Sox's tryout in 1945 and stands practically untouched today. It was first reported in 1979, some 34 years after the tryout, that *Boston Globe* baseball writer Clif Keane, present during the Robinson tryout as a spectator, claimed someone yelled from the stands, "Get those niggers off the field."[35] Speculation hinted at Cronin, Collins or even Tom Yawkey. No one knows if it was any of these individuals. As to Collins, it seems completely out of character.

There is even less to support the charges that Collins was anti–Catholic and anti–Semitic. When he and Yawkey took over the Red Sox in 1933, they essentially cleaned house. Boston is a city with a large Catholic population. Since many of the stadium workers and team employees were Catholic, that group suffered greatly by the personnel moves. As stated earlier, Bill Gavin, who worked for the Red Sox in the 1920s, declared that the reason for the changes was religious since Collins was Episcopalian.[36] There is little else regarding these charges. On the other hand, there are the comments of Tom Dowd, the Red Sox's traveling secretary, who spoke about Collins' contributions to a local Catholic church. "Each year," said Dowd, "Collins made contributions to the church. In fact, he and Tom Yawkey and Duffy Lewis, the Braves' road secretary, gave the organ to the church."[37]

In all this it must be remembered, Collins was not the majority owner of the Red Sox. He was a minor partner in the venture, an officer, a trusted advisor for sure, but still a soldier subject to command. In time, Collins would head to pasture, then pass on, but the Red

Sox's policy regarding African-American ball players, a costly one since the team suffered on the field for not taking advantage of the array of black talent available, post-dated Collins by some ten years. And if in later years Joe Cronin could explain away his inaction by saying his hands were tied since he was not the boss, Collins had that argument, too. However, he never used it. He never spoke publicly about his reasoning or the integration of the game in general.

In judging Collins' actions, one must be careful not to judge too harshly. Like most, he was a product of his times. In the context of these times, in 1945 and before, Collins was merely mirroring the actions of baseball's executives and its ownership, and even the vast majority of the players themselves. Until late 1945, so was Branch Rickey. What Collins and many others like him did in keeping baseball segregated can not be excused, merely explained. When examined by today's standards, the verdict seems simple. Collins' resistance to change and his rationalization for it are indefensible. Nevertheless, at the time, his lack of action and excuse making mirrored his fellow baseball leaders, nothing more, and nothing less. Only when Branch Rickey stepped up and did the right thing did Collins' impassivity and that of others appear truly shameful. Had Collins done the right thing, had he used his influence and opportunity to sign Jackie Robinson or one of the other black candidates to a contract in April 1945, we would honor Eddie Collins today as a baseball giant and a pathfinder in the American Civil Rights movement. Sadly, he did not and we do not. His intransigence not only cost him a much more esteemed position in baseball history, but it also probably cost his Red Sox's club one or more pennants in the ensuing years.

On the day of the Red Sox's tryout, the team was given the day off in preparation for the new season. As it turned out, once again ill-equipped to compete in a watered-down league, the Boston Americans took the whole season off, finishing seventh, even lower than in 1944. That nearly 100,000 more fans attended their games and watched a 71–83 team probably reflected a nation recovering from the initial shock of war more than a fascination with the quality of ball the Red Sox were playing.

There was one bright spot for the Red Sox in 1945. Rookie David "Boo" Ferriss, a 23-year-old right-hander from Mississippi, stepped into the rotation and immediately became the anchor of the staff, compiling a record of 21–10 and an ERA of 2.96. Ferriss, a product of the Red Sox's farm system, worked for $700 a month that year. He considered "Mr. Collins" one of his favorite people, a real gentleman, and found the general manager's new bride Emily "a lovely person." Money was not a motivator for Ferriss at that point, for he had recently returned from the service and was just happy to be in Boston.[38] Collins was happy to have Ferriss in Boston as well. As he watched news reports proclaiming an end to the war, he knew in his heart better days were ahead for his country in 1946 and for his Red Sox, too.

CHAPTER 23

Parting Shots

"I've lost the best friend I've ever had in baseball."
— Ted Williams[1]

Although the Red Sox's general manager was excited about his club's chances for 1946, few in the Boston press shared Eddie Collins' optimism. One in particular, Harold Kaese of the *Globe*, writing in April's *Saturday Evening Post*, minced few words. The article, entitled "What's the Matter With the Red Sox?" placed a great deal of the blame for the club's failures on Joe Cronin, but both Collins and Yawkey fell victim to a sharp word or two, as well.

Each spring Cronin is expected to lead the Red Sox to their first pennant since 1918 — a mere matter of twenty-seven years. Each fall Cronin is pictured by his critics as a man who could not win a pennant with an All-Star team. This will be a usual spring. The Red Sox will win the pennant in 1946. What will the fall bring? A championship or more abuse for Cronin...?

At first ... admirers gave him everything from Irish terriers to silver services. He was burdened with temperamental stars. Yawkey coddled favorites with hunting parties to his South Carolina island. General manager Eddie Collins wigwagged signals from his box on the roof.

Now the alibis are largely forgotten, except by those who love Cronin for his courage, by a few sympathetic analysts, and by some who would blame the Triple Alliance of Yawkey, Collins and Cronin *in toto*. Some dissidents say that Collins is about as active as a book end, and that Yawkey is a bemused example of inherited wealth. Even the Fenway Park pigeons are feathery bums to the sourest Red Sox critics.

But most Red Sox fans are sorry for Yawkey and most still have a solemn respect for Collins.... It is Cronin who meets the onslaught head on, his big chin a breakwater for a tide of complaint. Some Bostonians criticize art, some music, some Harvard, but many just criticize Cronin.[2]

The attacks came from within as well. In 1945 George "Pinky" Woods, a 30-year-old hurler who had completed his armed service, pitched for the Red Sox, finishing with a record of 4–7 and a 4.19 ERA. As the regular Red Sox players returned from war, a major reshuffling took place. Woods was a victim, sold to minor league Indianapolis in early 1946. He was unhappy, feeling that Red Sox management was insensitive to his medical conditions. When columnist Kaese asked what was wrong with the Red Sox, Woods had an answer. The Vermont native told his hometown newspaper that the trouble was the "powers behind the throne." Eddie Collins was the biggest "fly in the ointment."[3]

As usual, Collins shrugged off the criticism, for at the time he had more on his mind. In January he and his family celebrated the military discharge of son Eddie Jr. Hopes ran high for a quick return to baseball; the opposite had occurred. The younger Collins' ability to run, previously a strong point in his arsenal, was hampered by an Achilles tendon problem similar to that suffered by a number of servicemen who attempted to return to the sport. Coupled with a reported illness, the medical problems limited his spring comeback to a few innings. He was cut by the A's in early April.[4] Though he would bounce around in the upper minors for a while, Eddie Jr.'s baseball playing career was over. The senior Collins, who harbored high hopes for his youngest son, masked his disappointment well.

"I'm often asked if I have any regrets that my son, Eddie, Jr., did not develop into a great baseball star. I have none."[5]

The Boston press overlooked the Red Sox in 1946 and felt moved to predict continued failure because they expected the team's returning regulars to encounter a fate similar to Eddie Collins Jr. and others like him. Those "experts" were wrong. Out of the gate this newest edition of Boston's American League entry won five straight games, took first place, and remained there the entire season. This team owned by Yawkey, developed by Collins, and managed by Cronin, by now a full-fledged bench manager, the same "Triple Alliance" grilled in the spring by Kaese and many others became the city's conquering heroes on September 13 in Cleveland when the club clinched its first pennant since 1918. The final record of 104–50 was the franchise's second-best all-time. Over 1,400,000 fans, just part of a record-breaking year for baseball attendance in general, practically burst through the gates of Fenway Park to see them do it.

The charge on the field was led by Ted Williams, showing absolutely no rust from his time away as he constructed an MVP season. Virtually ignoring an over-shift of players to the right side of the infield, designed especially for him and tried previously by the wily Jimmy Dykes and now by Cleveland's Lou Boudreau, Williams hit .342, stroked 38 home runs and drove in 123 runners. In addition, Bobby Doerr (.271, 18, 116), Johnny Pesky (.335, 2, 55) and Dom DiMaggio (.316, 7, 73) were in mid-career form. A new acquisition, the former Detroit first sacker Rudy York, benefited from hitting behind Williams and added power to the lineup (.276, 17, 119).

However, it was improved pitching that thrust the pennant winners 12 games ahead of second-place Detroit at the finish. The leaders on the mound were Boo Ferris (25–6, 3.25) and 30-year-old Tex Hughson (20–11, 2.75). Mickey Harris added 17 wins and Joe Dobson 13 of his own.

What should have been exuberance on September 13 when the Red Sox clinched the pennant on the strength of a Hughson three-hitter and Williams' inside-the-park home run had been tempered by the loss of six straight games before they got there. Even the clubhouse celebration seemed anti-climactic, publicized more for the absence of superstar Williams, than for what it represented by way of accomplishment. Then the series was delayed when the Dodgers and Cardinals ended the National League regular season in a tie. While they waited, the Red Sox played an all-star team and Williams was struck in the right elbow by a pitched ball. To a superstitious Collins, it must have seemed like déjà vu 1914.

Nevertheless, as the World Series approached, the Boston press ate crow and lauded the architects of victory. Harold Kaese was particularly humble, sending a telegram of apology to Cronin. "Congratulations to a champ who made me a chump."[6] Later he gave Eddie a nod as well, not exactly waxing poetic, but refuting claims which had lingered since the mid-thirties about his interference in Cronin's managerial affairs.

"As a general manager, Collins may be a pygmy compared to his stature as a second baseman, but he has not interfered with Cronin's direction of the Red Sox on the field. The Red Sox did not win the pennant because Collins quit interfering, but because Cronin found the winning combination."[7]

But if Collins and the Red Sox thought winning the pennant would give them even a brief respite from the winds of controversy, they were wrong. On the eve of the series, their opponents, the Cardinals, now confirmed, rumors began circulating that Ted Williams was on the trading block. One such tidbit had him off to New York for Joe DiMaggio and a pitcher. Whether he was on the block — which seems unlikely — or he was not, the story and how the ball club reacted to it became more important than the truth of the matter. And, of course, the timing — the eve of a World Series — was crucial. For the Red Sox it could not have been worse.

Collins was visibly upset. When asked about the rumor, he repeatedly said, "Nuts to that."[8] A simple "No" presumably would have been better since that comment, and others from Red Sox officials, were considered non-denials and the story continued to fester. When Williams hit a meager .200 with no home runs and only a single RBI as the Red Sox lost the series in seven games, the last a 4–3 cliff-hanger involving a mad dash to the plate by the Cards' Enos Slaughter and controversy surrounding Pesky's handling of the relay throw; Collins' handling of the William's trade press debacle came in for its share of the blame. It did not help that Harold Kaese later wrote that the idea was Cronin's, vetoed by Yawkey, leaving Collins in the middle.[9]

By the end of 1946 Collins would have been happy just to be in the middle. At the start of the year, the Red Sox did some reshuffling at the top, including a redefinition of Eddie's job duties. Long-time club traveling secretary Phil Troy was named assistant general manager. His new job duties included handling of the business end of the club, as well as management of Fenway Park. This left Collins in charge of the handling of the players, as well as a growing and by now extensive farm system. If the intent of the division of the workload was to ease the burden on an aging general manager, who was approaching 60, it apparently did not. Exhausted by the ups and downs of a year which saw a son's baseball career take an abrupt downward turn and the ball club he helped build reach a crescendo peak, then fade, Collins fell ill the day before Thanksgiving. In mid–December, having skipped the minor and major league meetings in Los Angeles, he stopped by Fenway Park. His appearance was not good. Always a slender man, he had lost at least 20 pounds. Not one to sit around, Eddie visited the ball park for a few hours each day, but in his absence Joe Cronin handled many of his duties. Although information concerning the cause of Collins' health issues was kept quiet at the time, it appears from later information that Eddie was suffering from a heart condition.

In February 1947, perhaps recognizing the seriousness of Collins' condition, his alma mater Columbia awarded Eddie with a bronze medal for his standing as a "beloved and well-remembered graduate" and for his years of service to the alumni as the president of the school's local Boston alumni chapter.[10]

Although Collins was able to come to the office at least part-time in 1947, his duties were in large part assumed by Joe Cronin and to some extent even by Tom Yawkey. In late January the trio reluctantly agreed to the installation of lights for night baseball at Fenway.

One task Collins was still able to fulfill in 1947 was the signing of Ted Williams, the subject of all those distracting and headline-grabbing trade rumors the previous fall. On February 3 Williams sat down with Collins and signed for a reported $75,000. Collins was ecstatic, even though the figure was a hefty one.

"We have never had any trouble signing Williams. Almost always, we have let him name his own figure in the hope he would live up to what he thought he was worth. He has done so, and we are hopeful he will continue to do so. He's a great ball player but he's never tough to sign."[11]

Some baseball executives, including Sam Breadon of the Cardinals, Washington's Clark Griffith and even best buddy Herb Pennock of the Phillies, voiced opinions that Collins and the Red Sox were too generous with Williams. Upon learning of their criticism, Collins lashed back in an uncharacteristically caustic manner.

"I'm sick and tired of hearing the blasts.... We're paying Williams' salary; they're not....

"We are paying Williams what we think he is worth at the gate....

"I'm tired of hearing all this talk of Stan Musial [of the Cardinals] not getting as much as Ted. As far as I am concerned, Musial can't carry Williams' glove...."[12]

The response to Collins' comments about the extremely popular Musial was not limited to the participants. Griffith called Eddie "just a peevish old man. He can't stand criticism."[13] But it was Eddie's comments about Musial that struck the wrong piano key. The reaction was widespread and was practically all anti–Collins. There was almost a unanimous feeling Collins was wrong to make the comment in the first place. Almost as many felt he was also wrong about his assessment of the abilities of the two players. Although Musial, a terrific National League player that Collins had probably seldom seen, had not performed much better than Williams in the 1946 World Series, he garnered support from all sides. According to H.G. Salsinger of the *Detroit News*, "Perhaps Eddie Collins has the two players confused. At the conclusion of the last World's Series, it seemed to be the general opinion that Williams could not carry Musial's glove."[14]

Despite the acidity of the attacks, Williams, like Musial a totally innocent bystander, found some humor in it. "After reading the writer's comparisons between myself and Stan, I came to the conclusion that Williams stinks, but I've still got Collins on my side."[15]

Given Collins' history for trying to avoid even the hint of controversy, one wonders if his outburst in early 1947 was a result of his illness. At any rate in 1947, Williams, now more than ever living up to his nickname "the Splendid Splinter," had a banner year. Once again he captured his league's triple crown (.343, 32, 114), although Joe DiMaggio was named MVP by a scant margin. A number of other regulars did their part at the plate, too, including catcher Birdie Tebbetts, Pesky and Dom DiMaggio, but it was not enough. The Red Sox fell to third and ended the year 83–71. The pitching, so recently on the rise, fell back and once again became the Achilles heel as both Hughson and Ferris battled arm problems. Only 30-year-old Joe Dobson (18–8, 2.95) excelled. And once again the team suffered road woes, finishing 34–41 away from home.

Throughout the year rumors circulated that Collins, still quite ill, was out and Cronin in as general manager. Then in September Eddie celebrated his forty-first year in baseball with an announcement that he was feeling much better, ready to resume his duties. Therefore, it came as a bit of a surprise that just a few days later, on September 29, the Red Sox announced the hiring of a new manager by way of Joe McCarthy, the former highly successful manager of the New York Yankees. Joe Cronin now became the general manager replacing Collins, who would retain the title of vice president. In retrospect, the chronology of events makes sense. Tom Yawkey often stated that Collins would remain general manager as long as he wanted the job. He would, in other words, only leave on his own terms. By declaring himself ready to resume the position, Collins could now step down under his own power and turn the job over to Cronin. The hiring of a manager who had led the club's chief rival to seven world titles and an additional pennant in a little over 15 seasons seemed, at the time, like the move of the century.

The Red Sox responded to McCarthy during the 1948 regular season as they won 96 games and finished the pennant chase in a dead heat with the Cleveland Indians. All they had to do was win a playoff game with the Tribe at Fenway and they would face off in an all–Boston World Series against the surprising Boston Braves. That seemed a good bet since the Red Sox had started slow, but by the end of the year were operating on all cylinders. However, on October 4 the Indians, behind Gene Bearden — who garnered win number 20 — ruined the party, 8–3. Once again, the Red Sox club was a bridesmaid.

Although Collins' health seemed to be improving in 1948, his psyche took a crushing blow earlier that year when on January 30 Herb Pennock passed away from a cerebral hemorrhage, only days before his fifty-fourth birthday. Upon learning the news, Eddie was so overcome by grief he could not even talk about it. The pair had been friends ever since Pennock came to the A's as an 18-year-old rookie in 1912.

Now that Collins' management duties were greatly reduced, he had more time on his hands. In August the Red Sox's vice president and his wife Emily traveled to San Francisco on a business-pleasure trip. In September when Charles Graham, the current president of the Association of Professional Baseball Players of America, died, Collins, who at the time was vice president of the organization, agreed to serve as president. He was formally elected to the post early in 1949, winning the nod over former umpire-in-chief Bill Klem. The association, some 11,000 strong, was not a labor union, but rather a group whose purpose was to furnish financial aid to destitute former ball players and umpires. It was only to be used as a last resort. Eddie had served as a director for the organization over the years, joining other fellow ball players such as Mickey Cochrane, Joe Cronin, Rabbit Maranville, Gabby Hartnett and many others. More recently, he had become an officer and now its latest president. One issue on his early agenda was the matter of continued financing. Early on, the organization benefited from a share of the proceeds from the annual All-Star Game. When the war intervened and the funds were diverted to war charities, that funding stopped. As a baseball insider Collins seemed the perfect man to seek new resources. He quickly received assurances from the presidents of both leagues that they planned to make funds available.

If there ever was any thought the association Collins now headed might become a functioning union, it was clear it was not going to happen under his watch. Those who study Collins' early days might be surprised. He considered David Fultz, a former A's player and the man behind the Player's Fraternity — an early attempt in 1912 to unionize the players — one of the three most important men in shaping his early baseball career. Presumably Fultz, a lawyer with a Columbia law degree, had counseled young Eddie and taught him some of the tricks which made the budding A's star such an effective negotiator at contract time. Nonetheless, little of Fultz's union credo had rubbed off on his student. By 1946, if not before, Collins was definitely anti-union. That year, while Collins was still the general manager of the Red Sox, yet another attempt took place to form a players' union. When asked to comment on the American Baseball Guild formed that season by Robert Murphy and eager to get enough votes to represent the interests of the active players, Collins remarked, "Let him get a majority; he'll have a heck of a time doing it."[16]

As to those non-unionized players, the Red Sox were once again peddling them. In late 1947, shortly after Cronin was named to replace Collins in the front office, the Red Sox abandoned their policy of fiscal restraint and dealt six players and over $300,000 in cash to the money-starved St. Louis Browns for infield batting star Vern Stephens and pitcher Jack Kramer. Then a day later they sent three more players to the Browns and another $65,000 for infielder Billy Hitchcock and pitcher Ellis Kinder. These acquisitions, however, unlike the money-for-player deals of previous years, were not acts of desperation, but rather moves that met needs and strengthened positions that could not necessarily be filled from within. The difference from the past was that now the additions, when added to the roster in place, resulted in a competitive team. The ascendancy of players such as pitcher Mel Parnell, who would be a 25-game winner in 1949, and infielder Billy Goodman, who would lead the league in hitting at .354 in 1950, through the farm system was a tribute, in part, to the skill and wisdom of Eddie Collins. If he were to share the blame for the failures of the early Yawkey-Collins years, he must also share in the success of the 1946 pennant winner and the years of contention in

1948 and thereafter. Likewise, if the farm system, much improved in the 1940s, did not continue to produce quality talent, it was not Collins' fault.

According to Mark Armour and Daniel Levitt, who studied the Red Sox's player personnel of the post-war era, the franchise "enjoyed success in the late 1940s largely because their organization consistently produced quality players. Unfortunately, once Cronin replaced Collins as the team's general manager, the flow of talent slowed to a trickle."[17] This, plus the failure to sign black players, led to problems in the 1950s.

Dave Egan, the Colonel of the *Daily Record*, recognized Collins' contribution to the Red Sox as well. In lambasting the proposed move of Ted Collins' — no relation — professional football team from Boston to New York, Egan recognized Eddie's loyalty to the city through thick and thin, weathering criticism and a "vicious whispering campaign. Yet he never complained: he won first the respect of the public, and he lives here to this day, a highly respected member of our community.

"He had to build from the bottom no less than you [Ted Collins]. He more than any other person with the exception of Yawkey, is the creator of the Red Sox of today; the Red Sox who won the American League flag in 1946 and tied for it in 1948; the Red Sox who annually seem to set a new attendance record; the Red Sox who always can be depended upon to ... [finish] one — two — three in their league."[18]

The Red Sox of 1949 did not veer from that path. Picked by many experts to win the pennant and paced by one of their all-time best lineups and two 20-game winners [Parnell and Kinder], the Red Sox went into Yankee Stadium for a two-game series on October 1, leading the New Yorkers by one game. After losing the first game, 5–4, for the second straight year they essentially engaged in a playoff game for the pennant. They lost, 5–3, breaking the hearts of the players, the organization and their fans. Ted Williams had just completed another remarkable season (.343, 43, 159). He described the train ride back to Boston as "a damn funeral train." The next day a subheading in the *Boston Globe* bemoaned the fact there was "No Joy in Mudville."[19]

In March of that season, Collins, still feeling the effects of what now was certainly a chronic heart condition, gave up his team treasurer's duties, once again to Cronin. Still, he continued to make the trek to Fenway Park as often as possible.

According to sportswriter Gerry Hern of the *Boston Post*, "Eddie didn't fold easy." When advised not to climb stairs, "he arranged to have a friend drive him up the ramp of Fenway Park right to the door of the grandstand office so he could work in the sport he loved and lived for."[20]

His body might have been failing, but his mind remained razor sharp. Given a list of players who were active during one particular American League season, he saw an error; the player had not played until after Collins entered the league. He immediately corrected it. According to Hern, "Here he was, under medical treatment for a serious heart condition, and yet he still packed enough ambition and determination to correct a mistake that few people would have noticed."[21]

To the end Collins maintained a keen interest in the rules of the game, a hobby of sorts, regularly serving on various rules committees and maintaining a firm reputation as one of the leading experts in the field. In 1941 he had suggested the standardization of the height of pitching mounds.[22] At the time his suggestion was not accepted. In 1950, however, the idea was finally adopted, a uniform 15-inch height maintained throughout the major leagues. In 1969 the height was lowered to the current 10 inches. However, Collins' idea of a standardized mound height remains.

As the Red Sox prepared to renew the American League wars in 1950, still smarting from the final outcome of their last time in combat, there was good news on the business front. According to correspondent Lester Smith of the *Wall Street Journal*, the club had turned a corner financially, showing a profit in four of the last five seasons. Furthermore, after 17 years, the club's assets under the Yawkey-Collins partnership had tripled. The Red Sox were now valued at $4,891,683.[23]

All that mattered little to Red Sox rooters; they wanted a World Series championship. Once again in 1950 they did not get it, finishing third, one game behind second-place Detroit and four behind, of course, those damned pennant-winning Yankees. The Red Sox's record was, nevertheless, a quite respectable 94–60.

Although the Red Sox's finishes in both 1948 and 1949 were closer to the top, Collins took the team's final result in 1950 particularly hard. During the season he submitted to a number of lengthy interviews with Jim Leonard, a *Boston Post* sportswriter. The collaboration resulted in a series of fine articles of an autobiographical nature which appeared in *The Sporting News* in October and November of that year. During their sessions Collins expressed an unusual amount of frustration to Leonard at the outcome of the 1950 season. Perhaps he sensed time running out for his dream of a world title for his Red Sox. He had suffered a paralyzing stroke in August that affected one side of his body, including his sight. Maybe there was concern on his part that he literally would not see his beloved Red Sox perform again.

"This was the year they had to do it. This was the year the Red Sox should have won the pennant ... not next year ... or the year after. This was the year ... and they failed in the clutch."[24]

Nonetheless, Collins was preparing for another season in 1951. On the evening of February 1 at the Boston Baseball Writer's dinner, he was the recipient of the Paul Shannon Memorial Trophy, awarded for meritorious service to baseball. In the weeks preceding the event, Eddie's visits to his office had diminished to a few hours each. He felt good enough this night, however, to regale the crowd with baseball stories, take credit for bringing fellow attendee Joe Cronin to town, and toss his support to Happy Chandler, who was up for re-election as commissioner. Joining Collins on a dais which included Chandler, under whose watch baseball was integrated, were Boston players Birdie Tebbetts, Walt Dropo and Billy Goodman, as well as the newly acquired Lou Boudreau and the 1950 National League Rookie of the Year, Sam Jethroe of the Boston Braves. This was the same Sam Jethroe Collins watched from afar during the workout for the Red Sox in 1945. He was signed in 1949 as the first African-American member of the Braves. Collins, the vice president of the Red Sox, still an all-white organization, sat near Jethroe on the dais. During the evening he reportedly turned to the player, smiled and congratulated him on his success. The Braves' outfielder smiled back, trying not to exhibit the bitterness he obviously felt. "You had your chance, Mr. Collins. You had your chance."[25]

In many ways the sportswriter's banquet on February 1 was a glorious evening for Eddie Collins, surrounded as he was by many of the baseball people he dealt with and worked with for so many years. It was fitting that on such an evening he was guest of honor and received a thunderous ovation since, save a brief appearance in New York at the seventy-fifth birthday party for the National League, it was to be the last public appearance of his life.

On March 10 he suffered another stroke — the newspapers called it a "shock." He entered Peter Bent Brigham Hospital in Boston where he remained until his condition, aggravated by pneumonia, led to his death on the evening of March 25, 1951. Eddie's wife Emily reported that she had spent the majority of the day with her husband and he was quite alert and resting comfortably. Since the timing of his death came as a surprise, she was not at the hospital when he passed away.[26] Eddie was 63 years old.

When news of Collins' passing hit Sarasota, where the Red Sox were in training, it shocked the entire team. According to sources, Joe Cronin was too stunned to speak. Ted Williams wanted to return to Boston immediately to pay his respects. Confirming he considered Eddie his best friend in baseball, he told reporters, "Every time I talked things over with him he made me feel better. I shall miss him."[27]

One dear friend who took Collins' death particularly hard was Connie Mack, still steaming along but no longer managing at age 88, having just retired. "He was one of my finest boys," said the Tall Tactician, offering that Eddie "was the greatest second baseman who ever lived" and "my greatest friend."[28]

Mack's comments were echoed by Ty Cobb, who told one reporter, "[I]f anyone tells you he wasn't the greatest second baseman of all time you argue with him. Collins was a wonderful ball player. A better second baseman never lived and you can tell them Cobb said so."[29]

Countless other tributes poured in from baseball players, baseball executives, the press, and even politicians: Boston's mayor and the Massachusetts governor to name but two. Some of the most meaningful comments were from former teammates, including the "$100,000 infield," each of whom survived their second baseman and considered him a close friend. Of the many tributes that flowed from the press, one of particular note was written by the Colonel, never a soft touch when it came to Collins, particularly on the integration issue. In part it read:

> He was a cruel disappointment, when eyes that then were young first sought him out.
>
> He flopped around on the field like an old, beaten up rag doll on the end of a string. He was so slope-shouldered as to seem almost round-shouldered in a baseball uniform, and any physical culture expert worth his salt would have sniffed disdainfully at his posture. More than that, he was on the smallish side, and he moved without grace, and he was not my idea of what a living, breathing Frank Merriwell should look like but he was by far the greatest infielder I have ever seen or ever expect to, and now he has gone, taking some more of the golden yesterdays with him....
>
> Cobb and Collins ... were to baseball, I suppose, what Man O'War and Exterminator were to racing. They were the best of their time and, so far as I would know, the best of all time, and as Man O'War and Exterminator still run one-two in the races that are run at night down in the barn area when old men gather, so Cobb and Collins still run one-two in the book of those who know and follow baseball....
>
> You met him for the first time, and this was as rude a shock as seeing him for the first time. You assessed him as a cold man with a harsh voice that undoubtedly had been made harsher by a quarter of a century of bellowing, and you would find that you were completely and hopelessly wrong once again, as wrong in your original estimate of him as a man as you had been in your initial judgment of him as a ball player. As time passed, you'd come to respect him even more deeply as a man than you had as a ball player.... He would not stoop to glad-hand a baseball writer, or backslap a sports columnist, nor would he force himself to be pleasant when he felt unpleasant. He was Eddie Collins, and he insisted upon being his natural self at all times. So he pushed aside the social graces with an impatient hand, and he offered himself to you in his nakedness, and the day would come ... when you realized that here was a man of rare honesty and rare character, that here was one of the finest men you ever had known....
>
> He was a wonderful person to have known, and I count it a privilege that I knew him, and respected him, and came pretty close to loving him....[30]

Following a showing at the Eastman Funeral Home, the object of all this affection was laid to rest on March 28 at Lynwood Graveyard in Weston after a requiem mass at the Episcopal Church of the Advent in the Back Bay area. Pallbearers included the "$100,000 infield" of McInnis, Baker and Barry; Tom Yawkey, who flew in from South Carolina; Will Harridge, still American League president; and Joe and Frank Stevens of Stevens Concessionaires, supplier to Fenway and other ballparks. In addition to the second Mrs. Collins, son

Eddie was present but Paul, who was in Paris at the time, could not make it back in time for the funeral.

The list of those present at the requiem mass was a long one, including as expected a number of ball players and local officials. Meanwhile in Sarasota, a separate memorial mass was held at St. Martha's Catholic Church, the recipient of donations from Collins ever since his 1933 arrival in that city for the annual spring training rituals. In attendance were a number of Red Sox officials including Steve O'Neill, who had replaced Joe McCarthy as manager in mid-season 1950, and a number of Red Sox players, including Williams, Doerr, Pesky and Dom DiMaggio.

On the day they buried Eddie Collins, the Colonel, still obviously affected by his death, put the Collins years in Boston into perspective, telling readers the city owed the man its "everlasting debt," for "[h]e gave us Tom Yawkey...."

Describing the bleak situation surrounding baseball in Boston in early 1933, Egan continued:

> It was into this shambles that Eddie Collins walked with young Yawkey at his shoulder, to take over a down-at-the-heel ball park and a fly-specked franchise which were its only assets, and had he done nothing else in his career, this alone would have been sufficient to have established him as one of the best friends Boston has had in the last quarter of a century....
>
> These men took the Red Sox off the city dump and fashioned it into a powerful organization that draws hundreds of thousands of persons and millions of dollars into Boston every year, and if this is failure, as seems to be suggested by the criticisms, I want more such failures in other lines so that Boston once again becomes the metropolis that it should be....
>
> Now the man who brought Yawkey to Boston, and brought Cronin to Boston, and brought Doerr to Boston, and brought Williams to Boston goes to his rest, and I want to say, before he goes, that this adopted son of Boston has done well by our town.[31]

Egan obviously knew Collins well, having followed and written about him over many years. Another writer, one who watched and marveled at Collins' play over the years, but really was one of the last writers to know him well off the field, was Jim Leonard, who worked in concert with Eddie on the five-part series about his life that ran in *The Sporting News*. According to Leonard, "Eddie Collins wasn't the easiest person to know. He had a reserve that was hard to penetrate. He was extremely honest and, at times, brutally frank. Strangers didn't take to him. He had no disarming qualities.... [Y]ou accepted him as such — or rejected him....

"To some he appeared cold and distant. You didn't like him at first glance — nor did he show any evidence of liking you. But as the daily intervening sessions lengthened you grew to respect and admire him."

It took a long time for Leonard to extract a life story from Collins. He gave it up bit by bit, but always grudgingly. And on one subject he was particularly tight-lipped. A great deal of what we know of Collins' version of the Black Sox scandal came out during those interviews with Jim Leonard. Still we know much too little.

"Even to talk of that infamous chapter of baseball history seared the soul and singed the lips of the man who became the greatest second baseman of all time. It was a story that rankled his memory and troubled him constantly. It sought relief in telling, but never found an outlet....

"He resisted your every effort. 'I've said enough ... perhaps I've said too much,' he told you time and again. 'And I'm not going to say anymore,' he stated with finality."[32]

And that about did it for the Collins' saga, except that is for the never-ending statistical surveys and all-star lists comparing him to others. Although his ranking remains high, his lack of home run power and the perception that he lacked color kept him from gaining a permanent place at the forefront of baseball memories of players past. Even so every once in a while, eyebrows raise and the deceased second sacker becomes the topic of the day. Like the time in 1953 his former manager, Pants Rowland, called Collins a more valuable player to a team than Ty Cobb, or when someone uncovers new information or evinces new theories about the Black Sox.[33]

Still, by the early 1960s it is safe to say the name Eddie Collins was no longer on the lips of the average baseball fan, resigned to those who study the game in more detail. That was why it was particularly meaningful some 13 years after his death, on Labor Day, September 7, 1964, in the village of Millerton, Dutchess County, New York, the place of his birth, an Eddie Collins Day was held. A day described by the local media as "the biggest day in Millerton's history"; one in which Emily Jane Mann Hall Collins, Eddie Collins Jr., and Ken Smith, the director of the National Baseball Hall of Fame, attended the rededication of a renovated ball park on a five-acre tract of land, to be forever known as the Eddie Collins Memorial Park.[34] A ball park equipped with a lighted diamond, covered grandstand and a clubhouse remodeled in large part through the good auspices of Tom Yawkey and the American League. For it was then and there, located just a few miles from the place of his birth, where the spirit of Edward Trowbridge Collins, a ballplayer who scored a run 1,821 times in a 25-year playing career of sustained excellence that at times reflected brilliance, rounded third and touched home one final time.

Transcript of Eddie Collins' Statement to Leslie N. O'Connor, Chicago, February 19, 1921

[Page 1]

Q. Have you any recollection of the raising of a fund among the White Sox players in 1917?
A. Yes.

Q. When were you first approached on that subject?
A. As far as I recall it now, it was during the last series at home — in fact, I am not sure that the season had not been finished; but I am reasonably sure it was during our last series at home after our last trip east and after the pennant had been won. I know it was the ver [*sic*] fag end of the season, after everything had been decided.

Q. Where were you approached?
A. In the clubhouse in Chicago.

Q. After some game or before?
A. After a game there. As I recall it, it was during the last series and possibly the last game of that series, but I would not be sure about that.

Q. It was in the afternoon sometime, then?
A. Yes.

Q. Who talked to you on the subject?
A. Gandil.

Q. What did he say, as nearly as you can recall?
A. "We are taking up a little collection." He spoke collectively, as I recall, but without mentioning who, if there were others, were interested in taking up the collection. The impression he gave me was that each member of the Chicago club was supposed to contribute a certain amount and he figured it would total $45 apiece. That is the amount I gave him, as I understood as a remuneration for the Detroit pitchers. I am not sure whether he said "pitchers" or "players" — I think likely the pitchers for the way they had knocked off Boston either two out of the three or three straight.

Q. The impression you received was that a certain amount was to be collected from your whole club and that this sum had been proportioned among the White Sox players, resulting in a tax of $45 each?
A. Yes.

Q. Were you informed of the total amount to be raised?

319

A. No, I never was and I don't know to this day.

Q. Did Gandil state how the taking of the collection came to be suggested?
A. No.

Q. Do you know who originated the idea or who suggested it?
A. No. It was something new to me. I have never done anything like it before in my career or since.

Q. Do you know whether any others among the White Sox players were approached on the subject?
A. Schalk is the only one I know of, except that I received the general impression that all had been approached and that all had paid with the exception of "Tex" Russell.

[Page 2]
Q. Did you talk with anyone else about the collection?
A. I talked to Ray Schalk, who was my room mate at that time as I recall, though I am not positive about that.

Q. What was the subject of your conversation with him?
A. Why, that we regretted giving the money. It was something I had never done before and it looked strange. We looked on it askance, but did not think it was sufficiently important to refuse to contribute or to kick up a fuss about it.

Q. You are sure this collection was taken up after the White Sox had won the pennant?
A. Absolutely.

Q. For what were the Detroit players for whom the collection was taken up rewarded?
A. For the fact they had beaten Boston in a crucial series in Boston at the time previous to our having clinched the pennant.

Q. About what date was that series?
A. I can't tell you without a 1917 schedule, but it was the last series of the 1917 season between Detroit and Boston that was played in Boston.

Q. Was there any previous understanding or arrangement with any Detroit players that they would be rewarded by the White Sox if they beat Boston?
A. Absolutely not, so far as I know.

Q. Was the money sent to Detroit?
A. I don't know, except that subsequently one of the Detroit players wanted to know why he did not get some of it.

Q. Is there anything else you can add to what you have already said regarding this collection and its purpose?
A. Not that I can recall, only to state that it was distinctly as a reward to these Detroit players for knocking Boston off. As I recall, I would not say it was the common practice, but I do not think that our contribution to Detroit was a novel one. By that I mean I have heard or read where, if, for sort of an example, the New York Giants sent John Smith of St. Louis a check for a suit of clothes for beating Pittsburgh in a crucial game. [sic] That I can't substantiate with definite proof, except that I think it has been done before.

Q. Do you know whether that was the general impression among ball players — that the giving of small appreciations or rewards of a monetary nature to players on other teams was not improper and was not unusual?

A. I can't say as to that. It was not a usual practice so far as I know, but what I meant was that it was not a novel thing for a player to be given a suit of clothes or something like that. So far as players on a club taking up a collection, I never heard of it before. That was the reason Schalk and I looked at it as rather improper, but we let it slide because we thought we would not miss the $45 and we did not want to be the instigators of a row and took more or less the attitude "let George do it."

[Page 3]

Q. Is it the fact that the money was raised to pay Detroit for laying down in some games with the White Sox, so that the White Sox would be or were enabled to win those games and as a result the pennant?

A. Positively not. The proposition was never broached until [missing words — author's error] of the season and then it was put in the light that Detroit had assisted our position by beating Boston.

Q. Did Detroit ever lay down in any games with the White Sox, so far as you know?

A. Not to my knowledge.

Q. Was there anything in any of the games that the White Sox played with Detroit which might cause you to suspect that possibly the Detroit team or any particular members of it were not playing their best against the White Sox or were endeavoring in any way to assist the White Sox to win games from the Detroit team?

A. No, I don't think so. The last time that we played Detroit was early in Sept. — I think Labor Day — and my recollection, although I am not sure of it, is that at that time Detroit had some chance itself to win the pennant. I think Detroit was then in the running, but I would have to see a schedule to be sure of that.

Q. You did not see anything which would lead you to think that any Detroit player was trying to throw games to the White Sox?

A. No. Of course, it is hard to say whether anybody on a ball field is doing his best. As you look back on the games they might look peculiar, though at the time they were played there would not seem to be anything peculiar about them. That Detroit series we played I think we won the whole four games. I recall now that in that series one of the Detroit players was either taken out or did not play and they had a substitute and he made a couple of what — well, they looked like timely errors, for they enabled us to win that game. But whether you could say in all fairness that he did it deliberately would be difficult and unfair to the player and probably would not be true, especially in view of the fact that he was a substitute.

Q. Was there ever at any time since you have been on the White Sox team any other collection taken up for a purpose in any way similar to this Detroit collection?

A. Positively not.

Q. Neither before or since?

A. Positively not. This is the only time I have ever heard of it in Baseball.

Q. There is nothing else you can say on this?

A. The main point is that the first time I heard of it was after the pennant had been won and that any suggestion that it was given to Detroit for throwing any games to us is absolutely without foundation.

Q. Do you recall any other occurrence of what might be termed a suspicious nature during your connection with the Chicago White Sox?

A. No, I do not, other than possibly in 1919.

Q. What was the 1919 matter?

A. It was the last series of the year. We had clinched the pennant in Chicago with St. Louis. I do not recall positively now, but I think we cinched the pennant in the series with St. Louis and I think the first day we got home. It was one of the first games of the series. And as I recall, we sort of let down after

[Page 4]

that and St. Louis beat us. I mention this as showing the general feeling after the pennant. It was quite a strain. We had a pretty good Eastern trip. We went to Boston and won one game there and had to win another to win the pennant. We had a double header on Babe Ruth Day and they beat us both games. If we had won either of those games we would have won the pennant. I don't know that there was any danger of our being beaten out, but there is always a peculiar feeling about getting it over, even where you have a safe lead, and after you have won there is a general feeling of relaxation and indifference.

Q. Well, what is the point you desire to bring out?

A. Well, during the Detroit series which followed the St. Louis series after we had won the pennant, there was what might be termed a considerable lack of interest in the games on the part of the White Sox. Detroit was contending for third place. There was a mathematical possibility that they could make third place, provided they won all their games against us and provided Philadelphia beat New York one game. In fact they could win all their games with us and still not take third place unless Philadelphia beat New York in one game. There was also at that time some talk of throwing out the games in which Mays had participated, which would have given Detroit third place.

Q. What was there in the Chicago-Detroit series?

A. Detroit fought hard to win, while the White Sox played loosely, somewhat indifferently. We had won the title and the feeling was that it was merely a case of getting through with the remaining games on the schedule.

Q. Was this an individual feeling among the players or was there any concerted agreement to play listlessly or in such a manner that Detroit would win. [*sic*]

A. There seemed to be a sort of general feeling — about which I possibly might be wrong, as it is only my impression — that we would prefer to have Detroit beat out New York, but there was absolutely no prearranged agreement or understanding that they should win, nor any conference or arrangement between the White Sox players, individually or collectively, or with any Detroit players, that we should deliberately permit them to win.

Q. It was merely a case of letting down after winning the pennant?

A. As to the result of the games we did not give a whoop, but there was no feeling whatever that we should deliberately permit Detroit to win. That was not true of that series or of any game I have ever been in.

Q. Do you recall any other instance in which one club has played indifferently against another?

A. There are any number of such instances. It is just as logical for anyone to say that Philadelphia played listlessly against New York. I don't recall what their games were. In any number of games at the fag end of the season it is not unusual to see one club appear listless or indifferent to the outcome where it has nothing at stake. For instance, when I was with the Philadelphia club — I think it was in 1911 — we were to play the Giants in the World Series and Rube Marquard and Mathewson were in the stands watching us to get some pointers on us, and in that game our club deliberately played as we would not do under other circumstances, not for the sake of losing the game, but to throw off the scouts.

[Page 5]

Q. Is there anything you can add to your statement regarding this Chicago-Detroit Series in 1919?

A. No except that with reference to the allegation I have seen in the papers that I bet on that series, I want to say that I did not bet on it and so far as I know no money was bet on that series by any of the players on the club.

Q. Was it the practice for players to bet on games in which they participated?

A. Not to my knowledge. As far as I am concerned, I have rarely bet on a ball game in which I played and I never bet except that I would win.

Q. For any considerable amounts?

A. No. All the bets I have made on ball games, including world series games, would not aggregate $50, of which I don't believe I bet half on games in which I participated.

Eddie Collins' Career Statistics (as Player and Manager)

Eddie Collins
Edward Trowbridge Collins, Sr. (Cocky)

Bats Left, **Throws** Right
Height 5'9", **Weight** 175 lb.
School Columbia University

Debut September 17, 1906
Final Game August 2, 1930
Born May 2, 1887, in Millerton, NY
Died March 25, 1951, in Boston, MA
Father of Eddie Collins, Jr.

Inducted into the Hall of Fame in 1939.

Statistics courtesy baseball-reference.com   *All statistics are for American league only.*

Batting

Year	Ag	Tm	G	AB	R	H	2B	3B	HR	RBI	SB	CS	BB	SO	BA	OBP	SLG	*OPS+	TB	SH	SF	IBB	HBP	GDP	
1906	19	PHA	6	15	2	3	0	0	0	0	0		0		.200	.200	.200	24	3	3			0	0	
1907	20	PHA	14	23	0	8	0	1	0	2	0		0		.348	.348	.435	147	10	1			0	0	
1908	21	PHA	102	330	39	90	18	7	1	40	8		16		.273	.312	.379	118	125	15			3		
1909	22	PHA	153	571	104	198	30	10	3	56	67		62		.347	.416	.450	171	257	21			6		
1910	23	PHA	153	581	81	188	16	15	3	81	81		49		.324	.382	.418	152	243	22			6		
1911	24	PHA	132	493	92	180	22	13	3	73	38		62		.365	.451	.481	162	237	18			15		MVP-3
1912	25	PHA	153	543	137	189	25	11	0	64	63		101		.348	.450	.435	158	236	29			0		MVP-6
1913	26	PHA	148	534	125	184	23	13	3	73	55	30	85	37	.345	.441	.453	164	242	26			7		MVP-3
1914	27	PHA	152	526	122	181	23	14	2	85	58	30	97	31	.344	.452	.452	176	238	28			6		MVP-1
1915	28	CHW	155	521	118	173	22	10	4	77	46		119	27	.332	.460	.436	165	227	35			5		
1916	29	CHW	155	545	87	168	14	17	0	52	40	21	86	36	.308	.405	.396	140	216	39			3		
1917	30	CHW	156	564	91	163	18	12	0	67	53		89	16	.289	.389	.363	128	205	33			3		
1918	31	CHW	97	330	51	91	8	2	2	30	22		73	13	.276	.407	.330	121	109	22			0		
1919	32	CHW	140	518	87	165	19	7	4	80	33		68	27	.319	.400	.405	126	210	40			2		
1920	33	CHW	153	602	117	224	38	13	3	76	20	8	69	19	.372	.438	.493	146	297	33			2		
1921	34	CHW	139	526	79	177	20	10	2	58	12	10	66	11	.337	.412	.424	115	223	13			2		MVP-5
1922	35	CHW	154	598	92	194	20	12	1	69	20	12	73	16	.324	.401	.403	110	241	27			3		MVP-2
1923	36	CHW	145	505	89	182	22	5	5	67	48	29	84	8	.360	.455	.453	141	229	39			4		MVP-2
1924	37	CHW	152	556	108	194	27	7	6	86	42	17	89	16	.349	.441	.455	134	253	28			3		
1925	38	CHW	118	425	80	147	26	3	3	80	19	6	87	8	.346	.461	.442	135	188	17			4		
1926	39	CHW	106	375	66	129	32	4	1	62	13	8	62	8	.344	.441	.459	139	172	15			3		
1927	40	PHA	95	226	50	76	12	1	1	15	6	2	56	9	.336	.468	.412	124	93	8			0		
1928	41	PHA	36	33	3	10	3	0	0	7	0	0	4	4	.303	.378	.394	101	13	0			0		
1929	42	PHA	9	7	0	0	0	0	0	0	0	0	2	0	.000	.222	.000	-39	0	0			0		
1930	43	PHA	3	2	1	1	0	0	0	0	0	0	0	0	.500	.500	.500	151	1	0			0		
25 Seasons			2826	9949	1821	3315	438	187	47	1300	744	173	1499	286	.333	.424	.429	141	4268	512	0	0	77	0	
162 Game Avg			156	570	104	190	25	11	3	75	43	10	86	16	.333	.424	.429	141	245	29	0	0	4	0	
Career High				602	137	224	38	17	6	86	81	30	119	37	.372	.468	.493	176	297	40	0	0	15	0	
			G	AB	R	H	2B	3B	HR	RBI	SB	CS	BB	SO	BA	OBP	SLG	*OPS+	TB	SH	SF	IBB	HBP	GDP	

Batting Glossary

- Year — Year in which the season occurred
- Ag — Player age on July 1st of that year.
- Tm — Team they played for
- G — Games played
- AB — At Bats
- R — Runs Scored
- H — Hits
- 2B — Doubles
- 3B — Triples
- HR — Home Runs
- RBI — Runs Batted in
- SB — Stolen Bases
- CS — Caught Stealing (were counted in the AL after 1919 and after 1950 in the NL)
- BB — Base on Balls or Walks
- SO — Strikeouts or whiffs or K's (are available hit and miss between 1882 and 1912, but are available for all other seasons)
- BA — Batting Average H/AB
- OBP — On-Base Percentage (H+BB+HBP)/(AB+BB+SF+HBP) (SF and HBP are assumed zero if unavailable, see SF and HBP below)
- SLG — Slugging Percentage TB/AB (see TB below)
- TB — Total Bases (Singles + 2*2B + 3*3B + 4*HR)
- SH — Sacrifice Hits or Bunts (were first counted in 1895 and includes Sac Flies until 1953)
- SF — Sacrifice Flies (were first counted in 1954, prior to that they were included in Sac Hits)
- IBB — Intentional Base on Balls (were first counted in 1955)
- HBP — Hit by Pitch (are available for every season after 1887)
- GDP or GIDP — Grounded into Double Plays
- End Notations (SS, MVP, AS, ROY) — Tacked onto the end of the batting lines are notations if the player won the Silver Slugger (SS), was an All-star (AS), or received votes for the MVP or Rookie of the Year (ROY).
- OPS — It doesn't appear here, but OPS is On-Base Percentage + Slugging Percentage. It is a pretty good estimate of offensive ability.
- Adjusted OPS+ — It doesn't appear on the player pages yet, but OPS+ is OPS (see above) normalized for both the park and the league the player played in. See below for a full description.
- hmR/G and rdR/G — average runs per game scored by this team in home and road games.

Special Batting

Year	Ag	Tm	PA	Outs	RC	RC/27	AIR	BA	*lgBA	OBP	*lgOBP	SLG	*lgSLG	OPS	*lgOPS	OPS	psOPS	SB%
1906	19	PHA	18	15	1	1.80	77	.200	.259	.200	.315	.200	.332	.400	.647	24		
1907	20	PHA	24	16	3	5.06	73	.348	.256	.348	.312	.435	.321	.783	.633	147		
1908	21	PHA	364	255	38	4.02	74	.273	.253	.312	.311	.379	.322	.691	.634	118		
1909	22	PHA	660	394	106	7.26	75	.347	.255	.416	.316	.450	.323	.866	.639	171		
1910	23	PHA	658	415	91	5.92	74	.324	.249	.382	.315	.418	.321	.800	.636	152		
1911	24	PHA	588	331	103	8.40	94	.365	.279	.451	.345	.481	.366	.932	.711	162		
1912	25	PHA	673	383	106	7.47	88	.348	.268	.450	.336	.435	.352	.885	.688	158		
1913	26	PHA	652	376	105	7.54	86	.345	.262	.441	.333	.453	.344	.894	.678	164		
1914	27	PHA	657	403	106	7.10	79	.344	.252	.452	.324	.452	.330	.904	.654	176		65%
1915	28	CHW	680	413	104	6.80	86	.332	.259	.460	.337	.436	.339	.896	.677	165		60%
1916	29	CHW	673	437	87	5.38	83	.308	.258	.405	.332	.396	.337	.801	.669	140		65%
1917	30	CHW	689	434	79	4.91	81	.289	.257	.389	.328	.363	.333	.752	.661	128		
1918	31	CHW	425	261	44	4.55	83	.276	.262	.407	.333	.330	.334	.737	.666	121		
1919	32	CHW	628	393	83	5.70	95	.319	.276	.400	.342	.405	.371	.805	.713	126		
1920	33	CHW	706	419	130	8.38	106	.372	.291	.438	.356	.493	.400	.931	.756	146		71%
1921	34	CHW	607	372	92	6.68	113	.337	.298	.412	.364	.424	.419	.836	.783	115		54%
1922	35	CHW	701	443	96	5.85	110	.324	.293	.401	.358	.403	.411	.804	.769	110		62%
1923	36	CHW	632	391	103	7.11	107	.360	.289	.455	.359	.453	.399	.908	.758	141		62%
1924	37	CHW	676	407	111	7.36	109	.349	.294	.441	.363	.455	.404	.896	.767	134		71%
1925	38	CHW	533	301	86	7.71	111	.346	.293	.461	.363	.442	.411	.903	.774	135		76%
1926	39	CHW	455	269	75	7.53	106	.344	.285	.441	.356	.459	.399	.900	.755	139		61%
1927	40	PHA	290	160	44	7.43	116	.336	.300	.468	.369	.412	.422	.880	.791	124		75%
1928	41	PHA	37	23	5	5.87	111	.303	.292	.378	.358	.394	.415	.772	.773	101		0%
1929	42	PHA	9	7	0	0.00	116	.000	.297	.222	.364	.000	.429	.222	.793	-39		0%
1930	43	PHA	2	1	1	27.00	119	.500	.300	.500	.364	.500	.441	1.000	.806	151	0%	
25 Seasons			12037	7319	1799	6.64	93	.333	.273	.424	.342	.429	.366	.853	.707	141		

*Indicates the value is park adjusted

Special Batting Glossary

This area contains some additional statistics along with some advanced analytic or sabermetric stats. These stats attempt to give an in depth look at what the player's statistics mean within the context of the league and position they played in. These stats are subject to change and improvement as we flesh out this area.

- Year — Year in which the season occurred

- Ag — Player age on July 1st of that year.

- Tm — Team they played for

- PA — Approximate Plate Appearances — AB + BB + HBP + SF + SH

- Outs — (AB — H + CS + GIDP + SH + SF)

- RC — Runs Created — A runs estimator created by Bill James. A runs estimator attempts to quantify the entire contribution of a player's statistics to a team's total runs scored. It typically involves some positive value for things like hits, walks, steals, home runs, etc. and negative values for outs, caught stealing and GIDP. There are 24 different versions of RC depending on the stats you have and I am using the most basic here. (H + BB) * (TB)/ (PA)

- RC/27 — Runs Created per 27 outs — This is the number of runs a team of each player would score given their stats. RC * 27 / # of outs made by the player

- AIR — I call this AIR because it is how pumped up a player's stats are by the park and leagues they played in. I looked at the median league OBP and SLG from 1901 to the present and it historically is around .335 for league OBP and .400 for league slugging. Not quite, but those are the closest round numbers. Next I take, 100*((park-adjusted Lg OBP/ .335) + (park-adjusted Lg SLG /.400)−1) to come up with the player's AIR factor. 100 means they hit in historically average settings. Over 100 means higher offensive environment than usual. Under 100 means lower offensive environment than usual.

- BA and lgBA — Batting average and the league's batting (pitchers removed) average with the same home field.

- OBP and lgOBP — On-base percentage and the league's on-base percentage (pitchers removed) with the same home field.

- SLG and lgSLG — Slugging percentage and the league's Slugging percentage (pitchers removed) with the same home field.

- OPS and lgOPS — On-base percentage + Slugging and the league's on-base + slugging percentage (pitchers removed) with the same home field. This is a very good rough guide to a player's ability to get on base and also drive runners in. High OPS means lots of runs for the team.

- OPS+ — Adjusted OPS, see below. Essentially OPS normalized to the league. Think of it as a rate above the league average expressed as a percentage.

- psOPS — The OPS of a league average player of the same position as the player with the same home field (currently being developed).

- SB% — Stolen Base Percentage SB/(SB+CS)

Postseason Batting

Year	Round	Tm	Opp	WLser	G	AB	R	H	2B	3B	HR	RBI	BB	SO	BA	OBP	SLG	SB	CS	SH	SF	HBP
1910	WS	PHA	CHC	W	5	21	5	9	4	0	0	3	2	0	.429	.478	.619	4	2	1	0	0
1911	WS	PHA	NYG	W	6	21	4	6	1	0	0	1	2	3	.286	.348	.333	2	0	2	0	0
1913	WS	PHA	NYG	W	5	19	5	8	0	2	0	3	1	2	.421	.450	.632	3	0	2	0	0
1914	WS	PHA	BSN	L	4	14	0	3	0	0	0	1	2	1	.214	.294	.214	1	0	0	1	0
1917	WS	CHW	NYG	W	6	22	4	9	1	0	0	2	2	3	.409	.458	.455	3	0	0	1	1
1919	WS	CHW	CIN	L	8	31	2	7	1	0	0	1	1	2	.226	.265	.258	1	1	1	1	1
6 World Series				4-2	34	128	20	42	7	2	0	11	10	11	.328	.376	.414	14	3	6	2	1

WLser shows whether the player's team Won or Lost the series.

Fielding

FIELDING SORTED BY YEAR

Year	Ag	Tm	Pos	G	PO	A	E	DP	FP	lgFP	RFg	lgRFg	RF9	lgRF9	LF	CF	RF
1906	19	PHA	SS	3	8	10	2	0	.900	.934	6.00	5.40					5
			2B	1	0	0	0	0		.920	0.00	5.20					
			3B	1	1	1	0	0	1.000	.935	2.00	3.20					
1907	20	PHA	SS	6	11	9	4	1	.833	.951	3.33	5.43					
1908	21	PHA	2B	47	111	127	14	5	.944	.927	5.06	5.11					
			SS	28	60	61	10	7	.924	.954	4.32	5.42					
			OF	10	13	0	1	0	.929		1.30	1.80				3	
1909	22	PHA	2B	152	373	406	27	55	.967	.953	5.12	4.83			2		
			SS	1	2	4	0	0	1.000	.925	6.00	5.20					
1910	23	PHA	2B	153	402	451	25	67	.972	.945	5.58	4.91					
1911	24	PHA	2B	132	348	349	24	49	.967	.949	5.28	4.94					
1912	25	PHA	2B	153	387	426	38	63	.955	.945	5.31	4.75					
1913	26	PHA	2B	148	314	449	28	54	.965	.954	5.16	4.82					
1914	27	PHA	2B	152	354	387	23	55	.970	.953	4.88	4.78					
1915	28	CHW	2B	155	344	487	22	54	.974	.956	5.36	4.89					
1916	29	CHW	2B	155	346	415	19	75	.976	.964	4.91	4.88					
1917	30	CHW	2B	156	353	388	24	68	.969	.959	4.75	4.94					
1918	31	CHW	2B	96	231	285	14	53	.974	.958	5.38	5.31					

Year	Ag	Tm	Pos	G	PO	A	E	DP	FP	lgFP	RFg	lgRFg	RF9	lgRF9	LF	CF	RF
1919	32	CHW	2B	140	347	401	20	66	.974	.961	5.34	5.19					
1920	33	CHW	2B	153	449	471	23	76	.976	.962	6.01	5.54					
1921	34	CHW	2B	136	376	458	28	84	.968	.956	6.13	5.35					
1922	35	CHW	2B	154	406	451	21	73	.976	.966	5.56	5.49					
1923	36	CHW	2B	142	347	430	20	77	.975	.965	5.47	5.35					
1924	37	CHW	2B	150	396	446	20	83	.977	.966	5.61	5.39					
1925	38	CHW	2B	116	290	346	20	74	.970	.962	5.48	5.31					
1926	39	CHW	2B	101	228	307	15	53	.973	.967	5.30	5.33					
1927	40	PHA	2B	56	124	150	10	31	.965	.961	4.89	5.33					
			SS	1	0	0	0	0			0.00	4.90					
1928	41	PHA	2B	2	0	0	0	0			0.00	5.30					
			SS	1	0	1	0	0	1.000	.938	1.00	4.70					

FIELDING SORTED BY POSITION

Year	Ag	Tm	Pos	G	PO	A	E	DP	FP	lgFP	RFg	lgRFg	RF9	lgRF9	LF	CF	RF
Position Total			2B	2650	6526	7630	435	1215	.970	.958	5.34	5.10					
			SS	40	81	85	16	8	.912	.929	4.15	5.38			2		
			OF	10	13	0	1	0	.929	.954	1.30	1.80				3	5
			3B	1	1	1	0	0	1.000	.920	2.00	3.20					
Overall Total				2701	6621	7716	452	1223	.969	.957	5.31	5.09					

Fielding Glossary

- Year — Year in which the season occurred
- Tm — Team they played for
- POS — The position played
- G — Games played
- PO — Putouts
- A — Assists
- E — Errors
- DP — Double Plays
- FP — Fielding Percentage (A + PO) / (A + PO + E)
- lgFP — The fielding percentage a league average player would have in that many opportunities. (A + PO) / (A + PO + E)
- RFg — Range Factor by games played (A + PO) / G
- lgRFg — Major League Average Range Factor at that position that year by games.
- RF9 — Range Factor per nine innings 9 * (A + PO)/ Inn
- lgRF9 — Major League Average Range Factor at that position that year per nine innings.
- GS — Games Started (available for 2000 on)
- Inn — Innings Played (available for 2000 on)
- PB — For catchers, Passed Balls
- LF, CF, RF — Number of games played at each outfield position for years in which individual outfield stats are not available.
- End Notations (GG, AS) — Tacked onto the end of the fielding lines are notations if the player was an All-star (AS) or won the Gold Glove (GG).

Managerial Record

Year	League	Team	Age	G	W	L	WP	Finish	
1924	American Lg	ChicagoW	37	27	14	13	.519	6	Player/Manager
1925	American Lg	ChicagoW	38	154	79	75	.513	5	Player/Manager
1926	American Lg	ChicagoW	39	155	81	72	.529	5	Player/Manager
	TOTAL			336	174	160	.521		

Managerial Glossary

- Year — Year in which the season occurred
- Team — Team they played for
- League — League they played in (AL- American League, NL- National League)
- G — Games played
- W — Wins
- L — Losses
- WP — Winning Percentage
- Finish — End of season rank

Chapter Notes

Prologue

1. Eddie Collins (Sullivan) quoted in Stan Baumgartner, "Collins Went from Campus to A's," *The Sporting News*, August 16, 1950, 13.

2. Lee Allen, *The American League Story*, 36.

3. Ibid., 36–37. According to *Total Baseball (8th ed.)*, Waddell won 21 games in 1903.

4. Eddie Collins (Sullivan) quoted in Baumgartner, "Collins Went from Campus to A's," 13.

5. Eddie Collins as told to Jim Leonard, "From Sullivan to Collins: Colorful Life Story of Game's Greatest Second Baseman," Chapter I, *The Sporting News*, October 11, 1950, 14.

6. *Chicago Tribune*, September 18, 1906. The number of putouts and assists from the Tribune box score are consistent with Collins' (Sullivan) season totals. However, box scores in both the *Philadelphia Inquirer*, September 18, 1906, and *The Sporting News*, September 22, 1906, attribute two putouts and four assists to Collins' fielding performance.

7. *Philadelphia Inquirer*, September 18, 1906.

8. *Chicago Tribune*, September 19, 1906.

9. There is also some documentation that Collins (Sullivan) stole one base in his first game on September 17, 1906. See box scores of game carried in *Philadelphia Inquirer*, September 18, 1906, and *The Sporting News*, September 22, 1906, 5. This statistic is recorded in Collins' season totals for 1906 in *Total Baseball (8th ed.)*, but not in either Baseball-Reference.com or Retrosheet.com. A search at the National Baseball Library, Cooperstown, N.Y., of the day-to-day records for 1906 did not reveal a stolen base for Collins (Sullivan) for 1906.

Chapter 1

1. Eddie Collins quoted in *New York Herald*, January 1, 1911 (Magazine Section).

2. *The News*, Millerton, N.Y., May 16, 1985.

3. Pamphlet, *Welcome to Trowbridge House*, North East (N.Y.) Historical Society, August 28, 1999.

4. *Amenia* (N.Y.) *Times*, June 21, 1880.

5. *The Daily News*, Tarrytown, N.Y., January 18, 1929.

6. *The News*, Millerton, N.Y., February 26, 1942.

7. Ibid.

8. Eddie Collins quoted by Jim Leonard in *Baseball's Greatest Lineup*, 90.

9. F.C. Lane, "Collins the Great," 48–49.

10. Hugh Fullerton, "The Smartest Second Baseman," 36.

11. Joseph V. Poillucci, *Baseball in Dutchess County*, 6, 14–17.

12. Jeff Canning and Wally Buxton, *History of the Tarrytowns*, 13–24.

13. Ibid., 25.

14. Ibid., 72.

15. Ibid., 24.

16. *The Daily News*, Tarrytown, N.Y., January 18, 1929.

17. Eddie Collins as told to Jim Leonard, "From Sullivan to Collins," Chapter I, *The Sporting News*, October 1, 1950, 13.

18. *The Daily News*, Tarrytown, N.Y., March 19, 1955.

19. *Register for 1927–1928*, The Irving School, 7.

20. Ibid., 12.

21. Lane, "Collins the Great," 49.

22. *Press Record*, Tarrytown, N.Y., May 1, 1903. In an interview that appeared on page 5 of the Sunday Magazine section of the *New York Herald*, January 1, 1911, Collins stated that after a year of baseball at Irving, "(T)he Tarrytown High School invited me to participate in the sport whenever I could find the opportunity." Collins claims "the managers of both teams got together and arranged their schedules" to avoid conflicts. It was not a story Collins seemed to repeat in later discussions of that portion of his life.

23. Quoted in *New York Evening Telegram* article with handwritten notation "July 1918," Eddie Collins Clippings File, National Baseball Library, Cooperstown, N.Y.

24. Fullerton, "The Smartest Second Baseman," 36. See also Jack Wheeler quoted in J.G. Taylor Spink's column "Three and One," *The Sporting News*, February 12, 1942, 4.

25. *New York Times*, November 16, 1902.

26. *Turner's Hudson River Directory, 1906–7*, 24.

27. *The Daily News*, Tarrytown, N.Y., January 18, 1929.

Chapter 2

1. Eddie Collins quoted in *The Sporting News*, June 1, 1922, 4.

2. Eddie Collins as told to Jim Leonard, "From Sullivan to Collins," Chapter I, *The Sporting News*, October 11, 1950, 13.

3. *Columbia Spectator*, April 5, 1904.

4. Eddie Collins, "Twenty One Years of Baseball," Part I, *Los Angeles Times*, January 3, 1927. Some 23 years later Collins told a similar story but recalled the game was played in 1907 when he was a senior. At that time Collins was ineligible for college play but claimed he was permitted to play exhibitions. See Collins to Jim Leonard, "From Sullivan to Collins" Chapter I, 14. However, the box score from the 1904 game seems to support the earlier version. *New York Times*, April 14, 1904.

5. Review of the 1904 Varsity Baseball Season, *The Columbian*, 1906 Edition, 253.

6. *New York Times*, November 4, 1904.

7. F.C. Lane, "Collins the Great," 52. The other two were Billy Lush and David Fultz.

8. *New York Times*, April 16, 1905.

9. Newspaper article, "Eddie Collins Star at Columbia University on Diamond and Gridiron," publication unidentified, November 6, 1910, Eddie Collins Clippings File, National Baseball Library, Cooperstown, N.Y.

10. Mique (Mike) Martin quoted in J.G. Taylor Spink's column "Looping the Loops," *The Sporting News*, May 28, 1942, 1.

11. "Baseball By-Plays," *The Sporting News*, November 24, 1921, 4.

12. *New York Times*, October 12, 1905.

13. Ibid.

14. *Columbia Spectator*, October 17, 1905.

15. Lane, "Collins the Great," 50.

16. *New York Times*, October 29, 1905.

17. Ibid., November 5, 1905.

18. Quoted in Ray Robinson, *Speed Kings of the Base*, 166.

19. Collins, "Twenty One Years of Baseball," Part I.

20. Lane, "Collins the Great," 50.

21. Eddie Collins quoted in Bill Dooly, "Eddie Collins, Entering 26th Season, Says Baseball Would Be His Profession If He Had To Choose Again," *The Sporting News*, February 26, 1931, 5.

22. Ronald A. Smith, "Harvard and Columbia and a Reconsideration of the 1905–06 Football Crisis," 6–7.

23. *Columbia Spectator*, November 29, 1905.

24. Ibid., December 4, 1905.

Chapter 3

1. Edward T. "Eddie" Collins, "Connie Mack and His Mackmen," 13.

2. Newspaper article, "Eddie Collins Star at Columbia University on Diamond and Gridiron," publication unidentified, November 6, 1901, Eddie Collins Clippings File, National Baseball Library, Cooperstown, N.Y.

3. *The Sporting News*, June 8, 1944, 11.

4. *Columbia Spectator*, April 28, 1906.

5. Eddie Collins, "Twenty One Years of Baseball," Part I, *Los Angeles Times*, January 3, 1927.

6. Eddie Collins as told to Jim Leonard, "From Sullivan to Collins," Chapter I, *The Sporting News*, October 11, 1950, 13.

7. *Plattsburgh Press*, June 26, 1906.

8. F.C. Lane, "Collins the Great," 51.

9. Collins to Jim Leonard, "From Sullivan to Collins," Chapter I, 13.

10. Report from *Boston Herald* appearing in *Rutland Herald*, July 12, 1906.

11. *Plattsburgh Press*, July 12, 1906.

12. *Rutland Herald*, July 21, 1906.

13. Ibid., July 24, 1906.

14. Ibid., July 25, 1906.

15. Ibid., August 8, 1906.

16. Ibid., August 9, 1906.

17. Ibid., August 14, 1906.

18. Ibid., August 16, 1906.

19. Connie Mack, "The Stuff That Stars Are Made Of," *Saturday Evening Post*, 8. Mack's overall recall of the events leading up to Collins' signing seems cloudy. He relates here his courtship of the player involved two years. This is otherwise unsubstantiated, even by Mack himself. See Connie

Mack, "My 50 Years in Baseball," Installment No. 27, *Philadelphia Inquirer*, October 8, 1930, where Mack indicates his initial dealings with Collins occurred in 1906.

20. Eddie Collins quoted in Hugh Fullerton, "The Smartest Second Baseman," 37. Given the makeup of the Northern League, the Paddy Duff mentioned in Collins' quote could be Patrick Henry Duff who played one game for Washington in 1906, batting just one time in the majors.

21. Stan Baumgartner, "Collins Went from Campus to A's," *The Sporting News*, August 16, 1950, 13.

22. Fred Lieb's newspaper column "The Hot Stove League," publication unidentified, January 13, 1933, Eddie Collins Clippings File, National Baseball Library, Cooperstown, N.Y. In a slight variation, Mack indicates he first learned of Eddie from a "letter" from a "former player" who played that summer in a game in which Eddie played. Connie Mack, "My 50 Years in Baseball," Installment No. 27, *Philadelphia Inquirer*, October 8, 1930.

23. *Rutland Herald*, August 21, 1906.

24. Eddie Collins quoted in Lane, "Collins the Great," 51.

25. Ibid., 51–52.

26. *Hartford Courant*, August 28, 1906.

27. *Hartford Times*, August 31, 1906.

28. Ibid., September 3, 1906.

29. *Hartford Courant*, August 23, 1906.

30. William Holland quoted in Ibid., September 3, 1906.

31. Ibid., August 23, 1906.

32. Ibid., September 3, 1906.

33. Ibid., September 4, 1906.

34. *Hartford Times*, September 4, 1906. The same article incorrectly lists Eddie Collins as a University of Vermont player and states his teammate, one "Williams," was black. A review of Columbia records does not support the observation. No Williams is listed. As to Lush and black players, see also *Hartford Courant*, September 11, 1906.

35. Letter to Editor, *Hartford Courant*, September 4, 1906.

36. *Hartford Times*, August 31, 1906.

37. Ibid., September 1, 1906.

38. Edward "Eddie" T. Collins, "Connie Mack and His Mackmen," 13.

Chapter 4

1. *New York Evening Journal*, February 6, 1915.

2. Connie Mack, "*My 66 Years in the Big Leagues*," 32–33.

3. Collins quoted in F.C. Lane, "Collins the Great," 52. See also Connie Mack, "My 50 Years in Baseball," Installment No. 27, *Philadelphia Inquirer*, October 8, 1930.

4. Lee Allen, *The American League Story*, 7.

5. David M. Jordan, *The Athletics of Philadelphia*, 11.

6. Ibid., 8–16. See also Frederick G. Lieb, *Connie Mack*, 62–66; Allen, *The American League Story*, 1–12.

7. McGraw quoted in Ibid., 66.

8. Edward T. "Eddie" Collins, "Connie Mack and His Mackmen," 13.

9. Collins quoted in Lane, "*Collins the Great,*" 52. The agreement in Connie Mack's hand is dated [Monday] September 10, 1906. Since it appears the meeting between Mack and Collins took place on September 9, Mack probably did not want to date a contract on a Sunday. The agreement actually states that Collins shall not be loaned or farmed "without his consent." Ibid., 55. Thus, he technically could have been traded or sold to another club.

10. Collins, "*Connie Mack and his Mackmen,*" 13.

11. Eddie Collins with Boyden Sparkes, "Out at Second," 18.

12. Connie Mack, "My 50 Years in Baseball," Installment No. 27, *Philadelphia Inquirer*, October 8, 1930.

13. Phillip J. Lowry, *Green Cathedrals*, 209.

14. Eddie Collins as told to Jim Leonard, "From Sullivan to Collins," Chapter I, *The Sporting News*, October 11, 1950, 13.

15. Collins, "Connie Mack and His Mackmen," 13.

16. Edward T. Collins' contract and salary information, Transaction Card Collection, National Baseball Library, Cooperstown, N.Y.

17. *Columbia Spectator*, March 27, 1907.

18. *New York Times*, March 28, 1907.

19. Ibid., March 27, 1907. Collins added to the confusion, telling a reporter on at least one occasion that a Columbia professor noticed his photograph in a Chicago paper. The photograph showed him in action with the A's. He admitted it was his picture and this led to his ineligibility. Collins is quoted in *New York Herald*, January 1, 1911 (Sunday Magazine section).

20. Collins with Sparkes. "*Out at Second,*" 19. Although there is no reason to doubt Collins' claim that he coached the Columbia varsity, a report in the *Columbia Spectator*, April 4, 1907, states Collins "has been coaching the freshman."

21. *Columbia Spectator*, June 12, 1907.

Chapter 5

1. Eddie Collins quoted in *The Sporting News*, February 26, 1931, 5.

2. *Philadelphia Inquirer*, June 6, 1907.

3. F.C. Lane, "Collins the Great," 53–55.

4. Author unidentified, typewritten notes, Eddie Collins Clippings File, National Baseball Library, Cooperstown, N.Y.

5. Paul Krichell quoted in Ernest J. Lanigan's typewritten notes, Eddie Collins Clippings File, National Baseball Library, Cooperstown, N.Y.

6. Rich Westcott, *Philadelphia's Old Ballparks*, 16.

7. *Philadelphia Inquirer*, October 1, 1907.

8. Westcott, *Philadelphia's Old Ballparks*, 23.

9. Connie Mack quoted in Ibid., 24.

10. Eddie Collins, "Twenty One Years of Base Ball," Part X, *Los Angeles Times*, January 13, 1927.

11. Edward T. "Eddie" Collins, "Connie Mack and His Mackmen," 13.

12. Eddie Collins as told to Jim Leonard, "From Sullivan to Collins," Chapter I, *The Sporting News*, October 11, 1950, 13.

13. *Philadelphia Inquirer*, May 7, 1908.

14. Eddie Collins, "Twenty One Years of Base Ball," Part VII, *Los Angeles Times*, January 10, 1927.

15. Connie Mack quoted in *Philadelphia Inquirer*, May 7, 1908.

16. Ibid., May 29, 1908.

17. Ibid., April 15, 1928.

18. Ibid., July 7, 1908.

19. Ibid., July 12, 1908.

20. Ibid., July 16, 1908.

21. Collins, "Connie Mack and His Mackmen," 13.

22. Connie Mack quoted in Frederick G. Lieb, *Connie Mack*, 117–118.

23. Collins to Leonard, "From Sullivan to Collins," Chapter I, 13.

24. Lieb, *Connie Mack*, 117.

25. Collins, "Connie Mack and His Mackmen," 13.

26. Collins to Leonard, "From Sullivan to Collins," Chapter I, 14.

27. Andy Coakley quoted in Jimmy Powers' column "The Powerhouse," source and date unknown, Eddie Collins Clipping File #2, *The Sporting News* Archives, St. Louis, Missouri.

Chapter 6

1. Hugh Fullerton, "The Smartest Second Baseman," 36.

2. Harry Davis quoted in *The Sporting News*, January 7, 1943, 5.

3. *Philadelphia Inquirer*, March 12, 1909.

4. "The Old Sport's Musings," Ibid., March 17, 1909.

5. Donald Gropeman, *Say It Ain't So, Joe!*, 52.

6. Eddie Collins with Boyden Sparkes, "From Player to Pilot," 40–41. However, Collins' tale is inconsistent. In an earlier article that appeared on January 13, 1914, as part of a bi-weekly series he wrote in late 1913 and 1914 for a Philadelphia newspaper, Collins claims that in 1909 Mack borrowed the idea of meetings from his "Yannigans." This was the young group of players who regularly met each spring to strategize before their games with the A's "Regulars" and other opponents. Then only a few months later, in a June 1914 article, Collins credits the idea of daily meetings to "Uncle Sam" Erwin, a "picturesque ally" of the A's, stating that Mack adopted it. Edward "Eddie" T. Collins, "Connie Mack and His Mackmen," 14–16.

7. Collins, "Connie Mack and His Mackmen," 16.

8. David Fleitz, *Shoeless*, 29; referring to Jackson's description in *Cleveland Plain Dealer*, March 8, 1911.

9. Collins with Sparkes, "From Player to Pilot," 41.

10. Rich Westcott, *Philadelphia's Old Ballparks*, 103–107; Bruce Kuklick, *To Every Thing a Season*, 21–30.

11. Kuklick, *To Every Thing a Season*, 25.

12. Westcott, *Philadelphia's Old Ballparks*, 105.

13. Collins, "Connie Mack and His Mackmen," 16.

14. Collins with Sparkes, "From Player to Pilot," 41.

15. Eddie Collins, "Twenty One Years of Base Ball," Part II, *Los Angeles Times*, January 4, 1927.

16. Westcott, *Philadelphia's Old Ballparks*, 110–111.

17. Collins, "Connie Mack and His Mackmen," 16.

18. *Philadelphia Inquirer*, May 22, 1909.

19. Bob Broeg, *Superstars of Baseball*, 81.

20. *Philadelphia Inquirer*, June 1, 1909.

21. "The Old Sport's Musings," Ibid., July 5, 1909.

22. Ibid., July 13, 1909.

23. Ibid., July 18, 1909.

24. Ibid., July 31, 1909.

25. Eugene C. Murdock, *Ban Johnson*, 100–102. See also Tim Hurst entry in BaseballLibrary.com and entry for August 4 [*sic*], 1909 in Burt Solomon, *The Baseball Timeline*, 154.

26. *Philadelphia Inquirer*, August 4. 1909.

27. Frederick G. Lieb, "Dascoli Case Recalls Mid-Year Firings," *The Sporting News*, August 23, 1961, 3.

28. Editorial, *The Sporting News*, August 19, 1909, 4.

29. Murdock, *Ban Johnson*, 101–02.

30. Connie Mack quoted in *Philadelphia Inquirer*, August 27, 1909.

31. Ty Cobb with Al Stump, *Ty Cobb: My Life in Baseball*, 114.

32. Ty Cobb quoted in *Philadelphia Inquirer*, August 27, 1909.

33. Charles C. Alexander, *Ty Cobb*, 79–80.

34. Eddie Collins as told to Jim Leonard, "From Sulli-

van to Collin," Part II, *The Sporting News*, October 18, 1950, 13.

35. "The Old Sport's Musings," *Philadelphia Inquirer*, August 30, 1909.

36. Connie Mack quoted in Frederick G. Lieb, *Connie Mack*, 126.

37. Ibid., 127.

38. Connie Mack quoted in Ibid., 128.

Chapter 7

1. Johnny Evers quoted in W.A. Phelon, "After the Series," 5a.

2. Correspondence with baseball barnstorming expert Tom Barthel. His file shows this statement appeared in *The Sporting News*, October 14, 1909.

3. Paul Dickson, *The New Dickson Baseball Dictionary*, 36.

4. Mary Collins quoted in F.C. Lane, "Collins the Great," 49.

5. Connie Mack quoted in Frederick G. Lieb, *Connie Mack*, 129.

6. *Philadelphia Inquirer*, March 20, 1910.

7. Eddie Collins, "Twenty One Years of Base Ball," Part IV, *Los Angeles Times*, January 6, 1927.

8. Ibid.

9. *Philadelphia Inquirer*, March 28, 1910.

10. Ibid.

11. Eddie Collins, "Twenty One Years of Base Ball," Part III, *Los Angeles Times*, January 5, 1927.

12. Quote in Bill James and Rob Neyer, *The Neyer/James Guide to Pitchers*, 431.

13. *Philadelphia Inquirer*, May 3, 1910.

14. Fred Lieb, *Baseball As I Have Known It*, 21–23.

15. Eddie Collins, "Twenty One Years of Base Ball, Part XVI, January 20, 1927.

16. Eddie Collins, "Twenty One Years of Base Ball," Part XII, January 16, 1927.

17. Frederick G. Lieb, "Eddie Collins," 51–54.

18. Ibid., 54.

19. Hugh S. Fullerton, "Hitting the Dirt," 6.

20. *Philadelphia Inquirer*, May 21, 1910.

21. Connie Mack quoted in Lieb, *Connie Mack*, 131.

22. *Philadelphia Inquirer*, June 25, 1910.

23. "The Old Sport's Musings," Ibid., July 29, 1910.

24. Connie Mack quoted in Lieb, *Connie Mack*, 131–132.

25. Ibid., 133.

26. Fullerton, "Hitting the Dirt," 16.

27. Ibid., 6–7.

28. *Philadelphia Inquirer*, October 19, 1910.

29. Fullerton, "Hitting the Dirt," 10–11.

30. *Philadelphia Inquirer*, October 19, 1910.

Chapter 8

1. Frederick G. Lieb, "Eddie Collins," 54.

2. Various uncredited articles *Philadelphia Evening Bulletin*, Eddie Collins Clippings File, Urban Archives, Temple University, Philadelphia, Pa.

3. Edward T. Collins' contract and salary information, Transaction Card Collection, National Baseball Library, Cooperstown, N.Y.

4. *The Sporting News*, June 22, 1939, 18. See also January 17, 1959, 19.

5. Ibid., June 2, 1943, 10.

6. *Philadelphia Inquirer*, March 4, 1911.

7. Ibid., March 26, 1911.

8. Edward "Eddie" T. Collins, "Connie Mack and His Mackmen," 13.

9. Bruce Kuklick, *To Every Thing A Season*, 33.

10. Collins, "Connie Mack and His Mackmen," 18.

11. Eddie Collins, "Twenty One Years of Base Ball," Part XI, *Los Angeles Times*, January 15, 1927.

12. Eddie Collins quoted in unidentified news article, May 24, 1928, Eddie Collins Clippings File, Urban Archives, Temple University, Philadelphia, Pa.

13. *Philadelphia Inquirer*, June 8, 1911.

14. Eddie Collins quoted in unidentified newspaper article, June 25, 1928, Eddie Collins Clippings File, Urban Archives, Temple University, Philadelphia, Pa.

15. Connie Mack quoted in *Philadelphia Inquirer*, August 24, 1911.

16. Ibid., September 1, 1911.

17. Frederick G. Lieb, *Connie Mack*, 149–150.

18. Collins, "Connie Mack and His Mackmen," 17.

19. *Philadelphia Inquirer*, October 17, 1911.

20. Ibid., 11.

21. Tris Speaker article in *Boston Daily Globe*, October 17, 1911.

22. Eddie Collins as told to Jim Leonard, "From Sullivan to Collins," Chapter II, *The Sporting News*, October 18, 1950, 14.

23. Kuklick, *To Every Thing A Season*, 33–34.

24. Eddie Collins quoted in *Philadelphia Inquirer*, October 19, 1911.

25. Christy Mathewson writing in Ibid., October 21, 1911.

26. Christy Mathewson writing in Ibid., October 25, 1911.

27. Lieb, *Connie Mack*, 158–160.

28. *Philadelphia Inquirer*, October 26, 1911.

29. Edward T. Collins writing in *Boston Daily Globe*, October 29, 1911.

30. *The Sporting News*, October 19, 1949, 12.

31. Eddie Collins, "Twenty One Years of Base Ball," Part IV, *Los Angeles Times*, January 6, 1927.

32. Connie Mack quoted in Lieb, *Connie Mack*, 161.

33. Ibid., 161–162.

34. Collins to Leonard, "From Sullivan to Collins," Chapter II, 14.

35. Ibid.

36. Column "The Old Sport's Musings," *Philadelphia Inquirer*, August 19, 1912.

37. Otis Nixon quoted in *USA Today Baseball Weekly*, June 21–27, 1991, 14.

Chapter 9

1. John McGraw writing for *New York Times*, October 10, 1913.

2. Eddie Collins as told to Jim Leonard, "From Sullivan to Collins," Chapter II, *The Sporting News*, October 18, 1950, 14.

3. Edward T. Collins' contract and salary information, Transaction Card Collection, National Baseball Library, Cooperstown, N.Y.

4. *Philadelphia Inquirer*, April 26, 1913.

5. *The Sporting News*, May 23, 1912, p. 8.

6. Oscar Vitt quoted in Ibid., November 6, 1913, 6.

7. F.C. Lane, "The Greatest of All Second Basemen," 36–43.

8. Johnny Evers quoted in Ibid., 43–44.

9. Cy Young quoted in *The Sporting News*, August 23, 1950, 13.

10. *Philadelphia Inquirer*, June 12, 1913.

11. Eddie Collins with Boyden Sparkes, "From Player to Pilot," 41.

12. Eddie Collins, "Twenty One Years of Base Ball," Part VI, *Los Angeles Times*, January 8, 1927.

13. Ibid.

14. Frank Chance quoted in *Philadelphia Inquirer*, July 22, 1913.

15. Ibid., August 9, 1913.

16. Rube Oldring quoted in *The Sporting News*, October 29, 1934, 5.

17. John McGraw quoted in *Philadelphia Inquirer*, September 30, 1913.

18. Ban Johnson quoted in *Atlanta Constitution*, October 4, 1913.

19. *Washington Post*, October 13, 1913. See also *New York Times*, October 14, 1913.

20. Eddie Collins quoted in F.C. Lane, "Collins the Great," 58.

21. Eddie Collins writing in *Boston Daily Globe*, October 9, 1913.

22. Hugh Fullerton, "The Smartest Second Baseman," 38.

23. John J. McGraw writing in *New York Times*, October 10, 1913.

24. Eddie Collins as told to Jim Leonard, "From Sullivan to Collins," Chapter I, *The Sporting News*, October 11, 1950, 13.

25. Edward "Eddie" T. Collins, "Connie Mack and His Mackmen," 17–18.

26. Eddie Collins writing in *Boston Daily Globe*, October 11, 1913.

27. *Philadelphia Inquirer*, October 13, 1913.

28. *New York Times*, November 26, 1913. See also *Washington Post*, November 26, 1913.

29. Eddie Collins quoted in Frederick G. Lieb, *Connie Mack*, 171.

30. *Philadelphia Inquirer*, March 7, 1914.

31. Connie Mack quoted in Ibid., April 2, 1914.

32. Connie Mack quoted in Ibid., June 18, 1914.

33. Lane, "Collins the Great," 57.

34. Ibid., 56.

35. Lieb, *Connie Mack*, 174.

36. Lane, "Collins the Great," 57.

37. Edward T. Collins' contract and salary information, Transaction Card Collection, National Baseball Library, Cooperstown, N.Y.

38. Eddie Collins, "Twenty One Years of Base Ball," Part IX, *Los Angeles Times*, January 12, 1927. That Collins saw the Federal League as an opportunity — although a financially risky proposition — is clear from statements he wrote on February 10, 1914, in his semi-weekly column for a local Philadelphia newspaper. Telling readers he wanted the Federal League to succeed as "it would aid the player in the long run," he added that "the player has everything to gain and nothing to lose."

39. Eddie Collins, "Twenty One Years of Base Ball," Part XVII, *Los Angeles Times*, January 21, 1927.

40. Eddie Collins, Twenty One Years of Base Ball, Part XIII, *Los Angeles Times*, January 17, 1927. If, indeed, Collins was referring to the 8–8 tie on September 11, 1914, it was played in Philadelphia, not Boston. Also, the umpires in both games were Connolly and Chill.

41. Lane, "Collins the Great," 56.

42. Lieb, *Connie Mack*, 175–176.

43. Ban Johnson quoted in John E. Wray and J. Roy Stockton, "Ban Johnson's Own Story," Chapter XV, *St. Louis Post-Dispatch*, February 21, 1929.

44. Lane, "Collins the Great," 56.

45. Ibid., 57.

46. Ibid.

47. William C. Kashatus, *Money Pitcher*, 121–128.

48. Ibid., 124–125.

49. Ira Thomas quoted in *Los Angeles Examiner* article appearing in part in *Sporting Life*, December 5, 1914, 6.

50. Bob Broeg, *Superstars of Baseball*, 83. See also Stan Baumgartner, "*Signals,*" *Baseball Guide and Record Book 1947*, 128–129. Both writers allege the fee was paid for a series of ten articles in *American Magazine*. A review of monthly issues of that magazine reveals two articles, both written in the summer of 1914: Edward "Eddie" Collins, "Pitchers I Have Faced," 23–28, 74 and Edward "Eddie" T. Collins, "Mack and His Mackmen," 13–18. A more revealing article written by Collins about signal stealing appeared in Pearson's Magazine in June 1910. Eddie Collins, "Outguessing the Pitcher," 726–36.

51. Christy Mathewson writing in *New York American*, January 24, 1915.

52. Gabby Street quoted in *The Sporting News*, August 20, 1947, 2.

53. Unidentified newspaper article, December 8, 1914, Eddie Collins Clippings File, National Baseball Library, Cooperstown, N.Y.

54. William G. Weart's article reprinted in part in *Sporting Life*, November 21, 1914, 12.

55. Eddie Collins, "Twenty One Years of Base Ball," Part VII, *Los Angeles Times*, January 10, 1927.

Chapter 10

1. Lee Allen, *The American League Story*, 81.

2. "The Old Sport's Musings," *Philadelphia Inquirer*, October 10, 1914.

3. Connie Mack quoted in Bruce Kuklick, *To Everything a Season*, 36.

4. Ibid., 37.

5. Mabel Collins and others quoted in *Spokane Spokesman-Review*, January 5, 1915.

6. Ban Johnson quoted in John E. Wray and J. Roy Stockton, "Ban Johnson's Own Story," Part XVI, *St. Louis Post-Dispatch*, February 22, 1929. Actually the White Sox finished 1914 tied for sixth place. See also *The Sporting News*, December 19, 1956, 8, where Johnson is quoted that "one day when he [Comiskey] was mad at me" he repaid the $15,000 bonus Johnson gave to Collins in 1914.

7. Eddie Collins, "Twenty One Years of Base Ball, Part IX, *Los Angeles Times*, January 12, 1927.

8. Eddie Collins quoted in F.C. Lane, "Collins the Great," 58–59.

9. Correspondence with Dan Levitt, co-author of *Paths to Glory*. But see the *Sporting Life*, November 28, 1914, 6 and also December 19, 1914, which describes a November 19 meeting involving Ban Johnson, Mack and the prospective Yankee purchasers in which a Collins deal is discussed but fails due to the asking price of $50,000. See also comments of Dan Daniel who reports the asking price as $45,000 (*New York Sun*, January 7, 1920), as well as Jacob Ruppert's comments in his article, "The Ten-Million-Dollar Toy," *Saturday Evening Post*, March 28, 1931.

10. Eddie Collins quoted in *Philadelphia Inquirer*, December 9, 1914. See also Harry Davis' quotes in *The Sporting News*, January 7, 1942, 7. Davis states Collins consulted with him about the potential sale. Davis suggested Collins discuss it with his parents before meeting with Ban Johnson in New York City.

11. Connie Mack's quotes in *Philadelphia Evening Ledger* are set forth in Eugene C. Murdock, *Ban Johnson*, 79.

12. Frederick G. Lieb, *Connie Mack*, 182.

13. Connie Mack quoted in unidentified newspaper article, December 8, 1914, Eddie Collins Clippings File, Urban Archives, Temple University, Philadelphia, Pa.

14. Connie Mack quoted in unidentified newspaper article, September 25, 1930, Eddie Collins Clippings File, Urban Archives, Temple University, Philadelphia, Pa.

15. Collins, "Twenty One Years of Base Ball," Part IX.

16. "Right Cross's" column "From Ringside and Bleachers," *New York Evening Journal*, January 7, 1915.

17. *Chicago Daily News*, December 8, 1914, 1.

18. Charles Comiskey quoted in unidentified news article, dated December 1914, Eddie Collins Clippings File, National Baseball Library, Cooperstown, N.Y.

19. Charles A. Comiskey, "Why I Bought Eddie Collins," 15.

20. William A. Phelon, "A Gay Winter," 18.

21. William A. Phelon, "What I Know of Eddie Collins," 38–41.

22. J.C. Kofoed, "Collins and the Others," 71.

23. Eddie Collins quoted in Lane, "Collins the Great," 59–60.

24. Lawrence S. Ritter, *Lost Ballparks*, 29–32. See also Richard Lindberg, *The White Sox Encyclopedia*, 339–341.

25. Lindberg, *The White Sox Encyclopedia*, 340.

26. Christie [*sic*] Mathewson quoting from letter Eddie Collins wrote a "friend," *The Morning (Portland) Oregonian*, March 15, 1915.

27. Ibid.

28. *Chicago Tribune*, December 18, 1914.

29. Christie [*sic*] Mathewson quoting from Eddie Collins letter to a "friend," *The Morning (Portland) Oregonian*, March 15, 1915.

30. *Chicago Tribune*, December 12, 1914.

31. Ibid., December 20, 1914.

32. Column "Caught on the Fly," *The Sporting News*, January 14, 1915, p. 6.

33. Clarence Rowland quoted in *Chicago Tribune*, January 13, 1915.

34. Charles Comiskey quoted in Ibid., January 8, 1915.

35. Ibid., February 18, 1915.

36. Ibid., April 18, 1915.

37. Ibid., May 8, 1915.

38. Ibid., May 23, 1915.

39. Ibid., July 25, 1915.

40. For a good description of the trade, see David L. Fleitz, *Shoeless*, 102–104. For the article reporting the cash outlay of $15,000, see *Chicago Tribune*, August 21, 1915.

41. Eddie Collins, "Twenty One Years of Base Ball," Part XVII, *Los Angeles Times*, January 21, 1927.

42. Quote by unidentified Chicago Cubs player, *Chicago Tribune*, October 11, 1915.

43. Ibid.

44. *New York Globe and Commercial Advertiser*, June 16, 1916.

45. Eddie Collins quoted in *Chicago Tribune*, February 21, 1916.

46. Ibid., March 19, 1916.

47. Charles Comiskey quoted in Ibid., April 13, 1916.

48. Richard Carl Lindberg, *Stealing First in a Two-Team Town*, 69.

49. *Chicago Tribune*, May 15, 1916.

50. Eddie Collins quoted in F.C. Lane, *Batting*, 101.

51. Ibid., 99.

52. *Chicago Tribune*, September 10, 1916.

53. Ibid., October 8, 1916.

54. Charles Comiskey quoted in Ibid., December 20, 1916.

Chapter 11

1. Eddie Collins as told to Jim Leonard, "From Sullivan to Collins," Chapter Three, *The Sporting News*, October 25, 1950, 12.

2. *Chicago Tribune*, April 8, 1917.

3. Eddie Collins, "Twenty One Years of Base Ball," Part XV, *Los Angeles Times*, January 19, 1927.

4. Eddie Collins writing in *Chicago Tribune*, April 15, 1917.

5. Ibid., June 18, 1917.

6. Ban Johnson quoted in Ibid., June 18, 1917.

7. Warren N. Wilbert and William C. Hageman, *The 1917 White Sox*, 64.

8. Eddie Collins, "Twenty One Years of Base Ball," Part XV, *Los Angeles Times*, January 19, 1927.

9. Ibid.

10. Ibid.

11. Nor were any eyebrows raised in the direction of the White Sox the next day, September 4 in St. Louis, when the Sox beat the Browns, 13–6. After that game Browns owner Phil Ball accused two of his players, Del Pratt and Doc Lavan, of "laying down." The alleged lack of effort was attributed at the time to problems within the Browns' organization. Rick Huhn, *The Sizzler*, 66. See also BioProject.SABR.org for Del Pratt's biographical entry written by baseball historian, Steve Steinberg.

12. *Chicago Tribune*, September 18, 1917.

13. Eddie Collins quote appears in Wilbert and Hageman, *The 1917 White Sox*, 195.

14. Collins to Leonard, "From Sullivan to Collins," Chapter Three, 12.

15. Ibid. See also Richard A. Smiley, "I'm a Faster Man Than You Are, Heinie Zim," 97–103. The title of the article is taken from a poem by Grantland Rice referring to the "Zim" play. Smiley has reviewed photographs of the play which show Collins sliding across the plate and Zimmerman so close behind that he had to jump over Collins to avoid stepping on him.

16. *Chicago Tribune*, October 18, 1917. See also Smiley, "I'm a Faster Man Than You Are Heinie Zim," 103.

17. *Atlanta Constitution*, October 16, 1917.

18. Ibid., October 15, 1917.

19. John McGraw quoted in Wilbert and Hageman, *The 1917 White Sox*, 197.

20. Eddie Collins as told to Jim Leonard, "From Sullivan to Collins," Part Three, 11.

21. Ibid., 12.

22. Richard Carl Lindberg, *Stealing First in a Two-Team Town*, 98.

23. Wilbert and Hageman, *The 1917 Chicago White Sox*, 159.

24. See Eddie Collins' biographical entry by Paul Mittermeyer, *Deadball Stars of the American League*, 612, quoting Gandil teammate Clyde Milan of Washington that following the incident "for the rest of his playing career, Gandil was out to get even."

25. Robert C. Cottrell, *Blackball, the Black Sox, and the Babe*, 40–41. Weaver never forgave Collins for his alleged failure to sharpen his spikes. In John P. Carmichael, ed., *My Greatest Day in Baseball*, 44–45, Weaver claims Collins refused to sharpen his spikes because "he figured they might come back at him" and he might be hurt. Collins "was a great guy to look out for himself. If there was a tough gent comin' down to second, he'd yell for the shortstop to make the play." This type of public criticism of Collins' game was rare, even from the Black Sox players.

26. Clarence "Pants" Rowland quoted in *Chicago Tribune*, February 17, 1918.

27. Collins, "Twenty One Years of Base Ball," Part XV.
28. *Chicago Tribune*, April 27, 1918.
29. Ban Johnson quoted in *Chicago Tribune*, May 17, 1918.
30. Charles Comiskey quoted in Ibid., June 12, 1918.
31. Eugene C. Murdock, *Ban Johnson*, 146.
32. Ibid., 157.
33. *Chicago Tribune*, July 17, 1918.
34. Ibid., July 26, 1918.
35. Collins to Leonard, "From Sullivan to Collins," Chapter Three, 12.
36. *The Sporting News*, August 22, 1918, 5.
37. Collins to Leonard, "From Sullivan to Collins," Chapter Three, 12.
38. Ibid.
39. Ibid.

Chapter 12

1. Eddie Collins as told to Jim Leonard, "From Sullivan to Collins," Chapter Three, *The Sporting News*, October 25, 1950, 12.
2. Eddie Collins quoted in *Chicago Tribune*, January 3, 1919.
3. Eddie Collins as told to Jim Leonard, "From Sullivan to Collins," Chapter Four, *The Sporting News*, November 1, 1950, 13.
4. William Kid Gleason quoted in *Chicago Tribune*, September 25, 1919. See also Gleason's similar remarks in *The Sporting News*, December 19, 1918, 5.
5. Discharge papers of Edward Trowbridge Collins, United States Marine Corps Reserve, August 19, 1922, Eddie Collins Clippings File, National Baseball Library, Cooperstown, N.Y.
6. Collins to Leonard, "From Sullivan to Collins," Chapter Four, 13.
7. Eddie Collins quoted in Edward Grant Barrow with James M. Kahn, *My Fifty Years in Baseball*, 201. See also article in unidentified newspaper by Gerry Hern in which Collins is quoted that Gandil "despised" him, they did not speak, and during the entire 1919 season, Gandil "didn't throw the ball to me once during infield practice." Eddie Collins Clippings File #1, *The Sporting News* Archives, St. Louis, Mo.
8. Eddie Collins, "Twenty One Years of Base Ball," Part XV, *Los Angeles Times*, January 19, 1927.
9. Collins to Leonard, "From Sullivan to Collins," Chapter Four, 13.
10. Capt. Putnam quoted in *Chicago Tribune*, August 17, 1919.
11. Statement by Edward T. Collins to L.N. O'Connor of American League, 4, Box 1, Folder 10, Black Sox scandal (American League Records, 1914–1969), National Baseball Library, Cooperstown, N.Y.
12. Billy Evans writing in *Chicago Tribune*, September 25, 1919.
13. Ibid., September 30, 1919.
14. Quotes of Eddie Collins and Buck Weaver discussed in Gene Carney, *Burying the Black Sox*, 216, citing Joe Williams' article in *New York World-Telegram*, July 10, 1943, reprinted in *The Joe Williams Baseball Reader*.
15. *The Sporting News*, October 2, 1919, 1.
16. Eddie Collins writing in *Chicago Daily News*, October 1, 1919.
17. Ibid., October 2, 1919.
18. Collins to Leonard, "From Sullivan to Collins," Chapter Four, 14.
19. Ibid.

20. *Chicago Tribune*, October 3, 1919.
21. Eddie Collins writing in *Chicago Daily News*, October 3, 1919.
22. Collins to Leonard, "From Sullivan to Collins," Chapter Four, 14.
23. William A. Cook, *The 1919 World Series* , 44.
24. Bill Gleason quoted in *Chicago Tribune*, October 4, 1919.
25. Eddie Collins writing in *Chicago Daily News*, October 6, 1919.
26. Collins to Leonard, "Sullivan to Collins," Chapter Four, 14.
27. Ibid.
28. Eddie Collins writing in *Chicago Daily News*, October 7, 1919.
29. Eddie Collins writing in Ibid., October 8, 1919.
30. Collins to Leonard, "From Sullivan to Collins," Chapter Four, 14.
31. William Kid Gleason quoted in *Chicago Tribune*, October 8, 1919.
32. Ray Schalk and Eddie Collins writing in separate articles in *Chicago Daily News*, October 9, 1919.
33. Billy Evans writing in *Chicago Tribune*, November 2, 1919 and November 16, 1919.
34. William Kid Gleason quoted in Ibid., October 10, 1919.
35. Hugh Fullerton's column discussed in Gene Carney, *Burying the Black Sox*, xi and 11.
36. Eddie Collins writing in *Chicago Daily News*, October 10, 1919.
37. Charles Comiskey quoted in *Chicago Tribune*, November 22, 1919.
38. Charles Comiskey quoted in Ibid., December 15, 1919.
39. Ibid.
40. Ibid., December 31, 1919.

Chapter 13

1. Hugh Fullerton, "Baseball on Trial," 183.
2. *The Sporting News*, December 12, 1919, 5.
3. Collins' new contract was actually dated May 3, 1920. It called for $15,000 per year. Edward T. Collins' contract and salary information, Transaction Card Collection, National Baseball Library, Cooperstown, N.Y. Over the years there has been speculation that in 1918 or 1919 Collins' annual salary, along with that of others on the White Sox, was reduced by Comiskey to $14,500. See Collins' biographical entry in Deadball Stars of the American League, 612. Collins' transaction card does not reflect such a drop in pay.
4. Bill Gleason quoted in *Chicago Tribune*, March 19, 1920.
5. David L. Fleitz, *Shoeless: The Life and Times of Joe Jackson*, 209.
6. *Chicago Tribune*, April 15, 1920.
7. *The Sporting News*, May 6, 1920, 1.
8. Eliot Asinof, *Eight Men Out*, 144–145.
9. "The World of Sports," *The Chicago Whip*, March 27, 1920, 5. Cited in Robert C. Cottrell, *Blackball, the Black Sox, and the Babe*, 203–204.
10. *Chicago Tribune*, July 27, 1920.
11. Ibid., August 18, 1920.
12. Jim O'Leary's comment reported in Asinof, *Eight Men Out*, 148.
13. Eddie Collins quoted in Gerry Hern, "The Tipoff on the Black Sox," 12. Collins is incorrect about the timing of the game as far as team standings. When

there were seven games to go in the 1920 regular season, it was September 23, and the White Sox were playing in Cleveland. Their 10–3 win that day left them just one-half game behind the Indians. According to the box score, Weaver was not charged with an error in the game in Boston on September 1. *The Sporting News*, September 9, 1920, 5. Kerr was charged with an error, however, perhaps on the throw that Weaver allegedly dropped.

14. Joe Williams, "Black Sox Crooks Didn't Dare Approach Collins," March 27, year not identified, Eddie Collins Clippings File #1, *The Sporting News* Archives, St. Louis, Mo.

15. Byrd Lynn and Harvey McClellan quoted in *New York Times*, October 4, 1920.

16. Gene Carney, *Burying the Black Sox*, 225–226, citing Comiskey's testimony in *Joe Jackson vs. Chicago White Sox*, T 1545.

17. Article and letter from Fred M. Loomis in *Chicago Tribune*, September 19, 1920.

18. Hartley T. Replogle quoted in Ibid., September 23, 1920.

19. Ban Johnson quoted in Mike Sowell, *The Pitch That Killed*, 256. See also Johnson's quote in *Chicago Tribune*, September 24, 1920, where he says he heard a vague statement, repeated "more or less openly," that gamblers were saying they would tell all if the White Sox did not let Cleveland win.

20. *The Sporting News*, February 10, 1921, 4. On the other hand, the idea that Collins provided Johnson with information as early as September 1920 belies later attempts by Johnson to extract information about the White Sox conspiracy from Collins and Ray Schalk.

21. Sowell, *The Pitch That Killed*, 258.

22. *New York Tribune*, September 25, 1920, cited in Cottrell, *Blackball, the Black Sox, and the Babe*, 217.

23. *Chicago Tribune*, September 26, 1920.

24. Testimony attributed to Charles Comiskey and quotes of John A. Heydler in Ibid., September 27, 1920.

25. Asinof, *Eight Men Out*, 71–77.

26. *Chicago Tribune*, September 28, 1920.

27. Ibid.

28. Charles Comiskey's statement in *Chicago Daily News*, September 28, 1920.

29. See for example Carney, *Burying the Black Sox*.

30. *Chicago Tribune*, September 29, 1920.

31. Quotes allegedly by an unidentified White Sox player, Ibid.

32. Eddie Collins told to Jim Leonard, "From Sullivan to Collins," Chapter Four, *The Sporting News*, November 1, 1950, 13.

33. Hern, "The Tipoff on the Black Sox," 12.

34. Bill Gleason quoted in *Chicago Tribune*, September 29, 1920.

35. White Sox players statement printed in Ibid., October 5, 1920.

36. Eddie Collins quoted in *GRIT*, October 3, 1920.

37. Byrd Lynn and Harvey McClellan quoted in *New York Times*, October 4, 1920. See also *Chicago Tribune*, October 4, 1920.

38. Tom Shibe letter, Box 1, Folder 3, Black Sox scandal (American League Records, 1914–1969), National Baseball Library, Cooperstown, New York.

39. Eddie Collins quoted in *Collyer's Eye*, October 30, 1920, 1, 5.

40. Hern, "The Tipoff on the Black Sox," 12.

41. Eddie Collins to Jim Leonard, "From Sullivan to Collins," Chapter Three, *The Sporting News*, October 25, 1950, 12.

42. Carney, *Burying the Black Sox*, 234.

43. Ibid., 212, quoting Hugh Fullerton in article "On the Screen," *Atlanta Constitution*, July 11, 1921. In that article Fullerton mentions, without naming, four players on the White Sox "who had the guts and the honesty to denounce the crooks." (See Ibid., Footnote 10 to Chapter 8).

44. Timothy M. Gay, *Tris Speaker*, 226.

45. Harold Seymour's recollection of his interview with Joe Jackson in Dorothy Jane Mills, *A Woman's Work*, 101.

46. Joe Jackson as told to Furman Bisher, "This Is The Truth!" page unknown.

47. Dick Kerr quoted in *Washington Post*, February 15, 1937.

48. Collins to Leonard, "From Sullivan to Collins," Chapter Four, 13.

49. James T. Farrell, *My Baseball Diary*, 189. The Black Sox player Farrell refers to is probably Chick Gandil, who reportedly told one of the agents for the gamblers, "that's one guy [Collins] we can't get." Gandil's quote appears in an article by Joe Williams which was written on March 27, 1951, newspaper unidentified, Eddie Collins Clippings File #1, *The Sporting News* Archives, St. Louis, Mo.

Chapter 14

1. Richard Lindberg, *Who's on 3rd*, 47.

2. Kenesaw Mountain Landis quoted in *Chicago Tribune*, January 13, 1921.

3. Eddie Collins as told to Jim Leonard, "From Sullivan to Collins," *The Sporting News*, Chapter Four, November 1, 1950, 13.

4. Eddie Collins' Philadelphia interview mentioned in uncredited article, *The Sporting News*, February 3, 1921, 3. If reported accurately, Collins' reference to a "confession" is interesting. Over the years the term has been frequently used when referring to statements made by certain of the indicted White Sox players. Buck Weaver did admit sitting in on meetings with other indicted players where the subject of throwing games for money in the 1919 World Series was discussed and Jackson admitted actually receiving money at some point. However, both players repeatedly denied they threw any game during the World Series, insisting they gave their best effort at all times. Their statistics during the eight games arguably lend support to their position.

5. *Chicago Tribune*, January 30, 1921. The article attributes the "reports" of Collins' involvement to information which came from a south side (Chicago) establishment "frequented by Claude [Lefty] Williams and Joe Jackson." See also Buck Weaver's later allegations about certain games played in 1917 and 1919 in the *Lincoln* (Neb.) *Star*, May 12, 1922.

6. Judge Landis quoted in Ibid.

7. Ban Johnson quoted in Ibid.

8. Eddie Collins quoted in Ibid., January 31, 1921.

9. David Pietrusza, *Judge and Jury*, 297.

10. Letter dated July 15, 1921, from Leslie O'Connor to Honorable George F. Barrett (attorney for the American League in Black Sox criminal trial matters), Box 1, Folder 10, Black Sox scandal (American League Records, 1914–1969), National Baseball Library, Cooperstown, N.Y.

11. Quotes from statement by Edward T. Collins of Chicago Americans to L.N. O'Connor at Auditorium Hotel, Chicago, Illinois, February 19, 1921, in Ibid. The entire statement, pages 1–5, is set forth in Appendix One.

12. Letter dated February 24, 1921, from Eddie Collins to Judge Kenesaw Mountain Landis, Box 1, Folder 4, Black Sox scandal (American League Records, 1914–1969), National Baseball Library, Cooperstown, N.Y.

13. Rules on betting on baseball games were issued by and instituted at the behest of Judge Landis in early 1927.

14. See Buck Weaver's allegations in the *Lincoln (Neb.) Star*, May 12, 1922.

15. *Chicago Tribune*, March 27, 1921.

16. Ibid., March 13, 1921.

17. Letter dated May 26, 1921 from W. G. Evans to Ban Johnson, Box 1, Folder 7, Black Sox scandal File, (American League Records, 1914–1969), National Baseball Library, Cooperstown, N.Y.

18. Frank Navin letter to Ban Johnson dated June 30, 1921, Box 1, Folder 9, Black Sox scandal File, (American League Records, 1914–1969), National Baseball Library, Cooperstown, N.Y.

19. Letter presumably from Ban Johnson to Frank Navin dated July 9, 1921, Box 1, Folder 10, Black Sox scandal (American League Records, 1914–1969), National Baseball Library, Cooperstown, N.Y. It appears from a reply letter from Navin to Johnson dated July 10 that Navin was aware early on that his pitcher George Dauss was interviewed by Landis, but Navin neglected to tell Johnson about it. Ibid.

20. Letter from Leslie O'Connor to Honorable George F. Barrett dated July 15, in Ibid.

21. Henry Berger quoted in *Chicago Tribune*, July 9, 1921.

22. *Chicago American*, July 12, 1921.

23. Testimony of William Gleason and characterization of testimony of Eddie Collins and others in *Chicago Tribune*, July 29, 1921.

24. Testimony of Ray Schalk quoted in Ibid.

25. Ibid.

26. Daniel E. Ginsburg, *The Fix Is In*, 144. Citing *American Bar Association Journal*, February 1, 1988.

27. *Chicago Tribune*, August 3, 1921.

28. Ibid., August 4, 1921.

29. Statement of Judge Landis appears in Ginsberg, *The Fix Is In*, 144. Collins disagreed with the decision of Judge Landis in only one respect. He felt Joe Jackson was a "victim" and a "tragic patsy." ("I don't think he should have been judged as harshly as the others.") Collins quoted in article by Gerry Hern in the *Boston Post*, March 24, 1951, Eddie Collins Clippings File #1, The Sporting News Archives, St. Louis, Mo.

30. *Chicago Tribune*, August 27, 1921.

31. Hugh Fullerton writing in *New York Evening Mail*, October 31, 1921.

32. Eddie Collins quoted in *Chicago Tribune*, October 27, 1921.

Chapter 15

1. George Moriarty's column "Calling Them," *Baseball Magazine*, January 1924, 352.

2. *Chicago Tribune*, April 9, 1922.

3. Quotes of Eddie Collins to C. William Duncan, publication unidentified, March 9, 1933, Eddie Collins Clippings File, National Baseball Library, Cooperstown, New York.

4. Ray Schalk quoted in *Chicago Tribune*, May 12, 1922.

5. Buck Weaver quoted in the *Lincoln* (Neb.) *Star*, May 12, 1922.

6. Kid Gleason quoted in *Chicago Tribune*, July 11, 1922.

7. Hugh Fullerton writing in Ibid., August 4, 1922.

8. Colonel Jacob Ruppert quoted in Ibid., October 10, 1922.

9. Fred Lieb writing in *New York Evening Telegram*, December 12, 1922.

10. *Chicago Tribune*, December 10, 1922.

11. Fred Lieb writing in *New York Evening Telegram*, December 20, 1922. In agreement was Sid Mercer of the *New York Evening Journal*, December 26, 1922.

12. *Chicago Tribune*, December 25, 1922.

13. *The Daily News* (Tarrytown, N.Y.), January 18, 1929.

14. Captain T.L. Huston quoted in *Chicago Tribune*, February 3, 1923.

15. Colonel Ruppert and Kid Gleason quoted in Ibid., February 20, 1923.

16. Eddie Collins quoted in *The Sporting News*, November 30, 1922, 6.

17. Eddie Collins quoted in *Chicago Tribune*, March 16, 1923.

18. Eddie Collins quoted in Ibid., March 18, 1923.

19. Edward T. Collins' contract and salary information, Transaction Card Collection, National Baseball Library, Cooperstown, N.Y.

20. *Chicago Tribune*, April 2, 1923.

21. Ibid., April 6, 1923.

22. Eddie Collins quoted in *Boston Globe*, March 27, 1951.

23. Miller Huggins quoted in Ibid.

24. Shirley Povich, "If You Can Get Away With It!" 57.

25. Kid Gleason quoted in *Chicago Tribune*, October 17, 1923.

26. Eddie Collins as told to Jim Leonard, "From Sullivan to Collins," Chapter Four, *The Sporting News*, November 1, 1950, 13.

27. *Chicago Tribune*, October 26, 1923.

28. Ibid., October 28, 1923.

29. Eddie Collins quoted in Ibid., November 13, 1923.

30. Colonel Jacob Ruppert quoted in *New York Evening Telegram*, October 18, 1923.

31. Eddie Collins quoted in *Chicago Tribune*, December 11, 1923.

32. Ibid., December 13, 1923.

33. Ibid., December 16, 1923.

34. Eddie Collins with Boyden Sparkes, "From Player to Pilot," 8.

35. Ibid.

36. Eddie Collins quoted in *Chicago Tribune*, February 21, 1924.

37. Ibid., February 24, 1924.

38. Ibid., March 30, 1924.

39. Eddie Collins quoted in *The Sporting News*, March 27, 1924, 4.

40. Ted Lyons quoted in Ibid., September 19, 1935, 3.

41. *Chicago Tribune*, May 20, 1924.

42. Eddie Collins quoted in article by C. William Duncan, "Eddie Collins Talks of Player Days," source not identified, March 9, 1933, Eddie Collins Clippings File, National Baseball Library, Cooperstown, N.Y.

43. Collins with Sparkes, "From Player to Pilot," 8.

44. Eddie Collins' contract and salary information, Transaction Card Collection, National Baseball Library, Cooperstown, N.Y.

45. *Chicago Tribune*, December 12, 1924.

46. *Chicago Daily News*, December 15, 1924.

47. *Chicago Tribune*, December 25, 1924.

48. *The Sporting News*, January 8, 1925, 4. See also sportswriter Frank Menke's article in Ibid., May 12, 1925, 7, where he describes in similar terms the Comiskey-Collins relationship and hypothesizes the impediments such a relationship threw in Collins' path to success.

49. Collins to Leonard, "From Sullivan to Collins," Chapter Four, 13.

Chapter 16

1. Dan Desmond, "Second to None: The Life Story of Eddie Collins," First of multi-part series, source unknown, March 1951, Eddie Collins Clippings File #1, *The Sporting News* Archives, St. Louis, Mo.
2. Eddie Collins with Boyden Sparkes, "From Player to Pilot," 8.
3. Ibid.
4. Eddie Collins quoted in *Norwalk* (Ct.) *Hour*, May 20, 1933.
5. Ray Schalk quoted in *Chicago Tribune*, February 13, 1925.
6. Eddie Collins quoted in Ibid., April 14, 1925.
7. Eddie Collins to Jim Leonard, "From Sullivan to Collins," Chapter Four, November 1, 1950, 14.
8. E.W. Smith's remarks appear in "Scribbled by Scribes," *The Sporting News*, May 21, 1925, 4.
9. There is some question as to the actual date of Collins' 3,000th hit. In May 1958 Leonard Gettelson claimed that while researching for a publication of *The Sporting News* entitled *One for the Book*, he determined that Collins had four hits in 1906 rather than three and in 1907 was credited with three hits too many. He determined that Collins actually reached 3,000 with his first hit against the A's on June 11, 1925. *The Sporting News*, May 21, 1958, 8. Gettelson's numbers for 1906 and 1907 are not substantiated by this author's research. In addition, in calculating his totals Gettelson appears to accept that Collins had zero hits on June 3 as listed in the box score carried in *The Sporting News*, June 11, 1925, 5, when the *Chicago Tribune* box score shows three. The difference appears to be in the hit totals. Both box scores indicate 16 total hits, but *The Sporting News* box score shows only 13 hits in the hit column for the individual players. Collins' three hits are the only difference between the two box scores. The Hall of Fame and other sources accept June 3 as the correct date for Collins' accomplishment. In fairness to Gettelson, it should be noted that Collins himself often stated his early records were incorrect.
10. Collins with Sparkes, "From Player to Pilot," 9.
11. Collins to Leonard, "From Sullivan to Collins," Chapter Four, 14.
12. Collins with Sparkes, "From Player to Pilot," 9.
13. Ibid.
14. "The Observer" writing in his column "Casual Comment," *The Sporting News*, September 2, 1925, 4.
15. Eddie Collins' contract and salary information, Transaction Card Collection, National Baseball Library, Cooperstown, N.Y.
16. Eddie Collins quoted in *Chicago Tribune*, February 3, 1926.
17. James Crusinberry, "The Immortal Eddie Collins," 230.
18. Ibid.
19. Collins with Sparkes, "From Player to Pilot," 40.
20. Ibid.
21. Buck Crowe quoted in taped interview by Professor Eugene C. Murdock, November 1, 1974, Murdock Baseball Collection, Cleveland Public Library, Cleveland, Ohio.
22. Ted Lyons quoted in article by Joe Cashman, source unidentified, Eddie Collins Clippings File #2, *The Sporting News* Archives, St. Louis, Mo.
23. *Chicago Tribune*, June 21, 1926.
24. Ibid., July 25, 1926.
25. Ibid., August 3, 1926.
26. Ibid., August 7, 1926.
27. Collins with Sparkes, "From Player to Pilot," 41.

28. *Chicago Tribune*, August 15, 1926.
29. Ibid., September 22, 1926.
30. Collins with Sparkes, "From Player to Pilot," 41.
31. Eddie Collins quoted in *Chicago Tribune*, November 12, 1926.
32. Eddie Collins quoted in *Philadelphia Inquirer*, November 12, 1926.
33. Editorial in *Chicago Tribune*, November 13, 1926.
34. Column "In the Wake of the News," *Chicago Tribune,* November 14, 1926.
35. *Philadelphia Inquirer*, November 12, 1926.
36. Joe Vila's syndicated column in Ibid., December 19, 1926.
37. Editorial, *The Sporting News*, November 18, 1926, 4.
38. Don Maxwell writing a column "Speaking of Sports," *Chicago Tribune*, November 16, 1926.
39. Eddie Collins quoted in *Philadelphia Inquirer*, December 20, 1926.

Chapter 17

1. Will Rogers writing in *Washington Post*, January 23, 1927.
2. Eddie Collins quoted in *Philadelphia Inquirer*, December 20, 1926.
3. Connie Mack quoted in Frederick G. Lieb, *Connie Mack*, 174.
4. Connie Mack quoted in *Philadelphia Inquirer*, December 20, 1926.
5. Bob Warrington, "The Fight for Sunday Baseball in Philadelphia."
6. Eddie Collins quoted in *Chicago Tribune*, December 22, 1926.
7. Swede Risberg quoted in Ibid., December 30, 1926.
8. Ibid.
9. Connie Mack and Eddie Collins quoted in *Philadelphia Inquirer*, December 24, 1926.
10. Eddie Collins' contract and salary information, Transaction Card Collection, National Baseball Library, Cooperstown, N.Y.
11. Swede Risberg's statements to Judge Landis and quotes in *Chicago Tribune*, January 2, 1927.
12. Eddie Collins quoted in *Philadelphia Inquirer*, January 2, 1927.
13. *Chicago Tribune*, January 4, 1927.
14. Ibid., January 6, 1927.
15. Swede Risberg's testimony quoted in Ibid.
16. Pants Rowland quoted in Ibid., January 5, 1927.
17. Eddie Collins' testimony in Ibid.
18. Will Rogers writing in *Washington Post*, January 23, 1927.
19. Mabel Collins quoted in *Philadelphia Evening Bulletin*, January 10, 1927.
20. Ty Cobb's testimony in *Chicago Tribune*, January 6, 1927.
21. Chick Gandil's testimony in Ibid., January 8, 1927.
22. Chick Gandil's affidavit in Ibid., January 7, 1927.
23. Bill James' testimony in Ibid., January 8, 1927.
24. Eddie Collins' testimony in *Philadelphia Inquirer*, January 8, 1927.
25. Column "The Old Sport's Musings," Ibid., January 10, 1927.
26. Portion of decision of Judge Kenesaw Mountain Landis reported in Ibid., January 13, 1927.
27. Text of decision of Judge Kenesaw Mountain Landis in *The Sporting News*, January 20, 1927, 5.
28. Proposal of Judge Kenesaw Mountain Landis in *Philadelphia Inquirer*, January 13, 1927.

29. *Washington Post,* January 23, 1927.

30. *New York Herald-Tribune* editorial of January 14, 1927 quoted in David Pietrusza, *Judge and Jury,* 301.

31. Ban Johnson quoted in *Chicago Tribune,* January 17, 1927.

32. Pietrusza, *Judge and Jury,* 309–310.

Chapter 18

1. Eddie Collins with Boyden Sparkes, "Out at Second," 18.

2. Eddie Collins, "Twenty One Years of Base Ball," Part XV, *Los Angeles Times,* January 19, 1927.

3. Eddie Collins, "Twenty One Years of Base Ball, Part XX, *Los Angeles Times,* January 25, 1927.

4. Connie Mack quoted in *Philadelphia Inquirer,* January 28, 1927.

5. Eddie Collins quoted in Ibid., January 30, 1927.

6. Eddie Collins as told to Jim Leonard, "From Sullivan to Collins," Chapter Four, *The Sporting News,* November 1, 1950, 14.

7. Jim Kaplan, *Lefty Grove,* 105.

8. Connie Mack quoted in *The Sporting News,* December 29, 1927, 1.

9. Billy Evans quoted in Ibid., March 31, 1927, 2.

10. Paul Krichell quoted in column in source unknown, date unknown, Eddie Collins Clippings File #1, *The Sporting News* Archives, St. Louis, Mo. A different version of the incident, claiming Cobb directed disparaging remarks at the Braves pitcher, appeared in *Time,* March 28, 1927.

11. *Philadelphia Inquirer,* April 12, 1927.

12. Collins with Sparkes, "Out at Second," 18.

13. Collins to Leonard, "From Sullivan to Collins," Chapter Four, 14, 16.

14. *The Sporting News,* October 20, 1927, 3.

15. Eddie Collins' contract and salary information, Transaction Card Collection, National Baseball Library, Cooperstown, N.Y. There is indication that from the outset some of the younger A's players were upset with the large salaries paid Cobb and Speaker in 1928. Timothy M. Gay, *Tris Speaker,* 252.

16. Jimmie Foxx quoted in Bob Gorman, *Double X,* 25.

17. Collins with Sparkes, "Out at Second," 19.

18. Eddie Collins with Boyden Sparkes, "Coaching with Connie Mack," 10.

19. James C. Isaminger's column "Tips From the Sports Ticker," *Philadelphia Inquirer,* May 20, 1928.

20. The game is described in detail in Joseph J. Dittmer, *Baseball Records Registry* (Jefferson, N. C.: McFarland, 1997) which appears on the website BaseballLibrary.com. The Athletics fielded future Hall of Famers Ty Cobb, Tris Speaker, Mickey Cochrane, Al Simmons, Jimmie Foxx, Lefty Grove and Eddie Collins. The Yankees fielded future Hall of Famers Earle Combs, Babe Ruth, Lou Gehrig, Tony Lazzeri, Waite Hoyt and Leo Durocher. Also involved were future Cooperstown enshrinees Miller Huggins and Connie Mack (managers) and Tommy Connolly and Bill McGowan (umpires).

21. Eddie Collins quoted in *Philadelphia Evening Bulletin,* March 26, 1951.

Chapter 19

1. *Chicago Tribune,* October 2, 1929.

2. *The Daily News* (Tarrytown, N.Y.), January 18, 1929.

3. Eddie Collins quoted in *Philadelphia Inquirer,* March 1, 1929.

4. Eddie Collins quoted in *Philadelphia Evening Bulletin,* March 22, 1929.

5. Jimmie Dykes quoted in column "Playing The Game," by Ed Pollner, source unknown, March 27, 1951, Eddie Collins Clippings File #1, *The Sporting News* Archives, St. Louis, Mo.

6. Frederick G. Lieb, *Connie Mack,* 221–223.

7. Eddie Collins as told to Jim Leonard, "From Sullivan to Collins," Chapter Four, *The Sporting News,* November 1, 1950, 16.

8. Eddie Collins as told to Jim Leonard, "From Sullivan to Collins," Final (Fifth) Chapter, *The Sporting News,* November 8, 1950, 13. Ed Barrow confirmed that Donie Bush was his first choice in Edward Grant Barrow with James M. Kahn, *My Fifty Years in Baseball,* 152–153.

9. Connie Mack quoted in *Philadelphia Inquirer,* March 27, 1930.

10. Ibid., April 8, 1930.

11. Current record books show Collins appearing in three games, but batting only two times with one hit and one run. Thus, his appearance and out on either May 11 or August 5, 1930 is not recorded. See box scores in *Philadelphia Inquirer,* May 12, August 3 and August 6, 1930, as well as page 5 of *The Sporting News* issues of May 15, August 7 and 14, 1930.

12. *Philadelphia Inquirer,* August 29, 1930.

13. Connie Mack quoted in Ibid., October 9, 1930.

14. Eddie Collins interviewed in "Modern Baseball, the Greatest Ever!" 339–40.

15. Peter Morris, *A Game of Inches: The Game on the Field,* 465–66.

16. *Philadelphia Inquirer,* June 11, 1931.

17. Bill James, *The New Bill James Historical Baseball Abstract,* 481.

18. Eddie Collins with Boyden Sparkes, "Out at Second," 19.

19. Ibid., 80.

20. Eddie Collins with Boyden Sparkes, "Coaching With Connie Mack," 10–11.

21. Connie Mack writing in his syndicated column in *Philadelphia Inquirer,* October 4, 1931.

22. Eddie Collins quoted in Charles Bevis, *Mickey Cochrane,* 86.

23. *Philadelphia Inquirer,* October 8, 1931.

24. Earle Mack quoted in *The Sporting News,* October 29, 1931, 8.

25. James C. Isaminger's column "Tips From the Sports Ticker," *Philadelphia Inquirer,* September 4, 1932.

26. Connie Mack writing in his syndicated column in *Philadelphia Inquirer,* September 11, 1932.

Chapter 20

1. Eddie Collins with Boyden Sparkes, "Out at Second," 84.

2. News article, source unknown, September 2, 1929, Eddie Collins Clippings File, Urban Archives, Temple University, Philadelphia, Pa.

3. Bob Quinn quoted in *Philadelphia Inquirer,* February 26, 1933.

4. Ibid.

5. Eddie Collins as told to Jim Leonard, "From Sullivan to Collin," Final (Fifth) Chapter, *The Sporting News,* November 8, 1950, 13.

6. Eddie Collins with Boyden Sparkes, "Coaching With Connie Mack," 62.

7. Collins to Leonard, "From Sullivan to Collins," Final (Fifth) Chapter, 13.

8. Ibid.

9. Tom Yawkey quoted in J.G. Taylor Spink's column "Three and One," *The Sporting News*, January 30, 1936, 4.

10. *The Sporting News*, August 5, 1959, 16. See also Dan Daniel's column, "Over the Fence," *The Sporting News*, January 14, 1959, 10, which states Collins' interest in the Red Sox was $100,000 although it is not clear if that was the original value or the value when Yawkey later considered purchasing the New York Yankees.

11. Ernest Mehl's column "Sporting Comment," source unknown, .ca 1951, Eddie Collins Clippings File #1, *The Sporting News* Archives, St. Louis, Mo.

12. Mabel Collins quoted in *Philadelphia Record*, February 27, 1933.

13. Tom Yawkey and Eddie Collins quoted in *Boston Daily Record*, February 27, 1933.

14. Glenn Stout and Richard A. Johnson, *Red Sox Century*, 178.

15. Thomas Yawkey quoted in Ibid., 184.

16. Eddie Collins quoted in Ibid.

17. Eddie Collins with Boyden Sparkes, "Building a Ball Club," 18.

18. Daniel M. Daniel, "Tom Yawkey Rides His Hobby," 486.

19. Collins to Leonard, "From Sullivan To Collins," Final (Fifth) Chapter, 13.

20. J.G. Taylor Spink's column "Three and One," *The Sporting News*, July 6, 1933, 4.

21. Stout and Johnson, *Red Sox Century*, 187.

22. Collins with Sparkes, "Building a Ball Club," 43.

23. Paul Gallico's statement appears in column "Scribbled by Scribes," *The Sporting News*, December 28, 1933, 4.

24. Collins with Sparkes, "Building a Ball Club," 19.

25. Tom Yawkey quoted in F.C. Lane, "A Master Baseball Builder," 318.

26. Ibid.

27. Stout and Johnson, *Red Sox Century*, 185.

28. Jim Kaplan, *Lefty Grove*, 180.

29. Eddie Collins quoted in Lane, "A Master Baseball Builder," 318.

30. Interview with Eddie Collins, "It Takes Time to Build a Winner," 301.

31. Newspaper article by James B. Reston, source and date unknown, Eddie Collins Clippings File, Urban Archives, Temple University, Philadelphia, Pa.

32. Clark Griffith quoted in *The Sporting News*, July 30, 1952, 12.

33. See *The Sporting News*, December 20, 1934, 3, where Eddie Collins is quoted as saying, "You've never seen me charge down to the bench and that won't happen with Cronin in charge, either."

Chapter 21

1. Harold Kaese quoted in Peter Golenbock, *Fenway*, 91.

2. Column "Caught on the Fly," *The Sporting News*, October 3, 1935, 6.

3. Mark L. Armour and Daniel R. Levitt, *Paths to Glory*, 120.

4. J.G. Taylor Spink's column "Three and One," *The Sporting News*, January 30, 1936, 4.

5. *The Sporting News*, July 9, 1936, 5.

6. Editorial, Ibid., July 16, 1936, 4.

7. Gene Desautels quoted in Golenbock, *Fenway*, 92.

8. Tom Yawkey quoted in *The Sporting News*, December 3, 1936, 5. This was not the first time someone made

light of Collins' hunting skills. Babe Ruth related that Collins was "a queer hunter" who "likes to get out in the woods and tramp around with a gun, but ... never takes a shot at anything. Eddie is too tender-hearted." George Herman Ruth, *Babe Ruth's Own Book of Baseball* (New York: Putnam's, 1928, reprint, Lincoln, Neb.: Bison Books, 1992), 263.

9. Eddie Collins as told to Jim Leonard, "From Sullivan to Collins," Final (Fifth) Chapter, *The Sporting News*, November 8, 1950, 14.

10. Bobby Doerr, telephone interview with author, January 11, 2006.

11. Eddie Collins quoted in Bill Nowlin, ed., *The Kid*, 98; citing an article by Joe Cashman, *Boston Evening American*, July 13, 1941.

12. Ed Linn, *Hitter: The Life and Turmoils of Ted Williams*, 64. See also Michael Seidel, *Ted Williams*, 20. However, box scores in the *Portland Morning Oregonian* for August 8, 1936, show Williams played left field in the second contest and was 1-for-3 at the plate. This may have been the first time Collins saw Williams bat in a game.

13. Collins to Leonard, "From Sullivan to Collins," Final (Fifth) Chapter, 13.

14. Joe Wood quoted in *The Sporting News*, January 21, 1937, 6.

15. Ibid., January 14, 1937, 1.

16. Eddie Collins quoted in Ibid., March 18, 1937, 7.

17. Tom Yawkey quoted in Daniel L. Daniel's column "Rambling Round the Circuit With Pitcher Snorter Casey," *The Sporting News*, August 26, 1937, 4.

18. Seidel, *Ted Williams*, 22.

19. Eddie Collins quoted in Nowlin, ed., *The Kid*, 100; citing Arthur Sampson, *Ted Williams* (New York: A.S. Barnes, 1950), 17.

20. Letter from Samuel S. Williams to Tom Yawkey, January 1, 1938, American League files, National Baseball Library, Cooperstown, N.Y.

21. Letter from Eddie Collins to William Harridge, January 4, 1938, American League files, National Baseball Library, Cooperstown, N.Y.

22. Letter from Eddie Collins to Samuel S. Williams, January 7, 1938, American League files, National Baseball Library, Cooperstown, N.Y.

23. Letter from Samuel S. Williams to Edward T. Collins, January 18, 1938, American League files, National Baseball Library, Cooperstown, N.Y.

24. Memorandum correspondence from H.W. Lane to Ted Williams, January 5, 1938 and to Eddie Collins, January 20, 1938, American League files, National Baseball Library, Cooperstown, N.Y.

25. Ted Williams quoted in Nowlin, ed., *The Kid*, 101; citing Ted Williams, *My Turn At Bat: The Story of My Life* (New York: Simon and Schuster, 1969), 44.

26. Ibid.

27. Western Union Telegram, Eddie Collins to William Harridge, February 18, 1938, American League files, National Baseball Library, Cooperstown, N.Y.

28. Eddie Collins quoted in Nowlin, ed., *The Kid*, 101; citing article by Hy Hurwitz, *Boston Globe*, July 22, 1939.

29. Eddie Collins quoted in *The Sporting News*, February 2, 1939, 2.

30. Ibid.

31. Transcript of Eddie Collins' remarks, Hall of Fame Induction Ceremony, June 12, 1939, National Baseball Library, Cooperstown, N.Y.

32. Jim Reisler, *A Great Day in Cooperstown*, 130.

Chapter 22

1. Robert Peterson, *Only the Ball Was White*, 175.
2. Tom Yawkey quoted in Dan Daniel's column "Daniel's Dare," source and date unknown, Eddie Collins Clippings File, National Baseball Library, Cooperstown, N.Y.
3. Glenn Stout and Richard A. Johnson, *Red Sox Century*, 220.
4. Eddie Collins quoted in *Time*, April 10, 1950.
5. Ted Williams quoted in *Boston Daily Record*, March 26, 1951.
6. Bobby Doerr, telephone interview with author, January 11, 2006. Billy Werber, telephone interview with author, September 20, 2006.
7. Ted Williams quoted in J.G. Taylor Spink's column "Three and One," *The Sporting News*, July 17, 1941, 4.
8. Eddie Collins, Jr. quoted in *Daily Local News*, July 17, 1999, Eddie Collins Clippings File, National Baseball Library, Cooperstown, N.Y.
9. Eddie Collins quoted in Leigh Montville, *Ted Williams*, 100.
10. Henry Jones quoted in *The Weston Town Crier*, October 27, 2004.
11. *The Sporting News*, March 4, 1943, 10.
12. Stout and Johnson, *Red Sox Century*, 236.
13. Dave Egan's column "The Colonel," *Boston Daily Record*, January 26, 1943.
14. *Time*, September 6, 1943.
15. Herb Pennock and Eddie Collins quoted in column "On the Airlines," *The Sporting News*, December 9, 1943, 15.
16. Oscar Ruhl's column "The Ruhl Book," *The Sporting News*, November 11, 1944, 15.
17. Judge Kenesaw Mountain Landis quoted in David Pietrusza, *Judge and Jury*, 418.
18. Ibid., 419.
19. Excerpt from Eddie Collins' letter to Isador Muchnick, dated March 16, 1945, quoted in Dave Egan's column "The Colonel," *Boston Daily Record*, April 16, 1945. It seems the issue of denial of a Sunday baseball permit had been on the table since at least spring 1944. According to Glenn Stout in "Tryout and Fallout," para. 7–8, the issue was first raised by Muchnick in March 1944. The response Collins referred to in his March 16, 1945, letter was forwarded to the African-American community, then released nationwide. Ibid.
20. Wendell Smith, typewritten memorandum, p. 5, Wendell Smith Papers, Folder 1, National Baseball Library, Cooperstown, N.Y.
21. Letter from Sam Lacy to Eddie Collins et. al., March 3, 1945, American League files, National Baseball Library, Cooperstown, N.Y.
22. Letter from Eddie Collins to Sam Lacy, April 11, 1945, American League files, National Baseball Library, Cooperstown, N.Y.
23. Howard Bryant, *Shut Out*, 30.
24. Letter from Eddie Collins to William Harridge, April 11, 1945, American League files, National Baseball Library, Cooperstown, N.Y.
25. Letter from Eddie Collins to William Harridge, January 26, 1943, American League files, National Baseball Library, Cooperstown, N.Y.
26. Jules Tygiel, *Baseball's Great Experiment*, 45–46.
27. Dave Egan, *Boston Daily Record*, April 16, 1945. In "Tryout and Fallout," (see endnote 19 above) Glenn Stout attributes the timing of the tryout to Egan's column. The *Daily Record* was a "morning tabloid" and the trio of prospects, along with Wendell Smith, left for Fenway Park

at 10:00 A.M., after the paper hit the stands. See para. 29. He further states that in publishing the column Egan violated an "unknown" condition for affording the tryout. According to Stout, Collins required that Muchnick agree there would be no publicity about the workout. See para. 28. Stout believes this is why the Red Sox were easily able to delay the tryout and, until Egan's column, conceivably postpone it all together. Finally Stout writes that any excuse the Red Sox might use that the tryout was delayed from April 12 due to the death of President Roosevelt was a sham. The president did not die until later in the day, well after a tryout would have been held. See para. 21 and 27.
28. Jackie Robinson quoted in Bill Roeder, *Jackie Robinson*, 14–16.
29. Content of Collins' response to Wendell Smith and Collins' quote appear in Tygiel, *Baseball's Great Experiment*, 44.
30. Eddie Collins quoted in *The Sporting News*, November 1, 1945, 5.
31. Bryant, *Shut Out*, 28.
32. Eddie Collins quoted in Neil Lanctot, *Negro League Baseball*, note 47 at 445.
33. Photo in *Chicago Tribune*, August 23, 1925. See also discussion in Peter Morris, *A Game of Inches: The Game Behind the Scenes*, 256.
34. H.N. Hall quoted in Edgar G. Brand's column "Between Innings," *The Sporting News*, August 27, 1931, 4.
35. Clif Keane's report of the racial slur, as well as that Keane "always believed it was Yawkey," is related in Bryant, *Shut Out*, 32. The alleged slur itself, as related from Keane to writer Larry Whiteside, was first reported by Whiteside in the *Boston Globe*, July 22, 1979. See also Stout and Johnson, *Red Sox Century*, 242, quoting Keane saying, "People used to say it was Collins. But I really don't know." In his article "Tryout and Fallout," Glenn Stout ventures that it is possible Keane invented the incident "to deflect attention away from his own bigotry," adding that "[t]o be fair, Keane's own record on race is at best checkered." Para. 62. Then again Stout opines the delay in reporting might relate just as much to the *Globe*'s avoidance of racism issues regarding the Red Sox. Para. 63.
36. Stout and Johnson, *Red Sox Century*, 185.
37. Tom Dowd quoted in [Philadelphia] *Evening Bulletin*, March 27, 1951, Eddie Collins Clippings File #1, *The Sporting News* Archives, St. Louis, Mo.
38. Dave "Boo" Ferriss, telephone interview with author, September 18, 2006.

Chapter 23

1. Ted Williams quoted in *Boston Daily Record*, March 26, 1951.
2. Harold Kaese, "What the Matter With the Red Sox?" 10.
3. George "Pinky" Woods quoted in *Rutland (Vt.) Daily Herald*, August 9, 1946.
4. Charles G. Spink's column "Seventh Inning Stretch," *The Sporting News*, April 18, 1946, 10.
5. Eddie Collins to Jim Leonard, "From Sullivan to Collins," Final (Fifth) Chapter, November 8, 1950, 16.
6. Harold Kaese's telegram to Joe Cronin quoted in Frederick G. Lieb, *The Boston Red Sox*, 240.
7. Harold Kaese writing in column "Quotes," *The Sporting News*, November 6, 1946, 10. Kaese wrote that the rumors of Collins' interference stem from a particular game at Fenway Park in 1935. The public address announcer failed to announce a pinch-hitter. Collins came over to suggest he do so and the announcer said he would wait for

the umpire to give him the signal. An argument ensued at the plate involving Cronin. It concerned a pitching change he intended to make. While Cronin was at the plate and Collins was with the announcer, the umpire pointed to the announcer, signaling him to introduce the pinch-hitter. A reporter saw it, thought the new pitcher had been signaled in by Collins and took it from there. The announcer clearly denied that Collins had directed the change from on high. Kaese claimed that after that Collins avoided spring training or anything else which could be interpreted as his interference in on-the-field decision making.

8. Eddie Collins quoted in *The Sporting News*, October 16, 1946, 12.

9. Glenn Stout and Richard A. Johnson, *Red Sox Century*, 251.

10. *The Sporting News*, February 19, 1947, 24. Collins was also inducted into the Columbia University Sports Hall of Fame in 2006.

11. Eddie Collins quoted in Ibid., February 12, 1947, 7.

12. Eddie Collins quoted in Ibid., February 19, 1947, 11.

13. Clark Griffith quoted in Ibid., February 26, 1947, 21.

14. H.G. Salsinger quoted in Ibid., March 5, 1947, 5.

15. Ted Williams quoted in Ibid., March 12, 1947, 3.

16. Eddie Collins quoted in Dean A. Sullivan, *Middle Innings*, 209.

17. Mark L. Armour and Daniel R. Levitt, *Paths to Glory*, 152.

18. *The Sporting News*, January 5, 1949, 18.

19. Ted Williams and *Boston Globe* headline quoted in Stout and Johnson, *Red Sox Century*, 272.

20. Gerry Hern article, source and date unknown, Eddie Collins Clippings File #1, *The Sporting News* Archives, St. Louis, Mo.

21. Ibid.

22. *The Sporting News*, February 1, 1950, 3.

23. Ibid., June 7, 1950, 7.

24. Eddie Collins' quotes to Jim Leonard appear in Bob Broeg, "Quick Thinking Collins — 'Infielder Who Could Do It All,'" *The Sporting News*, August 30, 1969, 28.

25. Howard Bryant, *Shut Out*, 33.

26. *Boston Post*, March 26, 1951. See also *Boston Daily Record*, March 26, 1951, and *Boston Globe*, March 26, 1951.

27. Ted Williams quoted in *Boston Globe*, March 26, 1951.

28. Connie Mack quoted in article by Bill Cunningham, source unknown, March 26, 1951, Eddie Collins Clippings File #1, *The Sporting News* Archives, St. Louis, Mo., and in *Boston Globe*, March 26, 1951.

29. Ty Cobb to Jack McDonald, Sports Editor *The Call Bulletin*, source unknown, March 1951, Eddie Collins Clippings File #2, *The Sporting News* Archives, St. Louis, Mo.

30. Dave Egan's column "The Colonel's Tribute," *Boston Daily Record*, March 27, 1951.

31. Dave Egan's column "The Colonel," Ibid., March 28, 1951.

32. Jim Leonard, "Square–Shooter's End Seals Black Sox Story," *The Sporting News*, April 4, 1951, 16.

33. Clarence "Pants" Rowland quoted in *The Sporting News*, September 3, 1958, 20. Rowland claims the original report of his remarks was misinterpreted. It was originally reported that Rowland said, "Collins, in my time at least, was the standout player in the majors." Rowland quoted in Ibid., February 18, 1903, 26.

34. *The* (Millerton, N.Y. and Sharon, Ct.) *News*, September 3, 1964, 1.

Bibliography

Manuscript Resources

Al Hirshberg Collection, Central Library, Boston (Mass.) Public Library.

Black Sox Scandal, American League Records, 1914–1969 (microfilm), National Baseball Library, Cooperstown, N.Y.

Columbia University Archives and Columbiana Library, New York City.

Edward Trowbridge Collins, Sr. Collection, National Baseball Library, Cooperstown, N.Y.

Edward Trowbridge Collins, Sr. Collection, *The Sporting News* Archives, St. Louis.

Edward Trowbridge Collins, Sr. Collection, Urban Archives, Temple University, Philadelphia, Pa.

Eugene C. Murdock Baseball Collection, Cleveland (Ohio) Public Library, taped interviews of Red Faber, Buck Crouse and Ted Lyons.

Harold Kaese Collection, Central Library, Boston (Mass.) Public Library.

Major League Baseball Transaction Card Collection, National Baseball Library, Cooperstown, N.Y.

Wendell Smith Papers, c1943–1961, National Baseball Library, Cooperstown, N.Y.

Government Documents

Department of Public Health, Registry of Vital Records and Statistics, Commonwealth of Massachusetts.

New York State, Birth, Death and Marriage Indexes

Office of the City Registrar, Death Records, City of Boston, County of Suffolk, Commonwealth of Massachusetts.

Miscellaneous Resources

Columbian (Student Yearbook), Columbia University, New York City, 1904–1909.

Register for 1927–1928, The Irving School, Tarrytown-On-Hudson, N.Y.

Turner's Hudson River Directory, 1906–1907, W. L. Richmond, Publisher.

Internet Resources

BaseballAlmanac.com
BaseballHallofFame.org
BaseballIndex.org
BaseballLibrary.com
Baseball-Reference.com
Bioproject.SABR.org
Columbia.edu
Nlbpa.com
Philadelphiaathletics.org
Retrosheet.org
Time.com/time/archive

Personal Communications

Andres, Ernie. Telephone interview, September 19, 2006.

Batts Matt. Telephone interview, September 19, 2006.

Clark, Ruth Mack. Telephone interview, February 14, 2006.

Doerr, Bobby. Telephone interview, January 11, 2006.

Ferriss, Dave "Boo." Telephone interview, September 18, 2006.

Gutteridge, Don. Telephone interview, September 27, 2006.

Lefebvre, Bill "Lefty." Telephone interview, September 19, 2006.

Lucier, Leo. Telephone interview, September 19, 2006.

Mele, Sam. Telephone interview, September 19, 2006.

Pellagrini, Eddie. Telephone interview, September 21, 2006.

Stringer, Lou. Telephone interview, September 21, 2006.

Werber, Bill. Telephone interview, September 20, 2006.

Wright, Tom. Telephone interview, September 21, 2006.

Newspapers

Amenia (N.Y.) *Times*
Atlanta Constitution
Boston Daily Record

Boston Globe
Boston Herald
Boston Post
Chicago American
Chicago Daily News
Chicago Defender
Chicago Evening Post
Chicago Herald-Examiner
Chicago Tribune
Collyer's Eye
Columbia (University) Spectator
The Daily News (Tarrytown, N.Y.)
GRIT (Williamsport, Pa.)
The Hartford (Conn.) Times
The Hartford (Conn.) Courant
Lincoln (Nebr.) Star
Los Angeles Examiner
Los Angeles Times
The Morning (Portland) Oregonian
The News (Millerton, N.Y. and Sharon, Ct.)
New York American
New York Evening Journal
New York Globe and Commercial Advertiser
New York Herald
New York Sun
New York Times
New York World-Telegram
Norwalk (Conn.) Hour
Peekskill (N.Y.) Evening Star
Plattsburgh (N.Y.) Press
Rutland (Vt.) Herald
Philadelphia Evening Bulletin
Philadelphia Evening Ledger
Philadelphia Inquirer
Philadelphia North American
Philadelphia Press
Philadelphia Record
Press Record (Tarrytown, N.Y.)
The Rhinebeck (N.Y.) Gazette
Spokane (Wash.) Sportsman-Review
Sporting Life
Sporting News
St. Louis Post-Dispatch
USA Today Baseball Weekly
Washington Post
The Weston (Mass.) Town Crier

Newspaper Series

Collins, Eddie, as told to Jim Leonard. "From Sul-
livan to Collins: Colorful Life Story Of Game's
Greatest Second Baseman." The Sporting News
(Chapters One-Five): October 11, 18, 25 and
November 1, 8, 1950.
_____. "Twenty One Years of Base Ball (Parts I-
XXI)." Los Angeles Times (syndicated by North
American Newspaper Alliance, 1926): January 3–
8, 10–13, 15- 22, 24–26, 1927.

Books

Acocella, Nicholas, and Donald Dewey. The Great-
est Team of All Time: As Selected by Baseball's
Immortals, from Ty Cobb to Willie Mays. Holbrook,
Mass.: Bob Adams, 1994.
Alexander, Charles C. Breaking the Slump: Baseball
in the Depression Era. New York: Columbia Uni-
versity Press, 2002.
_____. Ty Cobb. New York: Oxford University Press,
1984.
Allen, Lee. The American League Story. New York:
Hill & Wang, 1962.
_____, and Tom Meany. Kings of the Diamond: The
Immortals in Baseball's Hall of Fame. New York:
Putnam's, 1965.
Anderson, Wayne. The Chicago Black Sox Trial. New
York: Rosen Publishing Group, 2004.
Armour, Mark L., and Daniel R. Levitt. Paths to
Glory: How Great Baseball Teams Got That Way.
Washington, D.C.: Brassey's, 2003.
Asinof, Eliot. Eight Men Out: The Black Sox and the
1919 World Series. New York: Holt, Rinehart and
Winston, 1963; reprint, Henry Holt and Com-
pany, 1987.
Axelson, G.W. Commy: The Life Story of Charles A.
Comiskey. Chicago: Reilly & Lee, 1919; reprint,
Jefferson, N.C.: McFarland, 2003.
Barrow, Edward Grant, with James M. Kahn. My
Fifty Years in Baseball. New York: Coward-
McCann, 1951.
Benson, John, and Tony Blengino. Baseball's Top 100:
The Best Individual Seasons of All Time. Wilton,
Conn.: Diamond Library, 1995.
Bevis, Charles. Mickey Cochrane: The Life of a Base-
ball Hall of Fame Catcher. Jefferson, N.C.: McFar-
land, 1998.
Bjarkman, Peter C. Top 10 Baseball Base Stealers.
Springfield, N.J.: Enslow Publishers, 1995.
Broeg, Bob. Superstars of Baseball: Their Lives, Their
Loves, Their Laughs, Their Laments. South Bend,
Ind.: Diamond Communications, 1994.
_____, and Bob Burrill. Don't Bring That Up!: Skele-
tons in the Sports Closet. New York: A.S. Barnes,
1946.
Brown, Warren. The Chicago White Sox. New York:
Putnam's, 1952.
Bryant, Howard. Shut Out: A Story of Race and
Baseball in Boston. New York: Routledge,
2002.
Burk, Robert F. Never Just a Game: Players, Owners,
and American Baseball to 1920. Chapel Hill: Uni-
versity of North Carolina Press, 1994.
_____. Much More Than a Game: Players, Owners, &
American Baseball Since 1921. Chapel Hill: Uni-
versity of North Carolina Press, 2001.
Canning, Jeff, and Wally Buxton. History of the Tar-
rytowns: Westchester County New York from Ancient
Times to the Present. Harrison, N.Y.: Harbor Hill
Books, 1975.

Carmichael, John P. *My Greatest Day in Baseball*. New York: A.S. Barnes, 1945.

Carney, Gene. *Burying the Black Sox: How Baseball's Cover-Up of the 1919 World Series Fix Almost Succeeded*. Washington, D.C.: Potomac Books, 2006.

Cobb, Ty, with Al Stump. *My Life in Baseball*. New York: Doubleday; reprint, Lincoln: University of Nebraska Press, 1993.

Cooke, William A. *The 1919 World Series: What Really Happened?* Jefferson, N.C.: McFarland, 2001.

Cottrell, Robert C. *Blackball, the Black Sox, and the Babe: Baseball's Crucial 1920 Season*. Jefferson, N.C.: McFarland, 2002.

Cox, James A. *The Lively Ball*. Alexandria, Va.: Redefinition, 1989.

Daniel, W. Harrison. *Jimmie Foxx: The Life and Times of a Baseball Hall of Famer, 1907–1967*. Jefferson, N.C.: McFarland, 1996.

Dawidoff, Nicholas. *The Catcher Was a Spy: The Mysterious Life of Moe Berg*. New York: Pantheon, 1994; reprint, Vintage Books, 1995.

Dellinger, Susan. *Red Legs and Black Sox: Edd Roush and the Untold Story of the 1919 World Series*. Cincinnati: Emmis Books, 2006.

Dewey, Donald, and Nicholas Acocella. *Total Ballclubs: The Ultimate Book of Baseball Teams*. Wilmington, Del.: Sport Media Publishing, 2005.

Dickson, Paul. *The New Dickson Baseball Dictionary*. Rev. ed. New York: Harcourt Brace, 1991.

Dittmar, Joseph J. *Baseball Records Registry*. Jefferson, N.C.: McFarland, 1997.

Dixon, Phil, with Patrick J. Hannigan. *The Negro Baseball Leagues: A Photographic History*. Mattituck, N.Y.: Amereon House, 1992.

Dykes, Jimmie, and Charles O. Dexter. *You Can't Steal First Base*. Philadelphia: J. B. Lippincott, 1967.

Farrell, James T. *My Baseball Diary*. New York: A.S. Barnes and Company, 1957; reprint, Carbondale: Southern Illinois University Press, 1998.

Fleitz, David L. *Shoeless: The Life and Times of Joe Jackson*. Jefferson, N.C.: McFarland, 2001.

Frommer, Harvey. *Shoeless Joe and Ragtime Baseball*. Lanham, Md.: Taylor Trade Publishing, 1992.

Gay, Timothy M. *Tris Speaker: The Rough-and-Tumble Life of a Baseball Legend*. Lincoln: University of Nebraska Press, 2005.

Getz, Mike. *Baseball's 3000-Hit Men: A Book of Stats, Facts, and Trivia*. Brooklyn, N.Y.: Gemmeg Press, 1982.

Ginsberg, Daniel E. *The Fix Is in: A History of Gambling and game Fixing Scandals*. Jefferson, N.C.: McFarland, 1995.

Golenbock, Peter. *Fenway: An Unexpurgated History of the Boston Red Sox*. New York: Putnam's, 1992.

Gorman, Bob. *Double X: The Story of Jimmie Foxx— Baseball's Forgotten Slugger*. Camden, N.J.: Holy Name Society, Diocese, 1990.

Greenberg, Eric Rolfe. *The Celebrant*. Lincoln: University of Nebraska Press, 1993.

Gropman, Donald. *Say It Ain't So, Joe!: The True Story of Shoeless Joe Jackson*. Rev. ed. Secaucus, N.Y.: Carol Publishing, 1999.

Gutman, Dan. *Baseball Babylon: From the Black Sox to Pete Rose, the Real Stories Behind the Scandals that Rocked the Game*. New York: Penguin Books, 1992.

Halberstam, David. *The Teammates*. New York: Hyperion, 2003.

Hirshberg, Al. *What's the Matter with the Red Sox?* New York: Dodd, Mead, 1973.

Holtzman, Jerome, and George Vass. *Baseball Chicago Style: A Tale of Two Teams, One City*. Chicago: Bonus Books, 2001.

Honig, Donald. *Baseball When the Grass Was Real: Baseball from the Twenties to the Forties Told by the Men Who Played It*. New York: Coward, McCann and Geohegan, 1975; reprint, Lincoln: University of Nebraska Press, 1993.

Huhn, Rick. *The Sizzler: Baseball's Forgotten Great*. Columbia: University of Missouri Press, 2004.

James, Bill. *The Bill James Historical Baseball Abstract*. New York: Villard Books, 1988.

_____. *The New Bill James Historical Baseball Abstract*. New York: Free Press, 2001.

_____, and Rob Neyer. *The Neyer/James Guide to Pitchers: An Historical Compendium of Pitching, Pitchers, and Pitches*. New York: Simon & Schuster, 2004.

Jones, David, ed. *Deadball Stars of the American League*. Washington, D.C.: Potomac Books, 2006.

Jordan, David M. *The Athletics of Philadelphia: Connie Mack's White Elephants, 1901–1954*. Jefferson, N.C.: McFarland, 1999.

Kaplan, Jim. *Lefty Grove: American Original*. Cleveland: Society for American Baseball Research, 2000.

Kashatus, William C. *Connie Mack's '29 Triumph: The Rise and Fall of the Philadelphia Athletics Dynasty*. Jefferson, N.C.: McFarland, 1999.

_____. *Money Pitcher: Chief Bender and the Tragedy of Indian Assimilation*. University Park: Pennsylvania State University Press, 2006.

_____. *The Philadelphia Athletics*. Charleston, S.C.: Arcadia Publishing, 2002.

_____. *September Swoon: Richie Allen, the '64 Phillies, and Racial Integration*. University Park: Pennsylvania State University Press, 2004.

Kuklick, Bruce. *To Every Thing a Season: Shibe Park and Urban Philadelphia, 1909–1976*. Princeton, N.J.: Princeton University Press, 1991.

Lanctot, Neil. *Negro League Baseball: The Rise and Ruin of a Black Institution*. Philadelphia: University of Pennsylvania Press, 2004.

Lane, F.C. *Batting*. Cleveland, Ohio: Society for American Baseball Research, 2001.

Levy, Alan H. *Rube Waddell: The Zany, Brilliant Life of a Strikeout Artist*. Jefferson, N.C.: McFarland, 2000.

Lieb, Frederick G. *Baseball as I Have Known It*. New York: Coward, McCann & Geoghegan, 1977.

_____. *The Boston Red Sox*. New York: G.P. Putnam's

Sons, 1947; reprint, Carbondale: Southern Illinois University Press, 2003.

_____.*Connie Mack: Grand Old Man of Baseball.* New York: Putnam's, 1945, rev. ed. 1948.

Lindberg, Richard. *Sox: The Complete Record of Chicago White Sox Baseball.* New York: Macmillan, 1984.

_____. *Stealing First in a Two-Team Town: The White Sox from Comiskey to Reinsdorf.* Champaign, Ill.: Sagamore Publishing, 1994.

_____. *The White Sox Encyclopedia.* Philadelphia: Temple University Press, 1997.

_____. *Who's on 3rd?: The Chicago White Sox Story.* South Bend, Ind.: Icarus Press, 1983.

Linn, Ed. *Hitter: The Life and Turmoils of Ted Williams.* New York: Harcourt Brace, 1993.

Lowry, Phillip J. *Green Cathedrals: The Ultimate Celebration of All 273 Major League and Negro League Ballparks Past and Present.* Reading, Mass.: Addison-Wesley, 1992; reprint, 1993.

Luhrs, Victor. *The Great Baseball Mystery: The 1919 World Series.* New York: A.S. Barnes, 1966.

Mack, Connie. *My 66 Years in the Big Leagues: The Great Story of America's National Game.* Philadelphia: John C. Winston, 1950.

McGuire, Mark. *The 100 Greatest Players of the 20th Century Ranked.* Jefferson, N.C.: McFarland, 2000.

McMane, Fred. *The 3,000 Hit Club.* Champaign, Ill.: Sports Publishing, 2000.

Meany, Tom. *Baseball's Greatest Hitters.* New York: A.S. Barnes, 1950.

Mills, Dorothy Jane. *A Woman's Work: Writing Baseball History with Harold Seymour.* Jefferson, N.C.: McFarland, 2004.

Montville, Leigh. *Ted Williams: The Biography of an American Hero.* New York: Doubleday, 2004.

Morris, Peter. *A Game of Inches: The Game on the Field.* Chicago: Ivan R. Dee, 2006.

_____. *A Game of Inches: The Game Behind the Scenes.* Chicago: Ivan R. Dee, 2006.

Murdock, Eugene C. *Ban Johnson: Czar of Baseball.* Westport, Ct.: Greenwood Press, 1982.

Nathan, Daniel A. *Saying It's So: A Cultural History of the Black Sox Scandal.* Urbana: University of Illinois Press, 2003.

Neyer, Rob. *Big Book of Baseball Blunders: A Complete Guide to the Worst Decisions and Stupidest Moments in Baseball History.* New York: Simon & Schuster, 2006.

_____, and Eddie Epstein. *Baseball Dynasties: The Greatest Teams of All Time.* New York: W.W. Norton, 2000.

Nowlin, Bill, ed. *The Kid: Ted Williams in San Diego.* Cambridge, Mass.: Rounder Books, 2005.

Peterson, Robert. *Only The Ball Was White.* Englewood Cliffs, N.J.: Prentice-Hall, 1970.

Philadelphia: A 300-Year History. New York: W. W. Norton, 1982.

Pietrusza, David. *Judge and Jury: The Life and Times of Judge Kenesaw Mountain Landis.* South Bend, Ind.: Diamond Communications, 1998.

Poillucci, Joseph V. *Baseball in Dutchess County: When It Was a Game.* Danbury, Conn.: Rutledge Books, 2000.

Reichler, Joseph L., ed. *The World Series: A 75th Anniversary.* New York: Simon and Schuster, 1978.

Reidenbaugh, Lowell. *Cooperstown: Where Baseball's Legends Live Forever.* St. Louis: Sporting News Publishing, 1983.

Reisler, Jim. *A Great Day in Cooperstown: The Improbable Birth of Baseball's Hall of Fame.* New York: Carroll & Graf, 2006.

Ritter, Lawrence S. *The Glory of Their Times: The Story of the Early Days of Baseball Told by the Men Who Played It.* Rev. ed. New York: William Morrow, 1984.

_____. *Lost Ballparks: A Celebration of Baseball's Legendary Fields.* New York: Viking Studio Books, 1992.

Robinson, Ray. *Speed Kings of the Base Paths: Baseball's Greatest Runners.* New York: Putnam's, 1964.

Roeder, Bill. *Jackie Robinson.* New York: A.S. Barnes, 1950.

Sagert, Kelly Boyer. *Joe Jackson: A Biography.* Westport, Conn.: Greenwood Press, 2004.

Seidel, Michael. *Ted Williams: A Baseball Life.* Chicago: Contemporary Books, 1991.

Seymour, Harold. *Baseball: The Golden Age.* New York: Oxford University Press, 1971.

Smith, Ron. *The Sporting News Selects Baseball's 100 Greatest Players: A Celebration of the 20th Century's Best.* St. Louis: Sporting News, 1998.

Solomon, Burt. *The Baseball Timeline.* New York: DK Publishing, 2001.

Sowell, Mike. *The Pitch That Killed.* New York: Collier Books, 1989.

Sparks, Barry. *Frank "Home Run" Baker: Hall of Famer and World Series Hero.* Jefferson, N.C.: McFarland, 2006.

Spink, J.G. Taylor, ed. *Baseball Guide and Record Book 1947.* St. Louis: Sporting News, 1947.

_____. *Judge Landis and 25 Years of Baseball.* St. Louis: Sporting News, 1974.

Stein, Fred. *And the Skipper Bats Cleanup: A History of the Baseball Player-Manager, with 42 Biographies of Men Who Filled the Dual Role.* Jefferson, N.C.: McFarland, 2002. .

Stein, Irving M. *The Ginger Kid: The Buck Weaver Story.* Dubuque, Iowa: Elysian Fields Press, 1992.

Stout, Glenn, and Richard A. Johnson. *Red Sox Century: The Definitive History of Baseball's Most Storied Franchise.* Boston: Houghton Mifflin, 2000; reprint, 2005.

Sullivan, Dean A., ed. *Middle Innings: A Documentary History of Baseball, 1900–1948.* Lincoln: University of Nebraska Press, 1998.

Threston, Christopher. *The Integration of Baseball in Philadelphia.* Jefferson, N.C.: McFarland, 2003.

Total Baseball. 8th ed. Wilmington, Del.: Sport Media Publishing, 2004.

Tygiel, Jules. *Baseball's Great Experiment: Jackie Robinson and His Legacy.* New York: Oxford University Press, 1983.

Veeck, Bill, with Ed Linn. *The Hustler's Handbook.* New York: Putnam's, 1965.

Waggoner, Glen, and Kathleen Maloney, and Hugh Howard. *Spitters, Beanballs, and the Incredible Shrinking Strike Zone: The Stories Behind the Rules of Baseball.* Rev. ed. Chicago: Triumph Books, 1990.

Walsh, Christy, ed. *Baseball's Greatest Lineup.* New York: A.S. Barnes, 1952.

Warner, Bass Warner, Jr. *The Private City: Philadelphia in Three Periods of Its Growth.* Philadelphia: University of Pennsylvania Press, 1968.

Westcott, Rich. *Philadelphia's Old Ballparks.* Philadelphia: Temple University Press, 1996.

Wilbert, Warren N., and William C. Hageman. *The 1917 White Sox: Their World Championship Season.* Jefferson, N.C.: McFarland, 2004.

Pamphlets

Welcome to Trowbridge House. North East (N.Y.) Historical Society, August 28, 1999.

Unpublished Papers

Tunis, Elizabeth C. "Flaws in the Diamond: Major Leaguers Expelled from Organized Baseball, 1919–1922." Unpublished typescript, National Baseball Library, Cooperstown, N.Y., 1975.

Articles

Arnett, Jeff. "Jim Crow and Baseball's Julius Caesar." *Memories and Dreams* (Baseball Hall of Fame, May-June 2006): 30–31.

Arnold, William. "Are the Athletics Quitters?" *Baseball Magazine* (November 1910): 41–44.

Belding, David L. "The Athletics in Cuba." *Baseball Magazine* (March 1911): 69–70.

_____. "Cobb vs. Collins?" *Baseball Magazine* (June 1911): 58–59.

Bisher, Furman. "This Is the Truth!" *Sport Magazine* (October 1949).

Brandt, William E. "The Breaks." *The Saturday Evening Post* (July 19, 1930): 45–46, 150.

Carmichael, John. "The Chicago White Sox." *Sport* (June 1951): 58, 60–68.

Carney, Gene. "A Minor Mystery from the 1919 World Series." Society for American Baseball Research convention publication *Baseball in the Buckeye State* (July 2004): 22–24.

Collins, Edward T. "Alertness, the Watchword of the Major Leaguer." *Baseball Magazine* (March 1915): 23–24.

_____, with Boyden Sparkes. "Building a Ball Club." *The Saturday Evening Post* (August 25, 1934): 18–19, 41, 43, 45.

_____, with Boyden Sparkes. "Coaching with Connie Mack." *The Saturday Evening Post* (July 28, 1934): 10–11, 59–60, 62.

_____. "Connie Mack and His Mackmen." *The American Magazine* (June 1914): 13–18.

_____, with Boyden Sparkes. "From Player to Pilot." *The Saturday Evening Post* (June 9, 1934): 8–9, 40–41.

_____. "How It Seems to Take Part in a World's Series." *Baseball Magazine* (November 1911): 14–16.

_____, interview. "It Takes Time to Build a Winner." *Baseball Magazine* (December 1934): 301, 326.

_____, interview. "Modern Baseball, the Greatest Ever!" *Baseball Magazine* (July 1931): 339–340.

_____. "My Impressions of Connie Mack." *Baseball Magazine* (February 1911): 2a-3a.

_____, with Boyden Sparkes. "Out at Second." *The Saturday Evening Post* (June 23, 1934): 18–19, 80–81, 84.

_____. "Outguessing the Pitcher." *Pearson's Magazine* (June 1910): 726–736.

_____. "Pitchers I Have Faced." *The American Magazine* (July 1914): 23–28, 74.

_____, interview. "The Rejuvenation of Eddie Collins — Champion Base-Stealer." *Baseball Magazine* (September 1924): 449–450, 472.

_____, interview. "Sixteen Years as a Big League Star." *Baseball Magazine* (March 1924): 435–437, 468.

_____, interview by F. C. Lane. "Thos. Yawkey Turns from 'Buying' to 'Building.'" *Baseball Magazine* (July 1937): 339–340, 374.

_____, interview. "The Winning Temperament." *Baseball Magazine* (August 1932): 395–396.

Comiskey, Charles A. "Why I Bought Eddie Collins." *Baseball Magazine* (March 1915): 15–16.

"The Competitive Instinct." *Time* (April 10, 1950).

Crusinberry, James. "The Immortal Eddie Collins." *Baseball Magazine* (June 1951): 229–231.

Daley, Arthur. "Superfan." *The American Magazine* (June 1951): 110–115.

Daniel, Daniel M. "Tom Yawkey Rides His Hobby." *Baseball Magazine* (October 1939): 485–486, 523–524.

Drohan, John. "Boston's Shining Stars." *Baseball Magazine* (December 1939): 293–294, 330.

Editorial Comment. *Baseball Magazine* (November 1919): 96.

_____. *Baseball Magazine* (December 1919): 459–460.

_____. *Baseball Magazine* (February 1920): 519, 530.

_____. *Baseball Magazine* (December 1920): 314–316, 334.

_____. *Baseball Magazine* (October 1921): 488, 510.

_____. *Baseball Magazine.* (January 1927): 342.

"$800,000 Show." *Time* (September 6, 1943).

Evans, Billy. "The College Man as a Professional Ball Player." *Leslie's Weekly* (March 16, 1911): 292–293.

———. "Looking Them Over." *Harper's Weekly* (March 27, 1915): 292–294.

———. "Twenty Years a Big League Umpire." *Liberty* (July 18, 1925): 31–35.

———. "Twenty Years a Big League Umpire." *Liberty* (August 1, 1925): 32–36.

Frisch, Frank, as told to Charles Dexter. "Things You Never See in the Series." *Sport* (October 1954): 26–28, 91–93.

Fullerton, Hugh S. "Baseball on Trial." *The New Republic* (October 20, 1920): 183–184.

———. "Between Games." *The American Magazine* (July 1911): 321–332.

———. "Hitting The Dirt." *The American Magazine* (May 1911): 2–16.

———. "The Smartest Second Baseman." *Liberty* (April 25, 1925): 36–38.

Gettelson, Leonard. "The Spectacular Career of Eddie Collins." *Baseball Magazine* (September 1926): 459.

Girsch, George. "The A's That Were Too Good to Win." *Baseball Digest* (February 1958): 25–26.

Hern, Gerry. "The Tipoff on the Black Sox." *Baseball Digest* (June 1949): 11–12.

Jackson, Shoeless Joe, as told to Furman Bisher. "This Is the Truth!" *Sport* (October 1949): 12–14, 83–84.

Johnson, Ban B. "The Inside of the Collins Deal." *Baseball Magazine* (March 1915): 31–32.

———, interviewed. "What Baseball Needs Most." *Baseball Magazine* (December 1902): 325–326.

Kaese, Harold. "What's the Matter With the Red Sox?" *The Saturday Evening Post* (April 1946): 10–11, 32–34.

Kirby, James. "The Year They Fixed the World Series." *American Bar Association Journal* (February 1, 1988): 64–69.

Kofoed, J.C. "Collins — and the Others." *Baseball Magazine* (March 1915): 69–72.

———. "The Greatest Infield in the History of Baseball." *Baseball Magazine* (July 1913): 56–58.

———. "The Hero of the World's Series." *Baseball Magazine* (December 1919): 467– 468.

Lane, F. C. "Collins the Great." *Baseball Magazine* (March 1915): 47–63.

———. "The Greatest of All Second Basemen." *Baseball Magazine* (December 1912): 33–44.

———. "How Rath, the Discard, Equaled Collins, the Star." *Baseball Magazine* (December 1919): 461–462, 500, 502–503.

———. "Mack's Methods." *Baseball Magazine* (May 1912): 23–26.

———. "A Master Baseball Builder." *Baseball Magazine* (June 1934): 291–292, 318, 332.

———. "Where the Dope Went Wrong." *Baseball Magazine* (December 1914): 13–17.

———. "Why the Athletics Are the Logical Favorites In the Coming World's Series." Baseball Magazine (November 1914): 20–27, 98.

Lardner, John. "A Man Who Saw the Gamut Run." *Newsweek* (April 9, 1951): 74.

———. "Pals, Pals, Pals." *Newsweek* (September 9, 1940): 52.

———. "Remember The Black Sox?" *The Saturday Evening Post* (April 30, 1938): 14–15, 82, 84–85.

Leduc, Harry. "Brainiest Second Baseman." *Baseball Digest* (June 1951): 43–46.

Lieb, Frederick G. "Eddie Collins." *Baseball Magazine* (June 1910): 51–54.

Mack, Connie. "The Stuff That Stars Are Made of." *The Saturday Evening Post* (April 27, 1912): 8–10, 52–53.

Miller, Hub. "Famous Father a Handicap." *Baseball Magazine* (July 1948): 263–264, 282.

———."You Can Beat the Hours." *Baseball Magazine* (May 1950): 407–408, 427.

Moriarty, George. "Calling Them." *Baseball Magazine* (January 1924): 352, 374–375.

Phelon, W. A. "After the Series." *Baseball Magazine* (December 1910): 1a–6a.

———. "How the New World's Championship Was Won." *Baseball Magazine* (December 1919): 453–458, 492, 509–511.

———. "How the Reds and White Sox Compare." *Baseball Magazine* (November 1919): 392–395, 440–441.

———. "What I Know of Eddie Collins." *Baseball Magazine* (March 1915): 37– 45.

———. "Why the Braves Won and the Athletics Lost the Championship of the World." *Baseball Magazine* (December 1914): 18–28, 100, 102, 104, 106.

Povich, Shirley. "If You Can Get Away with It!" *Baseball Digest* (January 1960): 57.

Robert, Harry. "The Philadelphia Athletics." *Sport* (February 1951): 25–29, 87–94.

Robinson, Ray. "Columbia's Other Hall of Famer: Eddie Collins." *Columbia* (Spring 1991): 25–28.

Rumill, Ed. "A Half Hour with Eddie Collins." *Baseball Magazine* (March 1944): 329– 330.

Salsinger, H. G. "The Path to Baseball Fame." *Leslie's Illustrated Weekly Newspaper* (June 5, 1913): 600, 602.

Sanborn, Irving E. "The Recent Eclipse of the Player-Manager." *Baseball Magazine* (February 1927): 391–393.

Smiley, Richard A. "I'm a Faster Man Than You Are, Heinie Zim." *The National Pastime: A Review of Baseball History* 26 (2006): 97–103.

Smith, Ronald A. "Harvard and Columbia and a Reconsideration of the 1905–06 Football Crisis." *Journal of Sport History* (Winter 1981): 5–19.

"Soda Pop." *Time* (March 28, 1927).

Stout, Glenn. "Tryout and Fallout: Race, Jackie Robinson and the Red Sox." *The Massachusetts Historical Review* (Vol. 6, NA 2004): Para. 1–78, http://historycooperative.org/journals/mhr/6/stout/html.

Thomas, Jay. "From the Ivy League to the Big Leagues." *The National Pastime: A Review of Baseball History* 24 (2004): 59–61.

Ward, John J. "The Greatest of All World's Series Players." *Baseball Magazine* (December 1917): 213–215.

Warrington, Bob. "Connie Mack's First Book." *Philadelphia Athletics Historical Society* (website): 1–3.

_____. "The Fight for Sunday Baseball in Philadelphia." *Philadelphia Athletics Historical Society* (website): 1–6.

_____. "Shibe Park's Grand Opening." *Philadelphia Athletics Historical Society* (website): 1–3.

Weart, William G. "Connie Mack." *Baseball Magazine* (November 1911): 21–26.

_____. "The Keystone Kings." *Baseball Magazine* (October 1914): 43–48.

Works, Ralph T. "Baseball Plays That Might Have Been." *Baseball Magazine* (February 1920: 529–530.

Yawkey, Thomas, interview. "We'll Win That Pennant Yet." *Baseball Magazine* (October 1936): 491–492, 520.

Index

Numbers in *bold italics* indicate pages with photographs.

African Americans: American League surveying talent of 303–304; Collins' attitude toward 306; discrimination against 3, 300; whites playing against 34–35, 65–66, 306; *see also* integration, of baseball
Ainsmith, Eddie 135
Alexander, Dale 275
all-star games 293; after American League seasons 83–84, 309; as benefits 261, 276, 312; *see also* American League, all-star teams from
Allen, Lee 5
Almada, Mel 288
Altrock, Nick 7
American Baseball Guild 312
American League 83, 142, 175, 242; all-star teams from 73–74, *79*, 82, 276; attendance 112, 124–125, 218; batting average in 51, 62, 124, 194, 295; batting titles in 110; Collins' statistics compared to 91, 129, 146, 199, 204, 226; Federal League and 120, 125; Johnson's presidency of 164, 241–242, 248–249; maintaining competitiveness of 114–115, 272; National League and 39, 157; not permitting rosin use 222–223; presidency of 155, 264, 272–273; surveying African American baseball talent 303–304
Ames, Leon 87–88
Anson, Adrian "Cap" 75–76, 220, 260
Anti-Saloon League, Collins addressing 125
appearance, Collins' 2, 16, 293
Armour, Mark 284, 313
Asinof, Eliot 170, 176
Association of Professional Baseball Players 312
Attell, Abe "the Little Champ" 176, 179
Austrian, Alfred 177

Bagby, Jim 169
Bagby, Jim, Jr. 291
Baker, John Franklin "Home Run"
2, 52, 57, 60, 63, 99, 104, 125, 315; on all-star team *79*, 82; with Athletics 58, 62, 76, *93*; home runs 84, 86; Mack and 64, 245; in "the $100,000 Infield" 52–53, 60, 80, *81*, 88–89; in World Series 74, 84–88, 99–101, 106–107
Baker, Newton D. 144 146–147
Ball, Phillip DeCatesby 103, 125, 218, 275, 306
Baltimore Orioles 125, 273
Bancroft, Dave 227
Barnard, E.S. 264
Barrett, Bill 217, 221
Barrett, George 192
Barrow, Ed 222, 258
Barry, Jack 48–49, 57, 64, 91, 133, 315; with Athletics 76, *98*; in "the $100,000 Infield" 66–67, 80, *81*, 88–89, 96–97; as shortstop 52–53, 57; in World Series 75, 87, 100–101
Base Ball Association 29
base running, Collins' 62–63, 72, 74, 203, 225
base running, primacy of 72–73
baseball: Collins' interest in rules of 313; Collins' loyalty to game 305–306; controversy over pitchers' rosin use 222–223; dead ball *vs.* "lively ball" eras in 167–168, 250, 263–264; gambling on 110, 134, 183, 185; honest players *vs.* crooks in 169, 172, 181; increasing popularity of 85; industries fielding teams 144–145, 148; length of games 45; reward collections as common in 232; rules changes in 167, 169; segregation in 300; WWI's effects on 142–144, 146; WWII's effects on 296, 299–300, 307
Baseball Abstract (James) 2
Baseball Hall of Fame 292
Baseball Player's Fraternity 99, 111
baseballs, new construction of 167–168
bats, athletes endorsing 78
batting, advantage *vs.* pitching 167, 222–223
batting, Collins' 2, 59, 225; all-star
teams and 82, 84; for A's 7, 43, 45–46, 48, 50–51, 55, 57–60, 64, 68, 71, 83, 89, 93–94, 98, 105, 121, 259–260; balance of advantage with pitching 263–264; career statistics 265; Collins on requirements of 69–70; for Columbia 16–17, 27–28; improvement in 17, 19, 294; move to less lively ball 263–264; for semiprofessional teams 29–30, 32–34, 36, 44; superstitions about 121–122; 3,000th major league hit 220; for White Sox 124, 126–127, 133–135, 153–154, 168–169, 171, 179, 189, 197, 199, 203, 210, 212, 215, 218, 220; in World Series 74–76, 86–87, 100, 107, 109, 138–139, 159–163
batting average, Eddie Jr.'s 292
batting averages 73; in American League 51, 124, 194, 204, 292, 295; in American *vs.* National leagues 261; of Athletics 47, 51, 249, 253; effects of "lively ball" on 169, 250; Red Sox 292, 295; White Sox 169
batting averages, Collins' 7; with A's 70–72, 80, 94, 103, 109–110, 124, 249, 253; career statistics 265; at Columbia 28; effects of "lively ball" on 169; leading American League 62; on semi-professional teams 33; with White Sox 137, 146, 156, 189, 194, 199, 204, 212, 226; in World Series 88, 101, 109, 139
batting order: Athletics' 93–94; Collins' place in 17–19, 59, 153, 210, 246–247; White Sox 121, 172, 189
beanballs 133, 170–171
Bearden, Gene 311
Bender, Albert "Chief" 66, 68, 113, 220; in Athletics' lineup 48, *98*; as coach 215, *216*, 223; good pitching by 42, 58–59, 63–64, 66, 68, 78–79, 82, 106; weak pitching by 94, 96; in World Series 23, 74, 76, 84, 86–88, 99–101, 107, 109, 110

Bengough, Benny 222, 250, *263*
Benton, Rube 137–139, 175
Benz, Joe 120, 131, *138*
Berg, Moe 223
Berger, Henry 192–193
Beta Theta Pi, Collins in 16
betting *see* Gambling
Bishop, Max 279; batting 253, 257, 262, 267–268; playing second base 231, 248–249, 255, 259
Black, Doug *263*
Black Sox scandal 2, 191, 194; Collins not talking about 190, 316; Collins reporting fixed games to Comiskey 172, 174, 180–182, 207; Comiskey not responding 158, 172–173; Comiskey offering reward for information about 165, 176; effects on Gleason 185, 204; indictments for fixing games 176–177, 179–180; interest in what Collins knew about fixing of 179–180, 182; investigations into 173–177; lawsuits against Comiskey and White Sox after 197, 207; players' shares for World Series 174, 179, 189; punishment of indicted players 177, 189, 193, 196; response of honest players to 169, 181–182; response of White Sox management to 172–173, 213; rumors about 1919 World Series fix 158, 163–165; teammates and players suspected in 168, 170; trials for 189–194
Blackburne, Lena 120–121
Blankenship, Ted 198, 202, 215, 224–225
Boland, Bernie 236–237, 239
Boley, Joe 247, 252
Bostic, Joe 304
Boston 134, 302, 313, 316
Boston Braves 106–109
Boston Red Sox 172; accusations of discrimination by 280, 305–306; American League pennant and 309, 313–314; American League standings 275, 280–281, 285, 288, 291–292, 295, 298, 300, 311; attendance draw of 280, 283, 288, 292, 294, 301, 309; batting averages of 292, 295; blame for bad performances of 285, 308; buying players 275–276, 280–281, 284, 312; Collins' death and 314–315, 316; Collins' roles in 3, 271–272, 274, 310, 312; effects of draft and enlistments on 297, 299, 308; farm system of 284–285, 296, 310, 313; financial profitability of 313–314; "Golden Outfield" of 89; inability to win away games 295, 298, 311; integration of 3, 302–307; management discord of 277–278, 285–286, 288, 296; management of 275, 278–279, 308, 310–313; in 1946 World Series 309–310; rebuilding 274–275, 312–313,

316; strengths and weaknesses of 283, 288, 291, 294, 296, 298, 307–308, 311, 313–314; Williams controversy and 294–295, 297; Yawkey buying 270–275
Bottomley, Jim 267, 268
Boudreau, Lou 309, 314
Bowman, Emmett 65
Breadon, Sam 310
Bresnahan, Roger 18
Bressler, Rube 102–103
Broeg, Bob 58
Brooklyn Royal Giants 34–35
Brouthers, "Big Dan" 10
Brown, Carroll "Boardwalk" 93–94, 97, *98*, 101, 103
Brown, Lloyd 275
Brown, Mordecai "Three-Finger" 73–76
Brown, Warren K. 208
Bryant, Howard 303, 305–306
Bryant, William Cullen 12
Buckner, William "Doc" 215, 221, 306
bunting, by Collins 2, 50, 64, 137
Burnham, Walter 43–44
Burns, Bill "Sleepy" 176, 179, 189, 191
Burns, George 137, 232
Bush, Donie 63, 258, 291
Bush, Guy 257
Bush, Joe "Bullet Joe" 97, 171, 205; on Athletics 91, 94, *98*, 102; Collins hunting with 212, 222, 250; in World Series 100–101, 109
Byrnes, Jimmy 31–32, 36

Caldwell, Ray 169
Callahan, James "Nixey" 118
Camp, Walter 25
captain, Collins as: of Athletics 243, 256, 264; at Columbia 15, 28, 36; of White Sox 127, 130, 149–151, 181, 198–199, 202, 208; of Yannigans 55
Carney, Doc 33–34
Carney, Gene 181
Carrigan, Bill 133
Cascarella, Joe 283
Cassidy, Dan 191
Century of Progress Exposition (Chicago) 276
Chalmers Award 73, 83; Collins in running for 91, 98; Collins winning *108*, 110; MVP replacing 204
Chance, Frank 73–76 97, 204–209, 212
Chandler, Albert Benjamin "Happy" 302, 314
Chapman, Ben 288
Chapman, Ray 169–171
Chappell, Larry 123
Chase, Hal 105, 120, 182; on all-stars team *79*, 82, 84; in Black Sox scandal 179–180, 189
Chicago 125, 276; Collins and 116, 200–201, 206–207, 213; effects of *Eastland* deaths in 122–123
Chicago City Series 124, 199–200, 204, 212, 221–222, 226

Chicago Cubs 72–76, 173, 257–258;
Chicago Whales 125
Chicago White Sox 2, 133, 197, 218, 248; American League standings of 123–124, 127–129, 133–137, 153–155, 169, 171, 178, 189, 194, 198–199, 203–204, 210–212, 219–220, 224–226; attendance draw of 124–125, 127–128, 130, 141, 146, 154, 162, 168, 194, 204, 218, 226; batting as strength or weakness of 118, 133, 153, 215; batting averages of 154, 156, 169; Black Sox lawsuits against Comiskey and 197, 207; camaraderie on 136–137, 189; cliques and divisiveness on 141–142, 149, 151–153, 157–158, 168, 172, 177–178; collection for Detroit Tigers from 136, 191–192, 197, 230–233; Collins as manager of 204, 212–213, 215, 224–225, 227; Collins' contracts with 166, 202, 207–208; Collins denying anger toward 226, 229; Collins' future with 208–209; Collins in Marines and 147–148, 153, 155; Collins released as player for 227, 243; Collins sold to 113–116; Collins' statistics compared to 199; corruption among 172, 182, 185–186; efforts to rebuild 116–117, 119–120, 130, 178–179; European tour by 212; injuries in 144, 204; Jackson and 124, 207; leaving to play for industry teams 144–146, 151; lineups of 120, 126, 131, 134, 143–146, *152*, 189, 202, 209–210, 215–216, 224; loss of Black Sox players 177, 184, 185, 193–194; new uniforms for 218; in 1917 World Series 2, 137, *138*, 140; in 1919 World Series 156–164; pennant hopes of 130, 156, 175; pitching as strength or weakness of 144–145, 156, 220; playing against Babe Ruth 128–129; Rowland moving players around 120–121, 126, 133; salaries and 141–143, 166; spring training of 120, 126, 131–132, 143, 151–152, 166–168, 185, 189, 196, 202, 207, 217, 223–224; strength of lineup of 169–170, 243; Sullivan (Collins) playing against 6–7; trade negotiations with Yankees 190, 200–201, 206; wins and losses in 168–172, 196–198, 219, 221, 224; *see also* Black Sox scandal; Chicago City Series
childhood, Collins' 10–12
Cicotte, Eddie 2, 119, 143, 169; ban on freak pitches and 164, 168; in Black Sox scandal 158, 165, 175–177, 180, 190–192; in 1917 World Series 137–140, *138*; in 1919 World Series 157, 160–162, 165; pitching performance of 133–134, 145, 153–154, 171–172; in

purportedly fixed series with Detroit 234; salary of 142, 166; in White Sox lineup 120, 131

Cincinnati Reds 155–164, 192

City Series *see* Chicago City Series; Philadelphia City Series

Cleveland Indians 123, 169, 173–175

Cleveland Naps 7, 71, 82

Cline, Philo Reed (brother-in-law) 10; identified as Albert 77

coaching, Collins' 253, 276; evaluations of 252–253, 256, 269; line 249, 252, 260–261, 265; for University of Pennsylvania 143, 189

Coakley, Andy 32, 42, 50, 102

Cobb, Ty 2, 82, 90–91, 247; accused of spiking 62–64; accused of throwing game 230, 241–242; on all-star teams 74, *79*, 82, 84, 243; with A's 243–244, 246, 249, *251*; awards for 73, 83, 110; base stealing by 58, 70, 98, 203; baseball articles by 85, 99; batting averages of 62, 80, 83; Collins and 60, 90, 94, 201, 251, 315; Collins compared to 62, 64, 75, 116, 203, 315; with Detroit Tigers 45, 71, 236; endorsing baseball bat 78; honors and awards for 110, 292; as manager 189, 226; pay for 141; as player-manager 204, 218; records of 82, 259; retirement of 253; spring training and 67, 246; as troublesome 89–90, 94, 246–247, 249; Yawkey and 271–272

Cochrane, Mickey 2, 245, 249, 253, 257, 260, 262, 312; in Collins' hunting group 263, *263*, 269, 286; financial losses of 258; as manager 281; in 1931 World Series 267–268

"Cocky" Collins nicknamed 60, 96

code of the clubhouse 181

Coffey, Jack 29

Coffman, Dick 266

Cole, Leonard "King" 73, 75–76

Collins, Eddie, III (grandson) 300, *301*

Collins, Edward Trowbridge: on American League all-star team *79*; with Athletics 46, *81*, *93*, *98*, *244*, *251*; at Columbia University *16*, *20*; with family *130*, *271*, *299*, *301*; with hunting group *263*; with Red Sox *274*, *278*, *290*; with White Sox *126*, *138*, *150*, *152*, *199*, *211*, *216*

Collins, Edward Trowbridge, Jr. (son) 129, *130*, 195, 251, *271*, 287; baseball and 270, 292, 297, *297*; education of 261, 270, 283, 288; enlistment of 297–298; family of 296, 300; father and 315–317

Collins, Emily Jane Mann Hall (wife) 301, 312, 314–317

Collins, Grace Rossman (half-sister) 10

Collins, Jane Pennock (daughter-in-law) 300, *301*

Collins, Jimmy 30, 43, 134

Collins, John Rossman (father) 9–10, 13–14, 39, 66, 201, 255

Collins, John "Shano": Black Sox scandal and 175, 177, 179, 193; in 1919 World Series 157, 162, 179; White Sox and 120–121, *138*, 169, 172, 178, 189

Collins, Mabel Harriet Doane (wife) 70, 77, 125, 260–261, 263, 299, *299*, 301; on Eddie's career 113, 235–236, 274–275; Eddie's teammates and 91, 128, 251; sons and 82, 283, 287–288

Collins, Mary Trowbridge (mother) 9–10, 13, 39, 66, 201, 291

Collins, Paul Doane (son) 82, 125, *130*, 195, 261, 270, 316; as minister 283, 287–288; officiating at weddings 296, 301

Collins, Pete (grandson) 300

Collins, Rip 220

the Colonel *see* Egan, Dave

Columbia Park (Athletics' field) 45, 51, 55–56

Columbia University 102, 310; Collins' education at 14, 16, 27, 36; Collins playing baseball for 2, 16, *18*, 18–21, *20*, 27–28, 40, 101; Collins playing football for 2, 15–18, 22–23, *24*; football program at 21–22, 24–26; prestige of 14–15

Combs, Earle 269

Comiskey, Charles 2–3, 189, 232; acquisition of Collins by 103, 113–116; Ban Johnson *vs.* 145, *146*, 154–155, 164, 173–174; Collins' future with White Sox and 208–209, 226–227; Collins' relationship with 142, 213–214, 218; holding line on salaries 140–142, 151, 196, 198; illness of 198, 209; on industry teams as draft dodge 144, 151; making bad player decisions 116–117, 196, 198, 202, 227; managers and 118–119, 149, 205, 207–208, 212–213, 216; players' bonuses and 142; players' 1917 World Series shares 140; rebuilding White Sox 119–120, 124; Rowland and 118–119, 126–127, 129–130, 149; spring training and 126, 131–132, 143; wanting White Sox pennant 130; on White Sox finances 124–125, 194; on World Series changes 147, 155; *see also* Black Sox scandal

Comiskey Park 118, 126; "Eddie Collins Day" at 224–225

Connolly, Joe 107

Connolly, Tommy 75, 91, 106

Cook, William 160

Coombs, Jack: Athletics and 42, 48, 66, 83, 102; health problems of 89, 94, 113; hitting for "the $100,000 Infield" practice 88–89; pitching competence of 68, 70–

71, 94; in World Series 74–76, 86–87

Cooperstown, New York, Baseball Hall of Fame in 292–293

Cottrell, Robert 142

Coumbe, Fritz 187

Coveleski, Stan 91, 169

Cramer, Doc 284, 291, 295

Crawford, Sam 45, 60, 62, 70, *79*, 82

Cronin, Joseph Edward 312; Collins and 281–282, 285–286, 288, 310–311, 315–316; as manager 281–282, 296, 305, 308, 310–311, 313; as player 284, 288, 291, 295–296, 298; Ted Williams and 288, 310

Cross, Monte 42–43, 45

Crouse, Bucky 210, 224

Crowe, Robert E. 190

Crusinberry, James 136, 146, 168, 223; on Collins as manager 210, 213; on Collins' decline 223–225; on gambling and corruption 134, 163, 173

Cuba, Athletics' trip to 91–92

Cunningham, Bill 302

Cunningham, George 236–237, 239

Cuyler, Kiki 257

Cvengros, Mike 202, 220

Daley, Tom *98*

Daly, Tommy 177

Danforth, Dave "Dauntless Dave" 131, 140, 145

Daniel, Dan 288

Daubert, Jake 158, 161–163

Dauss, George "Hooks" 170, 186, 192, 237–239

Davis, Harry 45, 78, 84, 101, 223; with Athletics 42, 54, 57, 66, 68, *98*, 218; Collins boarding with 63, 69; as manager 80, 88, 97; "the $100,000 Infield" and 60, 88–89; as player 52, 80–81, 97; in World Series 74–76, 86

Davis, Ike 216

DeFoe, Frederick W. 273, *274*

Demaree, Al 101

Depew, Chauncey 13

Derrick, Claud 82

Derringer, Paul 267

Desautels, Gene 286, 288

Detroit Tigers: 1917 White Sox collection for 136, 185–187, 191–192, 197, 230–241, 231–232; Athletics' rivalry with 44–45, 47, 58–59, 61–64, 70–72, 80, 82–83; Cobb on 67, 82; player strike against 89–90

Dever, William 224–225

Devlin, Art 18

Devore, Josh 84

Dickey, Bill 269

DiMaggio, Dom 295, 309, 311, 316

DiMaggio, Joe 292, 295, 310–311

Dinneen, Bill 106

Doane, C.P. 77

Doane, Mrs. Charles P. (mother-in-law) 260
Doane, Mabel Harriet *see* Collins, Mabel Harriet Doane (wife)
Dobson, Joe 309, 311
Doerr, Bobby 292, 300, 309; Collins and 3, 286–287, 295, 298–299, 316
Donovan, "Wild Bill": as manager for New York Yankees 125; as pitcher for Detroit Tigers 45, 58, 63–64
Donovan, William J. "Wild Bill" 21–23, 223
double plays, Collins' 83, 87, 101, 247, 266
double steals 96–97, 139
Douthit, Taylor 266
Dowd, Tom 306
Doyle, Larry 66, 83, 87, 99
draft, for WWI 135, 144
draft, for WWII 135, 297, 299
Dropo, Walt 314
Duer, William A. 12
Duff, Paddy 31–32
Duffy, Hugh 305
Dugan, Joe 198
Duncan, Pat 158–160, 163
Dunlap, Fred 75
Dunn, Jack 101, 125, 142, 273
Durst, Cedric 287
Dygert, Jimmy 48, 59
Dykes, Jimmy 245, 249, 255–257, 259–260, 267, 309

Earle, Howard J. 16
Earnshaw, George 251, 257–258, 262, 264, 266–268
Ebbets, Squire 72
Ebling, Doc 251, 268–269
Eddie Collins Memorial Park (Millerton) 317
education, Collins' 11–14, 16, 27
Edwards, Jim 220–221
Egan, Ben 101, 223
Egan, Dave "the Colonel": Collins and 301–303, 313, 315–316; on segregation in baseball 300, 304–305
Ehmke, Howard 239, 250, 252–253, 256–258, 262
Elberfield, Kid 74
Eliot, Charles W. 21, 25
Elks, holding "Eddie Collins Day" 218
Eller, Hod 156, 159, 161, 163
errors, Collins' 7; with Athletics 43, 47–49, 248, 249; career statistics 265–266; at Columbia 17, 19–20, 28; for semiprofessional teams 30–31, 33, 44; with White Sox 172, 225; in World Series 84, 87–88, 100
errors, White Sox 160–161, 170
Europe, White Sox tour in 212
Evans, Billy 157, 163, 174–175, 250; farm system under 284–285, 291, 296
Evans, W.G. 190
Evers, Johnny "the Crab" 73;

coaching under Chance 207–208; on Collins 117, 163; Collins compared to 75, 94–96; as player 107, *108*; as White Sox manager 196, 202, 209–210, *211*, 212–213
exhibition games 35, 137, 140; Athletics' 56–57, 66, 78; barnstorming 65; Columbia University against pro teams 17, 27

Faber, Urban "Red" 186, 202; as 20-game winner 169; on accusations of fixed series with Detroit 197, 234; Black Sox scandal and 177, 179; enlistment of 144–145; illness of 133, 155–156; spitballs by 167; with White Sox 120, 128–129, 134–135, 140, 143, 153, 168, 178–179, 189, 194, 197–198, 224; in World Series *138*, 138–139, 162, 179
Falk, Bibb 179, 189, 194, 197, 200, 215, 224
farm system 290–291; development of 284–285, 288
Red Sox 310, 313
Farrell, James T. 183
Farrell, Joseph C. 127
Federal League: Collins and 102, 115; competing for star players 103–105, 113, 120, 123; end of 125, 184
Felsch, Oscar "Happy" 120, 171; batting by 153, 169; in Black Sox scandal 165, 175, 177, 191, 193; leaving to play for industry teams 145–146; on 1917 White Sox team 135, *138*, 140; in 1917 World Series 137, 139; in 1919 World Series 159, 161–163; salary of 142, 166; suspected of continuing to fix games 170, 172
Fenway Park (Boston): lights for night games put in 310; modifications to 294, 298; Yawkey's restoration of 279–280
Ferguson, Charles 96
Ferrell, Rick 275, 281
Ferrell, Wes 281, 283, 288
Ferris, George H. 77
Ferriss, David "Boo" 307, 309, 311
fights, in games 153, 160, 198–199
Fisher, Ray 156
Flagstead, Ira 247
Fletcher, Art 86, 140, 258
Fogel, Horace 63
Fohl, Lee 226
football: Collins playing 2, 13, 15–18, 22–23, *24*; Columbia University program 21–22, 24–26; Eddie Jr. playing 270, *271*, 283
reforms of 21–22, 25
Ford, Russell *79*, 82, 106
Foster, Rube 65
Fournier, Jack 120, 123, 126–127
Foxx, Jimmie 255, 257; with A's 245, 249, 253, 259, 262, 269, 279; Collins and 251, 269, 298; as MVP 284, 291; with Red Sox

284, 288, 292, 295, 298; in World Series 258, 262, 267
Franklin, Ben 190
Frazee, Harry 154–155, 167, 198, 205, 270
Friend, Hugo 190–194
Frisch, Frankie 261, 266
Fullerton, Hugh 140, 181; on Athletics 70, 74–75; on Collins 10, 75, 100, 195; on Collins slowing down 198–199, 202–203; on 1919 World Series 163, 165; on primacy of base running 72–73
Fultz, David 99, 312
Furman, John Myers 12, 273

Gallico, Paul 279
gambling 131; attempts to fix Cubs-Phillies game 173; betting by players 186–187, 241; Clean Sox accused of betting on fixed games 185–187; Collins admitting bet on Tigers Game 188, 241; heavy betting on 1919 World Series 157–158; influence on baseball 110, 134, 173, 183; Landis limiting scope of corruption investigations 188–189; odds on 1919 World Series 158, 160, 162; Speaker and Cobb accused of throwing game 230, 241–242; White Sox rumored to continue fixing games for 170, 172, 174; White Sox rumored to have thrown 1919 World Series for 163, 172–173, 189–190
games played, Collins 143, 199, 204, 226, 256, 259–260, 265–266
games-played records 143, 296
Gandil, Arnold "Chick" 2, 135, 143, 153; accusations of 1917 fixed series with Detroit and 232–241; Black Sox scandal and 158, 175, 177, 179, 191; dislike for Collins 141–142, 152; leaving White Sox 166–168; in 1919 World Series 159, 160, 162–163, 165, 237–238; salary of 142, 151; taking up collection for Detroit players 186–187, 231; with White Sox 131, *138*, 139–140, *152*
Gavin, Bill 280, 306
Gedeon, Joe 180, 194
Gehrig, Lou 32, 269, 276
Gehringer, Charley 58, 276
general managers, Collins as 3, 274, 286–287, 295, 310–311
Gibbs, Harry 30
Gilmore, James A. 102, 104–105
Gleason, William "Kid" 118–119, 168, 269; Black Sox scandal and 163–165, 173–176, 178–179, 183, 185, 190, 192–193, 204; coaching for A's 246, 251; coaching for White Sox 128, 143; Collins and 149–151, 204, 207–209, 256; fights and 160, 199; 1919 World Series and 158, 162–163; scouting opponents before World Series 137, 155–156; White Sox collec-

tion for Detroit players and 192, 232; as White Sox manager 149, *150*, 171–172, 196, 198, 201–202, 204

"Golden Outfield" of Boston Red Sox 89

golf 66–67, 142, 153, 194, 217, 223

Gomez, Lefty 269

Goodman, Billy 312, 314

Gordon, Joe 298

Gorman, George E. 192

Goslin, Goose 269

Gowdy, Hank 107, 109, 136

Grabiner, Harry 118, 123, 205, 212–214

Graham, Charles 312

Great Depression 258, 261, 270, 280, 295

Green, Pumpsie 304

Grey, Sam 250

Griffith, Clark 20–21, 244, 281–282, 310–311

Grimes, Burleigh 167, 262, 268

Groh, Heinie 156, 159, 161–163

Groom, Bob 133

Gropman, Donald 54

Grove, Lefty "Mose": in All-Star Game 276; with A's 247, 250, 253, 257, 259, 261–262, 265–266, 269, 279, 283; with Red Sox 279–281, 283, 288, 291–292, 295–296; in World Series 267–268

gum, Collins chewing 69–70, 121

Haas, George "Mule" 251, 257, 260

Hafey, Chick 261

Hageman, William C. 134

Hahn, Philip 175

Haines, Jess 262

Hale, Sammy 245, 252, 259

Hallahan, Wild Bill 262, 267–268

Harding, Warren G. 197

hardworking, Collins as 66, 70, 88–89

Harridge, William 270, 272–273, *274*, 289–290, 303, 315

Harris, Mickey 309

Harris, Stanley Raymond "Bucky" 212, 278–279, 281, 285

Hartnett, Gabby 312

Hartsel, Topsy 42, 47, 53, 57, 66, 71

Hasbrook, Ziggy *138*

Hauser, Joe 251, 255

Heilmann, Harry 204

Heitmuller, Heinie 53, 64

Hern, Gerry 313

Herrmann, August Garry 145, 164, 167

Herzog, Buck 84, 86, 137

Heving, Johnnie 263

Heydler, John A. 175

Higgins, Pinky 288

hit-and-runs, Collins' record on 2

Hitchcock, Billy 312

Hodapp, Johnny 252

Hodge, Clarence "Shovel" 178, 198–199

Hofmann, Fred 205, 212, 250

Holke, Walter 137, 140

Holland, William 34–35

home runs 45, 68–69, 72, 98, 105, 137–138, 167–168

home runs, Collins' 20, 67, 153–154, 169, 199, 203, 247–248, 265

homes, Collins': in Chicago 125; in Lansdowne, Pennsylvania 125, 128, 270, 283; in Weston, Massachusetts 283, 298–299

Hooper, Harry 204–205, 223; playing for White Sox 89, 135, 189, 194, 197, 202, 215

Hoover, Herbert 256, 258, 262

Hornsby, Roger 257, 265

Houck, Byron 96, *98*

Hough, Frank 38, 53, 63, 71, 89, 92, 112, 239

Hoyt, Waite 200–201, 253, 263, 266, 268

Hudson, Henry 11

Huggins, Miller 195, 200–201, 206, 222, 257–258

Hughson, Tex 298, 300, 309, 311

humor, Collins' sense of 223

Hunnefield, Bill 223–224, 226

hunting 127, 286; Collins' group for 101, 142, 212, 222, 250, 258, 268–269

Hurst, Timothy Carroll 57, 60–61

Huston, Tillinghast 114, 200–201

illness, Collins' 255, 260–261; heart condition 310, 313; pneumonia 48; stroke 314; tonsillitis 34, 143

industries, fielding baseball teams 144, 148

infield, White Sox 134, 140, *152*, 178, 202

injuries, among White Sox 123, 133, 135, 210

injuries, Collins' 80; arm 82, 89; face 83, 170; hands 190, 225, 248–249; knee 74, 143–144, 203–204; leg 122, 221–222, 224–225, 229, 246–247; responses to 97, 220

injuries, Eddie Jr. 308–309

integration, of baseball 300–307; *see also* African Americans

intelligence, Collins' 2, 37, 70, 94, 203

interviews, of Collins 68–70, 114–115, 286, 314

Irving, Washington 11–12

Irving School 12–16, 272

Isaminger, Jimmy 176; on Collins as manager 226–227; on Collins' coaching 252, 269; on Collins' play 49, 247

Jackson, "Shoeless Joe" 2, 98, 143; Athletics and 54, 67, 142; batting statistics of 83, 129, 153–154, 156, 169; Black Sox scandal and 165, 175, 177, 185, 191–192; with Cleveland Naps 71, 82, 115; on fixing of games 172, 182; homesickness of 54–55; lawsuit over

lost wages after Black Sox scandal and 197, 207; in 1917 World Series 137–139; in 1919 World Series 159–163, 165; salary of 142, 166; on shipyard team during war 144, 151; with White Sox 123–124, 130, 133, *138*, 140, 170

Jacobson, "Baby Doll" 218

James, "Big Bill" 107, 156, 186; in accusations of fixed series with Detroit 233, 237–239, 241; in World Series 108, 163

James, Bill (author) 2, 265

Jamieson, Charlie 252

Jenkins, Joe *138*, 153

Jennings, Hughie 63, 67, 71, 83, 99, 125, 250

Jethroe, Sam 303–305, 314

Johnson, Ban 57, 90, 218, 264; on accusation of Speaker and Cobb throwing game 230, 241–242; American League owners and 164, 241–242, 248; Black Sox scandal and 158, 173–174, 190; on Collins' sale to White Sox 113–115; Comiskey and 116, 130, 145, *146*, 154–155, 164; on gambling in baseball 134, 186; Landis and 191, 222–223, 241–242; Mack and 38, 63, 247; on 1917 fund to reward Tigers 194, 197; resigning as league president 249; support for military by 132–133, 136, 144, 300; trying to balance strength of teams 114–115; umpires and 60–61, 248; on World Series 99, 107, 147

Johnson, Ernie 189, 202

Johnson, Richard 275

Johnson, Walter "Big Train" 46–47, 68, 156; on all-star teams 66, 74, *79*, 82; awards for 98, 212, 292; changing leagues 115, 119; Collins and 203, 219; records of 98, 266

Jones, Fielder 125, 149

Jones, "Sad Sam" 171, 192, 201, 250, 261

Jones, Samuel "Butch" 38, 92

Joss, Addie 7, 68, 79, 82, 197

Jourdan, Ted *138*, 168, 178

Judge, Joe 264

Kaese, Harold 308, 310

Kafoed, Jack 117

Kamm, Willie 198, 202, 204, 215, 219

Kaplan, Jim 246

Kashatus, William 110

Kauff, Benny 137–138

Keane, Clif 306

Keating, Ray 106

Keeler, "Wee Willie" 292

Kelley, Henrietta D. 176

Kerr, Richard "Dickie": Black Sox scandal and 177, 179, 182–183, 193; holding out for more money 196, 198; in 1920 season 169, 172, 176, 178; in 1921 season 189, 194; in 1919 World Series 159–162; White Sox and 151, 153, 156, 189, 200, 220, 223

Kiefer, Joe 179
Killifer, William 103–104
Kinder, Ellis 312
Klein, Frank O. 180
Klem, Bill 87, 312
Klepfer, Ed 123
Kline, Bob 279
Kling, Johnny 73
Knight, John 42
Knode, Ray 219
Koenig, Mark 250
Koob, Ernie 133
Kopf, Larry 158–160
Kountze, Mabrey "Doc" 302
Kracke, John *263*
Kramer, Jack 312
Krause, Harry 54, 59, 62
Kreuscher, Phillip 221
Krichell, Paul 44, 246
Kuklick, Bruce 56, 86, 112

Lacy, Sam 303–304
Lajoie, Napoleon 73, 116, 123, 220;
   on all-star teams 82, 243; Collins
   compared to 58, 60, 75, 94–96
Landis, Kenesaw Mountain 125,
   184, 223, 302; on accusations of
   Speaker and Cobb throwing
   game 230, 241–242; barring
   Kerr from playing 196, 200;
   Black Sox scandal and 165, 184,
   189, 193–194, 196, 237; on
   charges of fixed series between
   White Sox and Detroit 194, 197,
   230–242; on Clean Sox accused
   of betting on fixed games
   185–186; death of 302; Johnson
   vs. 191, 222–223; limiting corruption investigations 188–189,
   240–241; Rickey vs. 231–232,
   306; spring training and 217,
   300
Lane, Bill 286, 289
Lane, F.C. 12, 94–96, 104–105, 165
Lapp, Jack 58, 78, 87, *93*, *98*, 102
Lardner, Ring 140
Lary, Lyn 282
Lauder, Billy 16, 18–19, 102, 215,
   216, 220
Lavan, Doc *98*
law, Collins considering career in
   16, 27
Lazzeri, Tony 269
Lee, Arthur, Jr. 77
Leibold, Nemo 122–123, *138*, 153,
   163, 169, 177, 179, 189, 193
Leonard, Dutch 135, 230, 242
Leonard, Jim 180, 314, 316
Leverett, Dixie 198, 202, 217–218
Levi, Ben 191, 193
Levi, Louis 191, 193
Levitt, Dan 284, 313
Lewis, Duffy 89, 135
Lieb, Fred 61, 69–70, 200, 257
Linn, Ed 287
Livingston, Paddy 58, 62, *79*, 82
Lloyd, John Henry "Pop" 65
Loomis, Fred M. 173
Lord, Bris 62, 71, 92
Louisville Colonels 291

Louisville Slugger, Collins endors-
   ing bat for 78
Lowdermilk, Grover 154
Lupien, Tony 298
Luque, Dolph 156
Lush, Billy 34, 37, 102, 306; semi-
   professional teams and 28–30,
   32–33
Lynn, Byrd *138*, 144, 172, 179
Lyon, William P. and Charles 12
Lyons, Ted 209–210, 212, 215, 224

MacFayden, Danny 260
Mack, Connie (Cornelius Alexander
   McGillicuddy) 2, 48, 63, 71, 77,
   92, 219, 247, 260, 276, 280, 300;
   appreciation for players 68, 70;
   Athletics' barnstorming games
   and 65–66; Athletics' lineups and
   56–57, 92, 269; with Athletics
   team *98*; background of 37; in
   Baseball Hall of Fame 292; Cobb
   and 62, 243–244, 249; Collins as
   adjutant to 96, 244, 252; Collins'
   contracts and 43–44, 77, 121,
   180, *244*, 262, 315; on Collins'
   prospects 32, 48, 58; Collins'
   relationship with 102, 229, 255,
   259; Collins wanting to manage
   A's after 258, 273; on competitiveness of leagues 103, 272;
   Eddie Jr. and 292, 296; Federal
   League vs. 105; finances of 92,
   112, 115, 258; intra-squad match
   53–54; Johnson and 242, 247;
   "the $100,000 Infield" and 81, 89;
   in origins of Athletics 38–39, 92;
   playing career of 37–38; reputation as judge of talent 50; role in
   developing Collins 45–49, 58;
   rumors of retirement 268; scouting semiprofessional teams 31,
   36; scouting World Series opponents 106–107; selling off players
   113–115, 122, 279, 283–284;
   shuffling players around 48–50,
   52, 58, 249; signing Collins for
   Athletics 5–6, 39–40, 231; simi-
   larity of A's teams in 1928 and
   1909 254; style with players 43–
   44, 54–55, 78, 125, 266; trying
   to rebuild A's 42, 242, 245;
   working with younger players 5,
   7, 54–55, 64, 91, 94, 97; on
   World Series 76, 83–84, 86, 99,
   180; World Series and 76, 87,
   99–101, 109, 257–258, 262, 267–
   268; on Yawkey buying Boston
   Red Sox 272–273
Mack, Earle 251, 268
Mack, Katherine Hallahan 77
Magee, Sherry 67, 78
Mahaffey, Ray 266
Maharg, Billy 176, 191
Mails, Walter "Duster" 174–175
Maisel, Fritz 125
major leagues: Collins agreeing to
   play 39; Collins' lack of interest
   in 31–32, 36; Collins' potential
   for 28, 31–32

Malone, Pat 257
manager, Collins as 206, 228; for
   A's 96, 258, 273; coaches under
   215, 223; effectiveness as 220,
   222; filling in 207–210, 260;
   possible Yankee post 200–201,
   258; praise for 224–225, 227; for
   White Sox 207–208, 212–213,
   216, 223, 226–227
managers: for A's 80, 93; Cobb as
   189; Mackmen going on to be 71;
   not eligible for MVP award 204;
   players as 204; for Red Sox 278–
   279, 281; Rowland as 118–119,
   121, 128–130, 149; for White Sox
   118–119, 149, 204–205, 207–210;
   for Yankees 200–201, 258; see
   also general managers; Mack,
   Connie; player-managers
Manchester, Connecticut, semiprofessional team of 33–36
Mann, Les 109
Maranville, Walter "Rabbit" 99,
   107, 312
Marcum, Johnny 284
Marines: Collins in 147–148, 151;
   support for White Sox 153, 155
Marquard, Rube 83–85, 87, 99–
   100, 137
marriage, Collins' see Collins,
   Emily Jane Mann Hall (wife);
   Collins, Mabel Harriet Doane
   (wife)
Martin, John "Pepper" 266–268
Martin, Mique (Mike) 20–21
Mathewson, Christy 182; on arti-
   cles about baseball 85, 99, 111; in
   Baseball Hall of Fame 292; in
   World Series 83–87, 100–101
Maxwell, Don 227
Mays, Carl 135, 154–155, 164, 170–
   171, 200
McAleer, Jimmy *79*
McAvoy, Tom 21
McCarthy, Joe 257, 269, 311
McClellan, Harvey 172, 178–179,
   202, 204, 216
McCullough, John 268
McDonald, Charles A. 173
McGinnity, Joe 17
McGraw, John 17, 39, 99, 137, 140,
   276; on Collins 100–101; World
   Series and 83, 87–88, 99–100,
   139
McGuire, Jim "Deacon" 90
McInnis, John Phalen "Stuffy" 2,
   52, 54, 57, 66, 84, 97, *98*, 104,
   210, 315; in "the $100,000
   Infield" *81*, 88–89; playing first
   for Davis 80–81
McMann, P.F. 30
McManus, Marty 275, 277–278,
   278
McMullin, Fred 134–135, 137, *138*,
   140; Black Sox scandal and 165,
   177, 191; salary of 151, 166
McNair, Eric "Boob" 284, 288
McPhail, Larry 302–303
McPhee, Bid 75
Merkle, Fred 83, 87

Meyers, Chief 84, 86, 99
middle infield combo, Collins and Barry's 66–67
Milan, Clyde "Deerfoot" 74, *79*, 82, 98
military: baseball teams drilling for 132–133, 136; enlistment of players in 136, 142; integration in 302; *see also* draft
Miller, Edmund "Bing" 269, 283, 286; with A's 250–253, 257–258, 262, 267–268
Millerton, New York 9–10, 317
minor leagues: Collins playing for Newark Bears in 43–44; disbanding during WWI 145
Minuit, Peter 11
Mitchell, Willie 238–239
Moeller, Danny 98
Moore, Jimmy 266–267
Moran, Pat 156–157, 159, 160–161
Morehart, Ray 225–226
Morgan, Cy 59
Morgan, Joe 2, 265
Morley, William R. 21–24
most valuable player (MVP) awards 73, 212, 297–298; Cochrane as 253; eligibility for 204; Foxx as 269, 291; Grove as 266; Joe DiMaggio as 295, 311; Ted Williams as 309
Mostil, Johnny 197, 199; with White Sox 147, 189, 204, 210, 215, 218, 224
Muchnick, Isadore 302–303, 305
Muesel, Bob 200–201, 212
Mulligan, Eddie 189, 202
Mullin, George 62
Murdock, Eugene 61, 145
Murnane, Tim 40, 76
Murphy, Charley 72
Murphy, Danny 45, 78, 82, 88–89, 93; with Athletics 42–43, 49–50, 57, 66, *93*, *98*; leaving Athletics 103, 111; second base for Athletics and 48–51, 53, *81*; in World Series 75, 100
Murphy, Eddie "Honest Eddie" 136; with Athletics 86–87, 91–92, 97, *98*; Black Sox scandal and 175, 177, 179; with White Sox 122, *138*, 189, 210
Murphy, Robert 312
Murray, Red 85, 87, 300
Musial, Stan 311
Myatt, George 286–287

Nasium, Jim 114–115
National Baseball Museum (Cooperstown) 292–293
National Commission 98–99, 140, 145, 167
National League 125, 155, 261, 276; on African American baseball talent 303–304; American League and 38–39, 157
Navin, Frank J. 190–191, 232, 241–242
Navin, Phil 148
Needham, Tom 210

Negro leagues 302, 305
Ness, Jack 126
New York, Collins' desire to play in 201–202, 208–209
New York Dodgers 304–305
New York Giants: Columbia University baseball players and 16–17; in World Series 23, 83–88, 97–101, 137
New York Highlanders 19, 20–21
New York Yankees 171, 225; failed trade of Collins to 206, 209; rumors of Collins trade to 195, 198, 200–201, 207; up for sale 294
Newark Bears 43–44
Newsom, Bobo 288, 291
Newsome, Dick 296
Nicholls, Simon 7, 43, 48–50, 57, 79
Niehoff, Bert *211*
night games 294, 310
Nixon, Otis 91
Northern League (semiprofessional) 29–31

O'Connor, Leslie 186–188, 233, 235
O'Donnell, Patrick 224–225
"Old Sport" *see* Hough, Frank
Oldring, Rube 45, 59, 96–97; with Athletics 53, *93*, *98*; 1910 season of 68, 70, 73; in World Series 87, 101
O'Leary, Jim 171–172
O'Loughlin, Silk 45, 96
on-base percentage (OBP), Collins' 83, 98, 109–110, 124, 129, 137, 156, 194, 199, 204, 212, 220, 226, 249, 253, 265
"the $100,000 Infield" *81*, 88–89, 261, 315
O'Neill, Steve 169, 316
Ormsby, Emmett 247
Orr, Billy *98*
Orwoll, Ossie 252
outfield, White Sox 140, 178
outlaw leagues 29, 102
Overall, Orvil 73–74
Owen, Frank 6
owners' meetings 275, 289
ownership: of Athletics 92, 245; of Baltimore Orioles 125; of Red Sox 3, 274–275, 306

Pacific Coast League 145
pain, Collins playing through 97
Parnell, Mel 312
Pass, Sam 177
Paul Shannon Memorial Trophy 314
Paulette, Gene 200
pay: Comiskey holding line on 151, 196; Comiskey's players complaining about 141–142, 183; for fixing World Series games 176–177; for "the $100,000 Infield" 89; players' shares for Chicago City Series 124, 212; players' shares for World Series 76, 101, 109, 140, 164, 174, 262–263

pay, Collins': with Athletics 41, 77, 92, 105, 121, 231; compared to other players' 2, 77, 141–142, 250; Federal League offer 102; for managerships 213, 228; as a Marine 147; with Red Sox 288; on sale to White Sox 114–115, 121; on semiprofessional teams 28–33; with White Sox 166, 202, 213, 222
Peckinpaugh, Roger 277–278
Pennock, Herb 296–297, 310; with A's 91, 94, *98*, 102–103, 109; Collins' friendship with 103, 296, 312; grandson of 300, *301*
perfectionism, Collins' 50, 52
Perkins, Cy 263, *263*
Perritt, Pol 137
personality, Collins' 13, 27, 114, 223; competitiveness 60, 225, 253; loyalty 232–233, 305–306; not approachable 116, 295; shyness/modesty 67–69; summaries of 315–316; *see also* hardworking; self-confidence
Pesky, Johnny 298, 309, 310, 311, 316
Petway, Bruce 65
Pfeffer, Fred 75
Phelon, William 117
Philadelphia 55; ban on Sunday baseball in 47, 64, 259; Collins leaving 114, 119
Philadelphia Athletics 65, 89, 96, 229, 256, 257; age of team 88, 250; all-star teams *vs.* 74, 84; American League standings of 83, 90–91, 103, 105–106, 125, 249, 254, 256–257, 260–261, 265–266, 269; attendance draw of 96, 112, 245, 254, 258–259, 268; coaching staff 251, 258, 269; Collins' contracts with 92, 121; Collins' desire to manage 258, 273; Collins playing for 2, 5–7, 39–40, 48, 102, 229, 231; Collins' roles with 252, 255–256, 265; Collins working under Mack on 243–244, 250, 258; "Eddie Collins Day" 249; Eddie Jr. and 292, *297*, 308–309; Federal League and 104–105; finances of 259; formation of 38–39; intra-squad match 53–54; Jackson and 54, 67, 71, 142; leading American League 70–72, 96–97; lineup changes in 48–50, 56–57, 122, 251–252; lineups of 53, 92–93, 102–103, 245–246, 250–252, 259, 263, 269; Mack rebuilding 89, 242, 245; Mack splitting squad to work with younger players 54–55; new ball park for 51, 55–56; new uniforms for 264; 1928 season compared to 1909 254; Red Sox buying players from 283–284; rise and fall of performance of 42, 80, 97, 106, 110, 244–245, 252–253, 255–256, 265, 269; rivalry with

Detroit Tigers 58–59, 61–64, 70–72, 80, 82–83; season statistics of 51, 64, 249–250, 257, 262; spring training of 52, 66–67, 78, 88, 92, 102–103, 246, 251, 259; trip to Cuba 91–92; in World Series 23, 72–76, 83–88, 97–101, *98*, 106–109, 257–258, 266–268
Philadelphia City Series 67, 78, 89, 91, 93, 103, 246, 251, 259
Philadelphia Phillies 67; *see also* Philadelphia City Series
Phillipse, Frederick 11
philosophy, Collins' 125, 127–128
pinch hitting, by Collins 43–44, 46–48, 252, 256
Pipgras, George 276
pitching: Athletics' 68, 70–71, 94, 245, 257; balance of advantage with batting 263–264; ban on freak pitches 164, 167; as Cincinnati Reds strength 156–157; by Collins 12–13; controversy over rosin use 222–223; with "doctored" baseballs 131; increasing importance in "lively ball" era 250; increasing of use of trick pitches 106; injuries from bean-balls 170–171; perfect games 196–197; as Red Sox weakness 275, 288, 292, 295; relief 131; shifting advantage to batting from 167, 222–223; in White Sox lineup 120, 131; as White Sox strength 140, 144–145, 156, 161, 168; as White Sox weakness 156, 178–179, 198, 202, 204, 220; World Series as contests of 84–87, 99–100, 107–109
Plank, Eddie 88, 91, 113; with Athletics 42–43, 48, 57, 66, *98*; excellence as pitcher 57–59, 64; in World Series 87, 100–101, 108–109
Plattsburg, New York, semiprofessional team of 4, 28–31
player-managers: advantages of 221; Cobb as 218; Collins as 213, 217–218, 227; Cronin as 281; Mack as 38; McManus as Red Sox 275; Schalk as 228
player strikes 89–90
Player's Fraternity 312
players' unions 312
Poles, Spottswood 65
Poole, Jim 221
Povich, Shirley 203
Powers, Doc 52, 57–58
product endorsements 78, 103

Quinn, John Picus "Jack" 145, 250, 253, 260, 262–263, *274*, 275
Quinn, Robert A. 205, 270, 272–274, 303

Rariden, Bill 139–140
Rath, Morrie 157–159, 161–163
RBIs, by Collins 7; on Athletics 58–59, 68, 72, 80, 98, 105, 109–110; career statistics 265; on White Sox 124, 156, 168, 189, 199, 212, 218, 226; in World Series 74, 76, 100, 161
Reach, Al 38
Red Hook, New York, semiprofessional team of 29
Reese, Harold "Pee Wee" 290–291
Reichow, Oscar 169
Reider, Jim 293
religion 12–13, 287–288
Replogle, Hartley L. 174, 176
Reulbach, Ed 73, 75
Reyburn, John 57
Rice, Harry *263*
Rice, Sam 200
Richards, Coach 15
Rickey, Branch 306; development of farm system and 284; integrating baseball 304–305, 307
Rigler, Bill 100
Ring, Jimmy 156, 160, 161
Risberg, Charles "Swede" 142; accusations of 1917 fixed series with Detroit 231–241; in Black Sox scandal 158, 165, 177, 191; in 1917 World Series 137, *138*; in 1919 World Series 158–161, 163, 165, 237; salary of 151, 166; suspected of continuing to fix games 170; with White Sox 131, 133–134, 140, 143, *152*, 156, 171
Robertson, Charlie 196–198, 201, 223
Robertson, Dave 137, 139
Robinson, Jackie 3, 303–305
Rockville, Connecticut, semiprofessional team of 33–36, 40
Rogers, Will 235
Rommel, Eddie 221, 245, 250, 253, 257, 260, 262, 269
Roosevelt, Theodore 21, 25
Root, Charley 257
Rossman, Claude 45
Roth, Braggo 123
Rothstein, Arnold 175
Roush, Edd 156–157, 159–163, 165
Rowland, Clarence "Pants" 118–119, 121, 126–127, 131, 133; on accusations of fixed series with Detroit 231, 233–234, 237; Collins and 128, 317; Comiskey and 126–127; 1917 World Series and 136–137, *138*, 139; respect for 122, 128–130; as umpire 219, 248; as White Sox manager 133, 136, *138*, 149
Rudolph, Dick 29–31, 107
Ruel, Muddy 222
Ruether, Lefty Dutch 156–158, 161, 193
runs, Collins' 82; for A's 68, 72, 89–91, 94, 98; career statistics 265; last 260; for White Sox 134, 137, 155–156, 197, 203, 226; in World Series 74, 75–76, 87, 100, 109–110, 139, 162–163
Ruppert, Jacob 114, 155, 200–201, 206, 222, 258, 294
Russell, Reb 116, 120, 127, 143; in 1917 season 131, 135, *138*, 139–140
Ruth, Babe 222; batting averages of 204, 269; in benefit games 276, 300; Collins playing against 103, 128–129, 133–134, 169, 269; home runs by 155, 169, 171, 248; honors for 204, 292; Huggins and 222, 257; as possibility for Yankee manager 258; with Red Sox 135; swing producing more home runs 167–168; with Yankees 167, 169, 194, 198, 225, 269
Rutland, Vermont, semiprofessional team of 29–33

St. Louis Cardinals: as National League champions 261–262; in World Series 266–268, 309–310
Sallee, Slim 137, 156, 158–159, 162
Salsinger, H.G. 88, 311
San Diego Padres 286–290
Sanborn, I.E. 126, 159, 165, 170–171
Schaefer, Herman "Germany" 74, *79*
Schalk, Raymond William 135, 142, 186, 202, 219; in accusations of fixed series with Detroit 187, 192, 197, 236; Black Sox scandal and 175–177, 183, 190, 193; Collins and 128, 201, 216; fights with teammates 158, 181, 198–199; injuries of 143, 210; in 1919 World Series 158–159, 161–163, 165; playing golf with Collins and Landis 217, 223; with White Sox 120, 140, 169, 175, 189, 215; as White Sox manager 204–205, 226–228
Schang, Wally: with Athletics 92, *93*, *98*, 102, 259; in World Series 100–101, 109
Schulte, Frank "Wildfire" 73, 75–76
Schupp, Ferdie 137–138
Scott, Everett 223
Scott, Jim "Death Valley" 68, 120, 122, 133, 135–136
season, length of 47, 72, 147, 155
second basemen, Collins as 117, 221; for Athletics 48–49, 52, 231; career statistics 265–266; for Columbia University 16–17; compared to other 75, 94–96, 315; improvement 50–51, 58; skill of 2, 68, 74–75, 133, 212; slowing of 202–203, 248–249; subs for 82, 116, 143, 147; for White Sox 66–67, 194; *see also* "the $100,000 Infield"
self-confidence, Collins' 23, 60, 96–97, 117
self-confidence, in good batting 69
semiprofessional teams, Collins playing for 28–36, 41
Sewell, Joe 219
Seybold, Socks 42
Seymour, Harold 182
Shannon, Paul 285

Shawkey, Bob 205; with Athletics 94, *98*, 102; with hunting group 101, 222, 250, *263*; in World Series 101, 109; as Yankee manager 258
Shea, Merv 275
Shean, Dave 5, 30–31, 33, 40, 42–43
Sheckard, Jimmy 74–75
Sheely, Earl 189, 194, 202, 215
Shellenback, Frank 145
Sheridan, Jack 89
Shibe, Benjamin F. 38–39, 55–57, 92, 180, 245
Shibe, John 54, 91, 258, 273
Shibe, Thomas 245, 258, 273
Shibe, Mrs. Tom 296
Shibe Park 56, 59, 64
Shores, Bill 262
shortstop, Barry as 52–53, 57, 66–67, 80
shortstop, Collins as 252; for Athletics 6, 42–43, 47–49; for Columbia University 16, 17; errors as 44, 47, 49–50; for semi-professional teams 31, 33
sign stealing, by Collins 85
Simmons, Al 247–249, 253, 257–258, 262, 264, 269; in A's lineup 245, 259; in World Series 267–268
Simmons, E. W. 9–10
Sinclair, Harry 102
Sisler, George 2, 133, 250, 300; honors for 169, 204, 292; as player-manager 204, 226
size, Collins' small 5, 15, 21
Slaughter, Enos 310
Smith, E.W. 220
Smith, Elmer 198
Smith, Frank 208
Smith, Jimmy 160, 163
Smith, Ken 317
Smith, Wendell 303–304
Snodgrass, Fred 66, 83–84, 86
Somers, Charles 38, 71, 115, 123
South Side Park (Chicago) 6, 118
Sowell, Mike 174
Speaker, Tris 2, 91, 141, 153, 253; accused of throwing game 230, 241–242; on all-star teams 74, *79*, 82, 300; with Athletics 243–244, 250, *251*; baseball articles by 85; batting by 204, 220; as center fielder 51, 57, 89, 197, 243; Collins' friendship with 201, 251; with hunting groups 263, *263*, 286; as manager 169, 204
speed, Collins' 28, 87, 139
Spink, J.G. Taylor 277–278
sporting goods 70, 78
The Sporting News, Collins' five-part biography in 286, 314
Square Sox/Clean Sox 178–179
Stallings, George 107
Stanage, Oscar 61–62, 72, 237–239
Stengel, Casey 289
Stephens, Vern 312
Stephenson, Riggs 257
Stevens, Joe and Frank 315

stolen bases: in accusations of 1917 fixed series with Detroit 237, 240; "lively ball" ending 250
stolen bases, Collins': for A's 58, 72–73, 79, 83, 89–91, 94, 98, 105, 110, 122, 124, 225–226, 249; Cobb's compared to 62, 70, 80, 82; at Columbia 27–28; records set for 91; trickery in 203; for White Sox 137, 146, 154, 156, 171, 194, 204, 212, 220; in White Sox *vs.* Detroit Tigers series 136; in World Series 76, 100, 138–139, 163, 265
Stout, Glenn 275
Stovall, George 60
strategy, baseball: Collins writing articles about 102, 110–111; Mack teaching younger players 54–55
Street, Gabby 74, *79*, 82, 111, 219
strike outs, Collins' 127, 175, 194, 199, 204; in emery ball controversy 106; in World Series 100, 161
Strunk, Amos: with Athletics 54, 57, 66, 68, 73, *98*, 106; with White Sox 177–178, 194, 210
Sugden, Joe 90
Sullivan, Billy 219
Sullivan, Eddie (Collins playing for Athletics as) 5–7, 39–40, *40*
Summa, Homer 255
Summers, Ed "Kickapoo Chief" 62, 82
Sunday baseball, bans on 47, 64, 229, 259, 302
superstitions 69–70, 121–122

Taft, William Howard 67–68
Tarrytown, New York 11–12, 220
"The Tarrytown Terror" Collins nicknamed 70
Tarrytown Terrors 13
Tebbetts, Birdie 311, 314
Tener, John 80
Terry, Bill 289, 295
Terry, Zeb 126, 177
Tesreau, Jeff 100, 137
Theobald, Robert A. 27
Thomas, Ira 89, 96; coaching for A's 246, 251; on Collins' articles 110–111; players' relations with 111, 115; playing on A's 52, 58, 84, *98*, 102–103
Thomas, Ray 143
Thomas, Tommy 224
Thomas E. Wilson Sporting Goods Company 215
throwing, evaluations of Collins' arm 27, *53*, 58
Thurston, Sloppy 202, 210, 215, 221
Tinker, Joe 73, 125
Todt, Phil 263
Troy, Phil 310
Tyler, Lefty 109

umpires 62, 134, 167, 264; Collins arguing with 60–61, 89, 156; complaints about 46, 96, 248

uniforms 215, 264
University of Pennsylvania, Collins coaching for 143, 189

Van Graflan, Roy 248
Vanderbilt, Cornelius 13
VanZelst, Louis 78
Vaughan, Irving 200–201, 205, 208, 213
Vaughn, Manning 213
Veeck, William 173
Vickers, Rube 48
Vila, Joe 227
Vitt, Oscar 94, 232
Vosmik, Joe 291

Waddell, George Edward "Rube" 5–6, 40, 42–45, 48, 55, 103
Wagner, Honus "Flying Dutchman" 78, 220, 292–293
Walberg, George Elvin "Rube": with A's 245, 250, 257, 262, 266; hunting with Collins 269; with Red Sox 279, 286
walks, Collins' 129, 133, 194, 199, 203, 212, 220, 226, 249, 253, 265
walks, in allegedly thrown games 136, 158–159
Wallace, Bobby *79*, 82, 259–260
Walsh, Ed 6, 44, 71, 83, 100, 116, 120; as White Sox manager 202, 204–205, 207, 210
Walsh, Jimmy *93*, 97, *98*
Wambsganss, Bill 169
Waner, Paul 220
War Bonds game 300
Ward, Aaron 200–201, 206
Ward, John Montgomery 19
Ward, Robert B. 104
Warstler, Rabbit 279
Weart, William 56, 111
Weaver, George "Buck" 116, 135, 143; accusations of Clean Sox betting on fixed games 186, 188; asking Landis for reinstatement 237, 241; batting by 134–135, 153, 169, 172, 175; in Black Sox scandal 165, 175, 177, 180, 185, 191, 197; Collins and 120–122, 153; on fixing of series between White Sox and Detroit 197, 231–232, 237; in 1919 World Series 157, 160–163, 165; positions played 126, 131, 134, 137; Rowland and 126, 130; salary of 142, 151, 166, 168; suspected of continuing to fix games 170, 172; temper of 121, 134; value compared to Collins 170; with White Sox *138*, 140, *152*
Webster, Daniel 12
Weeghman, Charles 102, 125
Weiss, George 284
Werber, Billy 276, 295
Western League 38, 116; *see also* American League
Wheat, Zack 242, 246, 249
White, Doc 68
Wilbert, Warren N. 134
Wilkinson, Roy 156, 178, 179, 193

Williams, Claude "Lefty" 234; in 1919 World Series 158–159, 161–163, 165; in Black Sox scandal 165, 175, 177, 191–192; as pitching star 129, 131, 133, 143, 153–154, 168–169; playing for industry team 144–145; salary of 142, 166; with White Sox *138*, 139–140, 169, 171
Williams, Dib 259, 267, 283
Williams, Joe 172
Williams, Marvin 303–305
Williams, Ted: batting statistics of 292, 295, 309, 311, 313; Collins and *290*, 295, 298–299, 316; Collins impressed by 286–287, 310–311; Collins signing for Red Sox 3, 288–290, 295, 310; as controversial 294–295, 297–298; fans and 291–292, 296; rumors of trade 309–310
Williams family 286, 289–290
Wilson, Franklin 246
Wilson, Hack 257
Wilson, Jack 288
Wiltse, Hooks "Snakes" 17, 33, 87
Wingo, Ivy 157
Witt, Whitey 268–269
Wolfgang, Mellie *138*
Wood, Smokey Joe 68, 91, 266, 288; accused of throwing game 230, 242; on all-star team *79*, 82
Woodland Bards (White Sox fan club) 127, 137

Woodruff, Harvey T. 121
Woods, George "Pinky" 308
World Series 1905 23, 42
World Series 1909 65–66
World Series 1910 72–73
World Series 1911 83–88
World Series 1913 97–101
World Series 1914 106–107; A's quick loss of 109–110, 112, 115
World Series 1917 2, 137, *138*, 140
World Series 1918 147, 275
World Series 1919 157, 164; Cincinnati Reds *vs.* White Sox in 156–164; honesty of 192–193; players' shares for 164, 174, 179, 189; *see also* Black Sox scandal
World Series 1921 194
World Series 1929 257–258
World Series 1930 262
World Series 1931 266–268
World Series 1936 285
World Series 1940 294
World Series 1943 300
World Series 1944 300
World Series 1946 309–310
World Series, proposal to extend to nine games 155
World War I 135; armistice ending 148; effects on baseball 142–146
World War II 302, 308; effects on baseball 296–300, 307
writing, Collins' articles 70, 102, 119, 243, 263; Thomas' criticisms for 110–111, 115; on World Series

75, 85, 88, 136, 158–160, 165, 268
writing, of articles by players 85, 88, 94; about World Series 98–99, 136, 158, 160
Wycoff, Weldon *98*; in Athletics' 1914 lineup 102

Yannigans, Mack's 54–55, 66
Yawkey, Bill 271
Yawkey, Thomas A. 3, 308; buying Boston Red Sox 270–275, 316; buying players for Red Sox 275–276, 284, 288; Collins and 272, 296, 315–316; farm system and 291, 296; investment in Red Sox 279–280, 284; profitability of Red Sox under 313–314; purchase of Ted Williams and 288–290; Red Sox management and *274*, *278*, 278–279, 281–282, 288, 310; relationships with players 281, 286; Williams and 288, 310
Yerkes, Stan 31
York, Rudy 309
Young, Cy 43, 82, 96, 197
youth movement, Mack's 5, 7

Zelcer, David 191
Zimmerman, Heinie 2, 29, 73, 137, 139–140
Zork, Carl 190–191, 193